MARKETING

Contemporary Dimensions

MARKETING

Contemporary Dimensions

SECOND EDITION

ROBERT A. ROBICHEAUX

The University of Alabama

WILLIAM M. PRIDE

Texas A & M University

O. C. FERRELL

Illinois State University

Houghton Mifflin Company   **Boston**

Atlanta   Dallas   Geneva, Illinois

Hopewell, New Jersey   Palo Alto   London

To
Cyn, Scott, and Grant Robicheaux
Jim and Denzil Pride
James Collins Ferrell

Cover photograph by Michael Malyszko.

Printed in the U.S.A.

Library of Congress Catalog Card Number: 79-89125

ISBN: 0-395-28500-3

Contents

Contents by Author, Title, and Source

Preface

Marketing: Contemporary Dimensions, Second Edition, is an organized collection of fifty current, informative, and easy-to-read articles that focus on critical marketing issues. Although this collection of readings was prepared for use with *Marketing: Basic Concepts and Decisions,* Second Edition, by William M. Pride and O. C. Ferrell, it can be used as a supplement to most introductory marketing texts. A cross-reference table that correlates each selection with chapters in several other texts is included at the end of the book.

The articles included in this reader were carefully selected from a wide variety of marketing and related journals and magazines to accomplish the following objectives:

to describe actual, contemporary marketing decisions and activities in business and nonbusiness organizations that are familiar to most students;
to interest and excite students about the study and practice of marketing;
to develop the discussion of contemporary marketing concepts beyond that found in most introductory marketing texts;
to inform students of marketing decision frameworks that illustrate the logical relations among the various elements of marketing strategy development.

The fifty articles contained in the reader make up a comprehensive and representative collection from the contemporary marketing literature. The reader emphasizes decision-making and case-history types of articles to accomplish the purposes stated above. The first article, for example, "Corporate Strategy: A New Role for Marketers" by Philip Kotler, stresses the significance of strategic marketing decision making to corporate success in the 1980s. The second and third articles, "We Missed the Boat . . . We Were Outsmarted" and "Marketing Mistakes That Businesses Make," provide real-world examples of the consequences of inadequate marketing planning and operations.

The articles in *Marketing: Contemporary Dimensions* were drawn from a wide variety of traditional and nontraditional sources of marketing articles. For example, several articles appeared originally in *Journal of Marketing,*

Business Horizons, Harvard Business Review, and *Sales & Marketing Management.* However, several other articles appeared originally in *Marketing News* (AMA newsmagazine), *Feedstuffs* (a trade publication of the agribusiness industry), and *Handling and Shipping* (a transportation industry magazine). These, as well as articles from sources such as *Forbes, Dun's Review, Fortune, Advertising Age,* and *Distribution Worldwide,* should make marketing come alive and excite students.

The book is organized into seven parts. Each part is supplemented with text material that introduces and provides an overview of each general subject area and explains the rationale for the inclusion and ordering of the articles contained therein. The text material preceding each group of articles is spiced with real-world, contemporary illustrations of marketing practices and a brief discussion intended to help students gain a quick grasp of the types of articles contained in that part. Further, the questions for discussion included after each article challenge students to go beyond the mere recall of facts presented in the article and to integrate their text and instructor's lectures in formulating their answers.

We sincerely thank the authors and publishers whose talents, efforts, and generosity provided us the opportunity to reprint their materials in this collection. J. Barry Mason, Chairman of the Department of Management and Marketing at the University of Alabama, is due special thanks for supporting our efforts. We also wish to thank Pat Kessler, Cely Brown, and Theresa Malone, whose secretarial and typing skills were instrumental in completing this project.

Robert A. Robicheaux
William M. Pride
O. C. Ferrell

MARKETING

Contemporary Dimensions

PART ONE

The Nature of Marketing

When the U.S. Supreme Court ruled in 1968 to allow Bell telephone customers to attach "foreign" devices, such as non-Bell telephones, to the Bell network, competition began to seep into the residential telephone service industry. With that, the giant American Telephone and Telegraph Company (AT&T) had to learn how to market.[1]

During the three months after he was named the most valuable player in the 1978 World Series, Bucky Dent, the New York Yankees' shortstop, earned about $90,000 in personal appearance fees and guaranteed contracts. Jim Griffin, an agent with the William Morris Agency, had the responsibility for marketing "Bucky Dent."[2]

President Jimmy Carter prepared a marketing plan to "sell" a Strategic Arms Limitation Treaty (SALT) to the Congress and the American people. Presidential Assistant Hamilton Jordan was assigned the responsibility of "coordinating sales efforts," which included: plugs during the State of the Union address, White House briefings for newly elected senators, sessions at the State Department for women's groups and religious leaders, and State Department diplomat interviews on radio and TV stations.[3]

Marketing occurs whenever individuals and/or organizations perform any of a broad mix of activities to bring about effective exchanges. Marketing activities obviously are performed by business organizations that strive to make profits by selling products. Marketing practitioners have become increasingly aware, however, that the techniques that they have developed and successfully implemented in the business world can be used effectively to assist different types of non–business-oriented individuals and institutions to achieve exchange objectives.

1. Bro Uttal, "Selling Is No Longer Mickey Mouse at AT&T," *Fortune*, July 17, 1978, pp. 98–102, 104.
2. Tony Kornheiser, "Marketing Bucky Dent," *Birmingham Post-Herald*, January 29, 1979, p. B-1.
3. "Selling SALT," *Wall Street Journal*, December 22, 1978, p. 1.

Marketers blend, or mix together, a large number of interrelated activities to bring about desired exchanges. Planning, pricing, distributing, and promoting products (offerings) are the activities that characterize the marketing process. However, being technically proficient in these activities alone does not guarantee an organization marketing success. Nearly every day, products that were fairly priced, amply promoted, and readily available to almost everyone who could want them fail in the marketplace. To minimize the probability of marketing failure, management in many organizations has adopted the *marketing concept* as an operating philosophy. According to the marketing concept, every organization, business as well as non-business, should strive to identify and satisfy people's (customers', clients', or others') wants through a coordinated set of activities that allows the organization to achieve its goals. The philosophy stresses the interdependence of customer want satisfaction and organizational goal achievement and the importance of coordinating all organizational activities to accomplish these goals.

Part One consists of three selections that provide an overview of the nature of both the concept of marketing and the process of marketing management. In the first article, Philip Kotler predicts that organizations will rely on marketers much more heavily in future strategic planning efforts. Defining the organization's purpose, formulating objectives and goals, identifying feasible growth directions and planning the organization's product portfolio are the key steps in the marketing-oriented strategic planning process recommended by this leading marketing authority.

The second article in Part One, which appeared in *Forbes,* tells the story both of the rapid growth of the Miller Brewing Company from a 1972 sales volume of 5.4 million barrels of beer to a 1978 volume of 24.2 million and of the tough competition that Miller is posing for the "king of beers" company, Anheuser-Busch. How did Miller rise to within "striking distance of the king" over a period of only six years? Anheuser-Busch executives suffered a serious case of "marketing myopia" and were out-marketed by Miller's marketing team.

In the third article, Leonard L. Berry argues that, while all organizations market, not all are good at it. In "Marketing Mistakes That Businesses Make," Berry reviews some of the most common errors made by marketers and suggests how these might be avoided.

1

Corporate Strategy:
A New Role for Marketers
PHILIP KOTLER

The contemporary environment of business demands that corporate marketing executives chart a strategy for success in the 1980s. The role of marketing and of marketing managers is changing, according to a leading marketing philosopher.

Looking into the future of marketing management, Philip Kotler, the Harold T. Martin Professor of Marketing, Northwestern University, told the conference, "I see the following paradox:

"Marketing management will simultaneously become less important and more important."

It will become less important, he said, because it will be operating in a changing and more difficult climate; it will be more important because strategic planning will be more important and marketing skills will be essential to strategic planning.

"Looking back at the 1960s, we can safely call this period the Marketing Decade. Marketing finally came of age, and in many companies it became the driving force. Growth was the game, and marketers were its engineers.

"Marketers at Procter & Gamble showed that customer benefit-oriented marketing ideas could win a lion's share of the toothpaste, hair shampoo, potato chips, and baby diaper markets.

"Ford showed that a lifestyle marketing idea called the Mustang could capture a profitable share of the tough automobile market.

"IBM and Caterpillar exploited their customer-

Source: Marketing News, June 30, 1976, p. 4. Reprinted from *Marketing News* published by the American Marketing Association.

oriented marketing service systems to deepen their leadership in their respective markets.

"There was increasing talk about customer orientation, market segmentation, market targeting, market positioning, marketing plans, and marketing audits. We saw marketers rise to leadership positions in many companies. Sales and profits rose each year and much of the credit was given to the imagination and drive of marketing executives.

"How much of this growth was created by the energy of talented marketing people and how much was due simply to the momentum of a high growth economy? We didn't separate these possibilities at the time, but the slow growth economy of the 1970s leads us to raise this question.

"A cynic would say that marketing was easy in the 1960s. All that a marketer had to do was to work hard. In the 1970s, the marketer also has to work smart. In the 1980s, even the combination may not be enough.

"The 1980 scenario, Kotler said, will include such negative factors as:

1. A continued slow growth economy.
2. Continued consumerism and anti-business sentiment.
3. Increased government regulation and limitation of marketing activity.
4. High inflation.
5. Raw material availability problems.
6. Increased international protectionism.

"If this scenario continues, the marketer of the 1980s will have to be a sublime thinker and doer to produce rapid growth for his or her company in a slow-growth economy," Kotler said.

If the 1960s was the marketing decade, what is represented by the 1970's? The 1970s, he said, is the Strategic Planning Decade.

"Strategic planning has been moving into today's companies with the same rapidity and appeal as the marketing idea moved into the firms of the 1960s. It is happening so fast that many marketers still haven't noticed it. The idea of strategic planning has enough simplicity, beauty, and cogency to captivate business leaders.

"And as strategic planning takes hold, it will force a repositioning of marketing within the firm," Kotler said. "If anything, it threatens to demote marketing from a strategic to an operational function. Instead of marketing being in the driver's seat, strategic planning has moved into the driver's seat. Marketing has moved into the passenger's seat—and in some companies into the backseat. The position of corporate vice president of marketing has been eliminated in some companies and emasculated in some others, simultaneously with the installation of strategic planning.

"When a business function becomes successful, it is routinized, and it steps aside for a new function that claims salvation for the firm's problems," he said. "In the 1910s, inventors and engineers created a lot of enterprises: Henry Ford and his auto; the Wright Brothers and their planes; Thomas Edison and his many inventions.

"Financial types were strong in the 1920s, since there was a financial need and opportunity to consolidate, rationalize, and expand enterprises. During the 1930s, accountants took over leadership with their belt-tightening methods. In the 1940s, production people became our business heroes, producing first for the war, and then trying to catch up with consumer demand during the latter half of the decade.

"In the 1950s, the sales people had a heyday capitalizing on all of the unsatisfied demand coming out of the growth of the suburbs and rising consumer affluence, and in the 1960s, the marketing people had to create really good marketing ideas to increase their companies' shares of the market," he said.

"In the 1970s, the strategic planners have been entrusted with the responsibility of carrying the company forward. Any one of these functions may become central once again, depending on how the economy turns."

The recent ascendancy of strategic planning, Kotler said, is due to the growing importance of four factors: a highly volatile environment, high inflation, high cost of capital, and the high risk of new product developments.

"The company is forever trying to stabilize its position in the face of an ever-changing environment. It must find opportunities yielding a return exceeding today's cost of capital of 15%. The company has to use its money wisely, spending it on those business units that promise the best performance, and not squandering it on the weak performers. These ideas and needs have consolidated into the theory of strategic planning," Kotler said.

"The basic difference in results between running a company by marketing and running a company by strategic planning is that of undisciplined growth vs. disciplined growth.

"The marketer bubbles over with new product and marketing ideas. The company he leads will grow by accretion rather than by discipline.

"The strategic planner has a more systematic way to define the opportunities that make sense for the particular company. He needs the marketer's assistance in generating and appraising appropriate ideas but he defines the appropriate domain of ideas," he said.

"The marketer's skills will be essential in carrying out effective strategic planning. An article in the May–June, 1978, *Harvard Business Review* pointed out that strategic planning is not enough. Companies such as General Foods, Rohr Industries, Mattel, Outboard Marine, and Singer—all practitioners of strategic planning—had to swallow a lot of bad businesses which strategic planning led them to enter. Their marketing analysis was deficient. They didn't do strategic marketing research.

"Marketers will be relied on much more heavily in future strategic planning," Kotler said.

Strategic planning is the managerial process of developing and maintaining a viable relationship between the organization and its environment through the development of corporate purpose, objectives, growth strategies, and business portfolio plans for companywide operators, he said. The definition underlines the four steps in the strategic planning to which we now turn.

"Defining the corporate purpose should not be confused with defining corporate objectives and goals, for the latter are simply ways to realize the corporate purpose or mission. The corporate purpose is not to make money, since this is true of all companies," he said. "The company hopes to make money in the course of carrying out its purpose.

"Corporate purpose has to be defined in terms of accomplishing something outside of the organization. It should be defined in terms of business domains of operation—definable in terms of products, technologies, or markets," he said.

"Most companies have defined their purpose in terms of product—as an auto company, a steel company, or a toiletries company.

"Some companies define their domain in technological terms—as a chemical processing company or a foundry job shop.

"But marketers pointed out in the 1960s that businesses built on product or technological definitions of purpose are vulnerable to product and technological change. Even today some successful marketers persist in defining themselves in product terms—McDonald's defines itself as being in the hamburger business. The fact is that McDonald's is in the rapidly growing fast-food business and should have expanded into the fast-growing pizza business and Mexican fiesta business.

"Nevertheless," Kotler said, "many companies are moving to a market definition of their business domain. Xerox, for example, sees itself in the business of meeting companies' needs for improvement in office productivity.

"A market definition of purpose calls for stating the company's mission in terms of serving either a defined customer group, a customer need, or both.

"The marketer's contribution under strategic planning is to continue to press for customer-oriented definitions of purpose at the corporate, divisional, and product line levels of the company," he said.

The second step in strategic planning is to define the objectives and goals of the organization over the planning horizon, Kotler said.

"The company marketer makes a critical contribution to the determination of company objectives and goals by appraising their realism. It is easy for strategic planners to arrive at numbers, especially if they are consistent with past numbers. But will the environment and market permit the achievement of the stated sales and market share levels? Here the marketer provides essential data and assessment.

"The next step is to identify the most feasible growth directions for the company to achieve its objectives and goals," Kotler said. "In the usual circumstance, the company cannot reach its goals simply by further market penetration with its current products and markets. There is a 'strategic gap,' and the company must find new products and new markets."

Possible growth direction, he said, include

1. Market penetration,
2. Market development,
3. Product development,
4. Competitor acquisition,
5. Vertical backward and forward integration, and
6. Diversification.

"A marketing analysis is crucial to the choice of growth directions. The marketer must estimate how much remaining market penetration potential exists. If it is small, he has to imagine market development possibilities (new users, new uses, new usage levels). He has to imagine and plan product innovations and modifications. He has to examine possible competitor acquisitions and verticalization moves. Each of these moves call for appraising the size, growth, cost, and profitability of alternative growth thrusts," Kotler said.

"The fourth step in strategic planning is called portfolio planning, and in some ways, it is the most interesting and challenging to the marketer," he said. "More and more companies have become multiproduct, multimarket companies organized on a divisionalized basis. The modern company has become a collection of profit or investment centers.

"Unfortunately, not all centers are equally profitable. One can view the different natural units within a business, whether division, product lines, or products, as constituting an investment portfolio. As in any investment portfolio, some of the investments are strong, some moderate, some weak, and some clear losers. The job of investment management is to turn over the portfolio to earn the optimum return.

"To accomplish this, many companies have set up systems of identifying natural or strategic business units and then assigning a core objective to each. The objective may be to build, maintain, harvest, or terminate the business. This objective is determined by reviewing each business's performance and potential for sales growth, market share, and profitability," he said.

"The marketer contributes to the portfolio decision process in at least two ways. The first is to develop and appraise the market data necessary to estimate the business unit's future sales and profit potential. Suppose strategic management wants to harvest a business unit but the unit's manager wants to grow it. The key issue is how much sales and profit potential faces this business and this requires careful estimates of demand," Kotler said.

The second contribution of the marketing executive, he said, is to carry out the business unit's objective in the most cost-effective way.

"The marketer must carefully define the best target markets and cost-effective marketing mixes.

"But note that the marketer's job in the 1970s differs from the marketer's job in the 1960s. In the 1960s, marketers had to be good at growth. Marketing was the art of growthmanship. This art still applies, but not to all business units in the company. The marketer is told by the strategic planner what objective to pursue," he said.

He listed four types of future marketing managers:

1. **The growth marketer**
   1960 vintage. This marketer will "have entrepreneurial talent and a flair for creative marketing ideas."
2. **The maintenance marketer**
   This marketer will be good at maintaining the momentum of a going business. "He or she will know how to track customer and competitor behavior and evolve new product features, prices, communication appeals, and promotions to keep the product strong. This marketer will know the theory of mature products and how to prepare financially sound marketing plans."
3. **The harvester marketer**
   "This marketer will be good at drawing out cash from a business without killing it. He or she will be adept at cutting plant, equipment, and research and development costs; reducing advertising, promotion, sales force and customer service; and possibly raising price. This marketer will be good at finance, since the task is to extract the maximum cash from the business over a period of time."
4. **The terminal marketer**
   This marketer will be good at running the business either toward liquidating its assets or making it look attractive for acquisition. In some companies, such as General Electric, and also among consultants, can be found the beginnings of such a marketing specialty."

Questions

1. *What are the major differences between the business environment of the 1980s and that of the 1970s?*
2. *Describe the new role(s) envisioned by Philip Kotler for marketing managers during the 1980s.*

We Missed the Boat . . .
We Were Outsmarted

ROBERT J. FLAHERTY

Anheuser-Busch was scornfully aware of every move its rival, Miller Brewing Company, was making. But by the time it woke up, its once insignificant rival was calling the shots and the St. Louis giant was merely reacting.

John A. Murphy, the big, joking, energetic head of Philip Morris' Miller Brewing Co. (*Forbes,* July 10) keeps a voodoo doll named "August" in his Milwaukee office. Under his desk is a small foot rug bearing Anheuser-Busch's eagle trademark. Figuratively, if not literally, every time Murphy pricks the doll or steps on the rug, Anheuser-Busch Chairman and President August Adolphus Busch III winces.

For six years now, Murphy's Miller has been walking all over St. Louis' Anheuser-Busch, Inc. In 1972 Miller sold only 5.4 million barrels of beer to Anheuser's 26.5 million. By last year the gap had narrowed amazingly. The score: Miller, 24.2 million; Anheuser, 36.6 million. The gap is still narrowing. For 1978 Miller is probably going to sell at least 32 million barrels, a 33% gain, to Anheuser's 41 million, a 12% gain. A smiling Murphy tells everyone: It's not a question of "if" but of "when" Miller will pass them.

Caught in the middle of the battle between the two companies, Schlitz, Pabst and Coors have been major victims. Their market shares as well as earnings have declined.

Source: Forbes, August 7, 1978, pp. 36–38. Reprinted by permission of FORBES Magazine from the August 7, 1978, issue.

But while competitors were being mauled, Anheuser-Busch failed to launch an effective counterattack against Miller, being satisfied with merely defensive measures. As every player of war games knows, a good offense is the best defense.

"We didn't take Miller seriously but we do now," says Dennis P. Long, who heads Anheuser's beer business. "Their goal to become number one is the kind of thing you post on the locker room wall—and we do around here. This threat has united employees and management to fight a common enemy.

"They say Miller is innovative, that its ads are creative, that it brings out new products to create new market segments, that it's gaining market share." Long almost shouts this. "Aren't we doing all these things, too? In the last 12 months we have introduced more new products, more new ads, added more new marketing people and worked harder than in any similar time in the history of Anheuser-Busch."

Stupid, no. Complacent, yes. A classic case of self-deception. Trim, young (now 41) August Busch, who took over as chief executive in May 1975 from his father, Gussie, now retired, seemed to be doing all the right things. He developed a whole new team of younger, hard-driving executives, many of them M.B.A.-educated. Nor was August III himself untested when he got the top job. His training, in fact, began almost at the moment of his birth. "A couple of hours old, the first thing I ever had in my mouth was five drops of Budweiser," he says. Thus did his father begin to dedicate his oldest son to the beer business which had been in the family since 1873. But the son never had a sure thing. As Gussie told *Forbes* in 1971, his son would "not necessarily" succeed him. "He has to measure up and prove he can do the job."

After two years at the University of Arizona, August III settled down to the beer business, going to Chicago's Siebel Institute of Technology to become a brewmaster. To save the two years it would have required to become an M.B.A., he had the company engage as a consultant the great authority on operations research, Professor Russell Ackoff of the Wharton School. Ackoff and Busch became fast friends. Says a top Anheuser executive: "We owned the St. Louis Cardinals and Busch Gardens and all that, but we also developed a solid underpinning of scientific management and planning."

Meanwhile, rival Schlitz was getting scientific, too. It followed the Boston Consulting Group theory, which advised that the way to dominance in beer, as in other businesses, was through becoming the low-cost producer. Schlitz shortened the brewing cycle, while Anheuser stuck with a 30-day-or-longer cycle and with the more costly rice it used rather than the cheaper corn that Schlitz and others used. The Schlitz move was a failure. Some of the faster-brewed beer suffered a taste change if it stayed on the shelves too long. Either because of marketing problems or a reaction to the taste, sales slumped. Now Schlitz is going back to the lengthier brewing process.

So Anheuser was still king of beer, and its leader was surrounded by the best management talent money could buy. Schlitz was humbled and Miller wasn't worth thinking about. "We'd whipped the price enemy," says Dennis Long. "Now it was time to face our union: the Teamsters. Miller's sales seemed so minor we didn't really think much about them."

Young August was determined not to give in to the union the way his father always had. Old Gussie loathed strikes; they might cost the company market share. "But now," August says, "the union pushed us to the cliff. They wanted written into the contract that they would have the right to approve or disapprove any changes in production before we could implement them. They would manage our production, not us. It was a test of me. It was the first time they had dealt with me on the front line."

The result was a 100-day strike in the spring of 1976. Anheuser lost 12 million barrels of production, plus a lot of goodwill among union members. Sales for the full year were just 29 million barrels, a 6-million-barrel decline from 1975.

Meanwhile, Miller was coming up on the inside track. But the Anheuser team didn't recognize it. Why—with all its depth of management? The best answer is: arrogance, which led to complacency.

Anheuser had always concentrated its marketing fire on Joe Sixpack: male, a heavy beer-user, blue collar. Meanwhile, Miller's Murphy, recognizing that the beer market, like other markets, could be segmented, brought out Miller Lite and domestically made Löwenbräu.

Miller was also hitting Budweiser where it really hurt: right in the Joe Sixpack market. In 1974 Miller had bought up virtually all of the top network sports shows: *Monday Night Football, College Football Game of the Week.* Out the window went Miller's tired, effete old slogan, "The champagne of bottled beer." In came a jock image with black footballer Bubba Smith ripping off the top of a can of Miller with his bare hands.

While Miller was stealing a marketing march, Busch was worrying about his frayed profit margins, narrowed in the Anheuser price competition with Schlitz. "To hold our margins," he now concedes, "we de-marketed. We got rid of our brand manager system. While we were doing this, a supermarketer was laying the seeds of his success. *We* created the atmosphere for that success."

While Anheuser was skimping on marketing and neglecting new products, Miller made quick inroads among blacks, college students and at-home drinkers who liked sports. "We were perfectly aware of when they bought the *Monday Night Football* package," says Busch. "Perfectly aware. We looked at the cost of that on a total dollar basis, but not on a cost-per-thousand-beer-drinkers' basis. That's where we missed the boat. We were simply unsmarted."

What made this so galling was that Busch had forgotten the operations research lessons Professor

Ackoff taught him: Don't concentrate on any single aspect of your business, but make sure you consider all the factors in relation to one another. Concentrating on labor and finance, Busch had ignored marketing, had, in fact, penalized his marketing in order to improve the labor and financial pictures.

Sure, Busch saw that Miller was pushing hard with its Lite beer. But what the hell, Gablingers and Meister Bräu had tried that low-calorie stuff and failed. But times had changed, and Miller learned from the others' mistakes. "Miller ended up with 65% of the light beer market, which is now over 7% of the total beer market," laments John H. Purnell, Anheuser's director of planning.

When Miller brought out a U.S.-brewed Löwenbräu to compete with Anheuser's Michelob, Anheuser's response was to file a complaint with the Federal Trade Commission, charging its competitor with misleading advertising. Now, Anheuser has decided to get on the bandwagon. "We will have an imported beer," Dennis Long told *Forbes*. But why did Anheuser wait almost a year?

In July 1977 Busch ordered his executives to develop a whole new marketing program. Spending was raised from a prestrike $30 million to $100 million in 1978. To get its new brand managers and a promotion team in place Busch hired a headhunter to bring in 100 men from places like J. Walter Thompson, PepsiCo, Coca-Cola, Procter & Gamble and General Foods.

Anheuser decided to go into the product-segmentation game with a vengeance with two light beers, Michelob Light and lower-priced Natural. "Natural Light came out with a name that was too damn long: Anheuser-Busch Natural Light Beer," says Busch. "Under the pressure of time, we had to get in that marketplace before it was solidified by Miller Lite."

All of Anheuser advertising was looked at critically. Anheuser decided to aim at ethnic groups it had ignored previously. While most beer is consumed at home, Anheuser's usually serious ads were often set in bars. Now Anheuser tried some ads featuring black singer Lou Rawls and comedian Norm Crosby—and a "Welcome Home" theme as well.

While Anheuser people still think beer should have that snappy rice taste, they have just started selling corn-sweetened Busch beer in New England at premium prices. "We concede there is a taste spectrum," says Dennis Long. He also will soon launch a near beer with under 1% alcohol.

In sports Anheuser has tried to counter Miller's network TV spots in ways that almost look like an overreaction. Anheuser is now sponsoring nearly 200 professional and college teams and some touch football, hydroplane racing, jogging and hot-air ballooning.

Of course, you can't write off Anheuser-Busch. It is still number one in beer, a company with $1 billion in capital and a powerful distribution system. "Right now, I could sell Budweiser in paper cups," says Long. Busch expects sales to be about $2.6 billion this year, an 18% gain. The company will probably earn $2.50 a share this year, a 22% improvement over last year's record $2.04. But even those rising profits are something of a humiliation. Here's why. When Schlitz was the main enemy, Anheuser-Busch was competing mainly on price. Miller, by contrast, sells premium-priced beers and competes with advertising and promotion. So Anheuser-Busch is raising prices again—under Miller's umbrella.

On the over-the-counter market where it trades around 24, Anheuser-Busch stock has recovered from the nine-year low of 18 to which it sank last year. But as recently as 1972 it sold for 69. Anheuser-Busch and its shareholders have paid for management's complacency.

Questions

1. *What should the Anheuser-Busch marketing people have done during the mid-1970s when Miller Brewing launched its "segmentation-oriented" marketing campaigns?*

2. *What was the major management lesson learned by Anheuser-Busch's top managers from competing with Miller Brewing during the 1970s?*

Marketing Mistakes That Businesses Make

LEONARD L. BERRY

Assessing market opportunities and developing appropriate marketing strategies are difficult tasks. The environment of the firm is complex and everchanging, and few marketing strategy decision tools are precise. Some of the more common marketing mistakes can be avoided if management will make the necessary planning efforts.

The discipline of marketing is much more complex than first meets the eye. Marketing is not "bottled magic" or a clutch of "formula answers" or a series of gimmicks. Rather, marketing is that function in the organization responsible for managing the market, that is, for initiating change within the organization's control (new products, changed advertising strategy, different sales training approach) to adapt to environmental change beyond its control [the technology of polyvinyl chloride (PVC) plastics, the energy crisis, consumerism] that nonetheless has an impact on its markets. Marketing is the function responsible for, among other things, continually reading the market's changing requirements, creating products and product systems to satisfy those requirements, and communicating the availability and benefits of these offerings.

Marketing is complex, and, yet, in volatile and fiercely competitive circumstances, superior execution is vital; it is prone to superficial understanding but requires deep understanding; it is inevitable in

terms of its practice in the organization, but not in terms of its effective practice.

The purpose of this article is to bring together a number of thoughts about marketing that might be helpful in fostering greater understanding of this complex discipline, in provoking more awareness of its essentials. I will discuss a number of common marketing mistakes that I have become increasingly aware of as a result of consulting and research experiences. Then we shall examine a variety of means for preventing these errors.

Although the items forthcoming represent, in my opinion, common mistakes, it is important to keep in mind that the avoidance of them is also common. Whereas this article is meant to be a catalog of commonly made marketing errors, it is not meant to be an overall indictment of marketing practice in the United States. The dramatically good marketing that has been continually demonstrated by Sears, Xerox, Delta Airlines, Whirlpool, and many other organizations, is remindful of the need to discriminate among organizations, rather than fall prey to the tendency for all-encompassing judgments. Nevertheless, my own experiences have pointedly suggested that certain marketing mistakes are commonly made, and, in this sense, it would seem worthwhile to attempt to communicate in summary fashion at least some of them.

One of the most common marketing errors is the failure to recognize the real substance of the business; namely, the quality of the experience the ultimate consumer or user has when interfacing with the firm and/or its products. A question asked me at a recent seminar on bank marketing is illustrative:

Source: Atlanta Economic Review, 24 (July–August 1974), 21–27. Reprinted with permission of Georgia State University.

"Are bank advertising slogans ('The Friendly Bank,' 'The Family Bank,' 'The Lifetime Bank') worthwhile?" My answer was that it is action that counts, not talk. When you have action, however, talk can be helpful in reinforcing and capitalizing on the substance of the action. In short, what really counts is not whether the bank labels itself as "The Friendly Bank," but whether the bank *is* "The Friendly Bank."

Marketing happens every time the bank interacts with the customer. The teller, whether she knows it or not, is practicing marketing when she meets the customer. If she is rude, then to the customer on that day the bank is rude! Every working day the teller adds to or detracts from a quality relationship between the bank and the customer. In banks where tellers are carefully selected, excellently trained, continually motivated, reasonably compensated, part of the real substance of the bank's business is being recognized. To merely label the bank friendly, but forgo the continuing and challenging marketing management task of making it friendly, is to overlook what real marketing is all about.

In short, when the chips are down, many executives in many industries really don't believe, as Drucker has pointed out, that "The Customer is the Business."[1] What actually happens to the customer when interfacing with the firm and/or its products is considered in the organization's decision making, but not in a "high-priority" sense. Even worse, the customer's interest may be overlooked entirely. The goal of producing a superb experience for the customer becomes a cosmetic concept, voiced perhaps by many, but believed in by few.

Consider the plight of Eastern Airlines, a troubled, money-losing company as this is being written.[2] Several years ago Eastern instituted a cost-cutting program that, in effect, came to severely jeopardize the quality of the traveler's experience with Eastern. Floyd Hall, Eastern's chairman, described what happened this way:

"You know the way it goes. . . . The word goes out that expenses have to be cut by so many million dollars next year and your contribution will be X.

So the poor station manager has no choice. He cuts back and the first place he cuts back is with the lowest-paid people, who theoretically matter the least. Except that very often they happen to be the people handling the baggage. . . . We just cost-controlled ourselves to death."[3]

To be sure, the result of this particular cost-cutting program is not the only factor in Eastern's troubles. Nonetheless, it seems an important factor. It is one thing to rid a company of wasteful extravagance; it is, however, quite another thing to restrict vital and expected customer services to the point that a company alienates its market and its employees, and, in the process, becomes increasingly vulnerable to competition. Thus it is not surprising that in Richmond, Virginia, a market in which major routes are exclusive to Eastern, the local business community recently mounted an aggressive and organized effort to persuade CAB examiners that there was a need to bring additional air service to Richmond on current Eastern routes. Richmond travelers are not the only ones who feel this way. In recent months, Eastern has stimulated more formal customer complaints to the CAB than any other airline.

What one can learn from the Eastern example seems clear: to think lightly of what happens to the consumer when interfacing with the firm and/or its products, is to think lightly about what really matters.

Short-Run Marketing Considerations

Closely related to the marketing mistake of jeopardizing the substance of the business and, in fact, often a contributing factor to this kind of mistake is the common practice of marketing in the "short-run" at the expense of the "long-run." The problem here is that the long-run eventually occurs. It is not surprising that short-run thinking should so dominate long-run considerations in many firms. After all, executives are often compensated and otherwise "rewarded" on the basis of short-run accomplishments, e.g., sales results in the next month or quarter. Overaggressive pursuit of the short-run result, however, often has untoward side effects that sooner or later come back to haunt the company, for example: disproportionate emphasis on making the sale rather than servicing the client after the sale is made; marginally ethical or outright unethical tactics in making the sale; selling marginally qualified prospects, having relatively low probabilities for ultimately being satisfied with the purchase made; or sacrificing long-range marketing investments (for example, the needed marketing research study or even the marketing research department) for short-run purposes (for example, another sales incentive contest or inflating next quarter's profit for the stock analysts by restricting needed expenditure).

The story of a midwestern company that nationally markets an audiovisual, point-of-sale system along with an associated correspondence course is instructive in the present context. This firm, which in the late 1960's grew from almost nothing to an annual sales volume of approximately $20 million, is at this writing near ruin. In effect, the long-run has occurred. In the late 1960's, with most sales being made to veterans because of substantial government subsidies available to them, the following practices occurred:

Commissioned salesmen would sell to virtually anyone willing to buy. Course entrance requirements and credit criteria were largely cosmetic.

Customers who were shipped malfunctioning equipment typically encountered substantial difficulty in getting repairs or replacements.

Customers having trouble completing the course itself were rarely followed up and counseled.

Frequent customer complaints about the course or the point-of-sale material were largely ignored.

In brief, the real ethos in this company, never articulated, but well understood by most, was that there was only one rewardable and important action—namely, make the sale. This short-run orientation became even more rampant once the company went public. Decision making was continually riveted to the goal of maintaining the price of the stock. The *real* market was ignored. Management seemed to become vitally interested in virtually any tactic that could make the next quarter appear to be better than it really was. Indeed, eventually, almost the entire headquarters marketing staff was fired and not replaced, apparently to reduce overhead and inflate short-run profit.

The eventual consequences of all this, of course, were predictable. The firm has developed an unusually bad reputation in the industry to which it principally sells and resistance to its offerings has increased.[4] A sizable proportion of customers sold have never completed the course, resulting in substantial lost revenue, since federal subsidies are tied to student progression through the course. Activities necessary to recover from the brink of disaster (for example, a well-conceived diversification effort) have not been forthcoming.

One consultant, in writing about industrial companies, expressed well the liabilities inherent in short-run marketing domination in the firm:

"Unhappily, only rarely does marketing succeed in getting the breathing room it needs to make a substantive contribution . . . I have seen cases where division management's overriding emphasis on the short-term prevented new products from being developed or effectively launched when they were clearly needed. I have also seen others where division managers resisted the weeding out of marginal products or customers so that the mix could be upgraded, when this was clearly the right move to make.

"In all of these cases, it is clear that the actions needed to be responsive to the market were blocked—because it would have led to a temporary drop in profits—without regard for the longer term impact."[5]

New Products—The Marketer's View

A common mistake contributing to new product failure is the tendency for marketers of all kinds to overrely on the intuitive process, even when research is done, as a basis for new product conception. The problem is that the intuitive process tends to be disproportionately biased in favor of one's own experiences, values, and needs, with the resulting possibility that product benefits perceived as real and important by the marketer will be seen as unimportant or nonexistent by the market.

"Empathy," a word commonly used in management textbooks, in the context of "how to manage subordinates," is rarely used in marketing textbooks when the concern is stimulating the market to action. And yet, more real empathy with the consumer might have been the essential ingredient for avoiding the approximately $15 million[6] lost in the late 1960's when the short-lived attempt was made to launch a national soccer league, complete with network television coverage, in the United States.

The point is this: The new product marketer must do everything feasible to view the new product idea from the viewpoint of the consumer, to "see" the concept as the consumer will likely "see" it, to, as the saying goes, "get in the shoes" of the consumer. This means valid research in particular, bending over backward to move from the "marketer" view to the "market" view in general.

This type of mistake seems especially frequent in technologically oriented industries where research scientists and engineers commonly engage in pure research. The outcomes of pure research are not necessarily marketable, however. Consider the development of a new product by a southwestern firm which allowed for the simultaneous transmission of voice and graphic communications, from one point to a second point, by means of the existing telephone system. Inasmuch as this device represented a major technical breakthrough, management seemed to assume that a simple presentation of the product to the prospect was all that would be required for meeting sales expectations. As it turned out, management was wrong. From the prospect's standpoint, the new product provided insufficient additional benefit over existing communications alternatives to induce purchase. The new product, an engineering feat, attracted atten-

tion and interest, but not sales.[7] In a competitive and increasingly sophisticated marketplace, a well-engineered product is not enough. What is required is a well-engineered product that people want to buy.

Sometimes the intuitive process as a basis for new product ideas leads to the tendency for the marketer to develop new products that are the easiest to provide and promote, but, in actuality, lack relevancy to the consumer. One illustration of the vulnerabilities associated with this tendency was the introduction of a new margarine designed solely for the frying pan rather than for the table. Although the product did provide a benefit to the consumer—it was better for cooking, since it didn't create a black residue at high temperatures—it nevertheless failed in the marketplace. Apparently, from the viewpoint of the consumer, the importance or relevancy of this benefit was insufficient to generate purchase. As the new margarine was a relatively easy extension of the marketing company's product line, and was a product that could be heavily promoted without undue difficulty, it is perhaps understandable that management came to be enthusiastic about potential market acceptance. By the same token, however, it seems plausible that this enthusiasm allowed management to overlook a most critical variable in predicting purchase—namely, true customer need.[8]

Sometimes, it is not so much intuition that leads the marketer away from the consumer viewpoint as it is urgently felt pressures to solve a certain problem facing a company or industry. Indeed, more than a few students of the 1969 midi-dress fiasco, for example, would probably agree that the quest of many producers and distributors of women's apparel for relieving recessionary problems resulted in an arrogance for the consumer view, rather than an empathy for it. The unusual market resistance that developed because of the mismatch between what the marketer wanted to sell and what the market was willing to buy has been widely publicized and does not need to be recounted here.

In sum, new product ventures are risky in any event. Failing to do everything feasible to view the new product idea from the customer viewpoint, however, is treading on very thin ice indeed.

Being Blinded by Tradition

Although an individual's experience in a given industry is normally looked on as an important ingredient to his success in that industry, such experience, when long and concentrated, does have its dangers. One such danger is the possibility of being "blinded" from uncharacteristic, yet potentially fruitful, alternatives in conducting the business. In short, sometimes executives learn too well how "it is done in the ABC industry." The wisdom of widely held assumptions in a company or industry about what should be normal procedure and what practices won't work are often eventually tested, not by those with "experience," but by those without it, not by those in the industry, but by those outside of it.

Consider the rapid growth in the early 1970's of budget, economy motels offering single-room rates between $6 and $10—e.g., Motel 7, Scottish Inns of America, Econo-Travel. What is particularly interesting about this fast-growing facet of the motel/hotel industry is that it has been largely inspired by non-hotel people. According to *The Wall Street Journal*, the four or five most active economy motel chains are run by individuals with backgrounds in construction rather than hotel management.[9] Some of the practices common in these chains illustrate the inventiveness that sometimes springs from minds unencumbered by tradition:

Rooms are designed to reduce cleaning time. For example, beds are built flush to the floor so that area under them need not be cleaned.

Motel 6 forgoes dresser drawers in its rooms, since many people don't use them, and they take time to dust.

Expensive site studies are avoided by locating near a competitor that has likely already done one, such as Holiday Inn. In addition, since economy motels commonly do without restaurants, patrons can conveniently use the eating facilities of the neighboring competitor.[10]

What the preceding story suggests is that dogmatism concerning how marketing should and should not be done in a specific industry has certain conveniences but also some very real drawbacks. The "magic formula" for success, to be used over and over again once discovered, represents an unreachable goal. Changed market conditions, new technology, and other environmental forces will soon diminish the magic. Just a few years ago it would not have been difficult to find hotel executives ready to claim the impossibility of making big money in the industry when charging under $10 per room. And, indeed, with expensive, elegant lobbies, convention facilities, and sauna baths, it would be impossible. But, as in any other industry, different segments of the market search for different benefits when selecting from motel/hotel alternatives.

Recent experiences in the retail furniture industry also illustrate the dangers in assuming that there is one right way to conduct the business. It is in this industry that Levitz Furniture Corporation has now shattered the "conventional wisdom" that too much capital is required to maintain large, brand-name inventories of styles and fabrics, and, therefore, it is necessary that the consumers often wait six or more weeks for delivery of purchases. At Levitz, the consumer walks through a huge warehouse, neatly stacked with upward of $1 million worth of furniture inventory, eventually arriving at dozens of model room "vignettes." Upon making a selection, the merchandise is available to be brought out from the attached warehouse. If the consumer transports his purchase himself, he pays less.[11]

In sum, long experience in a given industry, with all of its obvious benefits, often seems to give rise to aspects of blindness and to dogma. Fresh insights and hard questions concerning traditional practices and industry assumptions are sometimes difficult to come by, and, yet, marketing, given the task of managing the fast-changing market, is not amenable to formula answers, to assumptions not continually tested.

Behavioral Change by the Consumer

One factor that sometimes contributes to poor marketing results is when a new product requires a strong behavioral change on the part of the consumer, and any resulting psychological discomfort on his part is not sufficiently minimized.

Very innovative new products that succeed on a large scale tend to do so on the basis of filling previously unmet market requirements, not on the basis of simply being different. However, we should not expect large segments of the consumer population to give up those behavioral "guidelines" provided by past experience with existing products. Whereas the existing consumption alternative allows the consumer knowledge on how to use the product, how well it works, and, in general, how to "act," the markedly novel product presents the same consumer with new risks, new uncertainties. If the potential benefits to be derived from "consuming" the new product appear sufficiently attractive, then enough consumers to make the product a success may be willing to proceed with the transaction and confront the risks of novelty. Such success can be enhanced via marketing actions designed to allay the perceived risk of novelty and minimize associated discomfort.

In the context of this concept, it is interesting to consider the failure of a well-financed attempt to provide doctors and hospitals with a computerized, medical diagnostic service. Specifically, the product involved a console hookup to central diagnostic computers, rendering unnecessary the transport of samples to pathology laboratories and the poring over medical texts to diagnose patient symptoms. It has been suggested that the venture failed, despite the very real attributes of the product, because "The customer was compelled to suddenly make an enormous change in his accustomed way of doing things, and to employ a strange and somewhat formidable piece of equipment that required special training in its use and in the interpretation of its output."[12]

Sometimes, even when research suggests otherwise, intuition contributes to ill-conceived new products. A case in point is the high-rise condominium developer in an eastern city who neglected a consultant's report advising against the ultimate location. Now that the development is being marketed it is meeting with resistance. Among the major problems are the location and the lack of sufficient space in the kitchen to eat there. Unfortunately, no research whatsoever was done concerning such considerations as the latter one.

The potential resistance on the part of consumers to new products requiring major behavioral shifts would seem an appropriate consideration for bankers in the marketing of automatic cash dispensing and teller equipment. Despite the ostensible convenience benefits of the money machines for certain segments of the market, usage data remain decidedly undramatic at this point in time.[13] The reality that the new money machines require people to radically alter established procedure for making cash deposits, withdrawals, and fund transfers between accounts is undoubtedly pertinent to the market results achieved thus far. The following quotations, taken from the 1972 Bank Marketing Association report, illustrate the point:

"I'll never use the machine again unless the bank is very busy. I tried to use it and it withheld my card.

"The machine ate up my husband's card. He tried four different numbers, then it took the card away. He was frightened, mad, felt rejected.

"It kept my . . . card and didn't give me any money. They kept the card after the third try and somebody said I must be real stupid, wasn't using it right. That I remember.

"I was one of the first to do business with the machine. I use it to withdraw money from my checking account even when the bank is open. But for making deposits either in my savings or checking account I don't trust the machine to handle my money properly. I want to be there, see the teller do it, have it entered in my passbook. I do worry that the machine might not record properly and I'd lose my money.

"I will not use it for deposits. Don't trust it. The machine will probably work but if something goes wrong, the bank is more likely to believe the machine than me." [14]

In sum, when a new product involves substantial behavioral change on the part of the consumer, care should be taken to minimize his potential discomfort or "psychological cost." To ignore this marketing opportunity is to accept the risk that many prospective customers might choose to avoid the discomfort of the new product rather than take advantage of its supposed benefits. Such a risk would be especially acute in circumstances where the new product did not offer benefits perceived by the consumer to be of major importance.

Viewing Social Movements as Problems

Still another common mistake that many executives make involves their company's response to pertinent social movements affecting or potentially affecting the business—e.g., consumerism, environmentalism, or women's liberation. All too frequently, corporate responses to such movements range from apathy ("It's not our problem") to aggression ("If they want a fight, they have come to the right place") to despair ("If these consumerists aren't careful, they'll ruin the entire industry"). Perhaps the one commonality among all of these responses is that they are all premised on the social movement in question being a problem, rather than an opportunity. That this is not necessarily the wisest orientation has already been well-demonstrated by especially responsive firms. This is not to suggest that all socially oriented demands presented to business are legitimate and therefore worthy of corporate remedy. Nor is this to suggest that all groups pushing for more corporate social re-

sponsibility of one kind or another are, in fact, always socially responsible in their own actions. Rather, the point is that, where it exists, the "blanket," unthinking corporate response to the social movements of our times as representing unjust and damaging problems for the business is both naive and self-defeating. Moreover, such a response fails to acknowledge that aggressive corporate responsibility can significantly contribute to increased corporate profitability.

In short, in an era of real and substantive social change that is more "pro-people" in character than "anti-business," the sensible and pragmatic alternative facing business is to search for the opportunity afforded by the changing climate. For example:

"Become the activist in finding ways to give people what they need; that is, ways to create economic and social profit at the same time. Indeed, there is much potential in viewing this new age as reflective not of problems but of opportunities in market needs to be served." [15]

One example of the potential in viewing social movements as opportunities rather than problems is afforded by the supermarket industry where a small group of regional chains (King Soopers in Denver, Jewel in Chicago, and Giant Foods in Maryland, Virginia, and Washington, D.C.) have been outcompeting larger, national companies. A primary tool in the recent successes of these three companies has been sensitive and sincere investment in the changing climate of the 1970's, particularly consumerism and environmentalism. The three chains have consistently been the first in their respective markets to innovate on behalf of the consumer—e.g., unit pricing, open dating, nutritional labeling, and consumer education through advertising, booklets, and leaflets. In addition, King Soopers has maintained a vigorous role in the ecology movement by sponsoring tree planting and waste product recycling programs, among others. [16]

Recent market results achieved by the three chains are noteworthy. For example, in Denver, an annual market survey published by a major newspaper there reveals that with respect to "grocery store preference," [17] the percentage of shoppers naming King Soopers has risen from 24% in 1969 to 36% in 1972. In the same time frame, the percentages for all other major chains in the area have either dropped or remained about the same.[18] In Chicago, Jewel's market share has climbed from 21% in 1969 to 30% in 1973, while National Tea slipped from 16% to 14% and A&P from 11% to 7%.[19]

Whirlpool is another illustration of a company that has benefited substantially in sales gains because of its consumer response programs. Beginning in 1964 when Whirlpool began making appreciable investments toward upgrading its field service organization, and taking into account more recent actions, such as establishing the COOL LINE (a nationwide telephone system enabling Whirlpool customers to call the company free should problems arise), Whirlpool has clearly demonstrated that corporate responsibility and corporate profitability can exist at the same time, in the same organization.[20]

In sum, the changing social environment of business presents opportunities to business that are very often perceived as problems. The tendency for management to have this perception often leads to responses that are essentially nonexistent, defensive, or cosmetic. What is overlooked is the tangible market opportunity that is often available, given sincere concern for the consumer and the larger society in which he lives, and the willingness to invest in behalf of this concern. Just as Chrysler has probably done itself more harm than good with its poorly executed, but well advertised, "Your Man in Detroit" campaign featuring Byron Nichols, so has American Motors done superbly with its "Buyer Protection Plan." In 1972 and 1973, among other features, this plan offered new car owners virtually "no-questions-asked" repairs on anything during the first year or 12,000 miles. My own conclusion, having studied both programs, is that American Motors made an investment in consumerism, while Chrysler took the "cosmetic" approach. It is not surprising, therefore, that in 1973 American Motors had its best six-month period in 13 years, and at least one consumer organization

was receiving more consumer complaints about Byron Nichols than about Chrysler cars.[21]

Opportunities for Consideration

The preceding discussion has had as its purpose the bringing together of some commonly made marketing mistakes in the hopes that presenting them herein might contribute to the capacity for avoiding them in the future. A major assumption underlying an article of this type, of course, is that "recognition" of an actual or potential marketing flaw in the business is an important and necessary step toward overcoming or avoiding it. The following suggestions, relating to one or more of the marketing errors considered here should be of particular interest to readers who feel this article has "struck close to home."

1. *Do internal marketing to facilitate external marketing.* The management task has traditionally been thought of as getting things done through people. Perhaps a better way to view this task, if the substance of the business is to be protected, is ". . . getting people to achieve through work."[22] Importantly, if employees, whose actions impact on the customer, are to be exceptionally motivated, they must have a job worth being exceptionally motivated for. A sense of high purpose and involvement in the job, pride in the company, respect for management are results that can only be earned, and only over time. The marketing concept calls for serving the consumer need, but, to facilitate this, management must also serve the employee need. That is, effective internal marketing contributes to effective external marketing.

The president of A-P-A Transport Company, a highly efficient, medium-sized, New Jersey trucking company, is one executive who practices internal marketing by consistently demonstrating with deeds the importance of the individual worker and his achievements—e.g., holding regular breakfast meetings with his drivers to discuss whatever is on their minds, or building a $500,000 health and recreation center for employees and their families on land adjacent to the North Bergen Terminal. According to *Business Week,* the real key to A-P-A's success is that management has been able ". . . to motivate A-P-A workers to work consistently at a very high level of productivity."[23]

2. *Provide incentives to encourage long-run thinking.* As long as corporate managements talk about the long-run but, in fact, pay and promote people on the basis of the short-run, any thoughts about responsibly building strength and protecting freedoms for years ahead will in reality continue to be routinely compromised. The challenge was aptly stated by Ackerman when he wrote as follows:

"The directives from top management, couched in terms of appeals to long-term benefits and corporate responsibility, fail to provoke acceptable action or achievement. Heads nod in agreement, but the chief executive's wishes are largely ignored. Managers in the operating units lack evidence of the corporation's commitment to the cause; responsibilities are unclear, scorecards are lacking, and rewards for successes or penalties for failures are absent. The managers view as foolhardy any attempt to implement the policy at the risk of sacrificing financial and operating performance."[24]

To foster long-run marketing thinking in an organization, management must face up to the complex but necessary challenge of modifying the criteria used to evaluate and, in turn, reward, subordinates. For example, a section of a periodic, personnel evaluation instrument might refer to activities that specifically contribute to making the company stronger five years from today.

At the same time, management should perhaps give consideration to the potential benefits of keeping good executives in the same job longer. Although internal job-hopping has some obvious advantages, such a system does tend to make "fast results" an important goal for individuals in these jobs, while sometimes camouflaging the source of marketing misdeeds when the long-run eventually occurs and the company begins to suffer.

What has just been said in the preceding two paragraphs also applies to the top management of a firm. Appointing a new president with the mandate to quickly turn the company around often results in the cutting of necessary cost centers as well as unnecessary ones. Similarly, the 63-year-old president facing mandatory retirement at 65 may find it difficult to get too excited about preparing his company for the technology expected to "revolutionize" the industry by 1980.

3. *Bring outsiders into the business.* As an example, one suggestion I would make to larger soft-drink bottlers is to bring in a soft-drink "outsider" as a member of the management group. By "outsider," I mean someone with solid experience in industry, but not in the soft-drink industry. Curiosity, imagination, interpersonal skills, and pragmatism would be especially important qualities for this person to have. Properly slotted into the management group of a bottling plant, such a person could potentially bring keen insight and resulting innovation into a business that tends to be tradition-bound. Being tradition-bound is perilous indeed in an industry buffeted by the environmental movement and facing such issues as: potential "health" problems with sugar; a possible ban of saccharin, now used in diet drinks instead of cyclamates; severe competition for supermarket shelf-space; the emergence of competitive, direct-to-consumer soft-drink stores (such as Lolli Pop, Pop Shoppes); major brand price wars; and the inroads made by private label soft drinks (such as Safeway's Cragmont brand) and "energy"-oriented beverages (such as Gatorade), and so on.

The point of this example is that one way to help overcome the blind spots of too much experience in a specific industry is to combine it with nonexperience in that industry. The "outsider," if he's the right person for the job and if he is truly given access to top management, can be expected to pay for himself many times over in just the questions he raises. Naturally, once the outsider gets too much industry experience, he, too, must make way for a new novice.

4. *When confronting the consumer with extreme novelty, encourage a "trial" run.* One potentially fruitful approach for helping consumers overcome psychological resistance to new products requiring major behavioral shifts is to provide incentives encouraging a trial run. Such a trial run, if success-

fully dealt with by the consumer, should allow subsequent encounters with the novel product to appear psychologically less formidable. For example, one large savings and loan association introduced a new cash dispensing machine by mailing 30,000 cards to area residents offering rewards to those who came in and tried the machine out. With the special cards, users could try the machine, which was temporarily set up to dispense envelopes with two coupons instead of money. One coupon was for a premium and another was a ticket for a grand prize type of drawing. According to *Savings and Loan News*,[25] the S&L had a 10% response to the mailing, opened about 1,000 card accounts, and overall, has developed one of the higher machine usage totals in the savings and loan industry.

Similarly, several years ago Continental Airlines sponsored a program whereby consumers who had never flown before could, for a fare of $10, take a plane trip on any of the company's routes if (1) empty seats were available and (2) the return trip was made on the next available Continental flight. The stated purpose of the experiment was to help people who had never flown before get a "feel" for flying and, in the process, relinquish a resistance to flying.

5. *Prepare an annual social plan.* Just as the marketing educator now routinely stresses to his students the need for the firm to prepare an annual marketing plan, so will he soon be stressing the need to develop an annual social plan as well. Already, many firms could benefit from such a document, though relatively few seem to avail themselves of the opportunity. The same firm that will invest heavily in developing annual product marketing plans very often will spend minimal sums when it comes to planning for corporate social programs. And yet, the 1970's is quickly proving itself as an era in which the traditional business of business is being modified in the face of potent social change.

A major pharmaceutical company well illustrates the point. Each year, middle management teams present very extensive product marketing plans to higher management in an annual meeting. Social planning, however, is ignored. And yet this particular company actually or potentially faces a number of crises concerning such issues as unwise consumer use of their products, improper pricing practices, the repeal of anti-substitution laws, and so on. Rather than such issues as these being studied and analyzed in a plan, with action positions and contingency options developed, they are, instead, dealt with on a crisis basis, one by one, as the issue evolves to major proportions.

As the present decade continues to unfold, more and more executives will come to view social planning to be as important as they now regard marketing planning to be. The social planning that evolves will be far more encompassing than the more closely written affirmative action programs, or something similarly concentrated. Rather, such plans will analyze environmental forces having meaning to the business, and map out coordinated strategies to capitalize on these forces. Consumer, community-action, and related programs will be planned with the same care and precision taken for granted in other types of corporate planning.

Conclusion

This article has attempted to describe some commonly made marketing errors and to indicate some opportunities for avoiding them. Although marketing itself is inherent to organizations, good marketing is not. And yet, in a fast-changing and, for many firms, highly competitive environment, good marketing takes on special importance. Hopefully, this article will prove helpful to those interested in improving the marketing performance of organizations which they manage.

Notes

1. See Peter F. Drucker, *Managing for Results* (New York, Harper and Row, 1964), especially chap. 6.
2. See "Eastern Clips Its Troubled Wings," *Business Week*, October 6, 1973, p. 48.
3. "Floyd Hall's Problems at Eastern," *Business Week*, August 18, 1973, p. 61.

4. As documented by a national survey privately conducted for the firm.

5. B. Charles Ames, "Trappings vs. Substance in Industrial Marketing," *Harvard Business Review*, July–August 1970, p. 98.

6. This figure is derived from an advertisement sponsored by *Forbes* magazine and appearing in *Advertising Age*, November 10, 1969, p. 82.

7. Leonard L. Berry and James S. Hensel, "Why Some New Bank Products Fail," *Bankers Monthly*, July 15, 1973, p. 26.

8. Ibid., pp. 26–27.

9. "Economy Motels Lure Travelers with Prices as Low as $6 a Room," *The Wall Street Journal*, December 26, 1972, p. 1.

10. Ibid.

11. "Levitz: The Hot Name in 'Instant' Furniture," *Business Week*, December 4, 1971, p. 90.

12. Theodore Levitt, "Production-Line Approach to Service," *Harvard Business Review*, September–October 1972, p. 49.

13. See "Automated Tellers: A Report to the Banking Industry," *Management Practice*, a quarterly publication of Coloney, Cannon, Main, and Pursell, Inc., Management Consultants, April 23, 1973.

14. Sidney J. Levy and Shirly Greene, *Man's Interface with the Money Machine* (Chicago, Bank Marketing Association, 1972), p. 43.

15. Leonard L. Berry and James S. Hensel, "Public Relations: Opportunity in the New Society," *Arizona Business*, August–September 1973, p. 15.

16. For additional information on King Soopers' program, see ibid., pp. 18–21; for additional information on Jewel's program, see "Freeze II Puts the Squeeze on Jewel," *Business Week*, June 30, 1973, pp. 44–45; for additional information on Giant Food's program, see "Company Performance Roundup—Giant Food, Inc.," *Business and Society*, Autumn 1972, pp. 91–92.

17. "Grocery store preference" was determined by asking respondents "where do you buy most of your groceries?"

18. *The Denver Post 1972 Consumer Analysis of the Denver Metropolitan Market—Sixteenth Annual Report*, compiled and published by *The Denver Post*, 1972.

19. "Freeze II Puts the Squeeze on Jewel," op. cit., p. 46.

20. For a more detailed description of Whirlpool's consumer-response programs, see Juel M. Ranum, "Meeting the Demands of the Consumer," an address to the Conference "Corporate Social Responsibility: An Assessment," October 12, 1972, New York (mimeographed).

21. "More Talk Than Action on Consumer Complaints," *Business Week*, May 19, 1973, p. 66.

22. John Adams, Jr., "Put Profit in Its Place," *Harvard Business Review*, March–April 1973, p. 154.

23. "A-P-A Makes the Short Haul Profitable," *Business Week*, October 6, 1973, p. 118.

24. Robert W. Ackerman, "How Companies Respond to Social Demands," *Harvard Business Review*, July–August 1973, p. 92.

25. Based on Ralph W. Jones, "Management of New Products," *The Journal of Industrial Engineering*, September–October 1958.

Questions

1. *Why is marketing blamed for so many mistakes made by companies in their relations with customers? Marketing managers in many firms do not determine "the business" of the company, so why are they responsible if the firm is in the "wrong business"?*

2. *Why do many young executives make marketing decisions that promise good short-run results, even if they are not the best decisions for the long run?*

3. *Review the author's five suggestions for avoiding the most common marketing mistakes. Consider an organization to which you belong. How might those suggestions help your organization avoid making a marketing mistake?*

PART TWO

The Analysis of Marketing Opportunities

"If you can't decide what to do with your free time, you might spend part of it finding out what to do with the rest of it. For a small fee, a leisure consultant will help you out." [1] At a time when free time is seen as an increasingly valuable asset, one segment of America seems willing to pay for a service that recommends what to do to have fun!

In 1979, energy shortages threatened to disrupt the social and economic stability of the United States. To motivate Americans to practice energy conservation both assiduously and voluntarily necessitated effecting fundamental changes in their attitudes toward energy use. [2] This was a marketing task.

"Television was yesterday's miracle. Qube is today's. The age of passive viewing is over." [3] This message was declared on an oversized color brochure advertising the instant viewer-response cable TV concept that was introduced in 1977. Advertisers began to use Qube's interactive capability to disseminate information, for direct marketing, and to pretest commercials and concepts. A little black box, about the size of a hand-held calculator, next to viewers' TV sets allows cable subscribers to respond instantly to questions, polls, and advertisements.

The energy market of the early 1980s represents a multitude of targets of opportunity for high-technology companies. Unquestionably, there will be needs to satisfy. The "winners," that is, the companies that succeed in making profits by serving those needs, will be identified by superior marketing research and management as well as by technical superiority. [4]

1. Laurel Leff, "Leisure Consultants Are Part Dr. Freud and Part Dear Abby," *Wall Street Journal,* September 12, 1978, p. 1.
2. William L. Shanklin, "The Energy Crisis and Consumer Behavior," *Atlanta Economic Review,* May–June 1978, pp. 28–32.
3. Linda A. Gluck, "How Cable TV Provides Instant Answers," *Stores,* July 1978, pp. 44–45.
4. Harry M. St. John, "The Energy Market for High-Technology Companies," *Journal of Marketing,* October 1978, pp. 46–53.

It is the role of marketing in the organization to plan, price, promote, and distribute want-satisfying products to consumers and industrial users. To formulate marketing strategy, each organization must (1) select one or more *target markets* among persons identified as both having wants and being able, willing, and authorized to purchase available want-satisfying products; and (2) create and maintain a complete marketing mix that satisfies the wants of members of the target market and contributes to the attainment of organizational objectives.

Analyzing marketing opportunities is management's critical first step in preparing to formulate marketing strategy. Marketing opportunity analysis activities are undertaken to determine the character, magnitude, and location of potential demand for want-satisfying products. This task requires an understanding of consumer behavior. Marketers must know something about potential consumers' wants and desires and about their decision-making processes if they are to create a satisfying marketing mix. Each opportunity analysis should also include an assessment of the extent to which other organizations already serve any identified wants. It is the task of marketing research to provide marketing managers with information about potential consumers, competitors, and other facts that could influence the organization's success in the marketplace.

The selections in Part Two provide an overview of the nature of marketing research, consumer behavior, and marketing opportunity analysis. In the first selection, the success story of Agree Creme Rinse and Agree Shampoo is told. The secret to the Johnson Wax Company's successful maiden voyage in the personal care product business was solid marketing research and wise market segmentation. The second piece, by noted product management specialist C. Merle Crawford, reviews the reasons why most new products do not achieve commercial success.

Too many people view marketing research as an extremely complex business made up of computers, models, and statistical gymnastics. This need not be so, says Michael F. d'Amico in the third article. Small business managers can generate useful facts and data without computers and esoteric statistics. The next two articles in this part belong to a series of articles that appeared in *Feedstuffs,* a trade magazine of the agribusiness industry. These two articles illustrate some innovative and interesting marketing research approaches and findings.

The seventh article contains a systematic approach that managers may take in conducting a market opportunity analysis. And the sixth and the last articles focus on two specific market segments that promise opportunity for the astute marketer: working women and the elderly.

4

Key Role of Research
in Agree's Success Is Told

MARKETING NEWS

Marketing research cannot guarantee success, but it can improve a manager's chances of making correct decisions. Johnson Wax's successful use of marketing research in introducing Agree is the focus of this article.

"The most successful new product introduction in the history of Johnson Wax" was how two marketing research executives of the company (formally S. C. Johnson & Son, Racine, Wis.) referred to the debut of Agree Creme Rinse and Agree Shampoo.

The appraisal was made before the recent Midwest Research Conference sponsored by the AMA's Chicago Chapter. The joint presentation was made by Frederic D. Nordeen, marketing research manager, and Neil DeClerk, associate marketing research manager.

"Marketing research was involved every step of the way," Nordeen said, recalling that Agree Creme Rinse, launched in 1977, has taken a 20% share of the market for its category and is No. 1 in unit volume.

Agree Shampoo, for which advertising didn't start until last August, also is "on target and doing very well," DeClerk said.

Marketing research at Johnson Wax, Nordeen said, "helped identify the opportunity, define who our target user should be, define our positioning and strategy, and define the physical features and performance attributes" of the Agree products.

Source: Marketing News, January 12, 1979, pp. 14–15. Reprinted from *Marketing News* published by the American Marketing Association.

"As positions and strategies were fine-tuned, as formulas were developed, and as advertising was written, we tested to make sure that we stayed on track," DeClerk said.

"We did a lot of work. We fielded more than 50 individual research projects from late 1975 until national introduction of Agree Shampoo this past summer. There were focus groups, concept studies, concept product studies, product testing, advertising testing, extended use testing, a laboratory test market, and a test market.

"I can't tell you how much we spent, but two research suppliers retired. If Fred and I had been on commission, we wouldn't have to be here today," he said. "But we were serious, and we were thorough."

"Finally, when we were ready, we put it all together with finished product and a detailed marketing plan and we tested them—first in a laboratory test market, then in a controlled store test market," Nordeen said.

"Johnson wax had been flirting with the personal care business since the mid-1960s, when a technical breakthrough led to Edge, a truly superior men's shave cream," he said. "Today, Edge is a strong No. 2 brand in its field—and gaining.

"Edge, our first success, and even our personal care product failures, taught us two simple lessons:

"We could profitably market a personal care product possessing a 'product plus,' and
"We could *not* profitably market a 'me-too' product.

"This commitment to the 'product plus' philosophy by Johnson Wax means we will only market new products demonstrably superior to competitive ones and recognizable as such by consumers," he said.

"With Edge, we'd had our appetite whetted for the personal care business, and we wanted more.

"And, when we looked over the field, it quickly became apparent that women's hair care was an area of interest. It was big, growing, and it fit our R&D abilities and marketing skills. In 1970, we began to explore the area."

"Over the next three years, we explored and eliminated several hair care products," DeClerk said. "We considered:

"Hair dressings (the category wasn't growing),

"Hair coloring (we didn't have the technological base), and

"Hair sprays (but changes in style and practices were trending women away from hair sprays)."

"This left shampoos and creme rinse/conditioners, and work began in the early 1970s which has led to Agree Creme Rinse and now to Agree Shampoo," Nordeen said.

"Before we decided to develop these products, marketing research's part had been fairly passive. We were called upon to establish market sizes and trends and generally review the attitudes of users and nonusers. But, once targets were set, marketing research assumed a more active role."

"In 1971, before we had begun to concentrate on shampoo and creme rinse, a mail panel study of hair care practices was conducted among a large national probability sample of women," DeClerk said. "It provided a broad background of knowledge of hair care practices, characteristics of women's hair, and user and nonuser data.

"And it gave an early indication of some directions of change. Compared to some 1965 background data, it showed women were shampooing more frequently, were more likely to use creme rinses and conditioners, and to a greater extent than in the past, perceived themselves to have oily hair," DeClerk said. "Oiliness, the mail panel showed, was the No. 1 problem."

"Agree Shampoo and Agree Creme Rinse at first

were on parallel development paths," Nordeen said. "Originally it had been planned that the shampoo come first, with the creme rinse to follow.

"But, since you can't always schedule R&D success and the creme rinse was ready before the shampoo, it was introduced first, in 1977, and quickly was a success."

Both products, DeClerk said, were targeted toward "greasies."

"How did we get to 'greasies'?

"We knew patterns were changing, oily hair was a problem, and more a problem among the young: the prime target, the most frequent users, and the most receptive to new ideas."

"In 1973 and 1974, we fine-tuned our approach to this market," Nordeen said. "We conducted many focus groups among all types of women, but increasingly we came to zero in on the young.

"This was a new experience for us at Johnson Wax. We were used to researching the attitudes and behavior of the housewife," he said.

"Now we needed to talk to her daughter, to understand teenage girls—some as young as 13—and reach them with both qualitative and quantitative research. This was a new (and more expensive) approach for us.

"Using focus groups to further our understanding of users' problems and perceptions—and also to get early reactions to some product concepts—we found that we were on the right path. The oiliness problems were major, and our ideas were regarded as important by the potential users."

"But," DeClerk said, "while the marketing research was telling us that we were working in interesting areas, R&D wasn't having as much luck.

"After many months of trying, it became apparent that the new technology just wasn't going to work for the shampoo, and we returned to ground zero.

"And, in a major disappointment, the Agree Creme Rinse formula failed to beat its major competitor in internal R&D testing. It was back to the drawing board."

"Then R&D came through on the creme rinse, developing a formula with no oil except for the fragrance, less than 0.25%," Nordeen said. "This made our communication to the consumer easier.

"It was during this time that (over a long lunch) 'Helps stop the greasies' was born."

So Agree Creme Rinse took the lead and ultimately would beat the shampoo to market. But shampoo development continued. It had its own R&D team and was making good progress toward a formula. Since Agree Creme Rinse had established the brand's positioning, shampoo work became more focused, DeClerk said.

"Early in 1975 we were into copy development," he said. "Some focus groups conducted at that time gave us our first exposure to our ultimate theme. These groups gave us insight into the virtues of several alternative 'reasons why' a shampoo would keep hair cleaner longer.

"They showed that users would be uncomfortable with heavy 'scientific' reasons. The communication task was really a simple one—to talk about cleaning.

"But, we certainly didn't stop with focus groups," he said. "We conducted quantified concept tests among target users."

The two researchers showed a "good example of a bad concept," an ad with "a laundry list of benefits, something for everyone. And it turned people off with 'special ingredients,' " DeClerk said.

Creative development now began in earnest, and the first of the commercials was written, Nordeen recalled. In the summer of 1975, the first shampoo commercial was rough produced and tested.

"At that time," he said, "we were on an early wording of our ultimate claim. We promised Agree would help keep hair cleaner longer. But after testing, it was back to writing copy.

"With the successful introduction of Agree Creme Rinse and its establishment of the term 'the greasies' as part of the language, our claim was modified to 'helps stop the greasies—between shampoos,' " Nordeen said. "Actually 17 new commercials have been tested using copy testing methods that offer us the best blend of measures of communication, motivation, and diagnostic help.

"We are finding, as time passes, that the motiva-

tion and communication scores are falling into predictable ranges, but that the diagnostic analysis of the ratings and open-end responses are providing valuable guidance. The commercials have been getting better as we learn more.

"By late 1975, the lab was making progress on the shampoo. A first formula was blind-tested against a target competitor and was significantly preferred," he said.

"This was the first of what ultimately was a series of more than 20 of these studies among 8,000 women—testing Agree and its formula refinements against the nine leading competitors, which were doing about 60% of all shampoo business. We were determined to have a 'product plus.' "

"Our test design used a blind-paired comparison among members of a mail panel," DeClerk said. "We placed products with 400 women and had them use each for two weeks. At the end of the use period, a telephone interview determined their preferences overall and their ratings on 15 to 20 performance attributes. And we asked open-end questions for supporting diagnostics."

Nordeen emphasized that they "early established the strategy for Agree Shampoo, defined our target, and consistently tested against the strategy. Product tests made sure the product delivered the right benefits to the right people—that the product was superior in the areas we claimed.

"Ad development and testing always made sure we were expressing our strategy well to those we wanted to reach. With all this behind us, we were ready to put the package together and get our first reactions to the total brand," he said.

"Up to now marketing research had been testing elements of the total product—performance, positioning, advertising—but in the meantime product management was developing the marketing plan," DeClerk said.

"From now on our concern was mainly with the plan, not so much the individual pieces," he said.

The first real test of the plan, according to Nordeen, was a lab test market, a technique that simulates the awareness, trial, and repurchase sequences by using a finished commercial and final label product and by providing a shopping situation in a simulated store, actual use, and simulated repurchase.

"Various assumptions can be made for levels of distribution, levels of ad effectiveness in building awareness, variations in the purchase cycle, and effects on trial of different sampling plans. We find it a valuable tool to test the effects of different combinations of marketing assumptions. We have confidence mainly because of a good track record with the model," Nordeen said.

"For example, our model predicted Agree Creme Rinse's test market share almost dead on and was only slightly lower than the ultimate national share.

"Then, because we sweetened the national plan to include more media and more sampling, we got better distribution than we'd fed into the program. In fact, when the model was rerun with results from our national introduction it came within a point of the real share."

"The Agree Shampoo lab test market was conducted in Fresno, Calif., and South Bend, Ind., two of the markets in which Agree Creme Rinse had been test marketed," DeClerk said.

"By using these cities, where the first Agree had been sold for more than a year, we were able to simulate the real-world time lapse between the introductions. This was key, since much of the shampoo's story and its appeal would play off the creme rinse's image.

"Frankly, we were nervous," he said. "We had committed more money to Agree Creme Rinse than to any other product we'd introduced, and now we were planning to go even further out on the limb with shampoo.

"But, we needn't have worried. The model predicted a share which met the objectives of the marketing plan. We got good trial based on advertising. We had good repurchase and retention rates. Our sampling program worked. And the model let us test various mixes of two different size samples.

"We wound up using a lower-cost sample in a mass co-op mailing, reserving a more expensive 2-oz. trial-size bottle for individual mailings to smaller numbers of identified target users.

"We had a 'go' for our national plan," DeClerk said.

"But, we're a cautious bunch," Nordeen said. "The women had only used the product for four weeks. Maybe they'd tire of it. Maybe there were some negatives. Maybe the basic promise, 'Helps stop the greasies between shampoos,' would lose its appeal.

"So, just before we started the lab test market, we began an extended-use study. We went back to Fresno and South Bend, the markets where Agree Creme Rinse had been test marketed, and we placed fully labeled, market-ready product.

"We placed the product with women who had read a print ad describing Agree Shampoo and who were willing to pay real money to buy a bottle.

"These women were meant to simulate real-world triers. They understood the promise. They were motivated to buy and presumably would use the product with the same expectations as a real-world trier would," Nordeen said.

"These women were called back at four-week intervals over 16 weeks and resupplied with product during the test if they wished to continue.

"There were very few who dropped out—hardly any for product-related reasons. They rated the product at each of the four callbacks on a long list of attributes.

"The ratings never varied; the actual ounces used were measured, and there was no slowdown in use. No long-term negatives showed up; the brand even seemed to gain strength as time went by.

"Now we were ready for test market," DeClerk said. "Actually, we'd begun planning the test market months before—even before the lab test market. But the good lab test market results gave us the green light to spend quite a bit of money on bottle and cap molds and on making and filling equipment.

"But, we couldn't be ready for test market until late summer or early fall of 1977," he said.

"Caution told us not to start a test market late in the fall. Previous experience with holiday season test marketing made us wary, and we elected to start a test market in January, 1978."

"We had faced a basic decision months before on what kind of test market we needed—on what the test market objectives were," Nordeen said.

"Our decision was easy. We had a sales success with Agree Creme Rinse and we knew we'd have no trouble getting distribution of Agree Shampoo. So sales ability wasn't the question; there was no need to sell in.

"What we needed was carefully to measure consumer response to the execution of the marketing plan. Therefore," he said, "we elected to conduct a controlled store test."

"For a change," DeClerk said, "we had some time to plan. The delay from fall, 1977, to January, 1978, allowed us to gather good base data and to use it to specify store patterns of shelf location, facings, prices, and promotional support.

"In effect, we went—store by store—through the stores we were going to audit and executed in each store what the response to the Agree Shampoo marketing plan would likely be.

"We even built some inefficiencies into our test market," he said. "For example, not all stores had both sizes of all types, and not all stores would participate in promotions. So, in effect, we were simulating trade response to the marketing plan."

"The proposed national plan was translated to test market in South Bend and Fresno," Nordeen said. "Because we were in a controlled store test we got instant distribution, and the ad and promotion timetable could begin on the same day we stocked shelves.

"During the test market we duplicated the gross-rating-point (GRP) levels of the national television plan. We simulated magazine coupon ads via newspaper inserts. We dropped co-op samples to the proper number of households. And we mailed single trial-size bottles to a list of the younger target users.

"We were careful to not overkill. We were interested in the true share, not how high we could make it," Nordeen said.

"We test marketed in the two Agree Creme Rinse test markets because the shampoo and creme rinse are companions and we needed to test the shampoo in a mature creme rinse situation. We had food, drug, and mass merchandiser stores in our panel, and we ran a tightly controlled test," DeClerk said.

"In all of these stores, we maintained a specified shelf location, a specified price, a specified item array, and a specified number of facings," he said. "Each store was visited regularly, some as often as three times a week, to insure that the plan was being followed."

"Store audits," Nordeen said, "were conducted and reported monthly, with adjustments made to compensate for the 100% distribution of the audit panel and for the super-efficiency of controlled store shelf management.

"The reduction factor we use for 'controlled store effect' is 15% (that is, 85% of the volume achieved in this special situation). This number, we have found, accurately reflects this special attention," Nordeen said.

DeClerk added that the test market was not only a vehicle for measuring sales and share but also enabled the company to test elements of the marketing plan on the firing line.

"We conducted qualitative studies among both purchasers and nonpurchasers as well as quantitative studies to measure how many and what kind of households got our samples," he said. "We measured how many sample receivers used our sample and how many went on to purchase.

"We measured rates of awareness and trial at eight, 13, and 26 weeks, and we probed for the attitudes toward the advertising and the product. In each of these studies we were measuring performance against an objective, a goal detailed in the marketing plan," he said.

"The net of all of our test market experience was positive," said Nordeen. "We achieved our share goals, our rates of awareness and trial were satisfactory, and our sampling worked. We were ready to go. And we did.

"In our first year, we will spend more than $30 million in advertising, sampling, couponing, trade deals, and public relations," he said. There's a lot riding on Agree Shampoo, but early results are favorable.

"We got excellent distribution very early and the product is moving off the shelves at the rate we expected. We're confident we have a success."

"Marketing research will have had a real part in the success of Agree Shampoo. We helped identify the opportunity, helped define the target user, helped define the positioning and strategy, and helped define the attributes and features the product should have," DeClerk said.

"Finally we tested the marketing plan. We did all these things, maybe not in as neat an order as in the textbooks, but we did them."

Questions

1. *What is marketing research?*
2. *Based on the lessons learned from Agree's success, prepare a brief argument for the value of marketing research for decision makers.*

5

Marketing Research
and the New Product
Failure Rate

C. MERLE CRAWFORD

*The overall rate of new product failures is terribly high.
Why hasn't the rate of new product success climbed as
a result of the many advances in marketing research
technology over the past twenty-five years?*

This article is based on these two premises: one,
the overall rate of new product failures remains
high, perhaps as high as 25 years ago; two, most
causes of failure are (or should be) amenable to
marketing research.

Continuance of the Failure Rate

On the question of failure rate, a review of the literature turns up surprisingly little documentation for
the frequent claim that 80% of all new products fail,
but it does show a continuing failure rate of considerable dimensions. Available references, cited in
the Bibliography, offer the following:

New Food and Drug Items:
  Nielson: 53% failed in 1971 versus 46% in 1962
    [14]
  Business Week: 50–80% failed [4]
  Rosen: Over 80% failed [16]
  Dodd: Over 80% failed [7]
  Helene Curtis: 43% failed [9]
  United Kingdom: Over 40% failed [8]

Source: Journal of Marketing, April 1977, pp. 51–61. Reprinted from *Journal of Marketing* published by the American Marketing Association.

New Consumer Goods (Primarily Packaged):
  Angelus: Over 80% failed [2]
  Booz, Allen & Hamilton (1968): 37% failed [3]
  The Conference Board: 40% failed [10]
  Ross Federal Research Corp.: 80% failed [15]
New Industrial Goods:
  The Conference Board: 20% failed [10]
  Booz, Allen & Hamilton (1968): 30 to 40% failed
    [3]
New "Products":
  U.S. Dept. of Commerce: 90% failed [17]

These studies are difficult to compare because
they differ in their definitions of failure. One used
"Went into test market but never went national."
Another used "Disappearance from store shelves."
The best approach passed the responsibility of a
definition to marketing management, asking them
to say whether a product failed to meet expectations. Abandoned products fail, but so do many
low-profit products even though they are kept in
the line, since they would not have been marketed
had the outcome been predictable (granting the exceptions of service products such as rarely used
drugs and items marketed only to fill out a line).
Practical situational realities further complicate the
picture, of course, and other exceptions can be
found, as one study participant put it:

They may have introduced it as a diversionary tactic for someone else's new product . . . New flavors may cost almost nothing to bring to market,
add a little temporary interest to the line and are
then withdrawn.

Regardless of definition, all estimates would seem to indicate substantial room for improvement. It would be tough to argue that current failure rates are satisfactory, even though individual companies are sometimes content.

Indictment of Marketing Research

The second premise, that improper or inadequate use of marketing research is significantly at fault, also requires explanation and comment. Some of the studies of new product success rates referred to above also explored the causes of those failures. They looked at the reasons why selected items were withdrawn from the market or failed to meet profit goals. Several other investigators sought reasons for failure even when their research didn't attempt to assess failure rate.

Exhibit 1 tallies the reasons these investigators have cited for new product failure. (To facilitate comparison I have taken some liberty with terminology, but, hopefully, not with meaning or intent.) As is generally suspected (though perhaps equally disappointing) all studies point to lack of meaningfully superior product uniqueness as the predominant reason for failure. High on the list, also, are the factors of poor planning, poor timing, and the tendency to let enthusiasm override a more appropriate caution.

Comparing these reasons for failure with the claimed capability of marketing research, we can test the premise that the reasons offered for failure predominately indict attitudes or decisions which a good marketing research program could avoid.

One could probably argue that timing (Exhibit 1, #3) is not controllable. Ford Motor Co. could not stop the consumer's loss of interest in middle-sized cars during *Edsel's* last year of development (though they should have detected it). One firm rarely knows another's new product plans in any detail. And certainly the forecasting of major economic fluctuations defies expertise well beyond the capability of most firms' marketing research departments.

The other three top reasons, however, cannot be excused. Consider:

Technology presumably exists to measure product differences.

We claim to be able to measure and validate the effectiveness of various marketing strategies and plans.

All experienced corporate marketing researchers know it is predominantly their assignment to see that enthusiasm doesn't outrun the known facts.

In short, currently available marketing research capability does exist to avoid three of the four major reasons for new product failures.

Why Should a Sophisticated Technology Fail?

We have 50 years of technological developments, a growing body of psychological and mathematical hypotheses (if not theory or, in some cases, confirmed facts or laws), a reasonably complete literature, excellent journals, an eminently successful association (The American Marketing Association), a solidly established educational system, and a collection of practitioners which would compare favorably with that of any profession.

Why, then, do we have such a high rate of new product failures? Is it possible, as some of the research studies suggest, that the problem is one of people, not technology? If so, just what is wrong? Why do brand managers, product managers, and marketing managers ignore key data or refuse to finance research which would far more than recoup its costs? It would be ridiculous to suggest that they do so intentionally; the search for an answer has to lead elsewhere. Such, indeed, was the point of departure for this investigation, which has tapped the thoughts and (sometimes very strong) opinions of highly experienced and knowledgeable people.

A careful review of the available literature (books, magazine and newspaper articles, published speeches, company house organs, etc.), combined with my personal experience, produced a

Exhibit 1

Reasons for new product failures

	Abrams (1)	Angelus (2)	Booz, Allen, Hamilton (3)	Constandse (5)	Diehl (6)	Hopkins & Bailey (10)	MacDonald (11)	Miles (13)	TOTAL
1. Lacked meaningful product uniqueness[a]	X	X	X	X	X	X	X	X	8
2. Poor planning[b]	X	X		X	X	X	X		6
3. Timing wrong	X	X	X	X		X			5
4. Enthusiasm crowded on facts				X	X	X	X	X	5
5. Product failed	X	X				X			3
6. Product lacked a champion					X				1
7. Company politics					X				1
8. Unexpected high product cost						X			1

[a] In some cases there was, in fact, no difference, but in most cases there was some difference, whose value was overestimated by the marketers to potential buyers.

[b] Includes poor positioning, poor segmentation, underbudgeting, poor overall themes, over pricing, and all other facets of a plan.

series of first-approximation hypotheses, which were sent to five experienced marketing researchers.

Their response led to extensive revisions, additions, and deletions. It also led back to the literature for evidence to support this or refute that. The next version of the report was prepared as a working paper and was reviewed by sixteen more new product marketers. The result of this final round of review is the present report. Unfortunately, there seems neither solid fact nor unanimous opinion in support of any one of the hypotheses.

[For a list of the outstanding practitioners involved, see the notes at the end of the article.]

Consequently, it was decided to make this a preliminary or interim report. The answers to the basic question are offered as nine possible explanations. I prefer to think of them as hypotheses in the formal sense of the word. They are not yet theory, even though there is some empirical base for every one. Perhaps future experimentation and testing will provide a base for firm conclusion; most study participants think not. I myself give them, even now, the benefit of the doubt.

No significance should be attached to the order in which they are listed.

Hypothesis 1: Product Developers Fail to Define Their Decision Process Concisely and Completely

An effective, and efficient, role for any business research requires a reasonably clear decision process on the part of persons using the research results. That is to say, the research should produce data which relate to specific critical decisions. Every decision which moves a new product closer to market should have a time designation and should be integrated into an overall sequence. It should also have an understood importance designation, a mechanism for resolving the data into decision, and a clear indication of the risks (probabilities and costs) involved with various dimensions of error.

To clarify by example, this means that a decision on the trade incentive portion of a new product's marketing program has an ideal date and perhaps a latest time. The developer should also know how this decision relates to other decisions (e.g., pricing or channel choice) which precede or follow it. He should also be able to tell his researcher how critical this decision is, what criteria he plans to use (e.g., competitive margins, legal constraints, attitudes toward dealer premiums on this type of product), and some feeling as to the relative importance of these different facts.

Finally, he should know what danger dimension he faces—that is, how serious is an error, how likely is an error, and how correctable would one be. Thus he might know that the dealer incentive program is essential to stocking and that his overall push strategy requires prior distribution of high quality and quantity. But perhaps his experience warns him that companies typically err on the side of too little incentive, and he knows that once the opening trade program misfires, recovery is almost impossible over the near-term.

From all this a qualified marketing researcher can craft a research program that will be both effective and efficient.

Short of having such a decision process, the researcher must shotgun it—gather tons of data (or as much as he has budget for), not knowing which pieces are particularly relevant and useful to the decision maker. If he comes up with the needed data he's lucky, and he'll still be faulted for all the excess information compiled. His outside research suppliers are, of course, doubly in the dark—they are expected to make creative applications to decisions even their purchasing client doesn't know.

A particularly flagrant example of suboptimal research concerns remedial action plans, scheduled for implementation when and if troubles come after launch. If the product developer fails to anticipate the potential problems and establish appropriate action points for each remedial plan, he'll have researchers studying all facets of the market results rather than concentrating on the few pieces of data which are really key. Then when trouble does hit, panic actions will stem from the flood of disjointed research data.

If decision parameters are known, a researcher can creatively and selectively manage the research technology to bring to bear on each decision the research (and only that research) which the decision warrants. Unfortunately, this first hypothesis holds that marketing planners and other product developers all too often lack this decision sophistication. They stand caricatured by the chap who, when asked why he was taking a given item into test market, replied, "Why, to see if it will sell, of course!"

Nothing in this hypothesis should be construed as suggesting a lock-step, mandatory sequence of steps in the development of every new product. Some researchers have appeared to be seeking such a "system." Instead, this hypothesis actually takes the opposite stance—requiring that a *particular* decision sequence be developed, unique to the situation and responsive to its demands. A truly efficient marketing research program can then be assembled.

At least two of the reviewers believe this degree of disciplined thinking comes only with a boost from above, and they have both established standard hurdle systems for their firms' new entries. Still no lock-step, but the burden and initiative for skipping a key step lie with the developer—he must seek a variance. One of them concluded:

The CEO should insist that there is a "process" to be followed by his company . . . It will have appropriate safe-guards built in . . . The product will be in concert with pre-determined corporate goals and direction.

Hypothesis 2: New-Product Decision-Makers Really Don't Understand the Proper Role for Marketing Research

It is entirely possible that many managers of product development do not understand what marketing research can do for them. If they lack the ability to use marketing research efficiently, the entire new product development function is hobbled; marketing research directors are forced to accept a role for their function substantially less than optimum and then must sell their service against an unfavorable institutionalized misconception.

Are there *a priori* reasons why new product managers might not understand marketing research? Indeed there are, and *by far the most persuading is the non-marketing background* of many persons making the key intermediate new product decisions; they have never worked in a situation where an organized research function existed solely as a service to decision makers.

This fact is rarely noted, but it is real. Ultimately top marketing people are involved in a new product's development, but it is increasingly common to see organizational forms which put early and intermediate decision authority on people with back-

grounds in technical research, engineering, manufacturing, corporate staff, etc. Such persons rarely are trained in the use of a decision-support function.

A tragic consequence is that both research and researchers are occasionally ignored. It is quite perplexing to college students, for example, to read in new product case studies that the results of product trials were rather poor, that advertising seemed confusing to potential customers, that test market results had to be rationalized, and yet the management concerned seemed genuinely shocked when the product ultimately failed. They find it almost impossible to believe that otherwise capable managers become so masochistic.

Determining the proper role for marketing research is no doubt more of a problem in technical firms than in consumer packaged goods firms. Brand managers are customarily quite capable of stipulating a meaningful and positive role for research. Often times they are former researchers. But most firms don't have brand managers, and a great deal of early product-concept decision-making is done by persons who are quite naive (or even hostile) toward market research.

Participants in this study offered strong support for this hypothesis, especially if they work in fields with strong technical R&D functions. One research supplier said:

Moreover, it seems to me that much of the new product research is done after product concepts and/or prototypes have been developed. By that time a great deal of decision-making has already taken place, commitments have been made, and the jobs of people on the new product team are at stake.

Another reviewer, primarily a consultant, used almost the same words, and concluded:

People, their jobs, and their reputation have been committed (to the new products) by that time. As a result, far too much research is devoted to trying to make silk purses out of sows' ears.

Yet another said we need a lot more front-end research. "After all, good copy research can only select good copy if it has a chance to test good copy."

The role of a support function can be critical, and in this case probably is. Perhaps top managements should ask their marketing research directors to submit, in writing, what they feel their role *should* be in product development. There may be some surprises.

Hypothesis 3: Marketing Researchers Fail to Sell Their Services Effectively

There are probably more euphemistic ways of stating this hypothesis. But researchers understand it as written. One study participant put it this way:

After years of fighting those specific problems, I have come to the conclusion that the marketing researcher has but two choices—either accept as a responsibility the task of getting clear definitions of marketing research's proper role in the product development process or become isolated, ignored, and thus wither away.

Over and over the same idea is heard; marketing research people must share the blame for an inadequate role. Occasionally a particularly inept manager may thwart even the best researcher, but this manager won't last long.

This hypothesis was not on the original list, and I ignored reference to it on the first round of reviews. The full group of reviewers put it squarely on the list, and reasonably high in probability. If marketing research personnel are unable (by one method or another) to achieve a proper acceptance of their services, then the odds on product failure increase sharply, no matter what the inherent capability of the function.

One reviewer, head of marketing research in a large company, recently persuaded his management to compile a "war chest" of some $600,000 to research his research—to develop that list of sequential research data hurdles which a new product will have to pass. Few researchers are so fortunate, but any pro in the business knows the long

story of "selling" which preceded that management's decision. The researcher is justifiably proud.

Hypothesis 4: Organizational Rigidities Are Hindering the Type of Involvement Essential to a Successful Marketing Research Program

Hypothesis No. 2 held that marketing research is hindered from achieving a proper role because of the non-marketing backgrounds of many of the key decision makers in new product development. Hypothesis No. 3 put the blame on researchers themselves. But there are other reasons, and many of them cluster under the general heading of organizational rigidities. Four specific rigidities have been identified in this study:

1. A Distorted Concept of Loyalty

There is hardly a marketing research director who hasn't seen a young and impressionable analyst come under the (evil?) influence of a sales manager or product manager. The analyst is detected as losing objectivity, and soon there is a flap over some research report which allegedly misinterprets a situation.

The outgrowth of such experiences is often the overt or covert building of organizational or procedural fences designed to protect the "integrity" of the research function, and to guarantee the objectivity of marketing researchers assigned to new product work. Researchers shouldn't get caught up in the enthusiasm of the development process, this line of reasoning insists, even if they are serving as the marketing department representative on committees, teams, or task forces.

We all must grant the attractiveness of research independence, research integrity, and objectivity, but we may also ask whether the price of achieving these ideals is sometimes the marketing research representatives' entirely inadequate input into team deliberations? Though not researched, to my knowledge, it seems that successful product development requires intense personal involvement of the participants. Venture groups get this type of commitment. So do smaller companies and divisions. Shouldn't any product development team manager expect his marketing researcher to want team success? Isn't the absence of team loyalty actually a form of disloyalty? Is it a natural thing for a decision maker to give credence to the advice and counsel of persons who repeatedly proclaim their independence from the team?

Few statements in this paper will attract more emotional reaction than these. One highly successful research director said:

I pride myself on the objectivity of my group and strive in every way to assure and protect it. More importantly, I think it has established research in management's eyes as the one function from which a straight, unpolluted answer can be assured.

Perhaps another reviewer best recognized the dilemma:

. . . each marketing organization must find a way to encourage involvement, objectivity, and professionalism at the same time.

If one accepts the premise that a major commitment to team success significantly enhances the likelihood of that success, then any organizational mandate which tends to isolate the marketing researcher from the rest of the new product team would seem to be unwise. Perhaps it happens too often.

Ironically, this concern can operate only if the marketing researcher is actually assigned to a team. He may not be, at least not in the beginning of the development process, and herein lies the *second* of the four possible rigidities.

2. Marketing Research Is Not in the Action

If a new product development system locks the marketing research function out of the action, it obviously can play no substantive role. Involvement by marketing strategists (product managers or marketing directors) who typically serve on overall new product committees is by no means assurance that marketing *researchers* are involved.

One practitioner told me:

There is a major communications gap between marketing research management and product or marketing management. All too often the researcher is deemed an academic, unrealistic technician and not a marketing strategist. He is not involved in strategic thinking, and he is not brought into the strategic picture seen by top management before the decisions are made.

As a result, the researcher withdraws and views marketing management as pragmatic, opportunistic, and perhaps not very bright. His defensive reaction forces him into becoming increasingly academic, increasingly technically oriented, and he therefore misses the boat when it comes to the real issue of getting involved with the decision process and a correct decision.

These arguments support the need for more marketing research involvement at the time early decisions are made, but I would also suggest the desirability of greater involvement in early product development operations. It could be argued sensibly, for example, that all product testing, whether in shops, laboratories, hospitals, or wherever, should have the counsel of experienced marketing researchers, but historical organizational arrangements frown on this type of "encroachment." Every now and then we hear a proposal that early R&D testing be under marketing's control, but such thoughts attract more attention than action.

3. Exclusion of Non-Researchers

The third type of organizational rigidity operates entirely within the marketing department. It stems from an all-too-frequent conviction that product and brand people should not be permitted to participate in the execution of a research project once its purpose and method are decided . . . in group interviewing sessions, for instance, or in examining field interviewer reports.

Just as the first of these four rigidities showed the potential dangers in trying to keep the researcher himself from becoming contaminated, the point here is that some research departments go to great lengths to prevent the possible contamination of their research processes or their research reports.

It can be granted that the scorekeeping (control) activities of a research department justify such caution, but the marketing research in support of new product development serves quite a different function. Numbers are not as important as ideas. Nuances are more critical than conclusions, and researchers should probably help key development people establish close and personal market contact.

4. Researchers with the Wrong Characteristics

The last of the four organizational rigidities concerns persons, not decisions, and may be unavoidable. It relates to the characteristics seemingly required of marketing researchers assigned to new product work:

High risk acceptance
Ability to work with all types of company personnel and at all levels
Ability to act with little precedent
Acceptance of a high waste ratio (projects cancelled or research performed for products that are abandoned)
Creativity in applying research techniques in new ways or to new markets
Ability to work on hectic scheduling and under great pressures
Understanding and acceptance of what one of this article's reviewers calls *a basically irrational process*. (He described new product development as essentially an art form, and proposed that the thought might serve as a separate hypothesis.)

Risk aversive, thorough, and orderly personnel are *persona-non-grata* in new product development. Yet most assignments in the marketing research department call for caution, order, patience, persistence. Thus we can speculate that many (perhaps most) researchers assigned to new product work are precisely the wrong people unless the department has been permitted to staff up especially for this purpose.

Hypothesis 5: The Project System of Marketing Research Department Management Works Contrary to the Needs of New Product Development

The Golden Era of Marketing Research has produced (1) a cascading flow of new research techniques (linear programming, conjoint measurement, Markov processes, Bayesian analysis, multivariate analysis, factor and cluster analyses, network analysis, and scores more), and (2) a pleasing and opportunity-laden growth in research budgets.

These forces join to produce several effects, one of which is the research project system. The project is probably the most efficient mechanism for directing and controlling techno-bureaucratic operations; and although small research departments *can* use the project system, the larger, more professional, and technically complex marketing research departments probably *must* use it.

But, again, there is a price tag on efficiency. Early editions of marketing research textbooks stressed a phase of research Lyndon Brown called the "informal investigation." Its purpose was to expose the researcher to the full dimensions of thought and hypothesis on the part of people connected with the problem. What precise information gathering and analysis activities he later undertook were coincidental to the essential element of his task—bringing the research function to a problem that had yet to yield all of its realities.

Unfortunately the marketing research director who wants to maximize these values loses considerable managerial flexibility. He must assign a researcher to a new product and let him stay with it through the full stream of gestational activity. This assignment would cover busy periods and slack periods, and would span the full range of research problems and skill requirements. It would yield the ideal researcher-developer involvement and relationship.

It would also be expensive, because the marketing research director would lose the many advantages of the project system; so he resists the ideal. Researcher A runs an early attitude study; Researcher B runs a product placement test; Researcher C works with his agency counterpart on some ad testing . . . etc. Researchers laugh at the apocryphal story of a colleague who said, "I'm going to lunch . . . if my product manager calls, get his name." But developers have been heard to complain similarly about their marketing researchers.

What is lost is the intimate familiarization of research with background and people. The "quick and dirty" research is never feasible. Nor is the even more speculative action of simply asking an experienced marketing researcher what he thinks a customer's reaction would be to some relatively minor proposal. Unless a research need is worthy of a project, it's apt to get no research attention at all.

Reviewer reaction agreed with this hypothesis, but several indicated they have "paid the price" and now assign researchers to products, not projects. One reviewer said:

The company is now assigning a research supplier to a brand with the understanding that that supplier accomplishes all of the research for that brand from concept testing through test marketing support research.

Hypothesis 6: The Typical Director of Marketing Research Has Defaulted on His Responsibilities as Keeper of the Research Conscience

New products are terribly demanding (uncertain environments, time pressures, political sensitivities), and ideally they require the professional input of the department's top researcher, plus the strength of his presence on various interfaces within the company.

But how reasonable is it to expect such a continuing personal involvement? In the first place the sheer number of projects may force the top researcher to give each one an organizational approval that is budgetary, not professional. Second, he may not be able to follow each new product development activity closely enough to know when to blow the proverbial research whistle—to demand that research be started (or stopped), or to insist that research findings be reviewed and reinterpreted.

Furthermore, this conscience of the department is not an easily delegated function. Courageous acts are high-risk acts to anyone, but especially to younger researchers who may be hoping to get promoted someday to the very departments they should whistle down. Consequently, a critical role is lost.

It is entirely plausible, of course, that this hypothesis is so irrevocably in conflict with the earlier one suggesting more delegation of authority to the research members of new product teams that we can't have both. On the other hand, the apparent conflict may simply be a managerial opportunity for which at least two options come to mind. First, only seasoned, confident research people would be assigned to new product work; these persons would have little difficulty standing firm as conditions dictated. Second, the marketing research department could spin off the new product marketing researchers under their own leaderhship, possibly giving them the time and involvement essential to the task of research technique guardianship.

One reviewer commented:

I have been disappointed at a number of cases in which enthusiasm for the product has caused normally rational people to become more salesmen than analysts. The result—they become selectively inattentive to negative feedback . . . They shirk their basic responsibility to remain objective.

If this type of excessive enthusiasm is to be controlled, a strong person is required. On the other hand, how much of the "stop here!" behavior can one expect from a marketing research director? As one reviewer put it:

If he takes on the responsibility 60% of the time . . . there is usually no one there to take it on the other 40%. This is a problem that must not be left to the research director but somehow must be solved organizationally.

Hypothesis 7: A Firm with a Low Product Failure Rate Is Passing up Profitable Risk

Potential new products can be arrayed in a frequency distribution from the one most certain to succeed down to the one almost certain to fail. A simple two-by-two matrix of success probability vs. success payoff then produces one cell (sure-fire big winners) where action is mandatory. The opposite cell of sure-fire losers with small profit potential will normally be avoided.

But the other two cells produce situations which will almost certainly add to the general failure rate. High-probability low-payoff products will be marketed during lulls between major new entries, and low-probability high-payoff products will be marketed to the extent that "expected" profits are adequate. Even conservatives will occasionally bet on a long-shot if the pay-off is high enough.

As markets grow in size and pay-offs increase, it seems logical that the rate of new product failure will actually *increase,* unless the development and introductory costs grow even more rapidly.

One reviewer referred to this phenomenon as a sort of Peter Principle. A management will market continuously riskier new items until they fail, and will stop only when the "package" of successes and failures starts to decline.

Not everyone agrees with this hypothesis even though it sounds unchallengingly logical. Some feel that a company's resources limit its introductions: a sales force can handle only so many new items a year, only so much cash is available for investments in introductory advertising, and so on. Within these limitations, they feel, one should expect an optimally functioning system to reduce or even

eliminate failures. The theoretical limit, based on the previous risk analysis syllogism, is never even approached.

The disagreement is amenable to research, but has not been researched. Until it is, we must keep the hypothesis as one possible explanation for the new product failure rate.

Hypothesis 8: The System of New Product Development Inherently Produces Counterproductive Behavior

This is another hypothesis that wasn't on the original list sent out to the practitioners for comment. But response certainly put it there, and feelings are very strong on the point.

The essence of the thinking is that the very nature of the product development process combined with the importance of new products produces situations in which human beings take actions designed to optimize individual well-being rather than the company's well-being. Several different pressures and behaviors are involved here.

First is top management which says, "We want $X million of new products every year," or "X new entries every year," or "X% of sales from new products by year 19XX." If these are kept as orienting goals, there seems to be no problem. But once they become operational targets that "will be planned for," trouble starts. Pressures mount, and several predictable reactions set in.

First, because the "costs" of not marketing new products has been increased by the management dictums (your job depends on your achieving our new goals) there *will be* new products, even if just me-too's or even of a low order of probable success. Under this system, even a poor product is better than no product, and woe to the people down the line who don't see that.

Second, there are two groups of middle managers who offer special reactions to the greater pressures. The so-called High Risk Achievers see the pressure as justification for their confidence, and let it be known that they expect "favorable" research results. This needn't even be subtle and every experienced researcher has faced the dilemma.

As one reviewer put it:

No self-respecting manager these days doesn't have a drawer full of reports to support his decision. But that doesn't mean the decision was based on the research. Conforming to a style of management, rather than substance, is all too common.

The other group—the Risk Avoiders—are probably the bigger problem. No less than three reviewers went out of their way to make the point that every review step in the development of a new product offers the decision maker two choices—one where he may win or lose (let's go ahead on the project) and one where he can't lose though he can't win either (let's cancel the project). Which he chooses depends partly on his own risk posture but also partly on his perception of how management keeps the score.

Product failures thwart managements in their drive for fixed new product goals, and no one wins rewards for failing to meet those goals. But Risk Avoiders are a lot more interested in building defenses than extending them. In turn this reduces the chance for really big winners, diverts research dollars into projects designed to kill ideas not improve upon them and, in general, it hobbles the system's capacity to produce good new products.

Ironically then, this hypothesis says that if top management sharply accelerates a demand for new items, it will cause failures to be pushed along and/or cause marginal products to be cancelled. Either way, the firm loses.

Other aberrations in the overall process are less subtle. Some managements are naive and overbelieve marketing research's ability to forecast demand. Some have a very short-term focus and divert monies from high pay-off longer term developments into short-range sure-fire mediocre products. Some are simply dogmatic or myopic and

won't believe certain research findings, however well developed. Some get so enthusiastic that they literally don't see or hear the caution signals.

All of these behaviors are apparently rather common, and only exceptional managements have succeeded in setting up new product development systems with safeguards against them. In all other firms, marketing research people must watch while their enhanced technological capabilities are distorted to fit unworthy motivations.

Hypothesis 9: Predicting New Product Sales and Profits Is an Inherently Impossible Task

This hypothesis says, in essence, given the best marketing research we can conceive and execute there will continue to be product failures—colossal failures and unnoticed failures, surprising failures and not-so-surprising failures.

Why? Because every new product can succeed only as persons or firms in the market place modify their behavior. And, the hypothesis holds, we will never be able to forecast the milieu within which that behavior operates to a degree which permits more than a very low order of accuracy in decision-making. Thus it follows that product developers will continue to make mistakes and will continue the stream of failures that we have seen throughout history. Occasionally there will arise situations which permit easy prediction, but these are very rare exceptions.

One might suspect that this hypothesis violates one of the premises underlying this investigation, the one relating to progress in the development of marketing research techniques. Actually, there is no conflict. Certainly there has been progress in marketing research, but this progress may not have added significantly to our skills in the particular area of new product development. To the extent that major behavior and attitude changes are essentially unpredictable, it never will. It is also possible that research advances have been essentially peripheral—helping us make new product decisions, but not those decisions critical to ultimate market success.

Thus we may now be much better at assessing what consumers think of our marketed products, or what they think of a new advertising campaign, or where our sales are being made. These are progress, but they may not be of particular value to the development of truly new products. Similarly, our enhanced research skills may lead to better sizes, colors, or shapes of widgets, but still leave us guessing as to whether people will buy truly new widgets if introduced to the market.

As with all of the hypotheses, there is strong disagreement among the practitioner panel reviewing this manuscript. One simply said, "I totally disagree with this hypothesis!" He feels our research technology has the inherent capability but that decision makers abuse it. In a way, of course, this permits the point to stand.

Summary

Any one or a combination of those nine hypotheses could be principally responsible for the failure of marketing research to stem or stop the flow of new product failures. In sum, the hypotheses respectively blame:

1. Those who develop the decision-making process.
2. Those who utilize research services.
3. The marketing researchers themselves.
4. Those who make organizational decisions.
5. The nature of a techno-bureaucratic system.
6. The director of marketing research.
7. The economics of the system.
8. Abusers of the system.
9. No one; the situation itself is inherently self-defeating.

There may be other plausible explanations, but these nine offer both *a priori* logic and some empirical evidence from the everday realm of new product development. In my judgment, they are really more than hypotheses, but I prefer to call them that because I feel they deserve further study. Whether they are totally researchable is open to question, but some attempt should be made to verify or deny each of the nine.

Bibliography

1. George J. Abrams, "Why New Products Fail," *Advertising Age*, April 22, 1974, pp. 51–52. [Experience of a foremost new product developer.].

2. Theodore L. Angelus, "Why Do Most New Products Fail?" *Advertising Age*, March 24, 1969, pp. 85–86. [Intensive study of 75 product failures.]

3. *Management of New Products* (Chicago, Il.: Booz, Allen, and Hamilton, 1968), especially pp. 11–12. [Includes results of studies of industry practices.]

4. "An Outside Job Fills the Product Gap," *Business Week*, May 16, 1970, pg. 48. [A reference to claim by Franklin W. Krum, Jr., of N. W. Ayer & Sons.]

5. William J. Constandse, "Why New Product Management Fails," *Business Management*, June 1971, pp. 163–65. [Study by an IBM Product Manager.]

6. Rick W. Diehl, "Achieving Successful Innovation," *Michigan Business Review*, March 1972, pp. 6–10. [Experiences of a Continental Can Co. executive.]

7. John W. Dodd, Jr., "New Products—Policy, Strategy, and Sense of Direction," *New Products: Concepts Development and Strategy*. Robert Scrace, ed. (Ann Arbor, MI: U. of Michigan, Graduate School of Business Administration, 1967), pp. 18–24. [Experiences of a Campbell Soup Co. marketer.]

8. D. S. Dunbar, "New Lamps for Old," *The Grocer*, April 1965, pg. 31. [Results of a J. Walter Thompson study.]

9. "Helene Curtis Comeback Move," *Advertising Age*, May 13, 1974, pp. 1-ff.

10. David S. Hopkins, and Earl L. Bailey, "New Product Pressures," *The Conference Board Research* 8 (June 1971), pp. 16–24. [Based on a survey of 125 members of Senior Marketing Executives Panel.]

11. Morgan B. MacDonald, Jr., *Appraising the Market for Industrial Products* (New York: National Industrial Conference Board, 112 pp.). [A study of the practices and experiences of around 100 U.S. and Canadian firms.]

12. Virginia Miles, "Avoid these Errors in New Product Research," *Advertising Age,* July 15, 1974, pp. 26-ff. [Experiences of the Director of CONCEPTS, division of Young & Rubicon Advertising Agency.]

13. *New Products in the Grocery Trade* (London: Kranshar, Andrews, and Eassie Ltd., 1971). [Failure rates derived from a study of new products' off-shelf disappearance.]

14. "New Product Success Ratio," *The Nielsen Researcher,* No. 5 (1971), pp. 2–10. [A summary of several Nielsen studies.]

15. John T. O'Meara, "Selecting Profitable Products," *Harvard Business Review,* January–February 1961, pp. 80–88. [Cites a study made by Ross Federal Research Corp. for Peter Hilton Inc., entitled "The Introduction of New Products."]

16. Charles E. Rosen, "New Product Decisions— Creative Measurements and Realistic Applications," *New Products: Concepts, Development and Strategy.* Robert Scrace, ed. (Ann Arbor, MI: U. of Michigan, Graduate School of Business Administration, 1967, pp. 11–17). [Experiences of a research firm president.]

17. Steven J. Shaw, "Behavioral Session Offers Fresh Insights into New Product Acceptance," *Journal of Marketing,* Vol. 29 No. 1, January 1965, pp. 9–13. [Mentioned, but did not cite, a U.S. Dept. of Commerce study.]

Note: The following persons were involved in the reviewing process, although none has seen the final version of the manuscript and cannot be held accountable for anything in it. In fact, I'm sure each would find parts of it totally unacceptable, so strong are opinions on this subject: Lee Adler (then of RCA), Earl Bailey (The Conference Board), Oliver Castle (A. C. Nielsen), John Coulson (Leo Burnett), Irving Crespi (Gallup Robinson), David Hardin (Market Facts), Gerald Koetting (Lincoln St. Louis), Robert Lavidge (Elrick and Lavidge), Donald Leslie (Mead Johnson), Elmer Lotshaw (Owens-Illinois), Lawrence Gibson (General Mills), Arthur Pearson (Clairol), Ralph Pernice (Upjohn), Stanley Petzel and Dennis Ready (Green Giant), James Sammer (Walker Research), Stanley Shores (Procter & Gamble), Richard Smoker (Penn Mutual), Roy Stout (Coca-Cola), Dale Thomas (Pitney Bowes), and Robert Williams (Dow).

Questions

1. *Given the choice of introducing one new product, which has a reasonably good chance of being a moderate short-term success, or another product, which has an outside chance of being a major long-term success, which would you choose?*
2. *Of the nine hypotheses discussed as plausible explanations for the high new product failure rate, which ones do you think are most important?*

6

Marketing Research for Small Business

MICHAEL F. D'AMICO

Marketing research is not limited in use to large mul-tinational companies with corporate research staffs, computers, and million-dollar research budgets. There are tools and approaches that can be used by the small-firm manager in making more informed decisions.

The term "marketing research" covers a broad range of activities. It encompasses the gathering and analyzing of facts relevant to problems arising during the transfer and sale of goods and services. Thus it can be used to study and improve almost any aspect of a firm's operation, including trans-portation, packaging, display, advertising, sales, and customer satisfaction.

Unfortunately, marketing research is viewed by many people as a necessarily complex business made up of computers, models, and statistical gym-nastics. This is because large companies with access to sophisticated techniques and materials, and professors demonstrating advanced statistical tools, have made marketing research seem more complicated than it actually is. Their efforts may have made marketing research more exact and, in a sense, better. But they have also made marketing research often appear to be beyond the means of the small business manager.

It is a fact, however, no matter how complex a large-scale marketing research project might be,

that it is based upon some kind of logical, "com-mon sense" idea. It is also true that any small busi-ness manager can use that simple idea, or an idea of his own, to find out about his own market, generat-ing useful facts and data without using a computer or any exotic tools.

Scientific Method

Marketing is more of an art than a science. Success in this area depends upon the skill and judgment of the individuals running the business. It cannot be reduced to a strictly organized body of rules or principles, and thus marketing research cannot be as fully scientific as research in one of the hard sciences such as chemistry or physics. Despite this, marketing research should be carried out, to the degree possible, according to the tenets of the "sci-entific method."

Among the features which characterize the scien-tific method are careful and accurate observation and classification of important facts, observation of the correlation and sequence of these facts, attempt to discover rules which are of value in problem-solving, self-criticism by the researcher, and testing the validity of the results.

Marketing does not lend itself fully to the scien-tific method because even the simplest experiment or study involves great complexity of subject. The difficult-to-handle "human element" is always present. Accurate measurement is difficult, for the usual interviews and questionnaires—are subjec-tive tools used in subjective procedures. In fact, the

Source: Journal of Small Business Management, January 1978, pp. 41–49. Copyright © 1978 by the International Council for Small Business and the West Virginia Univer-sity Bureau of Business Research.

very process of measurement may influence the results, for when people realize that they are being tested they are likely to change from their "natural" selves. The investigator, similarly, may not be objective, but may alter views or methods as the study moves forward. An experiment generally cannot be replicated as it can in fields such as biology. Finally, because of all these problems, predictions can never be 100 per cent accurate.

It is apparent, then, that marketing is not a true science and can never meet all the criteria of the "scientific method." The best that can be done is to approach marketing research *as scientifically as possible*. The researcher can, initially, set up the research project in such a way as to eliminate some of the major difficulties. For example, much data can be generated without the use of questionnaires and surveys. Having set up the research program the researcher should strive for objectivity, attempting to eliminate preconceptions and bias. He should try to obtain the most accurate measurements possible, and investigate pertinent facts fully. In so doing, the marketing researcher is being as scientific and thorough as the field of study allows.

Why Bother with Marketing Research?

Many small business managers avoid any special efforts that might be termed marketing research. Their reasons for such aversion cannot be dismissed lightly. Let us look at some common complaints about marketing research, and investigate their validity.

"Marketing research is too expensive." This complaint probably results from the view that the research has to involve complicated and expensive procedures. Of course it does not. At its simplest, merely noting which products sell better than others is a form of marketing research. Below are some very simple and inexpensive marketing research tools, most of them involving no major investment of time or money. Marketing research is "too expensive" only when the researcher allows it to be by application of improper techniques or by going overboard in his efforts.

"I don't know anything about marketing research." This complaint can be shown to have very little basis in fact. Since most marketing research studies, no matter how they have been fancied up, have some simple goal and some logical method, the small business manager *has* to be able to handle marketing research. Who is better qualified to identify problem areas? Who knows the customers better? Who has more information available? It is true that the manager might be blind to these elements because of complacency or refusal to consider them. In such cases there is probably little to be done because the manager will not help himself. Still, many marketing research tools are so simple and obvious that any concerned manager could use them if he chose to.

"I know all that stuff anyway." Here the manager could very well be right. He may really know all, or nearly all, the things that simple marketing research could tell him. The problem, of course, is that he could be wrong. Perhaps there has been a subtle shift in the market served. Maybe fewer or different customers are being served even though total sales figures have remained the same. There could be trends with deadly consequence to the business. The simple tools discussed in this article might help the manager discern these things with very little additional effort before it is too late. Should it turn out that the manager was correct in his reading of the market, his research will have served him, at the very least, as an insurance policy, as a means to keep facts and figures in an ordered way, and as a proof of his own acumen.

"Marketing research is not worth the trouble." As has just been seen, the manager may already know the information marketing research might yield. Still, a reasonable person would quickly concede that the "trouble" is always worthwhile when the survival of the business might be at stake. Many marketing research techniques involve so little extra effort on the part of the small business manager that this complaint is hardly valid.

Closely allied to this matter is the notion that research is fine for large companies which "have a lot to lose." But again, the small businessman has proportionately much more to lose than, say, a member of management at IBM.

What Marketing Research Does Not Do

Before detailing some marketing research techniques that any small business might use, a word of caution is necessary. Marketing research does many things, but far too much can be expected of it. Here are some things that marketing research does not do.

Marketing research does not give "the answer." To begin with, there is seldom any one answer to a business problem. Even if there were, it would be unlikely that marketing research would provide it. First, there are too many intervening factors between the findings of a study and the response of the market place. For example, some length of time must elapse before research results can be implemented. The Edsel was one of the most heavily researched new products ever introduced, but the time needed to produce the car was so long that the data gathered was obsolete by the time it reached the market place. Further, marketing research can deal only with parts of problems. Though great advances have been made in simulation of business processes, no study or model can show all aspects of the market and all interrelationships between the firm and the elements which make up its environment. Price levels might be judged by means of a test market or other experiment. Advertising, or another factor, could be similarly investigated. But all factors affecting marketing success and failures cannot be scrutinized simultaneously. Also, the dynamic nature of markets and marketing would make even the most all-encompassing study of questionable value.

Lastly, as every businessman knows, the decision-making process involves many hunches, visceral reactions, personal beliefs, and the like. No amount of reasearch or data can ever replace that human element so important to the process of management. Marketing research can only provide help in making decisions; it cannot make decisions.

Primary and Secondary Data

It has been noted that marketing research entails the gathering and analyzing of data. Researchers usually divide data into two large categories, "primary" and "secondary." Primary data are those which the researcher himself generates, also known as "original research." Secondary data are those which have been gathered by someone other than the researcher or his associates. For example, if a store manager surveys his customers, even on an informal basis, as to the detergents they prefer, this is primary research. The retailer has done the research for himself. If, on the other hand, the store manager goes to the library and locates a study of consumer detergent preferences on which he might base a decision, he has performed secondary research.

Each type of research presents advantages and disadvantages. But before treating these, one point of great importance must be made. The researcher must identify and formulate the problem before any data is gathered or research undertaken. Such a clarification forces the researcher to deeply consider his firm's difficulties and serves to set him on the track to the goal he seeks, namely, data pertinent to the *real* problem.

Secondary Data

Despite the term, secondary data should be sought before primary research is undertaken. The reasons for this are clear. Perhaps the data needed can be found easily at the library or in a book or magazine at home. It is obviously cheaper, quicker, and less trouble to find the information in secondary sources than it is to set out to conduct a survey or enter on some other project. However, the researcher should be wary of secondary data. For one thing, the data are, by definition, not brand new. They have been gathered, processed, printed, and circulated. All this takes time. This is not to say that such data are of no value, but they should be used with some caution.

Another difficulty associated with secondary data is the problem of finding the precise information required. A manufacturer seeking market data for the Southeastern United States might find studies of the South or Middle South, or a few states, but not of the Southeast as he has defined it.

A further problem area in the use of secondary data is the source and validity of those data. The original researcher who developed the study might have had unknown purposes. The original author may have used questionable survey methods, or unverified information. In some cases, he may have been trying to prove some point not related to the present problem, and may even have slanted his findings to prove that point.

Sources of Secondary Data

The sources of secondary marketing research data are far too many to list here, for secondary data has been defined as those data collected by anyone other than the present researcher or his associates. Many commercial sources of data exist, the Nielsen Company and others like it being well known. However, the small businessman might find these firms too expensive to employ, or he may be trying to answer local matters that could be researched quickly without bringing in outside help.

Readily available sources of inexpensive secondary data include libraries, public or connected with a local college, university, or other institution. Public libraries are often good sources of small-business data because they seek to serve local interests. Most other libraries are depositories of business information and related data such as census reports. Whenever possible, the researcher should use original sources. These are usually more complete than derivative studies and less likely to contain printing or transcription errors. Figure 1 shows the wide range of market information sources available.

Though the small business manager should familiarize himself with local libraries and their contents and filing methods, most librarians are willing to provide valuable aid. Particularly helpful are librarians specializing in the area of government documents, since governmental units are the major sources of market information.

Additional sources of secondary data include the trade associations which serve the particular business, the trade press, texts and other books, and even the newspaper. There is an ancient bit of advice to the effect that the best thing a small business can do is to do what the big businesses are doing. While this is surely not always the case, there is enough truth to it to encourage the small business manager to use available secondary sources if only to discover what others in his industry are up to.

Primary Data

As we have seen, primary data are those which are generated by the researcher in the course of his current study. One of the biggest fallacies in marketing research is that the researcher should charge right out and "do a survey." Actually, the researcher should generate his own data only if he cannot get the data he needs in some easier way. Although the remainder of this discussion deals with primary research tools, it should be stressed that the economies of time, effort, and money associated with secondary data make it desirable to use such data whenever possible, especially for the small business manager who is likely not in a position to invest a good deal in any of those components, regardless of how valuable results might prove. Primary research should be a last resort.

Sources of Primary Data

Inasmuch as primary data are generated by the researcher's own efforts, the number of sources of such data is limited only by the researcher's own imagination. As the reader considers just some of the many tools that could be used by the small businessman, he should keep three things in mind. Notice, first, that the bases of the methods detailed are

Figure 1

Sampler of marketing information sources

Sources of information	Types of information obtainable

SECONDARY

Governmental sources

Censuses of population, housing, business, manufacturers, agriculture, mining, governments.	Count of individuals, socio-economic characteristics.
Registration data.	Count of dwellings, age of structures, information on occupants.
Small Business Administration.	Retail, wholesale, service businesses.
Government Printing Office.	Number of manufacturers, quantities produced.
Other governmental sources.	Details on minerals industries.
	State and local governments, employees.
	Births, deaths, marriages, etc.
	SBA data and helps to businesses.
	Books, periodicals, agencies' reports.
	Depts of Agriculture, Commerce, Labor and other agencies.

Non-governmental sources

Periodicals.	Reports of data and findings, some original research.
Books and texts.	How-to information.
Original studies.	Historical data.
Trade press.	Dissertations, studies, monographs, experiments.
Trade associations.	Data and current events pertaining to particular industries.
General business press.	Commercially gathered data, e.g., share of market information, special studies.
Marketing research firms.	

PRIMARY

Surveys, questionnaires by means of personal, mail, or telephone approaches.	Opinion studies, product usage studies, preference studies, concept testing.
Data from within the firm.	Company records, sales trends, individual salesmen's performance.
Certain external data.	Customer behavior patterns, reactions, choices.
Observation.	How changes in some areas affect customer behavior.
Experiments.	Testing of products, sales methods, other variables.
Panel studies.	
Test marketing.	

logical, even obvious, things. The methods are techniques that almost anyone applying himself to a research problem might have developed. Secondly, the research methods are simple in the extreme, bearing out the earlier statement that marketing research need not be complex or frightening. Lastly, anyone can develop his own research tools and, as his expertise increases, increase their exactness and complexity, if such fits his purposes.

Company records are sources of primary marketing research data. This internal source of information, along with others such as salesmen's predictions, should be tapped before external data are sought. Yet many small businesses keep such poor records that the manager cannot find the most basic bits of information. One college class in small business administration was assigned the problem of counseling a local small parts manufacturer. The businessman distributed his products through a system of several agents and wanted to know whether he should continue this practice, change agents, or take some other step. The class found that the manufacturer had no records of the sales performance of the various agents he used. He did not know which were selling his product successfully and which were not. Amazingly, the simple activity of recording sales in terms of who made the sale had not been performed. Yet this information was exactly what was needed to answer his questions.

In another case, a publisher of trade magazines sold advertising through a number of agents. One of his employees spent a few days breaking down the company records, showing the percentage of total sales credited to particular agents, indicating which agents were improving their sales, and which were declining. Other simple treatments of the records were also set forth. The employee showed the figures to the company president and found that never in the company's seventy-year history had even these basic research steps been taken. Incidentally, the president, though impressed with the employee's efforts, made no attempt to follow up on the results and put them to use. This points up the fact that research findings, including very important ones, are useless unless they lead to decisions.

Imagine that a retailer located in a given shopping center wants to estimate the area from which his customers are drawn. If this could be determined, it would influence, for example, where advertising should be placed. Should only the local newspaper be used, or should billboards be erected in suburbs? Any number of research tools could be used here; the most useful are basically simple.

The techniques known as "license-plate analysis" is exactly that. A license number generally reveals information about the owner's residence. Information on how to interpret the numbers is generally available from state government agencies. The retailer trying to estimate his trading area need only note the plate numbers of cars in the parking lot to get some notion of where his patrons live, what percentage of his customers are drawn from the immediate area, and so forth. The retailer would logically attempt to allow for on-foot traffic if this is an important factor. Naturally, the retailer would also interpret his findings with care. A car registered in Alaska noted outside a store in New Jersey does not indicate that the store's trading area covers a five thousand mile range.

The simple concept underlying license plate analysis can be applied to other information sources. Customer telephone numbers can be used to identify the geographic extent of a market. Many restaurateurs ask people calling for dinner reservations to leave their phone numbers. Since phone numbers, like license plates, are assigned on a geographic basis, a restaurant owner can quickly get some idea of the number of customers he is drawing from various areas. Or he could test the worth of the advertisements he had placed in various area newspapers.

Closely related to this would be the trick of placing coded dollar-off coupons in area newspapers. When the coupons are cashed in, the restaurateur need only note which areas are represented and which are not. He might find, for example, that ads in the suburban paper are the ones attracting customers.

Credit records and the checks cashed by customers are gold mines of marketing research data. Actual names and addresses of customers are at the business manager's fingertips. Credit records might yield such information as where customers work, what their jobs are, whether or not they are married, whether there is one income or two, how much the family earns, and so on. Thus, if a business grants no credit, it is cutting itself off from vast stores of market information, though there are often fine reasons for not giving credit.

Some of the data that can be gleaned from credit records may be obtainable even if credit is not granted. Customers might be willing to supply their addresses so that the sales slip "can be filled out properly." Many retailers ask their patrons to sign up for the shop's "newsletter," coupons, or special sale information. Merely the addresses of the customers can tell the merchant how wide an area is served, and what kind of neighborhoods the customers live in. Many other things become easier to estimate. Among these are income, social standing (class), and family responsibilities, e.g., is the neighborhood a "family" neighborhood? Too, when the customer leaves his name to receive the "newsletter," the retailer can record a guess as to the customer's age, note the car driven, observe a wedding ring, notice the quality of the customer's clothes, observe the accompanying children, and check other variables.

Experiments are another source of marketing information. They are sometimes overlooked in the real-world context of business because they may be difficult to develop and carry out. However, the businessman may wish to perform simple experiments, and in fact, does so often. For example, a series of advertisements may be run and checked, perhaps by means of coupons, to determine which advertisements drew best. Or a panel of customers might be asked to evaluate advertisements or new products. The common points here are that a group of people is being exposed, in a controlled environment, to some variable which is being tested while other variables are being held constant. Of course, the environment cannot be fully controlled, nor can all other variables be held constant. These are goals to aim for. The researcher should attempt to achieve, to the degree possible, internal and external validity. These are achieved when the results of the experiment are truly related to the acts that were carried forth in the experiment, and when the findings of the experiment correspond to what would have happened in the "real world." These two goals are seldom fully realized, but they are targets for which the researcher must strive.

Surveys and other data-gathering tools can be used effectively by the small business firm. While the details of surveying methods, sampling and questionnaire construction cannot be dealt with in this short article, many books dealing with these matters are readily available. The business manager may, of course, adjust techniques to fit the needs of his particular business. But again, common sense lies at the foundation of every research tool. No matter what the small businessman undertakes in the way of research, he should bear in mind at least these two things; that the purpose of the survey is to help the businessman meet the customers' needs; and, that the survey, or other tool, is essentially a simple device, and can be used as such.

There is a thrice-told tale which sums up much of what has been said here about common sense in marketing research. It is claimed that the first marketing research practitioner may well have been John Jacob Astor. In need of information to help him run a retail outlet, Astor is reputed to have hired an artist to patrol New York City's streets sketching the hats worn by women of fashion. Using the sketches, Astor was able to keep up to date on popular fashions and their trends. Perhaps nothing could be simpler and more reasonable than this early marketing research technique. There is no reason why the tradition of getting information without complicating matters cannot be kept alive by today's business managers.

Implementing Marketing Research

The central theme of this article has been the simplicity of marketing research techniques that the small business manager might employ. But as everyone knows, implementation of even simple notions can become complex. However, with care, the implementation will become only as complex as the manager wishes it to be.

For example, take the case of the publisher above who was presented with a break-down of sales demonstrating which of his agents were the most effective, which were increasing sales, and which were declining. Seeing this, the publisher then could have instituted a longitudinal study of this type of information. He could have continued to gather data from month to month so as to determine sales trends, projections, and other factors. Had this been the course selected, implementation could have been simple enough: write down the figures; perform some simple addition, subtraction, and averaging to determine, as an example,

"average sales" or "sales per territory"; and, lastly, act upon the data.

On the other hand, the publisher could have had special forms designed and printed. Sales office personnel could be asked to predict sales, these figures later to be compared with results. Advanced statistical techniques could be applied to the figures rather than the simple averaging methods mentioned. A consultant could be hired. The publisher or his associates could take courses in statistics or computer science, the better to juggle the data collected. Finally, the whole affair could be computerized and reams of number-covered paper generated. But before the thought of all this frightens the small business manager away, the point should be made that marketing research should be in line with the manager's interests, abilities, and financial resources. The big step is to

Figure 2

Steps in the marketing research procedure

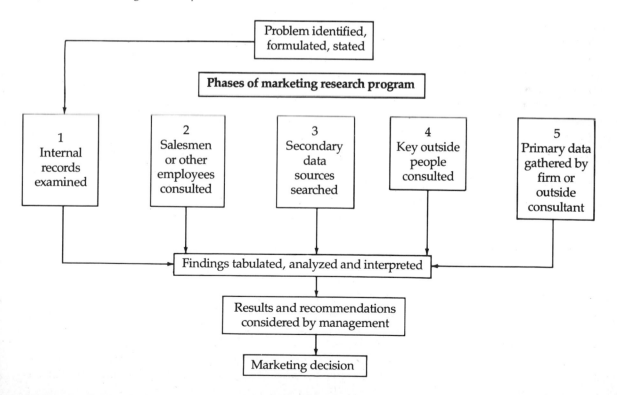

have *some* marketing research on which to base decisions. Moving the research beyond the point of initiation is, in most cases, a matter of far less difficulty than the initiation itself.

Summary

Figure 2 should help the reader to visualize the major components of marketing research and the general order in which they should be treated. It, in fact, summarizes much of what has been said in this necessarily short article. Note that at every step there is room for complexity or simplicity as suits the researcher and the problem faced. Note, too, that at each step the researcher can do too much, waiting for "all" data to be in before moving to the next step. As a general rule, some information is better than none, justifying the existence of even the most basic research program. But the delay involved in getting "all" the information (probably an impossibility anyway) makes heavily detailed study, if only because of the time element, as indefensible as no study at all.

Questions

1. *Based on the lessons you learned from this article, prepare a brief presentation, in which you argue persuasively in favor of marketing research to help solve problems, to be made to the owner-manager of a local retail store.*
2. *Suppose a bank in your town came to you with the following problem. The bank's market share among the college student population is declining. Design a research program to identify the causes for the declining market share and some appropriate remedies for the problem.*

7

New Tools for Marketing Research: Assessing a Company's Position

BRIAN F. BLAKE

LEE F. SCHRADER

WILLIAM L. JAMES

Analysis of customers' brand preferences can be very useful in describing a company's current position in relation to its competitors. Understanding why a company is viewed as it is by consumers may suggest how a company might improve its market share.

Have you, as the manager of a business, kept in touch with the needs and preferences of the customer?

Consider the case of a regional feed manufacturer who was earning an attractive return on a market share of about 10%. The firm decides to expand aggressively by going after an increase in market share. The strategy he adopts is to modify the product line, selling efforts and advertising to the approaches used successfully by the market leader.

After extensive discussion within the company's management, the changes are put into effect. Much to management's surprise, sales and market share nose dive! Too late it discovers that the changes did not attract new customers. Potential customers now saw the revamped company as just a pale imitation of the firmly established market leader. They see little reason to switch to the "substitute" when they could have the "real thing." Too late management sees that old customers have been lost.

The firm had been serving a segment of the market whose needs and preferences were different from the market as a whole. By changing, the firm left its previous segment to be captured by competitors. Too late did the manager realize that he should have sought more feedback from the market as a whole, both from present and from potential customers, rather than rely so heavily upon opinions of company's own management.

What do you know about the perspectives the customer uses in evaluating your company or its products? Does your information come only from your present customers who may not be typical of potential customers? Are your advertising and public relations efforts related to facts that really concern potential customers, or do they reflect only what management feels should be important to farmers?

These are difficult questions for any manager, but particularly for the business grown too large for personal contact with the customer. Once these direct contacts are lost, an independent check on the needs and preferences of customers becomes highly desirable, if not necessary, for survival.

Recently developed marketing research tools are now available at reasonable cost to assist the marketing manager assess the present position of his company or brand in the market, identify actions needed to move the company and its products toward that which customers desire, guide new product development, and evaluate product pricing alternatives. This series of four articles outlines the use of marketing research methods recently developed for each of these situations. Each article illustrates the main ideas with survey research completed for companies serving farmers. Products, firm names and data are disguised to protect the firms involved.

Source: Feedstuffs, December 26, 1977, pp. 19–20.

Assessing Company Position

Company or brand position represents more than market share. Position represents the place the company or brand holds in the eyes of customers and potential customers. More specifically, it is where your brand stands compared to other brands, and compared to what farmers perceive to be the ideal or best possible type of company.

Identifying the position your company now holds or the position that would be best for your company to hold is more easily said than done. Your brand share tells you the proportion of total volume which is represented by buyers who prefer your product, service and price: it tells little about the views of those who buy other brands. Changes in brand share indicate whether or not your marketing strategy is working, but tells little or nothing about why or what can be done to increase market share still more. Further, a traditional customer attitude survey may not be the answer. It does give more information than does brand share, but too often it provides just a mass of numbers difficult to translate into a marketing strategy.

What Must You Know?

Bruce Symonds (*Feedstuffs*, Sept. 26) lists "Where is my business today?" as the first question to deal with in building a marketing plan. To answer this question, the manager must grasp several issues. He must be aware of the perspectives or yardsticks the customer uses to judge competing companies. Let's judge the bait from the fish's viewpoint, not from the fisherman's!

The manager also must know precisely how the firm now differs from that type of company most preferred by farmers. Further, he must understand how these yardsticks and views of the company change from one market segment to another. Still further, he must consider how farmers evaluate other brands trying to serve the same market. Finally, if a marketing plan is to be carried out effectively, he must be assured that the company's mar-

keting and sales force realize where the company and its competitors stand in the eyes of farmers.

The manager needs all this information integrated into a single picture, one which shows actions that must be taken to achieve his marketing goals. The information is needed at reasonable cost and without requiring complex, time-consuming data gathering activities.

Multi-Dimensional Analysis of Brand Preferences

Multi-dimensional scaling (MDS) is a family of techniques ideally suited to the managerial needs outlined above. The most useful techniques can:

Suggest the yardsticks by which people judge some brands to be better than others.
Gauge how well people feel various brands stack up against each yardstick.
Estimate the type of brand which a market most prefers—even when that "ideal" brand is not yet on the market.
Find differences in the above among various market segments.

These results are condensed into an easily understood "preference map," as simple to understand as a road map. These techniques cost no more than traditional customer survey analysis—and may cost less.

An Actual Example

A company selling a production input to farmers in the eastern half of the U.S. was well into a major expansion effort. Its current market share was relatively low, about 10% of the market leader in much of the selling area. An MDS preference study was initiated to determine where its own brand and competing brands currently stood in the eyes of farmers, and to suggest how the company could best increase its future market share. Another objective of the study was to determine whether the company's sales managers were truly attuned to the opinions of farmers in their selling areas. Any attempt to expand market share would be undermined if the sales managers were familiar with their present customers, but were not aware of the views of potential customers.

A questionnaire was mailed to a representative sample of farmers. It asked them to rank various brands (companies) in order from most preferred to least preferred. Other questions asked farmers about the importance of various company characteristics (e.g., fast growing, research oriented, friendliness of dealers) and the extent each company displayed these characteristics. Finally, sales managers were asked to answer as they expected the farmers in their areas to respond. An MDS analysis of these survey data generated the following results.

Preference map

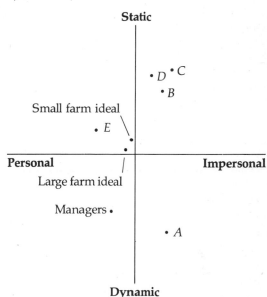

Results of Analysis

It appeared that farmers' evaluation of those brands studied could be adequately represented in two dimensions, or yardsticks, as shown in the accompanying figure. The analysts then used a combination of facts known about the companies and the company characteristics associated with particular brands to name these dimensions. The horizontal dimension appeared to reflect the extent dealers, product line and other aspects of the company were sensitive to the needs of farmers as individuals. Companies that were sensitive were more "personal," while those not seen as trying to accommodate the needs of the individual farmer were "impersonal."

The second perspective farmers used could be called "static" versus "dynamic." This yardstick was how predictable and unchanging were the products, dealer actions and policies of the company. A farmer knows what to expect from a static brand—but he doesn't expect innovation. Brands on the dynamic end of this yardstick are just the opposite. Their operations are very flexible, but perhaps a bit erratic and inconsistent!

The figure shows the type of company farmers most prefer to deal with and their evaluations of

five specific companies (A, B, C, D and E). As on a road map, the distance among points are important. That is, the closer together are points on the map, the more similar did farmers see them to be; the further apart are the points, the more different were they in the eyes of farmers. Next, as on a road map, the directions are important. The further right the location of an actual brand or an ideal, the more "impersonal" was it estimated to be; the further to the left, the more "personal." Similarly, the higher it was, the more "static" was it felt to be, and the lower it was the more "dynamic" it was perceived to be. Finally, to use a road map, one must know where the destination is located. Here, the "ideal brand" is the type of company with which a market segment would most prefer to deal. The ideal brand position was estimated separately for small farmers and large farmers. The closer a company is to the ideal brand, the more strongly is it preferred by that market segment.

The figure provides a great deal of information. First, the location of the ideal brands suggests that both small farmers and large farmers want to purchase from a company modestly personal and somewhat static. Second, we look at the distance between each brand and farmers' ideals. This shows that quite a few present brands were not even close to what farmers thought to be ideal. Company E, the actual market leader, was somewhat more static and personal than farmers desired. However, Company E was the closest of the five to what farmers wished and, so, emerged as the market leader. Companies B, C and D were far too hide bound for farmers' tastes. Company A, the sponsor of this study, was the furthest of the five from farmer ideals. It was seen as far too changeable and somewhat too impersonal. This observation certainly helps to account for why Company A's actual share of the market was the lowest of the five.

Actual share of market figures were available for all five companies and matched very closely predictions made by the preference analysis. This agreement of the two suggested that the preference analysis was providing a realistic picture of market conditions and, so, could give useful guidance about how the company might improve its market position. In passing, it should be noted that MDS preference analysis can be helpful when a company has little information about the share of some competitors. An MDS map can help to estimate the share of the market enjoyed by competitors when actual share of market figures are unavailable.

Third, we see that Company A's managers were not closely tuned into farmers' opinions. Although they may have been familiar with the views of their present customers, they were not in touch with views of farmers in general. The managers predicted that farmers wanted a company less static and more personal than actually was the case. Possibly the managers were basing their judgments too heavily upon the operations of their own company and upon the success of the market leader.

Implications for Action

What actions did this analysis suggest Company A take? Clearly, it should position itself close to farmer ideals. The company should demonstrate that it is more static and personal than farmers currently believe. An optimal position, in fact, would be to show that it is slightly more impersonal and somewhat more dynamic than the present market leader. The preference map, plus additional information gathered about various company characteristics, suggested that this repositioning would be helped by showing the predictability and stability of Company A's operations. The farmer should be assured that he knows what to expect from Company A in regard to dealers and products. Also, emphasizing company dependability, friendliness and service orientation would be in order. Product development, advertising, dealer activities, etc., should be coordinated to carry out this repositioning.

An alternative strategy, copying the marketing approach of the market leader, could be unwise. Here is yet another example of how a simple "copycat" market strategy can be self defeating. If Company A were to emulate the leader, Company E, it possibly may be seen as offering nothing more than does the already well entrenched brand. Just as important, this strategy would "overshoot the mark." Company A would then be seen as more static and personal than farmers desire.

Finally, the analysis suggests that staff need updating about what farmers currently think of the company and its competitors, and about the yardsticks farmers use to judge competing companies. The staff, down to the dealer level, should be informed of the position that the company will seek and the approaches that will be taken to reach that position. A more effective mechanism (e.g., regular surveys) should be developed to keep the staff abreast of future changes in farmers' opinions.

MDS preference analysis can be very useful in describing *what* is the present relative position of a company, *why* it is viewed this way in the market, and in suggesting *how* the company might improve its market share. Because it costs no more than standard surveys, it is available even to companies with limited market research budgets.

MDS is not a cure-all. Application of the technique depends on knowledge of the companies involved and the identification of company characteristics relevant to the customer. MDS is a tool to supplement the knowledge of the marketing manager, not a replacement.

The next article in this series will describe a method of identifying strengths and weaknesses in a company's image and product line. We call it the "action grid" approach.

References

Green, P., and Wind, Y. *Multi-attribute Decisions in Marketing: A Measureable Approach*. Dryden Press: Hinsdale, Illinois, 1973.

Wang, M. M., Shoneman, P., and Rusk, J. "A Conjugate Gradient Algorithm for the Multi-dimensional Analysis of Preference Data," *Multivariate Behavioral Research*, 1975, 10, 45–89.

Questions

1. *How does a company or brand position differ from market share?*
2. *"Let's judge the bait from the fish's viewpoint, not from the fisherman's!" Explain the significance of this statement in terms of a manager's need to assess his company's position.*
3. *Company A was positioned far away from its competitors and from small and large farm ideal points on the MDS preference map. What does this mean?*

8

New Tools for Marketing Research: The Action Grid

BRIAN F. BLAKE

LEE F. SCHRADER

WILLIAM L. JAMES

Marketers can identify features of their firm or product line using the Action Grid. This tool costs no more than standard surveys and is available to companies with limited budgets.

This article is the second of a series of reports introducing some recently developed tools of marketing research to agribusiness managers. The first article (*Feedstuffs*, Dec. 26, 1977) presented a method of assessing company position based on a survey of buyer preferences.

We now present the Action Grid, a tool to assist the marketing manager to select specific strategies for improving company or product position in the eyes of buyers. The Action Grid is the end product of a dual analysis; it identifies the relative importance of factors influencing buyer preferences and also indicates the degree to which a particular company or product possesses these factors. That is, the procedure tells us how important a factor is to the buying decision and where our company is perceived to stand relative to others on those factors.

The Action Grid presents information which is directly useful in the design of a marketing strategy—whether the goal is to reposition the company or simply to maintain one's current position in the market. One of the bonuses of the method is that Action Grids for competitors can be built from the same data. After all, it is well known that "one peek is worth two finesses."

Consider a marketing manager of a feed firm. He

Source: Feedstuffs, May 8, 1978, pp. 38–39.

is trying to improve his firm's image in the eyes of potential customers and thereby to increase the firm's share of the market. Based on reactions from his own staff and a handful of present customers, he decides that the firm's promotions should emphasize that the firm is a local, "down home" operation.

Much to his surprise, sales and market share drop. Looking back, he sees that he made two mistakes. First, he selected a feature of the company which was associated in customers' minds principally with the market leader. As a result, his decision pitted the firm "head-to-head" against the more firmly established leader and came out second best in the confrontation. Second, he discovers that this feature is not actually given much weight in people's decisions to deal with one company rather than with another. Individuals simply prefer to report it as important to their purchase decisions. Apparently this company attribute is like apple pie, motherhood or the flag: people say they are important, but often don't let them influence action. The manager's basic problem was that he erred in identifying his firm's real strengths and weaknesses in the eyes of customers.

Our manager can be forgiven somewhat for his error. It is very difficult to identify the strengths and weaknesses of a firm in the eyes of the buyer. As one tries to do this, he too often finds conflicting information. Frequently, he is swamped with a mass of facts and figures which are impossible to interpret. Too often he is unsure about the degree of confidence he can place in the information he receives. All of us would agree that accurately identifying a firm's strengths and weaknesses is essential to developing sound marketing plans. Yet we also would agree that identifying these is more easily said than done.

What Must You Know?

Selecting targets for marketing action depends upon having information which is comparative, which indicates the importance of factors to buyers, and which is presented in a decision oriented mode.

The information must first be *comparative*. Clearly, it must compare the various features of the company. Is the firm stronger in regard to the quality of dealer service, the quantity of the technical information provided customers, the price of the product, etc.? At the same time, the information must compare one's company with its competitors in regard to each feature. How strong is my firm compared to the competitors in the quality of dealer service? In the quantity of technical information? The key is to make both comparisons *simultaneously*. Whatever numerical scores are used must reflect the feature's strength relative to other facets of the company *and* to the same feature of other companies.

The next test of the information is critical. It must include an evaluation of the degree each company (or product) feature is *determinant* of product purchase. That is, how likely is a feature to increase or decrease the chances of product purchase? Without a numerical estimate of determinance, the manager cannot know how much emphasis to give a feature. Without an index of determinance, one can be misled, as was our hypothetical manager, by apple pie and motherhood types of responses. Without a measure of determinance, the manager may be undone whenever people are unaware of the impact a particular feature actually has on their purchase decisions.

Finally, the above information must be keyed to managerial decisions in a straightforward manner. The manager needs all this information integrated into a *single picture*, one which suggests actions that

can be taken to achieve one's marketing goals. Otherwise, there is some risk of losing sight of the forest for the trees! This information is needed at reasonable cost and without requiring complex, time consuming data gathering activities.

The Action Grid Approach

The Action Grid is a set of procedures to provide the manager with information which would have the characteristics described above. Basically, it is a six step operation:

1. Identify *potentially* important firm or product features.
2. Conduct survey of customer opinions.
3. Estimate relative success of firms separately for each feature.
4. Estimate determinance of each feature.
5. Compose Action Grid.
6. Take action on identified strengths and weaknesses.

Let us look more closely at each step and illustrate the Action Grid with data based on a recent analysis.

Step 1: Identify Features

The process begins by identifying a workable number of company and/or product features which may influence product purchase. This is critical. Only a limited number of features can be considered; yet omission of too many relevant factors can invalidate the analysis.

How does one select these features? Generally the analysis uses information from the firm's staff, particularly if some past marketing research results are available to confirm those views. Some caution is required here, though. As noted in the first article in this series, the company's marketing or sales staff may not be in tune with farmers' desires. In these cases, group interviews or other exploratory studies may be necessary to select features for study.

In the analysis referred to above, prior research had identified both the company and product features to be used in the study.

Step 2: Conduct Survey

Here we gather data to estimate the relative success of the firm and its competitors with respect to each feature, and to gauge the determinance of each feature. A secondary goal should be to gather supplementary information which can crosscheck the reliability of these estimates.

In our illustrative project, a mail questionnaire was sent to farmers in a multi-state area who were identified as buyers of the product of interest. The questionnaire asked respondents to rank the 15 features of a firm in order of how important they are to one's purchase. A separate question asked them to choose from a list of 10 firms the one that is best in regard to each feature. These questions were then repeated for 13 product features. Other questions asked the farmers to indicate their overall willingness to deal with each of the 10 firms listed.

Step 3: Estimate Success of Firms

Here we must estimate how favorably farmers regard the firm and its competitors with respect to each feature. Basically, the numerical estimate of a firm's success is based on percentage of mentions that firm receives as best on a given feature. By definition, such a "success score" compares one firm with another; comparing the success scores obtained by the firm for the various features allows us to see the relative strengths of the firm's features.

In our example, each of the 10 firms studied was given a success score for each of the 15 features. A separate set of success scores was calculated for each market segment of interest to the firm (e.g., large vs. small firms and different sales territories).

Step 4: Estimate Determinancy of Each Feature

A manager cannot devise a workable marketing plan without knowing how strongly each firm or product feature impacts customers' purchase decisions. Unfortunately, many market research studies fail to measure a feature's determinance when attempting to gauge the strengths and weaknesses of the firm or its product line. When they do try to measure determinance, these estimates are frequently based solely upon what people *say* is the importance of a feature to their purchase decisions.

The Action Grid approach suggests that a viable index of a feature's determinance must combine two aspects of a feature—its "felt importance" and its "estimated relevance." "Felt importance" is the extent customers say a feature is important to their purchasing from one firm rather than from another. The "estimated relevance" is the degree that peoples' reactions to a feature can predict their reactions to the firm or its products. That is, estimated relevance is how closely customers' preferences for dealing with competing firms agree with their views of how well those firms are rated on a particular feature.

For example, suppose people preferred to deal with firm No. 1 more than with firms No. 2 or No. 3, but thought that firm No. 1 was no better than the other firms on feature A. In this case, the estimated relevance of that feature would be fairly low. On the other side of the coin, suppose farmers preferred firm No. 1 to 2, and 2 to 3, and thought that the same order of firms held in order of excellence on feature B. The estimated relevance of feature B would be high.

Both felt importance and estimated relevance are necessary to gauge a feature's determinance. Felt importance cannot stand alone because too many biases can creep into a person's reports of his own preferences. People often answer in terms of how they *wish* to behave, rather than in terms of how they *do* behave. There is a second reason why indices of felt importance cannot stand alone. If the researcher is not careful, respondents may focus their attention on features which are not determinant because all major firms have these features.

For example, feed marketed by a feed manufacturer must meet claimed nutrient levels. Yet a feed's meeting claimed nutrient levels is probably not determinant. Since the feed of all major firms qualify, this is not a feature which will lead farmers to deal with one firm rather than with another. For these reasons, the marketing manager needs a crosscheck on felt importance, a way of finding reports that don't line up with farmers' actual decisions. Estimated relevance provides that crosscheck.

Nor can estimated relevance alone indicate a feature's determinance. People's reactions to a particular feature may be able to predict their over-all tendency to deal with those firms, yet that feature may not directly influence product purchase. An example of this is the case in which the leading brand is produced by the largest company. The size and market share coincidence may extend through several companies. Size of company may then predict market share for the particular product, but, obviously, it's not the size of the company that causes people to purchase that item.

When the felt importance and the estimated relevance of a feature are high, the feature is determinant and so is worthy of the manager's attention.

If both felt importance and estimated relevance are low, the manager can conclude that the feature is minimally determinant and so can be treated as trivial. If the two indices do not dovetail, however, we should conservatively conclude that the feature's determinancy is uncertain. In a majority of cases, however, we would anticipate that the uncertain features will not be strongly determinant.

In our illustrative study, felt importance was gauged from the questionnaire item asking farmers to rank various features of a firm in order of importance to one's purchase. Multidimensional scaling techniques similar to those described in our previous report (*Feedstuffs*, Dec. 26, 1977) were used to obtain a numerical index of importance.

Estimated relevance can be measured by the strength of the agreement between people's evaluations of companies on a particular feature and their over-all willingness to deal with those firms. In our illustrative project, the evaluations of companies on a feature were drawn from the survey item asking which firm was best on a feature. Over-all willingness to deal with a firm can be calculated from market share data, actual purchases by survey respondents, or from direct questions about one's willingness to deal with competing companies. We measured it by the survey items asking respondents to state their preferences for dealing with the firms listed. The measure of agreement between the two was obtained through a correlational analysis. Finally, the estimated relevance score and the felt importance score of each feature were combined to yield a single determinance score.

Step 5: Compose Action Grid

A firm's Action Grid shows the determinance of a feature on the vertical and the firm's relative success on that feature on the horizontal. Cross hairs dividing the grid into four sections are then added to make the Grid easier to read. A Grid is developed for one's own company and for each competitor of interest. Action Grids for two companies, the case firm (letters circled) and a competing firm (plain letters) is illustrated. In the interest of brevity, the analysis of only nine company characteristics, labeled A to I, is presented here.

The higher the determinance score, the more a feature is estimated to impact product purchase. Hence, the higher the score the more attention it deserves. In Figure 1, the manager should consider features A, B, C, D, and G in his marketing plans. Features H, I, E, and F can be given less consideration. The higher the success score, the more the firm dominates its competitors on that feature. Here, the firm is quite successful for features A, B, G, F, and E, but is relatively unsuccessful for the other features.

The closer is a feature to the upper right corner, the more is it a strength of the firm. The troublesome features are in the "Weakness" section. The closer is a feature to the upper left, the greater

Figure 1
Action grids

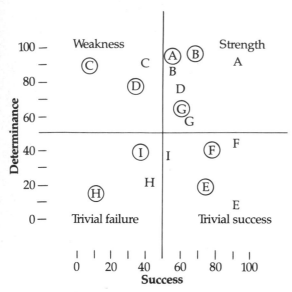

Letter indicates feature code.
Case firm Ⓐ   Competitor A

problem it represents. Since features near the bottom of the grid are trivial, they are best deleted from consideration as one lists his strengths and weaknesses.

Step 6: Take Action

Suppose one's marketing strategy dictates the presentation of a unique image, one which would optimally position the firm vis-a-vis the competitors. In this case the marketing manager would attend principally to those features pertinent to that image. In other cases maketing plans may strive to be outstanding in all crucial (i.e., determinant) features, whether or not those features coalesce into a unique image. Here the manager would focus upon all features which are substantially determinant. In either situation, though, one's marketing policies, product line and promotional themes could be coordinated to emphasize features in the upper right-

hand corner of the grid. Conversely, items in the upper left-hand corner should be evaluated to determine whether they represent a perceptual error or a real weakness.

The action implications of the grid are most easily seen when competing firms are considered. For simplicity let us treat the competitor shown *as if* this firm represented the majority of competitors.

Clearly, the case firm could emphasize feature B, in that the firm has a comparative advantage on this highly determinant feature. Features A and G may be less profitably stressed; although the firm is viewed favorably on these determinant features, so also is the competition.

The Achilles heels of the case firm were features C and D. These features appeared to be major stumbling blocks to enhancing the firm's market share. Management policies and product development priorities need revision in order to improve these features.

Finally, features E, F, H and I should not be the focus of the firm's marketing plans, for they are relatively unimportant to product purchase. Features E and H were interesting in this regard. A number of staff in the case firm had felt that E and H were important issues. They anticipated that E was a real strength of the firm, while H was a thorn in the firm's side. The survey, however, indicated that, although the firm stacked up well against the competition in E and was bested badly by other firms in H, both features were inconsequential and so could safely be dropped from consideration.

Conclusion

The Action Grid approach can be very useful in identifying features of one's firm or product line which are strengths in the eyes of customers and, so, can be emphasized in promotional and other marketing efforts. Conversely, it can point out features which are obstacles to increasing one's market share and, hence, should be corrected or, at least, deemphasized in promotional campaigns. The Action Grid is easy to understand and develop. It is based on a logical foundation and hence its implications for managerial decisions can be derived in a straightforward manner. Because it costs no more than standard surveys, it is available even to companies with limited market research budgets.

Like any technique, though, it is not without potential problems. On occasion, too many features may appear to have uncertain determinance. When this situation occurs, it may often be traced to the way in which Step 1 was performed. Inadequate attention to Step 1 can result in a poor selection of features for study. There probably is no technique available anywhere that can overcome a study's looking at the wrong things! An allied issue is that determinance must be inferred rather than directly measured in some situations. At these times data may not be available to check the assumptions of causality underlying the determinance measures. Another potential problem of the approach is that the technique depends to some extent on the user's qualitative judgment. Most obvious is the initial selection of features in Step 1. Thus, application of the approach depends on knowledge of the firms involved and their product lines.

Suitably used, the Action Grid can be a valuable decision aid for the marketing manager. Yet it is an aid, a tool to supplement the manager's knowledge; it is not a replacement for that knowledge.

The next article in this series discusses methods of evaluating alternative pricing strategies.

Reference

Martilla, John A. and John C. James, "Importance-Performance Analysis," *Journal of Marketing*, January, 1977, pp. 77–79. An earlier attempt at an Action Grid approach.

Questions

1. *When we select a bank in which to deposit our money, safety or security is important. However, safety is seldom a determinant factor. Explain.*
2. *Explain how the Action Grid can be used to identify and evaluate a firm's strengths and weaknesses.*

9

The Moving Target:
The Impact of Women's
Employment
on Consumer Behavior

RENA BARTOS

About half of the work force in the United States today is female. Working women certainly differ from full-time housewives in some of their market behavior. But there is no single stereotype that satisfactorily describes the working-women market segment.

The recent AMA conference, "Marketing Implications of the Changing Role of Women," signals recognition of a major demographic trend. That trend is a manifestation of profound social changes that might be called a quiet revolution.

The sheer increase in women's presence in the work force can be looked at two ways: *first,* the proportion of all workers who are women; and *second,* the proportion of all women who are workers.

In 1950 women represented 29.6% of all workers in the U.S. By 1975 their share had increased over ten percentage points to 39.9%.

At the turn of the century only 20% of all women went to work. In 1975 the proportion of women in the work force more than doubled to 46%.

The predictions are that women will continue to go to work at an unprecedented rate: 48.4% by 1980, 50.3% by 1985, and 51.4% by 1990. The Bureau of Labor Statistics predicts that by 1985 more than half of all women 16 years of age and over will be in the work force.

Source: Journal of Marketing, July 1977, pp. 31–37. Reprinted from *Journal of Marketing* published by the American Marketing Association.

Women as a Marketing Target

The definition of target groups is a basic step in marketing. The way we define those targets inevitably leads to marketing decisions relating to product development, product positioning, and communications strategies. Even research done to guide future strategic planning is directed or limited by the way we define the samples of those studies.

If the fact is that women's work changes them as consumers, then inevitably that knowledge should lead to at least some redefinition of women as a marketing target. If the women's market can no longer be assumed to be "any housewife 18 to 49," we may need to redefine that target or those targets. Is the working woman really a moving target? Are there any real differences between working women and their stay-at-home sisters when they go marketing?

The problem of simple comparison of the consumer behavior of working and non-working women implies that the situation is monolithic. It assumes that all working women are cut out of one pattern and that all non-working women are cut out of another. Once we define the two cookie-cutter patterns, we can determine not just how their behaviors differs, but how to communicate to them in the marketing place.

Differences in Quality

One of the most striking aspects of the increase of women in the work force is not their sheer quantity, but the changes in the quality of the women who work. What kinds of women have gone to work? And what are their reasons for doing so? Answers to these two questions provide some clues to the reality behind the cookie cutters.

There is not just a rise in the total number of women working, but a change in the kinds of women they are. Married women are responsible for the dramatic increase in the number of women at work. But the amazing news is the number of mothers of young children who have also joined the work force. (See Exhibit 1.)

Why are these women of all ages with all kinds of family responsibilities flocking to the work force? The obvious reason, of course, might be economic. Certainly as prices continue to go up, many women simply work for that second paycheck in order to help the family maintain its standard of living.

There are an increasing number of women who are working not just to get away from the limitations and drudgery of the household, but because of a sense of professional achievement and personal satisfaction that career-oriented men have always known. This is the move away from women finding their identities through the derived status of being wives and mothers to establishing identities of their own. This fact is most evident among better educated women and among younger women. And it seems to be a trend that will simply not go away.

Exhibit 1
Working wives (1950–1975)

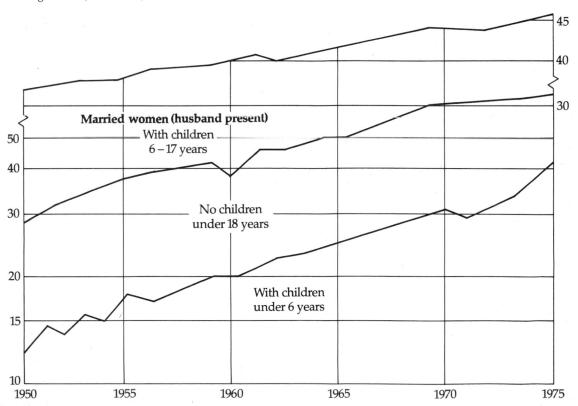

Another clue toward understanding how working impacts on the consumer behavior of women is to look at both working and non-working women, each in terms of their life situations. (See Exhibit 2.)

That single woman, without a husband or children, could be the young girl living at home, the young career girl just starting out on her own, or she could be an older widow or divorcee who has been married, had children, and is now alone in life.

The couple without children could represent the young couple just starting out or the older, empty-nest family. And with the move toward zero population growth and the wide acceptance of childlessness, this young couple may never have children, or could be a middle-aged couple without children.

At the other extreme, there are the increasing number of women who are mothers raising children without benefit of a father in the house.

The hypothesis is a simple one. In order to really understand the impact of work force participation on women as consumers, it is necessary to compare working with non-working women, within their situations in the life cycle.

However, there are attitudinal differences that go beyond the simple demography of whether or not a woman is married, or whether or not she has a child at home. When Yankelovich asked housewives in their sample group whether they ever planned to go to work, it was assumed that the answer to this kind of question in an interview situation would be a predisposition rather than a prediction of behavior. When we first encountered this question, approximately half of the housewives in the sample said they planned to go to work.

Yankelovich asked an equally intriguing question of working women: Do you consider the work you do "just a job" or a "career." This was not a question of what they did on the job, but how they felt about their work. At the time we first encountered this question, the ratio was roughly 70% "just a job" and 30% "career."

Exhibit 3 shows the size of each of the four segments forming the New Demographics, assembled for the J. Walter Thompson projection based on the

Exhibit 2

Life cycle profile of American women: 1974

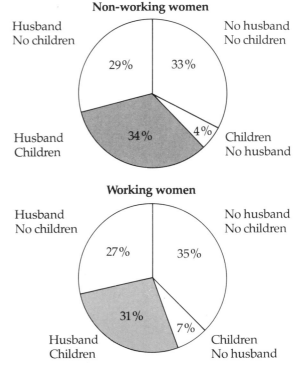

Source: Bureau of Labor Statistics, March 1974.

Exhibit 3

Size of the segments

	%	Number
Housewives		
Stay at home	29	20,803,781
Plan to work	20	14,260,803
Working women		
Just a job	32	22,584,223
Career	19	13,262,346
	100%	70,911,153

Source: JWT projection based on Yankelovich Monitor, 1975; Bureau of Labor Statistics, 1975; Target Group Index, 1975. Base: All women 16 & over in labor force or keeping house.

Yankelovich monitor, the Bureau of Labor Statistics (January 1975) and the Target Group Index (1975).

Differences in Buying Behavior

Until recently we had no way of knowing which of the housewives in our audiences or in our research studies were the "stay at home" variety and which ones were those who would say they "plan to work." Even if we had been innovative enough to talk specifically to working women, until now we haven't differentiated between the "just a job" and the career-minded types.

The real challenge in trying to make a connection between a fascinating clue like these data and marketing actions is to know whether these groups of consumers are really different in their marketing

behavior. Is the "plans-to-work" housewife a different kind of consumer than the "stay-at-home?" How do the career women and the "just-a-job" working women compare as customers? Who buys more? What kinds of products? Which brands?

Now let's consider some of the big-ticket products or services which are normally considered to be men's markets: financial services, travel, and cars.

Women and Money

How does working impact on women's financial activities? Working women are more likely than nonworking housewives to have savings accounts, regular checking accounts, and credit cards, as shown in Exhibit 4-A. The one area in which this pattern

Exhibit 4-A
Women and money

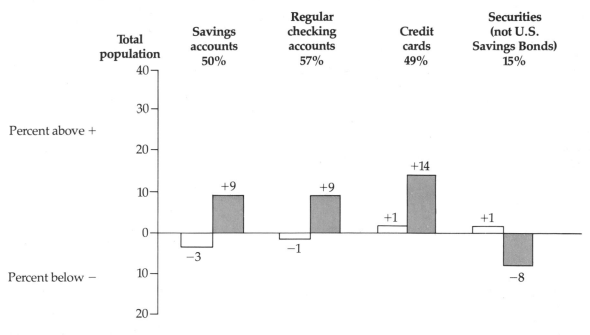

Women ☐ Don't work ■ Work

Exhibit 4-B
Married women: money

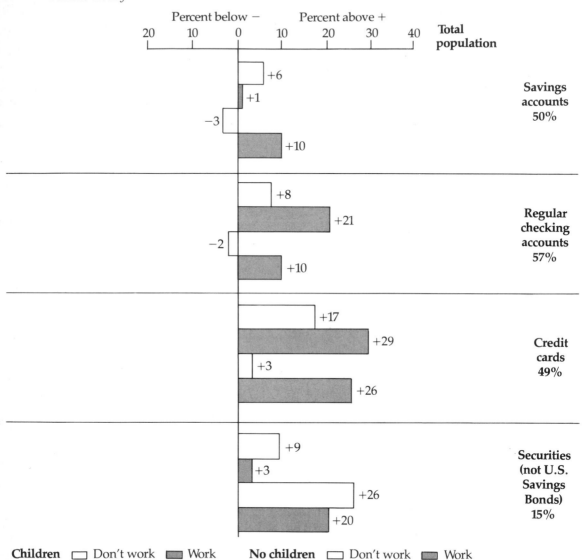

	Percent below −	Percent above +	

Total population

Savings accounts 50%: +6, +1, −3, +10

Regular checking accounts 57%: +8, +21, −2, +10

Credit cards 49%: +17, +29, +3, +26

Securities (not U.S. Savings Bonds) 15%: +9, +3, +26, +20

Children ☐ Don't work ▨ Work   **No children** ☐ Don't work ▨ Work

does not hold true is in ownership of securities beyond government savings bonds. Working women are somewhat below the norm in owning securities.

Now let's take a look at how this is affected by their stage in the life cycle as shown in Exhibits 4-B and 4-C:

The married housewife with children tops her working counter-part in having a savings account. But the childless married woman who works is more likely to have her own savings account than her "stay-at-home" counter-part.

The housewife with children at home is more likely to have a checking account than her childless

Exhibit 4-C

Unmarried women: money

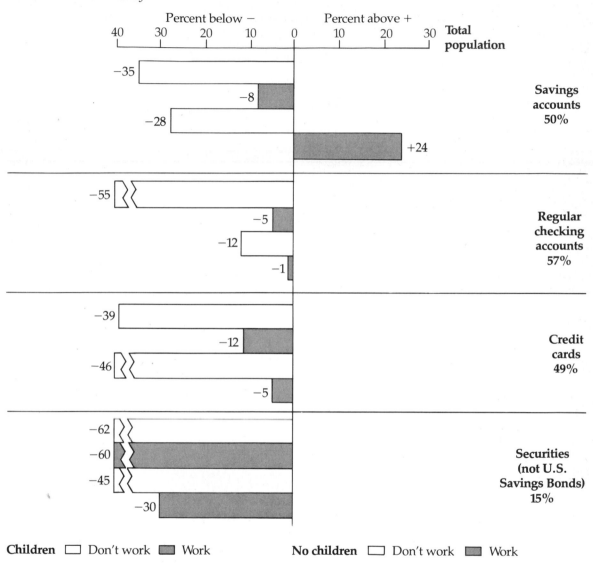

Children ☐ Don't work ▨ Work   **No children** ☐ Don't work ▨ Work

neighbor. However, in each case, their working sisters are more active checking account customers.

As depicted in Exhibit 4-D, the career-oriented working woman dominates financial activities. She is more likely than any group to have a savings ac-

count, to maintain a regular checking account, to have any credit cards, or to have investments. Among the housewives, the "plan-to-work" housewife does all of these things but to a far lesser degree than the career woman. The "just-a-job" working woman is at par in everything but investments, where she is well below the norm. The

Exhibit 4-D
New demographics: money

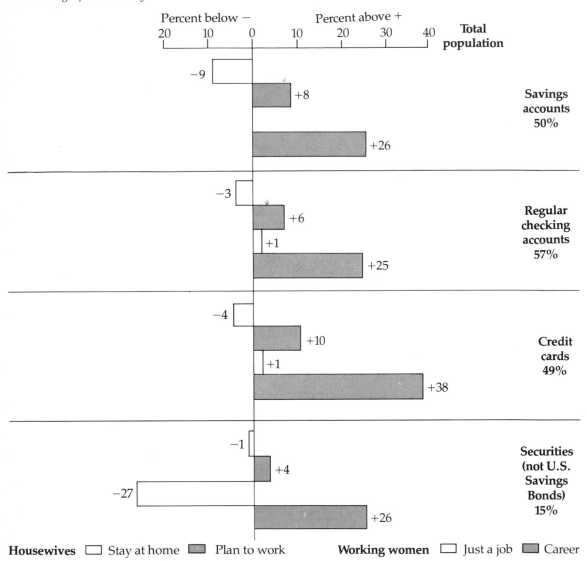

Housewives □ Stay at home ■ Plan to work Working women □ Just a job ■ Career "stay-at-home" housewife is far less involved in financial activity than any of the other groups.

Women and Travel

Is there any difference in the extent to which working and non-working women participate in travel activities? Exhibit 5-A shows that working women are far more likely to buy luggage, use travelers checks, have travelled in the United States by airplane, and to have stayed at a hotel. Are there differences in terms of their life situations? We can see from Exhibit 5-B that married working women without children at home are by far the best customers for travel services and products among all married women.

When we look at the unmarried women, as depicted in Exhibit 5-C, we see that the combination of no children at home and available income from a paycheck appears to provide the passport to women's travel activity.

In terms of the New Demographics, the career-oriented working woman is really the prime customer for travel. The "plans-to-work" housewife has bought some luggage, but she doesn't seem to have taken many trips recently. (See Exhibit 5-D.)

Women and Cars

One of the Detroit myths is that the only automotive decision that women make is to pick out the color of the upholstery. From Exhibit 6-A it can be seen that working women are somewhat more likely to have a driver's license and that they are slightly more likely to have two or more cars in their garages. The housewife is apt to have shared

Exhibit 5-A
Women and travel

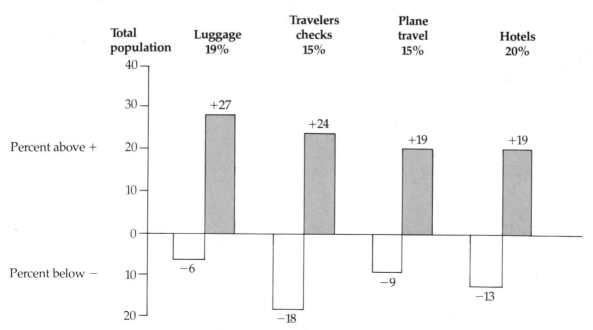

Exhibit 5-B
Married women: travel

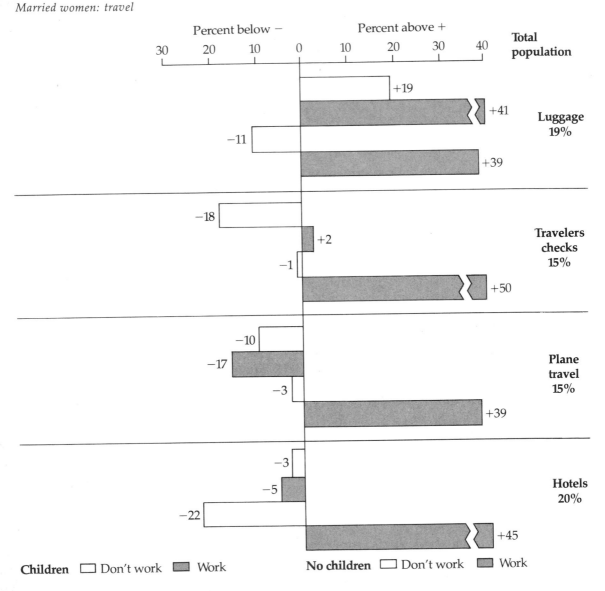

Exhibit 5-C
Unmarried women: travel

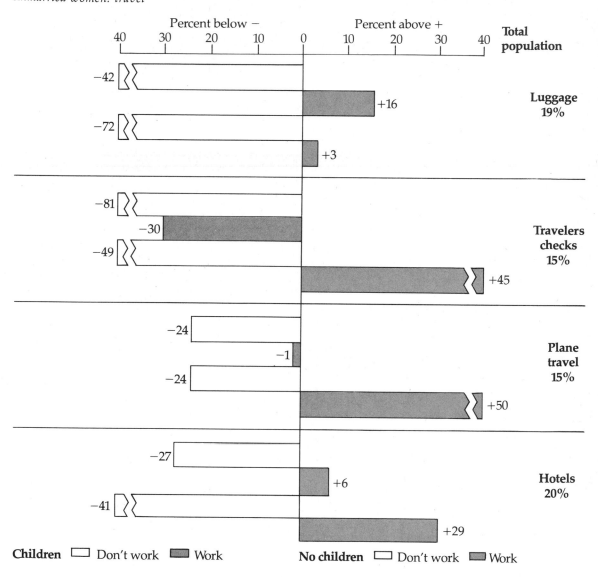

Children ☐ Don't work ■ Work   **No children** ☐ Don't work ■ Work

Exhibit 5-D
New demographics: travel

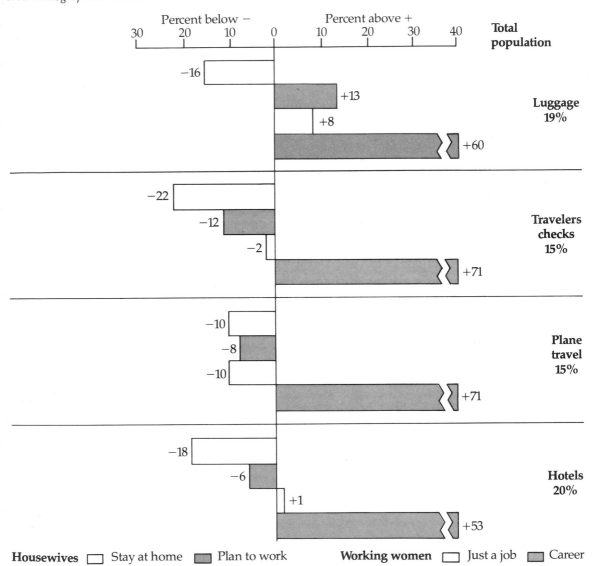

Exhibit 6-A

Women and cars

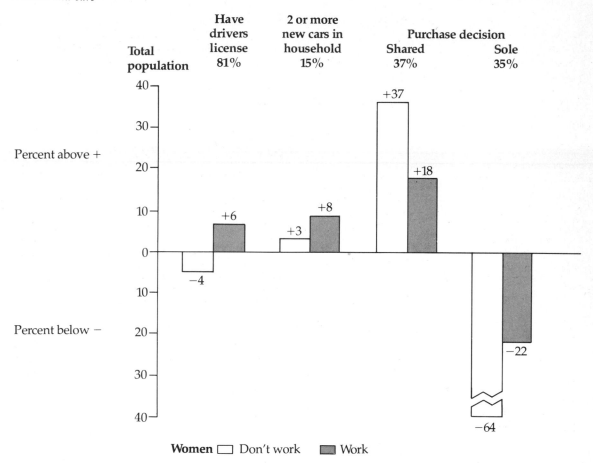

| | Total population | Have drivers license 81% | 2 or more new cars in household 15% | Purchase decision Shared 37% | Purchase decision Sole 35% |

Women ☐ Don't work ■ Work

in the car purchase decision, following the common experience that all women are more likely than the total population to report this kind of shared decision-making.

Both working women and housewives are below the norm in having selected a car totally on their own. However, the working woman is more likely than the full-time housewife to have bought her own car.

As Exhibit 6-B indicates, the married woman with no children under 18 at home is least likely of the four groups to have a driver's license. The

working mothers and the childless working and nonworking women are the most likely to have two or more new cars in their garages.

Conversely, all married women with and without children are far below the norm in buying cars on their own. But, in each case, the working woman is slightly more likely to buy her own car than her non-working sister.

Unmarried women are less involved in almost every aspect of car ownership than their married neighbors with one dramatic exception. The unmarried working women, both those with children

Exhibit 6-B
Married women: cars

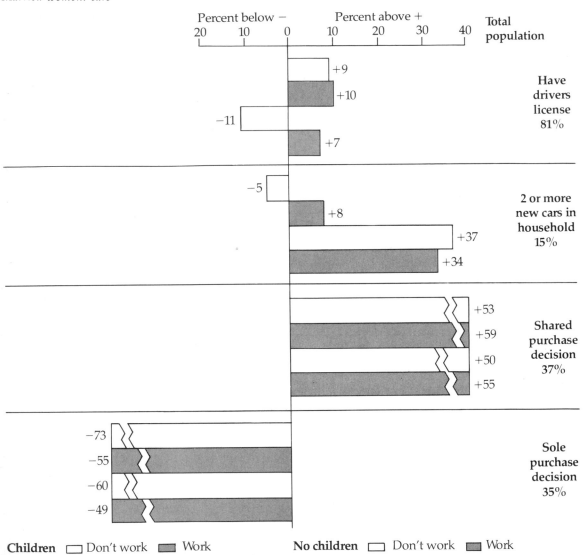

Percent below −   Percent above +   Total
20   10   0   10   20   30   40   population

+9
+10
−11
+7
Have drivers license 81%

−5
+8
+37
+34
2 or more new cars in household 15%

+53
+59
+50
+55
Shared purchase decision 37%

−73
−55
−60
−49
Sole purchase decision 35%

Children ☐ Don't work ▨ Work   **No children** ☐ Don't work ▨ Work

(divorcees and widows) and particularly those without, are clearly above the norm in selection and ownership of their own cars. (See Exhibit 6-C.)

Who is most likely to drive? The New Demographics again pin-points the career woman, followed by the "plans-to-work" housewife, as shown in Exhibit 6-D. But when it comes to having more than one car at home, through the purchase of a

new vehicle, although the career woman is the most likely customer, a substantial proportion of the "stay-at-home" housewives also report well-stocked garages. This skewing reflects income, but at two very different ends of the life-style spectrum.

Looking at the purchase decision for cars, all women are above the norm in having shared in that event. The two housewife groups are more likely to

Exhibit 6-C
Unmarried women: cars

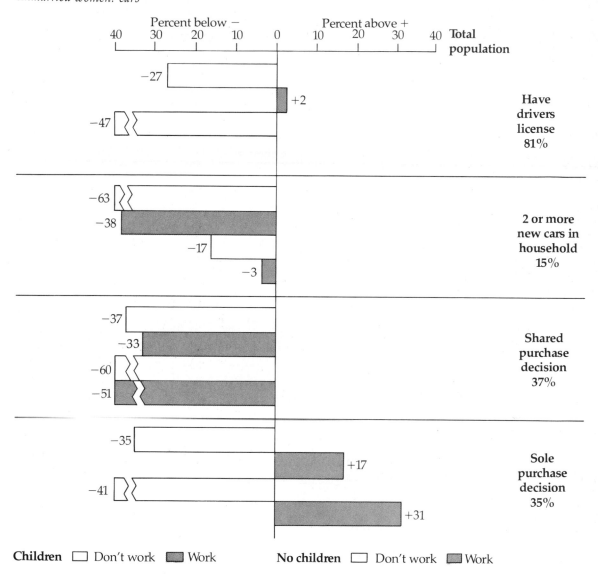

Children ☐ Don't work ◼ Work   **No children** ☐ Don't work ◼ Work

have done so, and the "plans-to-work" housewife took the most active part in that shared decision. Again, while all women are below par in their having made the decision themselves, there is a dramatic difference in this regard between the working women and the non-working women. The career woman is the most likely of the four groups to have bought a car herself.

Summary

We started out to learn whether or not working impacts on the consumer behavior of women. This brief look at some of the current data suggests that, yes, working women do differ from full-time housewives in some of their market behavior. We have also seen that we must go beyond a simplistic

Exhibit 6-D
New demographics: cars

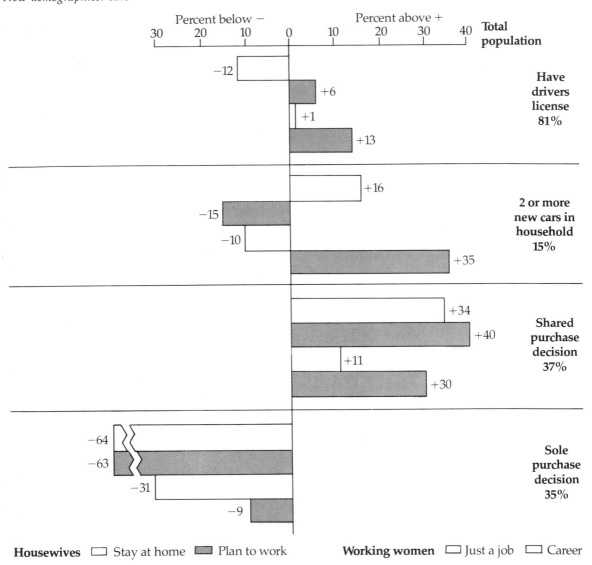

Percent below −   Percent above +   Total
30   20   10   0   10   20   30   40   population

Have drivers license 81%
−12
+6
+1
+13

2 or more new cars in household 15%
+16
−15
−10
+35

Shared purchase decision 37%
+34
+40
+11
+30

Sole purchase decision 35%
−64
−63
−31
−9

Housewives ☐ Stay at home ▧ Plan to work   **Working women** ☐ Just a job ☐ Career comparison of working women with housewives if we are to understand these two kinds of markets.

The contrast found in the investment behavior of career women and the "just-a-job" working women is dramatic evidence of the need to go beyond the perspective "working women" as a monolithic group.

There are two additional ways to give fuller dimension to our consideration of women who work. The first is to place any comparisons that we do of the market behavior of working and non-working women within the context of their life situations. The second incorporates the attitudes of women toward their present or potential roles in the work force—what we call the "New Demographics."

Very often when this kind of data is reviewed with marketing groups, they accept the evidence but they are troubled about its implications. This way of redefining the target does not necessarily mean that marketers need to develop sixteen separate strategies for the various life cycle and New Demographic groups. What it does mean is that we have a new way to dissect the market for a particular product and assess the value potential of all of these kinds of consumers. We can then build them

each into the marketing mix in their proper proportions and construct our strategies on the needs of our most promising prospects. This process takes the jigsaw puzzle apart and puts it back together again. Thus, we may uncover previously unmet product needs and fresh ways to communicate.

However, we might very well end up with a single strategy. But I guarantee that it will not be the same old cliché that would have occurred if we had defined our target as "any housewife, 18 to 49." Nor will it be the new kind of cliché that will develop if we assume that our target is "any working woman, 18 to 49."

Questions

1. *What are the major product categories in which working women's marketing mix preferences could be expected to differ dramatically from the preferences of full-time housewives?*
2. *What are some product categories in which working women's marketing mix preferences could be expected to be very similar to those of full-time housewives?*

10

Market Opportunity Analysis:
A Systematic Approach
for Practical Applications

ROBERT B. WOODRUFF

Conducting a market opportunity analysis is a critical stage in the marketing planning process. Woodruff proposes a systematic approach to assist corporate decision makers in developing and maintaining a base of knowledge about company market opportunities.

The thrust of the marketing concept applied to corporate management is that business decisions affecting market performance should reflect a sound understanding of the needs and wants of potential customers. This concept places the responsibility on marketing to communicate "the needs of the market to all major corporate departments."[1] Marketing managers have traditionally been expected to build and maintain a sound understanding of customers and markets in order to manage the selling activities of a firm. Now, the same market expertise is being recognized as a requirement for any corporate decision which affects market performance including new product development, corporate acquisitions, and distribution of products and services. The penalty for not bringing a knowledge of customers into corporate decisions is illustrated by an unsuccessful distribution decision made by Singer Company. Management attempted to expand the product mix sold in Singer's sewing machine stores by adding TV and audio products. Only later, after distribution had been established, did management discover that women who visit sewing machine stores are not the decision makers for TV and audio products.[2]

The importance of understanding customers and markets for corporate decision making is readily apparent. Yet, building and then maintaining the required market expertise is often quite difficult. Marketing managers may be prevented from frequent direct contact with customers by the corporate hierarchy and location which keeps them tied to a desk and away from the distribution points where products are sold. For many marketing personnel, the most intimate contact with customers comes during their first job as salesmen when decision responsibility is limited. As managers rise up the corporate ladder and are given more decision making responsibility the amount of time that can be devoted to meeting and interacting with customers becomes increasingly limited. Even sending corporate executives out into the marketplace to "press the flesh" by meeting potential customers firsthand is not sufficient to overcome the separation of management and customers.

Complicating the physical separation between managers and customers is the consistent tendency for markets to change—sometimes slowly, sometimes rapidly. Consider the challenge faced by

Source: Business Horizons, 19 (August 1976), 55–65. Copyright © 1976, by the Foundation for the School of Business at Indiana University. Reprinted by permission. (An expanded treatment of this topic by David W. Cravens, Gerald E. Hills, and Robert B. Woodruff appears in *Marketing Decision Making: Concepts and Strategy,* Homewood, Ill.: Irwin, 1976.)

1. Carlton P. McNamara, "The Present Status of the Marketing Concept," *Journal of Marketing,* Vol. 36 (January, 1972), p. 51.

2. "Why the Profits Vanished at Singer," *Business Week,* June 30, 1975, p. 106.

Gerber Products Company's management stemming from the "birth dearth" and changes in family structure. Declining birth rates and changes in attitudes toward the desirability of having children, timing of having children, and the number of children have led to a less attractive baby-food market.[3] Gerber and other companies dependent on baby-food products must find new strategies and expand into new markets in order to achieve corporate objectives.

The net effect of these problems is that managers must develop effective methods for building and maintaining an ongoing knowledge of customers and markets for use in corporate decision making. These methods cannot depend on any one source of market information such as periodic visits by executives to the marketplace, or even marketing research studies. Rather, methods must integrate customer information that may come from several different sources. The purpose of this article is to present a systematic approach for conducting market opportunity analyses which will provide the foundation for building the needed understanding of customers and markets. The first section defines market opportunity and discusses the requirements for effectively analyzing markets. In the next section, the major tasks included in market opportunity analyses are presented. The final section discusses the major outputs of market opportunity analyses and their uses in corporate decision making.

The Determinants of Market Opportunity

When evaluating possible market targets, management is often most interested in the potential size of demand in a market. This is appropriate because market size is an important indication of potential revenue flow that can be generated to cover costs and contribute to profits. Yet, the opportunity for a firm to achieve corporate and marketing objectives by serving a market is dependent only in part on

size. For example, selecting a very large market as a market target may not be a very good strategy. A large market that is being effectively served by competitors is often not an opportune market. Imagine trying to build another apartment complex in a city already saturated with apartments. Regardless of the size of housing demand available, the opportunity for a new complex may be very poor. Thus, market opportunity is partially dependent on how well demand is already being served by other firms.

Finally, market opportunity is also determined by marketing program requirements for a firm to effectively serve the wants and needs of the market. Assessing these requirements involves understanding the unique characteristics and demands of potential customers in order to determine what must be designed into marketing programs. The crucial link between market opportunity and the design of competitive, want-satisfying marketing programs is illustrated by the marketing strategy of American Motors Corporation. AMC depends heavily on "designing new-looking cars that can successfully compete with ones cranked out by rivals five to 165 times American Motors' size—Detroit's Big Three auto makers."[4] The success of the AMC Pacer demonstrates the rewards that can accrue to the company that meets market needs.

These three major determinants of market opportunity are shown in box B of Figure 1. To assist management in making market target and marketing programming decisions, a market opportunity analysis must help managers assess each one. Thus, the determinants of market opportunity offer guidelines for developing a practical approach to conducting analyses of market opportunities.

Analyzing Market Opportunities

Market Opportunity Analysis in Perspective

Market opportunity analysis is comprised of several interrelated activities that are shown in box A of

3. "The Baby-Food Market," *Business Week*, July 13, 1974, p. 45.

4. "Shoestring Styling: When Richard Teague Thinks Up a New Car, It's a 'Make-Do' Effort," *The Wall Street Journal*, June 18, 1975, p. 1.

Figure 1
*MOA activities for assessing the major determinants of
market opportunity*

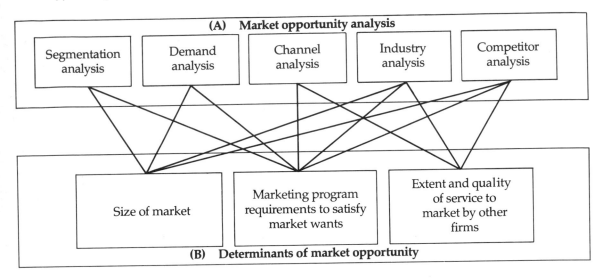

Figure 1. Each analysis activity is intended to provide management with a basis for assessing the key determinants of market opportunity. The lines linking MOA activities with the opportunity determinants in Figure 1 show which determinants are the focus for each MOA activity. For example, a contractor wishing to evaluate the market opportunity for a condominium complex in a city would use demand analysis to estimate the size of a market and to help determine whether the firm is capable of serving the market with a particular complex. The other MOA activities would be needed to more fully evaluate capability of serving the market and extent of market service provided by other firms since these determinants are not based solely on demand. Each of these MOA activities is briefly examined. To help visualize the purpose of market opportunity analysis, a MOA for a contractor evaluating whether to build a condominium complex will be used to illustrate each analysis activity.

Demand Analysis

The core activity of market opportunity analysis is the analysis of demand contained in a market. A market is a group of people or firms who are able and willing to buy a product or service for end-use purposes. First note that a market is comprised of final buyers of a product or service rather than intermediate buyers (those buying only for resale of the product). Demand analysis should concentrate on end users since there is considerable risk in only assessing intermediate buyers. For some products, such as condominiums, this guideline is obvious since there are no intermediate buyers. Condominium builders sell units directly to household end users. For other products, though, there may be a temptation to assess only intermediate buyers. For example, a small manufacturer of a food flavoring product focused its activities toward intermediate buyers, distributors and large retailers, of its products. This analysis caused management to become dissatisfied with the marketing effort of these resellers. However, management had no basis for proposing specific changes since they knew practically nothing about the consumers who were buying and using the product.

A market only exists when there is demand for some *product* or *service*. The mere presence of an unfulfilled want among some group of people does not constitute a market to a firm. So, analysis of demand must begin with a description of the product or service that people are able and willing to buy to satisfy wants. The product may be an already existing product or nothing more than a new product idea. There are varying levels of detail for describing a product using its characteristics. Consider again the analysis of the opportunity for a new condominium complex. The contractor must decide whether to assess demand for (1) all housing, (2) all condominiums, as well as (3) the firm's proposed condominium complex. In essence the "product" has been successively defined in greater detail in moving from a broad, generic description of housing to a more specific description of one

housing type, and finally down to the contractor's particular design of a condominium complex. Each market for a more specifically defined product is a subset of the market for a more broadly defined product. For example, the market for all condominiums is a subset of the market for all housing in a community. This is illustrated in Figure 2.

An important characteristic of MOAs is that the analysis of demand can be done at different levels corresponding to the degree of product description detail under consideration. For example, an analysis of aggregate demand for a product that has been defined rather broadly can help management determine the upper limit on the demand available to the firm. This is the market in which all firms in an industry are selling. Then, demand analysis can proceed to assess in more detail the portion of this total demand that is available for the firm's particular product or service offering. This latter step is necessary to determine whether the firm can establish a sufficiently profitable niche in the aggregate market to warrant taking advantage of the opportunity.

As an illustration of demand analyses performed

Figure 2

Illustrative markets for housing in a community

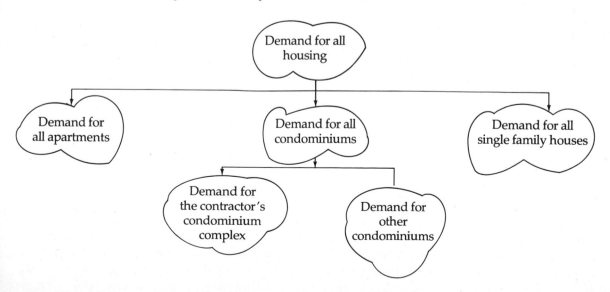

in stages at different product/market levels, suppose a contractor has purchased a large tract of land in an urban community. A market opportunity is believed to exist for a high priced, luxury condominium complex that can be built on this land. But, management has enough uncertainty about the nature and extent of this opportunity to make a MOA worthwhile. The demand analysis might begin by assessing the *demand for all housing* in the community. After all, the demand for the contractor's condominium will come from this housing demand. So, understanding the aggregate demand for housing will help management assess major trends and factors affecting people's housing decisions. For example, changes in mobility in combination with population growth in the community may suggest an expanding housing opportunity.

Since condominiums represent only one of several housing alternatives, the contractor will want to follow up with an analysis of the *demand for condominiums*. This assumes, of course, that the housing demand analysis has indicated a sufficiently attractive market opportunity to continue the MOA. Now, the contractor must determine the market opportunity for condominiums as opposed to other types of housing. Information on such factors as the type of person most likely to want a condominium; the extent of knowledge people have about condominium arrangements; interest rates, mortgage money availability and other financial considerations that affect people's choice between housing alternatives; and relative preferences people have for housing alternatives will help management assess whether demand for condominiums is attractive.

Finally, the contractor must assess whether the firm's particular condominium complex will be likely to generate a large enough *share of all condominium demand* within the community to meet company objectives. This requires a highly detailed analysis of the portion of the total condominium market that are potential customers of the firm's proposed offering. Information on the number and description of people able to buy a luxury condominium, their preferences for building type

(e.g., high rise vs. garden units) and location, amenities preferences, and so forth is needed to aid management in estimating the market opportunity for the firm. This kind of information will also help management determine what must be designed into the complex in order to attract customers.

Market Segmentation Analysis

Market segmentation is a strategic approach to selecting market targets and designing marketing programs appealing directly toward target segments. So, segmentation extends beyond the analysis of market opportunity into non-demand-related areas such as cost analyses. Yet, when a firm decides to employ a market segmentation strategy, there is an important overlap with market opportunity analysis. Demand analysis is needed to identify and describe profiles of segment buyers who will respond similarly to marketing program alternatives. For example, if a contractor wants to segment the multifamily housing market in a community in order to find a profitable "niche" for a condominium complex, demand analysis is needed to identify segments comprised of people who want the advantages of condominium living. One segment, for instance, might be elderly, high income, empty nesters who desire a condominium complex with elaborate security arrangements ensuring their safety. In this way, market segmentation provides direction for demand analysis in determining what management needs to know about product and/or brand markets. On the other hand, demand analysis may help management discover the potential for applying a market segmentation strategy. Demand analysis on a total market may uncover essential differences among market customers that can be used to form segments for the purpose of selecting market targets. For example, an anlaysis of housing demand may uncover important differences in the people who buy condominiums from those who rent apartments. These differences may suggest a market segmentation strategy.

Industry Analysis

Market opportunity for a firm depends as much on how well demand is being served by other firms as on the size and nature of demand. So, a market opportunity analysis should help management assess the extent and quality of service provided by competition. A useful starting point is to assess the entire industry that is serving a market. The task is not to examine individual firms, but to focus on an industry as a whole, where an industry is made up of the group of firms comprising direct competitors. For example, for a contractor doing a MOA for housing markets, the relevant industry is all other contractors serving the same market.

An industry analysis should help management determine how well demand is being developed by industry practices. Of paramount importance is assessing the directions in which the industry is moving during the time period covered by the MOA. This means that a MOA must provide information that will highlight industry trends. Such information should describe industry growth in terms of output, sales, number of firms and other factors that show how well the industry has been satisfying the potential that exists within a market. For example, an industry analysis of multifamily housing in a community, when compared with demand, may show that contractors as a group have been narrowing the gap between demand and supply. This indicates a declining opportunity for new units.

An industry analysis should also identify common operating practices of an industry. The focus is *not* on practices of individual firms, but on those practices which generally characterize the whole industry. This kind of information serves several purposes. Management is alerted to possible barriers to entering an industry or to staying within an industry. For example, our contractor considering entering the housing market in a community may discover that certain financial help (e.g., helping buyers to obtain loans) is typically given to prospective customers. Management may have to have working relationships with lending institutions already developed in order to compete for condominium customers. If these relationships have not already been developed or cannot be developed very quickly, then the contractor may not be able to penetrate this market.

Management also gains additional insight into the nature of the market being served through an industry analysis. Industry practices typically develop over time as the result of experience of firms in serving markets. So, there are often some important market characteristics that have caused particular practices to be used. The difficulty for certain kinds of individuals to obtain large financing would lead to the common industry practice of contractors helping condominium buyers obtain needed funds, for instance.

Competitor Analysis

Not all firms in an industry will present the same level of competition to a firm. Some firms may have selected different target markets or may have substantially different marketing programs that are not directly competing with a firm doing an MOA. Management may want to assess the strategies and tactics of only those firms that are most directly competing for the same customers. For example, our contractor will want to carefully evaluate those other condominium complexes that will also be trying to draw the same potential consumers. This may mean selecting for analysis only those condominium units in the same geographic area with similar amenities and price ranges since common product characteristics would indicate that target markets are similar. Analysis of other kinds of competitors, such as apartment complex contractors or single family housing contractors will typically not be necessary.

The analysis of individual competitors should include an assessment of their financial strength as well as their operating strengths and weaknesses. Financial strength information helps management assess the "staying power" of firms and provides insight into the level of resources that can be allocated to serving a market. This is illustrated by the competition between different size contractors in an urban community. Smaller contractors must try to build a market appeal and attract buyers even though they are being outspent by the larger contractors. Moreover, if and when the housing industry goes into the downturn of an economic cycle, a financial analysis will show which competitors are likely to have the ability to stay in this market and continue to be major competitors.

To fully analyze market opportunity, a MOA should also determine how well or how poorly each competitor is meeting the needs of markets. This task is dependent on already having done a detailed demand analysis to identify market needs. With this information management can concentrate primarily on operating practices that are specifically designed to serve these needs. The analysis does not have to go into as much depth on those operating practices not tied closely to serving particular market needs. If, for example, condominium buyers are unconcerned with the availability of certain amenities such as a club house or tennis courts, then a competitor analysis does not have to evaluate competitors for the quality of their offering of these amenities. More time and managerial effort can be concentrated on those condominium features that are important to potential buyers.

Channel Analysis

Finally, management should assess how well an industry is reaching a market through channels of distribution. A distribution channel refers to the collection of firms (e.g., manufacturers, wholesalers, retailers, etc.) that link the producer of some product with end-user markets. Of particular interest for analyzing market opportunities is the *demand channel*. This is the portion of a total channel comprised of just those types of firms that link the industry under analysis with its end-user markets. Since the relevant industry is defined as all firms at the same level in a channel as the firm doing a MOA, there does not have to be a demand channel

to assess. A contractor selling condominium units directly to housing buyers would not need a channel analysis since there are typically no other types of firms that link contractors with their markets. In general, a channel analysis is a necessary part of a MOA only when the industry is selling through intermediate buyers to reach a market.

The analysis should begin by describing the types of channel arrangements common for an industry. This requires identifying the types and number of intermediaries used by the industry to serve markets. Characteristics of typical channel arrangements can often provide management with insight into the nature of end-user markets. For example, many convenience products such as cigarettes and soft drinks are sold through a wide variety of retail outlets because consumers do not want to search or shop extensively for them. The description of channels can also help management assess the desirability of using existing channels or establishing new channels to reach markets. Some lumber companies, for instance, have been moving toward selling directly to consumers through company owned retail outlets rather than using the more common network of distributors and dealers.[5] This management decision was based in part on an analysis of the effectiveness of the traditional channel arrangements used by lumber manufacturers to reach consumer markets.

A channel analysis may be extended from assessing an entire demand channel to analyzing one or more particularly important levels. For example, a firm may want to concentrate on identifying and evaluating the practices of the next level in the channel closer to end-user markets. This is necessary if a firm wants to determine how best to enter existing channels by linking up with intermediate buyers. To establish working relationships with particular types of intermediate buyers may require a firm to meet certain requirements such as offering certain size profit margins, packaging design, cooperative promotional programs, training of salesmen and so forth.

5. "Marketing: Evans Products Cuts Out the Middleman," *Business Week*, July 31, 1971, p. 70.

Application of Market Opportunity Analyses

Performing all five of the analysis activities comprising a market opportunity analysis should provide management with two kinds of outputs. Management initially wants to know *the size* of market opportunity available to the firm. This requires making quantitative estimates of market demand and so, a MOA should provide management with market and sales forecasts. Moreover, for most marketing decisions, management also needs to understand the more *qualitative characteristics* describing the nature of a market including the service already being offered to customers by other firms. So, a MOA should provide market profiles and descriptions to help managment better visualize what the market is like as well as what must be built into marketing programs to serve that market. Each of these outputs and its application is discussed.

Figure 3
Demand forecasts provided by a MOA

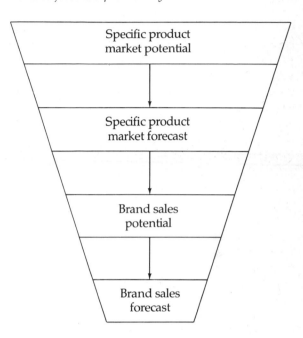

Market and Sales Forecasts

The size of a market must be estimated in order to assess the revenue that can be expected from serving a market's needs. Demand forecasts can be made that correspond to the levels of markets that have been identified during the demand analysis: (1) the size of demand for a specific product and (2) the size of demand for a brand of that product. Beginning with specific product sales estimates, management can determine the upper limit on demand that is available to all firms offering a brand of the product to that market. The task would then be to estimate the portion of total specific product demand that can be captured by the firm's brand of that product. In this way, the forecasting task is a funneling process of working toward a forecast of company brand sales by first determining the maximum level of sales that all brands of the same product will tap. This process is illustrated in Figure 3.

Market potential is the total sales that could be realized in a geographic area and time period if the industry were capable of fully developing all demand for a specific product. Of course, industries typically do not fully develop all potential demand due to weaknesses in industry practices (out-of-stocks, promotion that doesn't reach all potential users, etc.). So the level of sales that will actually be generated is some portion of the market potential. This portion is estimated by a *market forecast* which is the total sales that is expected to be achieved by all firms offering a specific product in a geographic area and time period with current industry operating practices. A market forecast tells management the upper limit of demand that can realistically be expected to be tapped by all firms in the industry. Market potential and market forecasts are derived from the aggregate level demand and industry analyses.

Management will also want to know the probable level of sales that the company's brand can capture. Brand sales will be determined by the relative effectiveness of the brand marketing program compared to the brand strategies of competitors. So, the forecaster must try to determine the share of the market forecast that a brand will capture. Management may want to begin this task by forecasting *sales potential*. This is the level of sales that a brand could capture if the firm's brand marketing program had no weaknesses. Thus, sales potential is the maximum sales that can be generated by achieving the highest possible market share given expected competitor marketing programs. In actual practice any brand strategy is unlikely to escape having some weaknesses. Perhaps insufficient funds are available for key parts of the marketing program, or distribution problems arise leading to stockouts. These difficulties will prevent a firm's brand from achieving 100 percent of sales potential. So, management must try to anticipate the actual level of brand sales that can be expected from a market. This sales estimate is a brand sales forecast which predicts the portion of sales potential that will actually be achieved by the firm's brand.

As an example of these forecasts, consider again the assessment of market opportunity for a condominium complex in a community. One forecasting procedure involves determining demographic characteristics of most likely condominium unit buyers and then using U.S. Census of Population Census Tract data to count the number (N_t) of people in the community having these characteristics for the forecast period t. Then an estimate of how likely it is that each of these people will buy one condominium unit during the forecast period t, assuming perfect industry practices, must be determined. This is usage rate, R_t, and could be developed from secondary sources on past condominium buying, survey data or managerial judgment. With these two estimates, market potential, MP_t, can be estimated by using the following relationship:

$$(1) \; MP_t = N_t \times R_t$$

A market forecast, MF_t, of condominium buyers requires estimating the portion of market potential that will actually buy a condominium unit during the forecasting period given current industry practices. Due to inadequacies in providing desired amenities, not having condominiums in all desired locations, or other circumstances, some of the market potential will end up not buying a con-

dominium who would have bought if these industry weaknesses did not exist. An estimate of the percentage of potential that will actually be converted into industry sales might be termed an Index of Industry Effectiveness (IE_t) and used in the following relationship:

$$(2) \; MF_t = MP_t \times IE_t$$

The market forecast sets the expected upper limit on the demand that will be tapped by all condominiums. Management now needs to know how much of this demand can be captured by their condominium complex as opposed to the portion that will be captured by existing, competitive complexes. Management can work toward this forecast by first estimating the maximum market share, MMS_t, that is possible. This estimate is based on management's understanding of market needs in the proposed area in the city in which the condominium will be built, an analysis of competitors' condominiums in this area, and a perfectly effective condominium marketing program (e.g., ideal number of units, a price range matching buyers' ability to pay, a promotional program reaching all potential users, and so forth). With this estimate, the firm's sales potential, SP_t, can be determined:

$$(3) \; SP_t = MF_t \times MMS_t$$

Finally, management recognizes that the initial condominium and supporting marketing program is not likely to be perfect. For instance, the firm may not have the resources to provide all amenities desired (e.g., tennis courts may have to be built at a later date due to lack of funds), all units may not be finished during the period, and local media may not be entirely effective in blanketing the entire market. While management will work on improving their marketing program, these initial deficiencies will keep the firm from achieving maximum market share. So, management must estimate a realistic market share, MS_t, that will be achieved given existing competitors and the actual marketing program that the firm will implement. To complete the forecast of expected brand sales, SF_t, this market share estimate is multiplied times the market forecast:

$$(4)\ SF_t = MF_t \times MS_t$$

These forecasts serve a dual purpose for management. The sales forecast is a key input to financial planning for the firm (expense budgets, cash flow statements, income projections, etc.) required to implement the proposed condominium marketing program. This is essential to decide upon appropriate target markets. In addition, the process of funneling down from market potential to a brand sales forecast allows management to assess the nature of the opportunity reflected by the *gaps* between each of the forecasts. For example, consider the illustrative forecasts developed by the condominium contractor as shown in Table 1. The gap between market potential and market forecast is very small (4,578.6 − 3,800.2 = 778.4 condominium units) which suggests that the contractor cannot count very much on developing the existing market for condominiums as a source of growth. Unless the entire industry introduces innovations that will increase market potential, the firm will have to look to expanding market share for growth. The gap between the firm's sales potential and sales forecast (456.0 − 342.0 = 114 units) shows the growth opportunity that can be expected from improvements in the firm's marketing program. Management attention should focus on those areas of the program in which improvements are most needed.

Qualitative Market Descriptions

Management needs far more understanding of markets than is contained in demand forecasts. Sales estimates do not provide much insight into *how best to serve* market targets. Management must build an understanding of the more qualitative nature and characteristics of markets including customers' needs, demographic profiles, satisfaction with existing products or services, non-demographic characteristics such as life style, and so forth. This kind of market information is just as important an output of a MOA as are the demand forecasts because it helps management choose between marketing program design alternatives. In turn, this task must be done to evaluate possible market targets and determine needed resource commitments.

Returning to the contractor firm attempting to invest in a condominium complex, management must decide what to design into the condominium marketing program that will compete effectively with existing condominiums. This may involve decisions on the design of condominium unit floorplans, pricing policy and methods, number of amenities, mix of amenities, building designs, advertising media and messages, and so forth. These kinds of marketing decisions are made to influence the housing decisions of consumers comprising market potential and sales potential. So, management must know who these people are, where they are located, what their housing needs

Table 1

Illustrative demand forecasts for condominium units in an urban community

Type of forecast	Forecast components	Component estimates	One year forecast
Market potential	$MP_t = N_t \times R_t$	$N_t = 5,870$ households $R_t = .78$ probability of buying one unit	4,578.6 condominium units
Market forecast	$MF_t = MP_t \times IE_t$	$MP_t = 4,578.6$ units $IE_t = .83$	3,800.2 units
Sales potential	$SP_t = MF_t \times MMS_t$	$MF_t = 3,800.2$ units $MMS_t = .12$	456.0 units
Sales forecast	$SF_t = MF_t \times MS_t$	$MF_t = 3,800.2$ units $MS_t = .09$	342.0 units

Table 2

*Illustrative qualitative market characteristics for two
potential condominium markets*

Market characteristics	Description of market A	Description of market B
Demographic profile	Young, moderate income, not married, manager or professional occupation.	Older, high income, children have left home, retired or near retirement, manager or professional occupation.
Primary needs for condominiums	Wants to live near employment, entertainment and shopping facilities; wants to own a home rather than rent.	Desires release from yard care and maintenance responsibilities; does not want to give up tax advantage of home ownership.
Geographic location	Now living in inner city, fringe areas of city, and some suburban areas.	Now living in suburban housing developments. Single family houses or older condominiums.
Existing housing	Apartments.	
Decision criteria for selecting housing alternative	Location near downtown, floor plan, price amenities.	Floor plans, security arrangements, convenience to shopping, maintenance services, parking, price.

are, how they now satisfy those needs, and how they decide between housing alternatives. For example, the illustrative customer descriptions shown in Table 2 for two different markets would help management build marketing programs tailored to serve market targets. Clearly the marketing program designed to serve Market A is different from that needed by Market B. The contractor would have to decide whether to design a marketing program aimed only at Market A or Market B or to target toward both markets simultaneously. The market target selection decision allows management to use these customer profiles to build into a marketing program those characteristics that will satisfy customer wants. For example to appeal to Market B would require well designed and implemented maintenance services, arrangements to provide owners with a feeling of security (e.g., enclosed garages, guards, alarms, locks, etc.) and nearby shopping facilities.

Figure 4 summarizes the application of the major MOA outputs to decisions faced by corporate and marketing managers. Market and sales forecasts show the revenue potential in alternative markets. So, these forecasts help management determine the profitability that can be expected by selecting a market as a market target. Revenue potential also helps management determine how much resources to allocate toward a market since resource allocation must be commensurate with expected return. Notice that demand forecasts are not much help to management for designing marketing programs. The qualitative market descriptions are much more useful to management for this task because these descriptions provide clues that show how best to influence customer decisions. Market descriptions are also useful for selecting market targets and allocating resources. Each of these decisions should be based on the requirements for satisfying demand in a market. A firm should not select a market as a target if management cannot design an effective, competitive marketing program to meet that market's needs and wants. For those markets selected as targets the resource allocation decisions should be based, in part, on the particular marketing program needed to meet a market's requirements. So,

Figure 4
The contribution of MOA to marketing decisions

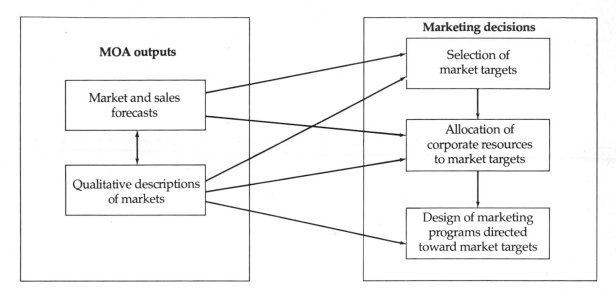

management must analyze qualitative market descriptions for all of the key marketing decisions.

Conclusions and Implications

Marketing decisions require management to analyze opportunities available to a firm in markets. It hardly seems necessary to build a rationale for the importance of understanding the nature and size of markets as a basis for making corporate and marketing decisions. Yet, it is not clear that many firms have a systematic approach to analyzing market opportunities. Management may not have the necessary understanding of the marketing process or the techniques and procedures for analyzing markets to determine market opportunity. This is most likely to characterize medium and small firms, though some of the largest firms also appear to lack this know-how.

This article has presented an integrated, systematic approach to conducting market opportunity analyses that can be applied to the assessment of new product opportunities and of opportunities for products already existing in a company's product mix. This approach represents a practical frame-

work to guide management in performing the activities, information analyses, and estimates needed to fully assess market opportunity by focusing on the major determinants of opportunity. Management alone is not likely to actually do all the information collection and analysis activities included in a MOA. Yet, as the sole user of the results of a MOA, management should have clearly in mind what must be assessed so that the proper direction and interpretation is given to the outputs of a MOA. For this reason, the essential starting point for developing market analysis capabilities is for management to have a sound, systematic approach to conducting MOAs firmly in mind. The approach presented here provides that starting point.

Questions

1. *Why is it more important than ever before for corporate managements to stay abreast of market conditions?*
2. *What factors are the primary determinants of market opportunities?*
3. *What are the major stages of the MOA process?*

11

Exploring the
Gray Market Segment

BETSY D. GELB

Cultivating retirement-age consumers could benefit alert retailers, but significant results would be likely only in unusual situations.

Teen market, working-women's market, black market—why not a gray market, focusing special marketing effort on 65-and-over consumers? A recent review of business journals concludes that the 65-and-over consumer is neglected in the marketplace.[1] This indifference is attributed to the belief by business that "the elderly want pretty much the same things as adults generally." Others have linked the low interest in marketing to "seniors" (the term now in vogue) with a belief that this group lacks purchasing power as well as distinct market characteristics.[2]

Are these views out of date? To answer that question, or to examine any population segment as a potential market segment a manager should evaluate whether it is feasible and profitable to market differently to these buyers and potential buyers. Ben M. Enis breaks this question down into a list of specific criteria for a useful market segment: identity, accessibility, responsiveness, and significance. In his terms, an organization would ask whether the members of a potential segment can be identified easily; whether the marketing organization can communicate with them; whether they will

respond to special effort; and whether that response will generate enough extra revenue to exceed the extra cost of adapting some part of the marketing mix.[3]

This article is intended to help managers analyze retirement-age consumers within this framework. The objective will be to relate the gray market to all four of Enis's criteria, using data on population and buying power from published sources and data on buying-related preferences and behavior from a study of Houston-area seniors.

The first two criteria justifying a market segment—identification and accessibility—appear to be increasingly easy for the retirement-age population segment to meet. Finding seniors and communicating specifically to them has been simplified by the growth of retirement communities. Furthermore, even those elderly who do not move to Sun City or to Sunset Acres in their own hometown are more likely than in past decades to live in their own households, rather than with younger relatives. Fully 96 percent of those in this age bracket live outside institutions. Of those, 47 percent are in husband-wife units, 43 percent live alone, and only 10 percent live with children.[4] Thus, it can be expected that they make their own buying decisions and can be reached by segmentation strategies aimed at their age bracket.

Would they respond to such strategies or resent them? Here, data are needed before conclusions concerning responsiveness can be drawn. Furthermore, even if the "responsiveness" criterion is met, would the marginal profit justify extra effort? Here, one issue is buying power. Another is whether

Source: Betsy D. Gelb, "Exploring the Gray Market Segment," pp. 41–46, *MSU Business Topics*, Spring 1978. Reprinted by permission of the publisher, Division of Research, Graduate School of Business Administration, Michigan State University.

physical and life-style characteristics of this age segment require more age-tailored, but also more expensive, marketing strategies.

To judge the buying power issue, it should be noted that population trends point to an increase in the proportion of seniors among the nation's buyers. Unless the birth rate spurts in the last quarter of this decade, the 1971–1981 total U.S. increase in population will be 13 percent, but the increase in the over-65 segment will be 17 percent. By the year 2000, it is reasonable to expect that the combination of a decreasing birth rate and longer life expectancy will bring the proportion of those 65 and over to 15 percent of the U.S. population.

A second consideration in evaluating this age group's buying power is the money they have to spend per person. Previous discussions addressing the viability of the older market have stressed spending as the critical variable. Such discussions have led to the conclusion that the existence of a retirement-age market was questionable, except for a few goods and service categories such as hearing aids, nursing care, and the like.[5] More recently, however, it has been noted that the propensity of retirement-age consumers to spend, rather than to save, means that for many kinds of products they are a significant buying force. The principal argument advanced by those holding that view is that assets, not income alone, should be considered buying power for an age segment whose propensity is to "dis-save."[6]

It also has been pointed out that even the income picture is changing for older Americans. Pensions cover an increasing percentage of the work force, although their impact is reduced by inflation. A Conference Board report estimates that the per capita income of those 65 and over is only 5 percent less than the per capita figure for the population as a whole.[7] Furthermore, one writer calculates that an over-65 household with a $5,500 annual income actually does as well as a younger family with $7,200 or more. Older people need pay no Social Security tax if retired; can claim extra exemptions on their taxes; are more likely to have their home paid for; and have Medicare to reduce health costs.[8]

However, Enis's responsiveness and significance criteria for a market segment suggest that issues in addition to spending power be considered. Clearly, special efforts would rest not only on the segment's ability to buy, but also on two assumptions outside the economic realm. They are:

(1) that attitudes in this age segment offer support for age-oriented products, promotional appeals, pricing, or distribution strategies—a "pro-age" mind-set;[9]

(2) that such strategies will be more profitable than nonsegmented strategies because this market has different needs, related to physical and life-style characteristics. Here life-style characteristics refer primarily to smaller household size and increased leisure time.

The Houston Study

To test these assumptions, a study was undertaken in Houston. A third issue also was examined in relation to the other two: Are age-distinct preferences, if any, a function of age *per se*, or do they stem from other variables? This third consideration was based on the realization that a disproportionate number of older consumers are women and, despite high assets, members of low income households. Thus, it would be possible to find preferences and buying behavior in this age segment that upon examination would relate to sex or income category as well as to age.

Data were gathered from 403 Houston-area seniors, a convenience sample of individuals present at regular monthly meetings of four retirement-age groups. Groups selected were: American Association of Retired Persons (AARP), International Brotherhood of Electrical Workers Retired Members, Service Corps of Retired Executives (SCORE), and Retired Senior Volunteer Program (RSVP). The individuals were in no sense believed typical; active group members simply were assumed to represent those elderly consumers whose views would be of most interest to business.

The seniors filled out questionnaires handed to them as part of the business of the meeting and completed them on the spot. Exceptionally large type was used, and assistance was available from university personnel familiar with the questionnaire. Therefore, at least some part of the form was filled out by more than 99 percent of those present. Respondents were not asked to sign the forms and were assured anonymity.

The questionnaire asked for check-off responses to 56 items. Among these, respondents were asked to scale their degree of agreement ("agree strongly" to "disagree strongly") with statements focusing on age-group identity. The statements included:

"I would pay a little more to shop in a store that went after the business of retirement-age people."
"Stores that sell clothing should have a special department for people of retirement age."
"I prefer to deal with sales clerks who are younger than I am."

They also were asked to scale frequency of behavior ("always" to "never") relating physical or life-style changes to shopping behavior. The statements included:

"I cut short my shopping trips because I get tired."
"Getting to the store is a bigger problem to me than it was a year ago."
"Someone younger takes me shopping when I go."

Conventional demographic data also were collected.

Results

Demographic data showed the convenience sample to be similar to the retirement-age population in several respects. Of the respondents, 31 percent were male, 69 percent female. They divided almost evenly between those 69 or younger and those 70 or older. About 45 percent were married; 45 percent were widowed; and 10 percent were single or divorced. One in five said he or she was employed. While 40 percent listed a household income of less than $400 per month, 30 percent checked categories between $400 and $699, and 30 percent listed household income of $700 or more.

The general notion that older buyers would welcome special treatment appeared to be supported by the majority of responses. Fifty-six percent agreed strongly or somewhat with the statement: "I would pay a little more to shop in a store that went after the business of retirement-age people." Fifty-six percent also agreed that clothing stores should have a special department for people of retirement age. The same percentage failed to agree even somewhat with the statement that "store owners are glad to see older people come in." Only 34 percent supported even somewhat the statement: "I prefer to deal with sales clerks who are younger than I am"—despite the fact that half the respondents were 70 or older. No relation was found between category of answer and either sex or income for any of these items.

The idea that special treatment would be appreciated was further supported by answers to a question asking what would attract the seniors to a hypothetical "new store in your neighborhood." Rating as high as a claim of low prices (Table 1) was the statement: "A sign in the window says 'Welcome, Seniors.' "

However, fewer than half the seniors reported buying behavior that could be attributed to the changes of retirement age. Concerning physical problems in shopping, for example, only 29 percent reported cutting shopping trips short at least half the time because of getting tired. A preference for small stores rather than large for at least half their shopping was expressed by 44 percent and may be associated with physical difficulties. Also, 26 percent agreed that at least half the time they found it "more of a problem to get to the store than it was a year ago."

About one senior in four said that at least half the time "someone younger takes me shopping." Furthermore, 37 percent agreed strongly, and 27 percent agreed somewhat, that to "shop around" at different stores is more trouble than it is worth. In general, the answers were the same across income groups and for both sexes, and thus appeared related to age rather than these other factors.

Is buying behavior affected by the life-style adjustments of retirement, smaller households, and

Table 1

Factors attracting seniors to a hypothetical new store

Reason	Percentage selecting (N = 403)
Ads say the store is inexpensive	57
A sign in the window says "Welcome, Seniors"	57
The store has someone to carry packages outside	56
It's a new kind of store	51
Ads for the store show people your age	33
Someone your age works at the store	32
The store has benches outside	29
The store looks "Old-Fashioned" from the outside	15

Note: Multiple answers possible.

increased leisure time? Three items dealt specifically with the issue of package size and quantity, since a controversy exists on this topic. Some writers see in the senior's smaller household a need for one-serving containers, while others see in his or her increased free time and decreased income a market for economy sizes or even case lots to be divided among households.

The Houston area seniors split on this issue. One-third replied that "always" or "most of the time" they bought in large amounts to save money, but 43 percent said they "hardly ever" or "never" did so, and low income correlated significantly with buying in small quantities. Also, 27 percent agreed "strongly" or "somewhat" that they would join a co-op buying group where members took turns shopping for the group and could buy in larger amounts. This percentage did not vary significantly between income categories but was significantly higher for men (53 percent) than for women (30 percent). On the other hand, 41 percent disagreed at least somewhat that they would participate in such a plan.

Limitations of the Houston study should be noted here: It involved only a convenience sample, was limited to one city at one point in time, and depended on self-reports of preferences and behavior. However, to the limited extent that its results

and other population/buying power data can be used to draw conclusions, it may offer useful insights for evaluating the 65-and-over age segment as a distinct market segment.

At the outset of this discussion, such an evaluation was linked to four criteria: identity, accessibility, responsiveness, and significance. Published data suggest that the segment meets the first two criteria. Responsiveness, a criterion which will be met only if age-directed changes in the marketing mix of an organization are welcomed by the elderly, seems supported by the data. The fourth criterion, significance, appears more questionable: It can be met only if enough more sales result in sufficient extra revenue to offset the cost of the segmentation efforts.

The study reported here viewed significance as a function of two factors: buying power and the proportion of the elderly reporting buying behavior distinct to their age group.

The reasoning is that a segmentation strategy—for example, a special package size or an extra retail location close to a retirement community—entails extra cost. If the gray market cannot afford the extra cost, the significance criterion is unmet. However, if the gray market can afford the extra cost, but has no age-related need for special treatment, then one of two equally unattractive possibilities awaits the marketer:

1. To cover the extra cost, the retail price is raised. Since the seniors did not need the special package (or whatever), they reach instead for the lower priced ordinary version.
2. The retail price is not raised; volume increases are expected to provide the incremental revenue. Unfortunately, these increases are accompanied by a volume decrease for the company's ordinary version, which seniors had been buying all along since no age-related characteristics precluded their doing so.

Therefore, the significance criterion can be met only if seniors report behavior suggesting a need for special treatment. The results of this study make that appear questionable for most seniors. It cannot be claimed that, by Enis's standards, the criteria to justify a market segment are met.

Recommendations

Nevertheless, several conclusions can be drawn from published data and from this study to assist marketers whose products are exceptionally sensitive to gray market purchase patterns. For such products, segmentation may pay off even if one-fourth or fewer of the elderly would respond differently to special marketing effort than to business as usual. These conclusions also lead to recommendations for the marketers of such products, to the extent that their particular markets make special action worthwhile:

1. The 65-and-over age segment is by no means homogeneous. Therefore, marketers will experience little success in learning the preferences of thousands of seniors by asking Great Aunt Jane.
2. To look at the 65-and-over group as low income shoppers can be misleading in two ways. First, it means overlooking the possibility that a senior with a $500-per-month income may be ready for a round-the-world trip. Assuming that income breaks down to $180 from Social Security and $320 from investments, the $320 may be a 5 percent return on about $77,000. Furthermore, the income may not be $500; it may, through a combination of pensions and transfer payments, be double that.
3. Surprisingly, perhaps, to feel valued as a *retirement-age shopper* has importance. The Houston respondents may not be typical in this respect, since they are members of retirement-age groups and thus have chosen to identify themselves with their age segment. Nevertheless, such groups are growing in numbers and membership; there seems no reason to doubt that such identification is on the upswing.
4. The majority of these seniors did not appear to need special treatment due to physical and life-style characteristics. More than one-third, however, do express agreement with statements indicating physical limitations.

Even such fragmentary conclusions as these can offer guidance for segmentation strategies directed to the gray market if a business expects the effort to be profitable. Such an effort may not be immediate, but managers who do not see seniors in their present customer mix should keep this age segment in mind; markets change. Therefore, the following recommendations can be seen either as examples that can be useful now, or as examples that will be useful if a marketing manager wakes up one morning to find that his or her buyers belong to "The Swingin' Sixties." From product design and promotion to the age of personnel employed, there are myriad marketing strategies available to those who see retirement-age buyers as a potential market segment.

Product Planning

For the senior market, physical and life-style changes point to an emphasis on services. Research shows car ownership for nearly 60 percent of households in this market segment, a high percentage of home ownership, and broad interest in health and gardening. Related services, then, may involve home security, auto maintenance and accessories, home remodeling, insurance, and perhaps lawn care services. The same homeowner who bought lawn fertilizer at 60 may be willing 10 years later to pay for a quarterly fertilizing service.

Based on some enthusiasm in the Houston study for buying co-ops and for economy, however, it appears that a substantial segment of the senior market seeks no-frills products and services. Perhaps after retirement the only way to "earn" money, with all the achievement that earning symbolizes, is to buy thriftily. Such an idea could be tested in further research by offering various product-service designs to buyers over a wide age range to see whether the demand for deluxe features drops off at retirement and to what extent the challenge of saving is significant for this age segment, independent of financial status.

Promotion

For promotion decisions, the findings of greatest interest appear to be those concerning physical limitations. Special events for seniors can include uncrowded Christmas shopping before a store's regular opening time. They can also include demonstrations, televised or in-store, on how to use products that the elderly might consider difficult to manage. Such demonstrations are not only useful, but also convey a message of corporate attention to the retirement-age consumer, a subtle but effective equivalent of the sign in the window that says "Welcome, Seniors." Furthermore, they are most effective when based on sound product research. Now being studied, for example, are kinds of doorknobs that are best for arthritic patients, and designs for cups, chairs, and mattresses.

Pricing

Conventional wisdom sees price as *the* salient feature in the senior marketing mix, but findings of this study suggest the possibility of interaction between pricing and a publicized effort to market to retirement-age customers. A marketer who offers discounts to this age group simultaneously can convey the messages of saving and special attention— both powerful attractions. Further research is needed in this area to test the possibility, for example, that discounts as rewards for long-time buyers are more attractive than the same discounts given because of diminished income in retirement.

Store Location and Staffing

For retailers interested in elderly buyers or for manufacturers appraising a current or proposed channel structure, store location and staffing may be rele-

vant factors. Proximity to public transportation and senior housing appears to be most critical. A location near a recreation center or a church with active retirement-age groups also may be desirable.

No clear-cut direction emerges from the Houston study for retail staffing decisions, but research in an individual community may yield different results. In this study, only one-third of the respondents said they preferred to deal with sales clerks younger than themselves. One-third said they would be attracted to a newly opened store in their neighborhood if someone their age worked there. This is a significant but hardly overwhelming percentage.

More relevant than rushing out to hire seniors as salespersons, however, may be the treatment that a firm gives to its own retirees, who will interact with potential 65-and-over consumers. In the present study, 56 percent of respondents failed to agree that store owners—representative of the marketing community—were glad to see them as customers. This perception suggests that more than staffing policies may be communicating indifference from marketers. Areas to be considered here include credit, support for public transportation, and the age mix of models used in advertising, in short, anything that represents the marketer to the retirement-age consumer.

In summary, the gray market may meet the three tests of identity, accessibility, and responsiveness as a market segment, but it may not for most marketers meet the fourth test—enough extra profit. For those who choose to target efforts to this segment, however, opportunities range from product design to the context in which retirement discounts are presented. Clearly, this study offers only a beginning, and the marketing community has many opportunities for research to improve its strategies for serving the gray market.

Notes

1. Joyanne Block, "The Aged Consumer and the Marketplace," *Marquette Business Reveiw* 18 (Summer 1974): 73–80.

2. R. Eugene Klippel and Timothy W. Sweeney, "The Use of Information Sources by the Aged Consumer," *Gerontologist* 14 (April 1974): 163.

3. Ben M. Enis, *Marketing Principles: The Management Process*, 2d ed. (Santa Monica, Calif.: Goodyear, 1977), pp. 243–46.

4. Fabian Linden, "Consumer Markets: Midlife and Beyond," excerpted from *Across the Board* 13 (December 1976): 2–3.

5. John A. Reinecke, "The 'Older' Market—Fact or Fiction?" *Journal of Marketing* 28 (January 1964): 60–64; and Sidney Goldstein, "The Aged Segment of the Market, 1950 and 1960," *Journal of Marketing* 35 (April 1968): 62–68.

6. Robert C. Atchley, *The Social Forces in Later Life* (Belmont, Calif.: Wadsworth Publishing Co., 1972), p. 123.

7. Linden, "Midlife and Beyond."

8. "The Over-65 Set: A Bonanza for Business?" *Nation's Business* 59 (November 1971): 34–35.

9. Betsy D. Gelb, "Gray Power: Next Challenge to Business?" *Business Horizons* 20 (April 1977): 38–45.

Questions

1. *What criteria should one use to evaluate the potential associated with individual market segments?*
2. *Might there be relevant segments within the gray (over-65) market segment? What might they be?*

PART THREE

Product and Price Decisions

Gillette Company spent two years and $18 million in preparation for the introduction of Dry Idea, its newest roll-on antiperspirant, aimed at women in the 20–45 age group. The stakes are high but so is the payoff for the winners in the $11 billion-a-year personal-care-products business. [1]

Generic products—no frills, no name, and brandless items—have been meeting with substantial consumer acceptance in U.S. supermarkets. As a consumer, how do you react to messages on labels such as this one that appeared on a facial tissue package: "These tissues are suitable for everyday use. Extra costs of colors, printing, or perfume have been avoided." [2]

Faced by severe competition from Japanese companies such as Ricoh, Canon, and Konishiroku which had dramatically seized about 25 percent of the $2 billion world market for "slow" photocopy machines, Xerox slashed its prices in retaliation. Its Model 3100, for example, was reduced 63 percent—from $12,000 to $4,400. Such price cuts had to be a stopgap strategy, however, because the price cuts left Xerox with unacceptable gross profit margins. [3]

U.S. public policy makers who wanted to curtail gasoline consumption in 1979 were faced with a perplexing problem. Economic theory suggested that demand could be cut if prices were raised. Political strategy suggested that voter-consumers would feel better about price hikes if they occurred gradually, in small increments. But consumers' perceptions of price changes and resultant changes in consumption behavior depend on both the magnitude and rapidity of price changes. For example, a 30 percent increase is likely to be more effective in dampening demand than a series of four incremental increases over a year that produce the same change in final price. "Thus, energy price increases cannot reasonably be expected to act as effective deterrents to consumption if they come only in small steps gradually over time." [4]

1. Neil Ulman, "Sweating It Out," *Wall Street Journal*, November 17, 1978, pp. 1, 41.
2. "Generic Groceries Keep Adding Market Share," *Marketing News*, February 23, 1979, pp. 1, 6, 7.
3. Bro Uttal, "Xerox Is Trying Too Hard," *Fortune*, March 13, 1978, p. 86.
4. William L. Shanklin, "The Energy Crisis and Consumer Behavior," *Atlanta Economic Review*, May–June 1978, pp. 28–32.

The first step that should be taken toward the development of an effective marketing strategy is an analysis of market opportunities. As described in Part Two, this analysis requires marketing managers to identify the character, the magnitude, and the location of potential demand for want-satisfying products. Along with identifying and describing demand, a market opportunity analysis should also assess the ability of an organization and its competitors to satisfy that demand. The identification and analysis of market opportunities prepare marketing management for intelligently approaching the formulation of successful marketing strategies. This requires, first, the selection of one or more *target markets* that present opportunities. Second, the creation and maintenance of a want-satisfying *marketing mix* is needed.

A marketing mix is a blend of product, price, distribution, and promotion efforts that the organization develops to satisfy the wants of the target markets. In Part Three, the focus is on the development of effective product and price decisions. Ford Motor Company's experience with the Edsel and Brown-Forman Distillers' experience with Frost 8/80 suggest that the mere identification and analysis of market opportunities does not guarantee market success for new products. In fact, the vast majority of ideas for new products—including goods, services, and ideas—either fail to make it through the preintroductory product development activities or fail to generate the desired consumer or user response upon introduction into the marketplace. The marketplace is liberally strewn with product failures. In addition to the Edsel and Frost 8/80, one might recall Colgate's Cue toothpaste, Bristol-Myers' Aerosol Ipana toothpaste, Gillette's Nine Flags Men's Cologne, and Warner-Lambert's Reef mouthwash. The failure of many new products in the marketplace can be attributed to ineffective assessments of market opportunities, inadequate organizational support (which is needed to achieve introductory success), and/or ineffective or inefficient marketing mixes.

The articles in Part Three are related to the development, management, and pricing of goods and services as integral parts of the organization's marketing mix. In the initial selection, "What's Really Wrong at Chrysler," Peter Vanderwicken underscores the importance of each organization's having a clear and generally accepted description of what its market is and what wants it wishes to satisfy before it develops products. Vanderwicken implies that Chrysler's long-standing product orientation and its failure to adopt a market orientation is at the root of its decrease in profits in the mid-1970s.

In "Hewlett-Packard: Where Slower Growth Is Smarter Management," *Business Week* describes the highly successful approach taken by a manufacturer of electronic instruments, minicomputers, and calculators. Hewlett-Packard is gambling its future on new product developments and has spurned the options of curtailing its expensive research activities and engaging in price competition to increase unit sales volumes for existing products.

Packaging and branding are the focal points of the third through fifth articles. Robert Lee Dickens discusses the major role that a package can play in product differentiation, segmentation, and communications strategies. Stanley R. Renas and Harold W. Fox cite the value of proprietary (private or distributor) brands to the independent seller. The *Dun's Review* article exposes the widespread practice of "counterfeiting" famous brand-name products like wrist watches, luggage, and cigarettes. The apparent capital of this illicit activity is Italy.

In the sixth article, C. Merle Crawford summarizes ten of the most common reasons why new products fail, while the seventh and eighth articles focus on test marketing. Saul Sands questions the value of test marketing new products. "The Middletowns of Marketing" describes the characteristics of good test market cities and identifies some of the more popular test markets in the United States. In the eighth article, "Diagnosing the Product Portfolio," George S. Day suggests a novel approach to marketing strategy formulation that is growing in use among managers of diversified companies.

Product pricing is examined in the final two articles. Robert E. Hempel examines the determinants of an effective price—some are recognized by economic theory and some aren't. The *Feedstuffs* piece is the third in this book. This article summarizes how marketers use buyer surveys to guide pricing decisions.

12

What's Really Wrong
at Chrysler
PETER VANDERWICKEN

In the summer of 1979, the Chrysler Corporation appeared headed for bankruptcy. Its future depended on management's ability to reach agreement on answers to three questions: (1) What is our purpose? (2) What are we trying to do? (3) Whom are we trying to serve?

This recession has been a tough one for auto makers generally, but for Chrysler Corp. it has been nearly disastrous. For the third time since he became head of the company fourteen years ago, Chairman Lynn Townsend has had to force it through a massive retrenchment.

Besides laying off a lot of workers temporarily, Chrysler has fired tens of thousands outright; at some Chrysler plants this spring, only people hired before 1965 still had jobs. Townsend has declared that he intends to get Chrysler's breakeven point down to a level where the company could make money even if the U.S. new-car market shrank to six million units (not counting imports). That is a sensationally austere goal, considering that even in dark-gray 1974 this market amounted to about 7.5 million cars.

With all the drastic economizing, moreover, Chrysler still lost $73.5 million in the fourth quarter of 1974 and $52.1 million for the year—by far the biggest quarterly and yearly losses in its history. And the company expects to keep losing money,

though at less hemorrhagic rates, at least through the third quarter of this year.

Despite widespread speculation that Chrysler may not survive, there is no serious basis for doubt that the company can weather its latest crisis. It has access to all the short-term loans it needs. Still, the belief that there is something wrong at Chrysler is certainly justified—there *is* something wrong.

None of the usual explanations of what is wrong, however, really gets at the central issue of why Chrysler continues to be such a marginal enterprise, such an erratically profitable business. It requires last-minute rescues every few years not because its costs are comparatively high (although they are) or because it is financially weaker than its competitors (although it is). Those factors are consequences of Chrysler's malaise, not the causes of it.

At bottom, Chrysler is in trouble because its management has never adequately answered the fundamental questions that confront any institution: What is our purpose? What are we trying to do? Whom are we trying to serve? Townsend and his colleagues have never been able to decide what kinds of cars they want to build or what kinds of customers they want to attract. They have no steady vision of what their company is or should become, and as a result they have continually shifted its gears, accentuating its weaknesses and failing to capitalize on its strengths.

Source: Fortune Magazine, 88 (May 1975), 176–179, 274–276. Reprinted from the May 1975 issue of *Fortune Magazine* by special permission; © 1975 Time Inc.

Long-lived Strategies

Any successful business is founded on a concept of a product it can make or a market it can serve. This idea becomes the company's central heritage. Over time it comes to dominate both the strategy and the spirit of the company, so that problems and opportunities are seen in relation to the fundamental principle. Organizations can often move beyond their original concept, but they can seldom abandon it.

Thus Henry Ford's idea, an inexpensive car for the masses, still dominates Ford Motor Co. Ford makes such expensive models as the Continental and the Marquis, to be sure, but most of its cars have been designed as low-priced models, and most of the time they have been inexpensively built. Since World War II, Ford has tried repeatedly to grow beyond that original concept. One of its attempts at a medium-priced car, the Edsel was a famous fiasco. More recently the company has had greater success in enlarging its product line and markets, but comparatively inexpensive cars are still the basis of its business.

G.M.'s concept, largely developed by Alfred P. Sloan Jr. in the early 1920's, was "a car for every purse and purpose." That is still G.M.'s strategy—a strategy that only G.M. is big enough to pursue. And American Motors has enjoyed revival in recent years after Chairman Roy Chapin decided that it would concentrate on exploiting its long-neglected heritage from Nash—innovative, superbly styled small cars.

The basic idea of Chrysler Corp. was quite different. Its heritage, says Townsend, was engineering. "What this company had in all of its products was more engineering breakthroughs and engineering differences than any other products being offered the American people." That emphasis was inherited from Walter Chrysler, who in 1924 designed the first Chrysler car around his new high-compression engine. The centrality of engineering at Chrysler, Townsend says, "has never changed from that day on." The result, he adds, is that "the engineering department is the most dominant influence in this company."

No from Below

The engineers don't control Chrysler by holding the top management posts. Few of the company's top officers have engineering backgrounds. Both Townsend and President John Riccardo were accountants before they joined Chrysler. The executive vice president, Eugene Cafiero, who runs the North American operations, came up through the manufacturing side of the company.

Engineering, however, does subtly determine how people at Chrysler think. When Townsend discusses a product, he describes it first in terms of its engineering features. When Chrysler executives wax enthusiastic about their company or its products, they are almost always talking about engineering. This state of mind is so strong, Townsend admits, that top management often accepts the engineers' judgments even in the company's most critical strategic decisions.

Engineering considerations, for example, dictate what kinds of cars the company makes. In the late Fifties, when the auto makers were developing their first compacts, Chrysler's management wanted to build a rear-engine compact to compete with G.M.'s Corvair. "We struggled here to do a rear-engined car," Townsend recalls, "and we couldn't. Our engineers were not willing to go with the weight distribution that it would entail. There was no way this management could have even ordered that engineering department to do a rear-engined car." A decade later, as Ford and G.M. were preparing subcompacts, Chrysler's engineers concluded they could not design one that would both be competitive in styling and meet their standards for interior comfort. As a result, Chrysler still does not have a U.S.-made minicar.

Engineering has provided Chrysler with a selling point over the years, but one that has often led the company astray. Chrysler's engineering probably has been significantly better than that of its competitors. Its transmissions, for example, are considered to be among the world's best. Its work on emission controls has been far superior to that of G.M. and Ford. Chrysler engineers have apparently made greater progress in controlling emissions within the engine, without using catalytic converters. In fact, they first warned eighteen months ago that converters might emit harmful sulfuric-acid mists, a danger that federal environmental regulators have only recently admitted.

Outside the River of Thought

Most of the time, however, Chrysler has been unable to obtain a competitive advantage from a new engineering feature. Its engineers' advances make the company's cars too different from those of its competitors. They break the boundaries of what Townsend calls the "river of thought" in automotive engineering. The course of that narrow stream is set by G.M., which holds half the market and can in effect dictate what will be acceptable design. Any innovation that moves Chrysler's cars outside the stream will probably fail in the marketplace.

In 1956, for example, Chrysler introduced a pushbutton transmission that eliminated the shift lever. The device was a flop because it made Chyrsler's cars too different. Every time Chrysler has tried any such major engineering advance, Townsend confesses, "it got clobbered."

The main difficulty with viewing engineering as Chrysler's dominant heritage, however, is that "engineering" offers no useful guidance to a product or a market. "Engineering" as a concept on which to build and run a company is quite different from "a workingman's car" or "a car for every purse." Each of the latter formulas offers a guide to what is to be produced and for whom. "Engineering," in contrast, does not define any product or marketing strategy.

To Townsend, however, engineering *is* Chrysler's strategy. The company, as he sees it, will compete in the market when and where its engineers believe they have a better product. And better engineering will allow it to charge a higher price. "We have traditionally sold our automobiles at prices above those of our competitors in each area of the market," Townsend says, "because we maintain our cars are worth more. They perform better; they've got better engineering."

An Unenviable Image

Overreliance on engineering as the company's strategy has had calamitous consequences. Chrysler responds to its engineer's inventions, not to the wants of its market. It has been unable to devise a sustained strategy for developing new products or for marketing them. The company has had no continuity of product design or marketing presentation. Its product development and marketing efforts have been disjointed and erratic. As a result, Chrysler has not been able to establish any sort of broad public image beyond engineering.

Image is a highly important matter to all the auto makers. The automobile industry is one in which the manufacturer's own corporate image can be crucial to the sale of its product. The industry has learned that the public's perception of an auto maker strongly influences whether people will visit one of its dealers. Indeed, if a company's image doesn't attract people, they might not even pay attention to its advertising. Accordingly, all of the auto makers do enormous amounts of research to discover the public's attitudes about them and their cars.

Chrysler's image is hardly cheering. Both the company and its cars are preceived as being more conservative than either G.M. or Ford—even downright stodgy. A Detroit marketing consultant who has worked for the auto makers says of Chrysler: "They are seen as years behind the other companies in styling, and even in engineering. If you ask, 'What's the last company to do anything?' people will say Chrysler."

Ask Any Schoolboy

But beyond that rather depressing image, people don't quite know what to think about Chrysler. The other auto companies have succeeded in implanting a firm impression of their cars and their character in the public mind. Both G. M. and Ford, for example, have succeeded in telling people how each car ranks in its hierarchy. Any schoolboy knows that a Pontiac is "better" (i.e., higher in price and prestige) than a Chevrolet. But not all schoolboys know that a Dodge is supposed to outrank a Plymouth.

The other auto makers have also done better than Chrysler at creating a consistent image for their cars. Researchers have found that most people can guess from its appearance alone whether a car was built by G.M., even if they aren't sure whether it is a Pontiac or a Buick. Townsend himself makes a remarkable admission of Chrysler's failure in this respect. "For as long as I've been here," he said recently, "it has only been in the full-size cars we came out with two years ago and the intermediates this year that we have been able to bring a consistency of style to the Chrysler product offering."

There is a very good reason why the auto makers work hard at creating a clearly defined image for themselves and their cars: Such a precise image is vital to car buyers. Says Leonard Piconke, Chrysler's director of marketing services: "The automobile is a piece of communication, and the automobile purchase is a very complex expression. When we do attitude studies we ask the question, 'Is that your kind of car?' The subject is deciding whether that car fits his image, the kind of personality he wants to project."

The Inner Car Buyer

To discover who buys their cars, and what kind of image the buyers are seeking, the auto makers study both the demographics and the psychographics of their customers—ages and income as well as attitudes and life-styles. About 70 percent of new-car buyers decide to purchase the same make again and again, so the customer corps of each company remains remarkably stable over long periods of time.

Ford's buyers are still basically workingmen seeking inexpensive transportation. But the company's use of bold styling over the last decade has also captured a large proportion of young, relatively affluent, style-conscious customers—the people advertisers call "urban upscale" buyers. G.M., with its Buick, Oldsmobile, and Pontiac divisions, is much stronger in the middle- and upper-middle income brackets. Its cars, especially its bigger cars, are symbols of success and prosperity. They are seen as all-American—not too stylish, not too dull, but good, sensible cars for everyone and a sound investment.

Chrysler's buyers as a group are discernibly different from G.M.'s or Ford's, and Chrysler executives are well aware of the differences. Generally, says Eugene Cafiero, "our buyers are a little older. Their incomes are a little lower in almost every category of car. In the lower end of the market, they are blue-collar workers." The demographics of its buyers have important consequences for Chrysler. Its customers are less likely than those of G.M. and Ford to buy cars that are "loaded" with expensive and profitable options. They tend to retain their cars longer, and thus are potential customers less often.

Last fall Lynn Townsend complained that half of the company's potential customers were unable to obtain credit, and that their inability to do so was aggravating the plunge in sales. Another reason Chrysler's sales declined so sharply last fall was that many of the blue-collar workers who buy its cars were among the first to be laid off. A lot of people who buy Chrysler's cars, says an executive at another automobile company, "are losers. These are people who didn't make it someplace."

Researchers have found that Chrysler Corp.'s customers are significantly more conservative, in both their sense of style and their self-image, than those of the other auto makers. They seek a feeling of security and stability from their car. "People who buy our cars worry about costs," says John Riccardo, "they worry about reliability, they worry about serviceability." Leonard Piconke describes the typical Chrysler buyer as "more rational than emotional, the guy who's looking for better quality and durability. He says, 'Maybe the Chrysler product isn't as stylish, but I don't want style. I want a car that will run.' "

Alienated Owners Remember You

While the people who buy Chrysler cars are not, on the whole, the ideal customers for an auto maker, they are nevertheless as important to the company's success as is engineering. Without its corps of pre-sold customers, Chrysler would have to win a new market for every new model—an impossible task. R. K. Brown, the group vice president for U.S. sales, says one of the first principles of the automobile business is that "you don't alienate and orphan owners. They remember you for a long time."

Yet Chrysler all too often has alienated its customers by ignoring their wants. A major demonstration of the company's confusion about its customers and purpose was the enthusiastic entry into the hot-car racing market in the Sixties. Early in that decade both Pontiac and Ford began to redesign some of their intermediate-size cars as racy-looking, souped-up vehicles for stock-car racing, and their victories began to attract customers from the burgeoning youth market. Chrysler's engineers were enthusiastic about their new 500-hp "hemi-head" engine, the most powerful engine then being produced by any U.S. auto maker, and the racing market provided a perfect opportunity to use it.

But unlike its competitors, who had turned only one or two models into racing cars with a hot-rod image, Chrysler marketed *most* of its intermediates with racing images—the Dodge Charger and Coronet, the Plymouth Road Runner and Satellite. For two or three years, that strategy worked wonders for Chrysler's sales. Its share of the intermediate market rose from 19 to 22 percent.

When the Hot-Rod Market Cooled

"We styled them for aerodynamics and we were doing just great," recalls Townsend. "That racing image brought youth to us. But when we hit the en-

vironmental years, our business in the intermediates just fell right on the floor." By souping up its intermediates, Chrysler alienated some bread-and-butter buyers, older and more conservative, who abandoned the company's cars and still have not returned. And when the racing fad ended, the young car buyers found that Chrysler had few other products to interest them, and they left too.

Only last fall did the company abandon its hot-rod cars, five years after the fleeting interest in them had waned. Partly because its intermediates were so out of date, Chrysler last year held only 12.4 percent of that market. Late in the year, however, the company began trying to recover its business in mid-size cars. In a model-juggling that was rare for Detroit, it dropped the popular Plymouth Fury from full size to intermediate. That step will make it easier for the people who have always owned a full-size car to save money, and gas, by moving down a notch.

A major advertising campaign in the middle Sixties, the "Dodge Rebellion," offered another piece of evidence that Chrysler Corp.'s management had misperceived its market. The campaign, replete with cowgirls and lots of hoopla, was part of a six-year effort to capture more young buyers for Dodge. "We have worked very hard over a number of years to move a youth image into the Dodge car," Townsend explains. "It's very, very hard."

One reason is that Dodge's traditional owners aren't very youthful—as Chrysler's management knew. "They're an older group than Plymouth owners," says Townsend, "and by and large, a more conservative group." The present owners of Dodge cars are about as far from "rebellious" as it is possible to be, and the unfortunate Dodge Rebellion campaign left them confused about their car's image and resentful of Chrysler's threat to their own image.

The campaign also failed to lure many youthful buyers to Dodge—it simply didn't match the public's idea of a Dodge. Chrysler was unable to make the huge leap from a stodgy image to a youthful image all at once. The unsuccessful effort left Dodge's present image unclear and its potential markets weakened for years to come.

The Voice of the Dealers

Chrysler's executives have failed to understand not only who their customers are but also what kinds of cars they want to buy. As a result, management has tried to cover a broader spectrum of the market than the company can handle. Reflecting its engineers' desires, Chrysler historically has emphasized its expensive, full-size cars. Its less costly or smaller cars have usually been grudgingly adopted stepchildren.

The first Plymouth, Townsend says, was introduced in the 1920's at the urging of the dealers "in order to take the customers that couldn't buy the higher-priced, better-engineered Chrysler car." For a good many years, he adds, the Plymouth "was just a peripheral product, because this company wanted to sell those Chryslers, DeSotos, and Dodges." As things turned out, however, the Plymouth became the company's best-selling product, and G.M. dominated the high-price market. The DeSoto line was dropped in 1961 for lack of sales.

Nevertheless, Chrysler continued to invest a disproportionate share of its money and effort in engineering, styling, and promoting its biggest and most expensive cars. When in 1970 the management decided to try to achieve an identity of style for all of the company's cars, it first restyled the full-size models, which were introduced in the fall of 1973. That happened to be just when the energy crisis hit, and sales of large cars fell sharply.

"We've taken a substantial amount of criticism for bringing out new big cars at that time," Townsend admits. But he argues that "we came with a new car into a declining market to preserve and improve our position in it—and it's still a substantial market." Despite all of Chrysler's efforts to sell big cars, however, it accounted for only 9 percent of the full-size cars sold in the U.S. last year—less than its overall market share of 14 percent.

sider peripheral—small cars. Its Plymouth Valiant and Dodge Dart are the best-selling compacts in the country, with 40 percent of that market. They are so strong that even without a subcompact, Chrysler holds 25 percent of the U.S. market for all small cars—far above its total market share. About one-fourth of all the new cars sold in the U.S. are compacts, and many automobile executives—including Townsend—think that by 1980 compacts may account for more than half of all sales.

Chrysler seems to have attained its enviable position in the compact market without really trying. When G.M. replaced its Corvair with the Nova, and Ford replaced the Falcon with the Mustang and Maverick, Chrysler's attention was riveted on its big cars and racy intermediates. The company just kept building its Valiants, and the virtually identical Darts, to keep its dealers happy. With little change from year to year, the cars improved in quality and gradually won a reputation for economy, reliability, and durability—exactly the qualities Chrysler's buyers were seeking. Their good quality and their bland but stable styling outweighed Chrysler's attempts to give them a livelier image. The Dart Swinger, for example, is bought mostly by people over forty-five.

Next fall, however, Chrysler will try a major gamble with its compacts. It will bring out a new, higher-priced line to supplement, and eventually replace, the Valiant and Dart. They will have styling similar to that of the company's current full-size and intermediate lines, and for the first time there will be a family resemblance among Chrysler Corp. cars in all size categories. Compact buyers in general, unlike most buyers of larger cars, are more interested in economy than in style. But that is beginning to change, and Chrysler hopes to attract new buyers with its somewhat more stylish compacts.

Succeeding Without Really Trying

Today Chrysler's greatest strength, astonishingly, is in a market segment it has always seemed to con-

And Now to "Distinguished Styling"

The company has already taken one leap into stylish cars, and it seems to have done so successfully.

Last fall saw the debut of a totally new, intermediate-size Chrysler, a "personal luxury" car called the Cordoba, and it is perhaps the best-looking medium-size American car on the road today. The Cordoba has what one marketing analyst calls "exactly the look of understated gentility that is ideal for a Chrysler car." It give Chrysler an entry in the growing, and highly profitable, market for luxurious but smaller cars that is now dominated by such imports as Mercedes, BMW, and Volvo. The car will help to restore Chrysler's position in the intermediate segment and might even bring it some new, style-conscious customers. So far, half the Cordoba's buyers have been trading in such competitive makes as Buicks and Oldsmobiles.

With a styling success in the Cordoba, and with more subdued but newly integrated styling throughout its line, Chrysler Corp. is setting off once again in a new direction. As Townsend puts it: "I think today probably most of the market wants distinguished styling." When he is reminded that Chrysler's cars are not noted for their smart styling, or its customers for their interest in it, he replies, "Yes, I know. But that's what the market is; we've had to get a high-style image."

Going for a high-style image, however, presents Chrysler with a considerable risk. In reaching for new customers, it could lose a lot of old customers. To succeed in its new "product policy," Chrysler will have to position its cars precisely in the public mind—something it has never been able to do very well. If the new, more stylish models are perceived as still being stodgy after all, they will attract few new customers. If they are perceived as being too stylish or too expensive, they could be rejected by many of the company's old customers.

A Value in Blandness

So it seems entirely possible that Chrysler is once again chasing a will-o'-the-wisp, much like its venture into hot rods a decade ago. It is true that "distinguished styling" is a lot closer to the character of Chrysler's buyers than hot rods. But changing an ingrained image, whether of a car or a company, takes years of careful and sustained effort.

In moving along in its new direction, Chrysler should take care to avoid losing more old customers than it gains new ones. Especially in the growing market for compacts, the company has a solid base of loyal customers, and its first priority should be to keep them happy, with economical, reliable, blandly styled cars. It should create the same stability of design and purpose in its intermediate and full-size cars and only gradually venture into a more fickle, style-minded market. Over time—a decade or so, perhaps—the company might be able to modify its image enough to attract a large group of more affluent, style-conscious buyers. Without such a consistent, long-term strategy, Chrysler will be condemned to remain a marginal and floundering enterprise.

Questions

1. *Critically assess the planning process at Chrysler Corporation between 1924 and 1974.*
2. *If Chrysler engineers have indeed developed better cars on occasion, why hasn't the company prospered? Is the logic of "build a better mousetrap and the world will beat a path to your door" valid?*
3. *Would you try to alter the orientation of Chrysler management? If so, how would you proceed?*

13

Hewlett-Packard:
Where Slower Growth
Is Smarter Management

BUSINESS WEEK

The Hewlett-Packard Company is a giant in a sophisticated engineering technology and marketing-oriented industry. Pricing for profits and keeping close to the market seem to have been two keys to that company's success.

David Packard, chairman of Hewlett-Packard Co., stretched his six-foot-five frame after lunching with a score of his middle managers recently and then proceeded to set the record straight on the company's strategy for survival in the fast-changing world of high-technology electronics. The leading producer of electronic instruments and a major force in minicomputers and calculators had grown too fast in the boom years of 1972–73, Packard declared.

He ticked off the disturbing results. Inventories and accounts receivable got out of hand, products went into production before they were fully developed, and prices were set too low. The problems were well in hand now, but Packard wanted to be sure that the lesson was understood.

"Somewhere we got into the idea that market share was an objective," Packard told his attentive audience, jingling a pocketful of coins for emphasis. "I hope that's straightened out. Anyone can build market share, and if you set your prices low

enough, you can get the whole damn market. But I'll tell you it won't get you anywhere around here."

Packard's feisty speech was part of a year-long campaign he and President William R. Hewlett have been waging to reemphasize the principles they laid down when they launched their unique partnership 36 years ago. The fact that Hewlett and Packard had to initiate and lead the drive personally shows clearly why some company watchers are beginning to worry about what will happen to the high-flyer once its two founders depart.

The style and leadership of the two men are intertwined with the major policies of their company to a far greater degree than are those of the top managers at most major corporations. Now both Hewlett and Packard are nearing retirement age, and they have started moving younger managers into positions that hint at a line of succession. A major task will be to make sure that their philosophies and strategies are deeply ingrained before they leave.

But it will be a tough act to follow. "Hewlett and Packard are unique people," declares Galen Wampler, who follows the company closely as an analyst for Creative Strategies, Inc. "The company needed a technology innovator like Hewlett, but it also had Packard, a man with a lot of business sense." Thomas J. Perkins, a venture capitalist who was once a top H-P executive, points out that Hewlett and Packard have been personally responsible for many of the company's new products and diversification moves. "They are extraordinary entrepreneurs," he says.

Pricing for Profit

The fundamental tenet on which they have built the company—and the point they have strongly reemphasized to their managers during the past year—is that rather than compete on price, H-P must concentrate on developing products so advanced that customers are willing to pay a premium for them. "After a few excursions in the opposite direction," says Hewlett, "we've found that this philosophy fits our style of operation."

So now, at a time when other companies are dropping prices to boost sales and cutting research spending to boost earnings, Hewlett-Packard is taking the opposite tack. It has raised prices by an average of 10% over the last year, and it has increased spending on research and development by 20% to an $80-million annual rate.

If the strategy works, H-P will slow the pace of growth that more than doubled sales in the past three years, but its profitability will continue to improve. So far, this is exactly what has happened. Last week, H-P announced that first-half sales were up to 14% to $460-million, while profits jumped 21% to $42-million. Several analysts now predict that H-P will reach $1-billion sales for the first time in the fiscal year that ends next October.

Even more dramatic than the first-half results was H-P's balance sheet turnaround. A year ago, net short-term borrowings totaled $118-million, and the company was planning to resort for the first time to long-term debt. Instead, Packard toured the divisions to impose new asset-management discipline. Reaction was quick: Inventories were slashed, accounts receivable were tightened, and hiring was frozen. As a result, H-P is now almost completely out of the banks. "This is nothing short of astounding," says Michael R. Weisberg, an analyst at William D. Witter, Inc.

To Spend or Not to Spend

The sail-trimming at Hewlett-Packard reflects one response to the unique dilemma that managers of high-technology companies must resolve in these days of accelerating technical change, intensified competition, and economic uncertainty. On the one hand, recession conditions create great financial dislocations for companies used to growing fast, and product development is a tempting area for temporary cutbacks. Notes Jeremy G. A. Davis, vice-president and general manager of the Boston Consulting Group's Menlo Park (Calif.) office: "The weaker the company, the more pressure there is to slash R&D spending."

On the other hand, some companies producing advanced electronic products feel that they must increase their research spending during a recession to be ready for the onslaught of price cuts and new products that will accompany the next upturn. "Our development spending is up 60% over last year," says Andrew S. Grove, executive vice-president of Intel Corp., a fast-growing semiconductor company that has prospered by introducing significant new products. "We are buying our position in the upturn," he declares. Packard agrees. "The main determinant of our growth," he says, "is the effectiveness of our new-product program."

In betting large sums on the inventiveness of their engineers, companies like Hewlett-Packard and Intel are counting on developing products that cannot be quickly imitated. The classic example is H-P's hand-held scientific calculator, the HP-35, which was introduced early in 1972 and did not have a serious competitor until Texas Instruments, Inc., introduced an electronic slide rule of its own last year.

In H-P's last fiscal year, according to estimates by Creative Strategies, the HP-35 and its later variations accounted for sales of $120-million and pretax earnings of $40-million. Whether that kind of success can ever be duplicated seems open to question in light of the increasing competitive pressures in virtually every niche of high-technology electronics. "The pioneer has very little lead time now," says Davis of Boston Consulting. "Instead of several years to get down that experience curve, he may have only a few months."

What is happening is that the management of technology—not only in electronics but also in pharmaceuticals, chemicals, and other specialties—

is no longer an art but a discipline that is becoming better understood by a growing number of companies. Furthermore, the specialization that once separated an instrument maker from a computer company or a component supplier has melted away in recent years as semiconductor devices have taken on new complexity and instruments have been combined with calculators and computers in an endless array of specialized systems. Semiconductor houses, such as Texas Instruments and National Semiconductor Corp., are integrating forward into end products, and instrument companies, such as Tektronix, Inc., and Varian Associates, are making their own data-processing equipment. The result is an open-ended array of potential competitors in almost every area of advanced electronics.

An increasingly common tactic to achieve dominance is to price a new product in relation to the manufacturing costs that the producer expects to achieve when the product is mature. Popularized by the Boston Consulting Group and exploited by such companies as TI and Digital Equipment Corp., "experience curve pricing" puts a premium on achieving market share early in the game. Other industries follow similar strategies, but one consultant points out: "Nobody is moving faster on the experience curve than the high-technology electronics companies, and the consequences of being late are most severe in that business."

A Good Strategy

Against that background, H-P's decision to eschew market share in favor of a concentration on profitability seems fraught with risk. But Packard and Hewlett do not see themselves as risk takers, and their philosophy makes sense for a company that can consistently produce truly innovative products. "If you have a new product that makes a contribution," says Packard, "it's easy to sell all you can produce at a respectable price. Then as you actually achieve cost reductions, you can lower the price accordingly."

H-P's leadership position in instruments has paid off handsomely as the company has diversified into computers, calculators, and components. "Measuring instruments have to be better than the products they measure," Packard explains. "From the beginning, we've had to keep a good base of technology." That is something of an understatement, says one former H-P executive. "Along with Bell Labs, they get the cream of the crop of bright young engineers," he claims. "And they provide an environment that is very rewarding."

Innovative products have been the cornerstone of H-P's growth since 1939, when Hewlett engineered a new audio oscillator and set up shop with Packard in a Palo Alto garage. The product was cheaper and easier to use than competing oscillators, and it was quickly followed by a family of test instruments based on the same design principles. During World War II, H-P developed some high-speed microwave instruments—"because we didn't know any better," Packard claims—and used that technology to ride the postwar boom in communications.

By the 1950s, H-P was churning out up to two dozen new products every year, including the first high-speed electronic counter and an oscillator that automatically swept through a range of frequencies. "Hewlett and Packard had the fortune or wisdom to get into the electronics business when it was just starting to boom," remarks one observer.

But H-P's strategy of product dominance did not always succeed. Despite heroic efforts, H-P has never managed to shake the grip held by Tektronix on oscilloscopes, the ubiquitous instrument used in every lab to display electronic signals on a cathode-ray tube. "We delayed our entry in that business too long," Packard admits, "and the first scope we introduced wasn't a better product." And in minicomputers, H-P missed an opportunity to catch up with Digital Equipment Corp. in the early 1970s by failing to move technology into the marketplace at a competitive pace. "Despite the fact that we are second in the market," says Paul C. Ely, Jr., general manager of H-P's Computer Systems Group, "our impact hasn't been felt."

Nevertheless, H-P's diversification has been a success by most standards. In the last fiscal year, the original test and measurement instruments accounted for only half of H-P's sales of $884-million. Data products, including minicomputers and calculators, brought in $326-million. Medical electronics, a field H-P entered largely by acquisition, added $76-million and analytical instruments another $39-million. Much of this growth has come in the last three years, spurred by both the world economic boom of 1972–73 and the success of new products, such as the minicalculator. Sales soared by nearly 30% in 1972 and to almost 40% the following year. "It was a seller's market," Packard says.

At first, growth was welcome. H-P had been sharply affected by the computer and aerospace downturns in 1970, while Packard was serving as No. 2 man in the Defense Dept. Earnings actually declined slightly in fiscal 1971 in spite of such measures as companywide pay cuts.

But the boom also brought problems, including a rapid increase in inventories and an unaccustomed influx of new employees. By the end of 1973, H-P's short-term debt load was big enough to force a decision. "Some of us thought we should convert to long-term debt," Packard says, "but I began to think about it, and I concluded that we hadn't been on the right track."

"The problem with debt," says Hewlett, "is that you eventually have to pay the piper. It's more comfortable to have zero debt when you have to increase inventories to keep people working." Adds Packard: "My philosophy goes back to the Depression. I don't want to be in debt if a downturn comes."

The situation came to a head while Packard was visiting H-P's German subsidiary in January of last year. "Somebody got up and said we should transfer more products to Europe to gain market share," recalls Ely. "Dave laid into that concept so hard that the audience was aghast." What troubled Packard, apparently, was the prospect that H-P would become so dependent on growth that it would slip away from the principles that he and Hewlett have expounded over the years.

As it happened, H-P's belt-tightening effort turned out to be the perfect preparation for the gen-

Figure 1

How Hewlett-Packard thrives on high technology

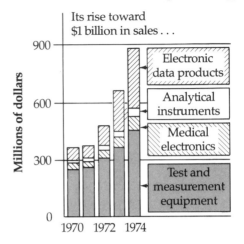

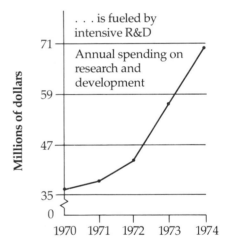

eral recession that hit last fall. With hiring virtually flat for most of last year, H-P's productivity improved rapidly.

The change in the cash position saved $5-million annually in interest charges, and prices on products such as oscilloscopes were pushed upward, offsetting price declines in calculators and computers. As a result, earnings jumped ahead in the face of slowing sales. "Packard put the emphasis on control at all levels," says Creative Strategies' Wampler. "That's the watchword for the future."

Choosing Heirs Apparent

But Packard was dismayed by the fact that he had to intervene directly in day-to-day management. "It bothered him that he had to do that," says one H-P manager. Packard will turn 65 in 1977 and Hewlett the following year, and their retirement would leave an enormous management gap. The two men still own about half the company stock and presumably could postpone retirement indefinitely. "Whether we will retire or not remains to be seen," Packard says. "But we want to be in a position to do so."

Last fall, Hewlett and Packard clarified the line of succession a bit by announcing a restructured corporate organization and moving three executives up to a new level of management. John A. Young, 43, who had headed the instrument group, was named executive vice-president and a director and given a joint mandate with Ralph E. Lee, 59, another executive vice-president, to oversee operations. Robert L. Boniface, 50, who has a marketing background, was made vice-president for administration.

This new troika is supposed to take a stronger hand in coordinating the activities of H-P's 23 operating divisions, but Hewlett and Packard are still reluctant to relinquish the reins. Corporate research and development activities still report directly to Hewlett, and one or both of the founders continue to sit in on annual management review sessions for each division. "They'll never retire," predicts one outsider. "They may drop in their tracks, but they will never really retire."

Even if Young and Lee, the obvious frontrunners, do step up to replace Hewlett and Packard, the result will hardly be an abrupt change. Both men are engineers who have come up through the ranks, and they project the same relaxed self-assurance that characterizes the founders. Young, who is more outgoing, would probably take the

high-visibility role played in recent years by Hewlett; Lee, who has a reputation as a troubleshooter, would concentrate on internal problems.

Both are committed to the H-P way of doing things, and Young likes to point to Harvard psychologist Michael Maccoby's division of technology workers into "craftsmen" and "gamesmen." Says Young: "Hewlett-Packard people tend to be more interested in making fundamental engineering contributions than in playing games."

The reorganization last fall also pushed some of the group managers into prominence, notably Ely in computer systems, William E. Terry in instruments, and Dean O. Morton in medical systems. Terry and Morton are both vice-presidents, but Ely's name is mentioned most often by outsiders because of his success in putting the computer operation back on the track.

Keeping Close to the Market

The new organization leaves intact H-P's basic strategy of approaching established markets through relatively autonomous product-oriented divisions. In any high-technology operation, a key problem is how to keep the engineers working on new products attuned to the needs of the market. Edward B. Roberts, David Sarnoff Professor of Management at MIT's Sloan School of Management, points out that many studies in the past 10 years have shown that 70% to 80% of all innovations were "market need based" as opposed to pure invention. "You still have to work hard in the lab," he says, "but merely coming up with technological niceties is no help."

In a company as large as H-P has become, engineers can easily get out of touch with the marketplace. H-P tries to avoid this by doing most of its R&D at the division level and by splitting up divisions whenever they seem in danger of getting too big. In instruments, for example, H-P now has 11 divisions, each with its own research and manufacturing facilities.

Each division also has its own marketing staff,

responsible for product management and promotion, but the actual selling is done through the six group organizations. "We have multiple factories competing for the attention of a central sales organization," says Edward McCracken, marketing manager for the Data Systems Div. "If we provide the easiest path for the sales engineer to make his quota, he's going to sell our product."

H-P's new-product efforts revolve around divisional project engineers, who organize the development effort, and product managers, who step in from marketing at an early stage and help specify the details of design and price. "The project manager has to be a little entrepreneur," says Richard Hackborn, who heads computer products development. "He has to have a handle on the technology and on how people use a product, and he has to take it right through to production." And the job is considerably more complex than it was a few years ago, Hackborn adds. "It used to be that the instrument desginer only had to satisfy the fellow at the next bench. Now H-P is in a lot of businesses, and that next-bench link has been severed."

A typical project team nowadays involves experts not only in instrument design but also in integrated-circuit processes, computer logic, and industrial design. A team from one division is likely to draw on help from others as well as from H-P Labs, the corporate research organization.

"At one time we split R&D and product engineering," says Bernard M. Oliver, vice-president for R&D. "But we discovered that the only way to get things done in a timely fashion is to have the originator of an idea carry it through to the end. We've tried to remove the fences between research and production and make a chute that starts in the lab and ends at the shipping dock."

An increasingly important tool for the H-P product-development teams is the company's growing network of semiconductor processing facilities. The HPA Div., a pioneer in light-emitting diode technology, sells displays and other optoelectronic components on the open market as well as to other H-P divisions. And many of the instrument and computer divisions have their own facilities for developing advanced semiconductor components. "The real advantage to this kind of vertical integration is in engineering efficiency," says Douglas C. Chance, general manager of the Santa Rosa Div., which makes microwave test gear. "If we make our own components, we can shorten the time it takes to get to the state of the art."

Semiconductor knowhow was vital to H-P's early development of the minicalculator—although, as is often the case, an outside vendor wound up making the production circuits—and it is rapidly becoming equally important to H-P's position in the minicomputer business. "With the advent of large-scale integrated circuits," says Ely, "engineers have to get right down to the cell level in semiconductor design. We want H-P to put its finger on the process and circuitry at the semiconductor level, rather than wait for the technology to filter down."

The Data Systems Div. is pursuing an ambitious program to develop a high-speed, high-density process known as silicon-on-sapphire (sos), which has stumped any number of semiconductor device makers. "We have prototype parts now," claims Hackborn, "and we could be in production by the end of the year."

Moving Fast Is the Key

Although H-P's divisions have considerable latitude in developing product strategies, they are not allowed to stray from their assigned markets. "If they go out in left field, they get a lot of scrutiny from topside," Hewlett says. An example is the division specializing in power supplies, which sought faster growth a few years back by getting into new markets. "They started to fall behind in their original product line," Boniface recalls, "and they had no success outside of it." The division was quickly brought back into step and now is making good profits again—in power supplies.

Even within the limits set by top management, new product proposals are carefully screened at the preliminary investigation stage. "We are very conservative in funding projects," says Oliver, "but our batting average is good. We're unhappy unless 80% of our projects pan out."

Once development of a new product is funded, the goal is to get it to market in a hurry. "We have a theory that sales lost during gestation time are never recovered," remarks Oliver. "There is a moment in history when a technology is available, and if you can conceive of a product, then others can conceive of it too."

Time is particularly important in the minicomputer business, where product generations are now only three years apart, and prices are dropping at an average rate of 30% per year. Until recently, H-P was floundering in that market, caught with the old-generation equipment at the low end of the price scale and unable to get its powerful new HP 3000 system out of the lab.

But Ely, who won his spurs as a developer of innovative microwave instruments, has turned H-P's computer business around in the last two years. "We've been cutting costs in marketing and reinvesting in product development," he says, "and it's starting to pay off." The 3000 is now the fastest growing part of the product line, and a gamble on using the new 4,096-bit semiconductor memory devices has given H-P a price-competitive entry at the low end as well.

But as H-P grows, it is faced with the added complication of transferring its sophisticated research and manufacturing operations away from home base in California. "The easiest thing to do is to grow right here," Hewlett says, "but it would be a mistake to put all our eggs in one basket." H-P has moved its microwave operation to a lavish new complex in rural Santa Rosa, north of San Francisco, and it plans to move the minicalculator group to Corvallis, Oregon. Chance, whose Santa Rosa Div. now employs some 800 workers, finds it easier to hire off the farm than in the heart of the high-technology industry. "We had 13,000 applications," he says, "and we didn't have to retrain anybody."

H-P has found it more difficult to move its concept of fully integrated divisions overseas. "We've encouraged all of our overseas divisions to develop a good R&D activity," says Packard, "but they have found it hard because our contribution here is so overwhelming."

Some progress is being made, however, at H-P's instrument plant in South Queensferry, Scotland, where about half the production now involves products designed there. An H-P operations in Germany, France, and Japan are building up product development skills. But even by relying primarily on U.S.-designed products, H-P's foreign sales now exceed domestic sales. "H-P is a very ethical supplier," notes one French competitor in explaining the company's powerful grip on the instrumentation business in Europe. "In the long run," he adds, "that policy pays."

A Remarkable Relationship

If there is one key to the success of H-P's strategy, it may be the unusual spirit of corporate loyalty that permeates the work force, particularly the 2,000-odd engineers working in R&D. Although their stock holdings now are worth some $700-million each, Hewlett and Packard still run an egalitarian ship. They draw salaries of only $156,000 each, and few top officers make more than $100,000. The company has distributed $64-million in cash profit-sharing bonuses in the last five years, and about half the 30,000 employees participate in a stock-purchase program. Rather than run the risk of big layoffs, H-P declines to bid on short-run government contracts, and when times are lean, everyone from Packard on down takes a pay cut. As a result, H-P is seldom afflicted with the migrations of people and ideas that most high-technology companies experience.

This strong esprit de corps is not only the result of how Hewlett and Packard manage their company but comes also from their own close relationship, which is remarkable on several counts. The two men have an almost uncanny ability to keep their thinking meshed, even when they are a continent apart. "They are almost totally in synch all the time," says Ely. "I often talk to them together, but when one is gone, the impact is no different." Hewlett and Packard even share their private lives. Together they operate—and brag about—a cattle-breeding empire that now takes in three ranches and 60,000 acres.

But there are differences in the way the two men operate. Packard, whose formidable height and rumbling baritone tend to intimidate new acquaintances, is actually a warm and sympathetic listener with a self-deprecating sense of humor. (Once, asked what his biggest accomplishment had been as Deputy Secretary of Defense, Packard thought for a moment and said, "I gave up smoking.")

Packard focuses on the management strategies that guide the company, and he was the driving force behind such key decisions as H-P's move into medical systems and its efforts to become a major factor in minicomputers. Hewlett, on the other hand, is known as a detached and analytical thinker whose great joy is in stirring technical ferment. "He leans toward conceiving product lines and needling people to get going on them," Oliver says. Some parts of H-P Labs, in fact, are considered Hewlett's personal research staff, and it was there that the HP-35 was nurtured, after several executives tried to shoot it down. But Hewlett also has a common touch, as he illustrated recently when he joined Young and another executive in a race to see who could assemble a new computer terminal in the shortest time. "Bill won," Ely reports, "but John's worked."

Both Hewlett and Packard are trying to pull back. "Their real role now is to build a second echelon of management," says one H-P insider. H-P has "a very broad base of fine management people," says Denny K. Paul, an analyst for Dataquest, Inc., of Palo Alto, who points out that the company has always pushed decision-making to the division level. "What concerns me," adds Paul, "is the question of what happens to esprit de corps if Hewlett and Packard leave."

That is obviously a concern that Hewlett and Packard share. "Motivation," says David Packard, "is the difference between a championship ball team and an ordinary ball team." The question for the future is whether players can stay motivated when their two coaches are no longer with the team.

Questions

1. *What characteristics of Hewlett-Packard's competitors have made that company's past marketing strategy very appropriate? What kinds of changes in H-P's competitive environment would dictate changing its marketing strategy?*
2. *Explain the concept of* learning curve pricing.
3. *What is the impact of learning curve pricing on market share?*
4. *What are the risks associated with learning curve pricing in a highly competitive industry?*

14

How Creative Packaging
Can Help You Position
Your Product

ROBERT LEE DICKENS

The role of the product package is multifaceted. It is a protector, an eye catcher, an information communicator, and a use facilitator. Its vital role in product positioning is stressed here.

How can package design help position your product? It can aid in differentiating a product from its competition, in focusing its appeal on a specific consumer segment, and in projecting and communicating the product's personality and performance claims in a persuasive and believable manner.

The past decades, with their steeply rising curve of discretionary income, have created a whole host of look-alike, act-alike brands. To the average consumer, a soap is a soap and a lotion is a lotion—until she tries them and gathers first-hand performance facts.

Today's more sophisticated consumers are more insistent and articulate about making sure that the product's promise is actually delivered. If your positioning makes the product seem something it isn't, you'll hear about it. Or, much worse, you won't hear about it.

Positioning starts with the product. What does it do? How is it perceived? Does it attack competitive market shares by doing the same thing, only better, or does it open up a totally new field and thereby additional buyers? What are, and who are, its potential customers?

How will the product be used? When? Where? By whom? What are the consumers' acknowledged feelings about the product and its use? What are their hidden, or subconscious, attitudes in that field of use?

Are these same feelings universally present and fairly uniform for your product's entire consumer population? Or do they shift and vary by region? By income? By age? By educational level? By ethnic origin?

The Challenge: Differentiate

Here's what we do with the answers to all these questions. We develop a concise, detailed product profile, a product performance cluster, a product character that will serve to guide us in positioning it. Thus, positioning is a precise description of the product's actual and perceived attributes, of the way it responds to consumer needs (whether conscious or unacknowledged), and most important, of the strategy that will differentiate it from competition and position it within the competitive market environment. If you do not differentiate, you have to rely almost entirely on pricing, distribution, display, sales promotion and advertising to sell the product. Display, sales promotion and especially advertising are severely handicapped without effective product differentiation.

Once you have determined the product's position, your research and development team knows what you want to sell, and can start developing product attributes. Let's say you see a significant need in soaps not fulfilled by competitors' products in a truly satisfying manner. Maybe the need is factual; maybe it is subconscious or entirely imagined (and, therefore, even stronger and more real). At this stage (your first planning session with R&D), it is not too early to invite your designer to participate.

I know that traditionally you first develop the product, and then call in the designer. But many of our clients discovered long ago these two facts:

1. Color, form, texture, fragrance, functional benefits envisioned by your designer can be built into the product more easily if he becomes part of the development assignment from the very start. Your designer can, for instance, develop a soap's shape, size, color (how about layered colors?), the way it handles (dry and wet), the way it can be molded.

2. Your designer is familiar not only with what is esthetically desirable, but also with what is attainable in costs, production limits, line speeds, distribution handicaps and packaging potentials. He can enhance brand name images—regal, aloof, folksy, commonsense, foreign, mysterious, sweet, acrid, young, childlike, businesslike, heady, delirious, precise . . . there is hardly an emotional appeal that cannot be conveyed by color and styling.

Once product quality and positioning have been tested, the brand name approved and package copy written in compliance with all legal regulations, the designer's role shifts to pure package design.

The Countless Options of Packaging

Package designers deal with glass or plastic molding or forming, wrap styles, can-making technology, materials, printing and embossing techniques, opening devices and other details that can provide additional consumer benefits as well as contribute to a healthy cost-of-goods structure.

In creating a bottle for a shampoo, for instance, you may want to market a product that imparts a sheen and luster to a teenager's hair: Should you take advantage of the extra polish a vinyl exterior surface can give you (provided you find a supplier), or should you forego the merchandising advantage of extra sheen for the profit advantage of lower cost resins? And if those smart teens are your market, what about vinyl's environmental implications?

Should you opt for that long, gracefully tapered styrene acrylonitrile cap which will lend verve and suavity to the bottle's contour, or should you choose the shorter, more pedestrian butadiene-styrene cap that will cost less?

Market Share or Profit?

You may compete more effectively with the "designer's dream": You may sell more units. But your profit, and that of the stores, will be lower. Which way do you go? How do you decide? Market shares or profits? Or both?

The package designer effects the tradeoffs by demonstrating the options and pointing out the assets and debits of each position. Custom mold vs. stock mold. One specific cap for each size vs. one cap for all sizes. Special pour spout vs. no pour fitment. Measuring dispenser vs. standard dispenser. Label vs. heat transfer, or pressure-sensitive Mylar polyester, or Kaumagraph in-mold decoration, vs. shrink band labeling, vs. silkscreen.

Transparent display of product (with possible visible sedimentation, or fill level fluctuation) vs. opaque. Angle-tilted neck and resulting uniqueness (with accompanying headaches of special fill-line cradles) vs. conventional straight neck (and a look very much like all your competitors). Centered parison vs. onesided; programed vs. nonprogramed.

The alternatives are endless, and each fork in the bottle design road can lead you closer or farther away from what was initially agreed upon as your objectives. The designer won't make these decisions for you—he does not have any dollars, market shares, or franchises involved, although he may well believe sufficiently in the quality of his work to be a stockholder in your company. But he will point out where the questions lie, and he will make sure that you can visualize the alternatives.

Questions

1. What key characteristics should a marketer consider when determining the shape, size, color, and other features of a package container for (a) cologne? (b) breakfast cereal? (c) industrial chemicals?

2. Select two competitive products in two distinct product categories that are available in a local retail outlet. Compare and contrast the critical marketing aspects of the packages of each set of competitive products.

15

Proprietary Brands: Boon for the Entrepreneur

STANLEY R. RENAS

HAROLD W. FOX

Proprietary brands offer an attractive advantage to industrial distributors, wholesalers, and retailers. However, their successful development is not without substantial risk.

Independence is a major goal of most entrepreneurs. But the ideal of independence is an illusion, many owners of small businesses discover. Beset by authoritarian customers, affluent vendors, acerbic officials, antagonistic workers, and avaricious bankers, "independent" businesspeople often scramble to placate these five sources of pressure.

Such subservience is reducible. One of the means is the proprietary brand, a distributor's own identification on products made by others. Proprietary brands, sometimes called private or distributor brands, offer the opportunity of substantial freedom for persons who lack much money, technical expertise, or salable ideas, but are energetic and efficient. Based on the authors' experience and research, this article discusses some critical factors for the small firm that buys standard or original formulations of a product line for distribution under its own name. Proprietary brands are pervasive in retail stores, mail order, and industrial marketing.

The proprietary brand is the key to relative autonomy. Dependence, even on customers, is somewhat tempered. Customers will tolerate some inconveniences if the proprietary brands and auxiliary services are otherwise satisfactory, because the firm is the sole source. As monopsonist, the distributor has a choice of vendors. If the products are standard, they have "commodity" status. If custom-made, the specifications are owned by the distributor. Either way, the proprietor's buying position is strong. As quasi-manufacturer, the proprietor has few dealings with regulators, avoids factory labor problems, and reduces conflicts with sales personnel. If his sales agents want exclusives, the proprietor can oblige them by reserving a separate brand for each. Moreover, since investment in fixed assets is zero or small, financial requirements are minor. Indeed, in the distribution of sanitary supplies, one-person firms are not uncommon.

Of course, interdependence is pervasive in a civilized society. Moreover, like most industries with ease of entry and deceptive simplicity of operation, the typical distributor constantly meets new challenges to survival. The fact remains, however, that distributors of products under their own brands can parlay modest resources into a large dose of independence. Ability to cultivate repeat business is crucial.

Product Tactics

One product line that lends itself well to this type of marketing is sanitary or janitorial supplies. Based on the needs of target industries, a distributor of sanitary supplies assembles a salable line of clean-

Source: Journal of Small Business Management, January 1978, pp. 27–30. Copyright © 1978 by the International Council for Small Business and the West Virginia University Bureau of Business Research.

ing compounds, disinfectants, and maintenance materials. A conscientious distributor analyzes the needs of prospects, recommends the best-suited grade, charges the same price as the competition, makes timely deliveries, offers usage instructions if desired, and reminds the purchasing agent when replenishment is necessary. The point is to protect the purchasing agent from any complaint.

An astute proprietor is not greedy. He or she realizes that premium prices could make an inexpert purchasing agent look foolish or worse. Costs and prices of the distributor's own line should be similar to competing proprietary brands, typically below manufacturers' brands. This saving from the list price of the nationally advertised counterpart makes the purchasing agent look efficient.

But a considerate proprietor also refrains from discounting, thus shielding the purchasing agent from worries about product quality. No wonder the owner of a sanitary supply firm described his business as "selling wholesale quantities at retail prices to indifferent purchasing agents who are unfamiliar with the goods they are buying."

The strategy of featuring proprietary brands allows various tactical options. For example, some sanitary supply houses establish their respectability by carrying well-known manufacturers' lines along with proprietary brands. Such names as Simonize wax, Easy-Off cleaner, Colgate soap, etc., help the distributor gain entry and book initial orders. They further enable the distributor to give buyers a continuing choice.

Alternatively, the proprietor may offer only the identical products that well-known manufacturers advertise nationally, but arrange to have the distributor's brand on the label instead. For example, suppose the proprietor uses the trade style, Renox Chemical Co., and registers the Renox brand with the United States Department of Agriculture. Instead of buying 300 one-gallon jugs of Purex brand bleach, the distributor could buy from Purex Corp. the same quantity and formulation of sodium hypochlorite, 5¼%, for sale under the name Renox. The same chemical and packing could also be bought from another manufacturer.

A superficial change in formula and package can

further differentiate the offerings. For example, the proprietor creates "Emerald Flood Cleaner" by asking a manufacturing chemist to embellish a common basic formula with green coloring and mint fragrance. In addition, the manufacturer is instructed to replace the usual plain black drum with a bright, multi-colored container sporting silk-screen overpaint. Then Renox has a generically standard product that is distinctive to the buyer's senses.

Another option is to vary the active ingredients. Say the proprietor orders a new "industrial strength" grade, because some prospects want it or can use it. A manufacturer supplies the requested formulation. The proprietor buys an impressive report from an independent laboratory, gives out some samples and collects testimonials, and merchandises this technological breakthrough along with the rest of the line. Such a brand extension is a routine tactic requiring little extra outlay or effort.

If, however, the proprietor wants to launch a completely new product, special procedures such as market-testing may be necessary. But first, who will invent the product, absorb the costs of research and development, apply for a patent, and so forth? The best safeguard of the proprietor's independence is to finance and control all phases himself. He either originates the idea or pays an inventor. The proprietor also rents laboratory services and retains a patent attorney. All this could be quite costly, at a high risk of failure. If the innovation succeeds, however, the proprietor can submit the patented specifications to competitive bidding, and have the product made by the cheapest acceptable producer.

Alternatively, a manufacturer may defray the research and development costs, but henceforth the proprietor would be dependent on this sponsor as the sole source for the new product. Prior agreements are necessary. How many units is the proprietor obligated to buy? What price will the manufacturer charge? Does the manufacturer promise not to sell the innovation to others? Between these polarities of full freedom and complete dependency a variety of arrangements exist in practice.

Procurement

The proprietor's suppliers are either well-known manufacturers which advertise their own brands (like forementioned Purex Corp.) or specialists in serving distributors. Fast-moving items are in stock. Others must be bought in minimum quantities and will be inventoried at the distributor's expense. The proprietor selects vendors according to the usual criteria of favorable quality, price, and credit terms, confidential dealings, speedy delivery, etc.

The proprietor is responsible for consistent adequate quality. Recent regulations such as the Occupational Safety and Health Act as well as judicial doctrines such as Strict Liability extend the responsibility of any businessperson dealing in products that injure somebody. Despite this increase in answerableness, the distributor often has no access to the manufacturing process because the vendor concurrently fills orders for competitors. Either a certificate of quality from an independent inspection firm or a sample of the run will have to suffice. The best assurance, of course, is to do business with reliable manufacturers.

On receipt of an order the contract manufacturer applies the proprietor's label to the goods and packs them together with the proprietor's packing slip into shipping containers bearing the proprietor's name. The contract manufacturer bills the proprietor, but often "drop-ships" the order directly to the ultimate user, thus eliminating extra transportation and handling. The bill of lading shows the proprietor as the shipper. Delivery should be by public carrier or a truck that does not reveal the contract manufacturer as the source. After all, the buyer and perhaps even the distributor's sales force regard the proprietor as the manufacturer, a fiction that the proprietor wishes to perpetuate, since the typical distributor harbors the fear that some of his contract manufacturers or sales personnel will compete on their own for his customers. A proprietary brand reinforces the distributor's posture as manufacturer and insulates him somewhat from new competition.

Problems

The most obvious difficulty in this kind of business is selling. The name of the line is unfamiliar and financial backing is weak. But many large companies and governmental units have a policy of dealing with small firms whenever possible, and their purchasing agents like to put a conscientious supplier on their roster.

Proprietary brands cause some additional challenges with which the small firm must grapple. Since goods are formulated or finished to the proprietor's specifications, special production runs or final assembly operations are necessary. As a consequence, inventories are larger than for standard brands. First, the cost of shiftover must be absorbed by a large number of units, but turnover is likely to be low. Second, delivery of customers' orders must be prompt. Third, demand may be seasonal or erratic. The proprietor must pay for all inventory-carrying costs. Excess inventory is almost unsalable. Out-of-stock may mean loss of orders and customers. All of these considerations put a heavy burden on forecasting accuracy.

More serious, perhaps, is the danger of cutoff from sources in case of shortages. Many manufacturers treat proprietary brands as fill-in business. When conditions are prosperous or materials are scarce, they stop accepting orders for proprietary brands. This happened to owners of service stations during the oil embargo. Their customers switched to major brands. But unlike the petroleum industry, in the sanitary supplies field the barriers to backward integration are not high. In fact, during some past periods of shortages, resourceful distributors found ways to deliver sanitary supplies that users could not get from large companies. If the proprietor cannot obtain an identical match of a previously marketed product, he or she extols a similar version as "new" and "improved."

Summary

Proprietary brands offer freedom and flexibility to an independent distributor, savings and services to the buyers, and extra volume to manufacturers. Margins for distributors are usually very wide, to defray various special finishing and carrying costs, to compensate for the difficult task of selling, and to allow a price inducement for the final buyer.

It is up to the proprietor to figure out each purchasing agent's requirements and make appropriate arrangements. The owner of proprietary brands has various options, from standard to unique products, from performing all the selling to administering several sales forces. The proprietary brand protects him or her somewhat from manufacturers and salespersons who would encroach on the distributor's established clientele. Thus a person who can sell to purchasing agents and can coordinate procurement and physical distribution has a vehicle to independence and profit.

Questions

1. *Just how does a proprietary brand give a distributor or retailer greater independence from suppliers?*
2. *Why would a supplier with a successful national brand be willing to supply a proprietary brand to a distributor or retailer? Wouldn't this simply reduce the supplier's brand's market share and reduce profits?*
3. *Identify at least two proprietary brands that are available in your local supermarket; department store.*

16

The Capital of Counterfeiting   JAMES HANSEN

Italian rip-off artists lead the world in pirating well-known trademarks and products, with American firms a favorite target. The problem is growing and the victims seem unable to stop it.

Robert Strauss, President Carter's chief trade negotiator, calls it "highway robbery of the consumer." French fashion designer Pierre Cardin considers it a "growing problem in international trade which requires urgent action." Both are talking about the widespread counterfeiting of famous brand-name products, and the world leader in this kind of rip-off is Italy.

Unlicensed copies of famous wristwatches, Ray-Ban sunglasses, Levi's, Vuitton luggage—even fake Marlboro cigarettes and counterfeit pharmaceuticals—are all widely available. And this world of shadow industries is not small time. Reasonably credible estimates put the turnover of Italy's illegal economy at 20%-to-25% of the country's official Gross National Product. The ripping-off of famous foreign trademarks accounts for a good part of that sum.

American firms are favorite targets of the trademarks pirates, and the whole business is beginning to hurt. A case in point is Bausch & Lomb Inc. The Rochester, New York, manufacturer believes that something like 25% of the sunglasses sold under its Ray-Ban trademark world-wide are phonies. Ac-

Source: Reprinted with the special permission of DUN's REVIEW, October 1978, pp. 68, 70, 72, 74. Copyright © 1978, Dun & Bradstreet Publications Corporation.

cording to the company's Rome lawyer, the fakes may cost the optical firm between $7 million and $8 million a year in lost sales in Italy alone, quite aside from any damage to the product's reputation. That's enough to make any manufacturer sit up and take note. Bausch & Lomb found that Italy was one of the centers of the traffic, and its response to the rip-off may serve as a model to any American manufacturer that finds it's getting burned by fakes in Italy.

Italy has laws forbidding the kind of piracy that the firm was suffering. The problem was to find someone interested in enforcing those laws because the Italian police are not very aggressive about the matter. The prevalent Italian attitude seems to be that the companies being ripped off are rich and can afford it. So B&L hired a smart Italian attorney and a group of investigators to go into the problem. The team tracked down the plants making the phony sunglasses and the print shops that were faking the labels. They identified the distribution networks and carefully documented everything. Then, in essence, they took the Italian police to court, demanding that the laws protecting the exclusivity of trademarks be enforced. The court issued a series of writs ordering the police to raid the factories and print shops that Bausch & Lomb believed were involved in the illicit traffic. At one printer's, police found an order had recently been filled for 46,000 adhesive labels with the Ray-Ban trademark, ready to be applied to the fakes. At retail prices in Italy, 46,000 pairs of Ray-Ban's are worth more than 1.2 billion lire, about $1.5 million.

Bausch & Lomb hasn't succeeded in clearing up

the problem, but it has struck an important blow. Other companies taking similar steps have not been even that fortunate.

Halfway Success

A well-known American trademark, "Fruit of the Loom," has become very fashionable in Italy as an item of decoration. It appears on T-shirts, purses, luggage, pocket mirrors—any of a thousand kinds of inexpensive consumer products. Almost none of these uses is authorized. When the Italian distributor took action to block the illegal use of the name and design, he had a kind of halfway success.

Many of the trademark pirates decided it wasn't worth the risk to steal the name directly, so they came out with an endless number of "slight" variations like "Fruit of the Moon," or "Fruit of the Gum" and even "Fruit on the Tee-shirts"—a nearly infinite chain of Fruits of This and That that took an expensively developed trademark and reduced it to garbage in the space of a few months. In an informal survey of nearly twenty retail distributors of T-shirts in Rome, it turned out that not one carried the genuine article, though all carried shirts that said they were. The T-shirts had been made in India or Red China and then imprinted with the fake trademark in Italy.

The quality of the T-shirts—and of just about every other counterfeited item—is uniformly bad. And while the prices are usually quite a bit lower than those for the genuine products, particularly for luxury items, in some cases they are about the same.

European houses producing extremely expensive goods for the luxury market are favorite targets of the rip-off artists—firms like Cartier (watches, lighters). Louis Vuitton (luggage), or Gucci (shoes and leather goods). The famous Cartier watch, flat with a rectangular case and a small ruby set on the stem, deserves a place in the counterfeit hall of fame. The watch—the real watch—retails in Italy starting at about $1,500. But throngs of street vendors outside train stations sell satisfactory looking imitations for a price starting at 9,000 lire, about

$10. From a foot away a person can't tell the difference. The watch face carries the Cartier name—and in certain chic circles in Italy, it's much more fashionable to wear the fake. Cartier has undertaken an expensive ad campaign warning against the copies, which don't keep very good time when they run at all, but retailers don't think the effort has had much effect. Most buyers are perfectly aware that they're not getting a real Cartier for the equivalent of $10 or $15. The problem from the French jeweler's standpoint is that the buyers just don't care.

Most managers are reluctant to talk about the counterfeiting problem for publication. They feel public discussion may damage consumer confidence in their trademark. Just as bad, from the managers' point of view, is that the home office, whether it is in the U.S., Germany or Great Britain, may not understand very clearly why the problem is still unsolved, since in most developed countries, illegal competition is the easiest to deal with.

One manager, blunter than most, when asked about what unauthorized copies are costing his firm in sales says: "It hurts, but we don't really know how much. Maybe that's a blessing, since we really can't do much to stop it." Another, representing a clothing manufacturer, sums up a common attitude: "It would cost more to stop than it costs us in sales. In a lot of cases, we'd wind up having to go after our own dealers." Many firms simply hope to keep the rip-off artists within tolerable limits and consider the whole thing just another expense of doing business in Italy.

Why Italy? What is there about sunny Italy that has turned it into the industrial counterfeiting capital of the world—a title that used to be a tightly held monopoly of low-labor-cost East Asian countries?

It has to do with a vast, if officially unrecognized, illegal economy whose production is equal to a big chunk of the government's formal GNP figure. In fact, judged by official figures, the continued survival of the Italian economy is a miracle on the order of flying rocks and snow on the Fourth of July. Investment levels are low and falling, unit labor costs are among the highest in the whole of Europe and getting worse, and endless strikes in all categories of the work force make production schedules hopeless dreaming.

Underground Economy

If the above-board economy survives, it is probably because there is a private, illegal and untaxed economy that is thriving. According to some estimates, as many as 2.5 million Italians work in the illegal economy in tiny shops and small factories that meet no safety standards, make no payroll deductions, pay less than minimum wages and pay no taxes. They tend to be financed by unreported income from other activities. A recent random survey by the Italian revenue authorities found that less than 3% of independently employed professionals had declared their true income when filing taxes.

These mini-factories at the fringes of the law can change their product lines the same day the owners change their minds about what they want to make. They are the backbone of the counterfeiting business. In addition, the borders are so open that Italy could be mistaken for a free port. According to obviously imprecise figures, as many as a third of the cigarettes and half the portable radios and tape players sold in Italy are smuggled in without payment of duty. A great many raw materials like cloth, leather and specialty metals enter Italy the same way. The government, it appears, is beginning to recognize the utility of all this and the rip-off occasionally seems to be tolerated more as a matter of policy than because of simple corruption.

To a degree, the Italian preeminence in the field may also be a question of tradition. One old Italian hand, interested professionally in the counterfeiting problem, recalls that in the late 1940s the Italians began counterfeiting the then extremely popular Parker pen. The copy was so good that the Parker people eventually found that the only answer was to buy out the plant in Bologna that was turning out the copies and make the whole thing official. They didn't even have to retool.

While Italy may be central to the question of the pirating of famous trademarks and products, the story does not finish there. Italian police recently raided a Milan print shop where they found more than 50,000 counterfeit "Levi's" labels ready to be stiched onto low-quality jeans destined for the Middle East. Similarly with fake sunglasses, whether Bausch & Lomb's Ray-Bans or other famous European marks, many are sold in Italy but most are intended to give a phony touch of class in some Third World country. Italian customers are often perfectly aware they're buying an imitation, but they like the price. In other countries, these products are often sold as genuine at the same price as the real thing.

By now it's no secret that American blue jeans enjoy a healthy market in Europe, and throughout the rest of the world for that matter. That makes them a natural target for the counterfeiters. It's no surprise that the market leader, Levi-Strauss & Co., should be the most heavily copied, though Blue Bell Inc.'s Wrangler, which plays Pepsi to Levi's Coca-Cola, comes a close second. Police in Rome recently seized 6,000 pairs of counterfeit Levi's already in retail channels, and they say the same action could be repeated in any city in Italy.

The counterfeits are excellent, nearly impossible to detect with the naked eye. Only one tiny, insignificant detail distinguishes them from the real thing. On a genuine pair of Levi's, one of the copper rivets on the hip pocket carries a number used for quality control purposes. The fakes don't have it. There is one other difference. The kids who take their new jeans home to launder a dozen times for the worn-in look are in for a surprise. The fake Levi's don't fade. The story has one more interesting twist. The phony labels and so forth were all put on in Italy, but rumor says the pants themselves were manufactured behind the Iron Curtain, probably in Rumania.

Inside Job

The jeans manufacturers have been particularly active in battling the counterfeiters. Levi Strauss, Blue Bell and Fiorucci, an Italian jeans maker with outlets in the U.S., are industry leaders in this respect. Since their investigators cover the same terrain, an informal system for exchanging useful information was developed. But this happy collaboration has been damaged by recent revelations that tie Fiorucci directly to the faking business.

The Italian manufacturer has been formally charged with commissioning cheap copies of its very own luxury items, which go for prices from $40 on up. Depositions filed by a disgruntled former employee charge that Fiorucci arranged to have the fakes made in South Korea. They were then brought into Italy and labeled as if they were originals. As if that weren't enough, part of the Fiorucci sales apparatus in southern Italy was caught funneling fake Levis and Wranglers to retailers. Though the firm's Milan-area headquarters was not implicated directly in that traffic, the situation did create understandable doubts on the part of the competitors.

There are persistent reports of an unauthorized, black-market factory in the Naples area that manufactures fake Marlboro cigarettes without ever having thought to obtain a license from Philip Morris, the trademark's owner. It is difficult for obvious reasons, to get precise information about this plant, but it was possible to find a small print shop in the same area that grinds out cartons bearing the famous brand name. Since no licensed Marlboros are made in Italy, these cartons must either be destined for the black market or enter into somewhat unusual export channels. What is clear is that some Marlboro packs purchased through illegal distributors in Italy differ markedly from the official Philip Morris packaging. The typefaces used in printing the packs is slighly different and the black-market product carefully shows Philip Morris' address as "Richmond, Virginia, U.S.A.," rather than just "Richmond, Virginia," as with the genuine article.

There is a certain temptation not to take all this very seriously. After all, no one is really getting hurt except a few companies with trademarks so successful they're worth copying. Right? Wrong. A Naples cardiologist who doesn't want to go into detail says that counterfeit heart pacemakers are circulating in southern Europe. They're excellent copies of a highly respected German brand, perfect in nearly all respects except quality control. These imitation pacemakers may have caused some deaths. The doctors don't like to talk about it because they feel they might be held liable for not recognizing the phonies at first glance.

There is another disturbing medical side to the counterfeiting business. Italian authorities are investigating what they believe to be the very widespread faking of well-known pharmaceutical products. The counterfeiters favor those drugs most commonly prescribed—antibiotics, vitamins and the steroid hormones. The medicines are compounded with stolen bulk chemicals in shadow factories and contain more or less the correct ingredients behind false famous labels. That "more or less" is the catch. When you're working completely outside the law, the most minimal quality control standards fall by the wayside. As in other similar cases, the pharmaceutical companies prefer to avoid public comment on the problem because they fear the publicity could undermine confidence in their products.

"La Siracusana"

So far, there haven't been any publicly reported cases of illness or other damage from the counterfeit drugs, but another rip-off product produced a wave of illness in Italy. The item involved: counterfeit stamps. The counterfeiters, in an apparent effort to keep costs down, backed the stamps with a glue poisonous to humans. The issue—called "La Siracusana," after the mythological figure whose portrait it carries—was finally withdrawn when postal authorities discovered that in some cities as much as 80% of the stamps circulating in that series were phonies. In the aftermath, one waggish editor suggested that the counterfeiters could have avoided detection if they simply had left the glue off the stamps, just as the government does (alluding to complaints that Italian stamps often fall off their envelopes).

There have been numerous proposals for reforms intended to stem the flood of counterfeits and pirated designs in Italy. A study made by the American Embassy in Rome, for instance, suggests one possible remedy. It notes that at the present time no mechanism exists whereby a trademark registered with the Italian Patent Office is also officially recognized by the Ministry of Finance. Theoretically, such recognition would enable Italian customs officials to seize phonies like the Rumanian jeans at the border. Another legal stratagem, technically possible but as yet untested, would permit manufacturers to have illegal copies seized on entry on the basis of copyright infringement. But this would require that the complainant petition the courts well in advance, specifying how, when and where the phonies would be arriving. Obviously, this would only be useful if the confiscated goods are in international commerce.

As far as international law goes, the major protection against trademark and design piracy comes out of the Paris Industrial Property Convention. The convention is aging and in need of revision. Aside from weakness in the counterfeiting area, the convention does not satisfactorily treat problems inherent in the buying and selling of computer software or other "know-how." Many governments think it's time to bring the convention up to date, and U.S. trade negotiator Strauss says that the sub-ject of commercial counterfeiting is being discussed at current trade talks in Geneva. In any case, a Common Market study commission will begin meeting soon on the problem. Some hopes are also pinned on a group with an unfortunate acronym, WIPO, for World Intellectual Property Organization. It aims to write model legislation to offer governments all over the world.

In the last analysis, though, the problem in Italy will continue, whatever the laws in the books, until the Italian government is politically, bureaucratically and economically able to do something about it. That may take some time, and until then it is likely to continue to be every man for himself.

Questions

1. *Why don't the executives of firms that are victims of counterfeiters simply publicize the problem and warn their loyal customers to be wary of imitations?*
2. *Which product classes are most susceptible to counterfeiting? Which are least susceptible? What factors cause the difference in susceptibility?*

17

Product Development: Today's Most Common Mistakes

C. MERLE CRAWFORD

Marketers play a major role in the development of new products. The failure rate of new products in the United States is appalling. Some common mistakes should and can be avoided.

Each year the marketing department at The University of Michigan Graduate School of Business Administration selects a group of organizations for an intensive study of how they plan and create new products and new services. Most of these organizations are manufacturing firms, but a few are wholesalers or retailers, some are producers of services, and some are from the public sector.

The purpose of the research is primarily educational with second-year MBA students conducting the field work, but an important by-product is an annual generalization about the "state of the art" in product development. And the state of the art right now could be a great deal better: Too many products fail needlessly and too much money is spent developing those that are successful.

From the micro (individual firm) point of view, the economics of new product success are such that an occasional stroke of good luck erases the costs of many mistakes, and everyone is forgiving. Without good luck, one merely changes managers and op-

timistically looks ahead—anything is better than pondering the sunk costs of a previous inept management.

But the public pays the price of new product failures; somehow those costs must be covered eventually. In the meantime, industry pays because profits were needlessly reduced, scarce resources were wasted and genuine growth opportunities were less well exploited.

Most managements sincerely want to improve the economic efficiency of their new product development programs, but most are far from optimally successful in the endeavor. In some cases firms simply don't know about, or don't care to use, those techniques successfully employed by others. The reasons for this are unclear, but there seems to be a feeling that "*this* time (or with *these* people or *this* idea) we will be successful on our own." Some well-known firms, for example, use organizational arrangements or marketing planning techniques which have been discarded by more innovative firms. One large food company had such a string of product development failures that, in 1974, it gave a consulting firm the task of complete overhaul. It turned out to be an easy task because the firm was years behind in its techniques.

Of course, not all answers in product development are so easy. Several of today's key operational headaches will require more research effort than they have received. The purpose of this report is to highlight areas of management weakness, the phases of product development where many of the firms we study are not taking advantage of proven techniques or policies.

Source: Reprinted by permission from the January 1977 issue (pp. 1–6) of the *University of Michigan Business Review*, published by the Graduate School of Business Administration, The University of Michigan.

Incomplete Overall Strategy

David Foster, president of Colgate-Palmolive Company, is currently leading that firm through its most successful new product development and marketing experience. A key factor in that success, Foster says, is a decision to avoid direct confrontation with Procter & Gamble in any market in which P&G dominates. This is a seemingly simple, understandable decision, but one which is difficult for many companies to accept.

With so many uncertainties in product development, it is understandable why managements resist closing off areas of activity. Who deliberately wants to stop employee interest in something which may be the firm's next bonanza? After all, many chief executives have weathered several crises because of the strength of one new product success.

But it is exactly this thinking which fills the Nevada tax coffers and which causes many firms to look back on a long array of "almosts" or "could have been's" and poor overall return from their efforts.

The evidence is clear: Every firm needs a precisely worded and carefully developed statement of the types of new products it wants, with an equally clear and firm statement of those it does *not* want. The distinction may be on lines of competition (a la Colgate), technology, risk, geography, distribution or whatever, depending entirely on the firm's situation and goals. But a statement there should be— regardless of the pain associated with rejection of opportunities in the excluded areas.

Our studies reveal that most firms simply have not reached this point of sophistication in their overall corporate strategy. It is true our interviews are not often with the chief executive officer and, therefore, these firms may have solid strategies which are not known to their product development people. But, if so, and I doubt it, what good are they? The corporate leaders in product innovation today almost inevitably know exactly where they want to go.

Inadequately Communicated Strategy

Even when management makes the thorough study and firm decision required for good product development strategy, the result is frequently classified as confidential and shared with no one beyond the board of directors or the executive committee.

Our researchers are appalled to talk to research and development personnel, sales personnel or marketing researchers who either don't know whether their firm has such a strategy or think the strategy is something quite different from what it really is. It is no accident that the world's most successful new product developers are not secretive about their strategies. Even business school students can discuss intelligently the strategies of P&G, 3-M, General Motors, DuPont, IBM, Xerox, etc. And now Colgate—though an earlier, unsuccessful strategy was apparently not known.

More than other corporate activity, product development is a team effort. It requires more cooperation, more delicate merging of efforts, more willingness to make concessions. One cannot visualize borax emerging from the desert with a request that twenty mules, driver and wagon try to work together.

But managements do exactly this when they decide to keep a strategy confidential. Operating in secrecy usually means there are scores of false starts and constant bickering between departments or that no one does anything without checking in at the top to see if it is "okay." We find numerous examples of these needless and sometimes fatal costs for new product development.

Large firms often suffer from organizational confusion, if only because they are so complex. Virtually all types of product development organizations are found in the large firm, and confusion may arise from sheer numbers and variety. This may be unavoidable and the firm consciously manages around the problem.

Organizational Confusion

But we also find unnecessary organizational confusion in small-medium or medium-sized firms. These firms usually have a traditional, functional form of organization, with an overall committee of some type to integrate the functions.

Unfortunately, as these firms grow, they cling to this relatively clean and simple arrangement too long. They use it for both established products and new products. When these firms had only one or a few products, and their product development activity consisted mainly of an occasional change in one of these products (or a close line extension), their regular organization worked well.

But the minute the growing firm moves to develop a product new to its management, trouble begins. The resource conflict between established and new products is under way, and at least a partial and perhaps temporary arrangement is required if the new development is to get the sustained effort it requires.

Yet, management typically resists a major organizational change for what seem to be valid economic reasons. As a result, product development languishes or dies, only rarely succeeding in fighting for proper attention. In those few cases, some functional executive may be a patron saint for the project or the president may be the inventor.

Things *may* work out. But all too often they don't, and third and fourth-level personnel pour out their frustrations as they describe the false starts, the resource shortages, the indecisive management. In general, front-line personnel wage a lonely and losing battle to bring forth new products for a management that usually is too busy on other matters to care.

Of course, management *is* busy. Growing firms of that size still face one crisis on top of another. It frequently is all they can do to handle these challenges to their near-term success, in spite of the fact they want and need the new products they feel forced to ignore.

As these firms grow, they will eventually establish a separate new product organization, giving someone the authority to act decisively and the resources to back up those decisions. Perhaps there will be a director of new products, or a task force, or perhaps an outside consultant. But our research shows that these growing firms usually wait too long and pay too high a price in new product delays at the very time in their life cycle when they most need new products.

Poor Communications Across the Marketing/R&D Interface

All functional interfaces can cause friction areas in the product development process, but our experience is that friction between marketing and R&D is the most damaging and, I might add, the most difficult to resolve effectively.

While the problem cannot be fully discussed here (the New York Chapter of the American Marketing Association recently held a day-long conference on this topic), the various solutions involve the obvious: special committees, retreats, personnel interfaces, and occasionally a change in authority to put full power on one side or the other. Fortunately, once top management recognizes the existence of the problem, sufficient remedies are available to make the interface operational.

It surprises us, however, to find so many firms apparently oblivious to the existence of this special problem. Research directors come up with products that marketing can't sell. Research fails to incorporate the special features which will make or break the product in the competitive arena. Research personnel are bitter in denouncing marketing for always changing its mind or chasing rainbows of the moment. Marketing people scoff at the isolation of their research staff, their impracticality, their irrelevance. The situation deteriorates to the point that there is little direct personal contact between the departments, even to the absence of coffee, lunch, or after-hours gatherings.

Groups who realize the need and value of close relationships and full understanding usually work hard to achieve them. Others, as the saying goes, "don't know what they're missing," but their product development program suffers accordingly.

Passive Idea Generation

Industry holds many beliefs about idea generation which are critically challenged by experts. These beliefs may sound familiar:

We always have more ideas than we have resources with which to evaluate them.

It's easy to dream up ideas for new products.

Our people work with our products all the time; they know the changes which could or should be made in them.

These concepts may be true in the quantitative sense but they are not true in the qualitative sense. Misreading the situation leads to the wrong conclusion: No formal idea generation program is needed. Accordingly, except for a few "eccentric" people around the firm, everyone takes a passive stance, ready to react to new ideas but not seeking them in any systematic way.

The opposition to formal programs may have resulted from experiences with brainstorming— that much-heralded Osborne creation which swept the business world in the 1950's and which re-emerges from time to time. But brainstorming is only one tool of the scores available; it is adaptable only to certain situations and is widely abused. It may work, but often doesn't, creating a negative reaction anytime formal idea generation is mentioned. Consequently, the typical marketing department has files of poor ideas and puts forth reluctant efforts to evaluate ideas that are marginally only "the best of a poor lot."

Great ideas, the ones which generate excitement and attract resources, are no trouble to evaluate— *difficult* to assess economically perhaps, but no trouble. Such ideas do not come easily. They can be sought optimally only by some systematic effort: attribute analysis, need assessment, matrix analysis or one of the many specialized techniques. Idea generation has come a long way from brainstorming and the check-list. Our research indicates that many firms are not aware of this.

Nothing is more surprising than the vast array of attitudes and policies on the financial evaluation of new product concepts and proposals. From firm to firm, practice is also unpredictable, apparently because it is often dictated arbitrarily by top executives and is not derived from meaningful variables in the different situations.

Wasteful Extremes in Financial Evaluation

Some firms do virtually no detailed financial evaluation; their managements are satisfied with what I call "threshold" criteria: "the market is larger than we need to be successful;" "our costs allow a gross margin well beyond that which we usually get;" "even one percent of the market will yield more sales than we need to break even." This approach can be faulted, of course, but perhaps we have reached the point where the burden of proof is on the accuser.

Ironically, the greatest waste occurs because of "ultra sophistication." Too many firms may have read too many accounting and financial journal articles about capital budgeting, discounted cash flow and net present value.

These are valuable concepts, strong additions to the technology of financial analysis, and they seem to apply perfectly to the evaluation of a new product proposal. There are even opportunities to apply the more sophisticated techniques of risk analysis and probabilities. Undoubtedly, the large firm can make use of all this. They have the personnel, the data and the computers to try. And if conditions permit, the resulting decision analysis is a beauty to behold. But our research shows a different outcome most of the time these techniques are used.

We see the tabular arrangements, the percentage-return figures, the physical manifestations. But we also see behind them, to the absolutely unquantifiable variables; to the charades that marketing people play to satisfy a controller or a division general manager trying to impress a corporate staff. We see assistant product managers laboriously completing forms with "manufactured" data because it's easier than trying to argue for exceptions to standard procedures.

In fact, most financial evaluations we see are

predicated upon one or two key judgments, usually of the "threshold" variety, which provide the real basis for judgment. The rest of the data and processing calculations are there because someone feels they should be.

New products are big risks. They produce wide swings in gain or loss. They are not really amenable to the fine-tuning techniques of analysis which were developed in other situations where hard data not only permits them but warrants them. Yet many firms are wasting the time of their best product development resource—people—on the compilation of these complex financial evaluation data sets.

Misuse of Marketing Research

Technological advancements in marketing research over the past twenty-five years have prepared it for a meaningful role in product development. Estimates of market potential should be more accurate, sales evaluations should be more complete and thorough, test marketing should provide more reliable indications of later market reactions.

Unfortunately, the full potential of marketing research is not being realized for several reasons. Many companies which should have marketing researchers do not. Nor do they call on outside experts for help. An agency may "do a study," trade association data may be compiled, the sales force may be polled, but no professional marketing research is actually undertaken. Even if there is an internal marketing group it is often hobbled by financial restrictions.

Apparently many marketing managements establish research budgets on percent-of-sales ratios derived from ongoing operations, whereas the *new product* budgets should be related to the risks and possible gains and losses of new products. Other ratios are irrelevant.

There is also evidence that many managements do not know or understand the proper role for marketing research or how it fits into the overall decision process.

Researchers, themselves, are not always properly organized or may be reluctant to "blow whistles," on dubious undertakings. Or, they may feel they are supposed to remain objective and remain apart from the actual developmental process.

Nevertheless, marketing research offers the capability for markedly increasing new product success ratios and should be better utilized in most companies.

In the late 1950's and early 1960's, several firms and research agencies developed the concept of "tracking" the launch of a new product. They had watched and envied the ability of the space program controllers to tell soon after a launch whether the projectile would ultimately achieve its intended goal, and if not, what actions could be taken to correct the problem while there was still time.

Poor Use of Tracking Concepts

Many leading marketing firms now track their new entries from the first day of test market on through the eventual national launch. To the extent their data permit, they try to emulate the techniques of the space program controllers.

But the practice has not spread very far. We still see firms launching new items and then sitting back to see how the sales will roll in. There is no attempt to measure product or concept awareness (even crudely); no measurement of trial purchases, no assessment of trial results. None, that is, until the sales fail to follow. Then the research effort is usually too little, too late.

Even if mistakes are ultimately diagnosed, our studies show that remedial action taken well after the fact is expensive and usually unsuccessful. Many firms simply go on to the next launch (and next failure) which is often well under way.

If the product development cost is low, the strategy of firing a steady stream of new items into the marketplace may be the best. One has only to watch for the winners to reveal themselves and write off the losers. But few firms are so fortunate, and better use of tracking analysis could pay handsome rewards.

Delusion/Self-deception/Over-confidence

Perhaps not the most common case of mismanagement, but certainly the most inexcusable, is the unwillingness of many in business to take an objective look at products under development. Product development *is* a gamble, certainly, and the fainthearted will score no Xerox or Polaroid coups. But real winners (like these) have only opinion or tradition against them in the early stages, technical advantage is with them.

We often find the opposite: Development going right along, even though a production facility can't meet cost objectives, customer groups say they don't like the product, or a test market fails. These are cases where hard fact in support of abandonment is refuted only by diehard opinion or, worse, the belief that "they *should* use this product and they will, even if they don't want it now."

There will be those instances where a "believer" will push a product to successful entry, against all odds, and there will continue to be "bootleg" products that everyone later claims to have supported when they did not. But this facet of product development risk still leaves something to be desired. For example, long-odds situations should get long-odds analyses and financial tests.

A geologist can be forgiven some emotionalism if he is pursuing what might be an entirely new oil bed; hopefully, he would stick closer to fact if deciding whether or not to re-open a copper mine in Michigan's Upper Peninsula.

Yet many businesses fail to make this distinction, and our evidence (obtained at different managerial levels in different firms) suggests that the primary reason is emotional. Too many people don't want to send negative information to top management, especially if someone there has made a personal commitment to the development, or if negative information is recorded as a negative attitude. There are many instances in which decision-makers do not get the facts or receive them carefully screened. They hear only what they let it be known they want to hear.

It takes careful and purposeful observation to spot these situations as they occur and it takes deliberate management action to avoid them. For example, a division management team was reviewing its progress with a group vice president. While discussing a particular item under development, the marketing research director almost casually mentioned there had been no customer test of the concept yet and there was some reason to expect negative reaction. He doesn't make such comments any more. His boss had on several occasions cited this particular development to the group executive as a strong plank in the division's future progress. Once the comment was made, the research director couldn't win, but it is his management which loses now.

A chief executive or a general manager is wrong if he believes the curse of delusion "can't strike *my* management team." It will, if he fails to take positive steps to avoid it, but then he will probably never know.

Every new product eventually becomes unprofitable and should be removed from the market. For some, the moment of reckoning comes in weeks or months; for a few, it is decades. But very few firms pursue this matter in an organized fashion. Occasionally, a period of financial duress forces an Operation Bootstrap, during which losing products are detected and dropped. Occasionally, a new marketing manager or a new product manager will take advantage of his "honeymoon" period to clean out a line.

Lack of a Product Abandonment Program

Unfortunately, these actions are almost inevitably taken *after* a product has become unprofitable. Even the recommended procedures in accounting journals call for past data, whereas the analysis should obviously use future data in a net present value calculation. The decision is a perfect analog to the new product decision. Shall we market this product in the future? Granted, the flow of investment is different, the validity of the sales estimates is different, and the risks much less. But the financial decision process should be the same.

The same managements which require a specific

internal rate of return on a proposed new product to insure that it significantly exceeds the firm's cost of capital or opportunity cost will permit older products to continue to the point where they are actually costing cash-out-of-hand. If non-dollar costs and returns are given full credence (and they should be in both cases), then the financial analysis for old and new products should be identical.

The reason they are not, apparently, is that product abandonment is not seen as the other half of the new product coin and therefore has neither person nor procedure, neither budget nor policy. This is surprising during a period of expensive capital, but there is continuous re-investment of large sums in products which could not get past a preliminary financial screening if they were treated as new products.

Conclusion

An annual trek through the product development practices of thirty to seventy firms has given The University of Michigan Graduate School of Business Administration a unique opportunity to assess the "state of the art." This paper has discussed the most common "mistakes" made by these firms; practices which generally are felt to be wrong based on the behavior of the most successful firms.

New product development is obviously a risky endeavor; it has far more failures than successes. It confronts management with a paradox: High risks should prompt the use of the most proven techniques, but high pay-offs prompt short cuts. Perhaps the rate of new product success is remarkably good considering the pressures of this trade-off.

Questions

1. *Select a product that has been recently introduced in the marketplace. Evaluate the product's chances for success.*
2. *If marketing research were properly conducted and if marketing strategy were soundly conceived, the chances of failure for a new product would be close to zero. Discuss.*

18

Can Business Afford
the Luxury of Test Marketing?   SAUL SANDS

Has test marketing been oversold? Have marketers promised too much? Or have contemporary conditions lessened the value of a once-valuable marketing tool?

Traditionally, test marketing is that stage in new product development where a finished product and its marketing program are actually tried out for the first time. The product is placed on sale in a select locality where consumer reaction to new product is observed and analyzed. The product's performance in this test market is expected to give an indication of how well the product will perform when it is introduced nationally or on a broader scale.

In the past, test marketing was done in a small number of specific, carefully chosen communities. These communities were selected because they were considered to have characteristics typical of the entire population of the country. Certain cities, such as Columbus, Ohio; Syracuse, N.Y. and Des Moines, Iowa, were chosen over and over again by many companies as the ideal sites to test their products.

Today it is generally accepted that no single city is typical of the entire country. Because of atypicality, a test market often gives little or no indication of how reaction to a new product would differ from region to region. The mixture of different kinds of people in small test areas is limited, mak-

ing it nearly impossible to achieve a true picture of how people with different attitudes, educational and social levels and ethnic backgrounds might react to a product.

Furthermore, cities frequently chosen as test markets had become test sophisticated. The residents came to realize that their cities were being used as test markets consciously or unconsciously. Accordingly, the behavior patterns of these people changed, often making the data obtained invalid.

Use of a test market leads to other problems as well. Companies usually directed more intensive media and sales force coverage to their test market than would realistically have accompanied national introduction of the product. Another major problem is the possibility that competition could confuse the results of your test by stepping up their own advertising and sales promotion in your test area.

These are just a few of the undesirable characteristics that have caused many companies to move from use of smaller test markets to larger test market areas, hoping to achieve more realistic results. Some companies, on the other hand, have ventured into different types of test marketing. Others have placed more emphasis on preliminary marketing research, while still others have either reduced the use of test marketing in certain instances or have dropped it altogether.

Questions can be raised concerning: a) the rationale behind decisions to test market new products; b) the alternatives in test marketing; and c) the rationale behind decisions not to test market new products.

Source: Reprinted by permission from the March 1978 issue (pp. 19–24) of the *University of Michigan Business Review*, published by the Graduate School of Business Administration, The University of Michigan.

Decision to Test Market

The decision to test market a new product is directly related to the degree of confidence the manufacturer has in the product. Test marketing is, after all, a form of risk control. The key motivation for test marketing is to produce useful estimates of future sales, however fraught with difficulties that may be.

A second motive for test marketing is to pre-test alternative marketing plans. Two or three different marketing approaches might be tried in a number of different cities to see which proves the most successful. Choosing the correct test markets is especially important in this instance.

A third reason for test marketing is a company's desire to consider the effect of the new product on its existing product line. A new product introduced into the market might cannibalize an existing and perhaps more profitable product of the company.

During test marketing, companies often discover weaknesses or faults within the product that escaped detection during the product development stage. They also gain the opportunity to gather important information about their channels of distribution for the new product. Existing distribution systems may not be set up to adequately handle the new product and it might be more profitable to sell the product outright to another firm or forget about it entirely.

Test Marketing Loses Favor

Why does test marketing appear to be falling out of favor with many companies and individual product managers, and why are people seeking alternative means of test marketing?

Everyone realizes there is tremendous opportunity in new products. There is also a very high failure rate. A study by one company, New Products Action Team, reported in 1969 that of 9,450 new products introduced the previous year, nearly 80 percent could be classed as failures because they didn't meet projected sales goals.[1] This company studied 75 of these new products in depth.

Theodore L. Angelus, president of the company stated, "If manufacturers do learn anything worthwhile from product testing, it seems to be that a successful product test should not be sufficient reason for a national introduction. After all, 90 percent of the brand failures in this study had successful product test results."[2]

This finding, along with the fact that it is difficult to find a true test market and project the subsequent test figures onto the national scale, leads one to wonder if the reverse is just as true. How often has a product which could have been successful failed its market test because the test area was not properly defined? And how often has a product that failed a well-planned market test found success in the national market?

Inflation has not spread the costs of test marketing. According to a recent Conference Board study,[3] soaring costs and a high risk of failure are convincing more firms to undergo early screening and tests to weed out losers before spending as much as $250,000 (in consumer goods areas) to test market.

Robert Roscoe, group manager of new products and acquisitions at Armour-Dial, Inc., has called test marketing, "the most time-consuming, expensive, worthless effort anyone can do in the new product area."[4] He then predicted that test marketing would be eliminated in the "not-too-distant future" and that it would be replaced by testing via computer simulation. This underscores a recent trend among a number of executives that test marketing in the traditional sense is outdated and no longer of practical value. There are others, however, who continue to argue that test marketing provides information that no other system can.

Decision Against Test Marketing

A number of circumstances could lead a company to choose not to test market a new product. First, there is the cost factor. As the cost of test marketing approaches the cost of larger-scale product marketing, it is, indeed, hard to justify the cost of the test.

It may be more justifiable to take a chance and enter the general market with the product.

A number of large producers of consumer packaged goods have cut back on or dropped test marketing completely. One company has decided to drop test marketing in instances where a product could be readily duplicated. The market research director of this company explains that if the product can be easily duplicated by the competition, the company might be beaten to the market place while it is still running market tests.[5] He added that secrecy is important in other special situations, such as when the first product introduced in a particular field can capture a very large share of the market and maintain a strong hold on that position. This situation makes it difficult for competitive products to break into the field and is obviously a condition where the company wants to be the first one into the market. He did, however, cite the value of market testing when there is need for information not obtainable through in-use tests: only test marketing provides information on the "absolute physical brand;" the distribution problems that might occur; the approach to be used by sales force as they handle the product, and the expected rate of repeat purchases.

Alternatives to Test Marketing

Many companies have never been able or are no longer able to afford the time and money involved in single and especially multi-city market testing. Alternatives have naturally been sought. Some are readily found in the structural procedure of product development (concept and in-use tests) while others have been created to fill this need by enterprising market research organizations. The alternatives include early-stage testing, mini-market testing, laboratory market testing, and computer simulations.

Early-Stage Testing

Early-stage testing includes any and all tests that are employed prior to the traditional market test, i.e., the available panoply of concept and in-use tests. Effective early-stage testing could either eliminate the need for a market test altogether or, at the very least, prepare the ground for a market test that would have a very high chance of predicting success or failure correctly for the product.

In this connection, Walter W. Faster, marketing director, Betty Crocker Division of General Mills, Inc., has said: "Time and money spent in the early stages are far more productive than that spent in the test market. And the test market is not the place to discover that the recipe directions are incorrect, the product tastes bad, or the package leaks."[6] On occasion, he adds, no market test at all is the simplest solution. Faster points out that General Mills is now placing its emphasis on this early-stage testing. It believes that this alternative will avoid costly and time-consuming mistakes.

Paul Johanson, then market research analyst for Ciba-Geigy's Agricultural Division, has stated that since each product is unique, you must have a good idea of its potential before even beginning to market it.[7] Ciba-Geigy uses many techniques in evaluating the potential of a new product. Every product must satisfy a need of a potential consumer; therefore, even before a new product is produced, marketing determines, in the market place with the potential consumers, the need for such a product. Ciba-Geigy believes it is in the business to fulfill needs of the American farmer, not merely to sell them products. If the product doesn't fit a consumer need, the product is not commercialized.

But, with need demonstrated, the next step is an experimental stage where the product is tested through use at Ciba-Geigy research farms, state and university research stations, and by cooperating farmers under controlled situations. Through this experimental use of products on the farm, Ciba-Geigy's commercial development group is able to monitor the use and performance of the new product under realistic conditions.

One of Ciba-Geigy's approaches in measuring the potential of a new product is to go directly to the consumer in order to determine the potential new product's place in the market.

Johanson explained that, following initial research work, a focus group may be set up. For example, new products for avocado growers (an interest group about which the company has very little knowledge) might be found or improved through a focus group. Company researchers would form a diversified group of avocado growers, try to find out just how they think and feel about their work, have them discuss insect and other problems, and then determine how particular products would meet their needs and fit into this market. Johanson stated that Ciba-Geigy gathers a considerable amount of information this way because the focus groups are set up so there are no simple "yes" or "no" answers. Instead, the focus is on a detailed, in-depth discussion by the participants on issues central to all members of the group. This information is then used to develop marketing concepts for the product.

Ciba-Geigy often tests these concepts with additional focus groups, or through the use of interviews to better quantify the information. In quantitative research, marketing concepts are pre-tested using a series of structured questions. The questions seek to determine whether the product is a viable one and whether the marketing approach is realistic: Is consumer interest in buying this type of product high or low? Is the concept meaningful to the consumer? How does the new product compare with existing products? What benefits and disadvantages do they see in it?

Johanson believes that consumers usually will be able to provide the information being sought. The main problem with the focus group technique is the need for a good group leader.

Establishing a focus group can be done in many ways—the company can contact prospective members directly, through its own people, through available mailing lists, or through an outside agency. In order to obtain objectivity and not prejudice the group, Ciba-Geigy uses either an independent research organization or its own research service, which is able to keep the sponsoring company anonymous.

The individuals to be included in the focus group are screened by telephone to determine whether they are appropriate for the research before they are invited to the meeting. Depending on the situation, an incentive such as a dinner, a gift or cash may be given in appreciation of the consumer's participation in the research. These groups can be set up with farmers, doctors, teachers, housewives, or any other homogeneous group. It is necessary for each person to feel comfortable with the others in the group and it is helpful if they know at least one other participant in the group. This peer group atmosphere opens a more natural flow of communications and makes people feel more comfortable with the topics being discussed. The participants in the focus group are told not to be afraid to disagree with anyone else in the group, since everyone has their own opinions and experiences to draw upon. It is always important to have participants in the discussion who are knowledgeable about the topics being discussed. The sessions are usually taped and may be even video-taped.

Before going into the group, Ciba-Geigy researchers carefully plan the meeting and determine the type of information desired. Indeed, this may be the most critical step of any research. After the session is over, it is explained to the participants of the focus group why the session was held and who was sponsoring it.

A series of focus groups provides information on how to market the product and whether or not it has the potential to be successful. Ciba-Geigy feels this is a viable alternative to other types of test marketing.

There are, of course, some drawbacks to concept-type testing. First, there is a risk of disclosing company plans to competitors. Second, the participants in the focus group may not fully grasp the idea of a non-existent product. The participants may also overstate their interest and encourage development of an unsound or undesirable product.

The company does, however, use more traditional or conventional means of test marketing to test new package designs. The purpose is to see what problems might occur in storing or handling a new size or new shape of package and to determine whether consumers will pay more for a more convenient form of package. The company will check the distributors and follow up with telephone or personal interviews with customers who are using the new package. Every product marketed by Ciba-Geigy is tested in both the laboratory and under actual use conditions by the consumer, years before it is marketed commercially.

Mini-Market Testing

Another alternative to traditional test marketing is mini-marketing (or controlled test marketing). This type of testing is normally carried out in a small- or medium-sized test market to allow for close control over the testing.

A distinct advantage of control testing over the traditional method of test marketing is speed. It is much simpler to set up a controlled test and, therefore, the results can be seen more quickly.

Bud Sherak of Market Facts, Inc., reports "the average length of a conventional test market was found to be 11 months, while the average length of a controlled test was six months."[8]

There is also an advantage of secrecy. It is more difficult for competition to find out about a controlled test market than for them to discover a conventional test market. Controlled test markets are also usually more economical than traditional tests.

This type of test marketing has only been used for about 15 years. If improvements continue in the field of projecting results onto the national level, it would appear that there is a substantial future in store for "controlled" or "mini-market" testing.

Laboratory Market Test

Robert Goldberg of Daniel Yankelovich, Inc., reports another direction market testing has taken in recent years. This is the laboratory test market. This approach was developed as an attempt to shorten the testing process and to provide better results rather than as a substitute for the traditional test market. Goldberg says:

We've been asked by a number of our clients who have been using the laboratory test market, whether we believe it can replace test marketing. At this point in time, our answer is that it cannot. It can, however, as one client said, 'eliminate test market failures.' We hope that the laboratory technique over time will become a shortcut for the new product marketer. A laboratory experiment, we believe, represents the right direction for such a shortcut.[9]

Basically, this system is an attempt to reproduce the real world within the confines of the laboratory. Consumers are brought into the laboratory and shown commercials for existing brands and the new product. The consumers are then led to a laboratory store, where they are given money that amounts to about one-fourth the purchase price of a product. They are then free to make or not make purchases, knowing they must use their own money to pay for the balance of the purchase price. This is followed by a group discussion. The consumers use the product at home. The follow-up consists of telephone interviews at some future date.

There are three objectives to the laboratory test market, according to Goldberg. First, it provides a total view of all the marketing elements operating together before the actual test market. It does this while keeping the test a secret from the competition. Second, once the test market is finally launched, results can be determined more quickly and more accurately. This saves both time and money. Third, it allows for the testing of many different marketing options in a short period of time. Once again, this saves time and money by eliminating many of these options and allowing only the best ones to be used in the real test market.

It would appear that as laboratory test marketing continues to be developed and refined, it, too, could become a valuable tool to the new product market manager.

Using Computers

The use of computers in recent years has gained wider acceptance in the test marketing field. At Phillip Morris, the computer was utilized to give management a much faster feedback on information obtained during test marketing. The typical six-month testing period in the tobacco industry was subsequently reduced to only two months. This gave Phillip Morris a greater head start on a new product introduction over its competitors.

Other companies, such as Du Pont, use computers to set up mathematical models to simulate the real market. Many observers feel that computers are another means of saving time and money but that they cannot fully replace test marketing. Others feel that someday computers will replace test marketing altogether. In any event, they are a valuable tool and more and more companies are beginning to use them as an adjunct to traditional test marketing.

Conclusion

For a successful market test program, research and management must work together with open lines of communication regardless of which avenues of market testing a company chooses to pursue.

Today, most companies are continuing to pursue the traditional means of market testing. Some companies are using larger test markets, at a considerably greater expense, in an attempt to duplicate more realistic test market conditions. Other companies are testing each marketing plan in two or more markets.

But in view of the large number of new product failures, and the tremendous expense involved, it is difficult to justify the loyalty some companies feel toward traditional market testing.

The author concludes that early-stage testing is the sounder approach. It avoids many of the pitfalls of traditional test marketing, keeps cost to a minimum, and could easily be combined with such methods as the controlled (or mini-market) test, the use of computers, or laboratory tests. It would enable the manager to gather the needed data with which to make a sound decision; keep cost to a minimum; maintain competitive secrecy so the company could be "first" in the market, and prevent the competition from "muddying up" test results by their own tactics. Early-stage testing is the best alternative available today in the author's opinion, and it is relatively inexpensive to boot.

Methods such as the laboratory test market, the controlled test market, and the use of computers are still fairly new. No one is really sure how good they are, or if they are an improvement over traditional test marketing. It would appear almost certain that they could be no worse.

Companies are now devoting much time, money and energy to the development of new products, the life-blood of industry. But, in spite of the high failure rate of traditional test marketing, many of these same companies seem reluctant to make a commitment to either develop new techniques or use the newer tools available to them in this field.

It is encouraging, however, that ideas on new marketing research techniques have begun to proliferate. Although they have not yet been wholeheartedly endorsed by marketers, they at least offer hope for more efficient new product development, thus freeing capital previously lost through new product failures.

Due to current economic conditions, increased cost for environmental protection and occupational safety, as well as increased operating costs, industry can no longer afford the luxury of unnecessary costs, among which may be the high cost of test marketing.

Notes

1. "Test Marketing: A Useful Function?", *Marketing Insights*, May 5, 1969.
2. *Ibid.*
3. "Weed Out Losers," *Chemical Spotlight*, November 23, 1973, Vol. XXIV, No. 99, Ridgewood, N.J.
4. "Test Marketing: A Useful Function?", *Marketing Insights*, May 5, 1969.

5. Personal interview by author.

6. Mr. Walter W. Faster, Marketing Director, Betty Crocker Division of General Mills, Inc., "Will Advance Testing Reduce New Product Risks?," Food Product Development, February, 1973.

7. Personal interview with author.

8. "Controlled Test Marketing and the Projection of Test Marketing Results," *Marketing Review*, February, 1973.

9. Robert Goldberg, Senior Associate, Daniel Yankelovich, Inc., "The Laboratory Test Market," *Marketing Review*, September, 1969, p. 10.

Questions

1. *What motivations or objectives might a marketing manager have for wanting to test market a product?*
2. *Why has test marketing fallen out of favor with some companies and individual managers?*

19

The Middletowns of Marketing

ROBERT LEVY

What makes a community a prime candidate for test marketing new products?

When consumers in Fort Wayne, Indiana, pop into their neighborhood A&P for some SOS, BVD or STP, they may well get the feeling that they are being watched by the FBI. Someone with a clipboard and uncommon curiosity may be taking notes on particular products they select from the shelves. At the checkout counter, they may be approached by a total stranger and asked why they purchased this detergent or that deodorant. And at day's end, data on their purchases may well be secretly telephoned to a distant headquarters for tabulation, evaluation and study.

It happens that the people of Fort Wayne are among the nation's most surveilled and surveyed shoppers. But they don't mind. In fact, the 373,700 residents of metropolitan Fort Wayne rather enjoy the attention they receive from many of the biggest consumer companies in the country. For Fort Wayne is a prime test market—a "Golden Zone" whose demographic and economic statistics so closely mirror those of the entire country that the buy or no-buy decisions of its Hoosier shoppers are immensely valuable to manufacturers.

What Fort Wayne represents to consumer companies is a national market in microcosm. The nation's 96th-biggest city with some $2 billion in retail sales, it is 67th in sales of home furnishings and

appliances, 72nd in retail sales per household, 76th in automotive purchases and 81st in department-store sales. More important to marketers, its $5,176 in effective buying income per capita deviates only slightly from the national figure of $5,003. And the city's two newspapers and three television stations provide advertisers with comprehensive media penetration that is easily measurable.

With its 25 shopping centers, Fort Wayne is such a favorite test market that as many as fifteen different products may be testing in the city at any given time. In recent years, the city founded by General "Mad" Anthony Wayne in 1794 has been the test tube for a frozen lemon juice, an ersatz bacon and sausage, a disposable diaper and a peanut butter-and-jelly spread and much more. Last month, Johnson & Johnson was trying out Fenjala, a new moisturizing bath essence, while Procter & Gamble was testing consumer acceptance of its newly packaged Moist & Easy cake mix.

From Boston to Fresno

Determining whether enough women in Fort Wayne will want to take a bath with Fenjala or bake cookies with Moist & Easy may seem like a piddling matter. But millions of dollars ride on the point-of-purchase decisions made by consumers in Fort Wayne and other frequently used litmus-test cities around the country: from Boston and Albany to Indianapolis and Kansas City, from Nashville and Dallas to Spokane and Fresno.

In these Middletowns of marketing, consumer reaction to a new product's appeal, packaging, pric-

Source: Reprinted with the special permission of DUN's REVIEW, July 1977, pp. 41–43. Copyright © 1977, Dun & Bradstreet Publications Corporation.

ing and advertising pitch pretty much determines whether a plant will be built to produce it in volume or if and when it should be "rolled out" regionally or nationally. Conversely, when a new widget bombs in Boston or Phoenix, it is a signal to its maker that the product is a potentially costly idea whose time has not yet come.

Much like producers of Broadway-bound shows trying out their offerings on the road, consumer companies were recently previewing their newest wares in test markets throughout the country. Among the most ubiquitous product categories: analgesics, specialized household cleaners, snack foods and soft drinks sweetened with new saccharine substitutes. The Nestle Co. was testing Sunrise instant coffee "mellowed with chickory" in Spokane and Grand Rapids and a dairy drink called Choco Chill in six different cities, including Milwaukee, Minneapolis, Des Moines and Davenport, Iowa. The Carnation Co. chose Omaha as a test market for its Moustache, a shaker-type drink. In Syracuse, New York, Combe, Inc. was trying out its All Day denture adhesive, while Denver and Detroit were the test cities for General Foods' Mellow Roast coffee. Phoenix was chosen to test at least seven new products, including General Mills' Apple Crunchies, Green Giant Co.'s Toast Toppers, Kimberly-Clark's Kotex stick tampons and Procter & Gamble's Bounce fabric softener.

The spirited action in test marketing has rebounded from the recession, when industry cut back on new-product introductions. This year, the big consumer companies that regularly use it, such as General Foods, P&G and Ralston-Purina are expected to invest a record $150 million (not counting media advertising costs) in market tests, about $30 million more than they spent last year. So keen is the competition for shelf space and so discerning the consumer, however, that only about 45% of new products succeed in market testing.

Nor is there any guarantee that the product that does well in a test city will wow the national marketplace. At best, market testing is an important indicator. It cannot predict absolute volume or share of market. Yet the big consumer companies that regularly use it, such as General Foods, P&G and Ralston-Purina, agree that test marketing has an impressive track record as a guide for arriving at a fundamental go/no-go decision.

The alternative, of course, is to send a new product to market regionally, back it with advertising and sales promotion, and hope for the best. But the dollars needed to develop, produce, package and distribute an untested product can run into the tens of millions—without a clue that the product will sell.

Although many large consumer products companies with vast sales organizations conduct their own tests, the procedure is tedious and time-consuming. A product is often tested in more than one city, and tests can last anywhere from six months to a year or more before the results are considered conclusive. Procter & Gamble, for instance, kept its Pringles Newfangled Potato Chips testing in Evansville, Indiana, for three years before distributing it.

Because of the demands, a big percentage of test marketing is handled by specialized service companies—such as Audits & Surveys, the Marketest division of Chicago's Market Facts and Cincinnati's Burgoyne Index—for fees ranging from $20,000 to $200,000, depending on the size of the job. Employing their own truck drivers, auditors, interviewers and invoice readers, the testing firms maintain warehousing facilities in test cities, stock stores with the product, arrange for its "facing" on the shelves and check sales daily in every store. "There is more time pressure in a product test than any other kind of market research," says Chairman David K. Hardin of Market Facts. "The client is always desperately anxious for the results because he's got to decide if a plant should be built to produce the product for a broader market."

Picking the Market

Needless to say one of the toughest problems is deciding where to test a product. Although Fort Wayne is the only city utilized by all three of the big test-marketing firms, there is no such thing as the ideal test market. If there were such a magic marketing town in America, so many products would be competing for consumers' dollars that the results would be meaningless. Procter & Gamble, for example, will not test more than one of its products in the same city at the same time and shuns any town in which competitive products are not represented.

Test cities are chosen with painstaking care on the basis of several criteria. It goes without saying that the site should have a demographic profile fairly representative of consumer buying habits throughout the country. "But you don't look for a mirror of America as much as a market environment comparable to that in which the product will compete when it is rolled out," says Carl Ravirca, vice president of Audits & Surveys.

A good test town is also one in which the manufacturer has established distribution lines and enjoys good relations with dealers. To monitor the effectiveness of the product's advertising program, companies also look for so-called "isolated" communities, whose media coverage is not "contaminated" by outside newspapers or radio and TV shows coming into the area from nearby cities. Too much cable TV, for instance, can water down broadcast testing and render results invalid. Similarly, too much newpaper circulation outside the primary test area can be nonproductive.

Another factor that can influence market tests is secrecy. As a General Foods marketing executive says: "We don't like the competition to know we're testing Brand X in City Z." Usually, the first inkling a company gets that a rival is testing a new product is when one of its salesmen happens to spot the product on a supermarket shelf. Invariably, the salesman buys the product, shipping it off to his company for study. A common gambit is for the company to then swiftly clog the distribution pipelines with its own similar product. It happened only last year when Calgon Corp. got wind of P&G's test for Bounce, a new product said to eliminate static cling from fabrics in the dryer. Calgon promptly plunged into the market with its own Cling Free, which was being readied for market, and, in effect, took a free ride on P&G's product push.

According to a study of the 25 most popular test cities by *Sales Management* magazine several years ago, Albany, Spokane and Fresno came closest to the U.S. average in population by age groups, deviating no more than a mere 5% from the national figure. In terms of effective buying income per capita and per household, Orlando, Nashville and Lima, Ohio, were the cities closest to the national average with a deviation of less than 7%. But in the important retail-sales category, measuring how much is spent for merchandise per capita and per household, the top three cities turned out to be Erie, Pennsylvania, Boston and South Bend, Indiana (100 miles from Fort Wayne), with a deviation of less than 1.8% from the national average. The only two test cities in the top ten in all three categories were Erie and South Bend.

Some marketers suggest that overuse of a test market breeds a city of professional consumers, who become conditioned to buying any new product that appears on the shelf because they feel it is expected of them. But Market Facts' Hardin calls such thinking "a crock of baloney." If a test is conducted properly, he argues, "the consumer doesn't even know he's involved in one."

Nevertheless, there are signs that the Eries and Fort Waynes may be overexposed, and companies of late have been looking around for new test markets. According to President Fitzhugh L. Corr of the Burgoyne Index, a number of Southern cities are growing in popularity, including Louisville and Lexington, Kentucky, and Knoxville and Chattanooga, Tennessee. Also part of the new trend, so-called mini-markets in the Southwest are winning test marketers' favor. Among them: Phoenix, Albuquerque and Lubbock, Texas.

Questions

1. *What major criteria should a marketing manager of a major consumer products company consider when selecting test market cities?*
2. *"The risks associated with test marketing may be greater than those associated with introducing new products without such research." Explain.*

20

Diagnosing the Product Portfolio

GEORGE S. DAY

Product portfolio management is increasing in popularity as an approach to marketing strategy formulation. The approach distinguishes among different classes of products and suggests relevant strategic management alternatives for each class.

The product portfolio approach to marketing strategy formulation has gained wide acceptance among managers of diversified companies. They are first attracted by the intuitively appealing concept that long-run corporate performance is more than the sum of the contributions of individual profit centers or product strategies. Secondly a product portfolio analysis suggests specific marketing strategies to achieve a balanced mix of products that will produce the maximum long-run effects from scarce cash and managerial resources. Lastly the concept employs a simple matrix representation which is easy to communicate and comprehend. Thus it is a useful tool in a headquarters campaign to demonstrate that the strategic issues facing the firm justify more centralized control over the planning and resource allocation process.

With the growing acceptance of the basic approach has come an increasing sensitivity to the limitations of the present methods of portraying the product portfolio, and a recognition that the approach is not equally useful in all corporate circumstances. Indeed, the implications can sometimes be

Source: Journal of Marketing, April 1977, pp. 29–38. Reprinted from *Journal of Marketing* published by the American Marketing Association.

grossly misleading. Inappropriate and misleading applications will result when:

The basic *assumptions* (especially those concerned with the value of market share dominance and the product life cycle) are violated.
The *measurements* are wrong, or
The *strategies* are not feasible.

This article identifies the critical assumptions and the measurement and application issues that may distort the strategic insights. A series of questions are posed that will aid planners and decisionmakers to better understand this aid to strategic thinking, and thereby make better decisions.

What Is the Product Portfolio?

Common to all portrayals of the product portfolio is the recognition that the competitive value of market share depends on the structure of competition and the stage of the product life cycle. Two examples of this approach have recently appeared in this journal.[1] However, the earliest, and most widely implemented is the cash quadrant or share/growth matrix developed by the Boston Consulting Group.[2] Each product is classified jointly by rate of present or forecast *market growth* (a proxy for stage in the product life cycle) and a measure of *market share dominance*.

The arguments for the use of market share are familiar and well documented.[3] Their basis is the cumulation of evidence that market share is strongly and positively correlated with product profitability. This theme is varied somewhat in the BCG approach by the emphasis on relative share—measure by the ratio of the company's share of the market to the share of the largest competitor. This is reasonable since the strategic implications of a 20% share are quite different if the largest competitor's is 40% or if it is 5%. Profitability will also vary, since according to the experience curve concept the largest competitor will be the most profitable at the prevailing price level.[4]

The product life cycle is employed because it highlights the desirability of a variety of products or services with different present and prospective growth rates. More important, the concept has some direct implications for the cost of gaining and/or holding market share:

During the *rapid growth stage,* purchase patterns and distribution channels are fluid. Market shares can be increased at "relatively" low cost by capturing a disproportionate share of incremental sales (especially where these sales come from new users of applications rather than heavier usage by existing users).

By contrast, the key-note during the *maturity stage* swings to stability and inertia in distribution and purchasing relationships. A substantial growth in share by one competitor will come at the expense of another competitor's capacity utilization, and will be resisted vigorously. As a result, gains in share are both time-consuming and costly (unless accompanied by a breakthrough in product value or performance that cannot be easily matched by competition).

Product Portfolio Strategies

When the share and growth rate of each of the products sold by a firm are jointly considered, a new basis for strategy evaluation emerges. While there are many possible combinations, an arbitrary classification of products into four share/growth categories (as shown in Exhibit 1) is sufficient to illustrate the strategy implications.

Low Growth/Dominant Share (Cash Cows)

These profitable products usually generate more cash than is required to maintain share. All strategies should be directed toward maintaining market dominance—including investments in technological leadership. Pricing decisions should be made cautiously with an eye to maintaining price leadership. Pressure to over-invest through product proliferation and market expansion should be resisted unless prospects for expanding primary demand are unusually attractive. Instead, excess cash should be used to support research activities and growth areas elsewhere in the company.

High Growth/Dominant Share (Stars)

Products that are market leaders, but also growing fast, will have substantial reported profits but need a lot of cash to finance the rate of growth. The appropriate strategies are designed primarily to protect the existing share level by reinvesting earnings in the form of price reductions, product improvement, better market coverage, production efficiency increases, etc. Particular attention must be given to obtaining a large share of the new users or new applications that are the source of growth in the market.

Low Growth/Subordinate Share (Dogs)

Since there usually can be only one market leader and because most markets are mature, the greatest number of products fall in this category. Such products are usually at a cost disadvantage and have few opportunities for growth at a reasonable cost. Their markets are not growing, so there is little new business to compete for, and market share gains will be resisted strenuously by the dominant competition.

The slower the growth (present or prospective) and the smaller the relative share, the greater the need for positive action. The possibilities include:

Exhibit 1
The cash quadrant approach to describing the product portfolio [a]

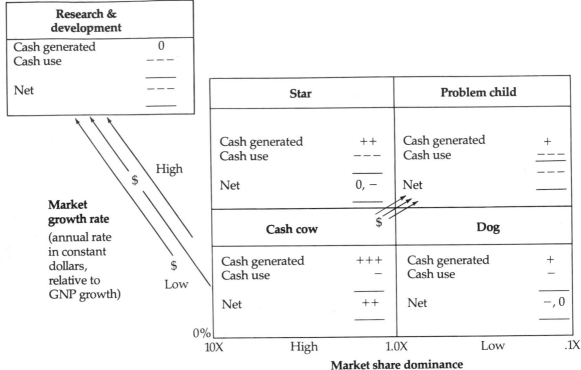

[a] Arrows indicate principal cash flows.

1. Focusing on a specialized segment of the market that can be dominated, and protected from competitive inroads.
2. Harvesting, which is a conscious cutback of all support costs to some minimum level which will maximize the cash flow over a foreseeable life-time—which is usually short.
3. Divestment, usually involving a sale as a going concern.
4. Abandonment or deletion from the product line.

High Growth/Subordinate Share (Problem Children)

The combination of rapid growth and poor profit margins creates an enormous demand for cash. If the cash is not forthcoming, the product will become a "Dog" as growth inevitably slows. The basic strategy options are fairly clear-cut; either invest heavily to get a disproportionate share of the new sales or buy existing shares by acquiring competitors and thus move the product toward the "Star" category or get out of the business using some of the methods just described.

Consideration also should be given to a market

segmentation strategy, but only if a defensible niche can be identified and resources are available to gain dominance. This strategy is even more attractive if the segment can provide an entrée and experience base from which to push for dominance of the whole market.

Overall Strategy

The long-run health of the corporation depends on having some products that *generate* cash (and provide acceptable reported profits), and others that *use* cash to support growth. Among the indicators of overall health are the size and vulnerability of the "Cash Cows" (and the prospects for the "Stars," if any), and the number of "Problem Children" and "Dogs." Particular attention must be paid to those products with large cash appetites. Unless the company has abundant cash flow, it cannot afford to sponsor many such products at one time. If resources (including debt capacity) are spread too thin, the company simply will wind up with too many marginal products and suffer a reduced capacity to finance promising new product entries or acquisitions in the future.

Exhibit 2
Balancing the product portfolio

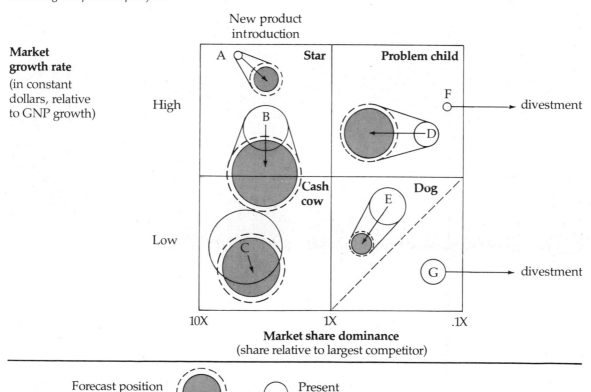

(Diameter of circle is proportional to product's contribution to total company sales volume.)

The share/growth matrix displayed in Exhibit 2 shows how one company (actually a composite of a number of situations) might follow the strategic implications of the product portfolio to achieve a better balance of sources and uses of cash. The *present* position of each product is defined by the relative share and market growth rate during a representative time *period*. Since business results normally fluctuate, it is important to use a time period that is not distorted by rare events. The *future* position may be either (a) a momentum forecast of the results of continuing the present strategy, or (b) a forecast of the consequences of a change in strategy. It is desirable to do both, and compare the results. The specific display of Exhibit 2 is a summary of the following strategic decisions.

Aggressively *support* the newly introduced product A, to ensure dominance (but anticipate share declines due to new competitive entries).
Continue present strategies of products B and C to ensure *maintenance* of market share.
Gain share of market for product D by investing in *acquisitions*.
Narrow and modify the range of models of product E to *focus* on one segment.
Divest products F and G.

Pitfalls in the Assumptions

The starting point in the decision to follow the implications of a product portfolio analysis is to ask whether the underlying assumptions make sense. The most fundamental assumptions relate to the role of market share in the businesses being portrayed in the portfolio. Even if the answers here are affirmative one may choose to not follow the implications if other objectives than balancing cash flows take priority, or there are barriers to implementing the indicated strategies.

What Is the Role of Market Share?

All the competitors are assumed to have the same overhead structures and experience curves, with their position on the experience curve corresponding to their market share position. Hence market share dominance is a proxy for the *relative* profit performance (e.g., GM vs. Chrysler). Other factors beyond market share may be influential in dictating *absolute, profit performance (e.g., calculators versus cosmetics)*.

The influence of market share is most apparent with high value-added products, where there are significant barriers to entry and the competition consists of a few, large, diversified corporations with the attendant large overheads (e.g., plastics, major appliances, automobiles, and semi-conductors). But even in these industrial environments there are distortions under conditions such as:

One competitor has a significant technological advantage which can be protected and used to establish a steeper cost reduction/experience curve.
The principal component of the product is produced by a supplier who has an inherent cost advantage because of an integrated process. Thus Dupont was at a cost disadvantage with Cyclohexane vis-à-vis the oil companies because the manufacture of the product was so highly integrated with the operations of an oil refinery.[5]
Competitors can economically gain large amounts of experience through acquisitions or licensing, or shift to a lower (but parallel) cost curve by resorting to off-shore production or component sourcing.
Profitability is highly sensitive to the rate of capacity utilization, regardless of size of plant.

There are many situations where the positive profitability and share relationship becomes very tenuous, and perhaps unattainable. A recent illustration is the building industry where large corporations—CNA with Larwin and ITT with Levitt—have suffered because of their inability to adequately offset their high overhead charges with a corresponding reduction in total costs.[6] Similar problems are also encountered in the service sector, and contribute to the many reasons why services which are highly labor-intensive and involve personal relationships must be approached with extreme caution in a product portfolio analysis.[7]

There is specific evidence from the Profit Impact of Market Strategies (PIMS) study [8] that the value of market share is not as significant for consumer goods as for industrial products. The reasons are not well understood, but probably reflect differences in buying behavior, the importance of product differentiation and the tendency for proliferation of marginally different brands in these categories. The strategy of protecting a market position by introducing line extensions, flankers, and spin-offs from a successful core brand means that product class boundaries are very unclear. Hence shares are harder to estimate. The individual brand in a category like deodorants or powdered drinks may not be the proper basis for evaluation. A related consequence is that joint costing problems multiply. For example, Unilever in the U.K. has 20 detergent brands all sharing production facilities and marketing resources to some degree.

When Do Market Shares Stabilize?

The operating assumption is that shares tend toward stability during the maturity stage, as the dominant competitors concentrate on defending their existing position. An important corollary is that gains in share are easier and cheaper to achieve during the growth stage.

There is scattered empirical evidence, including the results of the PIMS project, which supports these assumptions. Several qualifications must be made before the implications can be pursued in depth:

While market share *gains* may be costly, it is possible to mismanage a dominant position. The examples of A&P in food retailing, and British Leyland in the U.K. automobile market provide new benchmarks on the extent to which strong positions can erode unless vigorously defended.

When the two largest competitors are of roughly equal size, the share positions may continue to be fluid until one is finally dominant.

There are certain product categories, frequently high technology oriented, where a dominant full line/full service competitor is vulnerable if there are customer segments which do not require all the services, technical assistance, etc., that are provided. As markets mature this "sophisticated" segment usually grows. Thus, Digital Equipment Corp. has prospered in competition with IBM by simply selling basic hardware and depending on others to do the applications programming. [9] By contrast, IBM provides, for a price, a great deal of service backup and software for customers who are not self-sufficient. The dilemma for the dominant producer lies in the difficulty of serving both segments simultaneously. [10]

What Is the Objective of a Product Portfolio Strategy?

The strategies emerging from a product portfolio analysis emphasize the balance of cash flows, by ensuring that there are products that use cash to sustain growth and others that supply cash.

Yet corporate objectives have many more dimensions that require consideration. This point was recognized by Seymour Tilles in one of the earliest discussions of the portfolio approach. [11] It is worth repeating to avoid a possible myopic focus on cash flow considerations. Tilles' point was that an investor pursues a balanced combination of risk, income, and growth when acquiring a portfolio of securities. He further argued that "the same basic concepts apply equally well to product planning." The problem with concentrating on cash flow to maximize income and growth is that strategies to balance risks are not explicitly considered.

What must be avoided is excessive exposure to a specific threat from one of the following areas of vulnerability:

The economy (e.g., business downturns).
Social, political, environmental pressures.
Supply continuity.
Technological change.
Unions and related human factors.

It also follows that a firm should direct its new product search activities into several different opportunity areas, to avoid intensifying the degree of vulnerability. Thus, many companies in the power equipment market, such as Brown Boveri, are in a quandary over whether to meet the enormous resource demands of the nuclear power equipment market, because of the degree of vulnerability of this business compared to other possibilities such as household appliances.

The desire to reduce vulnerability is a possible reason for keeping, or even acquiring, a "Dog." Thus, firms may integrate backward to assure supply of highly leveraged materials.[12] If a "Dog" has a high percentage of captive business, it may not even belong as a separate entity in a portfolio analysis.

A similar argument could be used for products which have been acquired for intelligence reasons. For example, a large Italian knitwear manufacturer owns a high-fashion dress company selling only to boutiques to help follow and interpret fashion trends. Similarly, because of the complex nature of the distribution of lumber products, some suppliers have acquired lumber retailers to help learn about patterns of demand and changing end-user requirements. In both these cases the products/businesses were acquired for reasons outside the logic of the product portfolio, and should properly be excluded from the analysis.

Can the Strategies Be Implemented?

Not only does a product portfolio analysis provide insights into the long-run health of a company; it also implies the basic strategies that will strengthen the portfolio. Unfortunately, there are many situations where the risks of failure of these strategies are unacceptably high. Several of these risks were identified in a recent analysis of the dangers in the pursuit of market share.[13]

One danger is that the company's financial resources will not be adequate. The resulting problems are enormously compounded should the company find itself in a vulnerable financial position if the fight were stopped short for some reason. The fundamental question underlying such dangers is the likelihood that competitors will pursue the same strategy, because they follow the same logic in identifying and pursuing opportunities. As a result, there is a growing premium on the understanding of competitive responses, and especially the degree to which they will be discouraged by aggressive action.

An increasingly important question is whether government regulations will permit the corporation to follow the strategy it has chosen. Antitrust regulations—especially in the U.S.—now virtually preclude acquisitions undertaken by large companies in related areas. Thus the effort by ITT to acquire a "Cash Cow" in Hartford Fire and Indemnity Insurance was nearly aborted by a consent decree, and other moves by ITT into Avis, Canteen Corp., and Levitt have been divested by court order at enormous cost. Recent governmental actions—notably the *ReaLemon* case—may even make it desirable for companies with very large absolute market share to consider reducing that share.[14]

There is less recognition as yet that government involvement can cut both ways; making it difficult to get in *or out of* a business. Thus, because of national security considerations large defense contractors would have a difficult time exiting from the aerospace or defense businesses. The problems are most acute in countries like Britain and Italy where intervention policies include price controls, regional development directives and employment maintenance which may prevent the replacement of out-moded plants. Unions in these two countries are sometimes so dedicated to protecting the employment status quo that a manager may not even move employees from one product line to another without risking strike activity.

The last implementation question concerns the viability of a niche strategy, which appears at the outset to be an attractive way of coping with both "Dogs" and "Problem Children." The fundamental problem, of course, is whether a product or market niche can be isolated and protected against competitive inroads. But even if this can be achieved in the long-run, the strategy may not be attractive. The difficulties are most often encountered when a full or extensive product line is needed to support sales, service and distribution facilities. One specialized product may simply not generate sufficient volume and gross margin to cover the minimum costs of participation in the market. This is very clearly an issue in the construction equipment business because of the importance of assured service.

Pitfalls in the Measures

The "Achilles' Heel" of a product portfolio analysis is the units of measure; for if the share of market and growth estimates are dubious, so are the interpretations. Skeptics recognize this quickly, and can rapidly confuse the analysis by attacking the meaningfulness and accuracy of these measures and offering alternative definitions. With the present state of the measurements there is often no adequate defense.

What Share of What Market?

This is not one, but several questions. Each is controversial because they influence the bases for resource allocation and evaluation within the firm:

Should the definition of the product-market be broad (reflecting the generic need) or narrow?
How much market segmentation?
Should the focus be on the total product-market or a portion served by the company?
Which level of geography: local versus national versus regio-centric markets?

The answers to these questions are complicated by the lack of defensible procedures for identifying product-market boundaries. For example, four-digit SIC categories are convenient and geographically available but may have little relevance to consumer perceptions of substitutability which will influence the long-run performance of the product. Furthermore, there is the pace of product development activity which is dedicated to combining, extending, or otherwise obscuring the boundaries.

Breadth of Product-Market Definition?

This is a pivotal question. Consider the following extremes in definitions:

Intermediate builder chemicals for the detergent industry *or* Sodium Tri-polyphosphate.
Time/information display devices *or* medium-priced digital-display alarm clocks.
Main meal accompaniments *or* jellied cranberry.

Narrow definitions satisfy the short-run, tactical concerns of sales and product managers. Broader views, reflecting longer-run, strategic planning concerns, invariably reveal a larger market to account for (a) sales to untapped but potential markets, (b) changes in technology, price relationships, and supply which broaden the array of potential substitute products, and (c) the time required by present and prospective buyers to react to these changes.

Extent of Segmentation?

In other words, when does it become meaningful to divide the total market into sub-groups for the purpose of estimating shares? In the tire industry it is evident that the OEM and replacement markets are so dissimilar in behavior as to dictate totally different marketing mixes. But how much further should segmentation be pushed? The fact that a company has a large share of the high-income buyers of replacement tires is probably not strategically relevant.

In general the degree of segmentation for a portfolio analysis should be limited to grouping those buyers that share situational or behavioral characteristics that are strategically relevant. This means that different marketing mixes must be used to serve the segments that have been identified, which will be reflected in different cost and price structures. Other manifestations of a strategically important segment boundary would be a discontinuity in growth rates, share patterns, distribution patterns and so forth when going from one segment to another.

These judgments are particularly hard to make

for geographic boundaries. For example, what is meaningful for a manufacturer of industrial equipment facing dominant local competition in each of the national markets in the European Economic Community? Because the company is in each market, it has a 5% share of the total EEC market, while the largest regional competitor has 9%. In this case the choice of a regional rather than national market definition was dictated by the *trend* to similarity of product requirements throughout the EEC and the consequent feasibility of a single manufacturing facility to serve several countries.

The tendency for trade barriers to decline for countries within significant economic groupings will increasingly dictate regio-centric rather than nationally oriented boundaries. This, of course, will not happen where transportation costs or government efforts to protect sensitive industry categories (such as electric power generation equipment), by requiring local vendors, creates other kinds of barriers.

Market Served Versus Total Market?

Firms may elect to serve only just a part of the available market; such as retailers with central buying offices or utilities of a certain size. The share of the market served is an appropriate basis for tactical decisions. This share estimate may also be relevant for strategic decisions, especially if the market served corresponds to a distinct segment boundary. There is a risk that focusing only on the market served may mean overlooking a significant opportunity or competitive threat emerging from the unserved portion of the market. For example, a company serving the blank cassette tape market only through specialty audio outlets is vulnerable if buyers perceive that similar quality cassettes can be bought in general merchandise and discount outlets.

Another facet of the served market issue is the treatment of customers who have integrated backward and now satisfy their own needs from their own resources. Whether or not the captive volume is included in the estimate of total market size depends on how readily this captive volume can be displaced by outside suppliers. Recent analysis suggests that captive production—or infeeding—is "remarkably resilient to attack by outside suppliers." [15]

What Can Be Done?

The value of a strategically relevant product-market definition lies in "stretching" the company's perceptions appropriately—far enough so that significant threats and opportunities are not missed, but not so far as to dissipate information gathering and analysis efforts on "long shots." This is a difficult balance to achieve, given the myriads of possibilities. The best procedure for coping is to employ several alternative definitions, varying specificity of product and market segments. There will inevitably be both points of contradiction and consistency in the insights gained from portfolios constructed at one level versus another. The process of resolution can be very revealing, both in terms of understanding the competitive position and suggesting strategy alternatives. [16]

Market Growth Rate

The product life cycle is justifiably regarded as one of the most difficult marketing concepts to measure—or forecast.

There is a strong tendency in a portfolio analysis to judge that a product is maturing when there is a forecast of a decline in growth rate below some specified cut-off. One difficulty is that the same cut-off level does not apply equally to all products or economic climates. As slow growth or level GNP becomes the reality, high absolute growth rates become harder to achieve for all products, mature or otherwise. Products with lengthy introductory periods, facing substantial barriers to adoption, may never exhibit high growth rates, but may have an extended maturity stage. Other products may exhibit precisely the opposite life cycle pattern.

The focus in the product portfolio analysis should

be on the long-run growth rate forecast. This becomes especially important with products which are sensitive to the business cycle, such as machine tools, or have potential substitutes with fluctuating prices. Thus the future growth of engineered plastics is entwined with the price of zinc, aluminum, copper and steel; the sales of powdered breakfast beverages depends on the relative price of frozen orange juice concentrate.

These two examples also illustrate the problem of the self-fulfilling prophecy. A premature classification as a mature product may lead to the reduction of marketing resources to the level necessary to defend the share in order to maximize net cash flow. But if the product class sales are sensitive to market development activity (as in the case of engineered plastics) or advertising expenditures (as is the case with powdered breakfast drinks) and these budgets are reduced by the dominant firms then, indeed, the product growth rate will slow down.

The growth rate is strongly influenced by the choice of product-market boundaries. A broad product type (cigarettes) will usually have a longer maturity stage than a more specific product form (plain filter cigarettes). In theory, the growth of the individual brand is irrelevant. Yet, it cannot be ignored that the attractiveness of a growth market, however defined, will be diminished by the entry of new competitors with the typical depressing effect on the sales, prices and profits of the established firms. The extent of the reappraisal of the market will depend on the number, resources, and commitment of the new entrants. Are they likely to become what is known in the audio electronics industry as "rabbits," which come racing into the market, litter it up, and die off quickly?

Pitfalls from Unanticipated Consequences

Managers are very effective at tailoring their behavior to the evaluation system, *as they perceive it.* Whenever market share is used to evaluate performance, there is a tendency for managers to manipulate the product-market boundaries to show a static

or increasing share. The greater the degree of ambiguity or compromise in the definition of the boundaries the more tempting these adjustments become. The risk is that the resulting narrow view of the market may mean overlooking threats from substitutes or the opportunities within emerging market segments.

These problems are compounded when share dominance is also perceived to be an important determinant of the allocation of resources and top management interest. The manager who doesn't like the implications of being associated with a "Dog," may try to redefine the market so he can point to a larger market share or a higher than average growth rate. Regardless of his success with the attempted redefinition, his awareness of how the business is regarded in the overall portfolio will ultimately affect his morale. Then his energies may turn to seeking a transfer or looking for another job, and perhaps another prophecy has been fulfilled.

The forecast of market growth rate is also likely to be manipulated, especially if the preferred route to advancement and needed additional resources is perceived to depend on association with a product that is classified as "Star." This may lead to wishful thinking about the future growth prospects of the product. Unfortunately the quality of the review procedures in most planning processes is not robust enough to challenge such distortions. Further dysfunctional consequences will result if ambitious managers of "Cash Cows" actually attempt to expand their products through unnecessary product proliferation and market segmentation without regard to the impact on profits.

The potential for dysfunctional consequences does not mean that profit center managers and their employees should not be aware of the basis for resource allocation decisions within the firm. A strong argument can be made to the effect that it is worse for managers to observe those decisions and suspect the worst. What will surely create problems is to have an inappropriate reward system. A formula-based system, relying on achievement of a target for return on investment or an index of profit measures, that does not recognize the differences in potential among business, will lead to short-run actions that conflict with the basic strategies that should be pursued.

Alternative Views of the Portfolio

This analysis of the share/growth matrix portrayal of the product portfolio supports Bowman's contention that much of what now exists in the field of corporate or marketing strategy can be thought of as contingency theories. "The ideas, recommendations, or generalizations are rather dependent (contingent) for their truth and their relevance on the specific situational factors."[17] This means that in any specific analysis of the product portfolio there may be a number of factors beyond share and market growth with a much greater bearing on the attractiveness of a product-market or business; including:

The contribution rate.
Barriers to entry.
Cyclicality of sales.
The rate of capacity utilization.
Sensitivity of sales to change in prices, promotional
    activities, service levels, etc.
The extent of "captive" business.
The nature of technology (maturity, volatility, and
    complexity).
Availability of production and process opportu-
    nities.
Social, legal, governmental, and union pressures
    and opportunities.

Since these factors are situational, each company (or division) must develop its own ranking of their importance in determining attractiveness.[18] In practice these factors tend to be qualitatively combined into overall judgments of the attractiveness of the industry or market, and the company's position in that market. The resulting matrix for displaying the positions of each product is called a "nine-block" diagram or decision matrix.[19]

Although the implications of this version of the product portfolio are not as clear-cut, it does overcome many of the shortcomings of the share/growth matrix approach. Indeed the two approaches will likely yield different insights. But as the main purpose of the product portfolio analysis is to help guide—but not substitute for—strategic thinking, the process of reconciliation is useful in itself. Thus it is desirable to employ both approaches and compare results.

Summary

The product portfolio concept provides a useful synthesis of the analyses and judgments during the preliminary steps of the planning process, and is a provocative source of strategy alternatives. If nothing else, it demonstrates the fallacy of treating all businesses or profit centers as alike, and all capital investment decisions as independent and additive events.

There are a number of pitfalls to be avoided to ensure the implications are not misleading. This is especially true for the cash quadrant or share/growth matrix approach to portraying the portfolio. In many situations the basic assumptions are not satisfied. Further complications stem from uncertainties in the definitions of product-markets and the extent and timing of competitive actions. One final pitfall is the unanticipated consequences of adopting a portfolio approach. These may or may not be undesirable depending on whether they are recognized at the outset.

Despite the potential pitfalls it is important to not lose sight of the concept; that is, to base strategies on the perception of a company as an interdependent group of products and services, each playing a distinctive and supportive role.

Endnotes

1. Bernard Catry and Michel Chevalier, "Market Share Strategy and the Product Life Cycle," *Journal of Marketing*, Vol. 38 No. 4 (October 1974), pp. 29–34; and Yoram Wind and Henry J. Claycamp,

"Planning Product Line Strategy: A Matrix Approach," *Journal of Marketing*, Vol. 40 No. 1 (January 1976), pp. 2–9.

2. Described in the following pamphlets in the *Perspectives* series, authored by Bruce D. Henderson, "The Product Portfolio" (1970), "Cash Traps" (1972) and "The Experience Curve Reviewed: The Growth-Share Matrix or the Product Portfolio". (Boston Consulting Group, 1973). By 1972 the approach had been employed in more than 100 companies. See "Mead's Technique to Sort Out the Losers," *Business Week* (March 11, 1972), pp. 124–30.

3. Sidney Schoeffler, Robert D. Buzzell and Donald F. Heany, "Impact of Strategic Planning on Profit Performance," *Harvard Business Review* Vol. 52 (March–April 1974), pp. 137–45; and Robert D. Buzzell, Bradley T. Gale and Ralph G. M. Sultan, "Market Share—A Key to Profitability," *Harvard Business Review*, Vol. 53 (January–February 1975), pp. 97–106.

4. Boston Consulting Group, *Perspectives on Experience* (Boston: 1968 and 1970), and "Selling Business a Theory of Economics," *Business Week*, September 8, 1974, pg. 43–44.

5. Robert B. Stobaugh and Philip L. Towsend, "Price Forecasting and Strategic Planning: The Case of Petrochemicals," *Journal of Marketing Research*, Vol. XII (February 1975), pp. 19–29.

6. Carol J. Loomis, "The Further Misadventures of Harold Geneen," *Fortune*, June 1975.

7. There is incomplete but provocative evidence of significant share-profit relationships in the markets for auto rental, consumer finance, and retail securities brokerage.

8. Same as reference 3 above.

9. "A Minicomputer Tempest," *Business Week* January 27, 1975, pp. 79–80.

10. Some argue that the dilemma is very general, confronting all pioneering companies in mature markets. See Seymour Tilles, "Segmentation and Strategy," *Perspectives* (Boston: Boston Consulting Group, 1974).

11. Seymour Tilles, "Strategies for Allocating Funds," *Harvard Business Review*, Vol. 44 (January–February 1966), pp. 72–80.

12. This argument is compelling when $20,000 of Styrene Monomer can affect the production of $10,000,000 worth of formed polyester fiberglass parts.

13. William E. Fruhan, "Pyrrhic Victories in Fights for Market Share," *Harvard Business Review*, Vol. 50 (September–October 1972), pp. 100–107.

14. See Paul N. Bloom and Philip Kotler, "Strategies for High Market-Share Companies," *Harvard Business Review*, Vol. 53 (November–December 1975), pp. 63–72.

15. Aubrey Wilson and Bryan Atkin, "Exorcising the Ghosts in Marketing," *Harvard Business Review*, Vol. 54 (September–October 1976), pp. 117–27. See also, Ralph D. Kerkendall, "Customers as Competitors," *Perspectives* (Boston: Boston Consulting Group, 1975).

16. George S. Day and Allan D. Shocker, *Identifying Competitive Product-Market Boundaries: Strategic and Analytical Issues* (Boston: Marketing Science Institute, 1976).

17. Edward H. Bowman, "Epistemology, Corporate Strategy, and Academe," *Sloan Management Review* (Winter 1974), pp. 35–50.

18. The choice of factors and assessment of ranks is an important aspect of the design of a planning system. These issues are described in Peter Lorange, "Divisional Planning: Setting Effective Direction," *Sloan Management Review* (Fall 1975), pp. 77–91.

19. William E. Rothschild, *Putting It All Together: A Guide to Strategic Thinking* (New York: AMACOM, 1976).

Questions

1. *What criteria are used to classify products in the portfolio analysis approach?*
2. *Differentiate Cash Cows, Stars, Dogs, and Problem Children.*
3. *What is the objective of a product portfolio strategy?*

21

Pricing Policies and Profitability

ROBERT E. HAMPEL

Although economic theory provides a ready basis for arriving at a price, there are many variables that come into play in the marketplace.

The pricing activity of a firm can be divided into policy and actual pricing practice. Not too surprisingly, policy and practice may run close together or separate widely depending upon the industry, the firm's position within an industry, the strength of the individual firm, and the prevailing market conditions. This article will examine how the pricing problems can be approached and what benefits will accrue to a firm that approaches the pricing problem scientifically.

Pricing Policies and Goals

Pricing policies are statements of management's attitude toward pricing products. These policies do not determine prices, but they do set forth the factors to be considered and the ground rules to be followed. Policies can be many and varied and depend in a large degree on industry, company, product line, and the position of the product in the product life cycle.

Robert A. Lynn has defined eight goals for pricing.[1] Our discussion will center around these eight goals and his definitions:

1. Maximum profits
2. Target profits
3. Satisfactory profits
4. Market share
5. Sales maximization
6. Meeting competition
7. Image goals
8. Stability goals

Maximum Profits

Profits should, over the long run, be maximized in order to maximize the firm's value to its shareholders. Over the short term, however, this is not always justified. In the first place, the lack of exact knowledge of costs and demand makes it quite difficult to achieve maximization. In addition, it could be advantageous for a firm to price a product at less than the profit maximization price in order to develop a more broadly-based market and lessen dependence on a few customers. Broadening the market base is important to small concerns where, typically, 20 percent of the customers represent 80 percent of the volume. A significant example of short-term pricing contrary to the profit maximization theory was seen in the automobile industry of some 30 years ago. In mid-1948, late-model Chevrolets were selling on used-car lots for several hundred dollars above their list price. The manufacturers could have raised prices and achieved increased profits, but they did not. More than likely, they improved their public image at the expense of used car dealers.[2]

Target Profits

The target profit goal, which may also be interpreted as the goal of achieving a target return on investment, seeks to build up a price structure that provides a return on the capital employed for specific products, product groups, and divisions, so as to yield a predetermined corporate average return. In most cases, managements refer to stockholders' equity (net worth) plus long-term debt as the base upon which to calculate this return. Usually a standard cost system is used as a means of allocating fixed costs to various product divisions, with the standards premised on an assumed rate of production. Typically, when the assumed rate is about 70 to 80 percent of capacity, the product mix is assumed to be "normal." With this costing and pricing system, both costs and profit goals are based not upon the volume level, but rather on a standard volume. The margins added to standard costs are designed to produce the target profit rate on investment, assuming a standard volume to be the long-run average rate of plant utilization.

Satisfactory Profits

Some firms may not strive to achieve maximum profits or a target return rate. They may just strive to achieve satisfactory profits; but this pertinent fact may not be stated. When such objectives are not specifically stated, they can vary based on the subjective judgment of management. In researching management behavior, Herbert A. Simon contrasts "economic" man who "maximizes" with "administrative" man who "satisfices."[3] Administrative man is interested in satisfactory, or adequate, profits which may extend over a wide range. In firms where "administrative" man has the final authority, satisfactory profits will likely be the strategy.

Share of Market Goals

Many times, volume objectives, rather than profit objectives, are the guide to pricing policy. Al-

though this may not lead to optimum short-term profits, the benefits derived from increasing the customer base and resultant reduction in vulnerability can be beneficial for long-term financial objectives.

Sales Maximization

In this situation the firm seeks to maximize its dollar volume of sales subject to a constraint: some minimum level of profit (Exhibit 1). In this case, the firm's management know they could realize maximum profits ($1.5 million) by selling $10 million worth of product. They feel required to show only a $1 million profit, however, so they cut prices to the extent necessary to make total sales revenue equal $15 million. Management may well reason that the larger market will be of greater long-run importance than the higher profit. Many times, however, this may not be the case, and management is compensated (or receives industry acclaim) more on volume than on profitability.

Meeting Competition

Many firms have a pricing policy of meeting competition, which is to say they are followers in the industry rather than leaders. The price follower normally behaves rationally. His industry is such that a price increase by one firm—and only one

Exhibit 1
Sales maximization model

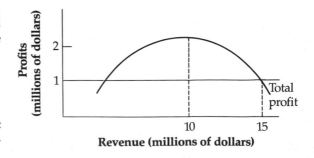

firm—can be disastrous to that firm. But a price rise by all firms can be beneficial. This is typical of the oligopolistic market situation. When a change is proposed by the industry leader, each firm in the industry must analyze the results of the price move in terms of cost to their firm. The potential follower must determine if the new price exceeds the extra cost that must be incurred to produce and sell a unit of the product. Next, he must determine if the profit figure, sales minus cost, will be greater in the new situation than it was in the old.

Image Goals

Firms often set prices to maintain a certain image in the marketplace. A price difference may have more than one meaning, and there is not always a negatively-sloped demand curve. Although many people have a negative reaction to high prices, there is a significant number of cases where high prices are thought to connote quality, value, or prestige. Accordingly, many people will buy such "quality" products merely because of the higher prices. On the matter of company image, one vice president of marketing remarks: ". . . it must be recognized that pricing policies are an integral part of a company's image. They help shape that image and, in fact, may be a major factor in determining it . . ."[4]

Stability Goals

Many customers prefer a stable price in order to ease future forecasting and expectations. Selling companies often try to maintain such stability as a pricing policy. They may fear that any change in any direction can lead to unforeseen and presumably unpleasant consequences.

Pricing Decisions

Once the pricing policy has been set for a firm, the managers of that firm must make the operating decisions regarding the pricing of its products. It should be noted, however, that although the single most important day-to-day management decision may well be pricing, the marketplace will to a large extent determine the price. For, even though price is determined by a combination of costs, competition, and demand, two of these factors involve the marketplace. The third—cost—will be the limiting factor on the seller. Obviously, if he cannot receive more for his product than the cost, his business will be short-lived. It can therefore be concluded that most pricing decisions will be made in terms of competition and demand. With knowledge of this, it then becomes important for a firm to know its cost in order to make a management decision about the firm's ability to sell its product in the marketplace.

Economic Demand Theory

One of the first factors to consider when setting price should be the analysis of the product-demand curve. A demand curve indicates what quantities of a particular product will be bought at various prices at any given time. Demand is elastic when a decrease in price yields higher revenue or an increase in price yields lower revenue. Demand is inelastic when a decrease in price reduces total revenue, or an increase in price brings in higher revenue. Whether demand is elastic or inelastic, however, in the short run, profits are maximized at the price where marginal revenue equals marginal cost. Because this price represents the firm's optimum level of operations, the firm should price its products accordingly.

Markup Pricing

Markup or cost-plus pricing is often used in manufacturing situations where projects or jobs are nonroutine and difficult to "cost" or estimate in advance, such as construction or military weapons development. Markup pricing is popular for several reasons: (1) there is less uncertainty about costs than about demand, (2) if all firms in a given industry use this pricing approach, their prices are likely to be similar if their costs and markup are similar, (3) there is the feeling that cost-markup pricing is equitable to buyer and seller alike because the seller does not take advantage of the buyer in periods of acute demand, yet nonetheless earns a fair return on his investment.

Costs to be used for cost-markup pricing are normally full-costs. The major advantage of the full-cost method is that it assures total cost recovery in long-run pricing. There are, however, a number of pitfalls to the full-cost method:

1. It ignores elasticity of demand. Since the full-cost method does not segregate fixed and variable costs, it is not possible to see what effect a price change will have on profits.
2. It fails to give consideration to competition. Pricing at full-cost tends to perpetuate existing inefficiencies by incorporating them into the price structure.
3. It does not distinguish between "out-of-pocket" and "sunk" costs. A firm using this method may be inclined to reject orders that do not at least cover the total costs involved. There are, however, conditions where acceptance of such orders will be profitable to the firm.
4. This method fails to recognize that all products may not be able to earn the same profit margin.
5. This method gives no consideration to the capital investment required to produce, finance, and distribute individual product lines.

Breakeven Analysis

The breakeven chart is an attempt to show the relationship between four variables: sales price, fixed costs, variable costs, and volume. The chart, by showing how profitable each level of output is, represents a basic attempt at cost-volume-profit relationship. The breakeven analysis can be a useful tool as one of the first requirements in measuring price in a cost-oriented pricing decision. It will allow determination of how many units must be sold at a given price to cover costs.

Marginal-Cost Pricing

From a pricing standpoint, the essential difference between marginal-costing and full-costing lies in the concept of cost recovery. Under full-costing, individual prices are expected to cover total costs, including fixed costs. Under marginal-costing, any contribution toward the recovery of fixed costs is regarded as better than none at all. Pricing under marginal-costing considerations is more flexible than full-cost pricing. The pricing objective is to discover the price and volume that will maximize profits, provided the price is at least greater than the marginal, or out-of-pocket, costs. Orders that might be rejected because they don't cover total costs or yield an adequate profit on full-costs might be acceptable under marginal-costing. The marginal or out-of-pocket costs, then, represent the price floor for a product or individual job in the short-term. Once enough revenue in excess of the out-of-pocket costs has been received to cover all fixed costs, the firm will begin to show a profit.

Summary

Pricing is a difficult and demanding function of management. Some firms make periodic price decisions on products and let them stand until changed. Others make price decisions on individual projects. It appears that the latter is faced with a more active pricing problem on an operating basis, because even though the marketplace will establish the general price for a product, it is up to the firm to determine if it is profitable, and then to market it at the going price.

Although economic theory provides a ready basis for arriving at a price, there are many variables that come into play in the marketplace. An established pricing policy appears necessary for a firm to reach its objectives. If we assume that a firm is in business to maximize its value to the shareholders, then its pricing policy should be based largely on target return on investment.

The marketplace will continue to fluctuate constantly based upon overall economic activity, competitors' reactions, and customers' demands. Each firm must maintain some posture within its pricing policy to make operating pricing decisions. This is especially true of those in the contract project business. The contribution concept or marginal-pricing concept is a valuable tool for daily price decisions. Care must be taken not to confuse contribution with profit, for profit comes only after all fixed costs are paid.

Notes

1. Robert A. Lynn, *Pricing Policies and Market Management*, Richard D. Irwin, Inc., Homewood, Ill., 1967.
2. *Ibid.*

3. See: Herbert A. Simon, *Administrative Behavior*, Macmillan & Co., New York, N.Y., 1957.
4. Otto Wheeley, "Pricing Policy and Objectives," *Creative Pricing*, American Management Association, 1968.

Questions

1. *What is the difference between a price policy and an operational price decision?*
2. *Define full-cost markup pricing. What are the pitfalls or problems with this approach?*
3. *Describe a situation in which marginal-cost pricing would be appropriate. Describe another in which it would be inappropriate.*

22

New Tools for Marketing Research: Product Pricing

LEE F. SCHRADER

BRIAN F. BLAKE

WILLIAM L. JAMES

Marketers can use buyer surveys to help guide pricing decisions. Surveys can obtain information at relatively low cost, without upsetting the market, but they require careful formulation and analysis.

New tools for assessing company position and for selecting strategies to improve company or product position were discussed in earlier articles in this series (*Feedstuffs*, Dec. 26, 1977, and May 8, 1978). In both these articles we discussed the use of surveys of buyer preferences to perform action oriented analyses. We now discuss methods to develop an appropriate product pricing strategy.

Price is one of the most important aspects of a company's marketing strategy. Yet pricing policy is often determined by "seat of the pants" methods despite the fact that methods are available which generate specific quantitative estimates of buyer response to price. Such estimates, while subject to error, can lead to better pricing decisions when combined with the judgment of the experienced marketing manager.

Pricing is only a part of one's marketing strategy, but it is critical. You all know of some firms who tried to "buy" market share with low prices and gave away the store in the process. You also know of some who priced themselves out of the market when they over-estimated the value of their products. If "cost plus a reasonable margin" were the appropriate strategy there would be few business failures. If "following the competition" were the

Source: Feedstuffs, May 29, 1978, pp. 18–19.

rule one would hardly expect to find gasoline selling for 5 to 7 cents more per gallon on one side of the street than on the other. The firm selling a branded (differentiated) product has some pricing discretion and the choices made have a dramatic impact on the bottom line.

What Must You Know?

To find the optimum marketing strategy one needs to know the impacts on sales which are produced by alternative combinations of price, product characteristics, services offered and company image. Unfortunately, such extensive knowledge exists only in dreams, but some progress toward that "impossible dream" is possible.

Key questions are: (1) How much will the general product price level affect total market volume? (2) How much will a change in your price affect your sales? and (3) What are the relative values of specific product characteristics or service differences to the buyers? An important aspect of the first question for many production inputs sold to farmers is the extent to which potential buyers use or make their own rather than use a commercially supplied product. The second question also has two dimensions; the effect of a change in your price when others remain the same, and the effect of a change in your price when other sellers react. Unfortunately, the methods we discuss are not capable of estimating the impact on other sellers' strategy. Our focus is on the response of the buyer to changes in one firm's marketing strategy.

What Can Be Done?

It is no accident that pricing decisions are often made without much supporting analysis. Price response data are particularly difficult to obtain.

One approach is to rely on the judgment of people in your own organization. But there are many problems with this tactic. Your sales people are likely to tell you that you are over-priced. At least, the complaints from the field are not likely to indicate that you are too low. As we demonstrated in the first article in this series, the sales organization may not be in tune with farmers' preferences. The staff may base their ideas on the word of those with whom they have most contact—the present customers. Your present customers may not be representative of the rest of the market—the source of added business.

A second approach is to talk it over with your competitors. Though that approach may be cheap and effective, it is illegal.

You might make some experimental price changes and observe buyer response, but that too presents problems. Price is an integral part of the image of a product in the market. An experimental price change may inadvertently alter that image unfavorably. Such a change may also stimulate undesired competitive reactions. The number of changes which can be made may be too few for adequate analysis. Whether a change in pricing policy on existing products or pricing for a modified product is involved, it is important that the initial decision be a good one.

Another alternative is to model the buyer's decision process to obtain insight into buyer behavior. This may be as simple as computing the value of additional output from an improved fertilizer or feed additive. More complex decisions may require a whole farm model, e.g., to evaluate the value of new combine size or livestock feeding system. Such models are expensive and may not properly represent buyer behavior. Buying is a human decision and may not follow the logic of the model. The typical profit maximizing model may be a more effective tool to demonstrate product value to the buyer than to forecast his behavior.

Some aspects of the total market demand for a product may be available from university or government research. Acreage response to crop prices (a demand for seed and fertilizer), or changes in animal numbers (feed use) as feed prices change are examples of the type of data available from these sources. These aggregate studies are of limited use to a firm concerned about a given geographic area or a more specific product line which are only parts of the larger market. Area or market segment differences may be critical.

The limitations of the above approaches have led to the development of methods to use a sample survey of buyers to estimate response to price and product characteristics. Despite a number of problems, we have found the analysis of survey data to provide useful information for pricing decisions. A well-designed survey can obtain information to estimate the demand for a product at relatively low cost and without "upsetting the market."

How Can It Be Done?

The first step in a pricing analysis is to determine precisely the aspect of demand to be investigated. One cannot design a single survey which will provide estimates of all the interesting dimensions of buyer response. Rather, it will be necessary to zero in on one for a few critical dimensions to get useful answers. As you know from experience, there is a limit to the patience of a survey respondent.

The appropriate questions may originate with management facing a current pressing problem, or they may be suggested by other marketing research. For example, the Action Grid (*Feedstuffs,* May 8, 1978) may have suggested that a product or service be modified. The particular modification being considered by the firm would increase its cost. The critical question would then be whether or not customer preference is sufficiently strong to justify this added cost. The focus could be on the price or perceived product difference which would be necessary to cause a buyer to change dealers or to buy a product or service rather than to make his own.

Once the problem is specified one must select an analysis technique appropriate to the problem. We limit our discussion to four approaches to obtaining answers expressed in terms of dollars and cents. These techniques represent only a few of those which might be used.

Simple Direct Question

The simplest approach is to ask the buyer directly for the value he places on a product, product concept, service, product variation, etc. For example, one might ask, "How much per ton would you be willing to pay for product X with feature Y?"

Although this approach is somtimes used in pricing studies, we cannot recommend it. The answers to such simple direct questions are far too difficult to interpret. For example, such questions may often reflect systematic bias to an unknown degree. Illustratively, significant numbers of buyers may report unreasonably low dollar amounts because they fear the survey may result in price increases.

These and other problems with simple direct questions are at least partially due to the unrealistic nature of the question. In actuality, buyer decisions are comparative. The buyer must choose among alternative products or brands. He must compare each product with the one he is currently using. He must trade off dollars to obtain desired product features. The difficulties emerging with the use of simple direct questions are basically due to their failure to adequately consider the comparative nature of buyer decisions. On the other hand, the three following approaches were developed to reflect these comparisons.

Direct Comparative Question

Such questions ask the buyer to indicate price differences he would be willing to pay for a particular product or attribute. For example, "How much more per ton than you now pay for product X would you be willing to pay for product X with feature Y added?"

Analysis of this type of data is straightforward. The average price difference may be determined by area or for selected groups of buyers (age, size of farm, etc.). An array of prices from high to low with a cumulative percentage of respondents indicating that price or higher provides an estimate of the market demand for the alternative analyzed. Illustratively, Figure 1 represents an estimate of the market demand for feature Y based on hypothetical answers to the question above.

This approach has several advantages; it is simple to ask and easy to analyze. It does consider the comparative nature of purchase decisions. On the other hand, it does have limitations. Only two points can be compared and so it is limited to analyzing single alternatives (here, product X with and without feature Y). It is appropriate only when the direction of buyer preferences can be presumed (e.g., purchase of certified seed vs. planting own seed, 1-year vs. 1-month guarantee).

A Dollarmetric Approach

More complex methods are required to explore buyers' responses to combinations of product features or to alternative features. For example, we may wish to explore buyers' reactions to feature X when it is combined with feature Z, or buyers'

Figure 1
Market demand–feature Y

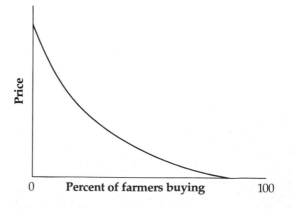

preferences for feature X over feature Z. The dollar-metric approach can be used to advantage here.

The survey respondent makes a series of choices between pairs of brands, products with different attributes, product-service combinations, or other aspects of the buying decision. After making a choice, the respondent is asked how much higher the price of the chosen alternative would have to be increased before the less preferred alternative would be chosen. Questions in a study of brand loyalty would be of the form:

If you had your choice of the following, which would you prefer? (Circle the preferred brand.)

Brand W at $10/100 kg or Brand V at $10/100 kg

Now how much would the price per 100 kilos of the brand that you chose have to increase before you would choose the other brand? (Place an X on the scale.)

```
: . . . . . : . . . . . : . . . . : . . . . : . . . . : . . . . . : . . . . . . . .
 0¢    50¢    $1   $1.50 $2.00 $2.50  over  $2.50
```

Analysis of the data yields estimates of brand preference in dollar terms plus a test of the reliability of these estimates. If a question on current brand usage is also included then the price difference needed in order to cause brand switching from the presently used brand for each brand user group can be calculated. Table 1 gives an example of the results of a dollarmetric analysis. The price differentials needed to induce switching for those who currently use Brand U are shown in the table. This table indicates that current users of Brand U

Table 1

Price change necessary to cause brand change for users of brand U*

Brand	U	V	W
U	0.00	1.50	1.00
V	−1.50	0.00	−0.50
W	−1.00	0.50	0.00

*Price differential required for column brand to be chosen over the row brand.

Table 2

Price change necessary to cause brand change for users of brand V

Brand	U	V	W
U	0.00	0.50	0.25
V	−0.50	0.00	−0.10
W	−0.25	0.10	0.00

would not switch at all as long as there was less than a dollar per 100 kilos price differential between U and W, and as long as there was less than a dollar and a half price differential per 100 kilos between U and V. Thus, depending on current pricing strategy, it may be possible to increase price without losing present customers. Table 2 gives an example of price differentials needed to induce switching for those who currently use Brand V.

This table indicates that the current users of Brand V actually like Brand V the least but find it cheaper than the other two brands. This would suggest an opportunity for either of the other brands to take customers away from Brand V if they wish to compete on price. Thus if Brand U were willing to lower its price to less than a 50-cent differential with Brand V, a substantial number of new customers might be attracted.

Thus, the dollarmetric analysis provides information on brand shifting and an estimate of other consequences of different pricing strategies.

Conjoint Measurement

Logically, every buyer would like the highest level of performance at the lowest cost. What is needed is a method of assessing the value that buyers place on various features of a product, and the extent to which they are willing to forego one feature to obtain a high level of another. If one of the feautres is price, then conjoint measurement (also called "trade-off analysis") offers a measure of the extent to which farmers are willing to pay a higher price in order to receive a higher level of a product feature.

Basically, a survey respondent is asked to rank in order of preference particular combinations of product features and price levels. The analytic technique then uses these rankings to estimate the relative utility (value, preference) buyers see in each product feature, in each price level, and in each particular combination of a price level and product feature. In addition, the approach can estimate the relative impact that price and product features have upon buyers' willingness to purchase.

For the sake of discussion, let us consider an analysis of just one product feature, gain per pound of feed, and one set of price levels. The approach, however, can be used with several product features simultaneously. For example, survey respondents can be asked to rank nine price-feature combinations for a ton of feed. Respondents would be given the grid in Figure 2. They would then write the number "1" in the box of the one they would most prefer to buy, the number "2" for their second choice, down to "9" for the one they would be least willing to buy.

The first and last preferences of the majority of respondents will be predictable; respondents would prefer most the feed offering a 2.4 conversion at $120 and least desire the feed costing $140 for a 2.8 conversion. Within these extremes, though, respondents' reactions to the other yield-price combinations are important.

Calculated utilities are shown in Table 3.

The numbers in each cell reflect the relative preferences for each price-feature combination. For example, feed costing $130 but offering a 2.6 conversion is considerably more desirable than is a $120 feed with a 2.8 conversion. As would be antici-

Table 3
Utility of price-feature combinations

Price per ton	Feed per pound of gain		
	2.40	2.60	2.80
$120	122	106	90
$130	116	100	84
$140	110	94	78

pated, more utility was seen in the lower conversion, lower cost alternatives. It should also be noted that the differences among the three levels of conversion are greater than the differences among the three price levels. This indicates that for those conversion and price levels considered here, conversion had more of an impact on willingness to buy than did price. In general, a price advantage moderately increased the desirability of the product. A decrease in conversion, on the other hand, strongly enhanced respondents' willingness to buy the item.

Conclusion

Estimates of demand useful for pricing decision can be obtained from buyer surveys. Surveys can suggest likely consequences of following particular pricing strategies. This information typically can be obtained without great cost and without adversely affecting one's market position. The methods though, have important limitations. One must rely on the respondents being able to project actions in hypothetical situations which may not be taken as seriously as the real decision and this may lead to biased estimates. Further, the methods outlined do not provide for the impact of the reactions of competing firms which may be a very important factor in specific situations.

Pricing decisions must be made whether or not all information desired is available. We have illustrated several approaches to obtain estimates which may not be available by other means. Information obtained from these analyses should be used to

Figure 2
Conjoint grid

Price per ton	Feed per pound of gain		
	2.80	2.60	2.40
$120			
$130			
$140			

supplement, not to replace, judgment based on experience in the market. Agreement between survey analysis and experience, on the other hand, suggests re-examination and a very careful approach.

References

Nevin, John R., "Laboratory Experiments for Estimating Consumer Demand: A Validation Study," *Journal of Marketing Research*, August, 1974, pp. 261–268.

Huber, Joel and Bill James, *The Monetary Worth of Physical Attributes: A Dollarmetric Approach*, Paper number 579, Institute for Research in the Behavioral Economic and Management Sciences, Krannert Graduate School of Management, Purdue University, November, 1976.

Pessemier, Edgar A., "An Experimental Method of Estimating Demand," Journal of Business, October, 1960, pp. 373–383.

Johnson, Richard M., "Trade-Off Analysis of Consumer Values," *Journal of Marketing Research*, May, 1974, pp. 121–127.

Questions

1. *Ideally, what should a manager know before attempting to set a price on a product?*
2. *Identify and describe several approaches that might be used to determine what a buyer might be willing to pay for a product.*

PART FOUR

Distribution Decisions

Just look at what you can buy in grocery stores today—a lot more than food. In most grocery stores you can find beach balls, hammers, motor oil, baby toys, antifreeze, corkscrews, hosiery, and many other products. Nonfood sales have been expanding faster than any other department in grocery stores. Part of the reason is the attractive margins. The Food Marketing Institute reports that the average gross margin for nonfood items is 33 percent compared to 21 percent or less for food products. Coffee is often sold at cost and sugar usually carries a mere 2 percent markup.[1]

The limited-assortment store may be revolutionizing retailing today as the convenience store did in the 1960s. These small stores (8,000 to 9,000 square feet compared to the average 25,000 to 30,000 square feet in supermarkets) with shallow product mixes (600 items compared to 8,000 to 10,000 in supers) can break even on sales as low as $15,000 per week (compared to $80,000 to $100,000 in supermarkets). These stores emphasize off-brands and low, low prices. Their appeal is primarily to the price-conscious grocery shopper.[2]

There appears to be a growing trend toward company ownership of outlets in the franchised fast-food industry. Franchisors owned 27 percent of the fast-food outlets in 1979 compared with 13 percent in 1969. McDonald's Corp. maintains a three-to-one ratio of franchised stores to company-owned stores but has been accused recently of converting high-profit locations to company units. Wendy's has increased its percentage of company-owned units to about 22 percent of its 1,300 outlets and has reported its motivation matter-of-factly: "We get a 4% royalty on franchised stores but we can pull down 17% to 20% pretax on company-owned stores."[3]

Penney's opened a giant 1.5 million square-foot regional distribution center just north of Reno, Nevada, in 1979. Penney's considered the state's low taxes, utility

1. Cheryl Blackerby, "Look What You Can Buy at Grocery Stores Now." *Birmingham Post-Herald,* March 1, 1979, p. B-6.
2. "Limited-Assortment Stores Multiply, Sell to Cost-Aware Market Segment," *Marketing News,* December 29, 1978, pp. 1, 3.
3. Stanley Penn, "Uneasy Alliances," *Wall Street Journal,* January 2, 1979, p. 1.

charges, and transport rates, in addition to its proximity to the major California consumer markets, in selecting the site. Of importance was the prohibition in the Nevada Constitution against state taxes on inventories that are in transit or storage but will ultimately be sold outside the state.[4]

The distribution responsibilities of marketing encompass the management of both physical distribution and marketing channel activities. Performed together, these two broad sets of activities link producers with consumers as well as with industrial users in our economic system. Marketing managers of manufacturers, wholesalers, and retailers must establish an operating relationship with their suppliers and/or resellers. A marketing channel consists of interdependent individuals and institutions that carry out the activities needed to bring about the exchange of products in the marketplace. The individuals and organizations that make up marketing channels engage in activities associated with the (1) physical storage and movement of goods, (2) transfer of title to goods, (3) communication among the various individuals and organizations in the system, (4) negotiation and ordering activities associated with exchange, and (5) payment for products exchanged throughout the channel.

The management of marketing channels consists of engineering (designing) channel structures, assigning functional responsibilities to all of the channel members, and coordinating and controlling the operation of the members to ensure that individual, organizational, and total channel goals are achieved. Some managers contend that these types of channel management activities are not possible in channels consisting of a large number of independently owned companies. They argue that authority is lacking in such channels, and no firm has the prescribed right to influence the decisions and activities of the other firms. Increasingly, however, the marketplace is exhibiting examples of companies that are legally exerting their influence far beyond the boundaries of their own organizations. By exercising their power over other channel members, these channel leaders are controlling some of the activities of their suppliers and resellers and are improving the performance (especially the profitability) of their own as well as these other organizations.

The second major set of distribution-related activities consists of the physical distribution functions associated with the physical storage and movement of goods throughout marketing channels. Determining and managing the level, location, and character of materials and finished-goods inventories; determining the schedules for and selecting methods of storing and transporting these inventories; and processing orders characterize the physical distribution activities of the firm.

Several selections in Part Four illustrate contemporary developments in

4. Herbert G. Lawson, "Redistributing the Distributors," *Wall Street Journal,* August 23, 1978, p. 54.

distribution. Very little is known by most people about manufacturers' representatives, for instance. In the first piece, Robert H. Collins reviews the characteristics of these "independent" businesses and the advantages and disadvantages they offer to small manufacturers who need selling assistance. The second selection, "The Leaning Tower of Sears," details the current plight of many of the firms that supply merchandise to Sears, the retailing giant that has fallen on hard times recently. The article illustrates how *interdependent* retailers and their suppliers can be. In the third selection, Trombetta and Page discuss how recent court decisions affect franchisor-franchisee relationships and the growing need for franchisors to restate some contract terms.

A warehouse retail outlet is a large-scale retail facility that incorporates warehouse operating techniques and has an attached warehouse facility. Levitz, the May Company, and Kennedy and Cohen all experienced great growth and then disaster with this type of operation in the 1970s. Al Bates offers a stimulating review of the past and speculates about the future of the concept in "Warehouse Retailing."

The final three selections in Part Four focus on physical distribution. Donald Bowersox speculates about the logistical "mission impossible" that many managers face and calls for a change in management attitudes in "The Need for Innovative Distribution Management." Then, in "Physical Distribution and Consumer Demands," Lambert and Stock charge that enlightened consumerism will force management to recognize the importance of physical distribution management to overall marketing success. In the last selection, public warehouses are described as supermarkets for distribution services. "Customers come to [them] and pick the service they want—space rental, help in billing, key management personnel. . . ."[5]

5. Gerry O. Patno, "Public Warehousing: Supermarkets for Distribution Services," *Handling and Shipping*, March 1977, p. 60.

23

Manufacturers' Representatives for Small Firms

ROBERT H. COLLINS

Small businesses often rely on independent field sales representatives to sell their products. Reps offer some companies a better trained and more efficient sales force at a lower cost than a company sales force.

Many times, the owners of small businesses face the problem of securing adequate sales coverage for their product line on a regional or national basis. When the business is just starting out, managing the sales function is easy. In most cases, either the owner or a partner does most of the selling. As business increases, small businessmen find that more and more of their time and energy has to be devoted to managing an increasingly complex business, leaving less and less time for selling the product. At some point in time, expansion forces the manager to face the decision of adding specialized sales personnel. In most cases, this decision becomes a question whether to hire a direct sales force or to contract out the sales function to one or more manufacturers' representatives.

Very little information on the use of the representative, or the rep, has been published, although much has been written on the subject of sales man-agement.[1] Using the same management techniques with a rep that one might use with a salaried salesperson will almost always lead to failure. This article is written to help small businessmen make that critical decision, and to provide guidelines for managing the sales function.

The "Rep"

Manufacturers' representatives may be known by one of many names: manufacturer's agents, sales agents, sales representatives, or simply agents. For our purposes, these will all be referred to as "reps." The rep is defined as an agent or firm which sells the related products of several companies in an exclusive territory, and is compensated on a commission basis.[2] It is important to note that reps are not distributors, and do not take title to the goods they sell; they are sales agents.

The rep has several characteristics which small business managers must keep in mind if they are to make use of this type of middleman effectively. One is that he typically is an independent small businessman or woman. Most rep agencies are one

---

Source: *Journal of Small Business Management*, Vol. 16, No. 1 (January 1978), pp. 13–18. Copyright © 1978 by the International Council for Small Business and the West Virginia University Bureau of Business Research. The author wishes to express special thanks to Ms. Marilyn Thomas, graduate student in business, Oregon State University, for yeoman service in assisting with the research for this article.

1. See Richard R. Still, Edward W. Cundiff, and Norman A. P. Govoni, *Sales Management: Decisions, Policies, and Cases,* 3rd ed. (Englewood Cliffs, New Jersey: Prentice-Hall, 1976) or William J. Stanton and Richard H. Buskirk, *Management of the Sales Force,* 4th ed. (Homewood, Illinois: Richard D. Irwin, 1974) as examples in this area.
2. William H. Krause, *How to Hire and Motivate Manufacturer's Representatives* (New York: AMACOM, 1976), p. 3.

or two-person agencies, generally consisting of five or fewer salespeople in total. Typical reps, like other small businessmen, are in business for themselves because of an entrepreneurial drive. The vast majority of successful reps were once successful direct salesmen for large firms, who went into business for themselves to escape the restrictions of a corporate organizational structure and environment. Reps work on commission and sometimes a bonus, hence their income is totally derived from their sales volume. They are also responsible for paying all of their own selling expenses. This results in a "different breed of cat" from the typical direct salesman. The successful rep is self-disciplined, independent, and an above-average salesman.[3]

Are Reps for You?

Many firms, both large and small, have found the rep to be a solution to their sales problems. Reps successfully sell both industrial and consumer goods, to final users and to distributors, and are especially useful in selling overseas. Major food manufacturers such as General Foods, Corn Products, and Heinz successfully market through food brokers, a form of rep.[4] A more typical consumer products application is Oregon Freeze Dry Foods, located in Albany, Oregon. This firm manufactures the *Mountain House* line of freeze-dried foods sold through retail grocery and sporting goods stores. The firm also produces products for institutional, government, and industrial markets, both in the U.S. and abroad. Annual gross sales are approximately $10 million. The greater part of the firm's output is sold by a network of forty-five reps operating throughout the United States and two U.S.-based reps who sell to U.S. and overseas commissaries and PX's. Each is paid a 7 percent commission.

A typical industrial manufacturer using reps successfully is Flomatcher of Corvallis, Oregon. Flomatcher manufactures a line of patented pumps and variable speed drives, ranging from five to 5,000 horsepower, which match pumping capacity with liquid flow. This equipment is used in industrial and municipal water and wastewater treatment plants. Annual gross sales run in the $3 million range, although a single sale may exceed $500,000. This firm markets nationwide through a network of thirty reps who receive commissions on a sliding scale, starting at 15 percent. Neptune-Micrifloc, another Corvallis firm, markets filter media, settling tubes, and biological waste treatment plants both nationwide and in ten foreign countries. Annual sales approximate $15 million. This firm uses a network of 38 reps whose commissions average 8 percent.

The rep is especially appealing to the small business for a number of reasons. Let's examine some characteristic advantages and disadvantages from the perspective of small business.[5]

Advantages

Fixed Sales Cost

The most important reason for using reps is their cost to the firm. When a firm hires a direct sales force a large part of its selling costs become fixed expenses in the accounting sense. Included are such expenses as salaries, company cars, travel and entertainment, fringe benefits, social security taxes, sales office expense, and sales training. Such expenses must be paid whether the direct salesman sells anything or not and are thus independent of sales volume. On the other hand, reps are paid a commission and are responsible for all of their own expenses, so that expense of selling through this channel is almost all variable expense. This fact

3. Krause, *How to Hire and Motivate*, Chapter 2, *passim*.
4. Benson P. Shapiro, *Sales Program Management: Formulation and Implementation* (New York: McGraw-Hill, 1977), p. 252.

5. Advantages and disadvantages adapted from Krause, *How to Hire and Motivate*, pp. 7–11 and Edwin E. Bobrow, *Marketing Through Manufacturers' Agents* (New York: Sales Builders, 1976), pp. 2–4.

Figure 1

Benefits to small business owner from using manufacturers' representatives

Advantages	Benefit
Fixed sales cost	Flexibility and lower risk
Incentive	Minimum compensation and incentive program required, results in lower overhead.
Trained sales force	Reduces or eliminates sales training expenses
Immediate access to new markets	Quicker penetration of markets, resulting in improved cash flow and conservation of capital
Permanence	Little turnover, local management

becomes particularly important to small businesses when the effect of cost structure on risk is considered. In most cases, the small business owner's selection of a sales force will be limited to only a few salesmen. A greater proportion of company business rides on an individual salesman than in the case of the large multi-line manufacturer; consequently the risk is greater. Changing the cost structure of selling expense from largely fixed to largely variable has the effect of lowering the breakeven point, thereby reducing risk to a more acceptable level.

Let's look at a specific example. Sales for a specific territory are forecasted at $1 million and sales force expenses at $50,000. If the company's sales personnel are used and sales fall short of the estimate, sales force expenses remain at $50,000. However, if a rep is used, and sales fall short of the estimate, sales force expenses as a percentage of sales, will also drop. Of course, if sales are higher than estimated, the rep's commission will increase proportionately, while the expenses of having a sales staff remain constant. While the result in this instance would be a smaller increase in profits, the protection provided in the opposite case makes this a risk most small businessmen will gladly take.

Incentive

The typical rep is a person highly motivated, some say driven, by the desire for money. For many, the opportunity for limitless income is what brought them into the business in the first place. Also, they have the financial pressures of overhead and expenses to keep them motivated to produce income. This largely eliminates the need for expensive and time-consuming incentive programs, such as sales contests.

Trained Sales Force

Reps are highly skilled salespeople in their own right. While a manager may expect to train the rep in the product knowledge and application skills needed to sell a particular product, training in selling skills *per se* is not required. The reduction in training expense can be a substantial contribution to profits, since costs for training new personnel will run in the $10–12,000 range.[6]

Immediate Access to New Markets

Depending on the type of business, development of the market, and a wide variety of other factors, a newly hired sales employee may take from two to four years to become fully productive. Valuable time must be spent in learning new skills, becoming familiar with the territory, and developing the territory. The capital investment may be as high as $100,000 before any significant cash flow is created to pay back the investment. For many small businesses, an investment of this size to develop a single territory is out of the question. Or, in many cases, the limited capital available might be better spent on improved plant and equipment or increased inventory. Reps are an attractive alternative for small businesses, getting them into new markets faster and with less capital outlay. In some cases, it may be only two or three months before sales result from hiring a rep.

Permanence

A risk inherent in the direct salesman is turnover. Large corporations face the fact that they will train a

6. *Survey of Selling Costs* (New York: Sales and Marketing Management, 1977), p. 90.

number of bright young people, only to lose many of them to other firms just as they become really productive. One has only to look as far as the ex-IBM and Xerox salesmen found in a wide variety of industries. A large firm employing hundreds of salesmen can absorb the loss of a salesman to a competitor much more easily than can the small businessman. To spend two years and $50,000–100,000 to train salesmen, only to have them leave for a better job with a competitor or distributor, is a risk that the small businessman cannot afford.

On the other hand, reps have financial and other ties to their territories which make it unlikely that they will leave it. The rep's major asset is his customer base; consequently, for most reps, it would be unthinkable to leave their home territory and set up shop in some other part of the country. Further, the rep's home office and base of operations is located in the territory, providing local sales management and a valuable knowledge of the territory.

Disadvantages

Loss of Control

The use of reps is not without its disadvantages. The major disadvantage of the manufacturer's rep is a certain loss of control. Once you turn the selling function over to a rep, you can expect to lose control over much of that function. The typical rep views any administrative task not directly related to selling the product as so much excess baggage.

Learning to Share

Your rep may be representing not only your firm in the market, but several others as well. As a result, you can expect not to have his full attention at all times. For many sales managers, this can be a disconcerting experience.

Administration

Each rep tends to have a unique system of administration. Therefore, if you use five reps, you may find yourself dealing with five different sets of administrative procedures. You cannot expect reps to adapt to your way, but rather you must adapt to theirs.

Overcoming the Disadvantages

The three major disadvantages of reps are generally less critical to the small business than to the large multiline corporation. Typically, their effects on the small business can be largely offset through the use of good management techniques, particularly with respect to recruiting, selection and training, compensation and incentive programs, and control techniques.

Recruiting, Selection and Training of the Rep

After you have determined that you intend to use reps, the first problem faced is that of finding the right one for your particular line. Since the rep is an extension of your firm, selecting the right one is critical to the successful sales program. Traditional sources of reps are referrals, trade publication ads, and directories Two excellent sources are:

Manufacturers' Agents National Association (MANA)
2021 Business Center Drive
P.O. Box 16878
Irvine, CA 92713
(714) 752-5231

Manufacturers' Agent Publishing Co., Inc.
663 Fifth Avenue
New York, NY 10022
(212) 682-0326

Once you have developed a list of reps which meet your needs, it is essential to select a limited number who can provide the necessary services, and place the one that best fits the needs of each territory under contract. Contracts should spell out the territory boundaries, commission and payment schedules, and the responsibilities and obligations of each party. Sample contracts are available from MANA for a small service charge.

As noted earlier, the rep can be expected to be an above-average salesman who has a working knowledge of the customers who might buy your product. He cannot, however, be expected to know your particular product line. Therefore, most of your training effort should be spent in making certain that he knows the particular advantages of your line. This will normally include time spent at the factory in getting to know your processes and people. It is essential that reps understand why your product is superior to the competition, and that they meet the people who will support their sales efforts.

Compensation and Incentives

The compensation plan and incentive programs are the basic tools used by sales managers to motivate their sales forces. In most companies employing a sales force, these programs can become elaborate; involving bonus and quota schemes, sales contests, recognition programs, etc. The typical rep is not motivated by such incentive programs. High commissions are the best motivators for reps, so the commission structure is the basis of any sales rep incentive program. Bonuses are also appropriate. This simplifies things for the small business, cutting down on overhead expenses.

Control

Perhaps the best advice, particularly to small businessmen just starting to use reps for the first time, is to learn to live with the problem. While reps are not beyond control, traditional methods normally used with direct salespeople will usually not work with reps. Perhaps the best advice is to treat these intermediaries as the professionals they are.[7] It is best to set goals jointly with them, leaving the details of implementation to them. They are working with you, not for you.

Will You Outgrow Your Rep?

Many small businessmen look on reps as a necessary evil. Their expectation is that sales volume will eventually grow to the point where a direct sales force is more economical.[8] This is not necessarily so. Current thinking on this matter seems to dictate some other choices. Some *Fortune 500* companies are actually switching from a direct sales force to reps. The basis for this move appears to be incentive and flexibility. Larger firms have found reps to be more aggressive and more flexible than a direct sales force. The small entrepreneur manages a "tighter ship," keeping costs down. Further, these firms have found reps to be especially effective in three areas: dealing with major and national accounts, seasonal products, and time and territory management. Highly skilled reps can deal more easily with national accounts than many direct salesmen. Reps offer a needed flexibility for seasonal products, and, since they present several products on each sales call, time is used more effectively.[9] In addition to all these considerations, protective legislation has been proposed which may make it more difficult to terminate a rep without "good cause."[10]

Conclusions

Many small businessmen feel that a direct sales force is essential to the marketing of their products. However, realizing that the average sales call costs over $71[11] (a figure which is increasing at a rate of more than 10 percent per year), they sometimes explore the manufacturers' representa-

7. Bobrow, *Marketing through Agents*, p. 55.

8. See Clyde E. Harris, Jr. and Jimmy E. Hilliard, "Switchover for Bigger Profits," *Sales and Marketing Management* (November 8, 1976), pp. 47–48, for a quantitative approach to making this decision.
9. Shapiro, *Sales Program Management*, p. 253.
10. John Y. McCollister, "Getting It All Together," *Sales and Marketing Management* (May 10, 1976), p. 9.
11. *Marketing Information Newsletter* (New York: Sales and Marketing Executives International), September, 1977, p. 4.

tive as an alternative. Compared to a direct sales force, the manufacturer's rep many times is better suited to the needs of the small business. By choosing this alternative, he is able to obtain a more highly trained and efficient sales force at a lower cost and with less risk. The use of reps can increase his firm's penetration of new markets, increase its cash flow, and reduce its capital requirements. While this approach may entail some loss of control over sales operations, specialized management techniques can normally overcome most of the problems encountered.

Questions

1. What is a "manufacturer's representative"?
2. How does a rep differ from a distributor?
3. What are the major advantages and disadvantages of reps for small businesses?

24

The Leaning Tower of Sears   CAROL J. LOOMIS

In 1978, about 12,000 suppliers sold $9.5 billion in goods to Sears. Many of those suppliers have long regarded selling to Sears as an excruciating blend of pain and pleasure. Sears' problems and strategic actions in recent years have given the suppliers much more pain than pleasure.

Among the many people befuddled by Sears, Roebuck these days is Federal Judge June L. Green, who in May dismissed the company's famous equal-employment suit against the government, postulating that "the notable skill and competence of Sears" could overcome even the toughest of problems. A legal expert Judge Green may be—up-to-date on retailers she clearly is not. The fact is that Sears, once renowned above all other merchandisers for its skills and competence, has for some years seemed out of stock on those items. Losing ground to such competitors as K mart and Penney's, Sears has floundered uncertainly from one merchandising strategy to another, none rewarding. Last year, the company's pretax retail profits (i.e., not including results of such operations as Allstate Insurance) ran even lower than in the recession year of 1970, when sales were only $9 billion, half of what they were in 1978.

The last merchandising strategy renounced—it was axed in early 1978—emphasized market share and was highly "promotional." Depending heavily on markdowns off regular price, the strategy produced spectacular sales increases but abysmal profits. The newest strategy, adopted later in 1978, is an about-face, disdaining market share unless it comes with acceptable margins. The company has said that markdowns are to be minimized and that it instead proposes to attract customers by offering better everyday prices and emphasizing quality and value.

The new strategy isn't working either, at least for now. The point is driven home by Sears' results for its first fiscal quarter, ended in April. Retail profits, though up somewhat from a disastrous first quarter last year (when the old strategy was still being wound down), continued to be embarrassingly low. And sales were a shocker, even for a company with modest ambitions. Budgeted to run about even with last year's first quarter, sales actually dropped by 11 percent—in a world in which a combination of inflation and real gains was producing increases for all of Sears' major competitors. May sales looked decent only in comparison with what went before: down 6.7 percent.

The first-quarter performance, says Senior Executive Vice President Joseph T. Moran Jr., was "terrible." He and other Sears executives supply the reasons: the company "overreacted" to its previous problems, developed "a bad plan" for the quarter, and made it worse through "a conservative execution." New tactics, if not a new strategy, are now going into effect: over the balance of the year, the company expects to be "more promotional."

Clearly, the weaves and bobs at Sears are impor-

Research associate: Richard I. Kirkland Jr.
Source: Reprinted from the July 2, 1979 issue of *Fortune Magazine* (pp. 78–85) by special permission; © 1979 Time Inc.

tant to its 472,000 employees and 324,000 share-holders (who have seen their stock sink from a high of 62, hit in 1973, to under 20 recently). But the world of Sears stretches also to about 12,000 suppliers, who last year sold the company $9.5 billion in goods. Imposing as that total is, it was drastically below what the vendors had been expecting. Many of them came under great pressure as Sears abruptly changed strategies, began to reduce inventories, and sharply cut back its promotional efforts. When some of the suppliers complained to Sears, they were advised publicly and testily by Sears' new chairman, Edward R. Telling, that the company had its own business to run and did not owe them a living.

That intelligence, transmitted by Telling at an analysts' meeting, was not totally a revelation to the suppliers: many have always regarded selling to Sears as an excruciating blend of pain and pleasure. This past year has been pure pain for most of them, and there are signs today of great turbulence within the suppliers' ranks. One major footwear vendor, a company in which Sears actually has an equity interest, has recently clashed bitterly with Sears (see box, page 183). Another supplier says he intends to sort out his problems as best he can—"and to hell with the general philosophy that comes down from the Tower." Some suppliers claim Sears has permanently damaged its vendor relationships, and almost all seem to be scrambling to add other customers. One of this crowd is Vermont American, a manufacturer of power-tool accessories. In its 1978 annual report, the company soberly noting lower sales to Sears, said it felt the year, for itself, had "ended an era."

For Sears, also, one era has surely ended. The days when it was the runaway leader in both sales and profit increases cannot likely be reclaimed; there are just too many smart, aggressive competitors around. The real question today is whether the company can even get itself back on a profitable growth track. The argument for an affirmative answer is that Sears is still a powerful institution, bent on getting its act together. The company has changed itself radically in the last few years, and today is in some ways unseasoned. Besides that

new strategy, the changes include a relatively new corporate structure, a four-man Office of the Chairman in which three members are new to their jobs, and some revised operating procedures proving very sticky to deal with. It could be that Sears is just on a learning curve, odd as the description seems for such a giant.

The weakness in that argument is that there are elements of the new strategy that seem confused and episodes of sloppy management in the last couple of years that are hard to explain away. In addition, there is just the tremendous difficulty of redirecting a monster like Sears. One man who perceives that problem, though he maintains firmly that it can be handled, is Sears' new head of planning, Philip J. Purcell. His appraisal: "Sears is *so big.* Until you've been in a huge institution like Sears—or, I suppose, G.M. or the Defense Department—you cannot understand how big it is."

For outsiders to understand this monster and its problems, light must be shed first of all on an arcane bookkeeping device known as "overbilling." Recently abolished, it was an institution run by the buying side of Sears but so influential that it virtually eclipsed the sales organization's plans for advertising and promoting its products. At heart, overbilling—known as Account 599 at Sears—was simply a mechanism (used by some other retailers too) by which Chicago built up a kind of corporate fund that could be spent for various purposes or brought down to the bottom line. The bankrollers of this fund were the stores, who coughed up the money by paying artificially inflated prices for the goods they bought.

Imagine, for example, a tool that a manufacturer was willing to sell to Sears for $10—the "raw cost." The Sears buyer ordering it might then direct that the tool actually be billed to the stores at a higher price, say $11. The manufacturer would accumulate the $1 overpayments and send a check to Chicago once a month. Or, in a variation, the manufacturer would bill Chicago for $10 and Chicago would extract $11 from the stores.

The overpayments went into a "kitty" that might then be used to finance suppliers' machinery (the original purpose for which 599 was set up many years ago) or to pay for national advertising. But by far the main use came to be the financing of markdowns on goods. That is, there would come a point at which the buyer would wish to offer the stores that same tool at a price below the $10 raw cost, perhaps because the tool was to be promoted at a cut price or perhaps because it was unlovely merchandise (a "buyer's mistake"). In either case, the buyer would offer the stores the tool at, say, $8 and would pay the manufacturer the remaining $2 he was owed out of 599 funds.

In general, overbilling money seldom crossed department lines—i.e., funds generated by the tool department were used for tools, and never mind that the dollars might have been more productively employed elsewhere. This system left each department with an annual 599 profit or loss, though a profit definitely got to be the buyers' goal, and was normally attained.

But in 1977 the company was just barreling into its "market-share strategy," and management decided it would be wise to try to spend most of the 599 money available. The underlying goal was to get the store managers to build traffic by enthusiastically pushing promotional goods. Sears had already devised a new compensation system that rewarded the stores for producing sales as well as profits. To this, it added yet another new system that gave a store manager increased discretion in accepting and promoting the cut-price goods the buyers were offering. Very significantly, it took several weeks for headquarters to learn how many markdowns a manager had actually taken (i.e., how much of the 599 account he had chewed up). As that implies, the system threatened to undermine management's "controls."

Certainly sales volume was no problem in 1977; it rose by a rousing 15 percent. The promotions were broad and lengthy affairs (items were sometimes kept on sale for more than thirty days), and the discounts were deep ("half price" was not uncommon). Charles C. Wurmstedt, senior executive vice president for field operations, remembers going into a Sears hardware department in New Orleans in those "opium days" and having the impression that every item had a "sale" sign on it. Questioned,

the department manager said there were thirty-six items on sale—only to correct himself minutes later to say he'd counted and there were actually eighty-nine.

For Sears, the whole year was a comparable miscalculation—except that management, getting those 599 reports only slowly from the field, was late in understanding that fact. What the record ultimately showed, particularly for the last quarter, were disproportionate sales of marked-down merchandise, produced, it appears, by the abundance of cut-price goods in the stores and by customers who "cherry picked," bypassing regular-priced merchandise to get at bargains. In December, the busiest month, the revenues given away via promotional markdowns amounted to an incredible 15 percent of realized sales. The 599 account available to finance the year's binge was very sizable: more than $1 billion. But the portion spent exceeded budget by nearly $100 million—a wallop that helped knock 1977 pretax retailing profits (before deductions for profit sharing) down to $860 million from $990 million in 1976.

That devastating news, accompanied by reports that other retailers were showing strong profit gains, hit Ed Telling, then fifty-eight, just as he was leaving his job as head of Sears' field organization and taking over from Arthur M. Wood as chief executive (hurdling A. Dean Swift, president then and now). Telling could not have taken the news well. Though an architect of the 1977 strategy, he had long resented overbilling, having described it to others as a "cancer" obscuring the store manager's true costs and interfering with his merchandising judgment.

It will no longer do either. A task force that Telling promptly appointed decided that overbilling deserved to die, which it did in February of this year. A task-force member, Joe Moran, says it is possible someone will miss 599, but he isn't sure who. "I can't find anybody who was for it. I've said to my wife, 'I wonder how in the hell that lasted for fifteen years, when all these people were against it.' "

Having begun so inauspiciously, Telling's term in office has since not got a whole lot jollier, and that perhaps helps explain his response when he is asked how he is enjoying his job. "The pay is good"—$563,000 last year—"but it's the worst job I've ever had." He then hastens to say he's kidding, but that is probably only half true. Other Sears executives say he is aggravated by the "outside" aspects of the job—dealing with government, analysts, the press—and it's clear he feels some frustration on the inside also. "You feel more responsible all of a sudden. But at the same time, you feel not able to *act* as quickly as you once would have."

Telling's impatience with the job might raise some questions about his aptitude for it. On the other hand, he possesses some highly visible assets, including a sharp intelligence, an engaging wit, and a rather extraordinary talent for inspiring almost fervent loyalty among people who have worked closely with him. One fan is William Bass, head of the New York group of stores, who pauses dramatically while describing his own Sears career to say, "And then I had something happen to me that should happen to everybody. I went to work for Mr. Telling." He continues: "If he said walk through that wall—and I'm serious—I would walk through the wall."

One could say that is just about what Telling has asked his organization to do since taking over: walk through the wall. The request was implied in his quick decision to abandon the promotional strategy and to ask the company to settle back to lower sales—about the last prospect any store manager can cheerfully face. But Telling obviously saw no choice. A retailer, he has since told analysts, cannot accept price promotion or sales growth as ends in themselves. The ultimate measurement of success, he said, must be profit.

Most of Sears' suppliers would no doubt agree; some, in fact, applaud Telling for having set Sears on what they feel is the right course. Some also have mainly good things to say about the way Sears does business. But there is a feeling, too, among many suppliers that the past year's events have demonstrated again what they see as Sears' classic flair for making their lives difficult.

Some supplier complaints concern Sears' hardnosed approach to prices, part of the discontent growing out of the company's frequent use of cost-plus arrangements called "known cost" contracts. In such deals, the supplier typically estimates his costs in advance for an amount of goods that Sears believes it will buy. Sears approves the estimated cost per unit and allows the vendor a specified profit on all units that Sears actually buys during a contract period (which may or may not be the number that was originally estimated).

There is usually a kicker: if the vendor ends up realizing lower costs than his estimate, Sears gets half the saving; if the vendor has cost overruns, he may in some cases have latitude to recover them from Sears in the next order period; in other cases he may simply be left out in the cold. An additional kicker is that Sears drives a very tough bargain in determining which costs can be charged against its contracts; it is prepared to pay only after its auditors have swarmed through a supplier's books. "They really get into your britches," says one longtime seller to Sears.

In some instances the company asks its suppliers to procure their raw materials through Sears; for example, Sears might buy corduroy in bulk from textile mills and then resell it to companies that make clothing for it. Sears' traditional justification of this practice is that it helps to ensure quality, supply, and the rock-bottom prices available to a volume buyer. "I've never believed that," says one apparel supplier. "I've always thought they were just trying to make a markup on the goods."

His opinion is perhaps supported by the account of a man who sells an item to lots of Sears suppliers. He and Sears' Department 806, a purchasing operation, work out the price he will charge. He says that for several years (until the practice was stopped earlier this year) he was directed by 806 to overcharge the vendors by a significant amount and to remit the amount of their overpayment to Sears once a month. Said one apparel vendor recently, hearing about this arrangement: "That doesn't sound very nice." Nor does it sound too sensible, since it must be assumed that Sears itself ended up paying a price inflated by the amount the vendor was overcharged, plus profit. Asked recently about this wondrous triangular affair, Jack F. Kincannon,

Sears' chief financial officer, said he could hardly be aware of all of the arrangements between Sears and suppliers, but that Department 806 had indeed had an "overbilling budget."

Probably the primary complaint of vendors is that Sears forces them to hold and finance "over-age" inventory—i.e., goods that Sears has ordered and is currently obligated to buy, but that it does not step up and take. One apparel manufacturer estimated recently that there is at least several hundred million dollars of over-age inventory in the hands of Sears suppliers today, including a large chunk he himself is holding. He says he can get Sears to pay for it only at the risk of future business.

Asked about such contentions, Sears' Moran, the top buying executive, supplies a skein of answers. The company, he says, has a "firm, ironclad policy" that suppliers will be paid when a contract expires (which, suppliers say, would typically be a year after goods were ordered). "I don't care about the legalities; it is a moral commitment, and we have had—without equivocation, without ifs, ands, or buts—a policy." *But*, he says, a buyer's report card is his skill in ordering goods in a quantity that closely approximates demand, and the buyer would be afraid to be way off for fear of looking incompetent. "You'd have to be the most naive person in the world to assume that there aren't buyers around who violate the policy. During our slowdown, there have to have been buyers who said to sources, 'Sit on it; I'll take it out when I get around to it. Don't send me any bills. If you do, I won't buy from you again.' If we find that out, the buyer won't be working for Sears any longer."

Moran consulted a report on his desk and found that, out of $2.8 billion of goods recently on order, the "over-age" goods amounted to $127 million, which seemed to him reasonable. *But*, he said, the figures didn't mean too much because a source and a buyer could always fudge the data. "A source could cancel the contract and write another one with a new date." Why would he want to do that? "Many sources are fearful of antagonizing a buyer, in this company or any other. And so they react to what they think the buyer will be pleased with, or

what, unfortunately, the buyer tells them he wants done."

Bringing this remarkable discussion to a close, Moran said that he was preparing to issue a "white paper" restating the company's policies about contract expirations and other matters. The effort seems overdue; surely the company could enforce its policy if it really wanted to. Just as surely, Moran's elucidation makes that apparel manufacturer's estimate of "at least several hundred million dollars in over-age goods" appear within the realm of possibility.

The obvious retort to any complaints vendors have is that no one is forcing them to sell to Sears. They do it, of course, because Sears can be such a gargantuan customer. One veteran supplier faces up to his contradictory feelings: "I've always hated Sears, but they've made me a wealthy man."

The glories of dealing with the company were never more evident than in 1977, when many suppliers ran flat-out making Sears goods. Some, says Moran dryly, even began to think their volume "was due entirely to their own genius and charm." Aware that Sears was driving for market share, many suppliers announced expansions in 1977, convinced they could not go wrong.

The news of cutbacks that began to filter down from Sears in 1978's first quarter therefore seemed almost unbelievable—and was indeed not taken seriously even by many of the buyers passing the word. In the spring of 1978, some big suppliers, such as Kellwood and DeSoto, were still publicly expressing optimism about their Sears business. (For data about how wrong they were, see the table.) One company catching on particularly late was Singer, which sells Sears close to $200 million worth of portable power tools and other products annually. In July, 1978, Singer was still announcing expansions of its tool facilities (which produce only for Sears); by January, the company had taken it all back, placing the blame on "volume adjustments" in its Sears business.

The prognosis for Singer's tool business with Sears, in fact, conveys a broadly important message about Sears, having to do with all of the products it has promoted very aggressively in the past. Porta-

Sales to Sears

Company (Percent owned by Sears)	Products	1978[1] (000)	Change from 1977	Proportion of total 1978 sales	Direction of company's 1978 profits
Whirlpool	Appliances	$1,062,270	+2%	51%	↓
Kellwood (22%)	Apparel, soft goods	*$385,000[2]	−8%	74%	↓
Roper (40%)	Kitchen appliances, mowers, luggage	*$266,000[3]	−17%	67%	↓
DeSoto (31%)	Paint, furniture, detergents	$211,756[3]	−13%	68%	↓
Singer	Power tools, furniture	$197,536	+8%	8%	↓
Armstrong Rubber (10%)	Tires, tubes	*$163,000[3]	+2%	42%	↓
Murray Ohio	Mowers, bicycles	$103,000	+12%	41%	↓
Easco	Hand tools	$101,652	+2%	32%	↑
Salant	Slacks, jeans	*$74,000[3]	−30%	34%	↓
Fieldcrest Mills	Bedspreads, blankets, towels	$66,350	+5%	14%	↑
Maremont	Shocks, mufflers	$65,023	+3%	20%	↑
Chamberlain Manufacturing	Home-improvement products	*$57,000[4]	−18%	28%	↑
Kleinert's (Sears owns 20% of a subsidiary)	Footwear, apparel	*$52,000[3]	−8%	60%	↓
Simmons	Mattresses, box springs	$46,000	−18%	9%	↓
Vermont American	Power-tool accessories, hand tools	$36,000	−20%	25%	↑
Oxford Industries	Apparel	*$33,000[3]	−18%	14%	↓
Mohawk Rubber	Tires	$30,684	−9%	14%	↓
Universal-Rundle (59%)	Plumbing fixtures, bathroom vanities	*$27,000[3]	−20%	32%	↓
Garan	Apparel	*$24,000[3]	−27%	21%	↓
Kroehler Manufacturing	Furniture	$22,385	−20%	16%	↓

"It's been an interesting year." That wry comment, from a Sears apparel supplier, refers to the private recession most Sears vendors began to experience in 1978 as the company's orders fell. The suppliers shown here are among the larger ones that break out Sears data in their 10-K's; some, as noted, are companies in which Sears has a sizable interest. Most companies whose figures have been updated into 1979 (i.e., all those not on a calendar year) show particularly poor results. Their "years" don't include the first quarter of 1978, when shipments were still strong, and do include this year's first quarter, which was a bummer. With Sears now getting more aggressive, the suppliers hope for better days.

*Figures and percentages are estimated.
[1] For calendar year unless otherwise noted.
[3] For fiscal year ending April 30, 1979.
[3] For twelve months ending with the most recently reported fiscal quarter.
[4] For fiscal year ending March 31, 1979.

ble power tools, carrying the Craftsman label, are among those. A giant in that business, Sears has engaged in a kind of price war with Black & Decker, the other giant, to the detriment of profit margins for both companies. Now things have changed: Sears executives say that though promotion of power tools certainly won't cease, they won't be promoted at the old levels ever again. This retreat has very broad implications, extending obviously to Singer, and to Vermont American, which makes many of the cutting parts used in the tools. But the implications extend also to Black & Decker, which has already begun to get improved margins because some of the pressure applied by Sears has been lifted. The tool customer, meanwhile, is not getting some of the bargains he used to. In short, this single move by Sears is remaking a market.

There are broad implications also, and more bad

tidings for some vendors, in a campaign Sears has on to reduce the number of its suppliers. The company's goal is to obtain manufacturing efficiencies by consolidating production. In power mowers, for example, AMF is losing out; Murray Ohio and Roper are survivors, with each to concentrate on one kind of mower. Roper is a company owned 40 percent by Sears. Do such Sears "affiliates" get preference? An answer comes from Robert E. Wood II, head man in the buying department for home-improvement products, and grandson of General Robert Wood, who ran Sears for twenty-six roaringly successful years, beginning in 1928. Today's Wood, forty-one years old, smart, and plainly a comer at Sears, says that, all things being equal, he would feel obliged to favor Roper over nonaffiliated suppliers. But Roper, he says, has got to prove itself in any buying situation and could conceivably lose, for instance, a battle it is currently waging with Emerson Electric for Sears' chain-saw business.

The move to cut suppliers was initiated by Joe Moran, who is playing a very significant role at Sears today. Though he has held his title as head of merchandising only a few months, Moran took on the job's responsibilities more than a year ago, when his boss, James W. Button, became ill (and subsequently stepped down). Moran very soon after began to translate the company's conservative new posture into a five-year merchandising plan, the first in Sears' history. There is no secret today about what the plan says, because a copy of a long summary was somehow obtained by the weekly, *Chicago Business*, which broadcast many of its details to a fascinated world last December. In addition, *Fortune* has seen large parts of the summary.

Moran's plan acknowledged that Sears' past policies had done nothing to enhance its reputation for delivery of value, and had actually eroded its reputation for low everyday prices. These problems were to be attacked by a new emphasis on quality, by a determination to be competitive at the lower end of a product line, and by renewed attention above the bottom prices to the "Good-Better-Best" standards that Sears made famous.

The plan also identified Sears' product mix of 70 percent durable goods and 30 percent apparel as just about right, and suggested the company's sales should grow roughly as fast as the rate of inflation in general-merchandise goods plus real growth in G.N.P. The plan went on to articulate what Sears is and what it is not. "Sears is a family store for middle-class, home-owning America. We are the premier distributor of durable goods [and] the premier distributor of nondurable goods that have their acceptance in function rather than fashion. We are not a fashion store . . . We are not a discounter, not an avant-garde department store."

Moran's plan contains seeming ambiguities. Though it appears to downplay fashion, some of the group merchandising plans appended make a call for more emphasis on fashion: the section for men's apparel, for example, says, "Our mission . . . is to invest/grow in the highly profitable fashion elements." Moran suggests that this contradiction arises from "a certain carelessness with words" that characterizes the plan, which he points out was intended only for internal use. Actually, he says, Sears is making a stronger commitment than ever before to "timely" styles and fashions. Studying all this, an outsider, or even an insider, might be pardoned if he did not understand exactly what Sears' approach to fashion is.

Other strategical confusions, some relating to that old villain, overbilling, were apparent in the first-quarter results this year. The quarter was planned last fall, at a time when management was struggling (very successfully) to keep expenses in line with declining sales. The plan called for national advertising expenditures to run $25 million for the first quarter, against $30 million spent last year. In deciding the level of markdowns to be pursued in the field, management held the line. Markdowns had run to 8.9 percent of sales in 1978; they were budgeted to come in between 8.7 percent and 9 percent in 1979's first quarter.

A lot of things then proceeded to go wrong with these plans. One kind of national advertising at Sears pushes its "image." As Joe Moran began to look at ads planned for the first quarter, he became convinced that many did not do much to promote the idea of quality and value that Sears wanted to get across. So Moran sent the company's ad agencies back to the drawing board.

Another kind of national advertising today pro-

A Big Problem in the Shoe Department

A few weeks ago, Kleinert's, a Pennsylvania footwear and apparel company, filed suit against Sears, its biggest customer by far. The charges included discriminatory pricing practices, breach of contract, and failure to purchase and give shipping instructions for finished goods. Sears, not to be outdone, sued also, charging Kleinert's with breaching its contracts by refusing to ship goods Sears ordered.

These salvos are particularly remarkable because the two companies have been tightly linked. Jack Brier, fifty-four, chairman of Kleinert's, and some associates got control of the company in 1969 after Sears' top footwear buyer, William H. Grant, urged Brier to get in the shoe business. At the time, Kleinert's was an apparel company doing $20 million in sales.

With Grant's constant encouragement, Brier bought a string of shoe companies, folding them into a subsidiary called Brierwood, of which Sears bought 20 percent. Brierwood became Sears' biggest U.S. footwear supplier—a "basic" source operating under a special contractual arrangement. By 1978, Kleinert's footwear sales, 80 percent of them to Sears, were $68 million. Apparel sales, some to Sears, were an additional $24 million.

There had been a run-in between Brier and Sears, however, in the early 1970's, when on the promise of business from a Sears buyer—not Grant—Kleinert's had bought a small Sears apparel supplier called Danoca. There was a double whammy after that. First, Sears did not deliver the business, a blow that sent Kleinert's reeling into heavy losses. Second, Kleinert's discovered through an audit that the Sears buyer had been accepting favors from Danoca. Brier took his grievances to Sears, which shored Kleinert's up financially. The buyer involved "resigned."

The footwear business kept going pretty well—until early 1978, when Brier got the bad news that Sears' orders would be well below projections. Stuck with carrying charges on some $20 million of Sears inventory and with a big overhead, Brier was in trouble. Sympathetic, Grant agreed to a plan through which Sears would pay Kleinert's a relatively small amount—say $1.50 per pair of shoes—for every pair cut from Sears' original projection.

The commitment was a departure; similar deals with "basic" sources everywhere would have saddled Sears with heavy costs. But Grant says he had made many important agreements before—starting and canceling contracts, raising and lowering profits, absorbing start-up costs—and nobody at Sears had balked. Claiming this time to have told people up the line at Sears about "the sense of the agreement," Grant says he again got no static.

But no agreement materialized. Finally, this March, after two quarters of losses, Brier wrote Sears Chairman Ed Telling a long letter including an explanation of Grant's commitment. The letter was bucked to Joe Moran, head of buying who says it was the first that Grant's superiors had heard of the promise. (The complaint filed by Kleinert's disagrees; it also claims that two Sears employees who sit on Brierwood's board were fully briefed.)

There has since been a meeting at which Moran told Brier that Sears would both meet Grant's commitment and pick up the Sears inventory, now grown to $32 million. But Moran also told Brier he was through as a "basic" source—that as of October, 1980, Brierwood would have to compete for business just like any other company. A few days later, Grant, who is fifty-five and had worked for Sears thirty-one years, got a telephone call from his boss asking him to take early retirement, which he has done.

As of early June, Kleinert's and Sears seemed to be involved in a test of wills. Kleinert's was refusing to ship shoes that Sears says it needs for the fall season; Sears was withholding the money that Moran had promised. About the only thing certain is that a partnership has been wrecked.

motes "Sears Super Values." In the old overbilling days, decisions about what to promote were quite easily made: the tool department, say, had the money, so tools got promoted. Last fall, with overbilling due to expire in February, the decisions looked harder; the buying side of Sears and the selling side couldn't even agree for some time what the Super Value items should be. There was a delay in preparing ads. The upshot is that only $10 million was spent on all kinds of national advertising in the first quarter, far below the $25 million planned.

Talk to about any manager in the field and he will tell you the shortage of national ads hurt business. But it is a fact that the field didn't stick to its first-quarter plans either. One reason it did not was that it was dealing with a whole new set of numbers. The stores' cost of merchandise fell as of February 1, because the cost no longer included overbilling. The stores' charges from headquarters, however, rose, since these were no longer being *absorbed* by overbilling. On balance, total costs did not change. Still the numbers looked different, and the field appears to have operated very conservatively while getting used to them. Besides, that was what Chicago wanted—a conservative stance, right? The field delivered, and then some; for the quarter, the markdowns-to-sales ratio fell almost to 6 percent, compared with the minimum of 8.7 percent planned. Says Moran: "It is a myth of management that orders, once given, are followed. It never happens that way."

Telling suspects Sears' failure to get where it planned in the quarter has to do with "the management of size." Shaking his head, he says: "It's a very difficult problem, and overreaction seems a part of it. I have no other answer."

The company is now busy reacting again, aided by the federal government, which in April weighed in with a helpful thought for sales improvement. The thought was advanced by the Council on Wage and Price Stability, which charged that Sears had raised prices last fall beyond the guideline limits; COWPS was reinforced by President Carter, who, in a fourteen-minute phone call to a Sears executive, demanded reductions. Catalogue sales were

then in a particular slump, and the government's demands, says one Sears executive, were perhaps a "happy coincidence." The company announced a 5 percent cut in all catalogue prices—and sat back to reap the publicity (and a jump in catalogue business also).

Sears now thinks of itself as "fine-tuning," trying to strike a prosperous balance between the excessive promotion of 1977 and the excessive caution of 1979. National ads for the company have begun to pop up, after months in which they all but disappeared from view; Sears says that by year-end it intends to spend all of the $115 million originally budgeted for national advertising. There is a lot of talk at Sears, also, about other promotional targets that, *this time,* are going to be met. Said one field executive recently, "We are just not going to accept sales decreases."

Whether that promise can be kept is uncertain. One former Sears executive expounded recently on the difficulties of getting customers back once you have lost them. "Your competitors are happy to help you when you're trying to cut sales; believe me, you don't get any help when you start trying to get them up." A supplier adds a related thought, having to do with the problems of "orchestrating" a plan that aims for very competitive prices and yet better margins. "In our product, Sears' prices are way up this year, and it looks to us as if competitors are just taking business away from them all over the place. I think it's very scary."

That is probably an apt description for a lot of things that have been happening at Sears—"very scary." The company obviously needs to recover its old skill and competence, and do it in short order. Whether it can is a matter of considerable doubt.

Questions

1. *Discuss the pros and cons of Sears' overbilling plan—Account 599.*
2. *Sears maintains equity interest (part ownership) in many of its suppliers. Discuss the advantages and disadvantages of these arrangements from the perspective of Sears. What about the suppliers' perspective?*

25

Franchisor Control vs. Franchisee Independence

WILLIAM L. TROMBETTA

ALBERT L. PAGE

Tying agreements, territorial restrictions, resale price control, and exclusive territory agreements often find their way into franchise contracts. The legality of these contracts is being questioned, and franchisors are being advised to rewrite their contracts.

The courts have recently delivered major pronouncements that are likely to have a significant effect on the degree of channel control that can be exercised by a franchisor on his franchisees. If the courts' recent rulings are any indication of future policy, franchise systems' attempts at controlling their franchisees, as well as their products/trademarks and distribution, are likely to be more and more restricted.

In recent years franchising has accounted for a significant sales volume. Franchise operations in the United States accounted for over $131 billion in annual sales in 1971, representing 35% of retail sales and 13% of GNP; at least 400,000 businessmen are franchisees.[1]

The need for businessmen to be more aware of possible infringements of the law as a result of their day-to-day operational activities is becoming more apparent.[2] Both franchisors and franchisees be-

come vulnerable to unexpected consequences resulting from decisions fraught with legal ramifications. Therefore, some insight into the legal interface with business should prove beneficial to franchise management and at the same time minimize potential confrontation with the courts.

The focus in this article is on the effect recent court decisions could have on a franchise agreement that defines the ability of franchise management to control the marketing and distribution of its product or service. The agreement analyzed here is modeled after an actual franchise agreement at issue in a case now pending at the trial court level and is presented as the "before" contract in Exhibit 1(A). The "after" contract, which has been rewritten where necessary to reflect the new realities of the contemporary franchisor/franchisee relationship as they have been shaped over recent years, is given in Exhibit 1(B).

The hypothetical franchisor in this article markets cosmetics, skin care and accessory items, toiletries, and also provides promotional and sales aid materials. On some of these materials it uses its registered trademark.

The products of the company are distributed throughout the United States by means of a four-level distribution system, at the top of which are franchisees called "field organizers." Field organizers purchase directly and exclusively from the company, which has developed an effective system for marketing its products. This system includes the sale in interstate commerce of certain exclusive territorial franchises to field organizers. The franchises range in price upward from $10,000. The sale

Source: Atlantic Economic Review, March–April 1978, pp. 28–34. The authors do not intend to set forth a franchise contract that might be accepted as legal. The exhibits and hypothetical contract construction given in this article are simply means to illustrate the analysis in terms of a legal environment that affects management's decision making within the constraints of the law.

Exhibit 1
XYZ Company franchise agreement, before and after

(A)
Before

1. Each field organizer becomes the head of his own organization and is an independent contractor.
2. All skin care products and beauty aids must be purchased directly from the company or a company-approved source of supply.
3. A field organizer agrees to carry sufficient inventory of sales aids, samples, prizes, and promotional items for his organization.
4. Each field organizer is required to purchase the current minimum requirement of sales aids, hostess gifts, and samples from the company or a company-approved source of supply.
5. For a field organizer to maintain his franchise, he must purchase skin care products and beauty aids having a minimum suggested retail price of $1,000 in volume each month.
6. A field organizer must obtain company approval prior to sponsoring any franchisee in the three levels below him and shall use forms of agreement furnished by the company for signing franchisees at the three levels below him in the chain of distribution.
7. A field organizer must maintain a product inventory and must supply the people below him in the chain of distribution with all products of the company, as needed.
8. Further requirements of field organizer to maintain his franchise shall be: (a) the field organizer shall handle no product or items except those manufactured, sold, or distributed by the company; (b) the company may, at its option, supply the affected zone organizer (2nd from the top of the distribution chain), division organizer (3rd from the top of the distribution chain), or area organizer (lowest level in the distribution chain) with the necessary products or items, or assign said zone, division, or area organizer to any other field organizer who will supply the zone, division, or area organizer with the necessary products or items.
9. A sound retail price policy is the basis of every good progressive business. In our distribution system, every area organizer can be assured that he or she will not be confronted with varying prices in the field. This assurance is made because of our definite policy on pricing. Regardless of where or to whom a retail or wholesale sale is made, it must be made in conformance with our policy. Under no circumstances can any deviation from this policy be made. Any infraction of this rule will constitute grounds for termination of any agreement with any franchisee.
10. Our company products cannot be sold to or in retail stores.
11. The field organizer agrees that, in addition to selling his zone organizer company products at 60% discount off of suggested retail price, the zone organizer shall be entitled to an additional discount for each calendar month that the zone organizer's monthly volume or purchases from the field organizer reach the following levels: the discounts apply to total volume of sales only in the skin care products and beauty aids, and require that, if this volume reaches between $2,000 and $3,000, the company will provide a discount of 1% which the field organizer must match. Similarly, if sales by the zone organizer in retail value exceed the last stated level, the company and the field organizer will provide matching discounts of 2%—yielding a total additional discount to the zone organizer of 4%.
12. While this agreement is in effect the franchisees will conduct the business of distribution of the company's products in the designated territory only.

(B)
After

1. Each field organizer becomes the head of his own organization and is an independent contractor.
2. The franchisee has a six-month option to purchase supplies, equipment, and promotional material from a source other than the company itself or company-approved sources of supply. In any event, the company reserves the right to evaluate and maintain that said material is of such standard and quality as not to bring discredit on the company, its merchandise, and its distributor; and merchandise purchased for resale from noncompany stores shall be merchantable and of commercially acceptable quality.
3. The company will work in continuous harmony with each of its distributors and pledges complete cooperation with these distributors whose actions are consistent with company policies. The company will not terminate a distributor without careful review by its Distributor Performance Appraisal Committee, of which the company president is chairman.
4. Effective management of inventory is an important part of the franchisee's managerial responsibilities. The company suggests that the franchisee maintain a product inventory in order to supply the people below him in the chain of distribution with merchandise as needed. Therefore, he should carry a sufficient level of inventory for his organization of sales aids, samples, prizes, and promotion items as well as skin care products and beauty aids. Failure to manage his inventory function adequately can be considered sufficient reason to seek termination of the distributor before the Distributor Performance Appraisal Committee.
5. All organizers at any level of distribution covenant and agree to use every reasonable means to encourage the use of company products throughout the chain of distribution and at home parties. Any distribution or sale of noncompany products shall not be undertaken without the prior written consent of the company, which consent the company agrees not to unreasonably withhold. The company hereby states that it relies solely on its requirement that its distributors recommend, promote, and encourage the purchase and sale of company products.

Exhibit 1(B) *(cont.)*

6. A field organizer must obtain company approval prior to sponsoring any franchisee in the three levels below him and shall use forms of agreement furnished by the company for signing franchisees at the three levels below him in the chain of distribution.
7. Under no circumstances can any deviation from company suggested prices and discount policy be tolerated. Any infraction of this stipulation will constitute grounds for *immediate* and automatic termination of any agreement with any franchisee.
8. In the company's judgment, we recommend that company products not be sold to and through retail stores. To prevent the cheapening of our products and the alienation of our distributors, we suggest that distributors consider the implications of identifying company products with their sale through retail outlets and how this sale could affect the distributor's self-interest. The company hopes that after such consideration it becomes clear that company products will be more successfully distributed through sole reliance on an established home party method.
9. Company distributors are expected to do business on the basis of service rather than price. The profit margins and discount policy suggested by the company are essential so that distributors can provide such important services as an ample arrangement and supply of company products proudly displayed at the home party, adequate safety stocks for exceptional demand, and an informed and enthusiastic distributor able to provide the customer with sound guidance and information, and at the same time enable the distributor to achieve a generous profit margin for such a high-quality service orientation.
10. While this agreement is in effect, the distributors shall conduct the business of distribution of the company's products in their primary geographic areas of responsibility. Any distributor infringing upon another distributor's area of primary responsibility shall be subject to a profit pass-over of 7% to the injured distributor, whereby the infringing distributor shall pay 7% of the gross receipts on a sale outside his area of primary responsibility to the distributor in whose area the sale is made. Said designated pass-over fee shall fairly compensate the distributor in whose area the merchandise is sold for his loss of advertising expenditures, sales efforts, and goodwill.

of franchises to field organizers has accounted for a substantial portion of the revenue of the firm.

The marketing plan of the company is to sell its products in private homes pursuant to the "party plan," a method somewhat widely used in the distribution of consumer products. Prospective customers who permit their homes to be used for these parties act as hostesses, and it is hoped that the hostesses and the guests invited by the hostesses will purchase various quantities of the company's products. The majority of the company's shipments, in quantity and in dollar volume, is done in interstate commerce. Each of the company's franchisees signs a standard franchise contract which contains, among others, those provisions shown as "before" in Exhibit 1(A).

At various meetings with the company management and field organizers present, the president made statements, in which other members of management concurred, that if any field organizer did not like the products that he was purchasing from the company or company-approved supply sources, he did not have to deal with the company at all. On the other hand, however, no individual franchisee has ever been specifically terminated or directly threatened with termination of his franchise because of purchases from nonapproved suppliers. Still, not a single franchisee has purchased more than $10 worth of supplies from a competing supplier in the last two years. And, for the most part, the small amount of purchases which did deviate were purchases of products such as promotional items and prizes to hostesses that are not manufactured directly by the company but are purchased by it and then sold, purportedly at a special discount price, to the franchisees.

Several franchisees have stated that, had they had the opportunity, they would have purchased some products, including cosmetic items, beauty aids, prizes and promotional items, from other sources that sell them for less than the company does, thereby increasing the franchisees' profits. The reason they did not do so, allegedly, was that they were afraid of losing their franchises. Other franchisees have been questioning other aspects of the franchise operation.

As for the value of the franchise, the following is a typical statement from a field organizer:

"I did not become disenchanted with the company's products until I realized that, as to the products other than the skin care and beauty aids (cosmetic items), I was getting ripped off by the company. I am talking about products such as eyeliner pencils, powder puffs, mirrors, and so forth, and the prizes and promotional items that do not have the company trademark. When I priced these items, I found that I could buy them cheaper at a discount store than I could buy them from my own company!"

Furthermore, one of the field organizers made an effort to purchase eyebrow pencils directly from the manufacturer from whom the company purchases them. He called the manufacturer and received a price quotation over the phone. He was asked to forward a certified check. But on receiving the check, the manufacturer returned it with a note explaining that he could not sell to the field organizer because he, like other manufacturers of products sold to the company, was prohibited from selling such products directly to the company's franchisees.

Tie-In Issues

From the facts given, it seems that some of the company franchisees are upset about the subtle pressure exerted on them when they consider the possibility of purchasing supplies and equipment from suppliers other than the organization or a company-approved supplier. They feel that the company possibly is making profits at their expense through the sale to them of supplies and equipment at higher prices than are available from other suppliers. A tying arrangement is an agreement by a party to sell a given product but only on the condition that the buyer also purchase a different (or tied) product, or at least agree that he will not purchase that product from any other supplier.[3] From a legal viewpoint, tie-in arrangements generally have been frowned upon because they deny competitors free access to the market for the tied product, not because the party imposing the tying requirements has a better product or a lower price but because of his power of leverage in another market. At the same time, buyers are forced to forgo their free choice among competing products.[4]

Clauses 2 and 4 in Exhibit 1(A) imply a tying arrangement by requiring the franchisee to purchase certain inventory, supplies, and promotional aids

directly from the franchisor or an approved supplier. This kind of arrangement has been looked upon unfavorably in previous litigation. The facts here suggest that the tying product would seem to be the franchise trademark and the entire bundle of benefits inherent in the franchise package. However, to gain access to this desirable package, the franchisee must purchase the tied product, namely, various supplies and inventory available from either the company or approved suppliers.

There may be a few situations that justify a tie-in arrangement, such as breaking into a new business or industry and attempting to preserve the market identity or quality of the franchisor's trademark. However, if there is a reasonable opportunity to purchase specified ingredients and inventory (such as display, order forms, and supply kits as we have here) in comparable quality or identity from nonfranchisor or nonfranchisor-approved sources, the restriction on the franchisee's purchasing discretion will be hard to justify.

The recent *Dunkin' Donuts* case offers some insights into possible actions of the franchisor to overcome, to some extent, the control restraint problems reflected in clauses 2 and 4 in Exhibit 1(A).[5] In clauses 2 and 4 of the new agreement, Exhibit 1(B), the franchisor now offers to meet the franchisee halfway. The franchisor can still reserve the right to stress standards of quality in the inventory and supplies his distributors sell and display, and the franchisee is given a reasonable amount of time, according to *Dunkin' Donuts* rationale, to shop around on his own to get a better deal on his purchase. Furthermore, clause 4 in Exhibit 1(B) expressly commits franchise management to work in good faith in reviewing any purchasing practices by the franchisee inconsistent or possibly harmful to the franchise system before taking any drastic action against the franchisee.

In a recent federal appellate decision, the *Dunkin' Donuts* case was reversed.[6] However, the reversal took place in only one circuit; and, as the district court pointed out in its opinion, there still is a great amount of disagreement among the various circuits with respect to the question of the degree of coercion that exists inherently, if at all, in the franchisor-franchisee relationship. The issues and im-plications brought out in *Dunkin' Donuts* certainly are not moot, and the chances are good that the case will reach the Supreme Court to resolve, eventually, the disagreement at the lower court levels. Hence, franchise management would be wise to operate on the assumption that the decision is not final on the issue of encouraging franchisees to purchase raw materials, promotional aids and displays, inven-tory, and so on from the franchisor or franchisor-approved sources.

At present, and certainly in the foreseeable fu-ture, tying arrangements represent an Achilles heel to the franchisor. For all practical purposes, tie-ins should be considered violations per se unless the franchisor is breaking into a new industry or at-tempting to maintain quality control or market identity that cannot be achieved through less re-strictive practices.

It would seem to be a wise policy for manage-ment to avoid obtaining revenue on any commis-sion or rebate scheme. If the franchise system requires a large input in terms of business supplies, equipment, and inventory, it may be dangerous to have any one supplier predominate because this might be construed as prima facie evidence of an illegal tie-in with an adverse impact on competi-tion. The *Dunkin' Donuts* case should make a fran-chisor wary of offering to supply such materials or of demanding approval of his franchisees' source of supply even under the most proper conditions.

Price Control

The channel control pricing issue appearing in clause 9 of Exhibit 1(A) is more complex than what might be characterized as the stereotyped concept of "price fixing in a smoke-filled room." The provi-sion announces in advance that the franchisor will not do business with anyone who does not adhere to the stipulated pricing policy. Is this illegal price fixing? Can a franchisor lawfully operate under such a pricing policy today?

A number of cases shed some light on this nebu-lous area. In *Klein v. American Luggage Works, Inc.*, a luggage manufacturing firm posted suggested re-tail prices in its catalogs.[7] Salesmen were told to in-struct retailers that strict adherence to the sug-gested prices was required. Complaints were sent to the manufacturer that an unidentified retailer was discounting the merchandise. A few months later in a field survey the manufacturer's salesmen were visiting retail outlets and found the discounter to be Klein. It was made clear to the store that it would be dropped as an outlet for the manufacturer's goods unless it adhered to the manufacturer's pric-ing schedule. The lower court decided in favor of Klein, reasoning that the manufacturer had gone beyond a simple announcement of its policy to re-fuse to deal with price cutters. The court of appeals reversed, reaffirming the Colgate Doctrine,[8] stating it found no conspiracy, only a simple announce-ment of the circumstances uner which the manufac-turer would deal with prospective middlemen. (The Colgate Doctrine holds that where there is no agreement by the parties, a manufacturer may law-fully attempt to maintain prices by announcing his policy beforehand and then simply refusing to sell to those who do not adhere to it.)

A case illustrating the difficulty a franchisor can get into by not adhering strictly to the Colgate Doc-trine is the *Coors* decision.[9] Price-cutting retailers were on notice that they would be refused sales if they did not adhere to the prices suggested by Coors. The following examples illustrate how Coors exceeded the Colgate Doctrine and suggest what our hypothetical franchisor might avoid doing in order to stay within the ever-narrowing confines of the Colgate Doctrine:

An area representative threatened to refuse sales to an offending retailer unless he adhered to the prices suggested by Coors.

Coors used its distributors to secure retailers' ad-herence to suggested minimum prices.

An area representative reported that a distributor planned to take appropriate action against a re-tailer who refused to sell at suggested prices.

A distributor stated that beer was not delivered to a retailer who cut prices.

A retailer testified of warnings and of being cut off, with deliveries being resumed after he sold the business.

Assuming that our franchisor seeks to control price throughout the distribution channel, it is clear that he cannot act in such a manner that manifests conspiracy, agreements, warnings, or post-termination dealings with offending distributors.

However, the *Coors* decision goes much further. The Federal Trade Commission (FTC) ordered that Coors refrain from providing any information or suggestions concerning what Coors believes to be an appropriate or proper markup or profit for Coors beer or a markup or profit below which the distributors are advised not to sell Coors beer. In addition, Coors was ordered to cease and desist from refusing to sell beer to any Coors distributor or from terminating or threatening to terminate any Coors distributor because the distributor had in the past or might in the future sell Coors beer at prices, markups, or profits different from those approved or recommended by Coors.

This ruling appears to pose problems for those implementing the discount scheme appearing in clause 11 of Exhibit 1(A). If the franchise company were to reconsider its desire to set prices and adopt what the authors perceive to be a more enlightened approach to pricing in general and discount and markup policy in particular, the franchisor could achieve some degree of pricing leverage by phrasing his contract language in a positive manner as appears in clause 9, Exhibit 1(B). This wording is patterned after that of the *Scott* decision [10] and achieves pricing policy objectives without the dubious value of relying on the ever-fading powers of the Colgate Doctrine. In *Scott*, the court even characterized the dealers' exercise of individual free choice in opting for Scott's suggested prices as "acting in their own self-interest." Hence, the court could find no coercion, conspiracy, threats, or warnings here. In the contract, Scott never even threatened to terminate a distributor for failure to adhere to its pricing policy. The net effect of Scott's loose approach to getting its way on the pricing issue was a completely unilateral, independent decision on

the part of Scott's distributors to price as Scott convincingly *reasoned* in its pitch to dealers.

If the franchisor persists on a hard line approach to pricing, the authors offer the language in clause 7, Exhibit 1(B). This language, omitting some of the "before" terminology, would seem to be sufficient to remain within the shelter of the Colgate Doctrine as a simple, unilateral announcement of the franchisor's pricing policy.

Franchisors' pricing policy discretion thus would appear to be restricted. They will want to think seriously about any kind of pricing agreements between themselves and their franchisees, even on discount policies. To remain within the safety of *Colgate*, the franchisor must do no more than announce his price policy. If a franchisee deviates from said policy, an example can be made of him, but that is the end of it. The franchisor must not approach or discuss the pricing problem with the franchisee, especially after the franchisee's termination but also before the franchisee's refusal to sell at the stated price, lest the discussion or possible subsequent adherence to the price policy by the franchisee be construed as an agreement or contract removing the franchisor from behind the shield of *Colgate*. The franchisor should avoid working with disgruntled third parties in order to monitor suggested prices lest the effort be construed as a conspiracy to fix prices. Above all, any pricing investigation on the part of the franchisor must be completely unilateral and independent. After the initial statement of price policy, the franchisor would be wise to avoid any subsequent promotional literature to his franchisees that emphasizes the desirability of pricing at the level suggested by the franchisor. Following the *Coors* holding, suggested resale prices are likely to be sanctioned if they are not accompanied by price checking by the franchisor or any discussion between the franchisor's representatives and franchisees as to the merits of adhering to the franchisor's pricing policy.

A viable alternative to the Colgate Doctrine might be found in the *Scott* rationale, which places the burden of adhering to a designated or suggested pricing policy on the franchisee in terms of his acting in his own economic self-interest as a result of his unilateral, independent pricing decision, with no interference whatsoever from the franchisor.

Franchise management also might consider a number of other options in its attempt to exercise some control over pricing in its relationship with franchisees: (1) premarking the price on the product or the package,[11] (2) advertising the price of the product,[12] and (3) suggesting price.[13]

Channel Control

The four-level distribution system employed by the company and manifested in clause 8 of Exhibit 1(A) is remarkably similar to the distribution scheme used by *Schwinn*.[14] The issues surrounding the nature and complexity of the distribution system suggest a possible effect on competition and raise questions as to its necessity to accomplish the company's objectives.

The *Schwinn* decision emphasized the importance of ascertaining who has title to the merchandise as it passes through a channel of distribution. In our hypothetical situation, holder of title is not specified. If the company ships the cosmetics and beauty aids directly to the home hostesses to distribute to their party guests, it would seem that the franchisees are merely brokers who take orders and do not assume title. If this is the case, because of the consignment nature of the distribution process, the franchisor could impose territorial and customer restrictions (price fixing still would be unlawful), according to the *Schwinn* rationale. On the other hand, if the franchisor transfers title or sells the goods to field organizers, who in turn transfer title, and so forth, the franchisor could not impose any channel control restrictions on his distributors. Therefore, *Schwinn* appeared to imply that if the franchisor wishes to maximize his ability to control the franchisee, consignment is the logical vehicle to employ.

In *Continental TV v. GTE Sylvania*, the Supreme Court reasoned that location restrictions have less potential for competitive harm than the restrictions

approved in *Schwinn*.[15] Therefore, in overruling *Schwinn*, the Supreme Court held that vertical restrictions will be judged under a rule of reason standard rather than the per se rule.

Restricted Distribution

In section 8(a) of its franchise agreement, the company presented here requires its franchisees to handle no products or items except those manufactured, sold, or distributed by it. This restricted distribution arrangement will lead to some complications, illustrated in the following questions: (1) Is it possible to sell at the same home party the products of two competing purveyors of cosmetics and beauty aids? (2) Indeed, can a home party be called a "(company trademark) Party" if the products sold at the party include items either not manufactured by the company or not bearing its trademark or, in the case of prizes and promotional items, not manufactured specifically for it?

A number of court decisions suggest that the company may be violating Section 3 of the Clayton Act in its attempt to restrict its franchisees from handling competitive products. One of the reasons why the *Schwinn* court looked approvingly at Schwinn's distribution process was the fact that its franchised retailers were free to handle other brands even though they were obliged to promote Schwinn bikes and to give them at least equal prominence with competing brands.

Recent decisions seem to support the notion that it is risky for a franchisor to restrict the franchisee's discretion in selling competitive merchandise. In *American Motor Inns, Inc. v. Holiday Inns, Inc.*,[16] American Motor Inns contended that the rule against Holiday Inn franchisees having an interest in a non-Holiday Inn hotel or motel substantially lessened competition. Holiday Inns countered that without this clause the franchisee could suggest other lodging to customers. The court rejected this argument, pointing out that other motels are not as restrictive and apparently are still able to accomplish their objective. At best, Holiday Inns could only request that its franchisees do their best to promote other Holiday Inns. In *Coors,* the FTC ordered that Coors cease and desist refusing to sell and threatening to terminate and refusing to sell to distributors who dispensed a competitive brand of beer.

Thus the more recent decisions indicate that the franchisor should take a cautious approach to the issue of stipulating what products a franchisee may or may not handle. At present, it appears that the best type of condition the franchisor can hope to impose on the franchisee is that he devote at least an equal effort in displaying and promoting the franchisor's products as those of another. Where the franchisee's activities result in a clearly adverse interest to the franchisor, the latter's case will be much stronger in refusing to deal with one who can be called, literally, an in-house competitor. Therefore, our hypothetical company, in rewriting its franchise agreement, has modified its stance on restricted distribution. Now, the requirement is only that the franchisee devote at least fair and equal effort to the company's products. In this regard, the franchisor would do well to keep abreast of the course of performance and trade practices in his field. The *American Motor Inns* decision shows the courts' willingness to study how similar enterprises can have satisfactory promotion of their merchandise without having to resort to restricting the variety of the franchisee's brand assortment. Clause 8 is rewritten in Exhibit 1(B) to reflect the recent posture of the courts toward limiting the franchisor's control to merely encouraging his franchisee to give his primary efforts to the franchisor's products.

Exclusive Dealing

Exclusive dealing is a vertical restraint wherein the buyer purchases his requirements exclusively from a single supplier or supplier-approved source, as indicated in clause 2, Exhibit 1(A). Exclusive dealing is a franchising control area that has not been drastically affected by recent court rulings.

There are two approaches to the issue of whether an exclusive dealing arrangement constitutes an antitrust violation. The first may be categorized as the substantial dollar-volume approach. It dates from the classic *Standard Oil of California* case,[17] in which the Supreme Court held that when a seller's exclusive dealing arrangement comprises a substantial dollar amount of volume, the required harmful effect on competition is established. In the *Tampa Electric* decision [18] the court devised a second approach, one which emphasized the percentage of market share foreclosed. The dollar amount could be substantial in itself and yet the market share could be minuscule.

The franchisor may face an additional threat in regard to exclusive dealing. Recall the company president's statement that if any field organizer does not like the products he has purchased from the company, he does not have to do business with the company at all. And recall further that the record shows that no single individual franchisee was ever specifically terminated or directly threatened with termination of his franchise because of his purchases, or requests for opportunity to make purchases, from other suppliers. The *Texaco* rationale, given as follows, would appear to be resilient enough to cause problems for the franchisor by virtue of the exclusive dealing implied in the president's statement. Once again the franchisee's inferior bargaining position vis-a-vis the franchisor is the pivotal factor:

"While the evidence in the present case fails to establish . . . overt coercive acts . . . we think it clear nonetheless that Texaco's dominant economic power was used in a manner which tended to foreclose competition in the marketing of TBA [tires, batteries, and accessories]. . . . A service station dealer whose very livelihood depends upon the continuing good favor of a major oil company is constantly aware of the oil company's desire that he stock and sell the recommended brand of TBA. . . . With the dealer's supply of gasoline, his lease on his station, and his Texaco identification subject to continuing review, we think it flies in the face of common sense to say, as Texaco asserts, that the dealer is 'perfectly free' to reject Texaco's chosen brand of TBA."[19]

This decision suggests at least the possibility of antitrust reaching anticompetitive franchise purchasing restrictions, even where there is no overt coercion but where the disparate economic power of one of the two parties is such that a de facto restraint is created by implicit threat of cancellation. The *Perma Life* decision also would favor the company's franchisee when he is thwarted in his attempt to purchase supplies directly from the company supplier.[20] In that case the dealers challenged as illegal restraints of trade the terms barring them from purchasing from nondesignated sources of supply. This would appear to be applicable to a situation similar to that of the company whose franchisee tries to purchase directly from the franchisor's source of supply.

Clause 2 in Exhibit 1(B) can remedy the franchisor's approach to the exclusive dealing problem. Clause 5 in that section allows the franchisor at least to reason with his distributors on the issue of selling nonfranchisor products.

Exclusive Territories

Section 12 of the "before" contract grants each field organizer an exclusive geographic territory where he may sell the company's products free from intrabrand interference. Section 10 prohibits the sale of the products to and by retail outlets.

Thus the exclusive territorial franchise issue manifests itself in two ways in the company's agreement. Clearly there is an attempt to protect each franchisee's territory. There also is an attempt to restrict where the product can be sold. Although *Colgate* allows a franchisor to pick and choose, within reason, the ones to whom he will sell, he encounters less discretion on where and to whom the product can be sold once the product leaves his hands, especially if he has passed title. A 1972 decision involving a retailer-sponsored cooperative severely limited the power to restrict sales by co-op

members to specified territories under penalty of possible termination of license.[21]

The rationale behind an exclusive territorial franchise generally favors competition. Especially for a start-up or developing firm, it may be necessary to offer an exclusive territory to build dealer morale and offer some measure of security to a dealer who feels safe and snug in his very own territory. If legal complications arise, the courts would employ a balancing test and sacrifice intrabrand competition where interbrand competition is fostered. Generally, exclusive territorial franchises are not unlawful per se but are subject to the rule of reason. The franchisor must be aware of the degree of market foreclosed and whether effective competition exists at the buyer and seller levels. The exclusive territorial franchise must not have as its purpose a scheme to monopolize.

The franchisor often requires that the franchisee agree not to sell the merchandise through retail outlets. Because for all practical purposes *Coors* and *Dunkin' Donuts* have made this kind of vertical restraint virtually illegal per se, this contract provision is not likely to be enforced successfully by the franchisor unless he retains title to the merchandise. If title is passed to the franchisees, the only other recourse available to the franchisor is to prove that territorial and customer restrictions are necessary for the maintenance of quality control. *Coors* explicitly states that the marketing of "standardized products" should not need the benefit of restrictions on where and to whom the product can be sold.

Prior to *Schwinn* there were court decisions that indicated territorial and customer restrictions could be justified on the grounds that the firm was a failing company and the restrictions were necessary to strengthen its distribution network, or the restrictions served as protection against aggressive competitors, or they represented the only practical device available to a small competitor for breaking into or staying in business. *Continental TV* has now enlarged management's discretion on where, to whom, and by what means a product can be distributed.

Clauses 8 and 10 of Exhibit 1(B) allow the franchisor to recoup some of his discretion with respect to where and to whom his products are sold. Clause 8 is phrased in the spirit of the *Scott* rationale, emphasizing an independent franchisee decision that redounds to the franchisee's benefit. Clause 10 is salvaged by the *Superior Bedding Co. v. Serta Associates* decision.[22] *Superior Bedding* enabled a supplier to exert some pressure on territorial allocations by using a profit pass-over. Although not as effective as an absolute order to stay out of a fellow franchisee's territory, the profit pass-over takes some of the incentive out of making a sale outside of the franchisee's "area of primary responsibility." The infringing franchisee is charged a certain percentage of the gross sales revenue to compensate the injured franchisee for his wasted advertising, selling effort, and goodwill. The reasonableness of the profit pass-over percentage is likely to be a question of fact, implying the need for effective cost accounting to justify the amount of the penalty. Assuming the profit pass-over device is not abused by the franchisor, the courts are likely to sanction this means as a method whereby the franchisor can exert some degree of control over territorial allocations.

Conclusion

In the analysis of the numerous control problems in the context of one franchisor's contract, a modified agreement has been developed. The authors believe that the rewritten agreement, in Exhibit 1(B), tends to reflect the franchisor's position in relation to the current legal environment within which he must operate. A comparison of the before and after agreements indicates that there has been a fundamental shift in the law's views on the control a franchisor can exercise over his distributors.

Recent court decisions relevant to the area of franchise control are likely to result in a franchise agreement that reduces the franchisor's overall discretionary control over his franchisees. A possible consequence of this more contemporary view of the franchisor/franchisee relationship is the proposition that the franchisor should seriously view his franchisees as truly independent businessmen. If an attempt to control infringes unreasonably and unnecessarily upon this independent businessman's freedom to make his own decisions, the franchisor proceeds at his own risk.

Notes

1. Ungar v. Dunkin' Donuts of America, Inc., 68 F.R.D. 65 (1975).

2. "Price-Fixing: Crackdown Under Way," *Business Week,* June 2, 1975, pp. 45–46.

3. Northern Pacific Railway Co. v. U.S., 356 U.S. 1 (1958).

4. Times-Picayune Publishing Co. v. U.S., 345 U.S. 594 (1953).

5. Ungar v. Dunkin' Donuts of America, 68 F.R.D. 65 (1975).

6. "Dunkin' Donuts, Inc. Antitrust Conviction Is Upset on Appeal," *The Wall Street Journal,* March 9, 1976, p. 36.

7. Klein v. American Luggage Works, Inc., 323 F. 2d 787 (3rd Cir. 1963).

8. U.S. v. Colgate, 250 U.S. 300 (1919).

9. Adolph Coors Co. v. FTC, 1974 Trade Cases Par. 75,090 (10th Cir.).

10. U.S. v. O.M. Scott and Sons, Co., 303 F. Supp. 141 (D.D.C. 1969).

11. Ibid., p. 143.

12. Cokely v. Tandy Corp., 1973 Trade Cases, Par. 73,342 (N.D. Cal.). The court upheld as legal national price advertising.

13. Adolph Coors Co. v. FTC, 1974 Trade Cases, Par. 75,090, at p. 96, 850 (10th Cir.).

14. U.S. v. Arnold, Schwinn and Co., 388 U.S. 365 (1967).

15. Continental TV, Inc. v. GTE Sylvania, 53 L. Ed. 2d 568 (1977).

16. American Motor Inns, Inc. v. Holiday Inns, Inc., 365 F. Supp. 1073 (D.N.J. 1973).

17. Standard Oil of California v. U.S., 337 US 293 (1949).

18. Tampa Electric Co. v. Nashville Coal Co., 365 US 320 (1961).

19. FTC v. Texaco, Inc., 393 US 229 (1968).

20. Perma Life Mufflers, Inc. v. International Parts Corp., 392 U.S. 134 (1968).

21. U.S. v. Topco Associates, Inc., 405 US 596 (1972).

22. Superior Bedding Co. v. Serta Associates, 353 F. Supp. 1143 (N.D. Ill. 1972).

Questions

1. *Define each of the following: (a) tying agreement; (b) restricted distribution; (c) exclusive dealing; (d) exclusive territory.*

2. *The* Continental TV v. GTE Sylvania *case that was decided in 1977 by the U.S. Supreme Court is having a great impact on franchisors' abilities to control franchisees. Discuss the Schwinn Doctrine and how it has changed in light of the* Continental TV *case.*

26

Warehouse Retailing: A Revolutionary Force in Distribution?

ALBERT D. BATES

The excitement generated about the unlimited potential of warehouse retailing in the 1960s and early 1970s has turned into disappointment. What happened? Why? What's the future like for warehouse retailing?

Warehouse retailing has a short, but certainly spectacular, history. In fact, probably no other retail concept has generated as much initial excitement among retailers and merchandise suppliers or has fallen into disfavor quite as quickly. Today, the warehouse concept remains a subject of controversy and confusion.

In the simplest terms a warehouse outlet is a large-scale retail facility with a large attached warehouse facility and incorporating a variety of warehouse operating techniques. In the early 1970s, a number of different warehouse retailing concepts were hailed as major strategic innovations, including the furniture warehouse showroom, the catalog showroom, and the food warehouse. Spurred on by the initial success, high visibility, and enthusiastic stock market acceptance of warehouse retailing innovators such as Levitz and Best Products, a variety of major firms made major commitments to the warehouse approach. These included Wickes and Unicapital (Rhodes) in furniture warehouse showrooms, The May Company (Consumers Distributing) and Grand Union (Grand Catalog Showrooms) in catalog showrooms, and Oshawa

Source: Copyright © 1977 by the Regents of the University of California. Reprinted from *California Management Review*, volume XX, number 2, pp. 74 to 80 by permission of the Regents.

(Hypermarché) and Jewel (Grand Bazaar) in large-scale food warehousing. In addition, a number of manufacturers made extraordinary commitments to their warehouse accounts, including direct financial support.

Today, much of the excitement generated by warehouse retailing has vanished, replaced in too many instances by a virtual deluge of red ink. To comprehend the frustrations inherent in warehouse retailing at present, consider the following examples:

Levitz, the largest furniture warehouse showroom, experienced declining sales volume during the mid-1970s. In the 1975 fiscal year the firm incurred a before-tax loss of $721,000, before rebounding somewhat in 1976.

The May Company experienced losses from its catalog showroom operations of $3.9 million during its first two years of operation, including a write-down of the catalog showroom investment to net asset value.

Kennedy and Cohen, by far the largest appliance warehouse, recently filed for Chapter 11 bankruptcy and closed all of its outlets.

All of these firms are large, highly visible organizations, and their difficulties have been discussed in laborious detail in the trade press. As a result, there is a natural tendency among many executives to view warehouse retailing as a failed concept which will receive only token interest in the future.[1] However, such a viewpoint overlooks the continued strengths of the warehouse approach, the important reasons for warehouse retailing's initial success, and several existing environmental conditions which could work in reestablishing the growth and excitement of the warehouse approach to retailing.

The purpose of this article is to review the current status of warehouse retailing. Particular attention will be given to the latent strength of existing warehouse retailing firms. It will be argued that these firms still possess the ability to make obsolete many conventional channels of distribution. Consequently, they represent a force that should continually be monitored by both manufacturers and retailers alike.

The Warehouse Concept

Before trying to analyze the present strengths and weaknesses of warehouse retailing, it is first necessary to have a detailed understanding of exactly what the concept involves, since there is some debate on this point. In its most basic dimensions, warehouse retailing incorporates five key characteristics: a very large and low-cost physical facility; emphasis on warehouse operating approaches and materials-handling technology; the maximum use of vertical space in merchandise display; an exceptionally large on-premise inventory; and the minimization of customer services. Each of these factors plays an indispensable role in creating a true warehouse retailing operation.

Physical Facilities

Central to making the warehouse concept work is a physical facility which is several times the size of conventional outlets. For example, a furniture warehouse showroom may occupy between 100,000 and 150,000 square feet of space and feature 250 room settings, compared to 10,000 to 25,000 square feet for most furniture stores. Such major size differentials usually hold true for other forms of warehouse retailing as well.

The use of a very large physical facility produces some economies of scale in construction. In addition, much more substantial savings arise from building a somewhat spartan warehouse-oriented outlet rather than a more conventional and expensive retail outlet. The savings per square foot in building costs can usually be translated quite directly into an important operating cost advantage.

Beyond cost savings, the large size of the warehouse retailer's facility presents the opportunity for more massive product displays. This tends to support the image of the warehouse retailer as being like a wholesaler open to the public and frequently produces a very favorable consumer attitude toward purchasing, particularly among some blue-collar market segments.[2]

Warehouse Operations

Virtually all warehouse retailers employ some sort of materials-handling equipment to facilitate more economical product movement. Such systems usually produce an important payroll cost savings, but at the same time they increase the overall investment in facilities and equipment. In firms with a real understanding of warehouse operating procedures, the trade-off between payroll expense and physical facilities investment is clearly in favor of the warehouse-oriented approach, as total costs can be reduced substantially. However, some companies have had pronounced difficulties in cost justifying the equipment investment. In such instances, the warehouse equipment does nothing but reinforce the wholesale image, making the equipment little more than a very expensive sales tool.

Vertical Space

Most, but certainly not all, warehouse retailers attempt to make more efficient use of cubic footage by displaying merchandise in a vertical rather than horizontal format. With such an approach it is not unusual to have merchandise stacked fifteen to twenty-five feet high. The logic of vertical presentation is that the "rent-free" space above normal display levels can be used to reduce the required building size and to create a strong visual merchandising impact.[3] Most warehouse retailers are pleased with both the merchandising and cost advantages of using vertical space. However, a few feel that the increased handling costs necessary to retrieve vertically stacked merchandise negate much of the positive merchandising value.

Inventory

Warehouse retailers typically maintain an extensive inventory, displayed so that it is highly visible to the consumer. This not only supports the warehouse image, but also reduces out-of-stock conditions and helps build a reputation for product availability.

A high inventory level is far from cost-free. In fact, the level of inventory investment associated with many forms of warehouse retailing can most correctly be described as staggering. Since large facilities are being utilized, and since they are being filled to capacity vertically, there is really no way to avoid high levels of investment. A furniture warehouse showroom, as an illustration, will usually carry between $1.0 and $1.5 million in inventory, far in excess of the inventory for conventional furniture retailers. Financing such an inventory level is a difficult proposition for most firms.

In successful warehouse outlets the high level of inventory is matched by an equally high level of sales volume, resulting in a desirable rate of inventory turnover. In fact, the turnover rate may be well above that for conventional outlets. Regardless of how desirable turnover may be, though, the large total dollar investment remains, serving as a deterrent to many firms contemplating entering the warehouse retailing field.

Service Reduction

Like other mass merchandisers, warehouse retailers rely heavily on customers to perform a variety of functions which other retailers have historically performed for customers free of charge.[4] As illustrations, delivery service, order writing, product packaging, and credit are all customer services that have been eliminated by some types of warehouse retailers. As with other mass merchandisers, the cost savings in service elimination are usually quite significant, providing the warehouse retailer with a definite cost advantage.

By combining the five characteristics outlined above, warehouse retailers become powerful forms of competition. In fact, most warehouse retailers exist on operating expense percentages that are 3 to 7 percentage points below competitors in the same product categories. In addition, warehouse firms also produce levels of space and employee productivity that exceed competition by 20 to 30 percent. All of this results in a major competitive advantage, an advantage that remains despite the recent poor economic performance of many warehouse retailers.

The Diversity of Warehouse Retailing

Warehouse retailing is frequently talked about as if it were a homogeneous collection of retailers with almost identical operating characteristics. In reality, though, the warehouse retailing field is quite diverse. Only a limited number of firms employ all of the warehouse operating techniques in the precise manner identified above. Instead, firms in particular lines of trade modify the concepts to meet the competitive demands of their unique industry. The ability of the warehouse concept to succeed in modified forms in multiple lines of trade is a tribute to the inherent strength of the warehouse approach.

Some of the diverse ways in which the concept has developed are outlined briefly in Table 1. Specifically, the table highlights the major characteristics of furniture warehouse showrooms, appliance warehouse showrooms, catalog showrooms, food warehouses, and hypermarkets. In the following paragraphs, each type of outlet is reviewed in some detail.

Probably the most widely discussed form of

Table 1
The scope of warehouse retailing

Warehouse retailing concept	Primary merchandise categories	Representative firms	Estimated market significance		Unique characteristics
			Stores	Sales (millions)	
Furniture warehouse showroom	Furniture, home furnishings and accessories	Levitz Wickes Joshua Doore	150	$900	Room setting displays
Appliance warehouse showroom	Television, home appliances	Kennedy and Cohen	5	$25	None
Catalog showroom	Jewelry, housewares, small appliances	Best Products Service Merchandise H. J. Wilson	1,100	$3,000	Separate warehouse and the use of a catalog for advertising
Food warehouse	Food	Nash-Finch Pacific Gamble Robinson	300	$1,500	None
Hypermarket	Food, general merchandise	Carrefour (France) Wertkauf (Germany) Euromarche (France)	10	$200	Massive scale of operations

warehouse retailing is the furniture warehouse showroom pioneered by Levitz, Wickes, Joshua Doore, and others. As implied by the name, these outlets combine the warehouse operation with a showroom in which home furnishings are displayed in room settings to facilitate customer selection. In addition, the units provide a relatively full complement of services, featuring sales assistance, credit, delivery at a modest fee, and a number of other services. Given the relatively full-service orientation of furniture warehouse showrooms, their main advantage over conventional outlets is not a dramatically lower price, but a combination of modest price advantage, an extensive merchandise assortment, and the rapid availability of merchandise.

Closely related to the furniture warehouse showroom in terms of operating characteristics is the appliance warehouse storeroom. Kennedy and Cohen is probably the only nationally known firm in this line of trade, although Tipton Electric in St. Louis and some others have emulated the concept. In most instances these firms provide an even

greater array of services than their counterparts in furniture retailing. Consequently, the warehouse part of the business tends to be an adjunct rather than the primary focus of the operation.

The largest of the warehouse concepts, at least in terms of number of stores operated, is the catalog showroom, which includes firms such as Best Products, Consumers Distributing, Service Merchandise, and H. J. Wilson. These firms also operate in a combined warehouse and showroom format, and specialize in portable appliances, houseware items, photography equipment, sporting goods, and jewelry. Catalog showrooms have two unique characteristics which distinguish them from other warehouse-oriented concepts. First, almost all of the advertising budget is devoted to a large catalog mailed to existing and prospective customers. The catalog contains the pictures, descriptions, and prices of all items carried in stock and is the vehicle by which the customer "shops" the store, for the showroom usually involves only a very limited display. Second, the showroom and warehouse are clearly separated from each other and customers are not granted access to the warehouse sector. By not allowing customers to witness warehouse operations, merchandising impact is probably reduced, but this has never been viewed as a significant problem. With these exceptions, catalog showrooms are true warehouse operations.

The food warehouse is an extension of the supermarket concept. As such, food warehouses aren't truly warehouses but are actually relatively large supermarkets with a slimmed-down product assortment, warehouse-oriented fixtures, and a drastically reduced set of customer services. For example, food warehouse customers may price mark their own merchandise with a marking pen, package their own purchases, provide their own carry-out service, and even bring their own sacks or boxes for packaging. With the reduced services the outlets operate almost exclusively on a price-competitive basis. To date most of the interest in the food warehouse has come from wholesalers anxious to develop their own retail networks. In particular, Pacific Gamble Robinson and Nash-Finch have been quite active in the food warehouse area.

The final major type of warehouse retailer, the hypermarket, is probably the most exciting in that it comes closest to employing all of the warehouse retailing concepts in their purest form. Hypermarkets, which are still almost exclusively confined to western Europe, are massive outlets—up to 300,000 square feet of selling area—selling both food and general merchandise. They can be reasonably characterized as a warehouse-oriented combination of the supermarket and the discount department store. In using this technique, companies such as Carrefour in France and Wertkauf in Germany have attained substantial market shares and have completely altered the nature of distribution in their respective countries. North American activity has been limited, although Oshawa in Canada and Meijers Thrifty Acres in Michigan both have prototype units in operation. If successful, they could be major factors in retailing in North America.

In summary, warehouse retailing has taken many forms and in a few instances has moved quite a ways away from the true warehouse approach. To some extent this experimentation and diversity explains the mixed success pattern of warehouse outlets. A more complete explanation of the problems in warehouse retailing probably lies in the fact that warehouse retailing has not adequately adapted to a changing environment.

Warehouse Retailing and the Environment

To a large degree the warehouse retailing concept suffered from drastic overselling, which created false expectations regarding potential sales growth and profitability. The overselling occurred because the first and most spectacular warehouse retailing successes occurred in the late 1960s and early 1970s, a time when economic conditions were especially conducive to new retailing developments. In particular, the era was characterized by low unemployment, high levels of discretionary income, controlled inflation, low capital costs, and relatively low construction costs. Today, almost all of these favorable conditions have shifted in such a way as to significantly change the basic operating economics of warehouse retailing. Yet warehouse operators have been either unable or unwilling to modify their basic concepts.

At present warehouse operations face an environment which still offers a number of strong supportive conditions, but which is also tempered by a relatively significant list of negative factors. By a careful appraisal of the new environment and by restructuring the warehouse concept in light of that environment, the initial promise of warehouse retailing may yet be reached.

Factors Favorable to Continued Warehouse Retailing Development

Warehouse retailers can rely on a boost to their competitive position by three factors which were important in the early development of the warehouse concept and which remain largely unchanged. First, and probably foremost, the warehouse retailing approach maintains an important

Table 2

Economic advantages of warehouse retailers over conventional retail outlets

Type of warehouse retailer	Conventional retail competition	Magnitude of the warehouse retailer's advantage			
		Operating expense percentage	Sales per man hour	Sales per square foot (selling area)	Inventory turnover
Furniture warehouse showrooms	Furniture and department stores	3–5 percentage points	Not available	$50 to $75 per foot	No advantage
Appliance warehouse showrooms	Appliance and department stores	4–8 percentage points	Not available	$100 to $150 per foot	No advantage
Catalog showrooms	Jewelry, discount and department stores	6–10 percentage points	Not available	$150 to $200 per foot	1 to 2 inventory turns
Food warehouses	Supermarkets	6–8 percentage points	$30 to $35 per man-hour	$100 to $125 per foot	4 to 6 inventory turns
Hypermarkets	Supermarkets and discount stores	5–7 percentage points	$20 to $25 per man-hour	$150 to $200 per foot	3 to 5 inventory turns

operating advantage, particularly in terms of labor savings. These operating advantages, some of which are shown in some detail in Table 2, allow the warehouse-oriented firm to create a substantial *potential* for underpricing competition. In fact, most warehouse retailers have the ability to operate on gross margins that are 3 to 10 percentage points below conventional outlets. With the near universality of price as a shopping appeal this could be quite significant.

So far, warehouse retailers have not been as aggressive as they might in capitalizing on their potential price advantage. Instead, they have emphasized customer services, fullness of assortment, and other nonprice variables. The lack of an aggressive price program is really quite alien to the warehouse concept. Warehouse retailers can probably be expected to reestablish a price position as they attempt to achieve their full potential.

A second factor which continues to support warehouse retailing development and growth is the advantage of warehouse retailers in terms of its merchandise position. One of the foundations for the success of the warehouse concept was the use of an extensive inventory to create a favorable merchandising effect and create a high in-stock position. In particular furniture warehouse showrooms and catalog showrooms were greatly aided by their reputation for merchandise availability.

This advantage was eroded somewhat by a combination of inflation and product shortages. Inflation made it more expensive to carry an extensive inventory and product shortages simply made it impossible to maintain a desired in-stock position. With both the inflation and product availability situations apparently returning to somewhat more normalized conditions, the warehouse retailer's merchandising position could again be a strong competitive advantage.

Finally, warehouse stores have typically been highly distinctive and fun places to shop compared to conventional retail stores. It is disquieting to admit, but many retail outlets are not really very exciting places to visit. There is a certain sameness of layout, decor, merchandise, and auxiliary services. In sharp contrast, many warehouse outlets use different merchandising and sales approaches, display items in a somewhat unique manner, provide an unusual set of services, and generally tend to operate in an almost bazaar-like atmosphere. This too represents a major strength.

Factors Unfavorable to Continued Warehouse Retailing Development

Aligned against future warehouse development are two significant factors, both of them having to do with changing economic pressures. These changed conditions are likely to continue for the foreseeable future. Consequently, they must be accounted for in warehouse operations.

First, because of inflation the investment associated with most forms of warehouse retailing is getting close to out of control. For example, the total asset investment associated with a new home furnishing warehouse is around $2.5 million and for a new hypermarket, approximately $5.0 million. Clearly, few companies can engineer this level of investment with ease. This means that in the future warehouse retailers are going to have to focus very heavily on ways to reduce the total investment and more creative financing techniques.

Second, most warehouse outlets are poor risks in a downtown economy. Given their size and high fixed costs, warehouse outlets tend to be more volume-sensitive than smaller stores. As a consequence, warehouse retailers will continue to perform poorly during economic recessions unless they can institute better cost controls or develop programs for stabilizing sales volume over the business cycle.

Warehouse Retailing: An Appraisal

In summary, warehouse retailing can best be described as still a relatively small (approximately $5.5 billion) and currently somewhat stagnant segment of the total retail marketplace, with the market

shares of the different types of operations not having increased appreciably in two or three years. If warehouse retailing is to regain its excitement and growth, the concept must be revised in light of changing environmental conditions. In developing a revised concept, several approaches seem especially noteworthy.

The underpricing advantage that is an intrinsic part of the warehouse approach must be employed in a more direct manner. An underpricing advantage is not especially significant if it is never actually employed. Since warehouse retailing is designed to be a low-cost mechanism, consumer expectations regarding price must be more directly fulfilled.

Warehouse retailers need to press their cost advantages even further by exploring new cost minimization programs. In particular, consideration should be given to becoming more self-service-oriented.

Warehouse retailers must think in terms of facility cost minimization programs. This would involve something of a slight reduction in typical outlet size coupled with a major review of all costs associated with building such outlets. Too many warehouse retailers have been moving away from a truly warehouse-oriented approach into more and more glamorous types of facilities. While this is a natural tendency among retailers, it must be avoided if the inherent cost advantages of warehouse retailing are to be maintained.

Inventory levels need to be controlled to minimize overall investment while maintaining appropriate in-stock levels. To accomplish this, warehouse firms should think more in terms of more intensive programmed relationships with key merchandise suppliers and the possible elimination of some fringe suppliers.

Product flows and materials handling procedures must be reviewed to insure that maximum productivity is being achieved. This is especially critical in the catalog showroom field where handling procedures leave ample room for improvement.

The warehouse concept should be more properly positioned in the market. Clearly, not every consumer is a potential warehouse shopper. Potential customers must be more precisely identified and appealed to more directly.

Executives in warehouse retailing organizations are well aware of the need for change and are actively moving toward restructuring their companies. If they are successful, the warehouse concept should reestablish its growth pattern and meet its initial potential.

Managerial Implications

For conventional retailers, the implications of a revitalized warehouse retailing concept are quite obvious. In the late 1960s and early 1970s warehouse operations took important hunks of volume from tradition-oriented firms. A repetition could be disastrous.

The implications for manufacturers are somewhat more subliminal, but equally important. Two implications are especially important considerations. First, warehouse outlets possess massive sales potential per outlet. As the concept grows the potential for sharp shifts in manufacturer output also exists. This is particularly true since most warehouse firms try to program extensively with key resources. For example, Kennedy and Cohen at one point was heavily committed to Sylvania in its television operation. This was a major assist to Sylvania in its efforts to reestablish market share. Given the volume sensitivity of most manufacturing organizations, the volume potential of warehouse retailers must be reckoned with.

Second, warehouse outlets have unique buying requirements which make it difficult for many manufacturers to deal with them successfully. For example, catalog showrooms need six-month price guarantees on merchandise so they can commit to a catalog; hypermarkets need special product packaging and containerization; and furniture warehouse showrooms need extended terms to help finance inventory. Merchandise suppliers need to be aware of these buying priorities if they are going to service warehouse retailers successfully.

In conclusion, it is impossible to predict exactly where warehouse retailing is going in the future. But if the major firms in the industry actively try to rethink and reposition their competitive offer, they can recapture lost market share and possibly reestablish the warehouse concept as one of the most exciting retail concepts for the 1970s. If they do so retailing will continue to be a turbulent sector of the economy for some time to come.

References

1. For a perspective on warehouse retailing in relation to other retail strategies, see Albert D. Bates and Bert C. McCammon, Jr., *Reseller Strategies and the Financial Performance of the Firm* (Norman: University of Oklahoma, 1975).
2. See, for example, Pierre Martineau, "Social Classes and Spending Behavior," *Journal of Marketing* (October 1958), pp. 121–130.
3. See Philip Kotler, "Atmospherics as a Marketing Tool," *Journal of Retailing* (Winter 1973–1974), pp. 48–64.
4. For more on service-elimination strategies, see *The Application of Supermarket Techniques to Other Lines of Retail Trade* (Columbus, Ohio: Management Horizons, Inc., 1975).

Questions

1. *What is a warehouse retailing outlet?*
2. *Describe the environmental conditions that most affected the rapid growth and eventual decline in warehouse retailing.*

27

The Need for Innovative Distribution Management

DONALD J. BOWERSOX

Physical distribution managers are living in an era of rapid change. Moreover, in many instances they are working with distribution systems that evolved in a haphazard, unplanned manner. Are they faced with a "mission impossible"?

When Peter Drucker called the last decade the "age of discontinuity," he was being modest. I really don't think that even Dr. Drucker anticipated the tempo and thrust of change that would materialize in such forces as price controls, energy shortages, appliance and automotive recalls, OSHA, regulatory instability, affirmative action, executive accountability, political upheaval, water shortages, and on and on. Let me review a few ways in which the changing times have impacted the distribution sector of our economy.

First, costs have risen continuously. We now experience a logistical cost that consumes approximately 20–22% of our gross national product. This cost is experienced from the practice of moving products from one place to another in order to have them in the right place at the right time to satisfy the consumer market.

Second, the logistical operating arena in the United States has become chaotic. There is nothing quite as disorganized and confusing as a distribution channel. It is labor-intensive. The higher the level of overall national employment, the lower the calibre of the work force available for employment in the distribution area.

Source: Distribution Worldwide, December 1977, pp. 27–30.

Third, what about these distribution channels? There used to be an old saying: you can eliminate the middleman, but you can't eliminate the function. In fact, all efforts to eliminate the middlemen have failed in the aggregate. We now have one retailer for every 100 consumers in the United States.

Furthermore, we have made scrambled merchandising a way of life. You can buy just about anything anywhere you want to buy it. There has been a shift in power in the distribution channel from manufacturers to retailers. The net result is that the process of distribution has become increasingly complex over the past several decades.

A fourth observation regarding today's distribution system is the vast amount of effort performed in anticipation of future transactions. We manufacture a product, ship it, ship it again, in the hope that it will finally arrive at a destination where someone will purchase it.

To a degree, anticipatory distribution cannot be avoided. However, our distribution system in the United States appears extreme with respect to the dollars expended to provide ready availability of merchandise. In the performance of this anticipatory distribution, managers who make the most important decisions are most often not held responsible for the consequences. Thus, marketing or manufacturing executives may initiate actions that result in anticipatory distribution, but logistical managers are held responsible.

Finally, we suffer from distribution system hangover. Very few of the distribution systems in place today are the result of a planned effort. Almost all of them are a combination of individual decisions made over the years with no attempt to evaluate the overall system design. The significant increase in system redesign studies currently underway by countless firms testifies to this basic neglect over the past decades.

A Look Ahead

If the system is suffering today, how will it cope with future requirements? Current projections are that the gross national product of the United States will exceed $2 trillion by 1980 and surpass $3 trillion prior to the end of the century. The areas of significant growth will be expenditures for goods and services.

Even more so than today, logistical systems will be required to support multiple product distribution to heterogeneous markets and through a variety of marketing channels. The return movement of inventory for recycling and/or recall will become a more integral part of future logistics. This rapidly increasing area of "reverse logistics" will require the logistical system flexibility of efficient two-way movement.

Ever-present in future society will be the continued problems and pressures of energy and ecology. The dependence of the logistical system upon a ready supply of energy is and will continue to be a critical concern. The cost of energy is projected to remain a serious problem for the logistical sector during the foreseeable future.

Distribution Solution

If you so wished, you could look at where we are today and what the future appears to have in store and conclude that we face a logistical "mission impossible." To further complicate the issue, it now appears that the rate of technological development directly applicable to the distributive trades may slow down during the decades ahead. Is there a solution?

In my mind, the solution is managerial innovation. Innovation to make the technology that is here

today work tomorrow. We have to find better ways of doing things, rather than resting upon technology to help us do the same old things in a better way.

Almost all innovations in the history of our civilization can be traced to people who didn't know it couldn't be done. In industry after industry, you see major innovations come from outsiders. One of the reasons is that within the industry there is always an experienced person who will tell you it won't work; this is the way we do it and that's the way it must always be done.

But experience shouldn't be a hitching post, it should be a guidepost. Most innovations don't just happen; they are planned through an organized utilization of information applied systematically to problems.

Logistics has evolved over a relatively short period of time from a fragmented operational effort into an integrated philosophy of strategic movement and storage management. During this developmental period, several basic concepts have emerged which have not been fully deployed in the logistical process. The following represent concepts which provide the foundation for innovative managerial action.

Systems Approach

The systems approach was and remains the cornerstone of the integrated logistical concept. Few question the logic that significant benefits can be obtained by integrated deployment of human and financial resources toward accomplishment of the logistical mission. The problem is one of application.

In far too many industrial and marketing organizations the systems approach is given lip service but not serious implementation. The identification and measurement of tradeoff potential within a logistical system is difficult without a serious reexamination of traditional procedures and practices. In most cases, organizational arrangements must be altered to focus accountability.

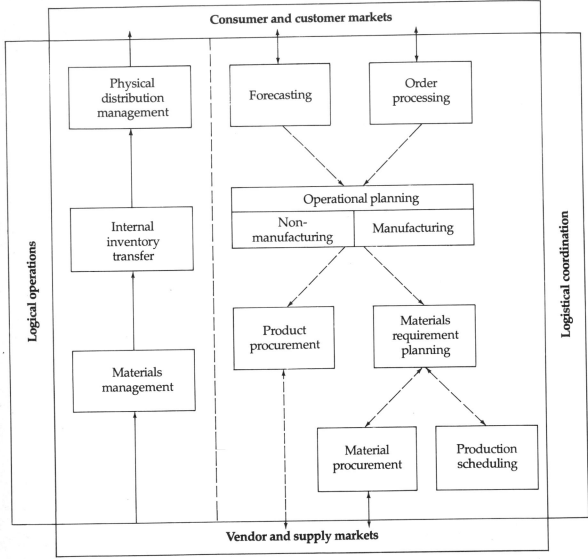

Integrated logistics consists of the operational direction and coordination of facility location, transportation, inventory, communication, and handling and storage. To achieve an orderly flow of products and materials, managerial attention must be devoted to the design of the logistical system and to the direction of its operation. Thus, logistical management is defined as: That managerial responsibility to design and administer a system to control the flow of materials, parts, and finished inventory to the maximum benefit of the enterprise.

In Fig. 1 (above) the boundaries of enterprise logistical activity as they relate to market interface points are identified by solid lines. The functional concerns of operations and coordination are separated by the vertical line of alternating dots and dashes. The left side of Fig. 1 reflects the operational or physical unit movements of logistics. The right side illustrates the process of logistical coordination. Coordination consists of information flow which is illustrated by vertical broken lines. Unlike physical movements which ideally flow toward the final sales destination, coordination communications represent a two-way process from and to both selling and buyer markets.

To accomplish the functions illustrated, transportation, inventory, and handling and storage must be fully coordinated between all facilities, customers, and vendors. Thus, integrated logistical management involves administration of all movement to, from, and between geographical locations that comprise the facility structure of the enterprise.

In many situations, new and innovative performance measurement devices must be implemented to open the door for the synergistic potential promised by the systems approach. Countless managers know *what* to do to improve logistical productivity but they don't know *how* to effectively implement systemic planning and management of logistical effort. In this sense, the systems approach offers new potential to many organizations because it has actually never been applied.

Data Transmission

One technological development of the last decade has been the significant increase in data transmission capability. The result is the capability to introduce time controlled information flow into planning and administration of a logistical system. By direct transmittal of customer orders to computer processing facilities, valuable time can be saved and deployed for the performance of other necessary logistical activities.

Perhaps the greatest untapped potential of data processing is the opportunity to improve control of the total performance cycle. Such control can eliminate a great deal of uncertainty which is so difficult to cope with when formulating safety stock policies. Implementation of control devices to increase speed of performance, could reduce dramatically the overall need for safety stocks in our national logistical system.

In fact, given performance consistency, a great deal of the logic used currently to formulate safety stock policy could be modified substantially. In data transmission we have a "here today" technological capability. The opportunity exists to improve overall performance because few firms are exploiting fully the many benefits attainable from time controlled information flow.

Consolidation

Two different forms of consolidation are fundamental to the design and operation of a logistical

system: (1) transportation, and (2) inventory. It is safe to generalize that few firms today realize fully the many benefits available from the two forms of consolidation.

Transportation consolidation results from the realization that movement costs can be controlled by fully coordinating shipping or procurement. Consolidation is essential to benefit from the quantity discounts structured into common carrier transportation rates. Such consolidation can be realized by grouping orders destined for a specific market, pooling through public warehouse distribution programs, and developing scheduled delivery programs.

Inventory consolidation relates to the number of locations at which inventory is held in anticipation of servicing customer orders. Few dispute that the total inventory necessary to support a logistical mission is directly related to the number of warehouses.

By consolidation of facilities, total cost can be lowered because inventory reductions or inventory availability for purposes of customer service can be increased given the same level of inventory. In spite of the undisputed benefits of inventory consolidation, countless firms continue to operate extensive field warehouses without justifying the network on the basis of total cost or customer service benefits.

Cost-Revenue Measurement

To a significant degree, failure to utilize a systems approach, lack of widespread use of data transmission capabilities, and failure to fully consolidate shipping or inventory locations are symptoms of inadequate measurement capabilities. Development of integrated logistics has long been hindered by the lack of standard functional costs. In particular, controversy exists concerning the appropriate measurement of cost tradeoffs.

Most practitioners agree that logistical plans ideally should be formulated on the basis of total cost expended in relation to revenue generated by customer service performance. Marginal cost-revenue measurement offers the necessary refinement over traditional forms of accounting. The total field of logistical controllership, while still in its infancy, provides a new perspective for measurement and control of the logistical process. The capability to set priorities and measure performance accurately offers a readily available way to improve logistical productivity.

Channel Separation

Substantial opportunities for improving logistical productivity can result from viewing the structure of overall distribution channels in terms of specialization of effort. Logistical channel relationships and performance plans should be formulated using specialists engaged in management of physical movement and storage. The concept of channel separation challenges the long-standing practice of using the same intermediaries for performing marketing and logistical functions.

For example, wholesalers traditionally have served as both marketing and physical distribution intermediaries. The tradition of a single channel structure is not based on inherent economic advantages or legal requirements. It evolved over time as a result of ease of development and for control purposes. The concept of channel separation offers a logical and practical alternative for the future given the control capabilities *now* available for use by logistical managers.

The channel separation concept is not new and has been tested. The technology to make it work is here today. The difficulty with establishing specialized channels is that long-standing and traditional business arrangements must be renegotiated and restructured.

Flexible Operations

Closely related to the notion of channel separation is the development of flexible operating structures. A flexible operating structure consists of a systems capability to service selected customer orders utilizing a variety of shipping locations and/or transportation methods depending upon the characteristics of the order. Thus, orders may be processed to customers in a combination of ways that achieve logistical performance objectives most effectively.

Operating flexibility eliminates the neat and rigid patterns of well-defined warehouse service areas which have become characteristic of countless enterprises. The procedure for meeting a customer's requirement at the lowest total cost using flexible assignment is now gaining an operational foothold.

Essential to flexible operations is development of selectivity in formulating inventory stocking policies and related safety stocks. It is not necessary and most often will not be desirable that all facilities have the same stocking policies. Using fine line item classification, policies should be formulated to meet specific performance standards.

The criteria for establishing such standards may be product profitability, customer profitability, importance of product delivery to customer or any other combination of standards critical to meeting operating objectives.

The important point is that stocking selectivity combined with flexible operating structure provides a way to realize high levels of output while reducing the level of assets deployed in support of the logistical mission. Similar to each of the concepts discussed, the technology is currently available to establish flexible operating capabilities.

Postponement

The traditional nature of logistical performance is that emphasis has been placed on movement of product in *anticipation* of future transactions. Anticipatory action is also characteristic of our manufacturing, wholesaling, and retail sectors of business. Generally, products are produced, transported, stored, handled, bought, and sold several times until they arrive at a location where they are offered for final sale. Providing all of the anticipatory work has been performed properly, final transactions are realized in an efficient and effective manner.

The concept of postponement is a risk-reducing approach to performing manufacturing and logistical operations. To the extent that final manufacturing or logistics of a product can be postponed until a final customer commitment is obtained, anticipatory action is reduced, resulting in little or no risk of error.

The attributes of postponement may be incorporated into a logistical system on the basis of *form* and/or *time*. Form postponement consists of holding the final manufacturing, assembly, or packaging until customer preference is identified. The classic example is mixing paints to customer specifications at retail stores. The potential for incorporating form postponement into logistical system design is almost unlimited.

The significant point about both form and time postponement is that they offer ways to reduce the anticipatory nature of today's business arrangements. Thus, to the extent postponement can be structured into a logistical system, reliance on forecasting and its related risk is reduced. The concept and the technology necessary to operationally benefit from postponement are available to management today.

Interorganization

Logistical operations extend beyond the traditional domain of a single enterprise to include many other organizations. The fact that no firm can be self-sufficient was the basic motivation behind the notion of channel separation. Since dependency exists, channel arrangements should be fostered to take maximum advantage of the specialization possible.

Coordination of interorganizational logistical performance provides an opportunity to eliminate duplication and minimize risk for the total channel.

The concept of interorganizational management creates opportunities for utilizing third-party specialists and shared distribution facilities.

While the track record of shared distribution facilities is not yet noteworthy, the expanded use of third-party specialists is extremely encouraging. The most serious problem confronted in the development of interorganizational arrangements is traditional practice. The concepts to guide the formulation of interorganizational arrangements are now available to management.

The Time Has Come

Projected logistical demands for the future are frightening. In the past, we have overpowered our productivity problems associated with growth and complexity by applying new technology. This does not appear to be a viable course of action for the future.

The key to overcoming the productivity gap is managerial innovation. Several sound concepts currently exist and can be implemented within today's technological capacity if management can foster operational and institutional change.

While many legal and/or regulatory barriers exist to hinder innovative change, the most serious problem is management attitude and inflexibility. The time has come to actually implement the philosophy of integrated logistics.

Questions

1. *Explain the meaning of the "systems approach" to logistics management and operations.*
2. *Differentiate the two forms of consolidation that are essential to the design and operation of a logistics system.*

28

Physical Distribution and Consumer Demands

DOUGLAS M. LAMBERT

JAMES R. STOCK

The consumer movement forced marketers to reconsider all aspects of business planning and operations. Consumer pressures have not bypassed the physical distribution manager.

Consumerism has a significant impact on the physical distribution function of a firm. Most business people would agree it is a force in society that affects the operations of every business firm. In fact, in a survey of 3,600 subscribers to the *Harvard Business Review*, 84 percent said consumerism is here to stay. One executive said "it is a factor which will not disappear in the near term, one which will even more strongly influence our decision making, and one which we need not fear."[1]

The U.S. Chamber of Commerce has made the following observation: "As American society changes, so do the wants and needs of consumers. In a world of ever-increasing complexity, consumers expect more help from both business and government—and greater understanding and fulfillment of the wants and needs that comprise consumer satisfaction. They also expect ever-higher performance levels of quality, safety, and integrity from business."[2]

In this article, the role of the firm in a consumer oriented society will be explored in terms of the

Source: Douglas M. Lambert and James R. Stock, "Physical Distribution and Consumer Demands," pp. 49–56, *MSU Business Topics*, Spring 1978. Reprinted by permission of the publisher, Division of Research, Graduate School of Business Administration, Michigan State University.

current and forecasted scope of the consumer movement and the impact of consumer demands on the distribution function. While most articles pertaining to consumerism concentrate on broad policy issues or on the obvious areas of promotion, product safety, warranties, and repairs, this article examines the impact of consumerism in the generally overlooked area of physical distribution.[3] The position is taken that business has placed too much emphasis on demand creation activities such as advertising and promotion and too little emphasis on the supply of that demand (physical supply or physical distribution). Within that context, both a descriptive and prescriptive approach will be taken. Implicit is the notion that while the physical distribution function is largely unknown to the consumer, it is critical to the satisfaction of consumerist demands.

As a preface to this discussion, a brief examination of consumerism is in order.

In recent years consumerism has become a major factor in the increasingly dynamic world in which the business firm must function. Consumerism has been defined as "the actions of individuals and organizations (consumer, government, and business) in response to consumers' dissatisfaction arising in exchange relationships,"[4] and as "the organized effort of consumers seeking redress, restitution and remedy for dissatisfaction they have accumulated in the acquisition of their standard of living."[5] Perhaps the most widely accepted definition is Philip Kotler's: "Consumerism is a social movement seeking to augment the rights and power of buyers in relation to sellers." Kotler argues that the rebirth of consumerism was inevitable because of "new conditions in the U.S. economy that warranted a fresh examination of the economic power of sellers in relation to buyers."[6]

The consumer movement is international in scope and is a dominant force in many of the highly industrialized Western nations. In fact, the International Organization of Consumers Unions reported 1974 year-end membership at almost 100 organizations in approximately 50 countries.[7]

In the United States, consumer protection has taken the form of laws. The Council on Environmental Quality extended government authority to protect the consumer interest in still another area, that of the environment, by giving the secretary of the interior the authority to conduct investigations, studies, surveys, and research relating to the nation's ecological systems, natural resources, and environmental quality.

Generally, government is assuming an increasingly active role in the regulation of industry. As a result, business is losing much of the flexibility it has enjoyed in the past. Through consumer protection legislation, the government is assuming the role of the silent partner who no longer wishes to remain silent.

The pervasiveness of the consumer movement is evidenced by the variety of government regulations and the concerted efforts of consumer protectionists and various consumer groups.

Much of what now exists or is proposed in the area of consumer protection has been brought about by business itself. The emphasis has traditionally been placed on demand creation for an increasing proliferation of goods, services, and ideas. Business has been extraordinarily successful— perhaps too successful. Consumers, caught in the financial pinch caused by inflation and recession, are beginning to question product costs and quality. Thomas A. Murphy, chairman of the board of the General Motors Corporation, made the following observation regarding consumerism and its results.

Every neglected service, every shoddy product, every reason for complaint is worse than bad business: it invites more regulation by government. Conversely, we counter the threat of government overregulation when we do what we must and should to satisfy our customers, when we get back to what competition in business is all about.[8]

The worldwide trend toward more government intervention in business led David Leighton to the conclusion that business ultimately will be reduced to a quasi-public utility structure with government not only regulating prices, product offerings, and distribution, but also determining what is in society's best interest.[9] Whether or not this projection materializes depends to a large extent on how responsive business is to the needs of the consumer during the next decade and beyond. There are a number of factors which strongly indicate that the consumer movement will not dissipate but will be an important force in the future.

1. As the world and national economies continue to expand there will be increased institutionalization of the marketing process and a corresponding increase in potential for lack of trust by the consumer for members of the marketing channel.
2. Inflation is a problem that may be with us for years to come, a fact that will foster economic discontent in the consumer.
3. Consumers, as they grow more affluent and have their more basic needs satisfied, will become more critical as their concern shifts to more altruistic motives and to quality of life versus quantity of things.
4. As products become more complex it will become increasingly difficult for consumers to make a choice when they purchase a product. This will put greater pressure on the marketing function to deliver the promised package of benefits.
5. As recession and inflation continue to reduce consumer purchasing power, greater emphasis will be placed on product quality at reasonable prices. Marketing must be equal to the task.
6. As consumers reach higher levels of education, their increased awareness of rights and power will lead to less tolerance of marketing abuses.[10]

Marketing originally was conceived as the distribution of economic goods and services. Over the years, as the body of marketing thought has evolved, theory and practice have become concerned with demand creation. The consumer movement promises to force a reconsideration of the importance of physical supply as a component of the marketing process.

Consumer Demands and Their Effect on Physical Distribution

The rise of the consumerism movement has made adoption of the marketing concept a critical success factor for business firms, government bodies, and others. The marketing concept states that the basic objective of an organization is to satisfy customers and society. This implies that marketing encompasses much more than the selling of goods and services. Marketing includes, among other things, research, product planning, inventory control, buying, and physical distribution. Because consumerism has had a direct impact on marketing, it follows that the elements of the marketing process—product, price, promotion, distribution— also must be subject to the pressure of consumerism. This can be seen in the areas of product availability, product quality, product costs, and environmental concern.

Product Availability

In the area of product availability, consumers demand products when and where they want them and in sufficient quantities to satisfy their needs. This requires that firms develop efficient distribution systems, able to service diverse consumer markets with products desired by consumers. Items especially important to the firm are customer service levels, time in transit, consistency of service, routing and scheduling, warehousing, and inventories.

Product Quality

The manufacturing arm of the firm is primarily responsible for maintaining acceptable product quality. However, once the product is produced, it is the responsibility of the physical distribution system to maintain that level of quality from the point of production to the point of consumption. Consumerism demands the highest quality products which the distribution system can offer. Therefore, the distribution network must attempt to minimize product mishandling, poor routing and scheduling, and delays in transit. In addition, when products fail to perform and must be returned through the channel of distribution, it is the responsibility of enterprise management to see that these returns are handled in the most efficient manner.

Product Costs

Higher prices are generally criticized by consumerists, especially if the rise in price is not associated with a commensurate benefit to the buyer. For example, consumerists are extremely critical of the high prices charged for various food products. The food retailer and others in the supply route bear the brunt of this criticism. Since it is generally felt that the farmer is not receiving high enough prices to justify the increased cost at the retail level, the retailer or someone else in the channel is held responsible. One possibility for the higher prices at the retail level is evidenced in a typical food distribution channel. A number of product movements and product handlings occur, and a variety of storage facilities are employed. The costs for this movement, handling, and storage have a direct impact on consumer prices. Inefficiencies in physical distribution result in higher costs throughout the channel of distribution. Typically, these inefficiencies will take the form of small orders, less than truckload versus truckload movements, and failure to use pallets. It can be speculated that consumers, their real incomes reduced by inflation, are becoming intolerant of system inefficiencies and short-comings since they are being forced to pay for these faults at the retail level.

Environmental Concern

In addition to intolerance of increased costs due to system inefficiencies, consumerists have doubts about intangible costs in the areas of energy, ecology, and urban congestion. Individuals, businesses, and governments are demanding efficient and productive distribution systems which move products with a minimum of pollution, the maximum in energy efficiency, and with a minimum of system delays such as those caused by transportation congestion. It is imperative, then, that the distribution system operate in the most efficient and productive manner from a macro (societal) and a micro (the firm) perspective.

Related issues are recycling and reuse of containers. Oregon and Michigan laws banning nonreturnable containers are evidence that consumers will accept the associated higher costs (in price or convenience).[11] Therefore, the distribution system has a responsibility to provide the most effective network possible to handle movement and storage of these containers.

Implications for Distribution Management

Specific implications for dealing with consumer demands on the physical distribution function can be categorized in terms of general management, customer service, transportation, inventory management, order processing and information control, warehousing, and packaging and material handling.

General Managerial Implications

Management must orient itself toward a total systems approach in order to minimize interdepart-mental conflict and the resulting inefficiencies. This will require new and better forms of distribution cost information and new standards by which to judge performance.

More efficiency in all areas of distribution may be necessary to reduce costs and reach the best cost-benefit ratio possible. All activities of physical distribution, including transportation, inventory management, order processing, storage, and materials handling, should be viewed as interrelated and integrated.[12] Successful management of these activities should result in synergistic results for the firm and its customers.

In addition, management must develop improved costing systems so that distribution cost trade-offs can be implemented. Also, the cost trade-offs that are made must be communicated to the consumer. Too often, the costs associated with consumer legislation are not made known to consumers. Many times, business has not adequately presented its case. In other situations the lack of adequate accounting information may have resulted in the evolution of inefficient channels of distribution.[13]

Customer Service

The customer service area represents the distribution system's most visible contact with the consumer. Its elements can be segregated into those that directly affect the purchase decision (the transaction elements) and those that support use of the product (the post-transaction elements). The transaction elements include product stockout levels, ability to handle backorders, elements of the order cycle, ability to expedite shipments, accuracy of order filling, and customer convenience in placing an order. The post-transaction elements include product installation, warranty, parts and repairs, product tracking, customer complaints, claims and product returns, and temporary replacement of the product for servicing and repairs.[14]

The Oregon bottle laws initially placed heavy demands on the distribution networks of beer and soft drink distributors and bottlers. The existing distribution channel had to be modified so that the return of containers would have minimal effect on the consumer in terms of product cost. It is estimated that the Oregon legislation will cause a $12 million hardship for beverage marketers in that state over the first ten years.[15] Business must react to these hardships in a positive manner. One method might be for the industry to establish a standard bottle or bottles so that individual brand labels could be glued on and washed off. This would reduce the return problems associated with multiple bottle shapes and sizes. Other methods might include the use at the retail level of machines to compress returned aluminum containers for easy storage and transportation. Creative responses are required.

Both consumer goods and industrial goods manufacturers can reduce friction between producer and consumer by developing a product-customer mix (see Table 1). This classification parallels the ABC analysis commonly used in inventory management. ABC analysis has been defined by Donald Bowersox.

Classification by sales volume is one of the oldest methods employed selectively to establish safety stock policy for an inventory line. In most marketing situations a small percentage of products account for a large percentage of sales. This generalization is often called the 20/80 rule, wherein 20 percent of the products account for 80 percent of the sales. The most common basis for sales classification is to rank-array and then group products into categories labeled ABC or similarly.[16]

Briefly, every company has customers that can be classified on the basis of such criteria as class of trade, profit potential, or urgency of need. Different distribution service standards can be applied to various customers and products. Table 2 shows one way of making the product-customer mix operational. The overall criteria for establishing these priorities and their corresponding service levels should be determined by corporate management, giving full consideration to the capabilities of the firm's distribution system. Although a manufac-

Table 1

The product-customer mix

Customer classification	Product			
	A	B	C	D
I	1	2	6	10
II	3	4	7	2
III	5	8	13	16
IV	9	14	15	19
V	11	17	18	20

Source: Bernard J. La Londe and James R. Robeson, "Corporate Strategy and Organization for Distribution," *Journal of Business Policy* 2 (Spring 1972): 51.

Note: Classifications I through V represent groupings of customers based on such criteria as class of trade, profit potential, geographic area, or size of order. Groups A through D represent groupings of products based on profit contribution or importance to customer. Priorities 1 through 20 represent importance of cell to overall corporate long-run profitability.

Table 2

Making the product-customer mix operational

Priority range	In-stock standard	Delivery standard	Order completeness standard
1–5	100%	48 hours	99%
6–10	97.5	72 hours	97
11–15	95	86 hours	95
16–20	90	120 hours	93

Source: Bernard J. La Londe and Paul H. Zinszer, *Customer Service: Meaning and Measurement* (Chicago, Illinois: National Council of Physical Distribution Management, 1976), p. 182.

turer of industrial products does not deal directly with the public, management may want to consider the impact of its priority system on the ability of the company's customers to satisfy the ultimate consumers. That is, the dollar profit contribution of an account may not be the only consideration when setting priorities, especially if such a decision could ultimately lead to consumer unrest. As stated by Bernard La Londe and Paul Zinszer,

customer service standards should: (1) reflect the customer's point of view; (2) provide an operational and objective measure of service performance; and

(3) provide management cues for corrective action.[17]

The customer service standards established by any firm are specific to that firm. It should be noted that firms giving different service levels to customers similarly situated in the same market may be violating the Robinson-Patman Act. However, markets can be classified by service levels on the basis of profitability, geography, or lines of trade.

Transportation

Better management of the corporate traffic department can be realized by improving the use of existing equipment and using more efficient forms of transportation in terms of energy consumption and pollution. The former could be accomplished by making better use of railcar space by consolidating shipments, and the latter could take the form of increased use of rail or water transport or diesel powered vehicles.

In addition, firms can ensure that key customers are monitored regularly by special personnel and are provided higher levels of service. This may require the use of premium transportation, for example, air freight. The company can ensure that its transportation carriers are competent, efficient, and dynamic. Specifically, firms should require, at a minimum, certain services from its carriers (thus ensuring higher levels of service to its customers).

1. Manual or computer systems should be used to trace, reroute, and expedite shipments efficiently and to provide accurate rating and billing of accounts.
2. The firm and its customers should obtain reports of all inbound and outbound freight being shipped/received during a specified period.
3. Carriers should work with the firm and its customers on claims prevention through carrier sales people or claims representatives.
4. Carriers should work with the firm and its customers on the development of new services,

such as automatic billing and auditing, shipment tracing, and new equipment. For example, Spector Motor Freight has developed a system whereby a shipper's distribution personnel have direct access to Spector's computer for the purposes of shipment tracing.

Improved routing and scheduling procedures may result in a reduced number of product shortages as well as reduced in-transit loss of perishables. These steps, plus any equipment improvements that would decrease the amount of loss and damage in transit, would ultimately reduce the cost to the consumer.

Inventory Management

The area of inventory management holds significant potential for cost reduction. Wendell Stewart has estimated that inventory carrying costs represent about one-third of the total distribution costs of a company.[18] In a recent study in the food industry, inventory carrying costs were calculated to average approximately 30 percent, with individual carrying costs ranging from 14 percent to 43 percent of the average annual inventory valued at variable cost delivered to the distribution center.[19]

It is conceivable that pressure to increase inventory levels will occur as corporations attempt to satisfy increasingly divergent consumer markets. The ABC method of providing customer service levels is one way to reduce inventory. Other inventory control systems such as IBM's IMPACT (for wholesale operations) and COGS (for consumer goods manufacturers) could be used to satisfy service requirements at a reasonable cost. Jefferson G. Summers, director of management information systems at Sterling Drug, Inc., reported favorably on the adoption of such a system. "The range of benefits from this system at Sterling Drug includes cost savings in seven figures and greatly improved production and distribution operations."[20]

Order Processing and Information Control

"Order processing constitutes a significant portion of the time, and in some cases the cost, required in a logistics system . . . a day saved in order-processing time may be as significant in reducing necessary inventories as a day saved in material handling or transportation. And it may be much less costly to accomplish time savings in information as opposed to physical flows."[21]

The adoption of on-line order processing systems can be used to ensure prompt delivery and to eliminate late deliveries and stockouts. Systems that can provide a timely and direct linkage with the customer (and hence the ultimate consumer) should be adopted to provide fast response time to shifts in consumer demand and to provide information about problems in the field.

One *Fortune* 500 firm has accomplished this by requiring that customers place orders with customer service representatives, located at corporate headquarters. The representatives are equipped with remote cathode ray tube terminals. This system not only reduces the order cycle time but also gives the customer immediate feedback on product availability and delivery dates.

Warehousing

The proliferation of product offerings and shortened product life cycles have resulted in increased stockkeeping units. This, combined with changing consumer demands, points to the major advantage of public warehousing over private or leased facilities—flexibility. With public warehousing facilities, the user can adapt to changes in buying patterns by adding or deleting storage space or storage locations at low cost.

1. The contemporary warehouse philosophy of using materials handling systems combining storage and handling for maximum efficiency should be maintained.

2. Where economically feasible, warehousing should be employed to reduce overall distribution costs and provide the highest possible service levels to the firm's customers.

3. Warehousing decisions should be determined, first, by customer demands and, second, by the needs of the firm.

The use of automated warehousing facilities offers the potential for creating true distribution centers as compared to storage locations. Automated warehouses could improve inventory turnover and lower inventory carrying costs.

Shared warehouses and consolidation terminals also represent opportunities for improved efficiency and reduced costs. Urban freight consolidation terminals have the added feature of reducing urban congestion and pollution.[22]

Packaging and Material Handling

Improved packaging can reduce damage and increase the efficiency of material handling. Efficient material handling equipment, pallets, standardized pallet sizes, and containerization all offer potential cost savings to the firm and its customers.

It should be noted that the area of packaging and materials handling is becoming more difficult to manage, particularly for manufacturers of hazardous materials. This is due primarily to increased government regulation of such materials. One distribution executive in the chemical industry foresees the day when he will be unable to fill some customers' orders because (1) they will want a quantity (for example, 20 gallons) of a particular product that cannot be delivered safely in that size container, or (2) they will not possess the necessary equipment to handle and store the product safely once it has been received.

If this projection is valid, much effort will be required by industry to strike a reasonable balance between consumer-employee protection and the levels of service, availability, and cost demanded in the marketplace. Failure to deal effectively with this problem will cut corporate profits and could result in more government regulation. Failure to comply with government regulation has even greater risk—

possible fines or jail terms for the managers involved.[23]

Overview and Concluding Note

As consumerism becomes more widespread in the United States and throughout the world, the demands on physical distribution will increase. Consumerism will not disappear. Since physical distribution is an essential element in a firm's product offering, and a significant contributor to the marketing concept, distribution strategy necessarily must adapt and change to meet the growing needs of consumers. Firms must increasingly become aware of their responsibilities in the physical supply of consumer demand. Consumerism promises to affect all aspects of the physical distribution process. Consequently, it deserves the attention of the physical distribution manager.

Consumerists will demand higher levels of customer service from business in the years ahead. Physical distribution is ideally situated within the corporate system; it offers the unique advantage of being able to increase efficiency without substantial expenditure. In fact, in some instances it may be possible to improve customer service levels at no additional cost. Integrating physical distribution activities so as to achieve synergistic results provides the firm with a straightforward approach to satisfying the increasing demands of consumerism.

Notes

1. Stephen A. Greyser and Steven L. Diamond, "Business Is Adapting to Consumerism," *Harvard Business Review* 52 (September–October 1974): 39.
2. Policy Declaration, 1970–1971, Chamber of Commerce of the United States (Washington, D.C.: 1970), pp. 9–12, in Ralph M. Gaedeke and Warren W. Etcheson, *Consumerism: Viewpoints from Business, Government and the Public Interest* (San Francisco: Canfield Press, 1972), p. 358.
3. David A. Aaker and George S. Day, "Corporate Responses to Consumerism Pressures," *Harvard Business Review* 50 (November–December 1972): 114–24; and Norman Kangun; Keith K. Cox; James Higginbotham; and John Burton, "Consumerism and Marketing Management," *Journal of Marketing* 39 (April 1975): 3–10.
4. William J. Stanton, *Fundamentals of Marketing,* 4th ed. (New York: McGraw-Hill, 1975), p. 671.
5. Richard H. Buskirk and James T. Rothe, "Consumerism—An Interpretation," *Journal of Marketing* 34 (October 1970): 61–65.
6. Philip Kotler, "What Consumerism Means for Marketers," *Harvard Business Review* 50 (May–June 1972): 49 and 50.
7. John Calascione and David R. Calhoun, "Consumerism," from *1975 Britannica Book of the Year* (Chicago: Encyclopedia Britannica, Inc., 1975), p. 189.
8. Thomas A. Murphy, "Businessman, Heal Thyself," *Newsweek,* 20 December 1976, p. 11.
9. David S. R. Leighton, "Consumerism in Canada: The Future," in David A. Aaker and George S. Day, *Consumerism Search for the Consumer Interest,* 2nd ed. (New York: The Free Press, 1974), p. 446.
10. See "U.S. Consumer Groups: Livelier Than Ever," *U.S. News and World Report,* 6 December 1976, pp. 90–91; "The Cries of Angry Consumers—What They're Telling Officials Now," *U.S. News and World Report,* 18 April 1977, pp. 61–62; and "America's Angry Consumers—What They're Telling Officials Now," *U.S. News and World Report,* 10 May 1976, pp. 56–58.
11. Pat Murphy, "A Cost/Benefit Analysis of the Oregon Bottle Bill," *1974 Combined Proceedings* (Chicago: American Marketing Association, 1975), pp. 347–50.
12. Donald J. Bowersox, *Logistical Management* (New York: Macmillan, 1974), p. 18.
13. Douglas M. Lambert, *The Distribution Channels Decision* (New York: National Association of Accountants, and Hamilton, Ontario: The Society of Management Accountants of Canada, 1978).
14. Bernard J. La Londe and Paul H. Zinszer, "Customer Service as a Component of the Physical Distribution System," working paper, The Ohio State University, 1975.

15. Murphy, "Oregon Bottle Bill," p. 351.

16. Bowersox, *Logistical Management,* pp. 204–05.

17. Bernard J. LaLonde and Paul H. Zinszer, *Customer Service: Meaning and Measurement* (Chicago: National Council of Physical Distribution Management, 1976), p. 180.

18. Wendell M. Stewart, "Physical Distribution: Key to Improved Volume and Profits," *Journal of Marketing* 29 (January 1965): 65–69.

19. Douglas M. Lambert, *The Development of an Inventory Costing Methodology: A Study of the Costs Associated with Holding Inventory* (Chicago: National Council of Physical Distribution Management, 1976).

20. Jefferson G. Summers, "A System to Roll Back Inventory Levels," *Transportation and Distribution Management* 13 (October 1973): 33.

21. James L. Heskett; Nicholas A. Glaskowsky, Jr.; and Robert M. Ivie, *Business Logistics,* 2nd ed. (New York: Ronald Press, 1973), p. 514.

22. For a detailed report on the potential of urban consolidation terminals, see James R. Robeson and Dennis R. McDermott, *The Economic Feasibility and Social Desirability of an Urban Consolidation Terminal* (Washington D.C., U.S. Department of Transportation, July 1974).

23. Tony McAdams and Robert C. Miljus, "Growing Criminal Liability of Executives," *Harvard Business Review* 56 (March–April 1977): 36–40.

Questions

1. *Explain the impact of the consumer movement upon physical distribution managers in the areas of product availability, product quality, product costs, and environmental concern.*

2. *Give examples that illustrate specific implications of growing consumer demands for improved service upon physical distribution activities.*

29

Public Warehousing: Supermarkets for Distribution Services

GERRY O. PATNO

The most current trend in public warehousing seems to be a shift from the old, entrepreneurial job of selling space for the storage of goods to offering a service for the distribution of goods. The difference is tremendous.

Last December, at Ohio State University in Columbus, Ohio, a group of professionals in the public warehousing industry gathered to discuss the pros and cons of using a public warehouse or building a private one. Two or three years of graduate-level finance and cost accounting would be necessary to fully understand the factors involved with building a private warehouse. But to understand the factors involved with using a public warehouse, talk to professionals in the business.

Distribution Supermarket

Ted Hermann, president of Pacific Freeport Warehouse in Sparks, Nevada, phrases it perfectly: "Customers come to us and pick the service they want—space rental, help in billing, key management personnel—and we give it to them. We are a supermarket for distribution services."

John Juzaitis, president of John-Jeffrey Corp. in Camden, New Jersey, elaborates, "Customer service is very critical. Not only is warehousing a deposit of merchandise, it's service in and out. It's

Source: Handling and Shipping, March 1977, pp. 59–61. Reprinted from HANDLING & SHIPPING, March 77, and copyright ©, 1977, by Penton/IPC, Inc.

consolidation programs. It's good, dependable service tailored to the operations of the customer."

What they're talking about, of course, is public warehousing and the direction it has taken the last 10 (or so) years. Almost without exception, experts in the field say you've got to please the customer, meet his every demand, no matter how specific, to stay competitive.

At one time, "customer service" was unloading goods, storing them, and shipping goods out. Today, public warehousemen offer their customers a wide range of distribution services: freight consolidation, labeling, billing (customers and customers' customers), managerial services, consultation, and just doing more for the customer to help him keep costs low.

Public vs. Private

True automation is a luxury only the private sector can afford, according to Don Horton, president of the American Warehousemen's Association (AWA). Private warehouses have complete control of products in and products out. Private warehouses have the financial security of a parent company. Private warehouses, for the most part, have only one customer—themselves.

Public warehouses must provide services for 15–20 different customers on a short-term (30-day) basis. Public warehouses need as much flexibility as possible, and can't automate to control one customer.

One semi-exception to this rule, however, is

Leaseway Distribution Centers' Holland Road Warehouse in Cleveland. Though a public warehouse, the facility has a semiautomatic roller system to accommodate the Ohio State Liquor Department account. The facility distributes 38 percent of all the liquor in the state of Ohio, handles 1,000 brands, and serves 17 outlets daily.

Leaseway landed the account on an exception to the public-warehouse rule: a long-term contract. But, says William Conn, president of the company, "We needed the security of a long-term contract in order to semiautomate. Without the security, the cost to the customer would be greater."

Other public warehouses have semi-automated in other ways. John-Jeffrey Corp. installed a wire-guided towcart system throughout its facility for fast material handling within the facility.

In Columbus, Ohio, Retail Merchants Consolidation and Distribution Center installed a magnetically-guided towline to speed up and facilitate cargo consolidations. In fact, Harry Cutler, Retail Merchants' president, has gone a step further—the company owns and operates its own fleet of trucks.

For the most part, however, public warehousemen cannot take the high-rise, computerized, full-automatic route. They could not justify the huge initial expense, and customers would certainly not pay for it.

Going Underground

In some areas of the country (those that used to be called deserted) the right natural ingredients exist for literally going underground. Large deposits of limestone mined out for construction materials yield a byproduct—dry, moisture-retardant caverns perfectly suited for the storage of goods. If such caverns have the good fortune of being in a not-too-off-track location, they make excellent (and economical) distribution centers.

Space Center Inc. of St. Paul, Minnesota, has two such underground warehouses (in Kansas City, Missouri and in Quincy, Illinois). Each offers a constant 55 degree temperature and a relative humidity

of 55 percent. Roger Carleson, vice president, says that the investment and operational costs are much less with underground caverns than with surface buildings. Though there is only a handful of underground warehouses, Mr. Carleson sees a trend to counteract the increased cost of surface buildings. "Physical growth," he says, "due to the high costs of construction will lead to more remodeling, using old buildings, and getting closer to the city. That's the real trend."

Other Costs on the Rise

Howard Way, president of Howard Way and Associates, Inc., of Alexandria, Virginia, says that public warehousemen ". . . do more for the customer—more split-function warehousing, more freight consolidation—because of the escalating costs of energy and transportation, and the desire to reduce empty backhaul."

Split-function warehousing[1] is an agreement between the warehouseman and his customer for the warehouseman to take custody of the goods (his normal responsibility) and possession (normally the responsibility of a buyer). In theory, then, the warehouseman buys the goods. He's responsible for goods in the warehouse, but is guaranteed reimbursement for those items not sold.

Owning the goods: (1) simplifies distribution. The warehouseman can take orders, price-mark and deliver goods, consolidate loads, fill backhaul trips, or allow pickup—all without common carrier regulations, because he owns the goods. (2) makes for efficient handling in and out fast turnover, and low risk of inventory. (3) achieves good customer service and cost savings.

Outlook on Labor

In most distribution center operations, the single biggest cost factor is labor. To get the most from

1. Originally formulated as the "March Plan," explained in *Handling & Shipping*, February, 1967, page 53.

labor, many distribution centers have computerized operations.

John-Jeffrey Corp. has two computers to discharge orders and picking sequence. The computers do not issue an order unless the product is in stock, and then issue picking orders according to the sequence in which the products are stocked.

Leaseway's liquor distribution center has an IBM computer that controls information on all inbound and outbound shipments. Using shipping detail cards with the computer enables management to know the total of cases by brand shipped to each store, to print daily shipment totals, to update inventory with new shipments received, and to pick orders in sequence from one of three designated areas (for fast, moderate, and slow movers).

Pacific Freeport's Ted Hermann says that his company is active in labor relations; i.e., studying the labor market with regard to wages and benefits, and acting accordingly. Employees are not only well trained, they are cross trained to learn several different jobs. Turnover is little, and management is brought up through the ranks via an in-house management training program.

The AWA's education committee also is striving to improve labor efficiency with its Standard Time Values (STV) program. Ed Starr, executive vice president of Dry Storage Corp. in Des Plains, Illinois, is an education committee member assigned to the STV program. He says that, "the industry must grab this program and use it to get reasonable labor costs and efficient use of labor."

The time standards are for the four major functions associated with operating a public warehouse: receiving, storing, picking, and shipping. The basic plan adapts to any situation; standard data is fed into situations to meet the needs of specific operations (manual or computerized) and to set standards for each function of each account.

With the STV program, warehousemen can determine shipping and picking demand, schedule pickup and delivery accordingly, and anticipate workloads. The resulting effect on labor and customer service indicate it—

Avoids idle time
Schedule workloads
Provides a system to price services
Provides a tool for handling accounts, storing goods, and choosing the proper equipment for the job
Helps determine the layout of a building
Assesses the value of different storage methods.

Presently, about 25 warehouses use the STV program, but, as Mr. Starr points out, "Because labor sometimes accounts for half the cost of operation, we must organize and discipline ourselves to use the program and get the results that can be achieved."

Where We've Been . . .

"Public warehousing has been riding the crest of a fairly long-term recession," says Ken Ackerman, chairman of Distribution Centers in Columbus, Ohio, "because of the big inventory liquidation from the fall of 1974 to the spring of 1975. Everyone unloaded inventories, and we have not yet bounced back."

As Mr. Ackerman explained at the OSU seminar last December, the American business ideal of cheap, abundant energy was shattered. That led to uncertainty and big business, for the most part, became nervous. It began building cash reserves (ask your local banker how business is) rather than inventory reserves, which had a damaging effect on public warehouses.

AWA's Don Horton says that the recession led to inventory reduction, but while business has increased, inventory has not. Stocks are not now in plentiful supply.

Ken Ackerman says that when businessmen realize the stock shortage and fear depletion of something, they'll start stockpiling. "That's what we need—to build inventories to the level of three years ago."

. . . **Where We're Going**

"The biggest problem," Ken Ackerman continues, "is forecasting what the future holds for warehousing. Customers just don't know how much space they'll need."

Regardless of space requirements, one thing's for sure—the public warehouseman will have to offer service, not just space.

Getting back to that December seminar at OSU, Jim Kennedy, Jr., secretary-treasurer of Cherokee Warehouses in Chattanooga, Tennessee, said, "Public warehousemen must anticipate and plan to satisfy the customer to achieve the goal of service with economy."

Dr. Bernard LaLonde, professor of marketing and logistics, OSU, pointed out that users tend to remember public warehouses by the last bad order. And furthermore, that "warehousemen commit sins of omission rather than commission. It's not that warehousemen don't want to give good service, it's just that they don't really know what customers want."

A study conducted by Dr. LaLonde, "The Public Warehouse Selection Decision," demonstrates a concern of public warehousemen for increased customer services. Asked to predict the most striking foreseeable change in the next ten years (the study was made in 1972), the majority of respondents said an "increase in level and types of services offered to customers" must occur.

Next were the "growing importance of large chains in multiple geographic locations," and "increased use of warehouse automation." Both of these trends have the end effect of better enabling warehousemen to serve customers.

Another trend which Dr. LaLonde says is more prevalent today than 10 years ago, and will be even more prevalent 10 years from now, is specialization in such industries as food, chemicals, etc. The FDA and EPA have set such stringent demands that in order to comply the warehouse must specialize in one particular field. Again, the end result benefits the customer.

Questions

1. *Compare and contrast the characteristics of public and private warehouses.*
2. *What environmental circumstances are causing public warehouses to become "supermarkets for distribution services?"*

PART FIVE

Promotion Decisions

Goodrich claimed, "We're the other guys!" Magnavox said, "Magnavox beats Zenith and RCA in 4 important ways." [1] *Other marketers followed suit in their advertising with messages like these. "Compare prices. If you like L'eggs at $1.39 a pair, you'll love StarCrest at 59¢ a pair!"* [2] *"Sorry Sears, PPG, Sherwin-Williams, Lucite and Dutch Boy . . . Spred Satin Wins!"* [3] *The Federal Trade Commission in 1971 began advocating such comparative advertising. Then, when concern rose that consumers were being confused because comparative advertising was being misused to purposely treat products in a careless and demeaning manner, serious questions were raised as to whether consumers were actually benefiting from or being harmed by the practice.* [4]

K-Tel became the dominant company in the fastest growing segment of the $2.8 billion record market by "putting together" a series of singles into "compilation albums," distributing those through mass merchandisers and discount stores, and saturating the marketplace with scores of millions of dollars of TV spot ads—$33 million worth in 1977. [5]

A Minneapolis bank advertised a free house plant for each deposit of $100 or more. A New York bank offered free carpeting to persons who took out a $1,200 home improvement loan. But the most interesting offer came from a Chicago bank which offered depositors of $150,000 a Mercedes 450 SL sports coupe as part of its prepaid interest plan. Today, banks are the largest users of direct-premiums among incentive-using industries. [6]

Procter and Gamble employs one of the largest sales forces in the United States. The firm employs career salespeople as well as individuals destined to be trained

1. *TV Guide*, September 7, 1974, p. 51.
2. *Parade*, April 7, 1974, p. 7.
3. *Woman's Day* March 1974, p. 123.
4. Peter M. Ginter and Jack M. Starling, "Issues in Comparative Advertising," *Atlanta Economic Review* September–October, 1977, pp. 23–28.
5. "K-Tel Grows by Selling Other People's Music," *Business Week* May 2, 1977, pp. 62–63.
6. Robert H. Preston, F. Robert Dwyer and William Rudelius, "The Effectiveness of Bank Premiums," *Journal of Marketing* July 1978, pp. 96–101.

and elevated to sales management positions in one of the largest consumer products companies in the world.

A firm's promotion mix may encompass a broad range of activities designed to communicate with individuals, groups, or organizations. These communication efforts are undertaken to facilitate exchange by influencing members of selected audiences to accept the promoting organization's goods, services, or ideas. A promotion mix is composed of advertising, personal selling, publicity, sales promotion, and/or packaging. Each organization blends some or all of these components into a promotion mix that allows the firm to communicate effectively with its target audiences. Thus, the promotion mix facilitates exchange.

For many people, marketing means advertising and personal selling. The discussions and articles contained in Parts One through Four of this book should certainly dispel this misconception. These two types of promotional activities are extremely important parts of many firms' marketing strategies. However, they are parts and do not, in themselves, represent any firm's total marketing efforts. Product planning, pricing, and distributing activities are the other marketing activities performed by marketers to satisfy market demand.

Several selections are included in Part Five to provide an overview of the process of promoting goods and services and to address some contemporary issues regarding promotion in our society. The first two articles focus on advertising's effectiveness. "Advertising's 'Holy Grail' " describes the advertising industry's search for the foolproof formula that will ". . . show companies how to get the maximum return for their ad dollars."[7] Says a top ad agency executive, "And when somebody comes up with the answer, he'll be a millionaire."[8] In "What Makes Advertising Effective?" Herbert E. Krugman considers the ticklish problem faced by every advertiser: how much advertising is enough? The answer to this question, of course, depends on the effectiveness of the advertising efforts. Krugman argues that managers require precise information about their audiences before they can develop effective advertising campaigns.

Using comparative ads to knock the competition and its sales generating effectiveness is the focus of the third article in Part Four: "How to Use In-Depth Trade Press . . ." stresses the value of a little used but extremely cost-effective communications tool. The successful use of sales promotion tools by Coca-Cola's Fountain Sales Department is documented in "Coca-Cola Puts Sparkle. . . ."

The final three articles in Part Four focus on personal selling and sales management. *Industrial Distribution* conducted a nationwide survey of dis-

7. Niles Howard, "Advertising's 'Holy Grail,' " *Dun's Review*, September 1978, p. 109.
8. Ibid.

tributor salespeople to find out how they really feel about their jobs. Findings are reported in "Let's Ask the Salesman." Three major conclusions drawn from another survey to determine how salespeople regard financial and nonfinancial incentives are presented in "Motivating Superior Outside Sales Personnel." Finally, in "Making MBO Work in the Sales Force," Hise and Gillett discuss the crucial issues that management must consider in order to implement an effective MBO program in the sales area.

30

Advertising's "Holy Grail"   NILES HOWARD

For years, companies have been searching for a fool-proof formula that will show them how much influence advertising has on sales. The answer has proved frustratingly elusive.

For years, giant Nabisco Inc. faced a problem common to many companies with long-established consumer products. Although such Nabisco brands as Ritz Crackers and Fig Newtons held solid positions in their respective markets, the cookie and cracker businesses were clearly maturing, and management was all but resigned to the prospect of negligible growth from these older products.

But five years ago, company marketing executives decided to try something new. Armed with some novel theories and sophisticated computer programs, they began varying the levels of advertising for the products in small, isolated communities and closely monitoring the effects on sales. The results surprised and fascinated management. Not only did sales of some products soar to unprecedented heights when advertising was increased, but, by repeating the tests, researchers were able to deduce some unusual statistical relationships between ad spending and sales volume. With those guidelines in hand, Nabisco set out on the biggest advertising push in its history, and sales of many once-stagnant brands have grown as much as 30% since 1975.

Source: Reprinted with the special permission of DUN's REVIEW, September 1978, pp. 109–110, 113. Copyright © 1978, Dun & Bradstreet Publications Corporation.

The Nabisco experience has been followed with great interest by just about everyone in the advertising business for the answers it may provide to one of the industry's most perplexing questions: How much influence does advertising have on sales—and, hence, profits—of a product? Although it is taken for granted by most companies that advertising is an important—if not the most important—single influence on the movement of goods and services, hard evidence has proven frustratingly elusive. As well-known retailer John Wanamaker used to lament: "I know that half the money I spend on advertising is wasted. The trouble is, I don't know which half."

But it is not for lack of trying. As advertising rates have soared in recent years, corporate marketing departments have been forced to give management better justification of the ad funds they shell out. Thus, researchers and ad agencies have been pouring millions of dollars into the construction of elaborate theories and computer models in an intense search for a foolproof formula that will show companies how to get the maximum return for their ad dollars. Such a formula has often been described as Madison Avenue's Holy Grail. "It is the impossible dream," says Paul J. Paulson, executive vice president of ad agency Doyle Dane Bernbach. "And when someone comes up with the answer, he'll be a millionaire."

Scanty Knowledge

The money at stake is staggering. A total of $37 billion was spent on advertising in this country last year, and 21 major companies spent more than $100 million each. But most ad budgets go through little of the cost-benefit scrutiny that is routinely applied to such other major expenditures as capital projects or payroll. Indeed, corporate executives will privately admit that they have only the vaguest notion of the point at which an additional advertising dollar ceases to pay for itself through increased profits; instead, most companies fall back on some rule of thumb—such as spending a certain percentage of sales or anticipated profits on advertising a product. Even in retrospect, it is rarely clear whether the decision was the right one, since it usually isn't known whether an increase or decrease in product sales is due to the level of advertising or to some other factor.

Companies, of course, do have some knowledge about the effects of their advertising. On the creative side, researchers have had considerable success in finding out from consumer studies the most persuasive kinds of written and broadcast messages. At the same time, most companies have been able to identify in great detail the kinds of people who use a particular product, as well as the kinds of advertising media these potential customers are most likely to see. Combined, those branches of research have been able to determine with impressive accuracy the type and amount of advertising required to influence the consumer's attitude toward a particular product.

The problem is that there is a large gap between consumer attitude and purchase. The decision to buy or not buy a particular product is based on a large number of factors besides advertising, and the ad industry has long recognized this as a major hurdle to the measurement of advertising results. Package design, for example, clearly has a powerful influence, as does price, position on the grocery shelf and product quality. The biggest difficulty marketing researchers have faced is figuring out how to isolate advertising from these other factors. Over the years, they have felt there must be some sort of universal formula that would work.

One area in which measurement has been possible is mail-order advertising, where pulling power can be figured simply by measuring the number of orders sent in. And there have been a number of attempts to transfer mail-order measurement methods to more general kinds of advertising. As early as the 1920s, adman Claude Hopkins, whom some consider the most successful copywriter of all time, claimed to have come up with ways to bridge that gap. Many companies, as might be expected, rushed to his door, but Hopkins' ideas eventually proved useless, as did a slew of other formulas and theories put forth by former ad agency executives, PhD candidates and university professors.

Then in 1961, General Mills Corp. asked Benjamin F. Butler Sr., an executive vice president of Marketing Research Corporation of America, to help it solve a communications problem that was impeding new-product development. The problem was that research and development executives knew so little about marketing, and marketing executives knew so little about physics and chemistry, that the two groups could not coordinate their ideas.

Butler came up with some suggestions to improve the flow of information, and in doing so became fascinated by similarities between the two fields and the possibility that physical science theories could be applied to marketing problems, particularly in the measurement of results. Using some case histories, a slide rule and a tabletop calculator, and working on his own, Butler soon came up with some general theories, and after a while quit his job to work on them full time. A short time later, he formed a consulting firm called Hendry Corp. to perfect and sell his new formula for predicting advertising effectiveness.

Theory of Entropy

Butler's formula was based on the thermodynamics theory of entropy, which states that when a system is left alone, its internal parts will reach an equilibrium; and by studying the relationships between the parts of the system, one can predict what will happen if the system is stimulated from the outside. Butler reasoned that a group of competing products constituted a system, and that if left alone they would achieve a stable market share. By determining the relationship between the market share of each product, Butler decided that he could predict how sales of each product would be affected if an external stimulus—a change in packaging, price or, most important, advertising—were applied.

He deduced, for instance, that the wider the market-share gap between a top-selling product and its competitors, the more likely consumers could be convinced to switch brands, and he came up with a formula to calculate the likelihood of that happening. Similarly, he reasoned that the more products there are that compete with each other, the greater the customer loyalty to a given brand; and he devised a formula to figure that, too. Thus, by gathering information about a product and its competitors, he claimed he could figure out precisely what would happen to sales and profits if advertising spending were increased or decreased by any specific amount. Subsequently, Hendry came out with a second model to calculate the earnings potential of new products; and later added a third, designed to forecast not just the immediate but the long-term impact of advertising. Results were issued in the form of a graph called a HendroGraph (see Exhibit 1.)

Butler was able to sell his formula to giant General Foods and, later, to Coca-Cola, Schlitz and other companies. But it was not until 1970, when Ogilvy & Mather bought the exclusive ad agency rights to the Hendry formula, that it finally won attention. After using the formula for a year, Ogilvy took out full-page ads to proclaim its success. "For the first time," Ogilvy maintained, "it is possible to find out in dollars and cents what you are getting for your advertising dollars."

But critics wasted little time in coming forward. The formula was faulted on technical grounds, and some agency executives and advertisers expressed bemused disbelief. The flap was brief, but while the Hendry formula continues to be used today by a number of companies, it failed to gain widespread acclaim as the magic formula everyone was looking for. For one thing, say the critics, Hendry has never told an outsider just exactly how the formula works. "It's a black box," says Stephens Dietz, a New York

Exhibit 1
Butler's "black box"

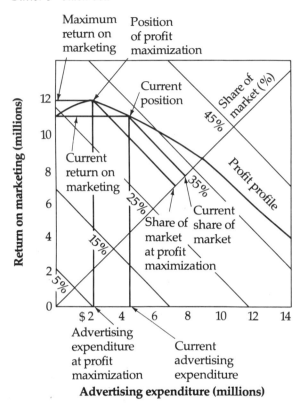

Of the numerous attempts to relate advertising to sales and profits, one of the most controversial is the formula developed by the late Benjamin Butler Sr. Although the formula remains a tightly guarded secret, the end result is easy to understand. This analysis, for example, charts what probably would happen to sales and profits of a particular product if its ad expenditures (bottom scale) were cut from $4.3 million to $2.4 million. At the lower budget level, the product's market share (diagonal line) falls from 33.5% to 30%, but its profit rises from $11.2 million to $12.1 million (scale, left).

marketing consultant. "You can see what goes in and what comes out, but I don't have the faintest idea what's inside, and neither, to my knowledge, does anyone else."

Comments Benjamin Butler Jr., who has been president of Hendry since his father's death in 1973: "People think that predicting results is impossible. But not only is it possible, we are doing it."

And others, too, keep trying. Since the late 1960s and early 1970s, the computer has spawned development of numerous programs to determine ad effectiveness. Most are meant to simply serve a particular company's needs, but several more ambitious ones have attracted industry attention. Rather than growing out of theoretical laws of behavior, they are generally based on field experiments. Ad agency Batten Barton, Durstine & Osborn, for instance, claims to have designed a computer model based on case studies that not only suggests how much money should be spent to advertise a brand, but the most effective way to spend it.

Nabisco's Success

One of the most ambitious and successful programs is Nabisco's. In the case of Ritz crackers, for example, the company selected communities representing 3.2% of the U.S. population and stepped up the level of advertising gradually until consumers were exposed to as many as three times more ads than normal. By tracking sales in every grocery store for a year, Nabisco learned how to increase sales by up to 15% without cutting into profit margins. In another case, the company varied advertising levels for nine brands at a time to calculate how advertising levels affected not only sales of those products, but other Nabisco products as well.

So far, Nabisco has about 200 million pieces of data relating advertising to sales on line. Soon, the company says, its computers will not only be able to pinpoint the ideal amount of advertising for a product, but will calculate the most profitable way to allocate ad dollars among products.

But even as such progress is made, most admen seem to agree that there is no foolproof answer and that the best a company can hope for is a formula that will provide a general guide to the proper amount of advertising, leaving the rest to human judgment. "The only way to find out how much to spend is to do it," says Stephens Dietz. "After about five years, you will have learned enough to make a pretty good judgment."

In fact, some of the most promising work now being done centers on the monitoring of advertising so as to permit more effective trial-and-error methods. For instance, New York marketing researcher Eric Marder says he has developed a questionnaire system that reveals not only who is watching every television commercial and what effect the commercial has on the viewer's attitudes toward the product, but whether the viewer eventually buys the product. He uses the system to prepare a syndicated report, which he sells to several national advertisers.

At the same time, the Advertising Research Foundation is conducting tests in Kansas City in which a computer is being used to gather information from electronic checkout systems in supermarkets and relate sales of a product to various levels of advertising expenditures.

Nevertheless, the appeal of a single formula remains. Says Jack Matthews, an advertising consultant in Chicago: "Companies call me constantly to ask, 'What kind of magic formulas do you have that you can sell us?' What can I tell them? There isn't any crystal ball. All you can do is look at what's happened, use your judgment and hope for the best."

Questions

1. *"The objective of an advertising campaign should be to increase _____." Fill in the blank and justify your answer.*
2. *Explain the relationship between sales, advertising expenses, and profits.*
3. *Explain, in general terms, Benjamin F. Butler Sr.'s formula to relate advertising effort to sales and profits.*
4. *What factors determine the effectiveness of an advertising campaign?*

31

What Makes
Advertising Effective?

HERBERT E. KRUGMAN

What makes an advertisement successful? How much advertising is enough? Many executives spend long hours trying to answer these two questions.

Any discussion of the effects of advertising must begin with the environment—a controlling factor that both defines and limits the possible effects. The environment of advertising consists of an intricate web of social, economic, and technological circumstances that direct an ad toward a particular audience through a particular medium. Obviously, the advertiser's primary concern in this environment is the consumer himself. How much attention does he pay to the advertising that surrounds him?

An answer to this question began in 1922 when a pioneer psychologist, Daniel Starch, devised a method for measuring readers' recognition of print advertising. In 1932 he established a readership research program that, through more than 240,000 interviews, annually surveys the readers of more than 1,000 issues of consumer and farm magazines, business publications, and newspapers.

To provide a reasonably precise answer to the question of how many people notice and read an ad, I chose the most common type of print advertising—the one-page, four-color ad—and totaled the Starch results for all such ads (20,347) in all

issues of 47 major magazines in 1970. I found that 44% of readers claim to have noticed a particular ad and 35% read enough to identify the brand, but only 9% say they read most of a particular ad. In other words, almost half of all ads are noticed—a third to the point of brand identification—but less than a tenth are of enough interest to be read. Naturally, the responses vary depending on ad size, content, and position, on the receptivity of the reader (sex, age, and income), and on whether the reader is in the market for the product advertised. At any rate, only a small portion of advertising is fully perceived at any time.

The situation in television is similar. In the 1960s George Gallup, another psychologist who pioneered in media research as well as in public opinion research, instituted a survey in which, for example, a cross section of Philadelphia was telephoned the day after an evening of television and asked to recall the commercials on the prime-time shows. On the average, only 12% of those who had seen a particular program could recall its commercials.

It has been demonstrated in many ways that people filter out much of the huge quantity of advertising to which they are exposed. For example, in a study conducted in 1968 by the American Association of Advertising Agencies and Harvard University, 1,536 participants, representing a national sample, were equipped with counters and asked to register every advertisement they saw. Each person enlisted for half a day. The number of exposures per person fell more often into the 11-20 category than into any other, which indicates that the respondents' perceptual screens were very effective indeed.[1]

I mention these findings not to suggest that advertising is ineffective or impotent, but to point out the terrific competition for the consumer's attention. The reader is, so to speak, shopping for information, and he is aware of much product publicity that he hears and sees. But he fully absorbs or perceives only the portion that interests him. These research findings on attention help define the nature of advertising's very special and *restricted* ability to persuade.

In view of this limitation, it may be useful to discuss what can be expected of advertising—that is, what processes produce what effects. It may also help to spell out the differences in impact among one, two, and multiple exposures to an ad. Finally, it may be helpful to show how to use industry figures to avoid use of too little or too much advertising.

What Makes a Successful Ad?

There seem to be three ingredients of successful advertising: information, rational stimulus, and emphasis. Few ads boast all three, but a good ad possesses at least one skillfully treated characteristic.

1. Information is the simplest ingredient. If your message contains news—such as the discovery of gold in California or a cure for cancer in spinach— the advertising skills brought to bear on it are not critical to the ad's success. The agency that first reported the American Dental Association's endorsement of Crest toothpaste had a rather easy job in producing an effective ad because the nature of the information almost guaranteed success. This is not a common phenomenon, but manufacturers of new products hope that their brainchildren will be accorded similar receptions.

2. Rational stimulus is the ingredient that pro-

vokes the consumer to evaluate, judge, and reach a decision. This response obviously is most common when the consumer happens to need or want the product or service in question. Involvement with the message is a prelude to, a substitute for, or a supplement to contacts with salesmen and stores. This rational process usually characterizes the reaction to ads for more expensive products and services; in such cases, an unwise purchase will haunt the shopper longer than if he had made a mistake buying a can of peas.

3. With the third ingredient, emphasis, the matter becomes more complex. Emphasis is particularly important in connection with less expensive products, products of relatively little importance to the consumer, and products with few differences among the brands represented. Consequently, the consumer is less interested in the advertising and is more likely to screen it out. The advertiser in such cases is more likely to emphasize a single theme or one aspect of the product. Also, he repeats frequently to gain attention and make his message familiar to the public. This, the most difficult type of advertising, seems to be the most appropriate for television and its so-called captive audience. In addition it contributes the most irritating and the most entertaining commercials of all.

It also, however, receives the most criticism from citizens concerned with taste. The amount of advertising and media effort in comparison with the seemingly modest increments in brand preference seems disproportionate to many observers, who charge that the effort is wasteful. Or, at the other extreme, they claim that the endless repetition of simple themes produces in consumers a witless compulsion to go out and snatch up the product— whether they need it or not.

The fact is, however, that inexpensive and, what seem to some, trivial products also have to be purchased. For many people such products do not merit enough concern to require involved comparison shopping; rather, consumers put them with little reflection into their shopping carts. The advertiser, who cannot hold a long discourse with the shopper when his ad is seen or heard, can only hope that a residual effect will still be operating at

1. Raymond A. Bauer and Stephen A. Greyser, *Advertising in America: The Consumer View* (Boston: Division of Research, Harvard Business School, 1968), p. 178.

the time of purchase. In short, advertising by emphasis aims for small, delayed effects, points that stick in the mind long enough to tip the scales in favor of Brand A over Brand B.

The exaggerated power that some critics attribute to repetitive advertising is based on an assumption that the consumer is being manipulated against his will by the message and "programmed" to buy the product immediately. It is not generally recognized that the advertising is designed primarily to produce an effect that persists after perceptual screening and forgetfulness have taken their toll. Most advertising has the modest goal of capturing attention and maintaining awareness; outright persuasion is a secondary consideration.

How Much Advertising Is Enough?

We spend a lot of money on repetitive advertising. Some experts explain this by noting that recall of an ad drops without constant reinforcement. Others note that members of the audience are not always in the market for the advertised product, but when they are, the advertising must *be there*. There's no choice but to advertise frequently.

I want to argue against single-exposure potency and also against much-repeated exposures. It is important to understand how communication works and how people learn, and before we can gain understanding, we have to examine the differences among the first, second, and third exposures. I stop at three because, as you shall see, psychologically there is no such thing as a fourth exposure; rather, fours, fives, and so on are repeats of the third exposure effect.

The importance of just two or three exposures, compared to a much larger number, is attested to by a variety of converging research findings based on different research methods.[2]

The first exposure is by definition unique. As with the initial exposure to anything, a "What is

it?" type of cognitive response dominates the reaction—that is, the audience tries to understand the nature of the stimulus. Anything novel, however unattractive it may be on second exposure, elicits some response the first time, even if it is only the mental classification required to discard the object as of no further interest.

The second exposure to a stimulus, if it is not blocked out, produces several effects. One may be the cognitive reaction that characterized the first exposure, if the audience missed much of the message the first time around. (This is most likely if the medium is radio or television, where the tape or film cannot be rewound or reversed.) More often, an evaluative "What of it?" response replaces the "What is it?" response; appreciating the nature of the new information, the consumer wonders whether it has relevance to him. If he absorbs the ad during the first exposure and finds it interesting, some of the "What of it?" response may take place then.

Another element of the second exposure, and unique to it, is the recognition response. "Aha, I've seen this before!" Such recognition permits the viewer or listener to pick up where he left off, without the necessity of repeating the cognitive step ("What is it?"). So the second exposure prompts an evaluation and consequently the "sale" occurs. This "What of it?" response completes the basic reaction to the ad or commercial.

By this time the consumer is familiar with the message, and the third exposure constitutes a reminder, if a decision to buy based on the evaluations has not been acted on. The third exposure is also the beginning of disengagement and withdrawal of attention from a completed episode.

This pattern holds true, I suggest, for any multiple exposure. Most people filter or screen out TV commercials, for example, by stopping at the "What is it?" response. But these same people, suddenly in the market months later for the product in question, may see and experience the twenty-third exposure to the commercial as if it were the second—that is, the twenty-third exposure will be only the second time it really commands their attention.

2. I discuss several of these studies in my article, "Why Three Exposures May Be Enough," *Journal of Advertising Research*, December 1972, p. 11.

Then the viewer is ready to absorb the message and evaluate it in terms of his or her needs. The twenty-fifth exposure, if not the twenty-fourth, will finish the sequence; subsequent exposures will arouse no further reaction. The viewer may still react to the commercial as entertainment or as an irritant, and while such a reaction may affect attitudes toward the advertiser, the industry, and the medium, these attitudes are probably irrelevant insofar as the response to the commercial message is concerned.

Industry Myths About Memory

Many people in and out of the advertising business, in looking at the enormous TV budgets and repeat scatter plans, assume that the agencies have evidence that consumers react slowly and gradually to commercials. That conclusion has made TV appear monolithic and successful on the basis of sheer mass and grinding momentum. To critics, it has made huge budgets seem especially advantageous and "unfair." Advertisers and their agencies, in using the television medium, have misused two common words in the English language, "remembering" and "forgetting."

There is a myth in the advertising world to the effect that viewers will forget your message if you don't repeat your pitch often. That myth supports large advertising expenditures and raises embarrassing and, to some extent, needless questions about unfair market dominance.

The myth is based primarily on the erosion of recall scores. Yet the inability to recall an ad or its message does not mean that the reader, viewer, or listener has forgotten it or erased it from memory. The acid test of forgetting is whether you no longer recognize the object. Few TV commercials seen at night can be remembered the next day. According to Gallup's prime-time survey, only 12% can recall the average commercial. But at General Electric we have shown photoscripts of TV commercials weeks after exposure and obtained a 50% recognition response. In my opinion, the public comes closer to forgetting *nothing* it has seen on TV. People just

"put it out of their minds" until and unless it has some use. And then one day, "Aha!"—the image of the product springs to life again and the response to the commercial continues.

I am not critical of large TV budgets that provide many exposures. I am critical when the advertising industry miconstrues the power of those large budgets. The large budget is often a worthwhile expense because it gives an advertiser the power to be constantly heard—and this is necessary since he never knows when the customer will be looking for his product. But the customer's reaction is independent, rapid, and decisive. Furthermore, while the customer may make up his or her mind more than once during a campaign, it occurs most frequently at some point in the second—or let's say psychologically second—exposure to the commercial.

How to Determine the Best Exposure Level

When evaluating proposed advertising budgets and media schedules, an advertiser can try to ascertain the optimal exposure level for a product, brand, and target audience. At the least, one should be able to recognize in each schedule what portion of the frequency distribution is inadequate and what portion is probably excessive—that is, wasteful and possibly irritating.

The relevant data are well illustrated in Telmar reports or in similar reports from Interactive Market Systems, Inc. Access to such information in a time-sharing computer service is included in an agency's or advertiser's contract with Simmons or TGI. Reports such as those shown here cost from $12 to $15 each. The type of report I shall discuss is based on the Beta Function Program; this program and the Metheringham formula are the two most widely used tools for estimating reach and frequency. For any given media schedule and target audience, the program provides a distribution of frequency of exposures as well as total impressions and reach.

Exhibit 1 is a skeletonized version of what is included in the program. First we have the target audience. This might be, for example, heads of households with incomes of $15,000 or more. Then there

Exhibit 1

Sample report showing frequency distribution of exposures

TARGET AUDIENCE
MEDIA SCHEDULE
U.S. POPULATION BASE (000)
GROSS IMPRESSIONS (000)

Net	% Reach		Average frequency	
	Reach		Cume	
Insertion level	%	People	%	People
0	—	_____	—	_____
1	—	_____	—	_____
2	—	_____	—	_____

is the media schedule, the specific vehicles used and the number of insertions. For example, this schedule might include two insertions in *Reader's Digest,* two in *TV Guide,* three in *Harper's-Atlantic,* four in *McCall's,* five in *Argosy,* and six in *Seventeen.* Next, there is the population base, in thousands. Gross impressions are also stated in thousands. The reach is estimated to be 73%, or 9,483 divided by the target base in the U.S. population (13,023). Thus 73% of the target audience is considered to have been exposed to the advertisement at least once. The average frequency of exposure in this case is high, 2.80.

The most important information is in the three columns at the bottom, which show (a) the number of exposures; (b) the frequency distribution, or the number of people reached *exactly* N times; and (c) the cumulative frequency distribution, or the people reached *at least* N times.

Now let's look at some actual cases, two small media schedules and then two larger ones. In Exhibit 2 we have a target of adult heads of households with incomes of $15,000 plus. The schedule consists of only one insertion in *TV Guide* and one in *Seventeen* magazine. About 31% of the target audience is exposed at least once, while almost nobody is exposed twice (1% of the target group). This small schedule is popular because it achieves 30% reach—almost one third of the target audience. I question, however, the value of one exposure; schedules as small as this are possibly a waste of money.

The next schedule (Exhibit 3), aimed at women, calls for two insertions in *McCall's* and two in *Seventeen.* This schedule is clearly more effective

Exhibit 2

Impact of smallest ad schedule

```
***REPORT                        (BETA-1)
ADULTS HH 115+
      1 TVG      1  17

BASE:     30422

                IMPRESSIONS              CPMG
GROSS              9707                  0.00

                 %       REACH           CPMN           AVG. FREQ.
NET            30.99     9429            0.00              1.03

INSERTION        REACH                          CUME
  LEVEL        %       PEOPLE           %              PEOPLE
    0         69.01    20993           100.00           30422
    1         30.08     9150            30.99            9429
    2          0.92      279             0.92             279
```

Note: "CPMG" and "CPMN" refer to cost per thousand subscribers or viewers, gross and net.

Exhibit 3

Impact of somewhat larger ad schedule

```
        ***REPORT                        (BETA-1)


        D
        WOMEN
            2 MC            2  17

        BASE:    68386

                          IMPRESSIONS          CPMG
        GROSS                35274             0.00

                      %              REACH     CPMN      AVG. FREQ.
        NET         31.93           21835      0.00         1.62

        INSERTION          REACH                  CUME
          LEVEL      %              PEOPLE     %          PEOPLE

            0       68.07           46551     100.00       68386
            1       14.57            9966      31.93       21835
            2       15.56           10641      17.36       11869
            3        1.29             885       1.80        1228
            4        0.50             343       0.50         343
```

than the first. While the reach is the same, the average frequency is significantly higher, and 16% of the audience is exposed twice.

The next schedule (Exhibit 4) is targeted for adult heads of households with incomes of at least $15,000. It lists two insertions in *Reader's Digest*, two in *TV Guide*, three in *Harper's-Atlantic*, four in *McCall's*, five in *Argosy*, and six in *Seventeen*. The reach is 75% and the average frequency, 3.4. More people are exposed twice (21%) than are exposed once (12%); 13% are exposed three times and 12% four times. It's a very solid schedule, but now, perhaps, we're beginning to overdo it a little. A few consumers have been exposed to the same message seven, eight, nine, ten, and more times.

In the last schedule (Exhibit 5), even more people are exposed ten or more times—and, mind you, I've been showing only schedules of print ads. I could show you many combined print and TV schedules where this frequency distribution gets very long indeed. In such cases the reach may be 90%. This is very gratifying; it means that nearly everyone in the target audience sees your ad at least

once. But there is a price that you, we, or the advertising industry pays: every tenth U.S. citizen sees the ad more than ten times.

Problems of Small and Large Advertisers

In the situations just examined, the small advertiser's problem is that he has to reach so hard for his single exposures—his "ones"—that he obtains few "twos" and "threes." He's getting less effectiveness than he thinks. On the other hand, the large advertiser is tempted to try to get everybody—that is, 100% reach. This is almost possible and is tempting when you already have 91% or 92%. If the advertiser gives in to this temptation, he inevitably subjects some of the audience to excessive exposure. So the advertiser also obtains excessive effects; he gets not just attention for his product and his advertising, but attention to the fact that the advertising is excessive. The consumer's reaction is "What do they think I am, a moron?"

The problem becomes complicated when the

Exhibit 4

Impact of large ad schedule

```
***REPORT                        (BETA-1)

ADULTS    HH115+
    2 RD        2 TVG        3 HA        4 MC        5 ARG        6 17

BASE:      30422

              IMPRESSIONS              CPMG
GROSS              77290              0.00

                 %       REACH        CPMN        AVG. FREQ.
NET          74.73      22733         0.00          3.40

INSERTION          REACH                      CUME
   LEVEL        %       PEOPLE           %        PEOPLE

      0      25.27      7689        100.00       30422
      1      12.22      3717         74.73       22733
      2      21.33      6488         62.51       19016
      3      12.59      3830         41.18       12528
      4      11.81      3592         28.59        8698
      5       6.16      1875         16.78        5106
      6       3.84      1169         10.62        3231
      7       2.17       660          6.78        2062
      8       1.34       409          4.61        1402
      9       1.25       380          3.26         993
     10       0.56       171          2.01         613
     11       0.72       218          1.45         442
     12       0.41       126          0.74         224
     13       0.13        40          0.32          98
     14       0.03         8          0.19          58
     15       0.13        39          0.16          50
     16       0.00         0          0.04          11
     17       0.04        11          0.04          11
```

small advertiser, observing the large one, decides that he too wants a high reach. But with a high-reach, low-frequency schedule, he loses impact. If he stepped up his one-exposure reach and made two exposures his practice, he might double his returns. At any rate, he should find out what he is buying and obtain a report on each proposed schedule.

What the large advertiser loses with a high-reach emphasis is more difficult to say. By irritating consumers, he may be substituting a public relations problem for a sales problem. He may even give the advertising industry, his own industry, and the media a bad name. But apart from that possibility, he may be indulging in a different kind of sin by paying for more than he needs. Does he really need a schedule in which half the exposures are reasonable—say, 50% of the target group is exposed up to five times—while the other half is exposed up to 20 times?

What Is the Effective Bandwidth?

There is a well-known story about the man who knew that half his advertising was good and half was bad, but he didn't know which was which. I suggest that the bad half is a combination of too little and too much, and the effective middle range involves a bandwidth that is determinable through

Exhibit 5
Impact of the largest ad schedule

```
***REPORT                    (BETA-1)

TOTAL ADULTS
    4 RD        4 TVG        4 HA        4 MC        4 ARG       4 17

  BASE:   130326

                        IMPRESSIONS       CPMG
  GROSS                   425968          0.00

                 %        REACH          CPMN        AVG. FREQ.
  NET          74.69     97339           0.00           4.38

  INSERTION         REACH                        CUME
    LEVEL      %         PEOPLE             %         PEOPLE

      0      25.31       32987          100.00       130326
      1      10.95       14266           74.69        97339
      2       9.76       12721           63.74        83073
      3       9.00       11727           53.98        70352
      4      15.30       19939           44.98        58625
      5       7.90       10301           29.68        38686
      6       6.18        8060           21.78        28385
      7       5.62        7323           15.60        20325
      8       4.72        6146            9.98        13002
      9       2.04        2655            5.26         6856
     10       1.20        1558            3.22         4201
     11       0.90        1177            2.03         2643
     12       0.72         944            1.12         1466
     13       0.22         282            0.40          522
     14       0.08         106            0.18          240
     15       0.06          78            0.10          134
     16       0.02          31            0.04           56
     17       0.00          13            0.02           25
     18       0.00           0            0.00           12
     19       0.00           0            0.00           12
     20       0.00          12            0.00           12
```

research. The lower limit of the bandwidth is clearly two exposures. The upper limit must be determined by tracking the target audience during a typical campaign to see when the upward slope of message recognition levels off.

You can start with a bandwidth objective on a judgment basis—one to be modified by research. Once, for example, I suggested to the advertising managers in a GE component that they start with the objective of exposing two thirds of their target group to at least two and no more than four exposures per month. While such an objective probably cannot be reached, it can be approached; and

setting it can sharply differentiate some proposed schedules from others. The process clearly calls for a closer look at schedules, instead of leaving everything up to the agency.

Not Too Much, Not Too Little

The effects of advertising on an individual are modest, but they are powerful in the mass and over time. Like erosion caused by shifting tides, little change occurs at any one moment, even though clear-cut effects appear eventually.

Good advertising gets attention, and its message lasts long enough through a few exposures to make one or two points. Optimally, these exposures should reach the target audience with an effective balance of a few exposures to most persons in the audience, rather than one exposure to many and many exposures to a few. Spillover exposures to nontarget audiences should be minimal. Ideally, the target audience should be exposed when it is in the market or during known shopping periods.

Advertising management needs precise information about audience attention and about patterns of reading, viewing, and shopping. But it is not enough to have great ads and fine media vehicles in which to place them; a good plan based on research is essential. Moreover, as in other areas of management, the numbers must be scrutinized with care.

Questions

1. *How does repeated advertising affect consumers?*
2. *Select a product that you purchased recently. Do you think that the seller advertised that product too much or too little?*
3. *What types of information would you need to determine whether a particular company was advertising too much or too little?*

32

How to Use In-Depth Trade Press Articles to Expand Your Markets

CAROLINE POH

DAVID APKER

Information that reaches customer markets via trade press articles and other publicity media can be managed effectively at a relatively low price.

In-depth trade publication articles, a little-used yet very cost-effective marketing communications tool, can help solve a common marketing problem—selling a new concept, which is a qualitatively different way of addressing an old problem, to a far-flung potential marketplace within the confines of a limited promotional budget.

"I classify all potential customers into three groups: KKs, KUs, and UUs," a long-time salesman told us in succinctly summing up this problem. "KKs *know* they have a problem and *know* there's a way to solve it. KUs *know* they have a problem, but are *unaware* there's an answer. UUs are *unaware* they even have a problem, although they surely do.

"KKs are easy to reach in print because they're busily scouring the trade press for ads and articles addressing themselves to this very topic," he said. "The trouble is KKs are few in number and competition is fierce for their business, which often makes it necessary to cut profit margins in order to get those orders.

"It's the KUs and the UUs who represent the most profitable source of potential business for us," he claimed. "Show us a way to find and educate *them.*"

Source: Marketing News, March 23, 1979, pp. 7–8. Reprinted from *Marketing News* published by the American Marketing Association.

The evolution of the successful work we've done over the intervening years began with that salesman's comments. What this industrial marketer needed was an educational effort targeted to a broad range of potential customers, who had to be persuaded to re-evaluate their whole outlook on how to handle some aspect of their manufacturing or distribution process.

In-depth trade publication articles proved to be a superb vehicle for this purpose. The space is free—often as much of it as you need to explain your concept clearly and convincingly—*if what you have to say is, legitimately, news.*

You don't have to make those hard decisions about which magazines are most important to you and allocate your limited ad dollars accordingly. One good story often can be adapted to fit the format and interests of many different magazines in many different industries.

Perhaps even more important is that having your company's story told in an article rather than an ad gives it important third-person endorsement, adding a high extra measure of credibility to everything you're saying. Anybody with enough dollars to spend can buy an ad and say nice things about his own product.

But your story has the implied endorsement of a knowledgeable editor, who, by printing it, is saying, in effect, "Listen to what these people have to say. It's valid and important to you."

There are also fringe benefits. When was the last time you bristled at a trade journal's round-up article that quoted your biggest competitors at length and never gave you so much as a mention? "It must be nice to have connections," you mutter. "They probably bought their way into that article with all the ads they've put into that magazine."

Well, that just isn't the way it works. Trade journal editors, like many of us, are underbudgeted, understaffed, and overworked.

Since they don't have the resources or the time to beat the bushes to find some little-known company that might have a big contribution to make to such an article, they call on the old reliables, the companies with which they're already acquainted. However, few better ways exist to become one of those firms than to work with an editor in his own area of expertise—the feature article.

Although we work for industrial companies with limited promotional budgets and almost nonexistent ad programs, we regularly get calls from editors of trade publications considered important in their fields. They ask, "We're planning an article on technology trends in this area, what can your client give us?"

In short, you become a valued information source simply by establishing your credibility, knowledgeability, and willingness to cooperate and help editors meet their deadlines with solid, factual, and understandable material.

Whenever you're selling a product or a service that has broken, or could break, new ground in solving problems for your potential customers, you may be sitting on a gold mine in trade press publicity. Never be too quick to consign your firm to the realm of "me-tooism."

For instance, one of our clients manufactured a very sophisticated line of automated sortation systems. It wasn't the only one in the business.

In fact, competition was intense for orders from the KK type of customers who knew they could not survive without it—postal systems, major catalogue distribution centers, and the like. Prices were being slashed.

But, the client told us, throughout a wide range of industries were hundreds of smaller operations, each of which could potentially save hundreds of thousands of dollars a year by automating its order-picking process. The problem was that these businesses had never even considered the possibility of automating.

They were unaware that they really had a problem, let alone that new technology had developed an answer to it. They wouldn't be reading the broad-based materials handling magazines, looking at ads for a system to meet their needs, because they didn't know they had such needs. In short, our salesman friend would class them as UUs.

The answer was to contact editors of magazines serving the specific industries our client had pinpointed. With each, we talked about the exciting possibilities for substantial cost savings to their readers by converting to automated handling.

We offered to prepare an in-depth article analyzing the benefits of such a conversion in terms of the needs of that industry. And we found the editors were as excited about the idea as we were.

The results: A number of six- and eight-magazine-page articles in a variety of publications, by-lined by the president of our client's company, including several cover treatments. Note well: The topic was *not* our client's specific systems; it was the whole *concept* of introducing automation in order handling.

But, of course, in illustrating the concept, we were able to use his specific systems as examples. And his company was clearly established as the place to call if you wanted to work with the leaders in the field.

Reprints of these articles became important sales-support materials for use in direct mail to target industries, for trade show handouts, inquiry responses, sales call door-openers, and the like.

How do you identify such topics for feature articles? Where do you look?

Begin by putting yourself into the shoes of the readers of the magazine because it's to them that the editor is ultimately responsible. What kind of information would you (the reader) like to have presented to you in order to help you do your job better?

That, obviously, will vary widely, depending upon the industry and the product being sold. But there are some general guidelines and broad categories:

The Concept Article: We've just touched on this. Is there a better way for you, the magazine's reader, to approach some aspect of your job? Have advances in technology opened up vistas that can save you time, money, chance for error, or aggravation? Wouldn't it make you, the reader, a hero of sorts to be able to lay out such information in front of your boss?

The How-To Article: This approach is appropriate when the concept is fairly well established in the minds of readers, but people are hanging back because they don't really feel confident about their understanding of how to implement it.

For instance, we're developing an article for one of the manufacturers of CAD (computer-aided design) systems for people such as those who design printed circuit boards. Most still design boards manually but are well aware of the better ways to do it and also of the substantial capital investment to go into CAD equipment.

They don't want to risk buying all that hardware unless they're sure they'll know how to use it fully. That's what we're telling them in this step-by-step article—"here's how to convert your design process from manual to automated so that you'll be able to take advantage of all the benefits that CAD offers. (And, of course, some of those benefits are unique to our particular system.)"

Once again, our client's by-line will appear. This is a generally accepted practice. We do the actual writing, but the ideas and all the information we're working with come from the client.

The Case History: This is a powerful tool for building credibility. Everything else we've talked about falls into the realm of theory: here's how things should work, in a logical universe, and here's why.

But, when one of your customers uses your product or service to achieve top results, that's the real world! It's the ultimate endorsement.

Ad people know this; many consumer and industrial ads focus on the satisfied customer and what he has to say about the vendor. Again, keep in mind the interests of the readers of the magazine.

There's something in all of us that's intrigued with what our counterparts in other companies are doing and achieving—because

perhaps we can learn from it. If your customer is a widget manufacturer, then the magazine that story should go in is *International Widget News*. And its title should be "XYZ Widget Makes a Killing by Using Automatic Widget Polisher." NOT "ABC Widget Polishers are Great."

The reader will get that message anyway, even if the ABC firm name is buried halfway through the article. But your customer (the XYZ firm) is what makes the story saleable.

The case history is particularly effective when it shows your firm providing extraordinary or innovative techniques in contributing to the end result. In fact, this factor can make the case history an exception to the rule that your product or service has to be new and newsworthy to rate feature treatment. If the way you've helped a customer to make use of it is new and interesting, that may be all you need.

One of our more successful case history articles involved another client, which offers computerized design of printed circuits to the electronics industry on a service bureau basis. This client worked with a customer firm to develop a computer program that could design the very difficult boards which use high-speed logic. Not only did the story spread the word that our client was now able to design this particular kind of board but it also showed them to be willing and eager to explore problem areas of whatever kind with customers and help them to find solutions.

Obviously, there can be a lot of overlap between these types of feature articles. You may well hit upon a concept article idea that includes a lot of how-to information, illustrated by appropriate case histories. But it does help in analyzing article potentials to think in terms of each of these approaches individually for each of the markets you'd like to hit.

How to Increase Your Productivity

As mentioned already, editorial space is free. However, the time that goes into developing and writing the articles for that space is not free.

If you are Mr. or Ms. Big (or a reasonable facsimile), be advised that you can make an immense difference in the success of the program simply by the input you're willing and able to provide.

You're the person who has a direct line to what's really happening in the business, what customers are concerned about, where the knowledge gaps are, what the questions are that a potential customer will be asking himself before he makes a buying decision, what alternatives he'll be considering, and what the relative significance is of the various technological factors involved. You also know where the problem areas are in your own process.

Find a person you can trust to charge with this article generation responsibility and then trust him or her. Keep him informed and updated. You may not see the direct relationship between any of this kind of information and those in-depth articles you're looking for; but be assured, it's there.

At some point in the preparation process, especially in dealing with high-technology businesses, it's been our experience that we hear an almost-audible "click" and everything falls into place. From that point on, ideas flow. When it happens is going to depend to a large extent on you.

But if you go about it intelligently, you can minimize unproductive time and put your dollars into work that's going to pay off. To begin with, evaluate carefully the very natural inclination to think "I don't have to pay somebody to do that. I can do it myself."

If your skills fall into the written communication area (a pretty big "if"), you probably can, but will you? And if you do, what other responsibilities will you put aside? How is your time better used? Shouldn't you be concentrating on your primary area of expertise?

Despite the best of intentions, no effective trade press feature program really gets off the ground unless it's made one of the primary responsibilities of someone who knows he or she will be evaluated largely on what he or she is able to accomplish in this area.

That person—whether in-house or an outside consultant—has to have a real vested interest in doing all the pushing, prodding, and nagging that's needed to get everybody working together and meeting deadlines. When this is just among the many duties of a busy executive, we've never yet seen it rise to the top of the stack.

The internal expert also may face the problem of understanding the technology all too well. As technical people learn more and more about less and less, they begin to talk and write in verbal shorthand and may assume a level of understanding on the part of the reader that he may not have. You may lose him after the second paragraph.

If you're that in-house expert, and you're doing the writing on your articles, find yourself a sounding board who typifies the average understanding level of the people you'll be writing for and who isn't afraid to say "Hey, I don't get it. How does this work? Why is it important?" Then listen to him: explain it to him 'til he does understand: And rewrite to incorporate that explanation.

Much of the writing to be done for these kinds of articles will of necessity be of a technical nature. You can't just skim the surface, learn the most important buyer benefits by rote, and get by on your fluency, charm, and graphic skills.

Here's a hard-earned tip for the outside consultant: somewhere within most companies is an "articulate spokesperson." And he isn't necessarily the president or even the vice president of marketing. Get to know, and talk with, as many of the line-level people, the salespeople, the production managers, as you can. Continue asking questions.

Eventually, you'll find the person who has an innate talent for putting things in context, in perspective, and in plain English; and then you'll have it made. If you limit your communications only to a few top people you may be fighting an uphill battle all the way.

The determined, intelligent, nontechnical person with good communication skills probably can do the job easier than a similarly motivated person already immersed in the technology. It's easier to pinpoint what it is you don't understand and set about learning it, than it is to try to guess what the less-initiated might have trouble with. You have to really understand the significance of what the company is producing, within the context of the end user's particular problems and all the other alternatives available to him.

The outside consultant has to hone his interviewing skills most carefully to achieve this. In other words, start asking questions and keep asking them until it all makes sense to you.

Never just copy down what someone else has written or said, unless you understand it. No short cuts. No faking it.

One of the most important assets we bring to a client is a level of "informed ignorance." It may take us awhile to understand a complex process; but by the time we do, we darn well know we can explain it in a way that every reader will be able to comprehend, too.

Key to Efficiency: The Query Letter

Now that you have someone assigned the responsibility, that person has immersed himself in the company and the product, and you've zeroed in one or more great article ideas, it's time to start writing the story, right?

Wrong. You do that with the simple things, such as new product releases or personnel changes, because if they're done properly and sent to the right places they'll be used. But you can save yourself a lot of unnecessary wheel-spinning on major features if you lead off with a query letter to the editor or editors of your choice.

This is basically salesmanship in print; and it's designed for one purpose: to sell your article idea. You describe briefly what your idea is, and why you feel it would be of great interest to that magazine's readers.

Put it within the broader context of what's going on in the industry and show where this particular topic fits. Be persuasive and a little bit excited about the value of this information to the readers.

Close by saying you'll call to see what he thinks. Then, within a week or two, do.

Don't try to sell the company in this letter. The editor doesn't really care how sterling its credentials may be—unless you have an article idea that turns him on.

If the company is obscure enough that he may not be familiar with it, include a separate background memo filling in those details.

Keep a clean copy of the letter. In many harried editorial offices, things like this get lost. You may have to resend it.

At the least, your query and call will open some dialogue. Perhaps this idea doesn't fit the editor's plans; but as you discuss it, you may discover another approach that does. And his new familiarity with you and the company may bear fruit later.

As you get to know various editors, you may be able to skip the letter and just call with an idea. But, in general, it's best to have it in writing, where he can refer to it.

The beauty of the query letter is that you put a minimum of time and effort into article development until you have something close to its guaranteed placement. No editor will give this unconditionally without seeing the manuscript.

But more often than you might expect, you'll get a response such as "Sounds good. Let us take a look at it. If it does what you say it will, we want it." We've been turned down on queries; but we've never yet reached the point of writing an article that was not ultimately published.

Tips on Working With Editors

1. You don't have to go hat in hand. When we began in this field, we thought we did; after all, we're asking this very important person for what amounts to (at current ad rates) perhaps $10,000 worth of free space.

   We dropped that idea when editors started thanking us—sometimes profusely—for the help we'd given them. They're darned nice people, thoroughly professional; and, if you are too, you'll be working with them as colleagues, not supplicants.

2. Observe deadlines. If you've agreed to supply a major story and he's planning on it, you'd better come through with it or forget about any future cooperation.

   How you get things done on your end is your

problem; excuses don't fill blank pages reserved for your article. That's why people charged with this responsibility, if they're good at what they do, do a great deal of nagging internally to keep the information flowing and the approvals coming forth on schedule.

3. Write in approved editorial style. Writing for somebody else's publication is a different ball game from ad copy or your own brochures and newsletters. Forget company puffery; let the facts and ideas speak for themselves.

    Read the publications you intend to write for until you have a good feel for their style. Sure, the editor is there to edit; but the less of it he has to do on your copy, the more receptive he'll be to your future contributions.

    That's one more good reason why it's usually more productive to teach a professional communicator about your particular business than it is to try to teach one of your technical experts to write.

4. Know what you can and can't expect of him. You have no right to approve or disapprove final, edited copy. Most editors in technical fields will, time permitting, let you review the text for technical accuracy before publication if they have made substantive changes or written parts or all of it themselves; you can ask, but not demand.

    You cannot specify date of publication. He may have every intention of putting it in the January issue, but something comes up, and you don't see it 'til November. It's frustrating, but it happens.

5. Don't give the same feature to competing magazines. Few surprises are more devastating to an editor than seeing the story he has on the press appear first in a competitive publication. (This is a switch from standard procedure on product releases, where you routinely blanket the market with the same release.)

    One of our early mistakes occurred when we sent the same query letter on a concept article idea to several magazines concurrently, figuring we'd do well to get one acceptance. Instead, we had four, almost by return mail. And we also

had a real challenge in finding ways to write them so that each was different from the rest.

How to Work With Your Company's or Clients' Customers

When you're writing about a customer of your company—typically for a case history article—there's one overriding rule to be observed, if you don't want the roof falling in on you: Get written approvals of absolutely everything you write for release!

The fact that your notes from your interview with the customer are very clear or even that you have his statements incontrovertibly on tape doesn't cut any ice if his boss hits the ceiling when he sees it in print.

Save yourself a lot of grief, and perhaps a customer for your company. Get it formally approved.

Prepare ahead of time; learn all you can about the customer company, what problem it faced, and how your company's product provided the solution. You may be hearing the same thing again from the customer; but thinking it through ahead of time will help you know what questions to ask.

Whenever possible, conduct your interviews with the customer in person, on site, where you can see the system, or whatever it is, doing its thing. It's far easier to understand.

And you'll get more natural, interesting quotes than over the phone. Obviously, since what the customer has to say is paramount, you never write a case history using input only from your company or client.

Get good photos of the product in action, preferably with people in them. Develop interesting charts and graphs where appropriate.

How to Merchandise the Articles

Publication of the article is just the first step. Unlike new product releases, which tend to generate a lot of inquiries, feature articles, surprisingly enough, aren't likely to create the same deluge. You're not pitching a piece of hardware to people who already know that's what they're looking for.

You're establishing a climate of understanding and credibility for your company. You're paving the way for your salespeople.

Take advantage of that momentum. Give them an arsenal of article reprints (we like to do them with the magazine's front cover as the cover of the reprint) to leave with prospects, hand out at trade shows, and the like.

Send them to your present customers. What you're doing is news—don't let anyone forget it.

Does It Work? A Case in Point

You're reading a prime example of most of the things we've been talking about. If you've read this far, you've proven the point.

This is a concept article ("You can enhance your promotional program immensely by going after in-depth feature articles in the trade press.") with a how-to emphasis and with a few capsule case histories sprinkled in to show how it works.

What's in it for us? Before you read this, you'd never heard of us. But now you know we're specialists in successfully formatting and implementing this kind of trade press program and we're for hire to help you analyze your position, get you set up to do it internally, or do it for you.

And, of course, we'll be merchandising lots of reprints of this article. Every present or prospective client of ours will know about it. We practice what we preach!

Questions

1. *Contrast publicity to the other forms of advertising.*
2. *Define each of the following types of trade press articles: (a) concept articles; (b) how-to articles; (c) case history articles.*

33

Coca-Cola Puts Sparkle into Foodservice Promotions

SALES & MARKETING MANAGEMENT

Coca-Cola sales promotion "adds life" to the company's marketing program that is satisfying and refreshing.

Around Coca-Cola U.S.A.'s Fountain Sales Dept. in Atlanta, talk of sales promotion flows as rapidly as Coke in a pizza parlor. The No. 1 soft drink syrup supplier to the nation's restaurants and institutional feeding operations spends much time and effort developing and testing promotion programs for its foodservice customers. Its objective, of course, is to increase gallonage sales of Coke syrup by helping fast-food operators, restaurant chains, and institutional accounts build their units' sales and profits.

The Fountain Sales Dept.'s promotional success is easy to document. For example:

Burger Chef's outlets increased their average sales volume 22% during a promotion offering a free *Star Wars* poster with every order of a large Coke, jumbo fries, and hamburger.

der Wienerschnitzel International, Newport Beach, Cal., increased its 275 outlets' average volume 20% during the weeks that it offered patrons a specially decorated 6.5-oz. glass free with a food-plus-Coke order, or for cash with the purchase of a 16-oz. Coke.

Source: Sales & Marketing Management, Marketing and Sales Promotion Special Report, August 1978. Reprinted by permission from *Sales & Marketing Management* magazine. Copyright 1978.

Krystal Co., Chattanooga, Tenn., increased its total soft drink sales by $385,000 during the four weeks its 192 units offered a reusable plastic cup free with every purchase of a 20-oz. Coke. Profits on the additional 20-oz. sales: $56,938.

For those promotions, as for others it cosponsors, the Fountain Sales Dept. spent thousands of dollars developing and testing the following:

The premium itself.
The advertising.
Point-of-sale materials.
The total offer. (For example, Coca-Cola might try to determine which of the following would be most likely to increase the food operator's sales and profits: a free poster with the Blue Plate special, a poster for 25¢ with a jumbo Coke, or a 39¢ poster with a medium-sized Coke.)

The company makes substantial outlays in this area because the stakes are high. Promotions are a basic part of the $93 billion foodservice industry's marketing strategy. Fast-food chains, in particular, run them 70%–80% of the year, and the lobbies in their headquarters are generally full of suppliers' salespeople waiting to present sales promotion proposals. A proposal has to be solidly pretested to merit consideration by the foodservice marketing executive, and the supplier that doesn't come up with good promotions can lose the operator's account to a more creative rival. Thus Coca-Cola's Bill Byrd, manager, advertising and sales promotion, for the Fountain Sales Dept., and his assistant manager, Robert M. Winnie, are continually working on new ideas for current and prospective foodservice accounts.

A promotion germinates from the ideas of one—or any combination—of four sources:

1. The premium vendor, such as Libbey Glass or Corning.
2. The Fountain Sales Dept.'s ad agency, McCann-Erickson.
3. A foodservice operator.
4. The department's staff.

Department staffers feel that they have a pretty good fix on the demographic and psychographic profiles of their customers' customers. They also believe that they know the marketing target each operator is focussing on and have a good idea of the types of promotions that the operator would go for.

Thus the department develops a preliminary program and pretests its appeal to the target audience, usually by means of what Stephen L. Freedman, manager of national marketing and sales programs, refers to as a "mall intercept test." Researchers employed by an independent research firm go into selected shopping center malls that cater to the types of shoppers that Coca-Cola research has shown are typical customers of the foodservice operator for whom the prospective promotion is designed. A researcher stops shoppers and asks if he may ask them a few questions. If the answer is yes, the researcher questions the shopper about her age, family, and types of restaurants that her family frequents. If she seems to be a target customer for the foodservice operator, she is shown a number of potential promotional offers—including, whenever possible, the actual glass, frisbee, or whatever would be part of the offer—and is asked how she'd react to them.

Because factors such as weather and individual mood tend to affect the level of consumer response, the company always includes a control offer among those shown to the consumers. The control is an offer that's been used consistently, so that Coca-Cola knows its relative performance and can use it to assess the consumer's reactions to other offers.

If the pay-out analysis following consumer testing is auspicious, department marketers present the program to the foodservice operator and propose that the operator test it in 15 to 20 of his outlets for the proposed length of the promotion (usually four to six weeks). If the operator agrees, in-store tests follow.

At this point, Coca-Cola relinquishes the sole financial burden for the promotion. For the store tests, it supplies the premiums at cost and shares the cost of point-of-sale materials and advertising with the foodservice operator. (Later, if the operator decides to roll with the promotion, it takes over the purchasing of the premiums and promotional materials, but continues to share the cost of the latter and the advertising with the Fountain Sales Dept.)

If the store test meets or surpasses the 10%–12% volume increase goals that Coca-Cola and most foodservice operators set for promotions, foodservice management has the option of rolling regional or national with it. In most cases, the operator handles the presentation to his company outlets or franchisees, but Coca-Cola's salespeople are sometimes called on to help.

Although the Fountain Sales Dept.'s pay-out criteria are confidential, it's willing to share some of the other criteria that Coca-Cola considers essential to achieve its promotional objectives:

1. The offer must always involve the purchase of a Coke or a Coke plus food.
2. The foodservice operator may not change any element of the tested offer, including the brand of the premium, the advertising mix, the point-of-sale materials, or the price of the premium, if applicable. The reason? As in the case of market-tested new products, any change in the offer can affect projected results.

Greed Doesn't Pay

For example, several years ago—before Coca-Cola adopted its no-changes rule—a fastfood operator insisted on raising the price of the premium when the promotion went national. Sales increased, but the operator was stuck with half a million glasses when the promotion ended because far fewer consumers than anticipated bought the premium.

3. The premium must:

Be a top-of-the line item, such as specially designed glassware, a National Football League or *Star Wars* poster, or a Wham-O frisbee.

Be exclusive to Coca-Cola within the foodservice industry.

Test high in consumer preference.

Have a specific value to the consumer.

Have a wide demographic appeal to consumers over 12. "We won't go with any premium aimed at the below-12-year-old," a spokesperson says. "We do not want to become involved in the controversy concerning promoting products—especially products containing sugar—to young children."

Because communications are the key to any successful promotion, department marketers also believe that foodservice management should offer its in-store employees (or "crews") an incentive to generate enthusiastic support for the promotion. The incentive may be a savings bond, luggage, clock, watch, week-end trip, or some other relatively inexpensive item. Coca-Cola Marketers suggest that the operator give awards to, say, crews of the top 10% of its units during the promotional period.

When all's said and done, Coca-Cola looks to sales promotion for more than just increasing its gallonage sales and maintaining close ties to current customers. It uses case histories of successful promotions, in its advertising to the trade and in tie-in sales aids, to help its sales force open still more accounts. A sure sign that, for Coca-Cola, promotions add life to marketing.

Questions

1. *What are the major sources of sales promotion ideas in the foodservice industry?*
2. *What makes Coca-Cola's foodservice promotions so effective?*

34

Let's Ask the Salesman RON KOLGRAF

The roles, satisfactions, and frustrations of inside and outside salespeople are highlighted here. Industrial Distribution *sponsored a real honest-to-goodness gripe session to gain insights into this area.*

"I don't get no respect." Comedian Rodney Dangerfield's characteristic line could have been coined for some distributor salesmen. Here they are dealing with all kinds of customers, handling all kinds of orders, in effect, creating the kind of image and all of the goodwill necessary for a distributor to run a successful operation, and you'll still hear salesmen complain that their opinions and suggestions are taken too lightly by management, if at all.

"I—and I can speak for a lot of salesmen I know in the industry—feel we just don't get listened to at all," complains one salesman out of New York City. "Distributors," he says, "are too overdeveloped at the top and aren't about to admit that salesmen have something to offer that can really make a difference."

It would appear that as the prime sources of customer contact and the direct witnesses to trends in supply and demand, the salesmen's suggestions and opinions on policies, inventories and on marketing would not only be heeded but appreciated. But in the majority of cases surveyed by *ID* [*Industrial Distribution*] for this Special Report, responses indicated that this simply was not the case across the industry. Among salespeople, morale is often

Source: Industrial Distribution, November 1977, pp. 35–42. Reprinted from *Industrial Distribution* magazine, a Morgan-Grampian publication.

low, particularly among inside salesmen who indicated some degree of resentment, feel unappreciated, unimportant, and as a consequence, underpaid.

The frustrations expressed in the survey by inside salesmen were generally less vehement than those expressed by outside salespeople. On the whole, there appears to be less detectable friction between management and outside salesmen due, in part, to day-to-day physical separation. Logically, there should be less friction between salesmen on the road and management than between management and salespeople restricted to the office.

"The inside salesmen take the orders, solicit more dollars, expedite, and take the guff. The outside salesmen get sales contests, bonuses, prizes, and the lunches and dinners as entertainment. The pay is the same if I do a lot or a little. What's my motivation—unless I like what I do?" questions a Cleveland inside salesman.

Many inside salespeople feel they "do the dirty work," and the outside salespeople get the credit with the accompanying salary increases and bonuses. Still, most outside salesmen reflect an equal degree of frustration. The feeling they express is one of futility. Salesmen would like to offer suggestions, they say, but feel they won't be considered anyway, so why try in the first place? Outside salesmen feel they're not backed up sufficiently by their managements, their inside salesmen, or their suppliers, yet both the outside and the inside salesmen readily admit they would be lost without strong support from each of them.

All in all, salesmen feel that they have a lot to say about distribution and its many facets but aren't given the opportunity to be heard often enough. Many feel that they and their roles are misunderstood by management. Significantly, where salesmen seem content, they appear to be respected and their opinions valued and, more important, their parent companies invariably show a long record of success.

How Salesmen View Suppliers

Question: How Good Are Your Suppliers' Reps?

When asked this question, most of the respondents to the survey were less than exuberant. They appeared to view the question subjectively, and indicated by their replies that the quality of the rep depended upon the individual making the judgment. Most salesmen pondered the question at length and responded much as one Atlanta, Ga., salesman did. "They're all right. Some do a tremendous job, and some don't give a damn." An East Coast salesman was more specific. "About 10% are extremely supportive. Another 30% are fairly supportive. Fully 60% are poor to unbelievable," A Hartford, Conn., salesman indicated, "The majority are excellent, but some of the new ones are not as good as the oldtimers." A Tulsa, Okla., salesman, on the other hand, had nothing but praise for reps. "They're very good," he said. "I have no problems with them. I set a date and they come in on schedule—they're consistent and helpful."

But a salesman out of Camden, N.J., felt otherwise. "Some are really good, some are awful. A lot of them only look out for themselves." Three New York City salesmen uplifted the image slightly with these statements: "Supplier reps are pretty good, hell they're only human like anybody else . . . On a scale of one to ten, I'd rate them a seven" and finally, "They're good, I guess. If you get a bad one, you raise cain and he's gone."

Overall, most of the terms used by the salesmen to describe supplier reps, bordered on "fair", "pretty good", "decent", "adequate", and "generally good but room for improvement." We then asked the salesmen this question:

Question: How Can Suppliers' Reps Improve?

What the salesmen would like to obtain from their supplier reps, overall, relates directly to improved service. A Clevelander bemoaned the fact that reps "Don't seem to be as concerned to serve us as we are to serve our customers." An Albany, N.Y., salesman and a Bridgeport, Conn., salesman would like to see reps travel with them on more sales calls.

"The personal contact gained by the customer and me when the supplier's rep comes along is invaluable. The good reps take care of you. They come in, go around with you to a customer, and gain a better understanding of everybody's needs." An Allentown, Pa., salesman concurs. "We need more service from the suppliers' reps. Most of them are simply order-takers, rather than service people. When we get a complaint, we want someone we can get a straight answer from." A Boston, Mass., salesman adds, "The people back at the factory know their apples from A to Z. But these men in the field don't have the answers. The reps need better product knowledge. Many of them use the older selling principles: a smile, and a lunch. Today, people don't care if you have two noses and are the ugliest guy in the world—they want service."

Aside from better service, the most common complaint about suppliers' reps is that they are deficient in technical knowledge. A Cincinnati, Ohio, salesman feels that "Reps should be 50% technical and 50% sales." A Detroit, Mich., salesman agrees, adding that "The reps are of no technical help and they don't return calls. They seem to feel just saying 'hello' helps me sell their products. What I want is facts, features, and advantages."

Salesmen feel the suppliers' reps aren't particularly loyal. "Hell, we have an investment in their products—they should come to us all the time, and not end-run us and go to our customers," says a

---

Suppliers . . .

What prejudices salesmen for or against suppliers? Here's what the survey showed.

Distributor salesmen LIKE suppliers who:

Keep adequate stock on hand ready to deliver
Are cooperative, help them solve problems
Will protect a territory

Distributor salesmen DISLIKE suppliers who:

Don't communicate regularly with distributors and their salesmen
Have multiple distribution in one area
Quote wrong or give misleading delivery dates
Won't respond to a user's problem
Don't give instant notification on shortages and price changes
Are vague on warranty, repair and return policies
Are tardy in responding to salesmen's letters requesting action

---

Tampa, Fla., salesman. "There should be no conflict between a distributor and a rep. They oughtn't sell lines that compete with us," adds a salesman from Newark, N.J.

Salesmen also feel the supplier reps should pay more attention to emergency needs, rather than serve clients on a first-come first-serve basis. "Even though we've been regular customers," says one from Cambridge, Mass., "they don't help us out in a real emergency—they don't always care. They certainly can be more prompt in answering emergency calls and dealing with shortages," a Mississippi salesman adds. "There is difficulty in getting some of these reps to follow up on problems after the sale," contends a man from New England.

The salesmen in general feel that supplier reps working for smaller suppliers and territories provide better service. The reason appears to be that reps for the larger suppliers simply have too much ground to cover. A Pawtucket, R.I., salesman puts it in perspective. "The supplier reps are just too thinly spread out. They have too much territory to cover." A Mass. salesman emphasizes this point: "Too many reps have too large a territory to give the necessary service."

Question: Are You Getting Enough Product Data and Training?

If the personal contact and service desired by distributor salesmen is too often found to be lacking among suppliers' reps, the amount of product data provided the salesmen seems to be pretty good, with exceptions. Some salesmen's comments:

"They keep us up to date very well with literature. . . . They're very helpful with product information if asked. . . . Most important lines come with decent literature, and more training programs are offered than we can realistically put to use. . . . It is either very good or only fair, no in between. You have to stay on them more and more to get specific details."

There were some complaints about the time involved in receiving information, and the type of data received, for example: "Some provide information in two days, and some in six months. It depends on how they feel that day, and usually the only info we get is price increases," says a Philadelphia salesman. A New Jersey salesman agrees. "Getting information is sometimes a problem," he says.

How Suppliers' Reps Can Improve . . .

Most suppliers carefully groom their reps to work with distributors. The survey showed that, according to distributor salesmen, there is still some room for improvement. Here's how some salesmen responded:

Provide sales training at the factory. Give us the knowledge we get from the reps through a home study course, for example . . . I'd like the reps to show more interest in what I do. If I need training to sell more, they should offer assistance.

They ought to keep us better informed on product changes whether they are in materials and design, or additions or deletions from the lines . . . And keep us informed on engineering, accounting and advertising changes.

Let them give me the same kind of service I give my customers. If an item's in stock, there's no reason for a shipping delay of two or more days, no reason at all. The reps ought to let us know.

Reps ought to be giving us more personal attention with user complaints and on orders. We like more human contact and not so much communication with computers.

By all means, let them tell us when their companies can't ship as planned.

Let us go directly to the supplier if necessary. Give us a toll-free number where we can get instant information direct.

Let the reps help us protect our territories and train people—ours and the users.

"Training sessions are available whether or not we take advantage of them," admits an upper N.Y. State salesman. The salesmen welcome training sessions, but feel they are too few and far between and could be improved in quality. The frequency of training sessions they described varied from once a month to at least once a year from each supplier. "I'd like to see more training sessions spread out among various products" was one response. An Indianapolis salesman stresses that "Inside salesmen should be the first to be informed of new product lines on changes." But a Boston salesman sees most training sessions "directed toward the outside salesmen; the inside guys trail along." These sessions are too valuable, the salesmen feel, to hold a session of "Let's look over a catalog." Says one: "We need clearly spelled out uses, advantages and applications. Just because the suppliers know doesn't mean I know." A Manchester, N.H., man put things into perspective. "I think," he says, "it's up to me as an individual to seek out what I want to know—areas I don't understand. I have to have the

initiative. Otherwise, especially with a national company, we can lose touch. I see one large bearing supplier rep once in every 40 years."

Question: How's Product Quality? Do Suppliers Make Good on Inferior Items?

Almost all of the salesmen *ID* talked to felt good about their product lines. A certain pride could be detected in many who felt their integrity was in direct proportion to the quality of the products they sold. They registered these statements: "I'm very proud of our lines . . . Very good—it has to be good or you just won't get back in the door . . . Excellent . . . In my experience, the suppliers have done very well . . . Top of the line . . . We only carry Cadillac items."

There are some problems generated among high-quality product lines. "Because of our tremendous stock volume, there are some lousy items," says a Hartford, Conn., salesman. "We have had two or three bummers," says a Pawtucket, R.I., salesman, "but we don't want to be associated with junk, so we switched products, but fast. For example, we sold plant furniture at one time. The customer got the material with parts missing, then got later shipments with the wrong parts. This creates resentment, and it hurts your reputation.

"We carry really good stuff, though the price squeeze in the motor industry has resulted in some real cheapos," says a man out of Providence, R.I. "We have some troublesome items," says a salesman from the Far West. "These are mostly with import screws."

"Imports are a very big industry," says one out of Chicago, "but there seem to be more product failures among them than among domestic items." Many respondents to the survey complained about the inferior quality of imported items. "We stick primarily with domestic manufacturing so our stock is excellent," says a Mississippian, "and they back up their products." A New Yorker disagrees. "Domestic product quality is definitely declining. This is especially true of products from companies no longer under original ownership. Mass acquisitions by holding companies and large conglomerates tend to lower the quality commitment."

Most salesmen indicated that the supplier would make good on inferior items, usually in the form of sales credits, albeit, in some cases, grudgingly. "The supplier will swallow a loss if need be, to keep the customer happy," says a Camden, N.J., salesman. "Yes, they do make good," says another. "If they didn't, I'd sell another brand."

Question: Do Your Suppliers Stay Ahead of Competition?

The consensus among the salesmen polled by *ID* is that their suppliers stay even, if not exactly ahead of the competition. "They're pretty much up with the competition. But they're all about the same anyway." "When one increases prices, the others will all follow suit in a week or so," says a salesman from southern California. Another pointed to a dis-

> **Productivity . . .**
>
> *I'm now more convinced than ever that the more useful support a distributor salesman gets from suppliers and management, the more he'll produce.* R.K.

crepancy between large and small companies. "The larger the company, the less they know about competition in the marketplace. They're too far removed."

"We look for suppliers of specials to stay with or ahead of the competition. Our major suppliers do stay ahead," adds a salesman from Michigan. "The suppliers can keep ahead of the competition if the feedback, the communication between us and them is good and we keep them abreast of what's going on," says one from Denver.

Respondents indicated that with good service and a willingness to bend, suppliers could easily stay ahead of the competition. Price is a big problem though. "We handle so many of the top lines that we seldom have recognition or acceptance problems, but we are often beaten on price," says a New Yorker. A Philadelphia salesman adds: "We're the middleman between the manufacturer and the end-user. Sometimes our position isn't competitively based enough to compete. By the time we find out the market is competitive and get abreast of the times, it's too late."

"Pricing in New England is getting brutal. Everybody is cutting everybody else's throat. A good supplier will provide you with a good price structure and you still make a profit. There's a lot of price cutting though. 'I'll drop you 20%' is an oft-heard typical comment. Severe price cutting erodes profits—somebody's not gonna make it in a highly competitive area," a N.H. salesman insists. Another New Englander agrees. "On very competitive items, it's you that takes the beating if you want to stay in the market."

"Pricing is a definite problem," says a St. Louis

salesman. "We carry high-priced, quality lines. A competitor who cuts prices 20%, and keep a very low overhead, gives us trouble."

"Some suppliers offer selling prices based on the realistic market, but most offer exaggerated prices in order to make discounts sound large," says a salesman from metro-New York. But other salesmen admit that the suppliers will work with them to some extent on special pricing. "Where the dollar volume warrants it, they are good on suggested prices," says a mid-Westerner. "If you have need for a competitive quote," says a Boston salesman, "occasionally you'll get it—but you'll lose some of your lunch money."

Distributor salesmen, like customers, shop around for the best prices. "If I think a quotation is out of line, I'll call around. First I go to my management who goes to our regular supplier who gives us a price. Then we'll compare other prices. If we get lower quotes, we'll go back to our regular supplier, and ask 'Hey, what's going on here?' Not that I play one against the other!," jokes a New Englander.

How Salesmen View Their Own Management

Question: What Do You Like Best About Your Management? The Least?

Salesmen hold strong views about their own management, some bordering on the euphoric, others on outright condemnation. Along with their comments to the survey questions, none were reluctant to offer bold, concrete suggestions about improving operations in their own companies.

On the plus side, good communication was the management plus cited most by the salesmen. Collectively, the salesmen pictured the ideal management as one that is accessible to salesmen, appreciates them, helps them solve problems, understands them as individuals, offers substantial incentives on the job and, as one salesman put it, "leaves the real job of selling to us."

"Trust, faith and fairness are the key principles of our management, and that's all to the good," said one obviously satisfied salesman. "Openness is the key—there's a constructive, relaxed atmosphere. Management doesn't pressure you to make 28 phone calls a day. They're receptive to the heartbeat of the marketplace." They set realistic programs and goals—"and they're ready to re-evaluate and readjust them if they don't turn out to be feasible," adds another.

"Our management is open to new ideas—they're constantly looking for ways to improve. Our top management exhibits strong ethics too, in all customer and employee relationships," another points out. "Honesty is important."

"The door's always open. These guys will talk things over with any employee. I like to think my opinions are worthwhile," adds a N.J. salesman.

Another attitude of management well-received by salesmen is one of *laissez faire,* or *hands off.* When management allows salesmen their head and avoids interfering, the better the results, most salesmen agree. "The freedom I have in dealing successfully with my customers the way I see fit is very important" one salesman says, adding that management will leave the salesman alone as long as sales are satisfactory.

To leave a salesman alone doesn't mean to ignore him completely. A number of them pointed out that they like to be appreciated by management, and like to receive an occasional compliment or two for a job well done. Closely related to this they said, are profit-sharing, awards, or similar incentive plans through which management recognizes sales achievements.

They revealed that they also like to be supported by a knowledgeable management, particularly those with strong backgrounds in sales and engineering. "When I have problems, they'll put aside whatever they're doing, and help me solve them fast. They're flexible in meeting the competition, and provide good leadership," a Philadelphia veteran notes. "They're OK," says another. "They get to know you as a person. They get down to your level, and understand your problems."

Salesmen and Their Own Management . . .

Assured that their names wouldn't be revealed, salesmen were only too happy to comment on how they feel their firms are being managed. Most were reasonably happy with their management. Here are some views from those who saw room for improvement:

They're not aggressive enough . . . They aren't organized, and they won't listen to problems or suggestions.

They're so damned old-fashioned. They'd run a lot better with new ideas.

The paperwork is killing me!

They won't spend any money or have anybody analyze the system here to make it more efficient.

They stay with bad programs too long.

They suffer from an inability to take advantage of market change and getting the whole team to adjust or improve.

Decisions are never firm.

I'd appreciate a better in-stock inventory, but they never want to spend any money on it.

They nit-pick too much and when they're doing well, they won't give you a pat on the back. When you do lousy, then they know you real well.

They're too lenient with non-producers in the company. Sometimes, poor performance and superior performance are equally rewarded. Our management accepts too many errors.

Departmental empires makes it tough for us.

We're too darned customer oriented to the point where we go overboard. We give until it hurts.

Officially, information flow between management and ourselves is lousy, but our grapevine is great.

I'd rather have a salary plus commission arrangement. If I work harder, I want to collect.

The favorites in this company get the best accounts, regardless of geography. I'd like to see a fairer division and quotas.

Education? The favorites go to school, the rest of us struggle to learn on our own.

Our marketing is poor. We've been in business a long time, but we're going to have to fight to keep up.

My management? I'll take the fifth on that one.

"It's the basic Peter Principle," says a third. "You demand responsibility, and they give you as much as you can handle until you can't handle it any more."

On the other hand, there were a number of things the salesmen did not like about their management. Many of the complaints, especially among the inside salesmen, referred to too little pay, a common gripe anywhere. Many inside salesmen feel their jobs to be dead-end positions. In many cases, outside salesmen felt their base salary was too low, especially in view of current economic indicators hinting at a possible downturn in the near future.

"Our management seems to be an organized chaos," said one. "They seem to know what's going on, but there's no reason behind the madness. It lacks structure."

"Many managers haven't been out enough to know what it's like to go against the competition," added another. "Having the boss come out once in a while would be a great help to me. Many times though, they don't know enough to be any help."

Salesmen and Their Jobs

No job is perfect and this holds true of distributor salesmen's jobs too. Here's how they responded to random questions about their jobs:

	Percent responding			
	Happy	Unhappy	Ambiguous	NA
Are you happy with your present form of compensation?	68	21	4	7

	Commission	Salary	Salary + bonus	Comm. & Profitsharing	NA
What type of compensation do you have?	12	8	34	42	4

	Yes	No	NA
Does your management motivate you?	63	32	5

	Excellent	Very Good	Good	Fair	Poor	NA
How do you feel about your company?	43	9	41	5	0	2

	Happy	Unhappy	NA
Are you happy with the way management assigns territories and quotas?	84	14	2

	Yes	No	NA
Is your management education minded?	78	19	3

	Excellent	Good	Fair	Poor	NA
How good is the information flow between sales and management, and sales and the warehouse?	9	46	28	13	4

	Yes	No	NA
Does your company maintain a large enough, saleable inventory?	93	4	3

	Yes	No	NA
Is your company customer-oriented enough?	74	21	5

	Good	Poor	NA
Is your firm a good or poor marketing organization?	79	17	4

How Salesmen View Customers

Question: What's Your Opinion of Today's PA's? Tougher, Fairer? More Knowledgeable?

The question appeared to make most of the salesmen surveyed uncomfortable but enough was gleaned from their comments to generate a pattern.

The distributor salesmen feel the purchasing agents they deal with, although tougher than ever, are not very knowledgeable about their products. They feel although they seem to be fully versed on prices, their actual product knowledge, in many (not all) cases, is limited to what is written on a piece of paper. Any time a salesman asks a PA for additional information relating to applications, alternate materials, etc., he feels he's asking for trouble, unless the PA has the answer at his fingertips.

"They could be much more knowledgeable about their products. They send wrong data to us which we get blamed for, but which really is their fault", moaned an Indianapolis salesman. "The good ones are very good, but there seems to be too few of them. It's tougher to get in the door, and your real work needs to be done with an engineer or foreman", laments a salesman from Phoenix. "They could be more knowledgeable", says a New Yorker, "and they could also ask the salesman for help in selecting the correct product for the job." "They tend to be office-oriented", says a salesman from Pittsburgh. "They lack shop and product experience and don't differentiate between first and second line commodities." PA's are a little frustrating at times. They're hard to relate to, because they don't know what they're talking about. They're only relays—they have to come back to you for more information if you ask them for specifics or follow-ups," says a Georgian. "A lot of them don't really know what they're doing. If you ask for more info, they get flustered."

"They're more price conscious than quality conscious anyway", says a Hartford salesman. "But if you buy a brand name end mill for $7 say, the same thing will cost $3 somewhere else, and he'll buy that. But you end up having to buy three of those

junk items in one week." "They're supposed to have the knowledge", says a Bostonian, "but they generally don't have the practical know-how. They read from a piece of paper—anything off the paper, they don't know.

"My first contact is with the PA. Then with the plant engineers. They (PA's) are becoming fussy though about sneaking in the back door. I never really had a super high regard for them—they're rubber stamp people," says a Providence, R.I. salesman. "They're order-takers—fillers really. I don't think they're very innovative. But maybe it's not their fault—they don't seem to have enough authority. I think they're fair though." "It depends", says a salesman out of East Texas, "on the day of the week, the month, and the year. But for any guy who wants to kick you out, there's another that'll let you in."

"Some just demand the world, but they seem to know what they're doing. There's not too much bull," a New Englander points out. "Some aren't knowledgeable enough to do the job they're doing. Others are, but don't have the time to do it thoroughly. Some care enough to take the time. They'll call in the order, and follow it up. They're all price conscious though." They're tougher today, says an eastern Pennsylvanian. A small handful of salesmen polled for the survey expressed doubts about the integrity of some PA's. Noting that PA's ethics were not a common problem-area, one upstate New Yorker admitted that "Occasionally, you have to take them out as a 'thank you' or to get an order." Another salesman appeared less convinced. "Competition," he said, "is rough and a few PA's will accept gifts of one kind or another. Without that, it's hard to break into some places."

Generally, though, most salesmen polled were adamant about having no part of it. Nor, they said, do most PA's. We've never *bought* business around here," declared one salesman. "Even if we could, it wouldn't work out very well. After all, who's obligated to whom? You're right up against the wall."

Says a New Hampshire salesman, "PA's are getting much more sophisticated. They're more reasonable than ever—now you can go in and talk business. I'm not a winer and diner with lunches,

Rapping with Distributor Salesmen

While this survey was still in the mail, *ID* went south to attend a supplier sales meeting at the supplier's invitation. After hours on the second day, *ID* loosened the tie, shed the jacket, rolled up the sleeves and rapped informally with four distributor salesmen attending the course. They came from Texas, Pennsylvania and Michigan. Their opinions were largely off-the-cuff and very revealing:

ID: *I invite you to "Tell it, like it is." Let's start with your suppliers. How good are your supplier reps today?*

Phil: I didn't mind working with the older ones, but a lot of these younger ones . . . well, we're teaching them.

Joe: . . . And there's such a heavy turnover, you can't keep up with these guys. I mean, you have one guy broken in, and he splits a week later.

Sam: OK, but the newer guys show a lot more aggressiveness. They come up with a lot more ideas.

Jim: But we're not getting any help with customer relations from them. They don't want to waste their time on some small account, you know, of no consequence to them.

Phil: That's right. With us smaller guys, he comes in and gets out as fast as he can. He's got his quotas, and he doesn't want to nickel and dime it.

Joe: These supplier reps get pressured, and when things get rough, they'll forget about distributors with small accounts. With guys like that, I just can't afford to waste my time.

ID: *Do these suppliers help you out at all with product information training, and all that?*

Sam: They're helpful, yes, but there's a certain amount of expense involved—I mean they can't hold these every week or two.

Phil: I tell you one thing: it's a real door opener when you have the factory man with you on a call.

Joe: It is—it's two against one—a real tool.

Jim: OK, but that's so damned high-pressure.

Joe: Right, but you're working closely together. It's like "Let's roll up the sleeves and see what the problems are here."

ID: *How do you compete against price wars?*

Sam: Secondary lines—you have to carry them. Because big companies are cutting quality to give better prices. It hits the consumer where it hurts, in the long run.

ID: *What more should your supplier reps do for you?*

Sam: Be quicker with their deliveries.

Jim: "Honest Jim" here always says to the customer he'll have the goods in 10–12 weeks. And I pad the real figure, which should be about 7–9 weeks. I look real bad when the actual delivery time ends up being around 16 weeks. I want honest delivery time from these guys.

Joe: . . . and get more stock in. I mean, the manufacturer is in a better position to stock more items than the distributor is. He's got more of a dollar outlay.

Phil: Also, it would be nice if those guys would update their catalogs. They list stuff they don't even carry, and they don't tell you—they just won't tell you. It's embarrassing.

Rapping with Distributor Salesmen *(cont.)*

Jim: They really should tell us when items are discontinued or added.

ID: *Let's give the suppliers a break for a minute, and talk about management.*

ID: *No really—what do you like about your management?*

Sam: I like the fact that you can talk to anyone. The door's always open, you know.

Jim: . . . and they know when to support you, and when to leave you alone.

ID: *What's the biggest problem?*

Joe: I guess the salary structure. Straight salary for an inside guy is hardly motivating.

Phil: I'd like to get a company car. If you're on salary plus commission, you should have a car.

Sam: I think the inside salesmen don't bust their guts to make the customer happy.

Jim: Yeah, but their attitude is that "We get you outside guys 75% of your business—we should get a piece of the action."

Joe: I think they're right.

Jim: They think they're unsung heroes, but you know, the customers hate being put on hold all the time.

ID: *Speaking of customers, let's talk about them. First, before we get into that, what do you think of today's PAs?*

Jim: They're about 50-50, young and old, good and bad.

Phil: If they eat well, they're agreeable.

ID: *Do you guys often find yourself making excuses for your firm, or for your suppliers?*

Joe: Are you kidding? That's all a salesman does. I haven't been wrong yet this year. I agree with the customer.

Sam: If you disagree, you're using poor psychology. You have to side with, and sympathize with the customer.

Jim: Inside salesmen suffer here. You know, with making excuses, they really get blasted sometimes.

ID: *Does that old myth about customer loyalty still exist?*

Joe: No . . . well, yes, it still exists, but it's different, you know. Today it means giving you the chance to match an offer they got somewhere else.

Jim: A loyal customer will tell you when your service starts to get bad. He just won't leave you like a jilted bride.

Phil: All prices being equal . . .

Joe: . . . and they aren't.

Sam: Loyalty means—this sounds like something out of *Love Story*—not shopping around. The customer comes directly to me without a lot of comparing prices. Someday if he's told he's getting overpriced, I'd rather have him know he's getting the best quality.

Jim: Loyalty: a good relationship, is where the customer knows he's not getting ripped off.

Joe: You only lose the customer once, and that's it. You don't get a second chance.

ballgames, golf and the usual standards. I don't want to do business with such guys. It's more than a matter of ethics. We're all growing up in this business. The WWII slap-on-the-back guys are dying off. Now, we're dealing with a much younger and smarter bunch of PA's."

Question: Are Customers Asking for Too Much? Or Are They Generally Satisfied as Long as They Get Their Orders Filled and on Time?

Most salesmen polled did not feel their customers were unjustified in asking for service, especially in light of today's prices. After all, several pointed out, distribution is a service industry.

Nevertheless, service cuts into a distributor's profits. But does service suffer?

"Service is the name of the game" says a salesman from Vermont. "They're satisfied if they get what they need, when they need it." "Our customers are service-oriented," says another from across the country. "We generally keep them happy with good service and reasonable prices. We pick up more customers due to our service than for price." "They're spending money with you, and deserve what they get!", says another Westerner. "Customers are usually satisfied," a downstate Maine salesman contends. "Some want the moon as far as price, but as long as they get an order on time, they're happy." Concludes a N.J. salesman: "For the prices we charge, we'd better give them a lot of service. If a PA knows you're telling him the truth on prices, you're OK. Too many customers have been burned by inferior items bought at cheaper prices. They come back to me to avoid all that."

Some salesmen do feel customers ask too much. "They call me at 3 pm, and want an order out by 5 pm," says a man from Denver. "And sometimes they want it yesterday," a New Yorker chimes in. "They always want the material soonest. That's my major complaint. We try to get it to them today instead of yesterday," a Boston salesman says.

"Sometimes they ask for too much," complains another. "They think you should have special tools right there on the shelf. They don't consider the manufacturing or delivery time." "Customers do ask for too much," echoes a general liner from Texas. "They demand and expect too much of us because of our broad product line and large inventory. No one can offer 24-hour delivery on everything made," concludes another.

Question: Do You Often Have to Make Excuses for Your Firm or Your Suppliers?

Most replied that they do not need to offer excuses for their firms or their suppliers. However, there are exceptions:

"I have to make excuses, but often the customer's expectations are unreasonable. We do, however, respond to justified complaints of system deficiencies," a Midwesterner points out. "Quite a bit of the time I make excuses—especially since the supplier no longer has an expediter. Today, we use Excuse #23 from a list of about 100 other excuses. We should be making sales instead of excuses," a Southerner grumbled. "I'd rather admit mistakes than make excuses," says another.

More often than not, the excuses salesmen make to customers relate to longer-than-promised or anticipated delivery time by the suppliers. This often requires involving management to pressure suppliers.

Question: What's Your Opinion of Customer Loyalty? Are They More or Less Loyal Than They Were?

In the good old days, the relationship between customer and salesman was a close one, built on mutual trust, respect, and understanding. In the age of allegedly impersonal big business, computers and Watergate, does customer loyalty still exist? According to the salesmen surveyed, it does.

"Customers are still loyal to us. Personnel changes pose problems for a while, but they gener-

---

How Salesmen See Customer Loyalty

What role does the salesman have in gaining and maintaining customer loyalty? The salesmen have some very strong opinions on how you build customer loyalty:

By being truthful, dependable, and on time for appointments.

By offering much more than just a product. Provide good service, good knowledge, and be willing to work at all levels and offer free advice when apropos.

By dropping in on the customer regularly.

By selling the company, by presenting your realistic strengths, and minimizing weaknesses. By selling your customers on realistic expectations in service, price, quality, etc.

By stocking his every requirement, and offering him a savings in cost where quality doesn't enter the picture. By making shipments on time, and delivering rush items, if necessary, in your own cars.

By finding the material he wants, and shipping it directly.

By introducing new products to him.

By talking to the customer face to face.

By being honest all the way, because the salesman is the company.

By selling yourself and your technical abilities.

By showing application of products to a customer's needs, and providing seminars.

By providing service, service, and more service.

"Whatever the customer wants, it is the distributor salesman's responsibility to either fulfill his desires or alter his expectations."—NY distributor salesman

---

ally continue to rely on us," states a Camden, N.J., salesman. "Their loyalty is in direct proportion to our service. Therefore, it's the salesman's problem, not the customer's" insists a Providence, R.I. salesman. "Most are more loyal, with the exception of the large corporations," adds another Easterner. "They're loyal if you give them a good, fair price. You don't give them a high price because you have them in the bag. They'll give you a chance to compete if you treat them well. If you're not out to hurt them, they won't hurt you", a Philadelphia salesman says bluntly.

"They're loyal in the respect that they'll come back to you after they've been burned somewhere else. Or, if they're price shopping, they'll give you a chance to match their best offer," says a Chicago salesman.

"Loyalty definitely still exists. The little guys could buy from anybody, because they don't get a big price discount like the big guys who buy a lot of stuff. Even if they can't get the stuff right away, they'll come here. They like the people—the personal contact," comments a specialist from Minneapolis. "They're loyal as far as price goes. If the price is too high, they'll mention the competition, instead of just dropping you," adds another from Minnesota. "Nowadays, taking a guy out to lunch once in a while is common. But some guys don't feel they're in debt. That's loyalty. If they won't go out to lunch with you, and still buy your product—that's real loyalty," says a sales engineer from Tennessee. "Not with the larger corporations", says a Chicago salesman. "The smaller companies—where you can get credit, and you're familiar with the personnel, and deal with people rather than computers—is where you find loyalty. If GMC wants to buy 12 screws, they'll send out quote requests to three or four people, for example, and get the lowest bid. That's who gets the order. There's no loyalty there," laments another.

"They are loyal," says a salesman from neighboring Alabama, "as long as you can supply fairly well. If they fail to receive often enough, they switch—understandably." "Our opinion of customer loyalty," retorts another, "is one that won't change sources because someone offers him a small savings in price."

A small handful of salesmen felt there was no customer loyalty left. "I've gotten burned a couple of times by guys I thought were loyal," says one. "I've been subjected to a few letdowns because I'm selling myself first, my company second, and the product third."

"Today, price and costs are so bad," says a Boston salesman, "they've (customers) got to go the cheapest place for the same quality. Imports are giving us trouble. Japanese roller chains, for example, are knocking the daylights out of American chain sales. Costs supersede loyalty, in the end. The customer has to sell and make a profit too. He has to get his best deal, and make the best living for himself that he can."

A Michigan salesman indicated that "During the recession we saw a decline in loyalty in favor of better pricing. During the shortages we saw a decline due to delivery and availability. Loyalty is stronger in good times." "Low price equals high loyalty," is how a Camden, N.J. salesman put it. "Customers will go where the price is right."

Questions

1. *Why is it logical to assume that outside salespeople are more likely than their inside sales counterparts to be dissatisfied with management?*
2. *What clues did you learn from this article that should help you in motivating inside salespeople? Outside salespeople?*

35

Motivating Superior Outside Sales Personnel

ELEANOR BRANTLEY SCHWARTZ

What do you, the manager, do to motivate your outside salespeople to work a little harder and sell a little more? The problem is particularly acute when you have to encourage high-level performers to do more.

The classic economic theory that man is motivated to "maximize his economic gains" has caused some managers to believe money is our prime motivator. Sales personnel, even more than others, have been thought to be motivated by greed for money and material success. They have been described typically as having:

. . . a nagging need to make more money than that paid in a structured job. Making more money shows he excels. Any waiter knows that salesmen are invariably the best tippers . . . Also, since the good salesman is only mildly interested in the abstracts, he likes things he can feel, touch, and see . . . He needs to purchase bigger homes, fancier cars . . . In short, a good salesman is acquisitive. Needless to say, if one deeply wishes to acquire, he needs money. To get money you need sales and high commissions.[1]

The basic contention among many sales managers has been that sales performance can be improved simply by increasing the financial rewards.

Perhaps sales management has also favored financial incentives because managers can correlate the high income of sales personnel with high sales. The inference is that sales volume is a direct result of compensation.

Social scientists, on the other hand, contend that nonfinancial incentives motivate as much as money. Although financial incentives satisfy the basic physical needs, they do not meet social and ego needs. Moreover, intrinsic motivators (achievement, challenge, responsibility, advancement, growth, enjoyment of the work itself, recognition, and involvement) have a longer-term effect on employee attitudes than extrinsic motivators (e.g., contests, prizes, quotas, and money). If intrinsically satisfied in his job, the employee works willingly at high performance levels.

Research was undertaken to determine how high-achieving outside sales persons in small businesses view financial and nonfinancial incentives and their impact on performance. Specific objectives were to:

1. Determine what financial incentives these sales personnel feel affect productivity the most.
2. Discover what high-achieving sales personnel expect of an incentive plan.
3. Isolate the factors that cause better-than-average sales people to terminate relationships with a firm.
4. Evaluate high-producing sales people's attitudes toward sales contests as a motivational device.
5. Evaluate major types of fringe benefits in terms of their motivational influence.

Source: Journal of Small Business Management, Vol. 16, No. 1 (January 1978), 19–26. Copyright © 1978 by the International Council for Small Business and the West Virginia University Bureau of Business Research.
1. T. H. Hartman, "Start Right by Hiring Right," *Sales Management*, April 30, 1973, pp. 76, 78.

6. Examine "motivated" sales people's attitudes toward non-financial incentives.
7. Based on the opinions of these achieving sales people, define the specific areas in which managers did the least effective motivational job.

The Sample

Forty-three small business managers from all parts of the United States were invited to submit names of up to five outside sales personnel who had been with the firm a minimum of three years and were considered "much better than average" in terms of sales performance. The study was limited intentionally to achieving sales people rather than either average or low achievers. The sales persons were not characterized by age, education, sex, geographical location, or other demographic factors. Included in the study were sales personnel of both consumer products and industrial products.

Of the 43 companies invited, 37 participated and provided names of 176 sales personnel. Seventy-three of these completed responses to the mail questionnaire.

Key Findings

Importantly, because the study was confined to high-achieving sales personnel, it cannot be construed to represent all sales people. The findings may be especially useful to owner/managers who feel motivational and other sales management programs should be designed to meet the needs and expectations of the best sales people rather than be aimed at average or below-average performers.

Finding #1. Low salary combined with high commission was perceived as the strongest compensation arrangement to encourage above average sales personnel to produce more. They were motivated by incentives over which they had control.

Discussion: In rating five forms of financial incentives on the basis of "weak," "significant," "considerable," and "strong," as they affect productivity, 87.7 percent of the responding sales people perceived the most important financial incentive as "low salary and high commission" followed by a "bonus based on individual performance" (see Table 1). This indicates that better-than-average sales people tend to want the incentives of high commissions. Bonuses based on *individual* performance rather than *group* performance were favored by most (71.2 percent) of the respondents. Bonuses based on company profits were viewed as weak incentives by more than half of the respondents. High achieving sales people appear to be motivated by incentives over which they have a direct and personal control through their own individual effort and talent.

Finding #2. "Fairness" was the most important expectation sales people had of a financial incentive plan followed by "reward for meeting preset goals," and "reward for performing good customer service."

Table 1

Perceived motivational effect of incentive plans upon productivity of high-achieving outside sales personnel $(n = 73)$

Type compensation	Weak		Significant		Considerable		Strong	
	No.	%	No.	%	No.	%	No.	%
Bonus based on group performance	59	80.8	9	12.3	3	4.1	2	2.7
Bonus based on individual performance	5	6.9	5	6.9	1	15.1	52	71.2
High salary and low commission	5	6.9	8	10.9	14	19.1	47	63.1
Low salary and high commission	0	0	4	5.5	5	6.8	64	87.7
Bonus based on company profits	39	53.4	21	28.8	11	15.1	2	2.7

Table 2

Expectations of high-achieving outside sales personnel for an incentive plan (n = 73)

Expectations	Sales people who expected this		Sales people with expectations met		Sales people with expectations not met	
	No.	%	No.	%	No.	%
Financially competitive with other companies within industry	50	68.4	42	84.0	8	16.0
Rewards sales personnel for good customer service	60	82.2	41	68.0	19	32.0
Fair (e.g., considers such differences as sales potential among various territories)	73	100.0	52	71.2	21	28.8
Financially rewards for meeting preset goals	69	94.5	60	86.9	9	13.1
Rewards length of service	8	10.6	4	50.0	4	50.0
Stimulates challenge (e.g., encourages sales people to go beyond preset goals)	52	71.2	34	65.4	18	34.6
Rewards achievement by advancement and/or more responsibility	50	68.4	30	60.0	20	40.0
Provides income stability and security	27	37.0	15	55.6	12	44.4

Length of service definitely was not considered an expectation of an incentive plan by better-than-average sales people.

Discussion: A significant majority of the 73 sales people, representing different industries and geographical regions, had similar expectations of a sales compensation plan (Table 2). They felt it should be financially competitive, reward good customer service, be fair, reward sales people for meeting preset goals, as well as encourage them to exceed preset goals, and reward achievement by advancement and/or more responsibility. Although all respondents felt a sales compensation plan should be fair, 21 (or 28.8 percent) of the sales people stated this expectation was not being met. The next most frequently anticipated expectation of a compensation plan was financial reward for meeting preset goals (94.5 percent of respondents). Most respondents (60 of 69) felt this expectation was met.

Finding #3. The two most important "demotivators" for better-than-average sales people were (a) a "better" job offered by another company, and (b) dislike of the job.

Discussion: In pinpointing demotivators, the majority of the 73 respondents indicated the major reason for leaving their last sales position was for either a "better position with another company"

(69.9 percent) or "dislike of the work itself" (53.1 percent), rather than the amount of pay or the type of compensation plan (see Table 3). By "better position" and "dislike of the work itself" the sales personnel indicated such things as "desire for more freedom, less routine, more compatible (agreeable) clientele, and greater challenge."

Finding #4. Generally, high-producing sales people liked sales contests. The observation most frequently made was that "prizes should be merchandise, not money."

Table 3

Reason high-achieving outside sales personnel left last sales position (n = 73)

Factor	Responding	
	No.*	%
Better position with another company	51	69.9
Dissatisfaction with pay benefits and/or compensation plan	22	30.1
Dislike of work itself (job content)	39	53.1
Unhappiness with management (supervision)	24	32.9
Dissatisfaction with promotion policies	18	24.7
Other reasons	17	23.2

*The total exceeds 73 because some respondents gave more than one explanation for leaving the previous position.

Table 4

How high-achieving outside sales personnel regard contests as motivators (n = 73)

Question	Very weak		Weak		Strong		Very strong	
	No.	%	No.	%	No.	%	No.	%
Based on your experience with your present organization and in past situations, how do you regard contests as a motivational influence?	7	9.6	10	13.7	42	57.5	14	19.2

Discussion: A significant majority (56 respondents or 76.7 percent) believed contests were either a strong or very strong motivational influence (see Table 4). Only 17 respondents or 23.3 percent considered contests as weak or very weak in terms of motivational impact. Respondents were asked also to give recommendations for making contests more effective as a motivating influence. Sixty-seven respondents replied and gave a total of 254 recommendations. Those given ten or more times are listed below:

	Times Mentioned
1. Prizes should be merchandise, not money	63
2. Prizes should be money, not merchandise	34
3. Contest goals should be realistic and attainable (neither too high nor too low)	26
4. Contest should not last more than two or three months	18
5. Contest should be fair with respect to equalizing chances to win.	17
6. All or most participants should win something	13
7. Sales people should participate in planning contest	12
8. Contests should be simple; they are often too complex	12
9. Manager should let each sales person know how he's doing at least every week or two	11

Finding #5. The consensus among the respondents was that fringe benefits are necessary to attract sales people but, presumably since they are now widely used, are not really important as motivators. High-achieving sales people take them for granted, and do not work harder because of them.

Discussion: As shown in Table 5, most of the sales people surveyed enjoy a rather full range of traditional fringe benefits, such as vacation with pay, life insurance, hospitalization insurance, major medical insurance, a pension plan, and some use of

Table 5

Fringe benefits available to surveyed high-achieving sales personnel (n = 73)

Benefits	Company coverage					
	Full		Part		None	
	No.	%	No.	%	No.	%
Vacation with pay	67	91.8	4	5.5	2	2.7
Life insurance	50	68.5	20	27.4	3	4.1
Hospitalization insurance	39	53.4	31	42.5	3	4.1
Major medical	39	53.4	31	42.5	3	4.1
Pension plan	37	50.7	26	35.6	10	13.7
Personal use of company car	41	56.2	18	24.6	14	19.2
Tuition reimbursement	15	20.5	24	32.9	34	46.6
Profit sharing	15	20.5	19	26.1	39	53.4
Stock options	4	5.5	9	12.3	60	82.2

a company car. Other fringe benefits, such as tuition reimbursement, profit sharing, and stock options, were much less popular. Fringe benefits tend to be more useful in attracting new sales personnel to a company than for motivating them to perform once they are on the job. They were viewed more as prerequisites to recruitment since a company cannot compete for good sales talent without them.

Finding #6. Among nonfinancial incentives, "enjoyment of work" were the most important as viewed by better-than-average sales people. Recognition and personal encouragement were not considered important motivational factors.

Discussion: Respondents were asked to evaluate the importance of six factors that are regarded generally as effective motivators (see Table 6). Enjoyment of work, followed by challenge and achievement, and involvement in decisions, were considered very important by more than half of the respondents. Opportunity for advancement was considered very important by about two-thirds of the respondents. Recognition and personal encouragement were considered important but not very important by a majority of the respondents. More than one-third of the respondents considered personal encouragement to be unimportant, contradicting motivational experts who place great reliance on personal counseling as a motivator, at least insofar as high-achievers are concerned.

Finding #7. "Is unable to communicate effectively" and "doesn't include sales personnel in the decision making process" were considered the two largest motivational errors committed by management.

Discussion: To round out this inquiry into how sales people viewed the effectiveness of various motivational tools and techniques, respondents were asked to relate what they felt was the *one* biggest motivational mistake made by their immediate supervisor. The 69 replies were classified into six categories:

	Times Mentioned
1. *Cannot Communicate Effectively* (e.g., "Unclear instructions," "Doesn't listen," "Can't explain things in writing")	21
2. *Doesn't Include Sales Personnel in Decision-making Process* (e.g., "No voice in territorial decisions or product modification," "Manager tells me what he wants—doesn't ask," "Never consults me in advance but expects miracle solutions when things break down")	17
3. *Frequently Criticizes, Rarely Praises* (e.g.,	

Table 6

Importance of nonfinancial incentives as motivators among high-achieving outside sales personnel (n = 73)

Motivator	Degree of motivational importance					
	Very important		Important		Unimportant	
	No.	%	No.	%	No.	%
Challenge and achievement	56	76.7	11	15.1	6	8.2
Opportunity for advancement (responsibility and growth through training, education, use of initiative)	43	58.9	20	27.4	10	13.7
Enjoyment of work itself	61	83.6	10	13.7	2	2.7
Recognition (awards, publicity in company publications, clubs)	24	32.9	44	60.3	5	6.8
Involvement in decisions about sales goals and other performance requirements	53	72.6	13	17.8	7	9.6
Personal encouragement and counseling (Management's expressed confidence in one's ability to succeed)	8	11.0	40	54.8	25	34.2

Times
Mentioned

"Stays on my back," "Takes credit for what I
do," "No personal interest in me")   14

4. *Negativism* (e.g., sarcasm, lack of trust,
abruptness, and discourtesy)   6

5. *Tells Me to Do a Better Job But Doesn't Show
Me How* (e.g., "Conducts meetings that are
a pure waste," "Isn't really qualified to help
me," and "Often wonder how he got his
job")   3

6. *Miscellaneous* (e.g., "My manager is too ego-
tistical," "Procrastinates," "Blames me instead of himself when things go wrong,"
Gives conflicting orders," "Insists on doing
everything the way it used to be done.")   8

Conclusions

Three major conclusions resulted from this study:

*Financial rewards appear to be significant incentives
among high achieving sales personnel.* Money is the
most important financial incentive, not to motivate
but to prevent demotivation and to maintain a favorable job attitude. While pay was not a major factor in turnover among these respondents (perhaps
because they are high-achievers), other studies
have shown that pay does affect retention rates of
sales people.[2]

*From a motivational standpoint, fringe benefits tend
to meet a set of individual needs different from those
met by direct compensation.* Basically, fringe benefits
meet security needs—*i.e.*, protection from the vicis-
situdes of fate (unemployment, ill health, old age)
as does also an incentive plan based mostly on salary. The paradox is that, according to some social
scientists, the more security that is provided to
those to whom security is of primary importance,
the more these individuals tend to maintain status
quo performance. The need is the motivator, not
the fulfillment of the need. Implications of an at-

tractive security package is that it tends to appeal to
the security-oriented rather than to the achieve-
ment-oriented persons.

*Monetary incentives alone cannot inspire most sales
people to higher levels of productivity.* An impression
that financial incentives constitute the only incentives to which sales people respond is incorrect.
There are periods in a person's career when desire
for and expectation of more financial reward for his
efforts has high priority; but, as these needs are
more and more satisfied, management should be
more attentive to non-financial needs. As achieving
persons grow in competency, they expect fair compensation and look to other rewards for motivation:
self-fulfillment through respect (ideas heard and accepted, etc.), involvement, and challenge of meaningful work. Financial incentives do not do a complete motivational job; nonfinancial incentives are
needed to fulfill psychic needs that money cannot.

Implications for Management

An incentive plan designed by a management sensitive to aspirations that motivate and frustrations
that demoralize sales people can use the salesperson's desire for reward and recognition, increase
his productivity, achieve the company's marketing
objectives, and maximize the company's profits.[3]
To stimulate sales personnel to make more sales
calls, change selling habits, display greater enthusiasm (the keys to successful selling and attainment
of marketing goals), management's motivational
strategy should include—in addition to a flexible financial plan that rewards sales personnel for meeting sales objectives—a creative atmosphere in
which management anticipates the social and psychological aspirations of sales personnel and then
helps them attain these goals through their work.
Financial incentives have a progressively less positive inducement to improve performance. The accumulation of financial rewards leads eventually to

2. Milton J. Stark, "Turnover: Pay Does Make a Difference," *The Conference Board Record*, April, 1970, p. 49.

3. Mathew J. Murphy and Richard C. Smyth, "How to
Harness Money Power to Increase Sales Power," *Industrial
Distribution*, September, 1970, p. 54.

a saturation point. In fact, a person's desire for financial reward will be satisfied long before he has achieved full psychological fulfillment. A creative atmosphere provides the opportunity to grow, to develop, to achieve personal and professional goals.[4] For management, then, the building of a creative environment conducive to releasing a person's potential for extraordinary achievement is one of the most important keys to motivation.

4. "Eight Keys to Motivation," *Sales Management*, November 3, 1975, pp. 46–56.

Questions

1. *What relationship is there between sales incentive programs and Maslow's hierarchy of needs theory?*
2. *"Financial rewards often have to be used not to motivate but to prevent demotivation." Explain.*

36

Making MBO Work in the Sales Force

RICHARD HISE

PETER L. GILLETT

Applying a management-by-objectives approach to sales force management can be tricky—but successful. Examples highlight this discussion.

Management by objectives (MBO) is an approach to management that has gained acceptance across a wide spectrum of American institutions. Business and industrial firms have apparently extensively embraced MBO, and evidence exists that acceptance is occurring in such diverse areas as government, hospitals, and other non-profit organizations.

Given the ubiquitousness of the MBO concept in industry, it is surprising that the literature does not have much to say about its value for marketing operations. Recently, however, several articles have appeared which strongly suggest that MBO would be an appropriate tool for managing sales force operations,[1] and some case studies describe how it was installed and implemented in existing sales forces.[2]

These discussions have been helpful in demonstrating the general MBO process. However, in order to make MBO as effective as possible in sales force operations, there must be an understanding not only of the basic MBO process, but also of MBO's behavioral underpinnings, the results firms have experienced, and the problems they have encountered. These, in turn, must be *integrated with the unique characteristics* of the selling job and mi-

lieu, especially the type of selling tasks, compensation plans, supervisory styles, and degree of autonomy for salesmen. Unfortunately, the aforementioned articles do not provide this integration; they assume that an MBO program can be superimposed on sales operations without modification from usage in other areas. Such is not the case, however. Only when those who develop MBO programs are aware of the peculiarities of the sales management function will it be possible to (1) determine those types of selling situations in which MBO is most likely to be successful, (2) delineate the major obstacles that are likely to occur, and (3) develop recommendations that are likely to achieve the results desired from the MBO program. Together, these three areas form the major focus of this article.

MBO is a *basic philosophy* of management that provides an integrating mechanism for the major management functions of planning, organization, and control.[3] As such, it is of integral importance in establishing goals in motivation, performance appraisal, supervision, management development, manpower planning,[4] communications, and individual growth and development.[5]

Several basic tenets appear to support the MBO philosophy. First, a *Theory Y* approach to management is presumed; that is, employees want to work, want to be successful, and thus do not have to be coerced. Second, *participative management* (involving subordinates in the decision-making processes) will result in a greater commitment to the goals since subordinates have had a say in developing them.

Source: *Atlanta Economic Review*, July–August, 1977, pp. 32–37.

MBO, as a process, should involve four major steps. First, superiors and subordinates jointly decide on the *specific objective* that the subordinates will try to achieve within a designated time period. Overall company objectives serve as a framework within which these specific goals must be developed. Second, the superior and the subordinate develop a *plan of action* to achieve the objectives determined in the first step. Third, *periodic reviews* are conducted in order to ascertain if these goals are likely to be achieved. If not, the action plan may have to be revised or the initial objectives changed. Fourth, at the end of the prescribed time period, an *appraisal of the subordinate's performance* is necessary. This phase involves a comparison of results with objectives.

Benefits of MBO Programs

What kinds of benefits are likely to result from MBO programs? A number of summaries of the various benefits of MBO exist.[6] Exhibit 1 capsulizes those benefits of MBO programs for which the greatest consensus exists. This exhibit indicates that MBO appears to be positively related to a number of highly desirable company objectives of a behavioral nature. To date, however, there is insufficient evidence to suggest that MBO results in higher levels of productivity for subordinates, for superiors, or for companies.[7] Until future studies of MBO conclusively demonstrate that improved per-

Exhibit 1

Benefits of MBO programs

1. Greater subordinate acceptance of decisions reached
2. Increased intrinsic job satisfaction
3. Improved planning
4. Better coordination
5. Greater flexibility
6. Improved superior-subordinate relationships
7. Improved attitude toward the content and challenge of the job
8. Effort more clearly directed to organizational goals
9. Provides clear standards for control purposes
10. Reduces role conflict and ambiguity
11. Provides objective appraisal criteria
12. Increase in level of goals set

formances are likely to result. MBO systems contemplated by sales managers probably should be justified on the basis of these expected behavioral improvements.

MBO in Sales Force Operations

Little is known about the extent to which the sales management area in general is utilizing MBO. However, brief comments on the few previous studies may prove helpful.

A Sales Planning by Objectives program at General Electric's Apparatus Service Division was instituted in 1971. Salesmen and sales managers developed sales volume objectives to be realized from major accounts. Dates were established for these objectives and salesmen submitted plans for achieving them.[8]

The EMCO Company, a pharmaceutical firm, used an MBO approach for its sales personnel that involved eight major steps:

1. A review of the overall marketing plan by top management.
2. Familiarization of home office personnel and field sales supervisors with MBO.
3. Field sales managers establish their goals and objectives.
4. Familiarization of field salesmen with MBO.
5. Statement of objectives from field salesmen.
6. Review of field salesmen's objectives with their sales manager.
7. Periodic feedback as to how well the objectives are being achieved.
8. Reestablishment of objectives by field salesmen who now possess additional experience and information.

Salesmen at EMCO believe that their MBO program resulted in a better feeling of accomplishment, provided direction, and made them profit-conscious.[9]

MBO at the Southern Sales Division of the CIBA Pharmaceutical Corporation involves two major phases. In *goal setting sessions,* district managers and sales representatives mutually determine goals for the sales representatives. In setting these goals, overall company objectives are recognized and the district manager answers the sales representatives' questions. An important part of these sessions is for sales representatives to develop the means for achieving their goals. During *progress review sessions*, sales representatives are provided feedback on how effectively their objectives are being achieved and new goals are established for the next cycle.[10]

While broad-based knowledge is lacking about the degree to which formal MBO programs currently exist in sales force operations, we should point out that to a large extent many sales managers have long practiced an integral part of MBO, that of appraising salesmen on the basis of their performance on hard performance measures. These measures include sales volume objectives, percentage of quotas obtained, market share, number of sales calls made, expense budgets, and others. This should not suggest, however, that formal, full-scale MBO programs have been instituted, nor should it imply that MBO can be indiscriminately adopted without careful consideration of the selling environment.

Selling Environment Aspects

We believe that four major components of the selling environment should be recognized when an MBO program is being adopted. These are (1) the type of task performed, (2) the degree of control existing for the salesman, (3) the supervisory style in existence, and (4) the compensation plan for salesmen.

Type of Task Performed

The type of selling task performed is an important factor to be considered. It is easier to institute MBO in the highly structured kinds of selling tasks incorporating definitive, easy-to-measure goals. In straight selling situations, salesmen and sales managers may readily agree on the goals to be achieved when such goals as sales volume are clearly the most appropriate measure of the salesman's performance.

For other kinds of sales positions, concrete measures of performance are not readily available. Some examples include: (1) missionary salesmen who attempt to build goodwill, (2) salesmen who provide technical assistance, (3) detail salesmen for pharmaceutical firms, (4) salesmen who are essentially order takers as opposed to order getters, and (5) salesmen whose primary mission is marketing intelligence. Although the absence of hard performance measures for these kinds of selling tasks may be a problem, MBO can exert a positive force because it requires superiors and subordinates to give more careful consideration to what the salesmen should accomplish. Management by objectives, as a philosophy, thus can provide motivation as well as a plan for achieving important goals.

Many companies are now encouraging their salesmen to broaden their responsibilities so that they are operating essentially as marketing managers. When this occurs, MBO is beneficial because it provides purpose, direction, and structure for these more complex, creative, and less-constrained tasks.

Degree of Control

By degree of control we mean the extent to which the salesman is free to organize his efforts toward definable goals and the degree to which these efforts directly result in achieving these goals. Several factors affect the degree of control:

1. For many branded consumer products, elements of the marketing mix other than personal selling account for a large percentage of the sales generated. Advertising is a good example.

2. Many salesmen require the help of other specialists in their firms. Industrial salesmen, in particular, may need to consult engineers, value analysts, production experts, and installation personnel.

3. Some areas of the firm may detract from the salesman's effectiveness because they are not performing acceptably. For example, traffic and distribution may be consistently guilty of late deliveries, resulting in cancelled orders.

4. Cataclysmic changes in the markets, competition, or demand affect control. Clearly superior new competitive products or drastic shifts in the market's tastes are examples.

When salesmen have a high degree of control, MBO is particularly appropriate because a salesman's performance results largely from his own effort. Even where control is minimal, MBO helps clarify potential problem areas. In addition, it forces management to isolate the contribution of salesmen toward the achievement of desirable goals.

Supervisory Style

The effectiveness of MBO depends largely on the human relations skills of supervisors. They must be effective communicators and listeners and must know how to provide feedback and encourage subordinates. Most importantly they need to be comfortable with a participative (democratic) management style.

Many sales managers lack these requisite skills. Being line managers, they tend to be somewhat autocratic in their dealings with subordinates. If they have been promoted to management positions directly from the sales ranks, they may not have had to develop these interpersonal skills. For sales managers lacking these skills, appropriate training is advisable before implementing an MBO program.

Compensation Plan

Salesmen under incentive compensation plans are more easily integrated into an MBO program than are those under straight salary plans. Salesmen paid a straight salary may not be as highly motivated as those whose compensation is largely incentive-based, as they may not see as direct a relationship between their efforts and earned rewards. To overcome this problem, salaried salesmen need to be shown how their achievements under MBO will be more clearly recognized by management and how this ultimately will affect their salary.

Making MBO More Effective

The four major steps in the MBO process mentioned earlier are shown in Exhibit 2. Drawing on

Exhibit 2
Major steps in MBO for sales management

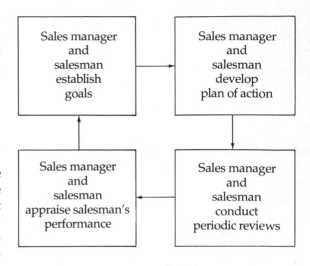

the experiences companies have had with MBO, the behavioral science literature dealing with each of these steps, and the peculiarities of the sales function, it is possible to develop a number of specific recommendations for making each phase work better. Before this is done, however, an important point needs to be made about the process depicted in Exhibit 2.

In each step, the sales manager and salesman need to *work together*. Only through their cooperative efforts throughout the entire process can MBO be made effective. Each individual needs to bring his particular strengths and expertise to the sessions so that *both* the organization and the individual will perform as effectively as possible.

Establishing Goals

Exhibit 3 contains the specific recommendations regarding goal establishment in an MBO program for sales management. Although many of these are common sense in nature, most of them also have solid empirical support.

Relatively new goals should be established by the sales manager and the salesman. Obviously, these should be the most important goals, the ones that significantly contribute to the company's success. A

Exhibit 3

Effective MBO goal-setting in sales force management

1. Establish few goals
2. Set priorities
3. Goals must be explicit
4. Write goals down
5. Encourage high-level goals
6. Determine when goals are to be achieved
7. Modify goals as conditions warrant
8. Integrate company and individual goals
9. Use group goal setting

concentration on relatively few goals provides salesmen with sufficient direction so that they can make the best use of their time and effort. It also minimizes the possibility of the salesman working at cross pusposes, that is, attempting to achieve one goal which results in the nonachievement of another. Henderson indicates that no more than three objectives were established in the Southern Sales Division of the CIBA Pharmaceutical Corporation. In many cases, one was sufficient.[11]

Even more direction can be provided salesmen if *priorities are agreed upon* for the goals that are established. When analyzing an MBO program at Black and Decker, Carroll and Tosi found that setting goal priorities was one factor that resulted in more favorable attitudes and better performance.[12]

Goals must be *explicit*. They should not be couched in general terms that are subject to interpretation. This is an important aspect of the MBO process, as there is clear evidence that its presence can have a number of desirable benefits. At Black and Decker, goals were more likely to be achieved if they were specific rather than general.[13] In the same firm, specificity of objectives was positively related to more favorable attitudes and higher performance.[14] A clear statement of objectives has also been found to result in higher levels of satisfaction for superiors and a more positive attitude toward the MBO program on the part of subordinates.[15] Also, it has been documented that clear, specific objectives are more important to performance than a sense of participation.[16] In a laboratory experiment Locke and Bryan found that spe-

cific goals produced higher performance than "do your best" goals.[17]

Goals need to be *written down*. Written goals reduce the possibility of any subsequent misunderstanding. They can also serve as a mechanism for the salesman to indicate his enthusiasm for the goals, thereby leading to a greater commitment to achieve them.

High-level goals should be encouraged in the MBO process. (The evidence in a highly controlled experiment demonstrated that performance increased as the level of the goal increased.)[18] They should not be overly difficult to obtain, however, and the sales manager needs to realize that not all of his salesmen may be capable of achieving them. It was found at Black and Decker that individuals who were less confident, less mature, and less career-oriented tended to be discouraged by difficult goals.[19]

The sales manager and salesman need to agree on a time schedule for attaining the goals. Generally, MBO programs specify a one-year period. Where time limits are perceived by the subordinate as being fair, goals are more likely to be achieved.[20]

Goals should be flexible; they will need to be *modified* by the sales manager and salesman to accommodate shifts in the market's tastes, changes in the level of competitor activity, changes in territorial assignments, ups and downs in the economy, and so on. This is one of the major advantages accruing from a planned program of periodic reviews, to be discussed later.

Every effort should be made to *integrate company and individual goals*. Here, the sales manager needs to take the initiative and show how the salesman can satisfy his own needs through achievement of the agreed-upon objectives, which, in turn, should contribute positively to the overall company objectives. Since all salesmen will not be motivated via the same needs, it is incumbent upon the sales manager to identify the most important motivators for each subordinate and show explicitly how achievement of the objective will result in a satisfaction of these needs. This phase of MBO is significant since it probably is the most effective way to reduce the resistance to change that is often encountered in MBO programs. Integration of individual and company goals is a must, according to Levinson, who has sharply questioned various aspects of the MBO process.[21]

A *team approach* to goal setting has exciting possibilities, even though it is a departure from the normal one-on-one situation usually associated with MBO. It appears that two types of team effort are appropriate for the sales area. First, the sales manager needs to meet with other executives *outside* the sales area whose responsibilities have an impact on his operations. These meetings should enable him to have a better idea as to how viable various goals may be. For example, he may learn that obtaining a 10% increase in sales may be inappropriate because of production problems which the production foreman may share with him. In this team effort, the interdependent nature of the sales job is recognized, and thus there should be better coordination of the overall sales effort[22] and less danger of *suboptimization*. In the second type of team effort, the sales manager meets with his salesmen in group goal-setting sessions. It was found that when this was done in insurance sales offices, the salesmen provided each other with more technical sales assistance and shared more openly and quickly new, effective appeals, the existence of new markets, and new strategies of selling.[23] The salesmen in these groups tended to set higher goals and apparently were more motivated to achieve them. Another report of group goal setting in a European chemical company indicated that better integration of individual and organizational goals occurred and the traditional barrier between superior and subordinate was reduced.[24]

Developing the Action Plan

Perhaps the most important aspect of the action plan is that it should be the combined effort of *both* the sales manager and salesman. The sales manager has valuable information and experience that he needs to share with his salesmen. Frequently, he is privy to aspects of the market and competition about which the salesman is ignorant.

An action plan needs to be specific. Thus it should include who, what is to be done (the objec-

tive), where, when, how, and how much is required (i.e., resources to be utilized).[25] An action plan that includes these elements is: For salesman Tom Smith to obtain a 20% market share for No. 10 sized envelopes in the southeast Pennsylvania territory by December 31, 1976, by increasing his average number of calls per week to 25 within a sales expense budget of $20,000.

Periodic Reviews

The research evidence is fairly conclusive as to the importance, nature, frequency, and benefits of the review process in MBO. Feedback has been identified as a critical factor in determining the success of MBO programs. Feedback needs to be specific and relevant. It needs to be periodic, frequent, and prompt.

Review sessions should be held several times a year. During these meetings, the sales manager and salesmen should come to an agreement as to the degree to which they believe goals are being satisfied and what needs to be done if they are not.

Appraising the Salesman's Performance

At the end of the time period stipulated in the action plan, the sales manager and salesman need to appraise the salesman's performance. This involves comparing results with the stated objectives. If results have been achieved, the salesman should be praised for his successes. However both parties also should determine if it would have been possible to have done better and, if so, how this might have been accomplished.

If the salesman has not been successful in achieving his goals, the sales manager should not dwell on the lack of accomplishment, nor should negative criticism be utilized. Negative criticism by itself is not likely to lead to improved results.[26] Instead, a specific action plan should be developed that, hopefully, will result in an improved performance. Thus the emphasis should be on *why* the objectives were not achieved and *how* they might be obtained in the future.

There seems to be general agreement that this appraisal session is *not the appropriate time* to discuss overall performance, salary increases, and promotion possibilities as the appraisal process detracts from the action plan for improving objectives.[27]

Problems

Firms with MBO systems have consistently encountered a number of administrative and implementation problems. The following problems appear to be particularly germane to MBO in the sales management area.

1. Some MBO systems have not had the *enthusiastic support of top management*. Without it, MBO is not likely to be successful.[28]

2. Some MBO programs have engendered a great deal of *resistance to the changes* required, and the companies involved were unable to develop suitable change strategies.[29] Resistance in the sales area can be minimized by explicitly showing salesmen how MBO will enable them to better achieve their own individual goals.

3. A frequent problem is that MBO is not integrated effectively with other systems in the company such as budgeting and forecasting.[30] A group approach to MBO, in which sales managers interact with managers in other areas of the company, may reduce the probability of this occurring.

4. Very frequently, managers *lack the necessary interpersonal skills* vital to the success of MBO, such as coaching, counseling, giving and receiving feedback, and interpersonal communications.[31] Additional training may alleviate this problem.

5. An *increased amount of time* needed by managers in implementing MBO was encountered at Purex[32] and the CIBA Pharmaceutical Corporation. At the latter company, 50% of the sales manager's time was required for the MBO program.[33] It can only be hoped that as a firm becomes more skilled with MBO, it would become less of a drain on management time.

6. *Excessive paper work* has occurred in a number of firms, including Purex.[34] Since nonselling activities may already account for a significant percentage of the salesmen's time, the specter of additional forms to fill out may cause some resistance. Firms should explore ways to minimize this burden by integrating it with already required work.

Conclusions

Before any company's executives institute an MBO program in the sales function, they need to ask themselves a number of crucial questions. Have we carefully analyzed our selling environment? If salesmen's objectives are difficult to pinpoint, if salesmen lack direct control over the achievement of objectives, if a salary-type compensation plan predominates, and sales managers lack interpersonal skills, have we recognized and accounted for these potential problems? Are we willing to use MBO even though we cannot be sure that it will result in greater productivity? How important to us are those areas in which MBO has been found to show immediate improvement, such as better superior-subordinate relationships, more favorable attitudes toward the job, or reduced role conflict? Do we feel that the benefits resulting from MBO will clearly outweigh some of the negatives, such as possible resistance to change, more supervisory time involved, and increased paper work? Do we have the resources and patience to give sales managers the necessary interpersonal skills? Are we prepared to wait three or four years to find out if MBO is really for us? Thoughtful executives will look long and hard at these and other questions before reaching a decision. They will resist the temptation to adopt such a program merely because MBO is a popular "buzzword," or because salesmen are already judged on concrete objectives and thus MBO would be easy to adopt.

A major deficiency of many ongoing MBO programs is apparently the failure of management to clearly specify what it expects MBO to achieve. It seems foolish to waste thousands of dollars and man-hours and not do so. In this regard, it would be helpful if we had a better understanding of the relationship between MBO and performance. But since this is not the case, sales managers must resist the temptation to become enthusiastic about MBO because they believe it will improve the productivity of their salesmen.

Sales managers need to carefully consider the benefits of the team approach to MBO. It appears to overcome some of the problems inherent in "one-on-one" MBO systems, such as poor coordination, possible suboptimization, and lack of information for proper goal setting. More importantly, there is some evidence that the team approach may result in increased productivity.

Any firm that decides to employ MBO in its sales operations should develop a number of sequential steps to be followed. The four that we suggest (setting goals, action plans, periodic review, and appraisal) may prove useful. The recommendations made in association with these should be helpful for firms instituting MBO.

Finally, MBO in sales force management will be effective only if it has the enthusiastic support of the salesmen involved. We submit that the best way to achieve this support is to show salesmen how the MBO system will enhance the possibility of their achieving their own personal objectives. Achieving this support involves the crucial task of integrating company and individual goals, a difficult task, but one we believe is crucial to the success of MBO in the sales function.

Notes

1. Donald W. Jackson, Jr. and Ramon J. Aldag, "Managing the Sales Force by Objectives," *Business Topics*, Spring 1974, pp. 53–59; and Michael J. Etzel and John M. Ivancevich, "Management by Objectives in Marketing: Philosophy, Process and Problems," *Journal of Marketing*, October 1974, pp. 47–55.
2. James O. Leathers, "Applying Management by Objectives to the Sales Force," *Personnel*, August 1973, pp. 45–50; Robert A. Else, "Selling by Measurable Objectives," *Sales Management*, May 24, 1973, pp. 22–24; and Richard I. Henderson, "MBO: How It Works in a Sales Force," *Supervisory Management*, April 1975, pp. 9–14.
3. William E. Reif and Gerald Bassford, "What MBO Really Is," *Business Horizons*, June 1973, p. 24.
4. Ibid.
5. Harry Levinson, "Management by Whose Objectives?" *Harvard Business Review*, July–August 1970, p. 126.
6. Etzel and Ivancevich, "Management by Objectives in Marketing"; Reif and Bassford, "What MBO Really Is"; Herbert H. Meyer, Emanuel Kay, and John R. P. French, "Split Rules in Performance Appraisal," *Harvard Business Review*, January–February 1965, pp. 126–129; Stephen J. Carroll, Jr. and Henry L. Tosi, Jr., *Management by Objectives* (New York, The Macmillan Co., 1973); and Anthony P. Raia, "Goal Setting and Self-Control," *Journal of Management Studies*, February 1965, pp. 35–53.
7. Dale D. McConkey, "MBO—Twenty Years Later, Where Do We Stand?" *Business Horizons*, August 1973, p. 27.
8. Else, "Selling by Measurable Objectives."
9. Leathers, "Applying Management by Objectives to the Sales Force."
10. Henderson, "MBO: How It Works in a Sales Force."
11. Ibid.
12. Carroll and Tosi, *Management by Objectives*, p. 41.
13. Ibid., p. 5.
14. Ibid., p. 40.
15. Henry L. Tosi, Jr. and Stephen J. Carroll, Jr., "Managerial Reaction to Management by Objectives," *Academy of Management Journal*, December 1968, pp. 415–426.
16. Etzel and Ivancevich, "Management by Objectives in Marketing," p. 48.
17. Judith F. Bryan and Edwin A. Locke, "Goal Setting as a Means of Increasing Motivation," *Journal of Applied Psychology*, 1967, pp. 274–277.
18. Carroll and Tosi, *Management by Objectives*, pp. 4–5.
19. Ibid.
20. Ibid., p. 5.
21. Levinson, "Management by Whose Objectives?"
22. Wendell L. French and Robert W. Hollman,

"Management by Objectives: The Team Approach," *California Management Review*, Spring 1975, p. 14.

23. Rensis Likert, *The Human Organization* (New York, McGraw-Hill, Inc., 1967), p. 57.

24. French and Hollman, "Management by Objectives: The Team Approach," p. 21.

25. Anthony P. Raia, *Management by Objectives* (Glenview, Illinois, Scott, Foresman and Co., 1974), p. 68.

26. Meyer, Kay, and French, "Split Roles in Performance Appraisal"; and Carroll and Tosi, *Management by Objectives*.

27. George S. Odiorne, *Management by Objectives* (New York, Pitman Publishing Corp., 1965), p. 79; and French and Hellman, "Management by Objec-

tives: The Team Approach," p. 16.

28. Raia, *Management by Objectives*, p. 149.

29. Ibid., pp. 149–151.

30. Ibid.

31. Ibid.

32. Ibid.

33. Henderson, "MBO: How It Works in a Sales Force."

34. Raia, *Management by Objectives*.

Questions

1. *Explain the basic tenets of the MBO philosophy.*
2. *In which types of sales organizations is MBO likely to work best? not to work?*

PART SIX

The Marketing Environment

Unquestionably, the 1980s will be a period of increased change and uncertainty. "To a major extent, the future economic well-being of people, the prosperity of industry, and the quality of life will depend on efficient and effective marketing systems that are responsive to the changing environment." [1]

"The world economy has been transfigured by shortages of important raw materials and products manufactured from them. Shortages along with spiraling inflation and pollution problems are forcing U.S. consumers and marketers to reevaluate their conception of an affluent economy." [2]

A 1975 national survey by the Opinion Research Corporation revealed that a majority of the American public believes that "the average manufacturer's after-tax profit is 33 per cent—over 20 times the actual. The estimate of oil companies' after-tax profit is 61 per cent—over eight times the actual." [3]

Beginning in the 1950s and continuing through the early 1970s, large anchor stores that attracted customers into suburban shopping malls often reserved for themselves the power to "veto" or block the entry of "undesirable" mall tenants. Too often, the veto power was used to control competition. Thus the FTC began labeling the practice as unlawful and in restraint of trade. [4]

In 1978, sporting goods retailers were losing 4 to 5 percent in sales each year due to shoplifting; that was $40,000 to $50,000 on a $1 million-a-year business. New electronic article surveillance systems were able in many cases to cut losses to about 1 percent. Importantly, the system also proved that sporting goods shoplifters were not mostly teenagers or minority group members but were like the average customer. In fact, one retailer found that his average shoplifter was "a

1. Gene R. Laczniak, Robert F. Lusch, and Jon G. Udell, "Marketing in 1985: A View from the Ivory Tower," *Journal of Marketing*, October 1977, pp. 53, 56.
2. Stephen W. Brown, Zohrab S. Demirdjian, and Sandra E. McKay, "The Consumer in an Era of Shortages," *MSU Business Topics*, Spring 1977, p. 49.
3. Ralph de Toledano, "Something Called Socialism," *The Knoxville Journal*, July 29, 1975, p. 5.
4. "Antitrust Action in the Shopping Malls," *Business Week*, December 8, 1975, p. 51.

white, female, 23 years old, had one child and a husband who made 15 grand a year. . . ." [5]

The environment poses threats and opportunities for businesspeople. As the linking pins between an organization and its environment, marketers must stay abreast of environmental conditions and must develop and implement strategies that are appropriate for those conditions.

The U.S. market economy is an open system. As such, it is subject to the influences of a wide variety of environmental forces. The individual business organization is affected by changes in the political, legal, technological, economic, and social environments. Managers make decisions in light of these forces, which are in a constant state of flux. Marketing managers, in particular, find themselves constrained by laws and regulations that limit their pricing, promotional, distribution, and even product development decisions. Of course, since it is the job of marketing to plan and implement the organization's exchange offers, marketers must be acutely aware of changes in the consumer, industrial, and nonbusiness organization markets for their company's products.

Also important to marketers are changes in the number, age, education, income, and other demographic characteristics of current and potential customer markets. Changes in buyers' attitudes, interests, and opinions can make once very appropriate marketing strategies very ineffective. For example, the women's movement of the 1970s led marketers of cosmetic or beauty aids and personal care products to redesign their marketing programs entirely. With more women working, a different variety of products was demanded. New promotional appeals were needed to sell to the new woman. With her radically increased income, price began to play a different role in the woman's purchase decision. Finally, her shopping patterns changed with greater restrictions on her time, and marketers were forced to modify their distribution channels to meet her demands.

Several dimensions of the environment of marketing are highlighted in the articles in Part Six. In "The 1980s and Beyond: A Perspective," William Lazer, a preeminent marketing scholar, discusses some of the fundamental factors and forces that will shape, not curtail, business opportunities during this decade. In "Retailing Executives View the 1980s," J. Barry Mason and Morris L. Mayer report the views of a sample of owners and managers about the key issues of the 1980s and their probable impacts on strategic and operating retail management.

The next articles in Part Six deal with the legal environment of marketing. The issues surrounding charges that the cereal companies monopolized the ready-to-eat breakfast cereal industry during the 1970s are discussed in "The Cereal Companies: Monopolists or Super Marketers?" The

5. "Scorecard," *Sports Illustrated,* December 1978, p. 8.

impact of antitrust laws on smaller companies is evaluated in "Antitrust Compliance for Small Business," by James E. Inman.

The impact of technological change on marketing management is explored in "Managing Xerox for Technological Change," from the *Conference Board Record*. Finally, in "Merchandise Shortages and Retail Policies," Stanley C. Hollander identifies alternative strategies that might be implemented if merchandise shortages become serious at the retail level in the 1980s.

37

The 1980s and Beyond:
A Perspective

WILLIAM LAZER

Shifts in demographic factors and social trends will shape business opportunity, not curtail it. There will be numerous opportunities for success—for those who think ahead.

The decade of the 1960s witnessed a most remarkable and extended period of continuous business growth.[1] The "soaring sixties" reached unprecedented heights in the expansion of population, income, employment, housing markets, business investments, and profits. It led to consumer expectations of a bigger and better future.

In striking contrast, the 1970s have been marked by rising unemployment, inflation, scarcity, declining productivity, contracting markets, a sharp recession, and a climate of considerable self-doubt and retrenchment. The following paraphrases of statements made in business publications about our economy in the last two years are examples:

The United States is steadily sliding down the path to decline.

Our long-term growth trend has slowed and we are confronted with permanent stagflation.

We are entering a period of scarcity in energy and raw materials.

The United States will have difficulty generating

sufficient economic growth to satisfy consumer demand.

Our economic and political system is designed to cope with short-term problems, and it cannot cope with the long-term demands placed upon it.

We are entering a new period of our history—a no-growth economy.

The good life and high living brought about by the affluence of the 1960s have now come to an abrupt halt.

Consumers in the future will be forced to lower their life-style expectations.

By conquering nature, Americans have squandered their natural resources. Soon they will have to live austerely.

There seem to be three tendencies on the part of business prognosticators. First, forecasts of future markets and business opportunities seem unduly influenced by the most immediate events, especially when those events show a sharp break with the recent past. This was the case with double-digit inflation, high unemployment levels, the quadrupling of petroleum prices, and our falling productivity levels. Second, greater weight seems to be given to negative market forces and economic difficulties than to positive or supporting factors. One need only review the lack of emphasis on declining interest rates, moderate levels of inflation, and increasing productivity of 1976, as compared to the notice given to their opposites during 1974. Third, American events do not seem to be placed in a balanced perspective. Our economic problems, difficult social issues, and disturbances are not viewed

Source: William Lazer, "The 1980s and Beyond: A Perspective," pp. 21–35, *MSU Business Topics,* Spring 1977. Reprinted by permission of the publisher, Division of Research, Graduate School of Business Administration, Michigan State University.

as happenings. They are treated as crises and are presented as precursors of a rapidly deteriorating future. For example, in the past few years in the United States, attention has been given to our energy crisis, environmental crisis, unemployment crisis, population crisis, international monetary crisis, hospital crisis, pollution crisis, medical crisis, food crisis, urban crisis, farm crisis, housing crisis, gun crisis, water crisis, credibility crisis, and, of course, Watergate crisis.

What do the basic shifts in demographic factors and social trends portend? What are the myths, and what are the realities? This article presents a perspective of some fundamental factors and forces that will shape business opportunities during the 1980s.

Declining Births or Another Baby Boom?

There seems to be as much misunderstanding about actual births, zero population growth, the desire to have children, and fertility rates as there is about any aspect of demographics. Such mistaken statements as the following are illustrative:

We have now reached zero population growth (ZPG), and our population is declining.
The young people no longer wish to have children.
Ours is an era of the childless marriage.
Young marrieds desire freedom, not entrapment with family responsibilities.
Given the pill and abortion, the number of babies born will continue to decline rapidly.

Our population growth depends on the rate of births, deaths, and migration. Death rates are quite predictable, and net migration to the United States averages about 400,000 persons per year. The controlling factor is the birthrate. Misconceptions about actual births and birthrates stem from a misunderstanding of technical terms used in reporting birth statistics, such as total fertility and zero population growth (ZPG).

In the United States, ZPG is estimated to occur when a rate of birth of 2.1 children per woman of

childbearing age—women aged 15–44—is maintained over a considerable period. At that rate, our population growth will eventually level off or just replace itself. Moreover, our current birthrate is below ZPG, being approximately 1.8 to 1.9. As a result, an erroneous conclusion is often drawn that the number of babies born is decreasing and our population is declining.

For our population to level off, it is estimated that a rate of 2.1 children per woman of childbearing age must be maintained for several decades. Will this occur? It could, but that may be unlikely. Even if it did occur, this would not mean that the number of babies born over the next 15 years will decline. In fact, the potential is present for a *second baby boom.* But it should also be recognized that if the current tendency to defer marriage and births is maintained, eventually the United States will have an excess of deaths over births.

During the late 1950s and early 1960s the postwar baby boom generated an average of about 4 million births per year, reaching a high point of 4.3 million births in 1957. That factor helped stimulate the growth years of the 1960s, leading to rapidly expanding markets and levels of great economic accomplishments. A second baby boom is likely to occur even if the birthrate remains at a low rate of 1.9 children per woman of childbearing age. The actual number of live births in the United States from 1940 on, with projections for 1980 and 1985, using a 2.1 birthrate, is given in Table 1. Ob-

Table 1
Live births in the United States

Year	Births (000's)
1940	2,570
1945	2,873
1950	3,645
1955	4,128
1960	4,307
1965	3,801
1970	3,725
1974	3,160
1980	4,000 (estimated)
1985	4,250 (estimated)

Source: Based on data from Bureau of the Census, *Current Population Reports*, Series P-25, using Series E for projection purposes.

viously, the 1980–1990 total occurs on a larger population base.

The next baby boom, however, will have some marked differences from that of the 1960s. The previous boom resulted from relatively fewer women having large families, almost four children each. The new baby boom will comprise about twice the number of women having one-half the number of children. A larger proportion of babies of the second baby boom will be firstborn. That, of course, has significant market ramifications.

Considerable attention has been paid by the news media to the childless couple. This is sometimes highlighted in terms of the two-career family. But such families are very small in number, and while they are expected to grow in the 1980s, their overall impact on births will remain insignificant. The main reasons for our relatively low birthrate are: (1) smaller families, (2) later starts for families, (3) postponement of marriage by the young, and (4) a decline in the proportion of women of childbearing age in the population. We should note that the proportion of all women represented by the 15 to 44 age group increased steadily from 40.7 percent in 1970 to 43.2 percent in 1975 and is expected to reach 45.8 percent by 1985.

But even if the number and proportion of women of childbearing age are increasing, the question is whether women have changed in their desire to bear children. Survey results continue to indicate that married women want to have children. The expected number of children for wives 18–24 in June 1974 was reported to be: 0 or one child, 17 percent; two children, 55.7 percent; three children, 19.4 percent; four or more children, 7.8 percent.[2]

The average number of children desired, however, has decreased significantly, and families are smaller. The norm now seems to be a matched set—a girl and a boy. Given the uncertainty associated with predetermining the sex of children, the birth of several children will be required by many couples to achieve the desired mix. Hence, it seems likely that a birthrate of more than two children per woman of childbearing age may be realized in the near future, contributing to the second

baby boom. Also, it should be noted that more babies are being born to unwed mothers.

Some of the characteristics of the second baby boom of interest to business are:

1. An average of about 4 million babies per year will be born between 1975 and 1990. This parallels the baby boom of the 1960s.
2. Previously, 25 percent of all babies were firstborn. By 1980 this may reach 40 percent. Thus, expenditure on children's furniture, clothing, housing needs, baby foods, and accoutrements will be affected.
3. Family size will be smaller.
4. Declining birthrate will result from fewer higher order births and not from childless couples.
5. The proportion of families expecting no children will continue to be small, and this will not be the norm.
6. Women aged 15–24 will have three-fourths of the firstborns, while women aged 20–29 will account for two-thirds of higher order births. These groups are increasing absolutely and proportionately.
7. Families will realize higher per capita income.[3]

Population Increase or Decline?

Related to the major misunderstandings about births are some of the general statements made about changes in our total population. For example:

Since our birthrate is below ZPG, our population has leveled off.
Our population has peaked and is now declining.
Ours is becoming more of a child-centered and teen-aged population.
Senior citizens are becoming less significant as a proportion of the total population.

Table 2 presents an estimate of expected growth in population from 1970 to 2000 using the assumption of a ZPG birthrate. While our population is increasing at a lower rate than it did during the 1960s,

Table 2

Population shifts in the United States, 1960–2000

Age	Population in millions					Percentage change			
	1960	1970	1980	1990	2000	1960–1970	1970–1980	1980–1990	1990–2000
Under 20	69	77	73	77	81	+11.1%	− 5.2%	+ 5.7%	+ 4.3%
20–24	11	17	21	18	19	+54.3	+22.6	−15.4	+ 7.8
25–34	23	26	37	42	36	+10.4	+46.1	+13.1	−14.6
35–44	24	23	26	37	41	− 4.5	+ 9.6	+45.5	+13.0
45–54	21	23	22	25	36	+13.3	− 3.9	+ 9.9	+45.1
55–64	16	19	21	20	22	+19.4	+13.0	− 3.4	+10.6
65 and over	17	20	24	28	29	+20.4	+19.8	+15.4	+ 3.9
	181	205	224	247	264	+13.4%	+ 9.4%	+10.0%	+ 7.2%

Source: Based on data from Bureau of the Census, *Current Population Reports,* Series P-25, using Series E for projection purposes.

it is still showing substantial gains. Conservative census projections indicate that the United States will add over 19 million people, more than four-fifths of the Canadian population, for example, during the 1970–1980 decade. It will add a little more, about 23 million, roughly the total Canadian population, between 1980 and 1990. By the year 2000 our population is expected to reach 264 million.

To gain perspectives on future market opportunities, a most important factor to note is the varying growth rate of different age groups. During the 1970s the relative rate of growth of the 25–34 age groups stands out. This group is expected to account for 46 percent of the growth over the decade.

The decade of the seventies is an era of the young marrieds. Their proportionate growth does not portend a revolution in values or upheaval in our society, as is often projected. Rather, the young marrieds are interested in establishing themselves in their communities, homes, families, and jobs. They support extended market growth for such items as houses, home furnishings, cars, appliances, and furniture. They are net borrowers, not net savers.

In gross terms, each of the decades from 1950 to 2000 may be characterized according to a "core market thrust"—that market which reflects the largest proportional growth. This trend is shown in Table 3. Obviously, there is some overlap between

Table 3

Characterization of decades

Decade	Core market focus
1950–1960	Babies and young children
1960–1970	Teen-agers and young adults
1970–1980	Young marrieds
1980–1990	Early middle agers
1990–2000	Middle agers

decades, but the table illustrates the ripple effect as people move through the age cycle.

A few highlights of expected trends in the growth of various age categories during the 1980s are pointed up in Table 4.

Population statistics reveal that even with a relatively low birthrate, our population will realize substantial growth. The young marrieds and middle agers will become more important in the next 15 years. Both males and females are living longer, and the population is aging. The life expectancy at birth for women in 1974 was almost 76 years, compared to 68 years for men. This will result in an increasing number of women living alone. The proportion of senior citizens, which is increasing and will continue to do so through the year 2000, will make itself felt.

Table 4

Trends in age groups in the 1980s

Age category	Projected trends
0–4	Although they have been contracting since 1960, between 1980 and 1985 *they will grow almost four times as fast* as the average for the whole population.
5–15	They realized great growth during and since the 1950s and were one-fourth of the population in 1970. *They will decline relatively* and account for less than 20 percent of the population in 1985.
18–24	They are currently expanding and represent the age category of first marriage and first child for many Americans. *They will decline relatively* during the 1980s.
25–34	The young marrieds *will continue to realize the greatest growth rate of all groups* through 1980. They are expected to grow by 46 percent over the decade of the 1970s.
35–44	The early middle-agers have high income, high home ownership, and teenagers at home. *They will expand at a rate of four times that of the general population from* 1980 to 1985.
45–54	The middle-age group is the one which enjoys the highest income and rate of savings. *It has been contracting* since 1970 and will continue to do so during the 1980s but will expand greatly in the 1990s.
55–64	The late middle-agers and younger senior citizens have high savings and buying power. They are empty nesters and *will grow at about the same rate as the general population* during the 1980s.
65 and over	The senior citizens present a growth market. Their incomes are lower than those of other adult population segments. The growth rate through 1985 is expected to *be twice that of the population rate,* and the proportion of women in this category is increasing.

Let us highlight some of the characteristics of two age groups of interest to business people; those aged 25–34 (young adults) and those 65 and over (senior citizens).

25–34—Young Adults

1. Single most important market to 1980.
2. A generation raised in affluence.
3. Expect bigger and better.
4. Will number about 31 million or 21 percent of the adult population in 1975.
5. Are in major growth phase of family.
6. Are married (over 75 percent).
7. Are in best educated population segment.
8. Included 12.7 million family heads in 1975.
9. 24 percent of family heads have college degree.
10. 45 percent of heads have white-collar job.
11. 80 percent of homes have children.
12. 23 percent of homes have three or more children.
13. Have one-third of the nation's children.
14. 38 percent of families earn $15,000 and over.
15. Over 50 percent of families own their premises.

65 and over—Senior Citizens

1. Are "younger older," not decrepit.
2. Amount to 10–12 percent of population in 1990.
3. Have considerable resources—pensions.
4. Have more active and full retirement.
5. Political power will increase.
6. Are interested in maintenance of self.
7. Have more surviving children.
8. Family ties remain.
9. Live apart from children.
10. Higher proportion of women will be evident by 1990.
11. Are relatively free of work and want.
12. Are not disadvantaged, unskilled, uneducated, blue-collar.
13. Will become more visible.
14. Will live longer.

An Affluent or a No-Growth Economy?

A signal characteristic of our economy for the past 30 years has been the continuous and substantial increase in real family income. It has been estimated that the standard of living enjoyed by the average U.S. family during that time has almost doubled. In addition, there has been some redistribution of income from the wealthiest to the poorest population segments. Relatively, however, the poor have not gained ground.

Since the economic downturn of 1973, many statements have been made questioning the viability of our economy and its capability of delivering an increased standard of living. The following are typical of the comments that have been made:

Americans in the future will be forced to cut back on their standard of living.
The high growth rates of the 1960s are over, and we are faced with permanent stagflation.
Real income in the future will continue to decrease.
Productivity rates are now declining and will continue to decline.
Americans will no longer be able to enjoy the good life of the previous two decades.

The reasons for such dire statements are understandable and include our severe recession, the high rates of inflation with the erosion of real personal income, the oil and energy situations, and rising prices and high unemployment. But what of the future? Two important determinants will be the rate of productivity realized and the rate of inflation.

Estimates of productivity increases tend to be colored by the negative figures of 1974, which was an atypical year. It was affected by such factors as the quadrupling of oil prices, scarcity of some raw materials, and the extended and deep recession. In 1974, two-thirds of the selected industries studied by the Bureau of Labor Statistics recorded declines in output, and more than 85 percent of them also had decreases in productivity.[4] That year was a cyclical peak, a stage at which productivity gains usually have been hard to sustain. But all of these industries realized productivity gains between 1950 and 1974, with increases ranging from a high of 6.9 percent to a low of one percent. From 1950 to 1969 productivity grew at an average rate of over 3 percent. During the five years 1969 to 1974, however, covering a rather difficult and atypical period, productivity grew at only an average rate of 2.1 per-

cent.[5] In 1975, productivity was just 2.1 percent, but 1976 estimates are 4.5 percent, and estimates for 1977 are about 5 percent.

Increasing attention is now being given to productivity by government, labor, and business. Productivity is highly correlated with both educational levels and past expenditures on research and development. Both of these factors should add a positive thrust in the future. For projection purposes an average productivity increase of 3 percent per year has been assumed and used as a basis for income projections. While this seems realistic, some readers may be more comfortable assuming rates of 2 or 2.5 percent. This would affect the amount but not the direction of the increase in income and would not invalidate references to family affluence.

But what about inflation levels which erode income? In 1974, as measured by increases in the Consumer Price Index, inflation for the first time in modern history reached double-digit levels—12.2 percent. For 1976, it is estimated to be less than 5 percent. Table 5 presents data on inflation since 1960. Even with the 1974 rate, reflecting the impact of the fourfold increase in petroleum prices, inflation since 1970 has averaged about 6.5 percent a year. The rate for 1976 is estimated to be less than 4 percent. An average rate of 5.5 percent into the early 1980s has been assumed.

The actual income growth rates of the 1960s, which were quite high, are expected to slow a little. But even with a lower than average 3 percent pro-

Table 5

Inflation levels as measured by percentage point changes in the consumer price index

Year	Percentage point changes
1960	1.5
1965	1.9
1970	5.5
1971	3.4
1972	3.4
1973	8.8
1974	12.2
1975	7.0
1976	4.8 (est.)

ductivity increase per annum, and a rate of inflation of about 5 percent, real family income over the decade 1975–1985 will increase markedly. The following statements are indicative of the income perspective:

1. In the past decade, while households grew by 25 percent, families with incomes of $15,000 and over almost doubled.
2. A larger number and proportion of American families will move into the upper income brackets between 1975 and 1985.
3. Even if productivity increases do not reach their long-run average of more than 3 percent per year and decline to an average figure such as 2.5 or 2.75 percent, real economic growth will still be substantial.
4. Families in the income bracket $20,000 and over in 1974 included one out of every four families as compared with one out of 20 in 1945.
5. Families with incomes over $20,000 in 1974 averaged more than $29,000 per year.
6. A median income family today enjoys a standard of living realized by only the top 10 percent of families in 1950.
7. Factory foremen and operatives head more than one-fourth of the families in the $20,000 and over category.

Three major points should be noted. First, even with higher inflation rates, there has been a substantial increase in the real incomes of American

Table 6
Changes in family income 1970 dollars

Income	In percentages		
	1960	1970	1980
$15,000 and over	8.5	21	35–38
10,000–15,000	21.5	27	26–29
7,000–10,000	23.5	21.5	14.5
5,000– 7,000	17	11.5	8.5
3,000– 5,000	14	10	7
Under 3,000	15.5	9	6

Note: These estimates were made using Department of Commerce data and assuming an annual real growth in income of 3 percent.

families, and on the average they are much more affluent than in the 1960s. This trend is reflected in Table 6. Second, over the next decade this trend will continue. We are, in fact, fast becoming a nation of upper middle income families. Third, the market segments that will enjoy inordinate growth are those households with incomes over $25,000 headed by persons aged 25–44.

A *Conference Board* study using census data as a basis for income projections and assuming an average real growth in income of 3.5 percent per year noted the striking fact that by 1985 the income pyramid will be reversed.[6] This is shown in Table 7, which indicates that the largest proportion of family income will be controlled by upper income families—those in the $25,000 and over and $35,000 and over income categories. Note that the percentage of family income controlled by families with incomes less than $10,000 is reduced from 12 percent in 1975 to 6 percent in 1985. Similarly, families with less than $15,000 per year controlled 30 percent of income in 1975 but will control only 18 percent in 1985. Moreover, similar changes will occur if one assumes a real growth rate in incomes of 2, 2.5, or 3 percent.

These projections suggest that markets for luxury goods and services will enjoy above-average growth. At the same time, notice should be taken of the poor and disadvantaged families in our population. It seems likely that the bottom 20 percent will still have a median income less than one-half the median income of the population. Although the concept and definition of underprivileged families will change, the real income gap between the affluent and the poor may actually increase.

Business people are often concerned not only with family income but also with income per household. In this regard, it is important to note the rapid growth in primary individual households—those comprised of individuals not living with families. Such households have grown almost four times as rapidly as husband-wife households. Also, the former have realized a rapid rise in income, which by 1973 was about 43 percent of the total income of a typical family. Projections indicate that by 1985 the per capita income of individual

Table 7
Changing distribution of family income, 1975 dollars

Family income category	Percentage of family income	
	1975	**1985**
$35,000 and over	16	28
$25,000 to $35,000	16	26
$20,000 to $25,000	17	16
$15,000 to $20,000	21	14
$10,000 to $15,000	18	10
Under $10,000	12	6

Source: Fabian Linden, "Age and Income—1985," *Conference Board Record*, 13 (June 1976).

households will be approximately 60 percent above that of per capita family income. Thus, primary individual households represent growing affluent markets, with expenditures expected to rise from 5.3 percent of total expenditures in 1965 to over 20 percent in 1985.

Income 1975–1985 (in 1975 Dollars)

Among the income trends for 1975–1985 are:

1. An increasingly large number of families will shift into upper income brackets.
2. There will be substantial expansions in disposable personal income.
3. The real income gap between affluent and poor families may increase.
4. The multiearner family will become even more prevalent than it is at present.
5. More than 7 million families in 1975 have three or more members in the labor force.
6. The middle-age market, 45–64, will be among the most lucrative for luxury items.
7. An estimated one-fourth of discretionary buy-

ing power will be controlled by those 55 and over.
8. Families with incomes over $25,000 will account for approximately one-half of family income.
9. A big target market for the next decade is the family with income over $25,000. Such families will grow from 14 percent to 30 percent of all families over the next decade.
10. By 1985 the income pyramid will be reversed, with the largest proportions of family income in the $25,000-and-over category.

The Working Wife—An Economic Necessity?

The changing social and economic status of wives is pointed up most dramatically by their participation in the labor force. The working wife is a major phenomenon of the past decade, and in 1975 an estimated 45 percent of wives were in the labor force. The high proportion of wives entering the work force has been given as a major reason for our current high rate of unemployment, but this is not evident from the gross employment statistics. It is estimated that, of a total labor force growth of 1.5 million in 1975, women, not all of them wives, accounted for 1.1 million workers.[7] Statistics on working women are shown in Tables 8 and 9. They reveal that between 1947 and 1973, while the female population increased by 52 percent, the female labor force increased by 123 percent. Also, the proportion of working wives is essentially the same regardless of the employment status of the husband, and the steepest gains have occurred where husbands are employed. But a relevant question concerns the kinds of jobs single women and wives occupy and the degree of competition with men.

Table 8
Women at work

Year	Female population 16 and over in millions	Women in labor force in millions	In percentages
1947	52.5	16.7	.318
1951	54.9	19.0	.346
1955	57.6	20.6	.358
1959	60.5	22.5	.372
1963	64.5	24.7	.383
1967	69.0	28.4	.412
1971	74.0	32.1	.434
1973	80.0	37.1	.464

Source: John E. Smallwood and Ronald L. Ernst, *Distribution Demographics Research Report* (Management Horizons, Inc., 1975) pp. 37–38.

Table 9
Working wives

Year	Husband employed	Husband unemployed
1955	28.4%	37.9%
1961	33.9	40.6
1965	36.7	44.4
1969	42.3	44.5
1971	43.6	51.7
1973	45.8	48.4

Source: John E. Smallwood and Ronald L. Ernst, *Distribution Demographics Research Report* (Management Horizons, Inc., 1975) pp. 37–38.

A variety of incorrect statements have been made about working wives, for example:

Wives work for economic reasons only.
Wives work mainly to supplement the inadequate earnings of husbands.
Wives work during their early married years, then drop out of the labor force and return to work later in life.
Wives with preprimary school children are not likely to be members of the labor force.
Wives work when they have no school age children at home.
Wives with husbands in the upper income groups are not as likely to be gainfully employed as those with husbands in the lower income groups.

The percentage of working wives nearly doubled between 1950 and 1975. In 1960, about 30 percent of wives worked. By 1975, the proportion grew to 45 percent. An extrapolation of these figures suggests that by 1985 well over 50 percent of wives, a majority, may be in the labor force. In 1975, more than half of all married women with school age children held jobs. Families with more than one wage earner are now a common occurrence. A March 1974 study revealed that 49 percent of all husband-wife families had two or more workers (not always a wife) and earned a median income of $15,120. Surprisingly, 7.2 million families had three or more earners and attained a median income of $20,975.

What motivates the working wife? Is it the growth of the service sector with job opportunities for women, particularly part-time jobs? Is it economic necessity? Is it an escape from the home and duties that society does not value highly? Is it a matter of using vocational and professional talents? The question is a complex one involving political, legal, cultural, and economic factors as well as particular family situations.

Undoubtedly, the feminist movement and government efforts have had an impact. Changing mores have supported and even stimulated the trend. In previous decades the fact that a wife worked was considered an indication of economic need, of the inadequacy of the husband's earnings in providing for the family, and of the wife's neglect of her responsibilities and family. A working wife today frequently is considered to be a liberated woman with an understanding husband, a person who is realizing herself while taking care of her family. Previously, the working wife tended to justify why she was working; now it is more likely to be the nonworking wife who does so.

A good proportion of wives do work out of economic necessity. In 1975, 13 percent of all families were headed by women—divorcees, unmarrieds and widows—for whom a job may be very important. Also, 47 percent of all wives with husbands earning $3,000 to $5,999 per year in 1970 were in the labor force.[8] On the average, in 1974 working wives contributed between 26 and 30 percent of total family income. In more than one-fourth of the husband and wife families wives contributed 40 percent or more of the family income.[9] The earnings of working wives have tended to become a permanent part of total family income and a basis for life-style expectations. Even where it is not a necessity, the economic contribution of the wife is often important to the whole family.

On the other hand, there is a large proportion of wives who work as a matter of choice rather than economic necessity. Some enter the labor force to get away from the home and family for a regular period. Sometimes wives take jobs outside the home which yield very little by way of net monetary gains. Sometimes work outside the home is seen as glamorous, challenging, exciting, and personally rewarding in contrast to the ill-defined, unpaid work in the home. In any event, whether induced by economic pressures or by choice, work outside the home is becoming a vital part of many wives' lives.

Observers have often assumed that wives work when they are young and reenter the labor force later in life; that they work when there are no preschool or school aged children at home, and that they work to supplement the husband's income. None of these assumptions seems to be supported, as shown by the data in Table 10. Note that the age of the wife, the number of school children, and the amount of the husband's earnings have little if any

impact on whether wives are in the labor force. A higher proportion of wives with school aged children work than do wives without children of school age. Husbands with higher earnings have a greater proportion of wives who are working. The factor most directly correlated with labor force participation of wives is their education level. Increasing educational accomplishments, particularly of minority wives, portend a larger proportion of them entering the job market.

The life-styles and purchase behavior of working wives are only beginning to be felt by business. The full-time working wife may work an average of 60–70 hours each week both on the job and at home. This affects the products and services she wants and needs. Studies indicate that the working wife tends to be:

1. more conscious of her appearance and concerned with dress and fashions;
2. very interested in maintaining a youthful posture (the young get ahead in business);
3. more confident, sure of herself, secure, and individualistic;
4. more adept at dealing with the external world and making decisions;
5. more concerned with convenience and ease in performing household duties;
6. more cosmopolitan in tastes, more knowledgeable, and a more demanding customer;
7. interested in leisure, travel, and exposure to the world outside the home;
8. concerned with improving herself and her educational background;
9. concerned with equal rights;
10. less concerned with small price differences in purchases than with convenience, time, and service.

Business should consider the impact, current and future, of the working wife on the demand for one-stop shopping, repair service on weekends and at night, Sunday store openings, evening sales, prepared foods, convenience items, products that require little service, and products that stress

Table 10

Labor force participation rates for women with selected characteristics, 1975

Age*	Percentage of women in the labor force		Educational attainment	Percentage of women in the labor force
16–19	49.3		Not a high school graduate	31.6
20–24	63.2		High school graduate	52.5
25–34	52.4		1–3 years of college	53.5
35–44	54.7		College graduate	64.1
45–54	54.6			
55–64	40.7		Ages of children	Percentage of wives employed
65 and over	8.2			
			Less than 3 years	32.7
			3–5 years	41.9
			6–17 years	52.3
Total family income	Percentage of wives in the labor force		None under 18	43.9
under $2,000	21.03			
$ 2000–2999	17.21		Husband's income	Percentage of wives in the labor force
3000–3999	16.23			
4000–4999	20.33		$ 999 or less	46.11
5000–5999	20.17		1000–1499	50.58
6000–6999	25.91		1500–1999	51.85
7000–7999	31.61		2000–2499	46.94
8000–8999	32.07		2500–2999	54.35
9000–9999	37.89		3000–3499	56.72
10000–10999	34.47		3500–3999	62.47
11000–11999	41.31		4000–4999	62.29
12000–12999	41.89		5000–5999	57.69
13000–13999	45.19		6000–6999	62.10
14000–14999	48.08		7000–7999	61.79
15000–15999	46.58		8000–8999	62.72
16000–16999	52.91		9000–9999	62.87
17000–17999	51.21		10000–11999	59.29
18000–19999	54.37		12000–14999	57.93
20000–24999	57.83		15000–19999	53.43
25000–49999	58.70		20000–24999	47.43
50000 and over	29.80		25000 and over	36.55

*1974 survey
Source: Bureau of the Census, *Current Population Survey.* Series P-23, no. 58 (1976); Series P-60, no. 105 (1977).

youthfulness, individualism, maintenance of self, and self-improvement.

Marriages and Families in a Divorce-Oriented Society?

There is much discussion today about whether young people have given up marriage. Recently, marriage trends have declined slightly. Also, divorce has become more prevalent, reaching a high point in the United States in 1976. Typical of the comments made are:

The outmoded institution of marriage is being replaced by the commune.
Alternative life-styles to marriage have arrived.
Women are giving up marriage and families to further their own careers.

The young no longer choose to marry.
We now have more divorces than marriages.

The following quotation, which like the above statements is untrue, is humorously misleading: "All our traditions are crumbling. Look at the Catholic Church. The only people who want to get married today are Catholic priests."[10]

The Census Bureau has found that the number of unmarried persons living with a member of the opposite sex in a two-person household in March 1976 was 1,320,000, double the number reported in 1970. It appears that there have been important changes in marriage and living arrangements, that later marriages have gained general acceptance, and that a higher proportion of adults may never marry. However, despite the attention directed to singles, communes, and alternative living arrangements, marriage today is still very popular. Approximately 93 percent of all American adults marry at some time in their lives. It is true that the total number of marriages in the United States has declined slightly in the last few years, from 2,277,000 in 1973, to 2,223,000 in 1974, to 2,126,000 in 1975.

Accompanying this decline is the fact that the proportion of marriages among women ages 20–24, which have generally constituted about 43 percent of first marriages, has also declined. In 1970, almost 40 percent in this age group were single. Does this indicate a rejection of marriage?

The more likely conclusion seems to be that a postponement rather than an abandonment of marriage is occurring. Factors such as the current recession, inflation, and unemployment tend to encourage the young to postpone getting married. Postponement of marriage, rather than rejection, is supported by the fact that the percentage of single females 25 and over actually declined between 1970 and 1974, from 7.2 percent to 6.4 percent.[11]

The relevant statistics suggest that in the future there likely will be a continuing rise in first marriages resulting from the number of women now in the 18–24 age category, the pressure built up by the postponement of marriage in the past few years, and the central position that marriage, the family, and home still maintain in our society. It seems rea-

sonable to expect an increase to 2,500,000 marriages per year by 1985, an increase of about 20 percent from the 1975 level of 2,100,000.

The structure and way of life of the family are being affected markedly by such factors as birthrates, age at marriage, size of family, developments in contraception, and the working wife. As was mentioned, family size has fallen dramatically. The average number of children per woman (total fertility rate) has dropped from a high of 3.7 in 1957 to about 1.8 in 1975. The five-year average for 1966–1971 was 2.4 children per woman. The impact is now being felt of the decreasing number of children per family, increasing number of women living alone, higher life expectancy of women as compared to men, growing number of young people living away from their families, and rapid increase in the number of divorces.

Young adults have a later marriage age, declining birthrates with fewer children, and a later age for the birth of the first child. Yet, they are having their children in a shorter span of years and planning the number and spacing of children. This is coupled with a decline in the age at which children leave home. The result is that adults in the future, who are living longer, will spend less time as "full nesters" and more time as "empty nesters." Also, future grandmothers and grandfathers may be relatively young, in their late 40s and early 50s, knowledgeable, well educated, more financially secure, and well traveled.

Traditionally, the usual dwelling unit, or household, has been perceived as a husband-wife family. Of the total number of households in 1960, 75 percent were husband-wife. By 1974, however, this proportion had declined to less than two-thirds. During this 15-year period, primary individual households—those headed by people living with their families—grew almost four times as fast as husband-wife households. They now comprise 22 percent of the total. Some of the important shifts in the distribution of household classes in the 1980s are identified in Table 11.

A disproportionate growth is occurring in households headed by unmarried people. The average size of the household continues to decrease and is

Table 11

Distribution of households in the 1980s

Household category	Projected trends
Husband-wife households	They will continue to decline relative to singles' households. Most of their growth to 1980 will be in the under 35 age group. From 1980 to 1990, it will be in the 35–44 age group.
Female family heads	These households, headed by women where no husband is present, have realized a high rate of growth. They will continue to do so through 1985. Most of the growth is in the under 35 age group, which is expanding at a rapid 7 percent growth rate.
Male family heads	Families headed by men with no wife present comprise only about 2 percent of all households. They will continue to be a relatively small proportion.
Primary female individuals	These households headed by single women, divorcees, and widows were made up largely of women over 35 in 1970. While the over 35 group comprised over 80 percent of such households, the under 35 group has doubled in numbers over the last 5 years and will continue to grow at a rapid rate through 1985. However, women over 35 living alone will still represent 12 percent of all households in 1980, more than four times as many as those under 35.
Primary male individuals	Households with single and divorced men living alone have doubled since 1970. Much of the growth has occurred in the under 35 group. Whereas, in 1970, these households were mostly headed by men over 35, by 1980 the balance will start to move in the direction of men under 35.

expected to reach 2.8 people per household in 1980. As divorces increase, the number of individual households expands; as divorced people remarry, individual households contract. It is interesting to note that to just maintain the quality of our housing, not to improve it, it has been estimated that we will need a minimum of 2 million–2.5 million net new households each year for the next ten years. Delivering them will be a major economic challenge.

A discussion of marriage and household trends must consider statistics on divorce. Both the rate and the number of divorces have accelerated greatly in the last 10 years. From 1967 to 1975, divorces almost doubled. Divorces totaled 913,000 in 1973, 970,000 in 1974, and 1,026,000 in 1975. It is estimated now that one in three marriages will end in divorce.

Increasing divorce rates should not be misconstrued as indicating a decline in the desire for marriage. Divorce represents not a rejection of marriage, but dissatisfaction with a specific partner.

Some of the tendencies gleaned from a study of divorce statistics are:

1. Divorces are likely to increase substantially.
2. The rate of increase in divorce is likely to remain higher than the rate of increase in marriage through 1985.
3. The average duration of marriage that ends in divorce is six to seven years.
4. Divorced people tend to remarry.
5. Divorced people tend to remarry other divorced people.
6. Divorced women wait longer for remarriage than divorced men.
7. A higher proportion of second marriages, as compared with first marriages, end in divorce.
8. Lower socioeconomic groups tend to account for a large proportion of second divorces.

Concluding Observations

Projections of some of the fundamental population and income statistics suggest that the longer run business climate is a cautiously optimistic one. Despite declining birthrates, we are likely to realize a second baby boom. The population will increase by about 42 million over the 1970s and 1980s. Real family income will continue to increase significantly, and we will become an even more affluent society.

While the proportion of single women and wives in the labor force will grow and add to our productivity, the family will remain a central focus. By 1985, marriage will be more popular than ever, as will divorce. There will be a significant growth in households accompanied by shifts within household categories.

American society is often characterized as being in a state of flux with major pressures influencing and shaping totally new and different life-styles, wants and needs, and markets. The changes are described as crises and rebellions. But the most striking fact resulting from an investigation of trends and projections is that life-styles of Americans have, in reality, demonstrated great stability and are likely to continue to do so. The developments of the 1980s will continue to highlight the dominant characteristics of the existence of the core American values of permanence and stability.

This does not mean that demographic and social changes will not occur, or that unexpected trends will not evolve, for they will. Rather, the data, past and future, seem to suggest that our basic values and patterns of relationships will be adapted readily to new social, environmental, economic, and political situations that will present expanding markets and business opportunities. The result will be stability within change—a factor often disguised by the emphasis given when highlighting the disruptions and deviations that are caused by immediate events.

Notes

1. All of the statistical data for this article, except where specifically noted, have been selected from U.S. government sources. The basic references are the monthly *Current Population Reports* of the Bureau of the Census, the 1970 Census, and the new publication *Status;* the U.S. Department of Labor, Bureau of Labor Statistics publications; and reports of government surveys and vital statistics. Interested readers are directed specifically to the *1970 Census of Population,* vol. 1, Part IB; *Current Population Reports,* Series P-25, nos. 614 and 493; U.S. Department of Labor, *Manpower Report to the President 1975;* Bureau of Labor Statistics, *Marital and Family Characteristics of Workers,* March 1973, and *Employment and Earnings,* April 1973; and Bureau of the Census, *A Statistical Portrait of Women in the United States, Current Population Reports,* Special Studies P-23, no. 58.

2. Bureau of the Census, Series P-20, no. 277.

3. This was reported by a Gallup poll of 1,562 adults age 18 or over, in 1974, as mentioned in "A Study of the American Family and Money," in *The General Mills American Family Report 1974–75,* conducted by Yankelovich, Skelly & White, Inc.

4. Bureau of Labor Statistics, *Productivity Indexes for Selected Industries* (Washington, D.C.: 1975), Bulletin 1890, 1976, p. 3.

5. Ibid.

6. Age and Income—1985," by Fabian Linden, *Conference Board Record,* 13 (June 1976).

7. As quoted in the *Wall Street Journal,* 8 March 1976, p. 1.

8. Bureau of the Census, *U.S. Census of Population: 1970 Employment Status and Work Experience* (Washington, D.C.: 1972), pp. 182–84.

9. See Thomas F. Bradshaw and John F. Stinson, "Trends in Weekly Earnings: An Analysis," *Monthly Labor Review* 98 (August 1975): 25–26.

10. As quoted in *Business Week,* 10 March 1975, p. 60.

11. For data on marital status, readers are referred to Bureau of the Census, *Current Population Reports,* Series P-20 (Washington, D.C.), nos. 212, 225, 287, 144, and 87; and U.S. Department of Health Education and Welfare, National Center for Health Statistics, *Vital Statistics Reports* (Washington, D.C.: various years).

Questions

1. *Explain how demographics can be predicting both a declining birthrate and a baby boom.*
2. *How are the anticipated demographic and social trends likely to affect the auto industry? the clothing industry? the furniture industry?*

38

Retailing Executives View the 1980s

J. BARRY MASON

MORRIS L. MAYER

Facets of the 1980s' operating environments discussed here include personnel problems, management philosophies, management controls, legal dimensions, the environment, and managerial strategy shifts in response to these issues.

The retailing management concept requires a close and continuous monitoring of the various environments facing management. This enables management to adjust its operating philosophies to an ever-changing reality and, therefore, they can respond to change aggressively. Given rapid changes in the economy and society, to do otherwise would be simply management by crisis. Early warning signs of imminent changes in the operating environment of the firm often exist, and management must address these before thay become too powerful to manage.[1] Among the changes that have had an impact on retailing during the 1970s are materials shortages, the oil crisis, rapid inflation, consumerism, an avalanche of environmental legislation, occupational health and safety regulations, and a host of other problems. Clearly, retailing is a dynamic sector of the economy and, thus, is subject to the impact of many different variables. As noted by Philip Kotler, "The linear environment of the 1950–1970 period has given way to a turbulent environment which produces new strategic surprises almost monthly."[2]

Source: Atlanta Economic Review, May–June 1978, pp. 4–10.

What is in store for retailing in the near future as the assumption of an automatic growth era is subject to reappraisal? More than ever, the management of change will be the key to successful retail management, but guidelines for the transitional period are still ill-defined.[3] Retail management is just now adjusting to the reality of having to assess the effects of their actions from the perspective of the environmentalist and the consumerist. Increasingly, the management of rapid social change will be necessary, also. Within the next few years we are likely to see the futurist become important in the executive suite. This may sound a little farfetched, but 10 years ago who would have thought that there would be specialists in the environment, social responsibility, or consumer affairs occupying executive positions? Early efforts need to be made to determine the probable future environments facing management so that necessary changes in strategy can be made. As observed by John Keane, 1976–1977 American Marketing Association President, "the roots of changes to occur in the 1990's are burrowing now."[4]

The purposes of the research reported in this article were to determine (1) the perceived importance of selected issues facing retail management in 1977, (2) the perceptions of retailers about key issues in 1977 versus the probable importance of the same issues in 1985, and (3) management perceptions of changes in institutional structure and operating strategies by 1985 in response to perceived operating realities. The issues chosen are indicative of those currently being discussed in the trade and academic literature about the present and probable future environments facing retail management.

A questionnaire was mailed to 164 members of the Alabama Retail Association. A total of 73 responses were obtained, a response rate of 45%. The views of these owners and/or managers and the nature of the issues posed allow limited generalizations about the emerging realities of retailing in the 1980s.

Issues in 1977

A portion of the research sought to determine the perceived importance to retailers of selected issues facing them in 1977.

External Issues

Issues external to the firm were somewhat less important overall to management than the other categories of problems, which are at least partly under the control of the firm. The strongest overall concern expressed was for the need to effectively monitor competition and the economic forces affecting the firm (Exhibit 1). The bureaucracy of the local, state, and federal governments is viewed as a major problem, also. Indeed, it has been stated that "governmental regulation is *the* issue on retailers' minds."[5]

Technology continues to be important, though perhaps it is not as much of a problem as even a year or two ago. The bulk of POS (point-of-sale or point-of-service data collection systems, typically involving a terminal as the input mechanism) equipment sales to major general merchandise retailers were made by the end of 1976, even though major markets do remain, especially among retailers other than the giants such as Sears, J. C. Penney, and Wards. The level of management sophistication about this equipment now seems to be such that many retail managers can intelligently discuss the disadvantages and advantages of the various types of systems. Indeed, most of them

The composition of the sample

Kind of store:

Department	27.8%
Food	20.8
Apparel	25.0
Furniture and appliances	11.1
Other	15.3

Number of employees:

2–5	2.7%
6–10	9.6
11–20	15.1
Over 20	72.6

Company sales volume:

Under $500,000	13.7%
$500,000–$1 million	13.7
Over $1 million	72.6

Typical store size:

Under 5,000 sq. ft.	19.4%
5,000–9,999	14.9
10,000–19,999	25.4
20,000–49,999	26.9
50,000–99,999	9.0
Over 100,000	4.5

Number of stores:

1	22.5%
2–3	22.5
4–5	9.9
6–10	22.5
11–20	5.6
Over 20	16.9

have decided whether to adopt a system, the point in time of adoption, and perhaps even the brand of equipment to be purchased.[6]

Finally, social issues continue to be a major part of the reality of the retail manager, as has been true since the early 1960s and the emergence of the latest wave of consumerism. However, consumerism is now an institutionalized part of operating policy for many retailers, and thus it may not have the urgency for action experienced during the late 1960s and early 1970s. Management perhaps is now able to more rationally factor this variable into their strategy decisions than was previously the case.[7]

Exhibit 1

Perceived importance of various activity issues in 1977

Issues	Percentage of respondents			
	Not important or slightly important	Important	Very important	Extremely important
Macro environment				
1. Understanding the various governmental/ regulatory impacts on your business	13.7	23.3	32.9	30.1
2. Keeping up with technological developments which affect your business	13.7	30.1	28.8	27.4
3. Being aware of social changes which can affect your operations	16.4	31.5	34.2	17.8
4. Monitoring your competition and the economic forces which affect your business	9.7	22.2	29.2	38.9
Personnel problems				
1. Improving personnel hiring practices	9.6	24.7	30.1	35.6
2. Affirmative action	10.4	34.3	28.4	26.9
3. Improving employee relations	6.9	20.8	29.2	43.1
Issues of management philosophy				
1. Establishing a philosophy of management	16.4	30.1	23.3	30.1
2. Establishing long- and short-run objectives	5.5	23.3	35.6	35.6
Management controls				
1. Obtaining a better working capital position	13.7	26.0	19.2	41.1
2. Improving your profitability	1.4	11.0	20.5	67.1
3. Reducing shortages	11.0	13.7	21.9	53.4
4. Improving advertising effectiveness	6.9	16.7	31.9	44.4
5. Setting up a good merchandise control system	11.1	27.8	22.2	38.9

Personnel Issues

Historically, the personnel function has been a source of frustration to retail management and continues to be a problem today.[8] Of the three personnel functions evaluated in this research, affirmative action seems to be somewhat less of a problem than either improving personnel hiring practices or improving employee relations. The peak of management problems with affirmative action may have passed, as management has had sufficient time to adapt to the new requirements. In any event, improving personnel hiring practices appears even more crucial in this era of high inflation and rapidly rising wage costs. This is understandable since labor costs represent approximately 70% of every expense dollar in retailing.[9]

Improving employee relations was rated as the greatest source of management concern among the three issues evaluated. Some persons have observed that large organizations especially are characterized by a lessened sense of employee responsibility and that employees may feel alienated in a complex organization. This feeling may be compounded by union allegiance separate from the organization.[10]

Issues of Management Philosophy

Management today appears to be grappling more intensively with the realities of formulating long- and short-run objectives than with establishing an overall ongoing philosophy of management. Successful establishments likely have a firmly grounded philosophy, which undergirds their activities, but they may be having to modify objectives in the face of the operating realities of 1977–1978. Management does not have the luxury of waiting for public decisions in such areas as energy. Rather, they must make these types of decisions on a continuing basis and with an eye toward the future. During the first half of 1975, J.C. Penney, Federated, and others announced almost simultaneously that they were embarking on major long-run planning projects. In short, because of economic uncertainties, strategic planning has emerged as a central corporate concern in the field of retailing.[11]

Management Controls

Three management controls issues were rated as particularly important. Almost 88% of the respondents rated improving profitability as a key issue. This is understandable because after-tax profits of all retailing corporations declined by 50% during the 17-year period of 1950–1967[12] and continued to decline throughout 1968–1974.[13] Numerous innovations in retail distributive institutions have emerged in the past few years, at least partly in response to efforts to offset decreasing profitability. These include, among others, home decorating centers, furniture warehouse showrooms, and superstores.[14]

Reducing shortages is also a continuing problem. Estimates indicate that up to 35% of all shortages are a result of shoplifting[15] and that on the average 30% of employees will make a strong effort to steal.[16]

Working capital shortage also emerged as a severe problem of 1977. Some persons forecast that the demand for additional capital will exceed new capital availability by approximately $500–$700 billion during the 1975–1985 time period.[17] Thus it is no wonder that this should be a major source of worry to management. During 1977, for example, investor uncertainty of the future reduced the flow of new equity capital to a trickle.[18]

Finally, after many years of research on advertising effectiveness, it appears to remain as much a problem as has been true historically. The same can be said for establishing a viable merchandise control system.

Rank Ordering of Issues

As a second aspect of this part of the research, respondents were asked to rank order the 10 problems perceived from the literature to be of major importance to retail managers in 1977. Almost without exception, getting adequate profits after taxes was ranked as the top problem, as shown in Exhibit 2. This was followed closely by increasing salary costs and the problem of inefficient employees. Other areas of strong importance include rising utility costs and inadequate cash flow. Problems of lesser importance, at least relative to the others, include poor quality from vendors, uncertain deliveries, and decisions about the new retail technology. Ranking low in importance among all of the firms was conforming to Occupational Safety and Health Administration (OSHA) regulations. These regulations apparently are more of a nuisance than a problem of substance, even though their impacts on retail management have been widely discussed in the literature.[19]

Issues in 1977 vs. 1985

This portion of the research sought to determine trends in issues over the next five to ten years versus their importance today as management seeks to cope with what are perceived to be new emerging realities. The results appear in Exhibit 3.

Exhibit 2

Respondent ordering of retail problems

Problem	Aggregate ranking	Department stores	Food stores	Apparel stores	Furniture and appliance stores	Others
Getting adequate profits after taxes	1	1	4	1	1	2
Increasing salary costs	2	3	2	3	2	6
Inefficient employees	3	2	5	2	8	1
Rising utility bills	4	4	1	3	3	4
Inadequate cash flow	5	6	3	4	4	7
Establishing competitive prices	6	4	6	6	6	9
Poor quality from vendors	7	5	10	6	10	5
Uncertain deliveries	8	7	9	8	9	3
Deciding what kind of "new technology" to adopt	9	8	8	7	8	8
OSHA regulations	10	8	7	9	5	8

Note: In several instances, aggregate responses resulted in two factors having the same relative importance.

Exhibit 3

Management perceptions of the importance of selected issues in 1977 versus 1985

Issues	Percentage of respondents			
	Same importance in 1985 as now	More importance in 1985 than now	Less importance in 1985 than now	N.A.*
Societal ethics and values				
1. Consumer activism	26.0	64.4	6.8	2.7
2. Society's rejection of profit as the primary motive of retailers	50.7	38.0	9.9	1.4
3. The concern of society over ethics of retailers	43.8	45.2	11.0	
4. Concern of society about how decisions of retail management will affect "quality of life"	42.8	31.0	15.5	11.3
5. Retailing's involvement in pollution issues	38.4	28.8	16.4	16.4
Governmental regulation				
6. Governmental regulation of retailing	19.2	75.3	5.5	
7. Paperwork associated with governmental regulation	23.2	72.6	4.1	
Operating issues				
8. Shortages of energy resources	5.5	94.5		
9. Energy costs as a percent of total costs	8.2	90.4	1.4	
10. Cost of capital	28.8	71.2		
11. Inflation	26.0	72.6	1.4	
12. Relationships with suppliers	65.3	30.5	4.2	
13. Revolutionary technological changes affecting retailing (e.g., POS, EFT)	21.9	67.1	5.5	5.5

*N.A. = Not applicable, thus of no importance now or in 1985.

Societal Values and Business Ethics

The role of the consumer activist is perceived by the respondents as being more important in 1985 than today. Retail management is becoming increasingly responsive to this issue,[20] even though some research has shown that retailers have made less progress on this issue than have other segments of the business community.[21] Apart from consumer activism and social responsibility issues, management perceives a continuing strong interest by society in the ethics of retailers. This issue is probably closely tied to consumerism. Approximately half of the respondents perceive that society's rejection of profit as a primary motive of retail management will remain at about the same intensity in 1985 as in 1977.

Environmental Issues

Of slightly less importance is retailing's perceived future involvement in pollution-related issues and the concern of society about how the behavior of retailers will affect the quality of life. The effects of environmental regulations particularly such factors as water pollution from parking lot runoffs, the effects of large shopping centers on air quality, and site selection problems continue to be important concerns, but apparently many feel these issues will have been more nearly resolved by 1985.[22]

Governmental Regulation

No letup is foreseen in governmental regulation. Many retailers already complain that they are drowning in a sea of paperwork. Among the issues that have to be resolved are metric conversion, a federal consumer-protection agency, comprehensive antitrust reform, and others. Many of these issues are currently being debated by Congress. Their diversity and potential for having a forceful impact on retailing reveal why management is convinced that additional government intervention and control is a reality for the future.[23]

Operating Issues

Management also overwhelmingly believes that there will be shortages of energy resources and that energy costs as a percent of the total cost structure of the firm will be much higher in 1985. Likewise, they believe that inflation will be worse and that the cost of capital will be higher. Relationships with suppliers are not perceived as changing greatly. However, technological change will be even more of a factor in 1985 than today. One of the greatest changes may be in adopting the concept of electronic funds transfer (EFT) systems.[24]

The Environment of 1985

Management also was asked to respond to questions about the various issues most likely to characterize the business environment of 1985.

Shifts in Institutional Structure

A strong consensus emerged that the variety store will continue to lose market share, as shown in Exhibit 4. Management is uncertain about the future growth of catalog showroom stores, but appears to believe that remote retailing will not be of major importance by 1985. Over 86% of the respondents perceive that the period of most rapid growth for the discount department store will be over by 1985, as it reaches a stage of stability and maturity.

Two new types of institutions are foreseen to be major institutional factors. The first is the expertly managed chain book store as opposed to the traditional stationery and book store. Already appearing on the scene is the Walden Book Company, a subsidiary of Carter Hawley Hale stores with sales in 1976 of $125 million from 400 stores in 44 states. The B. Dalton Company, the fastest growing segment of Dayton Hudson Corporation, achieved $106 million in sales in 1976 for 255 stores in 38 states.[25] Second, outlets specializing in sports equipment and apparel for outdoor sports and various recreational ac-

Exhibit 4

Management perceptions of the retail institutional structure of 1985

Possible trends in institutional structure	Percentage of respondents				
	Strongly agree	Agree	Neutral or no opinion	Disagree	Strongly disagree
1. Services retailing will continue to grow as a percentage of total retail sales	11.1	50.0	22.2	16.7	—
2. In supermarket retailing the trend toward superstores (self-service stores combining food, drug, and general household and family convenience items) will continue	16.7	62.5	15.3	4.2	1.4
3. The growth potential for the convenience store in the 1985 period is good, particularly with some major chains closing some of their smaller supermarkets as they open superstores	13.7	56.2	21.9	8.2	—
4. The conventional department store will remain a dominant retail institution	9.7	59.7	11.1	18.1	1.4
5. Discount department stores will maintain an important place in retailing but the period of rapid growth is over	5.6	80.6	2.8	9.7	1.4
6. The old-fashioned variety store will continue to lose market share	19.4	72.2	4.2	4.2	—
7. Some smaller junior department stores will convert to the fashion-oriented specialty apparel-type store (e.g., contemporary fashion apparel stores)	12.5	47.2	33.3	6.9	—
8. A strong likelihood exists of further growth in stores specializing in equipment and apparel for outdoor sports and activities	19.4	63.9	15.3	1.4	—
9. The older stationery and book store will be substantially replaced by chain book stores	11.1	47.2	36.1	2.8	2.8
10. Further development of the warehouse furniture stores is expected	8.3	56.9	26.4	8.3	—
11. The future of the catalog showroom store is problematic	4.2	41.7	48.6	2.8	2.8
12. By 1985 remote retailing will be well advanced. Customers will make many routine purchases without leaving their homes	8.5	32.4	15.5	38.0	5.6
13. The peak of the construction of the very large regional mall (1–2 million sq. ft.) has passed	6.9	52.8	13.9	22.2	4.2
14. We will see an upgrading of older suburban shopping centers and a surge of new, lively marketplaces in the center of older cities	13.7	50.7	13.7	19.2	2.7
15. Tomorrow's shopping center will be more often compact, multilevel, and multifunctional	28.8	61.6	6.8	2.7	—

tivities also are expected to expand at a rapid pace.[26]

Other perceived areas of strong institutional expansion are services retailing and superstores. Slower growth of population and slow economic expansion will mean that larger portions of total output can be devoted to consumption—the ultimate purpose of economic activity. Thus it follows that increasing sums of money also will be spent on services as opposed to goods. Services contribute to a higher standard of living. This trend is in keeping with the moderation of pollution and the drain on raw material resources. Fortunately, this is a more or less natural trend for advanced economies.[27]

Efforts to increase productivity and reduce labor costs probably account for the foreseen rapid future growth of supermarket retailing as a merchandising philosophy of management. This is a possible response to the increased tendencies toward one-stop shopping as a form of aggregate convenience designed to reduce gasoline consumption.

Separate questions were posed about probable trends in shopping center development. The last three items in Exhibit 4 focus on this dimension of retailing structure. The majority of the respondents perceive that the peak of construction of large regional malls will have passed by 1985. Consequently, they foresee an upgrading of older centers and a surge of new marketplaces downtown. Virtually all see the shopping center of 1985 as compact, multilevel, and multifunctional.[28]

Managerial Strategy Shifts

The respondents foresee that managerial strategy shifts will be necessary in several areas of retailing to meet the operating environment of 1985.

Product Offerings

As shown in Exhibit 5, product line simplification is foreseen as an increasing reality by 1985. Likewise, categories of department store services such as beauty salons, watch repair, and travel agencies, which are weak and costly, will be dropped if they cannot contribute significantly to the overall profitability of the firm.

Productivity

Apparently it will be necessary to invest heavily in the decade ahead to reduce the labor-intensive nature of retailing. A 10% increase or decrease in the selling expense ratio, for example, can have an impact on pre-tax profits of as much as 20%. It generally is the most flexible payroll expense item in a store, particularly in the short run.[29] The same productivity increases are possible by better space and inventory management.[30]

Other productivity-increasing measures foreseen include more space devoted to sales and less to storage and administration. Likewise, the application of central checkouts, self-selection, and low gross margins to areas of trade that have not experienced the use of these techniques before are foreseen. For example, we are beginning to see the emergence of toy supermarkets, home decorating centers, and self-service shoe stores that feature these concepts. They help keep operating expenses low and allow narrower margins on merchandise.[31]

Fixturing and Construction

Construction design and store fixturing also will be changing in the next several years, even though the changes will necessitate large capital outlays, putting even greater pressure on available capital.

An overwhelming consensus exists that retail management will be searching for better heating systems, new construction standards, and lighting innovations to help alleviate the problems of energy shortages and rapidly rising costs. Energy management apparently will have found a permanent place in both the line and staff responsibilities of the nation's retailers. Management will increasingly be seeking the most efficient and most readily available fuel. Roof insulation will be upgraded; the use of glass will be reduced; and exterior heat design will focus on reduced heat loss and solar gain. "Studies on solar heat, recycling the heat of

Exhibit 5

Management perceptions of changes in management strategy in responding to the environments of 1985

Possible changes in management strategy	Percentage of respondents				
	Strongly agree	Agree	Neutral or no opinion	Disagree	Strongly disagree
Product offerings					
1. Categories of services in department stores that are weak and costly will be dropped (e.g., beauty salons, watch repair)	20.5	45.2	24.7	8.2	1.4
2. Product line simplification will be a reality	11.0	54.8	19.2	12.3	2.7
Productivity					
1. To offset constantly rising costs, retailers will have to invest increasing amounts of money that will reduce the labor-intensive nature of retailing	30.6	50.7	8.2	8.2	1.4
2. The only way for management to battle inflation is to increase productivity	28.8	38.4	6.8	24.7	1.4
3. General merchandise stores will devote increasingly more space to sales and less to storage and administration	31.5	47.9	13.7	6.8	—
4. We will see the application of central checkout, self-selection, and low gross margins (supermarket concepts) to areas of trade where these techniques have not been used before	15.1	49.3	20.5	12.3	2.7
Store fixturing and construction					
1. Energy shortages and higher costs will cause retailers to search for better heating systems, new construction standards, and lighting innovations	71.2	28.8	—	—	—
2. We will see the replacement of the standard 4'6" high fixture with those at least 7' high—the cube effect	6.9	18.1	44.4	27.8	2.8
3. Curtailed expansion may be a real possibility	19.2	53.4	11.0	15.1	1.4
4. Stores of the 1980s will be smaller than in the 1960s and 1970s	11.0	31.5	9.6	37.0	11.0
5. Retailers will develop a flexible portfolio of different sized stores depending on the size of the market and existing competition	21.9	58.9	15.1	4.1	—

light and waste, ideal lighting and sources, use of natural light through skylights, and countermeasures for brown-outs and power shortages, all are needed to be versatile in overcoming the effects of depleted resources."[32]

Curtailed retail expansion may be a real possibility by 1985. Primary expansion is foreseen as occurring in secondary markets of less than 250,000 population as part of a market intensification strategy whereby more stores will be clustered in the same metropolitan area instead of expanding into new markets. Retailers are likely to have developed a more flexible portfolio of different sized stores depending on the size of the market and the existing competition. However, management does not strongly believe that the stores of the 1980s will be smaller than in the 1960s and 1970s in spite of some statements to the contrary.[33]

Discussion

The key issues of today that are perceived to be of continuing importance in 1985 include problems of shortages in energy resources, rising energy costs, major technology changes, consumer activism, government regulation, shortages of capital, and similar problems. The indications are that society and retailing are passing through a historical period in the economic, social, and political history of the United States as we move into what Daniel Bell calls the post-industrial era of the 1980s.[34] Management will be paying more attention to the dissatisfaction of consumers and apparently will be undergoing critical evaluation of programs and strategies.

Clearly, the professional character of management must continue to improve. The need for better and longer range planning, financial pressures, the increasingly conglomerate nature of retailing, and increased reporting requirements by an ever-increasing number of government agencies all will necessitate better skills in information collection and handling and communication. Continuing innovation will be required to offset declines in productivity.

Flexibility, initiative, and adaptability will be key words between 1977 and 1985, as retail management seeks to position itself to capitalize on emerging opportunities and to face successfully the continuing tumultuous environments of the near future. Sophisticated long-range planning will be an increasing reality. Yet retail management traditionally, as is true for many corporations today, is oriented toward short-run results. This is necessary to satisfy the demands of investors for yearly increases in corporate profitability and growth. Under these circumstances, a five-year planning horizon may be the longest time for which planning can occur. A critical need, however, is for effective, comprehensive long-range planning that

could be factored into the management philosophy of today's retail managers.

Notes

1. H. Igor Ansoff, "Managing Strategic Surprise by Response to Weak Signals," *California Management Review*, Winter 1975, pp. 21–23.

2. "Kotler Presents Whys, Hows of Marketing Audits for Firms, Nonprofit Organizations," *The Marketing News*, March 26, 1976, p. 12.

3. Joseph Barry Mason, "Developing Marketing Institutions for a Steady State Economy," in Jay Dixon White, ed., *The Science of Change and the Change of Science* (Washington, D.C., Society for General Systems Research, 1977).

4. "To Cope With Changes, Marketers Need Stability, Riskability, Accountability, Flexibility, and Adaptability," *The Marketing News*, July 1, 1977, p. 1.

5. "Chains Struggle With Government," *Chain Store Age Executive*, October 1976, p. 35.

6. Morris L. Mayer and Joseph B. Mason, "Point of Service Re-Examined," *Retail Control*, June–July 1977, pp. 2–24.

7. Ester Peterson, Satenig S. St. Marie, and Frederick Sturdivant, "The Future of Consumerism in Retailing," *Journal of Retailing*, Fall 1977, pp. 99–112.

8. Irving Bursteiner, "Current Personnel Practices in Department Stores," *Journal of Retailing*, Winter 1976–1977, pp. 3–14, 86.

9. "Return on Inventory Investment Is Vital," *Stores*, February 1977, p. 35.

10. Larry Rosenberg, "Retailers' Responses to Consumerism," *Business Horizons*, October 1975, p. 39.

11. Albert Bates and Bert C. McCammon, Jr., "Reseller Strategies and the Financial Performance of the Firm," in Hans B. Thorelli, ed., *Strategy Plus Structure Equals Performance* (Bloomington, Indiana, Indiana University Press, 1977), pp. 146–181; and "Long-Range Planning: Retailers Probe the Unknown," *Chain Store Age Executive*, October 1977, pp. 23–27.

12. National Cash Register, *The Changing Eco-*

nomics of General Merchandise Retailing (Dayton, Ohio, National Cash Register, 1970).

13. James Kenderdine and Bert C. McCammon, Jr., "Structure and Strategy in Retailing," in Henry Nash and Donald Robin, eds., *Proceedings* of the Southern Marketing Association, 1975, p. 118.

14. Bert C. McCammon, Jr., Robert F. Lusch, and Bradley Farnsworth, "Contemporary Markets and the Corporate Imperative: A Strategic Analysis for Senior Retailing Executives," paper presented at Seminar for Top Management in Retailing, Graduate School of Business Administration, Harvard University, 1976; and Albert D. Bates, "Ahead— The Retrenchment Era," *Journal of Retailing,* Fall 1977, pp. 29–46.

15. Amin El-Dirghami, "Shoplifting Among Students," *Journal of Retailing,* Fall 1974, p. 33.

16. "Employee Theft: A Billion Dollar Business," *Hardware Retailer,* November 1976, p. 126.

17. Albert Bates, "The Superstores: Emerging Innovations in Food Retailing," in Robert Robicheaux et al., eds., *Marketing: Contemporary Dimensions* (Boston, Houghton Mifflin Co., 1977), p. 207.

18. Robert F. Lusch and James M. Kenderdine, "Working Capital, Sales, and Profit in Chain Store Retailing: Some Empirical Observations," paper presented at the annual meeting of the Southwestern Marketing Association, New Orleans, Louisiana, March 1977.

19. "The OSHA Tangle," *Chain Store Age Executive,* April 1975, p. 16; "OSHA Chief Does Not See It the Way Chains Do," *Chain Store Age Executive,* April 1976, p. 17; and Joseph Barry Mason, "OSHA: Emerging Problems and Prospects," *California Management Review,* Winter 1975–1976, p. 21.

20. Leonard L. Berry, James S. Hensel, and Marian C. Burke, "Improving Retailer Capability for Effective Consumerism Response," *Journal of Retailing,* Fall 1976, pp. 3–14, 94.

21. Ronald J. Dornoff and Clint Tankersley, "Do Retailers Practice Social Responsibility?" *Journal of Retailing,* Winter 1975, pp. 33–42.

22. For further details, see Gordon L. Williams, "Environmental Legislation Affecting Retailers," *Stores,* April 1974, p. 19; "Malls Face EPA on Parking," *Chain Store Age,* December 1974, p. 14; "De-velopers Thrilled by EPA Regulations Delay," *Chain Store Age,* February 1975, p. 12; and J. Barry Mason, "Environmental Legislation: Impacts on Management," paper presented at the Macro-Marketing Theory Seminar, University of Colorado, August 1977.

23. Patricia Chapman, "Retailer Responsibility Extends to New Areas," *Stores,* April 1977, pp. 43–47.

24. "EFT Banking Into Clouds," *Chain Store Age Executive,* February 1976, p. 19; and "Key Court Round Is Bad News for EFT in Supers," *Progressive Grocer,* May 1976, p. 19.

25. "The Book Boom: Action in Paperbacks," *Business Week,* July 4, 1977, p. 50.

26. See also, for example, Malcolm P. McNair and Eleanor G. May, *The Evolution of Retail Institutions in the United States* (Cambridge, Massachusetts, The Marketing Science Institute, 1976), p. 139.

27. William R. George, "The Retailing of Services—A Challenging Future," *Journal of Retailing,* Fall 1977, pp. 85–98.

28. For additional views on these points, see James Rouse, "New Retail Projects: Go Downtown, Young Man," *Chain Store Age Executive,* September 1975, p. 31; and William Brubaker, "Tomorrow's Malls: Multi-Use and Better Looking," *Chain Store Age Executive,* September 1975, p. 33.

29. Steven P. Cron, "Control of Retail Selling Costs," *Retail Control,* August 1976, p. 60.

30. McCammon and Bates, "Reseller Strategies and Financial Performance," p. 152.

31. Albert E. Bates, David Kollat, and Cyrus Wilson, "Clearing Retailing's Upcoming Hurdles," *Chain Store Age Executive,* September 1975, pp. 24–25; and Albert D. Bates, "The Troubled Future of Retailing," *Business Horizons,* August 1976, pp. 22–28.

32. Charles R. Miller, "Energy and Material Woes Can't Be Marked Down," *Chain Store Age Executive,* April 1975, p. 36.

33. See, for example, Foster Sears, "Smaller Is the Word," *Chain Store Age Executive,* September 1975, p. 28; and Leonard S. Golden, "From Quantity to Quality," *Chain Store Age Executive,* September 1975, p. 29.

34. Daniel Bell, "The Post-Industrial Society—Ex-

pectations for the 1970's and 1980's," in Herman
Kahn, ed., *The Future of the Corporation* (New York,
Mason & Lipscomb Publishers, 1974).

Questions

1. *The survey findings reported in this article show that retail executives viewed improving profitability, reducing shortages and obtaining a better*

capital position as the most important issues they faced in 1977. In your opinion, will the relative importance of these issues change by 1985? Explain.

2. *Retailing productivity has lagged behind that of other sectors in our economy (manufacturing, agriculture, and so on). What might a retailer do in the 1980s to improve productivity? (Note: Productivity is measured in terms of a ratio of output to input, such as the ratio of net sales to personnel expenses.)*

39

The Cereal Companies:
Monopolists or Super
Marketers?

PAUL N. BLOOM

Widely accepted business practices have gone on trial, and the losers in the case could be entire industries. Kellogg, General Mills, and General Foods successfully used a wide range of common marketing practices and were accused by the FTC of engaging in illegal monopolization of the cereal industry.

Marketing is on trial in a courtroom in Washington, D.C. Three of the most prominent and successful marketing organizations in the world—Kellogg, General Mills, and General Foods—are being accused by the Federal Trade Commission of using a wide range of common marketing practices to help them establish and maintain a shared monopoly of the ready-to-eat breakfast cereal industry. Instead of seeing the cereal industry as providing numerous textbook examples (as it has, in fact, provided) of how marketing should be done by large-scale consumer products manufacturers, the Federal Trade Commission sees the industry as "a textbook example of the dangers of concentration and the evils of monopoly."[1] If the courts eventually rule in favor of the position taken by the FTC, then substantial portions of many of today's marketing texts and guidebooks may have to be rewritten.

This article contains a description of the FTC's antitrust case against the three largest cereal com-

Source: Paul N. Bloom, "The Cereal Companies: Monopolists or Super Marketers?" pp. 41–49, *MSU Business Topics,* Summer 1978. Reprinted by permission of the publisher, Division of Research, Graduate School of Business Administration, Michigan State University.

panies. The purpose is to spotlight the conflicts which exist between the interpretations given to certain marketing practices by the FTC attorneys and the interpretations given to these practices by most marketing scholars and practitioners. An attempt is made to show how a large number of marketers could find themselves in Catch-22 situations if the thinking of the FTC is upheld. These marketers could face the prospect of being damned if they used certain marketing practices and damned if they did not, as the FTC could attack them for choosing one course of action, and their competitors could attack them for choosing the other.

One warning must be offered. This article is *not* meant to contain an evaluation of the charges being made; it is primarily designed to give the reader a better understanding of the significance these charges have for marketing practitioners. A comprehensive evaluation of the case would require much more space than is available here and would require access to information submitted in the trial that has not yet been released to the public. Without doubt, a variety of complicated legal and economic issues must be resolved in this case.[2]

The trial of the cereal case before an FTC administrative law judge in Washington began in April 1976, four years after the FTC originally filed a formal complaint against the three respondents and Quaker Oats. The initial trial is expected to last into the 1980s. The FTC staff attorneys took until January 1978 to present their case (at which time the charges against Quaker Oats were dropped). The defense arguments of the three respondents should take several years to complete. A final determination may not occur until the late 1980s, since the law judge's decision could be appealed to the five FTC commissioners, and their decision could be appealed to a U.S. circuit court of appeals and to the Supreme Court.

The charges leveled against Kellogg, General Mills, and General Foods have evolved as the case has proceeded. The complaint filed in 1972 did not accuse the four original respondents of collusion or conspiracy, but instead placed considerable emphasis on how the respondents had used intensive advertising to help them establish a shared monopoly of the ready-to-eat cereal market. In fact, observers speculated that the case was being used to test certain economic theories about the anticompetitive effects of advertising.[3] These theories—which claim that advertising produces entry barriers by creating brand loyalties or by allowing large advertisers to achieve economies of scale—have received widespread attention in the economics and business literature.[4]

However, the pre-trial brief submitted by the FTC attorneys in 1976 gave only secondary emphasis to the argument that intensive advertising had produced anticompetitive effects. Instead, emphasis was given to the notion that an intricate tacit conspiracy has developed among the respondents which violates Section 5 of the Federal Trade Commission Act. The following paragraphs are devoted to discussing what the FTC staff sees as the dimensions of this alleged tacit conspiracy, based on what is said in the 524 pages of the pretrial brief. Apparently, the FTC staff has not changed its arguments substantially since publication of the brief.

The FTC staff seems to be saying that a tacit conspiracy consisting of four major components has been maintained in the ready-to-eat breakfast cereal industry. These components are:

1. the use of competitive monitoring procedures;
2. the use of noncompetitive pricing policies;
3. the *non*use of certain promotional techniques and other policies that could stimulate price competition; and
4. the use of exclusionary practices of shelf-space

allocation, brand proliferation, product differentiation, and intensive advertising.

The arguments of the FTC staff concerning each of these components of the alleged tacit conspiracy are presented in separate sections below. In each section, the interpretations given to certain marketing practices by the FTC staff are contrasted with the interpretations a marketing textbook might provide. A summary of these contrasting interpretations can be seen in Exhibit 1. The discussion and table should clearly point out that the FTC staff has mounted a fundamental challenge to marketing thought and practice.

Competitive Monitoring Charges

The FTC staff views the first component of the tacit conspiracy as being essential for holding the conspiracy together. Without a formal or written agreement, the respondents allegedly keep their conspiracy healthy by closely watching one another's activities. Firms supposedly will be afraid to do anything that would draw quick, retaliatory actions from observant competitors. They will, instead, restrict their actions to those that fall within the industry's permissible code of conduct—something which has been learned over the years with the help of competitive monitoring. Thus, competitive monitoring allegedly can permit a tacit conspiracy to develop and thrive without the benefit of any formal communications or agreements among the conspirators.

The competitive monitoring activities that have drawn criticism from the FTC staff include the following:

1. using salespersons to collect information on the prices, shelf locations, new product introductions, and promotions of rivals by observing shelf displays, consulting with buyers, or conversing with salespersons from competing firms;
2. using standard reports on industry marketing

Exhibit 1

A comparison of interpretations of the cereal companies' behavior

Behaviors	FTC staff's interpretation	Marketing textbook interpretation
1. Monitoring of competitors' activities through: 　a. Salespersons' reports 　b. Subscriptions to Nielsen, SAMI, etc. 　c. Participation in a trade association	1a, b, c. Policing actions designed to ensure compliance with a code of conduct.	1a, b, c. Marketing intelligence gathering.
2. Use of pricing policies such as: 　a. Prior announcement of increases 　b. Delivered pricing 　c. Offering "price protection" 　d. Suggesting retail price 　e. Making price changes at different times than cost changes 　f. Keeping high prices for failing brands	2. Avoiding price competition by: 　a. Reducing uncertainty 　b. Keeping wholesale prices uniform geographically (reduces uncertainty) 　c. Allowing instant retaliation to a price cut 　d. Keeping retail prices uniform (reduces uncertainty) 　e. Reducing uncertainty by cutting frequency of changes 　f. Avoiding price cuts	2a, b, c, d. Helping a manufacturer establish better relationships with retailers. 　e. Demand-oriented pricing 　f. A milking strategy
3. Nonuse of: 　a. Trade allowances and discounts 　b. Cents-off deals 　c. Private labels 　d. Vitamin fortification (until pressured) 　e. In-pack premiums (for 10 years)	3a, b, c, d, e. Avoiding actions that could stimulate price competition.	3a, b, c, d, e. Avoiding destructive, costly forms of competition. Also avoiding government accusations of using predatory or discriminatory practices.
4. Use of: 　a. Promotion of shelf-space plans 　b. Brand proliferation 　c. Product differentiation 　d. Intensive advertising	4. Excluding entry by: 　a. Allowing new firms only poor shelf locations 　b, c. Leaving no profitable positions for new firms 　d. Building brand loyalty and setting scale-economy barriers	4a. Helping retailers 　b, c. Serving diverse consumer tastes 　d. Stimulating primary demand, creating brand awareness, and reinforcing purchase decisions.

activities obtained from Nielsen, SAMI, and other widely used data reporting services;

3. using the A. C. Nielsen Company for several years as a clearinghouse for advertising data. (The respondents allegedly submitted data on advertising expenditures in each media for each brand to Nielsen and then received from Nielsen, as a supplement to the firm's regular reports, detailed information on the advertising expenditures of all the cooperating firms.);

4. using the results of studies on competitors conducted by advertising agencies and marketing research firms; and

5. participating in the activities of The Cereal Institute, a trade association.

As indicated, the FTC staff sees these activities as policing actions used by the respondents to ensure that no firm deviates from the accepted industry code of conduct. Of course, these activities (perhaps with the exception of the clearinghouse operation) could also be viewed as attempts to gather timely, useful marketing intelligence data. Business firms always have a need to know about their competitors and the rest of their environment, and the procedures cited by the FTC staff are commonly used to gather intelligence. Without this information, a firm could find itself unprepared for an initiative by a competitor or unable to make a timely response to a rapid change in the feelings of consumers or public policy makers. By keeping on top of things through the use of salespersons, reporting services, research firms, and trade associations, a firm can avoid a host of difficulties and probably keep itself *more* competitive than it might be otherwise.

Thus, the FTC staff is labeling as anticompetitive a group of activities which conventional marketing wisdom would tend to label as competitive. If the viewpoint of the FTC staff is eventually upheld in the courts, then firms in oligopolistic industries such as cereals will be confronted with the problem of determining how much marketing intelligence they are permitted to and should collect. Collecting too much intelligence could get a firm in trouble with the FTC, while collecting too little could get a

firm in trouble with its competitors and customers. Under these circumstances, the amount of intelligence a firm could collect would probably depend on how closely its behavior corresponded to that of its competitors. A firm that did things differently from its competitors could collect as much intelligence as it wanted, while a firm that followed industry marketing norms would have to limit its intelligence gathering or risk being labeled as a tacit conspirator.

Noncompetitive Pricing Charges

The second component of the alleged tacit conspiracy is an understanding among the respondents as to what constitutes permissible pricing behavior. The FTC staff seems to feel that the industry code of conduct limits the respondents to using pricing policies which encourage interdependence and leader-follower pricing, with Kellogg generally serving as the price leader. The pricing policies they allegedly have used to help them avoid competing with one another on a price basis include the following.

1. The announcement of price increases to the public well before they are to take effect. This supposedly helps the companies reduce uncertainty about one another's actions and thereby keeps the leader-follower pattern intact.

2. The use of delivered pricing systems which charge all customers the same price for a given shipment, regardless of location. This supposedly reduces uncertainty and reduces the chances of emerge since price differentials between brands will always be the same nationwide, and price skirmishes will therefore not occur as a result of attempts by some firms to keep differentials the same across locations.

3. The offering of price protection to retailers. This protects retailers by giving them an immediate credit if a price reduction occurs on goods that are in transit to them or are sitting in their warehouses. This supposedly discourages price cutting by a

manufacturer because it allows immediate retaliation by competitors. A firm that wants to meet a price cut by a rival would not have to wait until the next shipment eventually appears on retailers' shelves to have its response noticed by consumers but could use price protection to get a lower price on goods already in the retailers' possession.

4. The suggesting of retail prices to retailers, accompanied by considerable sales efforts to get the retailers to follow these prices. This supposedly reduces uncertainty and reduces the chances of price skirmishes resulting from inconsistent price differentials.

5. The changing of prices in a timing pattern inconsistent with (and more spaced out than) the incidence of cost changes. This supposedly reduces the frequency of price changes and thereby reduces the chances that price competition will emerge.

6. The charging of high prices for failing brands (a milking strategy), rather than price cuts to stimulate sales. This supposedly conveys a message that price cutting is not acceptable in the industry.

In sum, the FTC staff believes that firms interested in competing on a price basis would not use pricing policies such as these.

Clearly, there are logical alternative explanations for using these policies. For example, early announcements of price increases, delivered pricing systems, price protection, and suggested retail prices could be used as part of an effort by manufacturers to establish good relations with retailers. These policies could help reduce uncertainty for retailers, simplify their record keeping, and eliminate any concerns they might have about being victimized by price discrimination. The use of alternative pricing policies could put the cereal manufacturers in troublesome conflict with many of their retailers.

The failure of price changes to follow cost changes could be viewed as an attempt by the manufacturers to avoid the relatively unsound practice of cost-oriented pricing and to substitute demand-oriented or competition-oriented pricing. Similarly, the use of milking strategies for failing brands could be seen as an attempt to make the best of a situation in which even a lower price might not help the sales situation.

Marketers will face a serious dilemma if the thinking of the FTC staff about these pricing policies is upheld. Abandonment of these policies could seriously damage manufacturer-retailer relations and could complicate the price-setting task for manufacturers in innumerable ways. Nevertheless, a manufacturer in an oligopolistic industry with a history of parallel pricing behavior would probably find it wise to abandon these policies in order to avoid difficulties with the FTC. The firm would have to find other and potentially less efficient ways of pleasing retailers and setting prices. A manufacturer who was not part of a parallel pricing pattern, however, would probably be able to continue using these policies.

Passive Behavior Charges

The FTC staff sees the third component of the tacit conspiracy as an understanding to avoid or limit the use of certain marketing strategies that might stimulate price competition among the respondents. The industry code of conduct allegedly forbids or discourages the use of promotional strategies or product modifications that might lead firms to use lower prices as a means of drawing customers away from competitors. The FTC staff believes the respondents have behaved passively in the sales promotion and product modification areas, and have avoided taking aggressive actions that might stimulate price skirmishes or even price wars.

Several examples of passive behavior are cited by the FTC staff. First, it is claimed that trade allowances and discounts are relatively nonexistent in the cereal industry, as are cents-off offers to consumers. The FTC staff indicates that if more of these dealer-directed and consumer-directed promotional techniques were used, more variability in retail prices would exist, and more price competition would result (since parallel pricing would be more difficult to maintain). Second, it is claimed that the respondents have refused to produce or sell private labels, even when asked to do so by major super-market chains. This is viewed by the FTC staff as an attempt to stifle price competition. Finally, it is claimed that the respondents held back on the vitamin fortification of their products until they were pressured by the government to do so in the early 1970s, and that they maintained an understanding for more than ten years (1957 to 1968) to limit the use of in-pack premiums. The failure to act aggressively in fortifying brands and in using premiums is seen by the FTC staff as indicating a desire to avoid all competition that could eventually lead to price competition.

An alternative interpretation can be given for the reluctance of the respondents to use the cited practices. These practices could be seen as costly, inefficient ways of attracting customers when compared to the practices the respondents have tended to use—heavy advertising, brand proliferation, and product differentiation (discussed later in this article). It may not be wise for these firms to use *push* strategies (for example, deals, promotions) to get their brands on the shelves and favored by consumers, when *pull* strategies (for example, advertising, differentiation) might work more effectively. These widely known firms might not need to give retailers and consumers incentives to try their products. In addition, it might not be wise for these firms to manufacture private label cereals for retailers when a better return on investment could be obtained by manufacturing their own brands or by taking advantage of other investment opportunities. Furthermore, vitamin fortification and the inclusion of premiums may not have been of much concern to consumers during the time they were not offered.

If the FTC staff's arguments are accepted by the courts and marketers can get into trouble for *not* engaging in certain practices, numerous problems will emerge for top executives and legal staffs. These people will have to learn not only what their firms *cannot do* under the FTC Act, but also what they *cannot not do* under this law.

Moreover, the problems of business executives could become even more acute if the FTC staff is successful in two other antitrust cases it is pursu-

ing. In cases involving ITT Continental Baking (for its marketing of Wonder Bread) and General Foods (for its marketing of coffees), the FTC staff is, among other things, questioning whether the *selective* use of trade allowances and discounts where competition is more severe constitutes predatory conduct designed to injure competitors. Thus, a situation could arise in which large-scale marketers of consumer products could not choose to refrain from offering trade deals, but could also not choose to offer them on a selective basis. Trade deals would, therefore, have to be offered to everyone.

Exclusionary Conduct Charges

The last component of the tacit conspiracy view is the one that allegedly allows the respondents to keep any new firms from obtaining a significant market share. The FTC staff indicates that the respondents have informally agreed to engage in the practices of *shelf-space allocation, brand proliferation, product differentiation,* and *intensive advertising* to exclude entry to the industry and to retain their more than 90 percent share of the market. In other words, the industry's code of conduct allegedly permits these forms of competitive behavior because they hurt industry outsiders more than insiders.

By labeling practices such as product differentiation and intensive advertising as exclusionary, the FTC staff is questioning the essence of modern marketing. Therefore, the reasoning of the FTC staff deserves careful examination.

Shelf-Space Allocation

The FTC staff claims that the three respondents have promoted an exclusionary shelf-space allocation plan that has received widespread acceptance by retailers. The plan, promoted by Kellogg, gives each brand a share of the available shelf space in proportion to its share of the market. Although the other respondents offer shelf-space plans to retailers, the FTC staff says that these plans have been promoted lightly and that there generally has been acquiescence to the Kellogg plan. The other respondents allegedly have seen no need to challenge the Kellogg plan as long as they have gotten their share of the space, especially since Kellogg has a larger and more experienced sales force.

The Kellogg plan has, according to the FTC staff, managed to exclude entrants and discourage competition in several ways. First, the plan gives the brands of the three respondents better locations at the center of the aisles while relegating other brands to poorer locations at the ends of the aisles. Second, the plan has the brands of each manufacturer displayed in a separate grouping, making it difficult for consumers to compare similar items (for example, branded and private label corn flakes), and making it more likely that consumers will select second brands made by the company that manufactures their first selection. Third, the plan displays the respondents' brands in a billboard fashion (several facings are put next to one another), getting them more attention and impulse purchases. Last, the plan's fair-share concept of allocating space based on market share tends to stabilize market shares, since a brand's share depends to some extent on the amount of shelf space it receives.

Brand Proliferation

The respondents' practice of continually bringing out new cereal brands is the second major activity that has been labeled exclusionary by the FTC staff. Brand proliferation allegedly excludes entrants in the following way:

1. Virtually every profitable position in the product space of the ready-to-eat cereal industry is occupied by several brands belonging to the respondents.
2. With so many brands competing to let consumers know where they stand in the space, the costs of getting the attention of consumers and establishing just one new brand in a profitable position in the space are high.
3. With so many brands already established in

each profitable position in the space, it is extremely difficult for one brand (such as a private label) to create enough preference for itself to obtain a share of the total cereal market large enough to take advantage of economies of scale in production (approximately a 4 to 6 percent share).
4. Even if a new firm manages to establish a brand in some unoccupied, profitable position, it will not be able to maintain a high share for this brand for long. The respondents can be expected to bring out new brands immediately to compete in this location—as they did with natural cereals.
5. Thus, in order for a new firm to attain competitive production costs, it will need to establish several successful brands (industry experts consider a one percent brand share to be good) in multiple positions across the product space. The promotional costs needed to establish several brands in profitable positions, and to obtain adequate market shares for each, serve to deter entry.

In addition to the above argument, the FTC staff is also claiming that brand proliferation discourages entry by making less shelf space available to new firms.

Product Differentiation

The FTC staff's criticism of the respondents' product differentiation practices is tied closely to its argument about brand proliferation. The staff essentially sees product differentiation, supported by intensive advertising, as the means by which the respondents are able to place brands in profitable positions all across the product space. As discussed above, this positioning allegedly helps insulate the respondents from new competition—especially from private labels. In addition, the FTC staff argues that this positioning helps insulate the respondents from competition from one another—

since a brand only has to compete with the few other brands that are positioned near it.

The FTC staff defines *product differentiation* as "conduct which draws the consumer's attention to minor variations between products, thereby diverting his attention from a comparison of the basic similarities between them."[5] Practices identified in the pre-trial brief as constituting this form of conduct include the use of product symbols (for example, Cap'n Crunch and Tony the Tiger), unique package designs, trademarks, nutritional claims, premiums, and changes in the shapes, colors, textures, flavors, additives, or sugar content of old brands in order to create new brands. In essence, the FTC staff is arguing that these practices make it more difficult and time-consuming for consumers (particularly children) to make value comparisons between brands to discover their true similarities, and that, therefore, consumers start to prefer brands that are perceived to exist all across the product space.

Intensive Advertising

The FTC staff is charging that the respondents use intensive advertising not only to support brand proliferation and product differentiation, but also to discourage entrants in other ways. Intensive advertising is allegedly used to create consumer brand loyalties for the respondents' products, making it more difficult for new firms to acquire customers. The staff also claims that intensive advertising gives the respondents an advantage with retailers in getting shelf locations. In addition, it is argued that intensive advertising allows the respondents to obtain quantity discounts from the media, putting small firms that cannot obtain such discounts at a cost disadvantage. Finally, intensive advertising has allegedly allowed the respondents to obtain product protection from the television networks— isolating their advertisements in time (for a substantial period both before and after) from ads for other cereal brands. In sum, the FTC staff believes that newcomers to the cereal industry simply could

not afford the advertising campaigns needed to overcome the advantages the respondents have obtained through intensive advertising.

Alternative Viewpoints

A marketing professional might offer several explanations for use of the allegedly exclusionary practices.

1. Shelf-space plans are promoted to provide a service to retailers which can help them lower their costs and increase their revenues.
2. Brand proliferation and product differentiation are used to cater to diverse and rapidly changing consumer tastes.
3. Intensive advertising is used to stimulate primary demand for ready-to-eat cereals, to create awareness of individual brands, and to reinforce recently made brand choices of consumers.

If the courts fail to accept explanations such as these and find the practices to be exclusionary, then organizations in the detergent, paper product, automobile, cosmetic, and many other industries may have to redesign their marketing programs to avoid difficulties with the FTC. They may have to start marketing a smaller number of less heavily advertised brands with reasonably uniform characteristics. Needless to say, developing a profitable marketing program under these constraints would be a severe challenge.

Additional Case Details

The FTC staff is also offering a variety of back-up arguments, just in case the tacit conspiracy argument is rejected. These arguments basically say that the respondents should be found in violation of Section 5 because the *results* produced by the industry's concentrated structure and distinctive conduct (whether or not a conspiracy exists) have been poor for society. High profits, high selling costs, and infrequent innovations are cited as some of the signs which suggest that industry performance has been lacking. The FTC staff seems to believe there is legal precedent for this back-up argument in the decisions in several other antitrust cases.

The remedies sought by the FTC staff in the cereal case are designed to restructure the industry so as to prevent the re-emergence of the current situation. This means that in addition to prohibiting the respondents from engaging in certain practices such as allocating shelf space or exchanging advertising data, the FTC staff would like to create eight cereal firms out of the three respondents and require the three to license most of their trademarks on a royalty-free basis to any firm (except Quaker Oats) that is willing to maintain the necessary quality control standards.

The divestiture plan of the FTC staff would break three new firms away from Kellogg and one each from General Mills and General Foods. Each new firm would be given the exclusive rights to the trademark of at least one major brand (for example, Special K, Rice Krispies, Wheaties) in order to give it a sound basis on which to expand its operations. Royalty-free licensing of trademarks would be required for a twenty-year period for all the remaining brands of Kellogg, General Mills, and General Foods. In addition, during the same period, these three firms (1) would have to license the trademarks of any new brands they develop on a royalty-free basis after five years, (2) would have to provide licensees with formulas and methods of production, including quality control standards, (3) would have to license package design as part of the trademark licenses, and (4) would have to avoid acquiring any cereal firms. The FTC staff believes these remedies will restore workable competition to the cereal industry by discouraging brand proliferation, product differentiation, and intensive advertising and by encouraging new firms to enter the industry with low-price strategies.

Conclusion

Marketers will want to pay close attention to how the courts answer the question posed in the title of this article. If they decide that the three major cereal companies are monopolists, then many large-scale organizations may have to make substantial revisions in marketing policies and programs. Giant organizations such as General Motors, Procter and Gamble, Revlon, and Kodak may no longer be able to do a host of things textbooks have called good marketing practice, and they may be forced to use marketing strategies they avoided in the past. They may even have to *demarket* certain brands or employ other strategies that could reduce the risk of government antitrust action.[6]

On the other hand, if the courts decide that the major cereal companies are super marketers with sound competitive reasons for using the practices they use, then modern marketing will have won a victory. Product differentiation, intensive advertising, market intelligence gathering, and other common marketing procedures will be cleared of the charge that they are anticompetitive forces.[7]

Notes

1. FTC Complaint Counsel, *Trial Brief—In the Matter of Kellogg Company et al.*, Docket No. 8883, Federal Trade Commission, 1976, vol. 1, p. 1.
2. For an in-depth evaluation of a portion of the FTC staff's charges, see the author's monograph, "The Cereal Antitrust Case: An Analysis of Selected Issues," in *Research in Marketing: An Annual Compilation of Research, Volume 2,* edited by Jagdish N. Sheth (Greenwich, Conn.: JAI Press, forthcoming).
3. See Yale Brozen, "New FTC Policy from Obsolete Economic Doctrine," *Antitrust Law Journal* 41 (Issue 3, 1973): 477–87; and William E. Huth, "The Advertising Industry—An Unlikely Monopolizer," *Antitrust Bulletin* 14 (Winter 1974): 653–79.
4. See James M. Ferguson, *Advertising and Competition: Theory, Measurement, Fact* (Cambridge, Mass.: Ballinger Publishing Co., 1974; and Jean Jacques Lambin, "What Is the Real Impact of Advertising?" *Harvard Business Review* 53 (May–June 1975): 139–47.
5. FTC, *Trial Brief*, p. 325.

6. For further discussion of the strategies firms could be forced to use to avoid antitrust difficulties, see Paul N. Bloom and Philip Kotler, "Strategies for High Market Share Companies," *Harvard Business Review* 53 (November–December 1975): 63–72.
7. The author would like to thank William Nickels and Robert Spekman for their helpful comments. Financial support for this research was provided in part by the Bureau of Business and Economic Research of the University of Maryland.

Questions

1. *The FTC charged the cereal companies with a conspiracy consisting of four major components. Briefly define each of the components.*
2. *Can you make a distinction between companies that achieve monopolistic market positions by being "super marketers" and those that achieve monopolistic positions by being "unscrupulous marketers"? Should the courts make that distinction?*

40

Antitrust Compliance
for Small Business

JAMES E. INMAN

Antitrust laws and regulations apply to all companies involved in interstate commerce in the United States. These laws do not apply just to IBM, Procter & Gamble, and General Motors. More and more small business people are discovering the need for an antitrust compliance program.

What does antitrust law—literally law directed against trusts, as giant business combinations were once called—have to do with small business? The answer in brief is: all economic institutions in the United States do business under the protection and subject to the restraints of the federal antitrust laws. Legislated under the "interstate commerce" power of Congress, these laws are virtually allembracing. Hardly any business is so small or local that federal antitrust laws do not apply. They have been applied to retailing, to the rendering of services, and to manufacturing. For example, antitrust laws have been applied against motion picture exhibitors, bowling alley proprietors, and garbage collectors.

In the American business system competition is the cornerstone of our free enterprise economy. The purpose of the antitrust laws is to preserve the conditions necessary for competition and thus to protect the system itself. To the extent that the antitrust laws fail, governmental control of large aggrega-

tions of economic wealth and power may be expected to replace them. It is in the self-interest of American business, therefore, to be familiar with and abide by the antitrust laws. This is particularly important for smaller firms who are often the beneficiaries of antitrust law. Smaller business firms should not engage in practices which their own business community has collectively denounced as unfair when practiced by larger business units.

There are practical reasons for obeying antitrust laws also. Recently, antitrust enforcement officials have stated their intention to treat antitrust violations as serious criminal offenses to be punished by imprisonment more frequently than in the past. This change in attitude is also reflected in the 1974 Congressional increase of penalties for violation of antitrust laws. Violations which were previously misdemeanors have been changed to felonies with a maximum penalty from one to three years imprisonment. Fines were increased from $50,000 to $100,000 for individuals and $1,000,000 for corporations. Associated with such prosecution is the loss of public approval and esteem for the violator. Finally, there has been a sharp increase in the number of private actions, including class actions, by corporations and individuals claiming to have been injured by antitrust violations. Such victims are able to bring actions against antitrust violators and recover damages which the law allows to be trebled. Involvement in such litigations can obviously be expensive, time-consuming, and arduous to the small business firm. Consequently, minimum steps to avoid antitrust transgressions are

Source: Journal of Small Business Management, October 1977, pp. 10–19. Copyright © 1977 by the International Council for Small Business and the West Virginia University Bureau of Business Research.

imperative. Antitrust compliance programs are needed for all firms.

Company Antitrust Policy

It should be made clear that the purpose of a compliance program is not the avoidance of being caught. It is not concealment of activities involved in a violation of antitrust law in order to avoid detection. The attitude on the part of top management should never be, "Let's not tell our attorneys." Nor does an antitrust compliance program consist of the mere preparation of papers expressing a company attitude to conform with the laws.

In contrast, an antitrust compliance program must begin with a proper attitude and its expression by the top management of the firm. Top management must demonstrate its respect for antitrust through its leadership and its intolerance for even slight transgressions of the antitrust laws. Just as management dictates other policy and expects subordinate performance consistent with that policy, the same attitude should prevail in implementation and performance under antitrust policies of the company.

Part of the implementation of any policy entails the practical understanding of such policy. While antitrust laws have some complexities and even those areas in which the exact intent of the law may be in doubt, the point should be made that one need not be a lawyer to effectively stay clear of antitrust difficulties. Compliance programs are designed to help the company avoid breaches of those areas of the law which all can understand because of their clear meaning. Legal counsel can be secured to deal with the specific meaning of the more difficult areas of law, should that need arise.

Antitrust Compliance Programs

The more complete antitrust compliance programs are tailor-made for particular business firms. Individual fabrication of the compliance program is necessary because of differing company and industry facts. Legal counsel must be well briefed concerning the particular facets of the company's business. An antitrust compliance program normally includes five elements.

The first element of an antitrust compliance program is the formulation of a statement of company policy on antitrust. Such statements should indicate the reasons for complying with antitrust law and the obvious types of infractions of antitrust law that should be avoided. It should indicate that severe discipline upon company employees is to be expected if they violate company policy. The statement should receive wide circulation within the company to all appropriate personnel and should include the advisement of personnel that they have the privilege of circumventing channels to top officials or the company law offices for the purpose of reporting any perceptions of antitrust violations. In addition, it should be made known to all department heads that they are responsible for themselves and for their subordinates in being advised of the company antitrust policy and for maintaining consistent practices.

Secondly, the compliance program must contain some means of training personnel concerning the antitrust laws. The educational program should emphasize that portion of antitrust law which is well-known and subject to vigorous enforcement by the antitrust authorities. The program should not assert that antitrust law is vague and unfair. Emphasis of undue complexity or of vagueness in certain areas of the law would encourage only disrespect for the laws and for the company's policy on antitrust compliance.

The third element of a good compliance program includes the establishment of internal procedures to implement the company policy on antitrust. Company procedures concerning pricing, termination of dealers, marketing of new products, trade association activities or refusals to deal should all incorporate a recognition of the relevant antitrust laws in the formulation of those policies. In effect, the antitrust laws should be considered as an additional constraint in formulation of company policies on these matters. The decision-making process must be circumscribed by the rules of antitrust.

An additional element of antitrust compliance normally includes a documentation system. Documents should be developed which supply information that antitrust was duly considered in formulation of policies and in the decision making procedures of the company. For example, as the company develops its new pricing policies, documents should be prepared that indicate that the rules of antitrust were considered in the formulation of the pricing policy. Every effort to stay within the boundaries of antitrust should be noted within the documents. The documents are to be preserved for subsequent use in defending against charges of antitrust violations. Such documentation procedures could supply valuable evidence to convince a jury or court of the attitude of the company and its desire to comply with antitrust laws. Such evidence is pertinent to establish that no evil intent existed in the minds of company officials.

The last element of an antitrust compliance program would include periodic audits of existing company antitrust policies, educational programs, decision-making procedures and documentation systems. The audit should determine whether the compliance components are effective and whether any modifications are necessary. The changing aspects of the law and of company operations necessitate the periodic audit.

It is unlikely that many small business firms are able to spend the time and funds necessary to implement a wide-scale antitrust compliance program. In some cases, the only feasible program may be self-directed. In such instances, this article may be most helpful in enunciating company policy and modifying the operating and decision-making procedures of the firm. The essential element that a self-help program requires is a practical understanding of the antitrust laws. The outline that follows is an overview of the antitrust laws that are particularly relevant to the small business firm. This outline should help businessmen to identify antitrust issues when they arise in the course of their work. It is not a comprehensive presentation of the antitrust laws, but of those laws which may most likely be unwittingly violated by the small

businessman are included in a general discussion. By careful attention to this material, small business executives can minimize the likelihood of antitrust violations and identify instances in which they need legal counsel. In addition, they may learn when they are being victimized by other violators of antitrust laws and when to use the protection of these laws for survival of their own firms.

The Statutes

There are four principal antitrust laws and related federal statutes, which are written in broad and somewhat, vague language. However, the meaning of these statutes has been clarified and interpreted by numerous court decisions over the course of many years. These basic statutes are:

1. The Sherman Act, Section 1 of which prohibits "contracts, combinations and conspiracies in restraint of trade," and Section 2 of which prohibits "monopolization or attempt to monopolize" in any product line or geographical area of commerce.
2. The Clayton Act prohibits mergers and acquisitions which may substantially lessen competition in any line of commerce. Another section makes it unlawful to sell commodities on condition that the buyer will refuse to deal in the goods of competing sellers. Such "exclusive dealing" arrangements are illegal if they have the probability of substantially lessening competition in any line of commerce.
3. The Robinson-Patman Act generally restricts a seller from discriminating in price between buyers. This act also covers indirect discrimination by the unequal allocation of allowances for promotional services.
4. The Federal Trade Commission Act prohibits "unfair" methods of competition.

A more thorough description of these statutes and offenses thereof are presented in the following sections.

Relations with Competitors

The chief antitrust statute, the Sherman Act, prohibits conspiracies and understandings that unreasonably restrain trade. Some kind of *joint or concerted* action between two or more persons or companies must exist for Section 1 of the Sherman Act to apply. But there need not be anything so formal as a written contract; "understandings" are enough, and can be inferred by the court or jury from the way the parties have conducted themselves. Any kind of a mutual understanding which gives the parties a basis for expecting that a business practice or decision will be adopted by one and all, or at least not opposed by the others, is sufficient to establish a violation. Furthermore, the joint action need not be between competitors. Under some circumstances it can even by between members of the same family or wholly owned corporations.

For Section 1 to be violated the joint action must have as its *purpose or effect* an unreasonable restraint of trade. If the *purpose* is unreasonable, it does not matter whether the action taken by the parties is successful or not. Such restraints of trade that are in their purpose considered unreasonable are identified as *"per se"* violations. Federal enforcement policy allows *criminal* prosecution of these *per se* offenses which include the following:

Price Fixing

This agreement need not be on a specific price. The law is violated by agreements on maximums or minimums; or on a common sales agent; or on terms or conditions of sale such as credit terms or discounts; or even on the mere exchange of price information if there is a stabilizing effect on prices. The agreement of price-fixing schemes can be inferred from a course of conduct, or from a history of telephone calls, meetings and the like between competitors followed by uniform price action. Price-fixing, in whatever form, is the antitrust violation most frequently prosecuted criminally.

Dividing Territory

Competitors may not agree as to geographical areas in which each will or will not sell. Any course of action whereby competitors avoid each other's territory may be a basis for a court finding of such an illegal agreement.

Dividing Customers

Competitors may not agree that each will sell to a particular customer or class of customers and not to another. Neither may competitors agree on which of them will make any specific sales.

Dividing Products

Basically, competitors may not agree that one will not make or sell products made or sold by another.

Limiting Production

Competitors may not agree to restrict or limit production or production capacity. Violations of this form often involve a quota system.

Boycotting

Competing sellers must not agree among themselves not to sell to a particular customer or reseller, whatever the reason.

Suppression of Quality Competition

Competitors may not agree to restrict the development of improvements in the quality of their products. Nor may competitors agree to limit research for quality improvements. Most agreements of this type are, in effect, agreements not to compete and are contrary to the basic concepts of antitrust laws.

To avoid suspicion of a *per se* violation there should be no conversations or communications of any kind with competitors concerning the items above. If any communications are made, a document should be prepared indicating the extent of the conversation and how the conversation was limited to avoid any violation of antitrust laws. If one of these subjects comes up in conversation at a trade meeting attended by company employees, employees should terminate the conversation immediately or leave the gathering. Again, documentation of the incident should be recorded indicating the facts and the employee's non-involvement. In all the *per se* situations it makes no difference that an apparently sound business consideration may be involved also. There are no acceptable excuses nor such a thing as being just a "little bit" guilty.

Besides the *per se* offenses under the Sherman Act, the legality of other joint action by competitors turns on the reasonableness, under the circumstances, of any restraint on competition. Reasonableness of such restraints is measured in terms of both the purpose of the restraint and the effect of the restraint on competition. All of these potential restraints must be tested on an individual basis. However, one should remember that a reasonable business purpose will not excuse joint action which has an unreasonable effect upon competition.

Joint activities of competitors to present views or make recommendations to governmental bodies are exempt from antitrust laws if they are limited to good faith efforts to influence governmental policy. However, the courts have ruled that such action must not be a mere sham to accomplish an otherwise illegal purpose. Therefore, before engaging with other companies in joint presentations before governmental bodies, each proposal should be reviewed to make certain that the project cannot be asserted to be a sham and thus lose its antitrust exemption status.

Relations with Customers

The firm's relationships with its customers are subject to a number of antitrust statutes, each of which is keyed to particular types of transactions.

Resale Restrictions

The antitrust law advances the basic premise that someone who purchased a product should have the right to do with it as he chooses without restriction by the person who sold it to him. Thus, any agreement or understanding by the seller and the customer with respect to the price which the customer will resell the product violates the law. This in-

cludes any arrangement between seller and buyer by means of which the seller controls the buyer's resale price. A violation also occurs when a seller commits himself to one buyer on the price the seller will charge another buyer. Even complaints from one buyer about another buyer's low resale prices may, if the seller attempts to discipline or "speak to" the buyer with lower resale prices, support inferences of a vertical price agreement in violation of antitrust laws.

As a general rule, no restrictions on resale of any sort should be placed upon customers. Sellers should not restrict the customers to whom its buyers may re-sell, unless genuine safety precautions require it. A seller should not place territorial restrictions upon the buyer as to where he can resell his purchases. Although it is lawful to make a buyer responsible for adequately serving a given territorial area, such requirements should not actually support territorial restrictions by excluding buyers from resales in other territories. No coercion or threats of any kind should ever be used on a customer in an effort to impose price, customer or territorial restrictions on his resale policies, the only possible exception being the imposition of customer resale restrictions to prevent the goods from getting into the hands of one who, because of inexperience, would possibly be injured thereby.

Refusal to Deal

A company that does not have a monopoly on a product has the right to select the customers with whom it chooses to do business. This is a right that must be exercised by the company alone without consultation with any other party. The company cannot agree with one of its buyers not to sell to a second buyer. Such group behavior is an illegal boycott. Also, the right to refuse to deal may never be relied upon as a technique to achieve adherence to resale restrictions imposed on the customer. Threat of termination of dealings is the type of coercion typically employed to attempt to achieve resale restrictions on customers, and such techniques violate the law.

Exclusive Dealings

Selection 3 of the Clayton Act clearly applies to a seller (or lessor) of goods (not services) who gains a commitment from his buyer (or lessee) not to buy from a competitor of the seller. The commitment need not be formal; a short-term cancellation clause may supply sufficient "understanding." However, whether the particular agreement is prohibited by law depends in each case upon whether the probable effect of the agreement may substantially lessen competition. If the arrangement is urged by the seller, it is more likely to be unlawful. If it is arranged to meet the operational needs of the buyer, it may be proper. Of course, other factors are important also; such as the length of the arrangement and whether other retail outlets are available to competing sellers.

Requirements Contracts

A contract that requires a buyer to purchase all or substantially all of his requirements of a product from the seller may violate Section 3 of the Clayton Act if that contract, together with other similar requirements contracts the seller may have for that product, will foreclose to other competitive sellers a significant portion of the merchant market for that product. No "full requirements" sales contracts or those for 75 percent or more of the buyer's requirements should be executed where the "probable effect" of such contracts may substantially lessen competition.

Tie-in Arrangements

These are refusals to sell or lease one product or service unless a different product or service is also bought or leased. The courts have said ordinarily there can be hardly any reason for tying two goods together except to use one's power over the first product or service to gain a market for the other. For example, it is normally unreasonable to require

that a buyer finance his purchase through the seller or to require that lessees of equipment use the lessor's supplies in the equipment. In fact, the courts currently give tie-in's a *per se* status of illegality unless the seller can produce an exceptional justification. The tie-in may be justified if the seller can prove that his new and sensitive piece of equipment functions properly only if serviced by him. If this is true, and only as long as this is true, the tie-in service contract would not be unreasonable. "Package" deals are not tie-in's when the buyer is allowed to purchase the components separately if he so desires.

Price Discrimination

The basic purpose of the Robinson-Patman Act is the equitable treatment by the seller of customers who compete with one another in the use or re-sale of the seller's products. The act is intended to assure that in purchases of similar goods (not services) from the same seller one buyer will not be given a price advantage over another if the advantage *may* have an anticompetitive effect among the buyers or with competing sellers, or among the customers of either.

Consequently, it is illegal to charge two different prices to two different buyers for goods of like grade and quality where the effect of the differences in price *may* be substantially to lessen competition.

A competitive injury at the seller level is sometimes called geographical price discrimination. In such instances, the seller lowers his price in some geographical region to compete with a regional seller. If the high prices obtained elsewhere by the discriminating seller are subsidizing the low, below cost price in the regional sales, the geographical price discrimination is illegal because the purpose of the price discrimination is to injure a competing seller.

A buyer-level injury occurs when a seller favors one buyer with a lower price than another buyer who must compete with a favored one. An injury occurs at the third level when some favored buyer is able to pass lower prices on to other customers who at the third level are able to beat their competition which purchases from the seller at a higher price.

To determine whether a Robinson-Patman violation has occurred, one should ask whether the company had made sales:

a. At different prices;
b. Within a reasonable contemporary time-period (this may vary depending upon the competitive market; six months is a good rule of thumb);
c. In interstate commerce (price discrimination occurring totally intra-state may violate state laws; however);
d. Of products of like grade and quality (no significant difference from a commercial standpoint);
e. To customers where injury to competition at the seller, buyer or sub-buyer level will *probably* result.

If any of the above is absent, no Robinson-Patman problem should be present. However, if the above criteria are present, the price difference may, nevertheless, be defended under the law if the lower price was given in good faith to meet (but not beat) a price offered by a competitor. In addition, the difference between the prices charged to the favored and non-favored customer may be "cost-justified" on the basis of cost savings realized by the seller in its sale and delivery expenses in dealing with the favored customer. Of course, if the price change is occasioned by changes in the market or the marketability of the goods, no violation occurs.

The "cost justification" defense can be most difficult to establish to a court's satisfaction. Debates concerning the allocation of overhead costs or others may cause the seller to fail to carry his burden of proof that his lower price was cost justified. Hence, to rely upon a cost justification defense, only cost directly attributable to the sale or to the delivery should be used. The "meeting competition" defense is available only in individual competitive situations and is not available if the seller has good reason to know that the price he is meeting is itself unlawful. Hence, a seller should verify and document in advance the lower price being offered by a competitor before he grants his favored customer the lower price.

Finally, it should be noted that violations of the Robinson-Patman Act subject the company to potential treble damage suits by victims of the practice, but do not subject the violator to criminal prosecution unless he knowingly or with bad purpose attempts a buyers level or seller level injury.

Phony Brokerage

Brokerage may not be paid by a seller to the buyer or an agent of the buyer except for services rendered to the seller. Often buyers attempt to by-pass brokers of the seller and then seek the commission the broker normally earns from the seller. However, the buyer has not rendered services to the seller and is not entitled to such brokerage commission. The buyer has rendered services to himself in by-passing the broker. These phony brokerage allowances are illegal *per se*.

Equitable Promotional Services

Other provisions of the Robinson-Patman Act seek to afford equitable treatment to competing customers by requiring that a promotional payment, service or facility (such as an advertising display) extended by the seller to a customer be made available on proportionately equal terms to all of the seller's customers who are competing with the recipient of the promotional assistance. However, the seller may justify his failure to provide equitable treatment on promotional services on the ground that he was meeting in good faith a competing offer of assistance by a competitor. The law does not require the probable adverse competitive effect to be shown for a violation to occur concerning equitable treatment in promotional affairs.

Relations with Suppliers

The firm's relationships with its suppliers are subject to regulation by the antitrust laws as well.

Price-fixing

Just as with competitors, the firm may not agree with its suppliers to fix or maintain the price in their transactions. While individual transactions obviously involve a negotiation of a price, agreements on maximums or minimums over a series of transactions involves vertical price-fixing which is illegal *per se*.

Buying from Competitors

When the company buys from someone with whom it also competes, price discussions present special problems. In order to avoid any semblance of competitor agreement on prices, great care should be used to limit any communications on price to what is actually required by the transaction under consideration.

Group Boycott

Two or more persons may not agree that they will not do business with a third person. Consequently, a firm should not agree to or coerce its supplier to refuse to deal with a competitor of the firm. It has even been held to be an illegal boycott for a group to agree simply to give notice to each other before doing business with the third person.

Reciprocal Dealings

A seller who may also be a large purchaser may not use his purchasing power to promote sales of his product to his suppliers. The use of trade relations and reciprocity is illegal, whether by coercion or by way of mutual patronage ("you scratch my back and I'll scratch yours") as a result of an understanding to the effect that purchases by each party are conditioned upon purchases by the other.

The law does not prohibit a firm from purchasing products from companies which purchase from it, but any understanding or agreement conditioning purchases on purchases by the other is illegal.

Other Prohibitions

Section 2 of the Sherman Act outlaws monopolies or attempts to monopolize. "Monopoly" does not mean having all of the business, but simply enough to give power to control prices or to exclude competition. Generally, control of more than 50 percent of a product or geographical market would be necessary before any question of monopolization could arise. Most charges of a Section 2 violation by small businesses involve some misuse or abuse of existing economic power. The exercise of such monopoly power to effectively keep others from entering into competition, or the coercion of preferential treatment from suppliers are typical abuses of monopoly power.

Section 7 of the Clayton Act prohibits one corporation from acquiring all or any part of the stock or assets of another, where in some product market or geographical area of the country, the effect of such acquisitions may be substantially to lessen competition. This section may prohibit mergers between competitors, customers, or suppliers. Section 7 may be invoked long after the acquisition is made if subsequent events indicate the likelihood of the prohibited effect occurring at the later time. However, it should be noted that Section 7 does not apply when one of the corporations does a wholly intrastate business. While the Sherman Act may still be applicable, it is not likely to be employed to prohibit this type of merger.

The Federal Trade Commission Act of 1914 created the Federal Trade Commission, an administrative body of experts, to determine and prohibit "unfair methods of competition." The Commission can determine that anything that violates one of the federal antitrust laws is also illegal under the FTC Act. However, the Commission is also empowered to find that anything which violates the spirit, although not the letter, of the federal antitrust laws is unlawful under the FTC Act. For example, the Robinson-Patman Act makes a buyer liable for inducing discriminatory prices, but not discriminatory advertising allowances. The Commission, nevertheless, has successfully established that this latter practice is unlawful under the FTC Act. The Commission's duties also include prohibition of false and misleading material in advertising, warranties and promotional activities. In short, the Commission's responsibilities include attacking most types of unethical business conduct. However, under the FTC Act the Commission's enforcement is limited to a cease and desist order, and no private parties can maintain treble damage suits for a violation of the FTC Act.

Finally, small businesses should note that many states have enacted their own antitrust laws. State antitrust laws vary considerably from state to state. However, in spite of the diversity of approach, the practices prohibited at the state level are comparable to those covered under federal law. The business manager would be well advised to investigate his state antitrust laws, since they may well have a specific prohibition of some practice or a rule of interpretation that differs from the federal law.

Conclusion

The concepts of antitrust law are constantly evolving with new court interpretations and congressional enactments. Hence, one should not assume because a certain action was permissible in the past that it will continue to be so in the future. Constant checking is required. Businessmen are accustomed to accepting "business risk." However, businessmen should not treat antitrust violations as a business risk, for the penalties both on the company and on the individual can be severe.

The preceding discussion has concentrated on what the antitrust laws prohibit and how they are enforced, with theme of prevention of any antitrust violations. An additional aspect of prevention involves realization that whatever you do, say, or write may be reviewed by some enforcing agency

(or a treble damage plaintiff) sooner or later. As a consequence, business executives should do their best to ensure that their behavior is consistent with the antitrust laws and that their writings are not subject to damaging misinterpretations. For example, a businessman may write, "our prices are in agreement with our competitors," when he really means his prices are independently determined, yet similar to his competitors. These inaccurate expressions can be misleading, and unfortunately give rise to inferences of illegal joint behavior. However, the destruction of damaging memoranda is a dangerous practice because it lends itself to unfortunate inferences if subsequently disclosed (and multiple copies abound in this age). However, papers may be categorized and once the precategorized useful life of such papers has terminated, no stigma attaches to their routine destruction. Documents prepared specifically for antitrust compliance, however, should be categorized with those documents of longest useful life.

While it is not possible within this article to cover all areas with which antitrust is concerned, the limited discussion herein should serve to identify areas of business decision-making which are constrained by antitrust laws. The early identification of involvement with competitive restraints and subsequent consultation with professional legal advice should provide most small businesses with sufficient protection to comply with antitrust laws.

Questions

1. *Antitrust laws should be obeyed because they are the law. Beyond this, what are some additional, practical reasons for obeying antitrust laws?*
2. *What are the four basic antitrust statutes?*
3. *What are the essential ingredients of a sound antitrust compliance program?*

41

Managing Xerox
for Technological Change

D. R. McCAMUS

". . . one can only manage change effectively if it is anticipated. You cannot afford to be surprised." Xerox works hard to avoid being surprised.

If Xerox is to be relevant in the future, it cannot rely on the same kind of luck that occurred with the discovery in 1938 of xerography, unfortunately not a reproducible event. We have created, and must continue to create, a planning environment that is conducive to a continuing stream of technological innovation. Not just any old inventions, thank you very much, but just those we really want because they lead us in the overall business direction we have selected.

Companies like Xerox are an extreme example of the need all companies feel today to manage technological change. Our very existence depends on our ability to create new technologies and capitalize· on them in the marketplace.

The processes Xerox has in place in an attempt to ensure that this all happens may suggest many of the basic principles which, I believe, are universal in their application. Fundamental to this entire process, in our view, is an effective longrange planning system. It seems obvious that one can only manage change effectively if it is anticipated. You cannot afford to be surprised.

Is not every successful company haunted by the prospect of the fate they have just delivered to their competitor? The thought of some new company en-

Source: The Conference Board RECORD, August 1975, pp. 32–34.

tering your market with a new concept that will put you on the defensive is an ever-present threat to every company today.

Why do so many well-established companies often fail to continue to innovate and maintain their position within respective fields of endeavor while others continue year after year to maintain that leadership? Inevitably you will find that the companies which have *effective* long-range planning systems are consistently leading the way. I say effective with emphasis because I have yet to meet a businessman who fails to agree that long-range planning is important. But I haven't met very many who are satisfied with their company's performance in this area.

Escaping Corporate Terminal Illness

In my view the chronic inability to produce meaningful long-range plans will turn out to be a terminal illness for many currently-successful corporations before the end of the Seventies.

Deciding the period of the long-range plan is of critical importance. Too long a time frame can cause frustration and destroy the whole impetus of the process. Too short-range will result in a false sense of security because it won't allow you to contemplate radical changes in your business environment that could occur as a result of technological or socio-economic changes. Ontario Hydro, for example, is now able to make a very quiet transition to dependence on atomic power-generation over the next decade because 20 years ago I made some investments in this technology. Twenty years ago! We feel at Xerox that 20 years is a must if you aspire to creating new technologies.

We call this the research planning frame. That is the time span required to initiate research in new technologies and see these technologies become a factor in the current operation of the company. Or, expressed differently, from the time we decide that we want to engage a new technology until we can export some business impact from these efforts, about 20 years will have elapsed. That is, if we are successful.

How do you come to grips with the next 20 years in a meaningful way? This is very difficult and requires an almost ruthless pursuit of something called a corporate "game plan." It is absolutely essential that a very specific set of company goals extending down to the level of the kinds of products and services to be offered in this time frame be developed. In my experience, this process requires a great deal of involvement from senior management, and in our case has required establishment of special staff groups and program teams from time to time to create and refine these concepts. At Xerox, this took the form of studies which resulted in a business concept called "the office of the future."

This contemplates a range of products employing a broad spectrum of technologies integrated in such a way as to provide a complete administrative communications system. This scenario is more than a series of blue-sky concepts. It is a road map that describes the kinds of technologies and the product missions involved. It spells out the logical candidates for the solution of the technological requirements. From this road map we can determine the kinds of technologies we must engage and the priorities that must be established.

From the original technology base of xerography, we have expanded our interest to include digital computers, facsimile transmission, typewriter technology, microfilms, color reproduction, mailing systems, and many others. Obviously, these technologies are directed toward office automation. Our concept of the future direction of the company has led us to make huge investments in obtaining command of a broad range of technologies which we believe will allow us to create entirely new systems concepts far beyond anything available today. If we have invested wisely in our research efforts, we should begin to see a variety of product options emerge.

A Marketing Context

A product concept is essentially the marriage of a technological innovation with an identified market potential. Herein lies the critical role of marketing—to play a vital role in providing the context for the entire research effort. At some point marketing must accept the leadership in the development process and become committed to the "concept." We at Xerox formalize this process into a phased planning system which originates with a product concept which has a defined market opportunity. On average we believe we can expect to see these concepts emerge as viable product options in about 10 years.

The system provides a framework in which management can evaluate new product programs. This process, in fact, is designed to provide a vehicle for surfacing worthy product concepts and assisting management in evaluating their worth, assessing progress at critical points, identifying alternatives, and committing resources at each stage of development.

In the *concept phase,* we document product ideas originating from the research frame. The product concepts are aligned with marketing goals. Comments are made on the concept by all operating units within Xerox in relationship to its value as a potential marketing opportunity. The commitments at this stage extend only to spending the funds necessary to proceed to the feasibility stage, where it must be demonstrated that the technical objectives can be met—in other words, that we can make it work.

In the *feasibility phase* we are looking for a demonstration that we will be able to manipulate the system to achieve an optimum balance. We must in fact know that we have the technology under control—most products that fail will do so for that reason. During this phase refinements are made on production costs and on ultimate service costs. Marketing now has some idea of pricing levels and can now attempt to refine market opportunity projections and also to estimate market penetration. We are attempting at this stage to evauate capabilities and unique features against the cost of the product and the price we will have to charge for it.

Depending on our experience with the market involved or whether, in fact, the market even exists at this stage, our confidence level in these forecasts can vary dramatically. Market research is now of vital importance. We also consider what we know or can guess about our competitors and their ability to develop viable products within the same time frame. There is still no firm commitment to the product program, but each operating unit involved—and in a multinational corporation such as Xerox, we are speaking of a worldwide participation—agrees or disagrees with the criteria for going on to the *definition phase* where we will now finalize the precise product specification right down to final weight, operating characteristics, reliability, etc.

Planning to Create Change

Manufacturing units are involved and bid on the production of the unit. This process is very impor-tant as it acts as a cross-check on the production estimates and ultimately provides a balanced work-load allocation. During this phase each operating unit develops a full-blown business plan for the product. This process is repeated with a host of product and business opportunities. If we have achieved our goals in this process, by now management's task will be to select from a range of options in order to meet their growth objectives in each of the business areas that are identified as prime targets for the company. This selection process distills down into a detailed operating plan for the near term. In our system this is a five-year projection.

The process is one that we believe can effectively manage technological change. In fact it is possible, in our view, to *plan* to *create technological change*. If this is done effectively, it is possible to provide the options management requires in order to plan a consistent rate of growth in perpetuity.

Questions

1. *How does Xerox define the role of marketing in technological research efforts?*
2. *Which single characteristic of Xerox management allowed the company to thrive in a rapidly changing, high-technology environment?*

42

Merchandise Shortages
and Retail Policies

STANLEY C. HOLLANDER

Some say that shortages of a variety of products are imminent. The manner in which the situation is handled at the corner-store level will have a major effect on public relations and the business climate.

Predictions of forthcoming merchandise shortages are plentiful. For example, almost every article in a recent special issue of a retailing journal contained a forecast that merchants would soon be plagued by shortages of important resale commodities.[1] Many business people and consumers probably remain unconvinced that serious scarcities will occur. Yet few can escape a nagging fear that they may occur.

The policies and strategies that retailers use to meet any significant future shortages naturally will be important to the retailers themselves (one of our largest business sectors) and will affect their public relations. Retailers' behavior also will affect their suppliers, who may have to adjust their own practices to meet retailers' needs. Also, some manufacturers and wholesalers, particularly those who are closely identified with their dealer networks, may want to influence the way stores handle their products. The entire business community has an interest in retailers' responses to shortages, since retailing is the business sector with which the public most frequently deals and by which it is likely to

judge the business system. Finally, as consumers we all will be affected by the way goods become available to us in the stores.

If shortages are, at the least, a distinct possibility, retail stores and other business firms would be well advised to develop appropriate contingency plans. This is so for two reasons.

1. When shortages do occur, they are likely to emerge suddenly and confusingly. We can all remember the hasty and chaotic responses to sugar, coffee, and gasoline shortages in the recent past. One week the shelves are full, the next they are empty. After the fact, of course, we can all explain how the problem developed and how it should have been foreseen. But this is often an artifact of hindsight. Moreover, many specific shortages are triggered by unanticipated events—bad weather just before the harvest, a twist or turn in international relations, a disaster in an important manufacturing facility, a breakdown in labor relations, or a sudden expansion of demand (perhaps in response to rumors of shortages).
2. The public may become hostile toward business under shortage conditions. Surveys show that the oil industry, whatever the merits of its position, has not exactly gained friends among the public under present conditions. Other businesses, particularly in the retail trade, could face the same problem. Some advance thinking will help in developing appropriate responses and thus aid in reducing or avoiding damage to the firm's public relations.

Source: Stanley C. Hollander, "Merchandise Shortages and Retail Policies," pp. 27, 33, *MSU Business Topics,* Summer 1978. Reprinted by permission of the publisher, Division of Research, Graduate School of Business Administration, Michigan State University.

Retailers are particularly susceptible to public ill will in times of shortages and have special opportunities to gain goodwill. Stores are the points of contact between consumers and production-marketing channels. Breakdowns in supply become manifest through the disappearance of familiar items from the store assortments. Consequently, consumers are likely to feel the merchants are at fault, possibly through some nefarious plot to manipulate quantities and prices, if the normal varieties of goods are not available at what the public considers normal prices. Consumers are not marketing experts, and they are susceptible to the historic distrust of retailers and their suppliers. The merchants, for their part, may reasonably complain that such feelings are unfair and that storekeepers are often blamed for things over which they have no control. Nevertheless, the fact that some widely held belief is unjustified will not necessarily remove its potential for damage. So merchants must not only *be* responsive in times of shortage, they must be *perceived* as being responsive.

Yet that is also the retailers' opportunity. Since most merchants are engaged in multiproduct businesses, they are uniquely positioned to engage in what has been called demarketing, that is, redirecting consumer demand in accordance with supply realities.[2] They can implement their slogan of being consumers' purchasing agents by suggesting substitutes and alternatives.

In thinking about how to cope with the commercial and public relations aspects of shortages, merchants should consider the relative likelihood of at least two possible scenarios.

The Two Scenarios: Scouts and Street Fighters

The Boy Scout–Girl Scout Scenario

The usual discussion of shortages envisages a rather good-natured, stiff-upper-lip, belt-tightening sequence of events. This may be labeled the scout scenario. If matches become scarce, we save them for really critical needs. For other occasions,

we learn how to make fires by rubbing two sticks together or by preserving an ember from one fire to the next. All of this involves some inconvenience, but we have also saved some money, had some good healthy stick-rubbing exercise, learned to be closer to nature, and increased our happiness.

The commercial version goes as follows:

1. Companies expect their buyers to display great resourcefulness and ingenuity in developing alternative sources of supply and substitute products. Nevertheless, some demands remain unfilled.
2. Companies exert a fair amount of demarketing effort, persuading and educating customers on the use of substitutes, the preservation of present supplies, and the reasons for the shortages of new goods.
3. To the extent that new supplies are not made available and consumers are not convinced to accept substitutes, people simply do without. Supply and demand may be equalized through price increases, or management may allocate goods in terms of some strategic objective. The usual scenario suggests, always implicitly, never explicitly, that the unsatisfied consumers accept their lot more or less uncomplainingly.

The Street Fight Scenario

The alternative picture is less attractive. Potential consumers struggle to increase their shares of the pie. Much of this struggle will take place at economic levels preceding purchase and consumption as the different sectors strive to increase their relative purchasing power. Labor, old-age pensioners, and other economic groups will seek to increase their wages, allowances, and incomes.

Some of the struggle will, nevertheless, be between the consumers and the retailer. There may be hoarding and accusations of hoarding, charges of profiteering, and demands for government intervention.[3] Consumers and/or consumerists may call for rationing or public distribution of scarce items. (Many U.S. municipalities opened public markets or conducted public sales of foodstuffs during the post-World War I inflation.)

Which Scenario Will We See?

The prime determinants between the two scenarios probably will be the severity and abruptness of the shortages. Some element of scarcity will usually occur even in markets that appear oversupplied. Even in the midst of a general glut or period of overproduction consumers usually will have to search aggressively if they want something that is out of season, is the very latest fad, or has been removed from production. Both merchants and consumers can easily cope with such fragmentary and transitory shortages. But a sharp, general restriction of supplies may have a different effect. We have become used to abundance and may have a low tolerance for frustration. If the shortages are widespread and come quickly upon one another's heels before we have had time to develop lower expectations, we may react angrily or meanly.

Another major determinant of the public's reaction may well be its perception of business behavior. Retailers and other firms probably will not win many friends during shortages, but they can minimize the hostilities the shortages will engender.[4]

Small and Large Retailers

The trade's moral and commercial responsibilities for preventing adverse perceptions of business conduct will fall upon both small and large retailers. Small and medium-sized dealers will probably have better access to local supply markets and will be more flexible in handling small odd-lots of merchandise as they become available. Some manufacturers may divert raw materials and production facilities from low margin, private label goods that mainly go to the large chains in order to increase or maintain the output of higher markup, national brand lines. Small dealers can be more flexible and more closely attuned to local consumer opinion in

deciding how to handle scarce products. But they also are likely to be personally acquainted with a larger portion of their clientele and subject to more interpersonal requests for preferential treatment. They may particularly need well-formulated and well-articulated policies because so many customers and friends will want to make their merchandise allocation decisions for them.

The large retailers will probably have the greater supplies of scarce merchandise, despite the factors discussed above, because of their ability to scour primary markets and to deploy skilled buying staffs. Also, many vendors will be anxious to retain their goodwill. But the big retailers will certainly need policies to ensure consistent and equitable handling of scarce items throughout their organizations.

Policies

No special policies are needed in the event of normal shortages, transitory and minor in scope, as discussed above. But management should have a set of guidelines for merchandisers to use when the scarcities exceed some tolerable level. These policies should deal with the procurement, distribution, pricing, and promotion of the items in short supply.

Procurement

In view of the possibility of shortages, retailers may want to reappraise the wisdom of depending upon a single vulnerable merchandise category, such as phonograph records or paper goods. The merits of depending upon a single supplier, perhaps as part of a channel system dominated by that firm, also may call for review. Presumably, under such an arrangement the supplier feels a special obligation to the affiliated retailers, but those retailers do become vulnerable to the supplier's own production or procurement difficulties. Some large retailers that have been following a policy of concentrating their purchases with fewer and fewer vendors will want to add additional sources of supply.

When the shortages occur, the larger retailers will try to help their suppliers maintain or increase production, and all retailers will seek new sources of supply. These steps will be much more difficult and require much more intensive effort than establishing positions with alternate vendors prior to the shortages. Once the scarcity develops, the firms with the desired products will not be anxious to take on new, temporary customers. But no matter how vigorous the procurement effort becomes, some cautions should be observed.

1. Diversion—Diverting supplies from basic public needs to increase the supplies of more trivial products would raise both ethical and public relations questions. Retailers probably will have few occasions to worry about these questions, since such high-priority sectors as medicine and national defense usually can easily outbid the retail trade for scarce items. Moreover, under a free market system, retailers and other firms are at liberty to seek whatever goods they can find. But there could be instances, perhaps in trying to persuade a vendor to ship merchandise to a store rather than to a charitable institution, in which zeal might outrun wisdom.

2. Ersatz—Substitute materials or supplies may be less satisfactory than the ones they replace. (Such goods came to be called by the German term *ersatz* during World War II.) Both as a matter of fairness and to preserve goodwill, the retailers would be well advised to warn customers of any anticipated difficulties, shorter life expectancy, or need for extra care. Such information should, if feasible, be permanently labeled in or on the goods, since consumers' memories of warnings at the time of purchase may be fleeting.

3. Overstocking—Handling ersatz items involves many commercial as well as public relations problems. The goods can easily prove unsalable if, as will often be the case, regular-quality lines reappear in the market. Therefore, merchants should avoid overstocking the ersatz, thus reducing the

danger of markdowns and the danger of appearing to stock shoddy goods.

4. Monopsony and coercion—The smaller dealers and their wholesalers, as well as other claimants, cannot be expected to sit idly by if goods flow mainly to large retailers. They will actively seek out their own supplies. They will also protest in various forums and seek new methods of allocation if they consider themselves badly deprived by the existing supply arrangements. Also, vendors will be resistant to excessive pressure. Consequently, the chain buying staffs will face the difficult task of aggressively seeking to obtain as much of the scarce items as possible without overstepping the bounds of propriety.

Distribution

Several cautions should be observed in distribution.

1. Allocation to stores—The multistore company will be strongly tempted to send the best supplies of scarce goods to either the most profitable stores or those most severely pressed by competition. But several years ago some supermarket firms yielded to a similar temptation with very unfortunate results. As many readers will remember, during the waning years of the trading stamp boom, many supermarket companies replaced trading stamps with games of chance—actually forms of bingo in which customers had to assemble sets of specially marked cards, cash register tapes, or coupons that spelled out a preselected winning word. The chains that tried to use these games to manipulate demand allocated disproportionate quantities of one or two vital letters to the stores at which they were most anxious to encourage trade. The strategy was soon discovered. The public, which might have been mildly amused by similar tactics in a carnival tent, was apparently quite annoyed by this behavior in supposedly respectable and friendly supermarkets. In any event, there was a hue and cry, and the Federal Trade Commission issued stringent regulations

concerning games of chance in supermarket sales promotions. Management should not only think in terms of equitable allocation, but also should announce, publicize, and enforce an equitable allocation program. Management should anticipate consumer and government complaints and investigations; it should be able to document its own performance.

2. Time of sale—Philip Kotler has suggested an important point for gasoline refiners. He notes that dealers might be tempted, during periods of shortages, to concentrate on selling full tankloads of gasoline during the most convenient hours for themselves and close their stations for the remainder of the day. He urges that dealers be guided to sell in smaller quantities over a longer time span, in order to preserve long-run goodwill. The latter is more in accordance with motorists' expectations of service station availability and assistance throughout much of the day.[5]

Other time-of-day decisions also will shape the allocation of items that are in truly short supply relative to demand. Putting the merchandise on sale during the morning and afternoon hours will tend to penalize working consumers; evening hours may reduce availability (or possibly eliminate an advantage for) full-time housewives. Long lines outside the store in the morning are undesirable, tend to attract people who want only the scarce items, and increase the probability of disappointment (and resentment) if the line grows too long. Some variation in the times at which the scarce goods are first placed on sale is probably wise.

3. Mail and telephone orders—Retailers who sell most of their merchandise over the counter but who take some supplementary mail and telephone orders probably will, and should, depart from a completely even allocation policy in favor of those customers who visit the store. Advertising the scarce supplies, either in the mass media or by direct mail, to induce mail and telephone orders would be unwise since it would lead to more orders than could be filled. Yet, the store cannot accept standing orders from its external customers without discriminating against its regular in-store shoppers. Catalogue firms and other mail order sellers will, of course, have to try to find ways of satisfying their regular mail and phone customers.

4. Rainchecks—If some advertised or other desired items are not available when customers come to the stores, retailers sometimes issue rainchecks, that is, written commitments of their intent and willingness to complete the transaction at a future time. Overissuance of rainchecks has been censured as an unsatisfactory substitute for adequate supplies of advertised price specials. Also, consumers may be suspicious of the advertising and raincheck combination as a device to induce two store visits instead of one. Even at best the checks involve some consumer inconvenience and disappointment. Nevertheless, they can be helpful in some shortage situations. Many dealers used them during the 1977 Christmas season, when unanticipated heavy demands caused temporary shortages of the most popular toys and home appliances, yet the gift-givers wanted to offer recipients some tangible evidence that the items would eventually be forthcoming.[6] Obviously, rainchecks can be used only when additional supplies can be expected with a high degree of certainty. Otherwise, they may become empty promises that simply aggravate consumer annoyance.

5. Purchase limitations—Restrictions on the quantity that an individual can buy often are used to spread the available stock among more customers, but can be troublesome. During normal buyers' market periods, quantity restrictions often are interpreted as evidence of predatory sales below cost (why wouldn't the dealer want to sell as much as possible?) and so are held in some ill repute. A family shopping together may insist that each member be treated as an individual and so obtain two, three, or four times the quota of an unaccompanied shopper. This claim will be appropriate in some instances, inappropriate in others. Or a customer may make repeated trips through the checkout line, buying a single unit at a time. Such tactics, however, tend to be self-limiting because of the time and energy the shopper must devote to obtaining the goods, possible social pressure from other shoppers, and perhaps some judicious inattention from store salespeople. The store staff can-

not act as a bureaucratic rationing board and hold formal hearings on each customer's claim. Consequently, management should provide some instructions on how to handle the difficult situations, probably with a recommendation for doing nothing at all except in the most flagrant cases.

Also, rules should be established governing sales to employees. The store staff will feel that it has first claim on particularly desirable merchandise. Management must decide how far it wants to accede to such feelings, both as a practical matter (supervisory, receiving, and clerical personnel will know about the arrival of the goods in any event) and as an aid to store morale.

6. Special cases—From time to time the firm may be asked to help with some emergency or pressing chronic need, such as locating a critically necessary scarce food item for a child with a rare disease. The retail firm usually will try to help in such cases if it can. The main problem in large organizations may be to make certain that the requests are not curtly denied at subordinate levels. Such assistance may be publicized, but managements will differ in their preference for doing so.

Promotion

Several cautions should be observed in promotion.

1. Advertising—Scarce merchandise will need little advertising or special featuring at the point of sale. Advance announcements, in the appropriate media, that such goods have arrived and will be offered to the public at a specific time would probably be the fairest way of letting the general public compete for the products. But such announcements could also have dysfunctional consequences. They could attract crowds of single-item buyers who will simply clog the store. (Also, advertising supplies of scarce products will tend to allocate the goods away from the store's regular customers.)

Advertising should be used to explain the firm's policies for handling scarce goods. And as advocated under the demarketing concept, it also may be used to encourage the purchase of substitutes and to cultivate goodwill.

Catalogue retailers have a special problem because of the time lags between catalogue preparation and expiration. Prices, merchandise features, and availabilities may easily change during this lengthy interval. Disruptions of the supply markets complicate the difficulties. Yet, mail order customers are normally very disappointed, and sometimes seriously inconvenienced, if their orders are returned unfilled. The mail order sellers, for their part, not only lose business if they cannot fill orders, but also incur considerable postage and clerical expense. Some mail order firms have found that the most satisfactory solution is to send the customer a slightly more expensive substitute, along with a note that waives the price difference and explains the company's desire to avoid inconvenience for the customer. This solution, in effect, involves a markdown of the more expensive replacement. A certain percentage of the substitutes are returned at the seller's expense. Enough sales, however, are completed and enough customer goodwill is retained to make this, in many cases, the least costly response.

2. Display—As noted above, scarce items do not need special display for promotional purposes. Shoplifting could be an especially acute problem for such goods, and high security displays may be needed.

3. Personal selling—Salespeople and other store personnel should be well briefed about company policies for scarce merchandise. The training problem is complex because of the large number of temporary and part-time workers. Furthermore, many retail workers are not overly loyal to their companies and, unless well educated on the subject, may be expected to create and pass on all sorts of rumors about how such goods are being handled.

Some retailers will experience another personnel problem that also will create difficulties for many manufacturers and wholesalers. Retail sales workers in automobile dealerships and in appliance, furniture, shoe, and clothing stores often receive all or part of their pay in the form of percentage commissions on sales completed, as is also the case with sales workers at nonretail levels. The commission system is designed to provide a strong incentive under normal conditions of abundance or over-supply. However, no incentive is needed when customers are clamoring for goods. In that event each salesperson's commission becomes a simple function of the quantity that he or she is allowed to sell. If the total amount of goods available will not provide adequate remuneration, management must institute some other compensation system for the salespeople it wishes to retain. If the commission system is kept in use, perhaps because the short-ages affect only a limited portion of the total assort-ment, management must devise some appropriate method for dividing among the affected sales work-ers opportunities to sell the scarce goods.

4. *Pricing.* The factory costs of scarce goods are likely to be higher than normal. Vendors will be less susceptible to price pressures, they may have to use more expensive components, and they may try to concentrate production in the more profitable model ranges. Production runs may be shorter and economies of scale weaker. Substitute ingredients may be more costly or more difficult to handle, and substitute suppliers may be less efficient or simply higher priced than normal sources. Acquisition may be more difficult, time consuming, and expen-sive, and in-bound shipping may take place in smaller lots and at higher unit costs. Promotion and inventory-carrying costs should be lower than nor-mal, but the net balance may still be above the reg-ular level.

Special prices, clearance reductions, and bargain sales will be unnecessary and inappropriate. (J. K. Galbraith has commented that many retailers car-ried on traditional bargain reductions through the first year of World War II, out of force of habit, despite clearly continuing shortages of supply.[7]) But consumers may simultaneously fight to obtain the goods and be sensitive to the prices being charged. Eagerness to obtain the items may cloak a sharp awareness, and a deep resentment, of any price that does not seem right. Pricing scarce goods, in the face of cost increases, must necessar-ily become a fine art. Decisions will be complicated by the widely recognized fact that when and if price controls are imposed, they usually take the form of a base-date freeze. That is, sellers are held to the highest price they charged on some specific date or during some specific period before the imposition of the controls. Consequently, the retailers and other sellers who exercised restraint during the base period are penalized in comparison to those who advanced prices sharply.

Concluding Observations

Both large and small retailers face serious problems in trying to maintain their businesses and their goodwill when merchandise shortages develop. The normal tasks of business operation become more complex, and there is the added burden of trying to appease consumer resentment. Some of the problems discussed above would disappear (and many new ones would emerge) if the scarce commodities were allocated by government. Then the government could also serve as a scapegoat for consumer complaints. But few merchants, large or small, are likely to welcome such an eventuality.

The policy decisions of the retail trade alone will not be sufficient to avert the street fighter scenario. All segments of society will have to act sanely and responsibly. But the mishandling of scarce goods at the retail level could easily precipitate demands for rationing and other stringent controls. Wise re-tailing practices based upon well-considered poli-cies could be a major factor, quite possibly the key one, in establishing an orderly adjustment to what-ever supply difficulties we may face in the future. Of course, that which is everyone's business can become no one's business. But the concept of en-lightened self-interest will become relevant for each retail organization during periods of shortages. Those firms that win reputations as consumer ad-vocates rather than as opportunists should gain valuable dividends in customer goodwill.

Notes

1. Leonard L. Berry, special issue editor, *Journal of Retailing* 53 (Fall 1977).

2. The seminal exploration of demarketing is in Philip Kotler and Sidney J. Levy, "Demarketing, Yes Demarketing," *Harvard Business Review* 49 (November–December 1971): 74–80.

3. Neissim Hanna, A. H. Kizilbash, and Albert Smart, "Marketing Strategy under Conditions of Economic Scarcity," *Journal of Marketing* 39 (January 1975): 63–67, discuss governmental intervention as a factor to which marketers will have to adjust if shortages ensue.

4. Philip Kotler, "Marketing during Periods of Shortage," *Journal of Marketing* 38 (July 1974): 20–29, discusses long-term profit maximizing strategies, primarily in terms of suppliers' programs.

5. Kotler, "Marketing during Periods of Shortage," p. 26.

6. "Backlogging Cuisinarts: Filling Orders with almost Empty Boxes," *Retailing Home Furnishings*, 12 December 1977, Sec. 1, p. 32; and "The Great Toy Shortage," *Newsweek,* 19 December 1977, p. 58.

7. J. K. Galbraith, *A Theory of Price Control* (Cambridge, Mass.: Harvard University Press, 1952).

Questions

1. *The two scenarios envisioned by Hollander for merchants coping with shortages are labeled "scouts" and "street fighters." Describe each.*

2. *During our recent experiences with gasoline shortages, which operating policies were adopted by retailers in your area?*

3. *As a small retailer aware of probable future shortages of scarce products, what actions could you take today to secure your market position and your customers' satisfaction?*

PART SEVEN

Strategic Decisions
and Selected Applications

Emery Air Freight, a pioneer in the air freight forwarding business, took advantage of a "strategic window" and has prospered. Emery targeted all of its marketing energies on the "emergency" segment of the air freight transportation market.[1]

U.S. electronics firms that were seeking new end market applications for their semiconductors revolutionized the watchmaking industry with digital watches and created a whole new breed of companies—assemblers of digital watches. Swiss and Japanese watchmakers at first viewed the digital watch as a U.S. fad but eventually realized that the revolution was real.[2]

In the past two decades, over 500 U.S. firms paid bribes or made questionable payments that totaled billions of dollars to win sales abroad. For example, Exxon paid nearly $60 billion, Lockheed $55 billion, and Boeing $50 million. The Foreign Corrupt Practices Act of 1977 prohibited bribery of foreign officials, political candidates, and party leaders. But, because other nations have no such law, American executives are contending that they are losing business to their foreign competitors.[3]

Colleges are facing critical problems of resource acquisition and allocation. The institutions that will survive and, perhaps, thrive will be those that establish mutually satisfying relations with their key publics. In other words, the best marketed universities will come out on top.[4]

Marketing occurs whenever individuals or organizations perform any of a broad mix of activities to bring about *exchanges*. In a business firm, marketing managers analyze market opportunities and develop an organizational

1. Darek F. Abell, "Strategic Windows," *Journal of Marketing*, July 1978, pp. 22–23.
2. "Digital Watches: Bringing Watchmaking Back to the United States," *Business Week*, October 27, 1975, pp. 78 ff.
3. "Business Without Bribes," *Business Week*, February 19, 1979, pp. 63–64.
4. Leonard L. Berry and Bruce H. Allen, "Marketing's Crucial Role for Institutions of Higher Education," *Atlanta Economic Review*, July–August 1977, p. 24.

marketing strategy that they believe will serve the market and contribute to the accomplishment of the firm's objectives. A comprehensive marketing strategy consists of the selection of one or more target markets and the formulation of a set of product, price, distribution, and promotion plans. There are many analysis and decision techniques available to the modern marketing manager to help develop marketing strategy. Still, the manager relies on intuition and artistic talents as well to develop strategies that serve the needs of both the consumer and the organization in an unstable and, at times, unpredictable environment. It is the responsibility of the marketing strategist to integrate the marketing mix with the environment to reach organizational goals.

The articles in Part Seven were selected to explain and illustrate the formulation and implementation of marketing strategy in business as well as nonbusiness organizations and in domestic as well as international markets. In the first selection, David S. Hopkins reviews several strategic marketing options available to the business manager who identifies a problem product or line. In the *Dun's Review* piece "Can Sears Come Back?" the giant retailer's reorganization plan and back-to-basics retailing strategy, designed to correct past errors and recapture lost profitability, is summarized. Then, Coca-Cola's diversification beyond the soft drink market into table wines, fruit drinks and water desalinization equipment is recounted in "The Strategy That Refreshes."

In "Industrial Marketing: A Niche on the Aisle," Martin Everett tells the success story of the Raymond Corporation, a very profitable (although perhaps not so glamorous to some) marketer of industrial trucks.

Philip Kotler, in "Strategies for Introducing Marketing into Nonprofit Organizations," discusses how organizations that specialize in the delivery of social services that are not adequately provided by either business or government can apply marketing technology and processes. Next, in "Marketing: One YMCA Attacks the Problems," Jacqueline Janders reviews the experiences of the Milwaukee YMCA as it developed and implemented a marketing plan.

The final two articles in Part Seven deal with international marketing. In "Ethics in an International Business Context," Hans Schollhammer calls upon the international business community to develop and enforce a strict code of business morality to combat growing public distrust and burgeoning legal regulations which are restricting U.S. business growth and success in foreign markets. Finally, Peter Vanderwicken, in "When Levi Strauss Burst Its Britches," tells of the danger of expanding rapidly into international markets without the necessary control over international distribution of products.

43

New Emphases
in Marketing Strategies

DAVID S. HOPKINS

The best hope that a company has to avoid future problems of poorly performing products is to develop a sound strategy for the entire product line. New emphases in marketing strategies are highlighted here.

When management critically appraises the company's market offerings, it often finds individual products or services that are weak or ailing in certain respects. Some may be failing to achieve their potential, perhaps through neglect; or it may be that a problem product was the pet of a previous manager, and no one has yet had the courage to put it to sleep.

Sometimes the reasons for a product's weakness are notorious and evident to everyone. But neither symptoms nor causes are always obvious in their early stages. Troublesome symptoms that marketers look for include low profitability; stagnant or declining sales volume or market share; risks of technological obsolescence; entry into a mature or declining phase of the product's life cycle; and a poor fit with the company's strengths or declared "mission."

A textile executive speaks for many in stating: "Management is more likely to recognize 'problem' products today than in the past because of the extreme pressures of the middle 1970s on escalating material, labor and capital costs. Many products that may have been able to limp along are no longer able to do so, because of their difficulty in competing for capital and today's attention to return on assets."

A few companies with a very large number of products routinely make use of the computer to flag any items being sold which fail to meet predetermined criteria. More often, though, signs of trouble are spotted when annual marketing plans are being prepared, or when periodic audits of marketing performance are being conducted.

Having identified a problem product or product line deserving special attention, management may have several strategic options:

Revitalize

Whether and how a product can be revitalized depends on the nature of its malady. By redesigning, remodeling, or reformulating the product, it may be possible to ensure that it satisfies customer needs better. Or there may be promising possibilities for repositioning it to appeal more strongly to a particular segment of the market, or to find new uses for it (as, for example, the makers of Arm & Hammer baking soda were successful in doing). Or there may be an obvious need to beef up the product's advertising or sales promotion support. Or relief may come by cutting unnecessary costs with which the product may have been burdened.

Source: The Conference Board RECORD, August 1976, pp. 35–39.

This article is based on research in progress, including findings from a recent survey of the Board's Senior Marketing Executives Panel. It is adapted in part from a talk given at a joint conference of the Connecticut Chapter of the American Marketing Association and the School of Business Administration, University of Connecticut.

While the option of revitalizing a problem product is the happiest one of all, the cost-benefits of such action clearly need to be watched. It may not make sense to spend much time and effort trying to turn around a relatively minor product.

Simplify and Prune

Sometimes, over the years, line extensions have been added to the point where low-volume items are dragging down the profit performance of the line as a whole. One marketing head recently expressed his belief that *any* company with an extensive line could trim costs and add to revenues by culling 10% of the varieties being offered. He felt that even deeper cuts could often be made, though perhaps not so painlessly.

Pruning has been popular in recent seasons, and companies generally have two benefits in mind when they do it. One is potential cost savings from longer production runs and reduced inventories. Another is the possibility of concentrating marketing, R&D, and other efforts more forcefully behind a shorter list of products. As one manager puts it, the age of selectivity has arrived.

"Harvest"

If a product reaches the stage where continued support can no longer be justified, the practice in some firms is to accept the inevitable and try to pull in a short-term gain by raising the product's price or lowering its quality. In less extreme situations, consumer product manufacturers may be able to cut off advertising, and turn a going brand into a maintenance brand; or they may successfully go in the other direction, engaging in heavy couponing, dealing, and offering of special incentives to the trade. Either way, the momentum of the product may continue for years, with sales declining but useful revenues still coming in.

Eliminate

A proposal to abandon a problem product often meets opposition—especially from the sales department. Sales managers are optimistic by nature, and sometimes they develop a "Micawber syndrome"; that is to say, they express the perennial expectation that sales and revenues will turn up if only the product is allowed just one more chance. Sometimes, too, a kind of bonding seems to develop between a salesman and the established product he has sold for many years.

These days, however, the discipline of planning is making it harder to duck a painful decision to eliminate an old product fallen on hard times. In many firms, everyone has become more prepared, when necessary, to bite the bullet of product elimination or divestment.

One executive describes the changing philosophy this way: "We no longer can afford to be 'all things to all people.' We are looking at items which have been only marginally profitable for years, but which we have continued to manufacture in order to be a 'full service' supplier; and we are now saying 'no' to the customer's order for these items."

Divestment is a preferred alternative, of course, to completely abandoning a product or a business, in cases where there are tangible assets in manufacturing, distribution, or customer connections with potential value to the right buyer. But within the unit to be divested, anxieties—even trauma—often need to be overcome.

Anticipating and Forestalling Problems

Many managers in trend-setting companies say that routinization of formally conducted product planning has paid off handsomely. For one thing, it often helps to identify emerging problems and forces management to consider decision options such as those just described. But awareness has recently been growing that dealing with a product problem after it has surfaced is a poor second-best to anticipating and forestalling it. And there is widespread concern that too many product plans

---

"Don't Prolong the Agony!"

Nowadays our company's management is more likely to recognize problem products and to take remedial action than they were in the 1960s. One of the reasons: we have more sophisticated financial management tools and a lot of them are off the computer. They readily show management when a product line is not earning a good return on the investment of funds, equipment, space, and time. In recent years, our management has learned that it seldom, if ever, pays to prolong the agony with a declining problem product. Experience with several products has taught us a lesson.

Marketing manager
a heating equipment producer

---

lack the substance to withstand future shock. For example, an unexpected turn in the economy has quite often torpedoed remedial plans and sunk them in midstream.

So there is extra emphasis, these days, on incorporating *defensive* features into product plans. The first line of defense is usually to put in place a system to provide early warning of any variance from planned objectives. It has become standard practice to monitor performance against target at milestone intervals throughout the year.

Also, many more firms are trying to gain flexibility through contingency planning against events not necessarily expected but which—if they did occur—could have a substantial impact (for example, introduction of a new product by a competitor, or a change in the market at a turning point in the economy). Some firms are incorporating into their plans probabilistic forecasts and allowing for a variety of contingencies. Then, if a signal is triggered, operational responses can be more quickly implemented than before. An important element here is that this altered course may represent a total change in marketing strategy.

Forestalling a problem can, of course, go beyond defensive measures. Even in industries such as packaged foods, where marketers frequently grumble that product life-cycles are becoming painfully short, some firms reportedly have made a success of product "stretch-out" by recycling a mature or declining product to give it a new lease on life. Giving the product a "face-lift," or making cosmetic changes in packaging or promotion, can sometimes work wonders.

There are many other possibilities, managements have discovered. For example, a "me-too" product with no clear advantage over the competition can sometimes be respositioned into a niche where it can offer a wanted benefit to a significant segment of the market. Or a commodity product, perhaps in chemicals or metals, may be given an extra twist that will bring it closer to becoming a specialty.

Investment Returns and Cash Flow

Inflation, high interest rates, and resulting pressures on corporate funds have been accentuating the importance of winning a return on investment that is up to or above the company standard. Also, many firms have been trying to pay for growth out of earnings. Although product managers have always been concerned with the cost structures for their products, they are finding themselves pushed even more than before to find ways to trim costs any way they can—by economies in manufacture, packaging, promotion, or distribution. Reviews of pricing arrangements are more frequent, and product managers are expected to be prompt in recommending increases whenever the returns seem likely to fall below target levels. On occasion, a product's price may be increased even though it is recognized that the trade-off will be a measurable loss in sales or market share.

Marketing management in many firms is working much more closely than before with executives in finance and accounting. There is a tendency in some cases to make product managers more directly *accountable* for the profitability of their products, to a degree beyond the somewhat looser *responsibility* for profits that was always theirs. A few firms have made a different change, according to report, by establishing a new position—that of marketing controller, whose job it is to audit marketing costs and prices, thus ensuring product managers' alertness to profitability.

The growing influence of corporate planners and financial executives over marketing plans is tending to set these plans within a broader perspective than was usual a few years ago. More clearly a means to attain *business* goals, the marketing plan in many companies may nowadays be properly described as a business plan.

Market Share Considerations

There's nothing new, of course, in marketers desiring a high market share. Yet, increasingly, marketers and planners are saying their objective is to win a *dominant* market share, to go for a position of market leadership.

Some are setting very high objectives for an acceptable share of market. For instance, one large industrial company aims for market share equal to at least 1¼ times that of the nearest competitor in any product/market category. It acts on the assumption that problems are likely to gather, and that divestment should be considered in any situation where its share is only 25% to 50% of the industry leader. Another firm, a producer of specialized equipment, always strives to be "number one" with a 50% to 60% share, but will accept a 30% share provided it is still the leader in the market. Other firms often set lower thresholds for dominating the competition.

Minimum objectives for share of market are being widely discussed, and sometimes used as a guide to strategic decisions. Olin Corporation, for example, is reported to have divested its aluminum

---

Responding to a Product Problem

At a housewares producer, when a product appears to be in difficulty, management asks these test questions:

To what degree is there continued consumer acceptance for this product?

Is the product still a viable element of our overall marketing and product strategies?

Does the product still fit with our strengths in sales and distribution?

If the problem is one of profitability, is there any reasonable short-term alternative to dropping the product?

If answers to these questions are discouraging, management moves to eliminate the product in a way that will minimize financial loss and ill will in the marketplace.

"Our main thrust at present," declares the firm's general manager, "is to plan and establish strategies which will preclude problem products in the future."

Consequently, additional questions routinely asked of any product are concerned with:

The adequacy of profit margins, including examination of the price elasticity of demand in the light of rising costs.

The sufficiency of arrangements for sales, distribution, and after-sales servicing.

The nature and size of promotional expenditures necessary to sustain the product in the marketplace.

Realistic evaluation of such factors as the stage of the product's life-cycle, the extent of household saturation for the product category, and the outlook for competitive moves and countermoves.

business on the ground that just maintaining its small, 4% share would have required big capital expenditures which, it felt, could be better employed elsewhere in the company.[1] And Westinghouse Electric is said to have sold its major appliance line because it reckoned it needed at least an additional 3% beyond the approximate 5% share it held before it could compete effectively against the industry leaders—General Electric and Whirlpool, which divided about half the total market between them.[2]

In the same vein, a senior executive of Clark Equipment Company was quoted as saying: "You make money if you dominate or are a strong second in an industry, like Caterpillar or Ford, or if you specialize within an industry. But not if you're third or fourth, or even a poor second."[3]

This consideration may also apply to small businesses or products. It is widely held that a product's leverage on the market is positively correlated with market share. In particular, high market share can be vital for distribution. A company marketing packaged foods, for example, may find its brand squeezed off the supermarket shelf unless it is among the two or three leaders. An exception may be a large product category, such as coffee or cereals. Another exception may arise if a company can position its brand into a special market segment that is also large enough for sell-through at a volume acceptable to the supermarket manager.

There are some, however, who criticize setting a high market share as a principal objective. They point out that there is often a trade-off between market share and profitability; and that more important aims are to sustain a product's contribution margin at the highest possible level, and to concentrate the company's efforts on markets which are rapidly growing.

But even these critics accept that an increase in the volume of production and sales of a product will probably tend to reduce costs per unit—at least up to a point. And, while market share and product volume are not the same, they often march together. Recently the significance of volume was reconfirmed by The Conference Board in a technical analysis of marketing cost ratios (total marketing expenditures expressed as a percentage of net sales) among a cross-section of manufacturers during 1971.[4] It was found, for example, that a manufacturer's business unit with a low volume of sales tended to have a heavier burden of marketing costs than did a unit with relatively higher sales.

Doing What One Does Best

According to Peter Drucker, "The first step in planning is to ask of any activity, any product, any process or market, 'If we were not committed to this today, would we go into it?' If the answer is no, one says, 'How can we get out—fast?'[5]

This very tough-minded attitude is more often held now toward products in an established line than in the past. There are general tendencies, too, for managers to be more conscious of the interdependency of all the products or services in a company's portfolio; to be more discriminating and insightful in choosing marketing strategies; and to be more aware that searching only for market opportunities, without also being sensitized to external risks and threats, may represent a new form of marketing myopia. A strong lesson of recent years has been that resources should be directed mainly to those products with the highest return and the best potential, even when this means "red-lining" the others.

The search is increasingly for uniqueness, some winning advantage that competitors cannot match. In the expression favored by McKinsey: "Where is the *leverage* in the company?" Someone else once said: "If what you have is an abundance of lemons, make lemonade." But the leverage, the unmatched advantage, need not be in a company's physical

1. *Business Week,* August 10, 1974.
2. *Forbes,* May 15, 1975.
3. *Business Week,* March 17, 1975.

4. Earl L. Bailey, *Marketing Cost Ratios of U.S. Manufacturers. A Technical Analysis* (The Conference Board, Inc., 1975).
5. Peter Drucker, *Management: Tasks, Responsibilities, Practices* (Harper & Row, 1974).

resources. It may be in low production costs, in technology, in distribution, or in marketing expertise, or elsewhere.

"The function of strategy is the function of management," declares a marketing vice president. In his company, as in others, the imperatives of strategic planning are now being "imprinted" on management behavior, overlaying the imprint of the customer-oriented marketing concept that was so widely felt in earlier years. Whereas, formerly, product plans and strategies prepared at the operating level were likely to follow a marketing mandate, it is now becoming common practice for them to internalize the needs and resources of the corporation as a whole. One planner speaks of his role as that of a catalyst, "To persuade line managers not to think in terms of product for product's sake, but rather in terms of product for the sake of the business," and "to shift from examining the components of a product's position to examining its dynamics."

Perhaps because strategic planning came of age during the turbulence of the first half of the 1970s, a number of firms first began to apply its precepts for spotting threats and overcoming weaknesses. Recently, there has been a subtle shift of emphasis in some companies from concern over downside risks to more frequent weighing of upside opportunities.

"We are concerting our efforts where they will do the most good," declares another marketing vice president. "There is much opportunity for expansion and improvement. All we need are people, time and money, and it has become critical to spend these assets wisely."

In seeking answers to probing questions of strategy, it is widely agreed, lies the best hope of avoiding problem products in the future.

Questions

1. Compare and contrast the following strategies: a. Revitalize; b. Simplify and prune; c. Harvest; d. Eliminate.
2. What does it mean to incorporate defensive features into product plans?

44

Can Sears Come Back?   LYNN ADKINS

The leaders of Sears, Roebuck & Co., the world's biggest retail marketer, made some serious strategic mistakes during the last decade that cost the firm market share and profits. Whether Sears can recoup those losses remains to be seen.

"It is a staid old company that got more and more staid while the rest of the world was passing it by," says one security analyst.

"It is a very strong company, and I believe it will have even more market clout in the future," says another.

The company evoking such a diversity of opinion among analysts is none other than Sears, Roebuck & Co., the world's biggest retailer. And it is no wonder they disagree. Of late, the Sears Tower in Chicago has been emitting a barrage of signals that would confuse even the most experienced Sears watcher.

During its 92-year history, Sears has been a pacesetter in the retail industry and a financial innovator in the business world. But in the last decade, its leaders made serious blunders, not only in merchandising strategy but in the overall management of the company. As a result, Sears' pretax profit margins slipped badly—from a high of 11.1% in 1969 to 7.4% in 1977. And by 1977, with merchandising profits seriously eroding, the company was

Source: DUN'S REVIEW, February 1979, pp. 68–72. Reprinted with the special permission of *Dun's Review,* February 1979, Copyright 1979, Dun & Bradstreet Publications Corporation.

getting fully half its earnings from its Allstate insurance and financial services subsidiaries.

To reverse this precipitous state of affairs, Edward R. Telling, who replaced Arthur M. Wood as chairman and chief executive officer in February 1978, lost no time unleashing the most comprehensive reorganization in Sears' history. Telling, a 33-year company veteran who had risen through the merchandising ranks, directed executives to present five-year plans for their individual operations, and these sometimes conflicting proposals were then melded into a massive five-year plan for the company as a whole. Among other things, it calls for establishment of a new distribution network, drastic reductions in merchandising staff, a massive cutback in the number of suppliers and less spending on advertising and promotion.

In line with these changes, Sears also announced that it would be relocating its women's fashions buying operation from New York to Chicago. The move, which caused much consternation among the buyers in New York, is an obvious attempt to not only streamline the operation but place it under closer scrutiny by headquarters. When completed, in August, the fashion buying staff will be reduced from 2,000 employees to around 800.

Managing Size

The drastic changes now planned for Sears are an attempt to overcome two fundamental problems. The first is the basic merchandising problem of how and in what markets the company should compete in today's retailing environment, with its cut-throat competition, low profit margins and ever-changing trends. The second centers on how top management can more efficiently control and monitor the far-flung network of an $18-billion-sales giant. "The phenomenon of size makes these changes essential," comments Joseph T. Moran Jr., who takes over as Sears senior executive vice president of merchandising this month. "The management of size is probably the single largest managerial problem that faces most American business."

Whether or not these changes will work has created widespread discussion and analysis among journalists, security analysts and the business community. The sheer size of Sears gives it a marked impact not only on the retailing industry but the economy in general. Sears accounts for about 6.5% of the total merchandising sales in the U.S., or about 1% of the nation's Gross National Product. Three out of four Americans shop at Sears, and the Sears credit card is the most widely distributed in the country—26 million accounts. In 1977 alone, 54.3% of the company's sales, or $9.3 billion worth, was purchased on credit.

Sears' huge nonretail operations also make it an important factor in the financial world. Its wholly owned Allstate Insurance Co. is one of the largest and most innovative in the industry, while Allstate Enterprises offers financial services and owns a major savings and loan association in California. Sears Roebuck Acceptance Corp., organized in 1956, raises billions of dollars every year to finance Sears credit operations, inventory purchases and expansion programs through the issuance of short-term commercial paper. Sears is also engaged in real-estate development via its Homart Development Co., which operates fourteen regional shopping centers and is a partner in eight others. Homart ranks among the top ten real-estate developers in the country.

Under its new merchandising strategy, Telling recently told a group of security analysts, Sears will stress profit gains as opposed to increases in market share and concentrate on the broad Middle America consumer market for staple durable and nondurable goods. As he put it: "We are not a high-fashion store. We are not a specialty store. We are not a dis-

counter or an avant-garde department store."

That, of course, sounds like the old Sears. From its earliest days as a mail-order operation, Sears built its reputation on basic quality products at reasonable prices. The Sears catalog linked the farmer's wife in Nebraska to the garment district in New York. And when the automobile and super-highway allowed the American public to leave the cities and locate in the suburbs after World War II, Sears was one of the first major retailers to build stores in these areas. Moreover, its slogans "Shop at Sears and Save" and "Satisfaction Guaranteed or Your Money Back" were much more than rhetorical promotion gimmicks. Early on, Sears offered customers attractive service contracts and a policy of readily accepting and exchanging returned merchandise.

As it grew over the years, Sears became not only the nation's leading merchandiser but a major purchaser of manufactured goods. To serve its huge and multifaceted needs, it formed unique relationships with suppliers running the gamut from General Electric Co. to small one-product companies. When Sears needed more merchandise than a supplier could provide, it often took an equity interest in the company by providing the needed capital to expand capacity. Working closely with these suppliers to get products made to its specifications and quality demands, Sears built up a roster of products carrying its label. DieHard batteries, Weatherbeater paints and Kenmore appliances are all products exclusive to Sears—and household words to boot. Currently, Sears partially owns thirty companies, from which it buys about 25% of its merchandise.

But while Sears' position as industry leader created advantages, it also produced some big headaches. Providing customers with service guarantees and freely accepting returned merchandise was an expensive way to do business. Besides that, by the late 1960s, when the discounters and major department stores began establishing outlets in suburban malls, the Sears stores built years earlier often looked shabby by comparison. The wide diversity of merchandise it carried also saddled Sears with heavy inventories at a time when specialty stores, with their much smaller stocks, came into vogue. And many of Sears suppliers began relying too heavily on the company for their sales and earnings increases, as well as for their basic product planning and promotion. As one analyst notes: "Some of the suppliers just lost the ability to run their own companies because Sears had done so much for them for so long."

Sears organizational and retailing strategies were no longer in step with a fast-changing marketplace. But in trying to catch up, it made blunder after blunder. In the late 1960s, the company embarked on a strategy of upgrading its soft goods, particularly women's apparel and accessories. While Sears' stores still carried staple wardrobe items like white blouses and sensible winter coats, they were increasingly stocked with high-fashion clothing and accessories. To some extent, Sears' image as a retailer changed almost overnight to that of a trendy and sometimes overpriced department store. Unfortunately, though, the company found that women who could afford high-priced clothes did not want to shop at Sears for them; and even more damaging, shoppers at the lower end of the market, dismayed by the rising prices, turned to discount stores like K mart. After 1970, Sears' market share began slipping noticeably.

Given the changing American lifestyle and the rise in consumer spending power, most analysts agree that Sears' upgrading strategy was correct. It was the implementation that was faulty. Says retail analyst Stanley H. Iverson of Duff & Phelps Inc.: "They just moved too fast and too far with the program. When you have that broad 80% of the market in the middle, you have to move very, very gradually."

Expensive Experiment

Worse, Sears then compounded the error by trying to quickly buy back the market share it had lost at the low end of the market. Early in 1977, it embarked on a massive campaign of special promotions and reduced prices—spending a whopping $504 million on advertising—to lure shoppers into Sears stores all over the country. The company did indeed regain some of its lost market share, but it

was hardly worth it. Droves of shoppers walked past the regularly priced merchandise to the promotional items, and analysts estimate that the company actually gave away about half of its 15% sales gain with no profits to show for its effort. This unprofitable experiment was allowed to continue through 1977 because, as one analyst says, "Management didn't have adequate controls to monitor it." Sears' retailing profits for the year fell 17.5%.

Telling agrees that the tactic hurt Sears. "The market share really doesn't of itself have anything to do with generating profit," he recently admitted. "It can be a very expensive way to dissipate profits."

But many analysts wonder whether Telling's back-to-basics strategy will work either. With competition from both specialty and discount stores, they say, Sears will be hard-pressed to attract the number of customers it needs for future growth. Analyst Ed Weller of Sanford Berstein & Co., for one, believes that Sears is being overly optimistic in projecting sales of $28.7 billion by 1983 from retail and catalog operations. That works out to an annual growth rate of a little over 11% a year from 1978's estimated sales of $16.9 billion. "I don't think they have nearly as much growth in front of them as they think," Weller contends. "Despite all the proposed changes, there is no reason to believe they'll be able to do in the future what they have not been able to do in the past."

Many other analysts agree, and what particularly worries them is whether Telling and the new management team he has put together will be able to achieve the structural and organizational changes necessary to make the new merchandising plan work. For the first time in years, management is attempting to gain control over the layers and layers of bureaucracy that have grown up in an empire of almost 900 retail stores, 12,000 suppliers and 400,000 employees.

It will not be easy, given the widespread autonomy that had accrued to the Sears managers in the field and their almost total lack of communication with headquarters. For years, store and regional managers made the bulk of the merchandising decisions, and managers were known to drop whole sections from stores without informing headquarters. Even decisions on new sites for stores were made at the territorial level. And if the Midwestern territory, say, accounted for 25% of overall retail sales, it was likely to receive an equal percentage of expansion funds even if another region had greater potential for growth. To put a stop to all that, a department of logistics has been established at headquarters to centralize the planning and monitoring of everything from sales and inventory to store planning and distribution.

With the field managers running their own show, inventories also got out of hand. Many stores kept their stock at much higher levels than demand warranted, adding considerably to overhead costs. To control inventories, Sears is setting up a centralized distribution operation. Eleven new regional distribution centers will be built to receive all merchandise purchased and ship it directly to the stores. With this system, says Jack F. Kincannon, senior vice president of finance, merchandise can be shipped almost daily and the stores can operate with much lower inventory.

Independent Buyers

The company's elaborate buyer system was also out of control. Technically, the buyers were part of corporate staff, but they too developed an independence over the years because of their close contact with store personnel and suppliers. The buyers were responsible for providing the stores with merchandise and served as liaison between the stores and suppliers. But they were not held responsible for profits.

In their efforts to keep the stores and suppliers satisfied, abuses crept in. For example, if a long-time supplier came out with a new product, a buyer might encourage the stores to take the merchandise whether they needed it or not; the stores might then promote the product with cut-rate pricing, while regularly priced competitive merchandise sat on the shelf.

One practice that turned out to be particularly destructive was overbilling. Sears' buyers routinely overcharged the stores for much of their merchandise, putting the surplus over what the goods actually cost into a special account for advertising and promotion. As Sears grew, so did "account 599," as it was known in company parlance—hitting $1 billion a year recently.

But overbilling created pricing distortions to the point that store managers often never knew the true cost or profit on many items. On the one hand, the stores eagerly used the funds for greater and greater markdowns and more and more advertising. On the other, because the stores calculated their standard markups from the prices the buyers were charging them—which averaged around 15% above normal—many items in Sears stores ended up being overpriced compared with the competition. Account 599, too, has been eliminated at Sears. "What good there was in it was far outweighed by the evils that . . . had entered into it," Telling admits.

Under the reorganization, Sears' 640 buyers will be held accountable for the profitability of their operations. In concert with store managers and the corporate staff in Chicago, they will be responsible for formulating purchasing strategies and product development. And as the buyers take on more responsibility, the bureaucracy of sales coordinators in the field, which had mushroomed beyond control, will be considerably smaller and less important. According to *Crain's Chicago Business,* which recently published details of the five-year plan, Sears expects to drop 150 or so sales coordinators and assistant marketing managers, or almost half the current staff. The company has already simplified its field organization from 125 administrative units to fifty. And the number of merchandising groups that oversee the buyers have been reduced from 48 to nine. As a result, Sears has projected that it will more than double sales per employee by 1983.

Intrinsic to the mismanagement of the buying operation was Sears' complex relationship with suppliers. To some extent, buyers worked so closely with the suppliers that many of their purchasing decisions did not make good business sense—a problem that became compounded over the years. As Telling recently told security analysts:

"I've become a little testy with some suppliers and have suggested they get another customer, get two or three more customers. There's just nothing that I read in any of the fine print that says we have to build inventories we don't need so that they can happily earn great sums of money. I think that some of them probably should settle down and run their business and not expect Sears to run it for them."

One of the results of the system is the sheer number of suppliers, which seems to have just grown like Topsy. This happened, Joseph Moran explains, because many suppliers did not expand at the rate that Sears did and were not able to supply certain items the buyers wanted. So the buyers looked elsewhere, and the result was a proliferation of suppliers that sold perhaps only one or two items to Sears rather than whole product lines. This created added bureaucracy and paperwork. Worse, because Sears accounted for a very small portion of these suppliers' sales, it had a hard time enforcing its traditional quality controls.

Sears has already cut the number of suppliers from 14,000 to about 12,000 and plans further reductions. Much of this will no doubt come from natural attrition in line with the company's plan to drastically reduce the number of products it carries—from 60,000 currently to around 35,000. Its strategy, as noted, will be to concentrate on the most popular basic merchandise, leaving the frills to the specialty stores. "It may stock only nine bicycles rather than fifteen," says one analyst. "But those nine will cover all the important price points and be the most popular bikes."

More Diversification?

While Telling and his management team are busy trying to put Sears back on the course, there are also indications that the company plans to continue its long-time diversification policy with another major acquisition. Philip J. Purcell, vice president for corporate planning, will not elaborate on analysts' speculation that the company is looking into such areas as food processing and energy. But he does allow that Sears would "definitely consider putting its funds into a related or diversified area that would give it a reasonable long-term rate of return."

Meanwhile, the company can garner at least a glimmer of hope from an improved performance in 1978. In the third quarter, operating profit margins increased (to 8.5%) for the first time since the first quarter of 1976. And analysts estimate that Sears' earnings for the full year climbed at least 7% to $2.80 a share on a 4% increase in sales to an estimated $17.9 billion. With most economists predicting a softening in demand for mass merchandisers like Sears, the company is expected to show minimal sales growth this year but a continuing improvement in profit margins. And Purcell says that management expects retailing profits as a percentage of total business to increase steadily over the next five years.

In the coming years, of course, analysts will be scrutinizing Sears' results quarter by quarter for signs that its new strategy is working. Purcell admits: "It will be at least five years before it will be very clear whether we did or did not do it."

Questions

1. How do you perceive Sears's market position relative to other major department store retailers in your area? Are your perceptions consistent with the target position of Edward R. Telling?
2. What, in your opinion, were some of the reasons why Sears's executives may have led the firm away from its market position of the 1950s and early 1960s?

45

The Strategy That Refreshes?   BRIAN McGLYNN

The Coca-Cola Company earns nearly 75 percent of its profits from a single product—Coca-Cola. In light of the growing competition Coca-Cola faces from Pepsi Co and Seven-Up, is a change in Coca-Cola's strategy appropriate?

At the north end of Atlanta, far from the gleaming towers of that city's convention-center downtown, stands the low red-brick building that has served for more than half a century as world headquarters for The Coca-Cola Co. and as its local syrup-making plant. Built in 1920, the building is somehow symbolic of the company—solid, unchanging, in some ways even quaint. Soon Chairman J. Paul Austin, 63, will move his offices from that five-story office complex and plant building into a white 26-story high-rise office tower next door. Will Coke enter a new corporate age as well?

The question might be better put: *Should* Coke change anything? With revenues of about $4 billion this year and nearly $400 million in net earnings, Coke is still averaging the 9% to 10% net margin on sales and the 23% to 25% return on stockholders' equity it has been accustomed to for more than ten years. It produces nearly half the soft drinks sold in the world. Its 37% grip on the U.S. market has remained unshakable for decades, despite the rise of scrappy Pepsi-Cola, whose 318% growth since 1968 has come, not at the expense of its larger rival,

but at that of smaller companies like Royal Crown Cola and many local soft drink brands.

All of which leads to yet another question: Should *any* company, no matter how profitable and consistent, be getting nearly 75% of its profits, year after year, from a single product?

It's a nice kind of question to worry about. And if any company can afford to take its time coming up with an answer, it's The Coca-Cola Co. The answer, nevertheless, in Paul Austin's view, is a surprisingly urgent "No." Even without questions of long-range balance, Coca-Cola's old formulas for doing business no longer suffice. The world has changed around Coca-Cola, he argues, and the company is changing slowly to accommodate the new order.

Coke's biggest market, the U.S., is the most developed. This year, its margins were squeezed—through the end of the third quarter revenues were up 18%, net up 13%. Corporate overhead was up 20.6%, some of it from a reorganization of foreign operations, but some from an increased marketing burden to meet new competition. From Philip Morris, for example, which terrorized the beer business when it bought Miller Brewing and pushed it past Coors, Pabst and Schlitz to number two in the industry, and now owns Coca-Cola competitor Seven-Up. From Pepsi Co, which has become a conglomerate with a growing war chest for marketing battles aimed sharply and specifically at Coke. Problems are coming from Coke's 760 domestic bottlers (1,300 worldwide) as well. Never entirely docile, they are no longer small mom-and-pop operations, but rather growing conglomerates or multiplant companies, big in their own right, that

Source: Forbes, November 27, 1978, pp. 81–84. Reprinted by permission of FORBES Magazine.

are starting to flex their negotiating muscles.

Austin's biggest problem currently is getting those domestic bottlers to agree to a new contract to replace Coke's 58-year-old pricing formula for the syrup it sells to them. Coke's practices are unique in the business. Other soft drink makers, like Pepsi, Royal Crown and Seven-Up, sell concentrate—syrup without sugar—to their bottlers. Those bottlers put in the sugar themselves or sometimes use fructose, a less expensive sweetener. Coke does this overseas, too, but in the U.S. the only thing it allows bottlers to add is the carbonated water. The syrup comes complete with sugar, and fructose is out. "It produces a chemical reaction with the Coca-Cola which throws the flavor off," says Austin. "Why? Well, the chemists know, and I take their word for it."

Coke's bottlers would like to have the same freedom as Pepsi's bottlers to put in their own cane sugar or use an alternative sweetener should an acceptable one be found. They're also apprehensive about making any changes in the pricing structure.

Coke bottlers have the means and the motive to hang tough. A typical operation's margin, says William M. Williams, a member of the board of governors of the Coca-Cola Bottlers Assn., ranges between 14% and 18%—some of the best Pepsi bottlers are well below that. And many of Coke's bottlers now have size as well as profitability to bolster their hands. Coca-Cola Bottling Co. of New York, for example, is a $315 million company listed on the New York Stock Exchange. Coke of Los Angeles is a $219 million operation that is now a subsidiary of $1.9 billion Northwest Industries. As the bottling business consolidates more, their negotiating position can only strengthen.

"The contract negotiations should have begun when I took over," says Austin, who became the boss in 1962. "I had other things to do first, but in retrospect I should have gotten busy on this the first day."

Getting copacetic with its bottlers is crucial to Coke because it may soon be facing the kind of challenge it has rarely faced before, even from Pepsi. It's not Philip Morris' entry into the soft drink business that troubles Austin. "The Seven-Up Co. was well run before Philip Morris bought it," he says in the measured, softly accented phrases of a man born in LaGrange, Ga. "As far as I can see, nothing new has been added." Rather, it's the possibility of radical change in the entire franchise bottling structure that may be forced on Coca-Cola and other syrupmakers by the Federal Trade Commision.

Early this year the FTC ruled that exclusive bottler territories—a cornerstone of the present franchise contract with the bottlers—were anticompetitive and ordered the boundary lines erased. Austin believes the decision will be overturned. "It does not increase competition," he argues. "On the contrary, [it] will have the opposite effect." But, if it is not overturned by the courts, Coke may soon be facing a smaller number of bigger, stronger bottlers.

Austin must sort out relations with his bottlers at a time when the U.S. soft drink market is reaching close to a saturation point (which a Coca-Cola spokesman prefers to characterize as reaching "a more developed stage"). Last year, on average, each man, woman and child in this country drank 550 eight-ounce servings of soda pop. How much more can they reasonably be asked to swallow? Better growth prospects now lie overseas, where Coke has, of course, long been. "We're not multinational," Austin insists, "we're multilocal." Big pushes are being started in Japan and Brazil—both countries with relatively low soft drink consumption (*see chart*), high disposable income and large populations. Margins are high, too. In Latin America, including Brazil, Coke gets nearly 25% pretax; in the Canada and Pacific group, of which Japan is a part, margins approach 19%—lower than Latin America, but still better than the U.S. market corporate average of 13%.

In the Soviet Union, Coke will be the exclusive supplier of soft drinks to the 1980 Olympics in Moscow. But that's only a foot in the door at best. Once the Olympics are over, the company will be allowed to distribute only the relatively insignificant Fanta (fruit flavored) and Sprite (a 7 Up–type drink) sodas in Russia. Pepsi beat Coke to the punch with an exclusive contract signed in 1972, in the spirit of

Think global

Per capital consumption of soft drinks is higher in the U.S. than anywhere else. Holding 37% of the saturated U.S. market, Coca-Cola's best growth prospects in soft drinks obviously lie overseas.

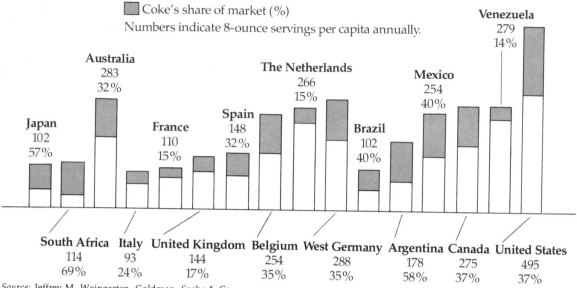

□ Coke's share of market (%)
Numbers indicate 8-ounce servings per capita annually.

Venezuela
279
14%

Australia
283
32%

The Netherlands
266
15%

Mexico
254
40%

Spain
148
32%

Japan
102
57%

France
110
15%

Brazil
102
40%

South Africa   Italy   United Kingdom   Belgium   West Germany   Argentina   Canada   United States
114   93   144   254   288   178   275   495
69%   24%   17%   35%   35%   58%   37%   37%

Source: Jeffrey M. Weingarten, Goldman, Sachs & Co.

detente, by Nixon confidant Donald M. Kendall, chairman of Pepsi Co.

"The competition has exclusivity until 1984," says Austin, not a trace of Orwellian portent in his voice, "and our contract is limited to serving the Olympic facilities only. In the future, we'll negotiate for Coca-Cola itself." Perhaps having Georgian Jimmy Carter, a Coca-Cola fan, in the White House will help.

Austin is also trying to stick a foot in Arab doors. Long on the Arab boycott list for continuing operations in Israel, Coke nevertheless is quietly talking with Egyptian leaders about resuming distribution there.

For Coca-Cola, then, the soft drink business promises a full measure of new stresses in bottler relations and old problems in competition. But it also promises ongoing profits of a high order, higher than most other businesses yield, and reasonable prospects for some growth. On balance, it could be argued, Coca-Cola continues to be sitting pretty and could not do better than concentrate on its syrup concentrate business, let others go crazy

trying to make an acquisition program work and make its already fat dividend payment (58% of earnings) even fatter.

Austin thinks otherwise.

"Coca-Cola must be a changing company," says Austin. "So must any large company. You can't sink anything in concrete because that attitude will slowly seep through to all levels of the organization and all of a sudden you're lying dead in the water."

Coca-Cola has, of course, been pushing beyond the pop business for some time now. It has acquired "market leaders," as they say in the business schools, elsewhere in the food business (Minute Maid, Hi-C fruit drink, among others). It is dipping a more than tentative toe into acquaculture. Through its Aqua-Chem subsidiary, bought in 1970, it now makes 90% of all the water desalinization equipment in use today in the world.

All told, Coca-Cola's nonsoft drink operations now add up to 24.1% of total revenues. That's quite a sum—about $858 million. But they contribute just 11.4% of total operating profits—about $72 million. Austin acknowledges the uneven profitability of some of the non-soft drink operations. But he continues to believe that for the long range the company must continue to deploy capital elsewhere. If others point to some past acquisitions as drags on overall profitability, he points to what is possible in the future. He cites Coke's burgeoning plastics business as an example. "We've started a plastics business by rolling together four separately purchased units," Austin says. "It's small, and we're still looking around, but it's the best return on investment we make."

Nothing, perhaps, makes Coca-Cola's ambitions clearer than its entry, in 1976, into the wine business with the acquisition of Taylor Wine Co. The Taylor deal represented not only a new market but, as it has turned out, a departure in style.

Once exclusively a New York State wine producer, headquartered in Hammondsport in the heart of the Finger Lakes grape country, Austin quickly moved to establish Taylor in California as well. "Our plan of action was to cover the spectrum," says Austin, "so we went to California and bought Sterling and Monterey Vineyards. Both of them are boutique wineries—very high quality."

In addition to Taylor, workhorse brands like Taylor Table Wines, average New York State table wines; and its Great Western Champagne, a top domestic brand; Sterling and Monterey give Taylor premium-priced California vintage wines as well. Advertising strategy for California Cellars, the new vintage line's common name, shows Coca-Cola in a new, startlingly aggressive mood. It wasn't so long ago that Coke-men like Austin did not deign to use the name of a competitor. (Pepsi was always referred to as "The Imitator.") The current Taylor's

California Cellars television campaign consists of a filmed wine-tasting test in which California Cellars' Rosé, Burgundy and Rhine were judged by an independent gang of tasters and found to be "better" than competing top-of-the-line jug wines from Sebastiani, Almadén and Inglenook, which are mentioned by name. (A film of the Chablis taste test, however, will not be seen: California Cellars' entry came in second to Inglenook.)

Austin's rationale for going after the jug wine market is simple—these wines are 54% of the growing domestic market. "They'll be the base of our pyramid," he says. The rest of the pyramid will consist of the even more expensive Sterling and Monterey vintage wines.

Clearly, wines don't fit the staid Coke way of doing things. If they go well—and perhaps if they don't—soon Coke will care even less for old styles, preferring to get on to new business.

Questions

1. *Coca-Cola limits its bottlers' sales activities to exclusive territories and sells them its Coke concentrate complete with sugar. This latter practice prevents bottlers from substituting fructose for sugar—a common practice among Pepsi, Royal Crown, and 7 Up bottlers. Should Coca-Cola be allowed to impose this limitation on the bottlers?*
2. *What if any changes in Coca-Cola's marketing strategy would you recommend in light of changing competitive, legal, and social factors in the environment?*

46

Industrial Marketing:
A Niche on the Aisle
MARTIN EVERETT

The Raymond Corporation pulled off an industrial mar-
keting coup when it was the first to market a lift truck
that could navigate the narrow spaces in warehouses.
The competitors are crowding in now, however, and it
is time for Raymond to explore new opportunities.

It's only a question of time before they make a blockbuster movie filmed entirely within the confines of a modern industrial warehouse. It will be called *Cube,* naturally, reflecting the current preoccupation with getting every last inch of storage space out of (or into) these sprawling structures. The heroine, a prematurely gray order-entry clerk in her thirties, will be spirited to the nether recesses of the building by the agents of Waste Space. The authorities from Materials Handling zip about, frantically beeping the horns on their electric trucks, but they are stymied. So efficiently has this warehouse been built that their squat vehicles can't get down the side aisles. This clearly is a job for a narrow-aisle specialist: the Man from Raymond.

Whimsical as this may sound, it points up some of the reasons why Raymond Corp., a $60 million company from Greene, N.Y., has acquired a reputation as a fearsome competitor in the $1.5 billion industrial truck business. Its products are best known to the public as forklift trucks, but that category includes such elaborate gear as specialized, $40,000 sideloaders used for hauling steel bars, and "wire-guided" systems in which computer-controlled vehicles make their rounds by following an electric circuit embedded in the concrete floor.

Raymond's claim to fame is that early in the game it recognized a dominant trend in warehouses and industrial storerooms: to get the most out of a building's cubic capacity, it was necessary to put the rows of storage racks as close together as possible. But before that could be done, someone obviously had to come up with a lift truck that could maneuver in closer quarters, so Raymond developed the first "narrow-aisle" lift truck and has been specializing in this segment of the market ever since. So successful has it been, in fact, that it is recognized for its achievements on several fronts:

Carving out a niche in the market that enables it to maneuver under the guns of much larger competitors.

Achieving sales growth that has consistently run ahead of the industry. During the last 10 years, its sales have climbed at a compounded rate of 12%, compared with 6.6% for the industry in general.

Compiling a record of profitability that is the envy of many of its larger competitors. Last year, for example, sales climbed 29%, to $60.6 million, and earnings rose 22%, to $4.6 million, or 7.6% of sales.

Introducing a string of product innovations that has allowed it to strengthen its hold on the narrow-aisle segment of the market.

Building up a franchised dealer organization capable of educating customers in the special benefits

Source: Sales & Marketing Management (March 1978), 39–43. Reprinted by permission from *Sales & Marketing Management* magazine. Copyright 1978.

of Raymond's line, as well as providing service to back up the sale.

Creating separate divisions for sales and marketing to provide better support for dealers. The reorganization, which took place last summer, has also strengthened marketing research and planning and made it possible to hew more closely to the ambitious financial goals set forth by top management.

"Our main strength is being able to provide a wide variety of truck configurations within each of our specialized product lines and produce them profitably in a reasonable time," says Rocco Nenarella, manager of Raymond's newly formed Marketing Div. "We are, in effect, a large job shop." Nenarella, an engineer who got into marketing through product development work, sees the reorganization as another step in the company's evolution in the marketplace.

"By having a separate marketing group, we will be able to provide better support for our own salespeople and for our dealer organization," he says, noting that there has been a general strengthening in all areas of his operation, which includes such diverse functions as marketing research, advertising and promotion, training programs and technical publications, systems engineering, and, thanks to the increasing role of the computer, systems software.

J. R. (Jay) Furgason, manager, Sales Div., thinks the reorganization also puts Raymond in a better position to pursue the long-term goals set forth by top management: "If we are supposed to be a $150 million company in five years, we need to function that way now," he says, observing that the step will also keep the sales operation from putting too many demands on various marketing functions. "Under the old set-up," he says, "if you had a training manual to be updated, it might not get done because everyone was concerned with making the next sale."

Furgason oversees a sizable in-house staff that is geared to helping the company's 42 franchised dealers achieve their sales objectives. "When we talk about long-term sales growth, what we are really saying is that the *dealers* have to do that. That being the case, we have to give them the wherewithal to get the sales."

Despite its small size, Raymond is capable of mustering considerable resources to serve the market sector that it has chosen as its oyster. "Our overall corporate strategy is to dominate those segments of the market where our large competitors are the weakest," says president George G. Raymond Jr. "We are not trying to replace them in their leadership position by entering areas where the major companies have great strength." Thus, although it obviously doesn't have unlimited funds, the company is increasing its budget for such things as advertising and promotion, product manuals, and dealer sales seminars, all of which will be directed at explaining the benefits of its specialized, narrow-aisle product line.

This still leaves the dealer salesperson with a complex sales job. Bruce Boldrin, manager, marketing training and technical publications, notes that "from the beginning, Raymond has operated with a two-step sales strategy: (1) Sell the concept. (2) Follow up with the product." Because even the humblest pallet-handler in its line represents a capital investment for the customer, Boldrin's department keeps dealers primed with information about how Raymond can help the customer save space and increase productivity.

As an example, he cites the Electote, an automated cart that hauls stacked pallets along a wire-guided course from the loading dock to the warehouse interior. "In our field training sessions, we teach salespeople how to position Electote as a product that's designed for a moderate level of activity," says Boldrin. "They have to be able to convince the customer that it requires less capital than the conveyor belt that's used for continuous operation and that its operating cost is lower than a manned machine."

Against the Giants

How long Raymond will be able to grow in its selected markets without getting stepped on by one

*How Raymond split Sales and Marketing so they could
work together*

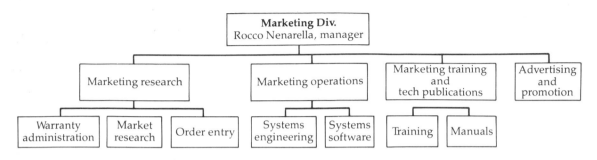

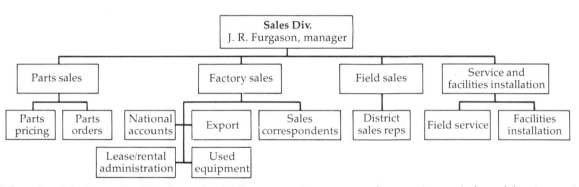

Where does Sales leave off and Marketing begin? Few companies can answer that question precisely, and there's a good reason: although each has its specific character, the two functions are so intertwined that they are in daily contact with each other. In a small industrial company like Raymond Corp., the distinction is even finer because instead of fielding its own sales force, the company has a network of 42 franchised dealers with a combined force of 325 salespeople. Thus the prime task for both the Sales Div. and the Marketing Div. is to support the dealer sales effort and monitor results.

The main difference between the two functions, of course, is that Sales maintains direct contact with the dealers. For major decisions, this will involve one of Raymond's four district sales representatives. "The district guy is our man in the field, and he's also the dealer's man at the factory," says Jay Furgason, manager, Sales Div. Daily contact with dealers, however, is the responsibility of sales correspondents, a corps of six young salespersons at the company's Greene, N.Y., headquarters.

Because industrial trucks represent a sizable capital investment for the customer, a sales correspondent may work with a dealer for two or three months on one sale. During that time, he is free to go virtually anywhere in the company to seek technical advice and other information. Often, this means calling on the people in Marketing Operations for guidance in systems engineering and systems software, but it could also entail putting the dealer directly in touch with engineers in the design and manufacturing departments.

One of the interesting aspects of this system is that Raymond encourages its correspondents to move out into the dealer network as soon as possible. "When one of our dealers needs a salesman, this is one place he looks first," says Furgason. "This works out better for everyone. If a person remains a sales correspondent for more than a year and a half, he has a problem and so do we."

Knowing where you stand in the market

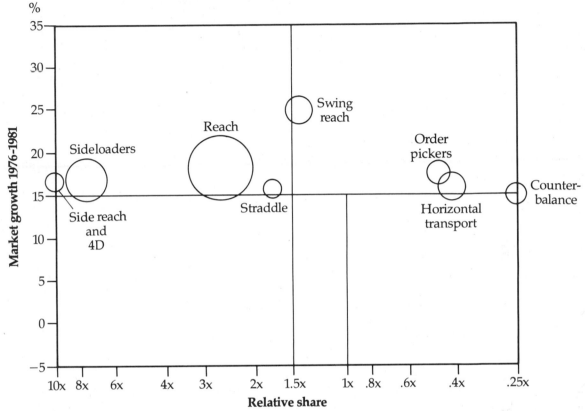

Source: Raymond Corp.
Raymond's marketing people use this grid to plot the relative strength of their products in the marketplace (these are approximate figures). The left-hand scale shows the anticipated market growth from 1976 to 1981, and the one at the bottom indicates how the company compares with its next largest competitor in specific product segments. The size of each circle reflects profit. Thus the largest circle shows that the reach truck is Raymond's leading profit-earner, with a market share two to three times that of its nearest rival. Similarly, it is possible to see that Raymond has little competition in specialized side-reach vehicles and that its impact is negligible on the market for counterbalanced trucks, which is dominated by Clark Equipment, Hyster, and Eaton.

of the industry giants is *the* major strategic consideration for the company. Not only do Eaton, Clark Equipment, Hyster, and Caterpillar control about 75% of the industrial truck market but they show signs of wanting to cash in on the brisk growth of the narrow-aisle sector. Eaton, which has two divisions that compete with Raymond in some product areas, has introduced a number of narrow-aisle vehicles and is counting on such entries to play an important part in its product strategy. Says Alan F. Bethell, vice president of Eaton's Materials Han-

dling Group, "Last year, 80% of our industrial truck sales came from models that were less than five years old, and this trend is likely to continue."

Hyster, too, is chomping at Raymond's territory. "We have to spread our capabilities over a wide product line, but we'll do everything in our power to dislodge Raymond from its dominant position in narrow-aisle trucks," says Jack P. Greer, vice president, marketing, for Hyster's U.S. industrial truck operations in Danville, Ill. An unabashed admirer of Raymond's achievements, Greer, nevertheless, questions whether his feisty rival can offer as much job-shop custom designing as it once did. "Any of us can build highly specialized equipment for a customer, but he pays more for it and he waits longer to get it," says Greer. "My impression is that Raymond has long since outgrown the stage where it designs the product in some guy's warehouse on a sheet of brown wrapping paper."

Such talk is naturally disputed by Raymond's Nenarella, who claims that in some cases his engineers can make basic design changes to suit a customer and still deliver the goods in a shorter time than the 9 or 10 months that it generally takes a larger manufacturer. In selling systems, which are gradually becoming a more important part of Raymond's business, the dealer is often invited to bring his customer to Greene so that he can discuss design requirements with the company's systems engineering people.

Basically Trucks

When it comes to making money, however, Raymond relies not on elaborate systems but on sales of its basic line of reach trucks, 80% of which are not sold as part of a system. In fact, because research about five years ago showed that there was strong demand for the basic Model 20, half of the production run today is devoted to turning out a standard model. Thus a certain number of these "commodity trucks" are put into the pipeline in anticipation of demand, even though there are no firm orders for them. Although Raymond does not carry an inventory of any of its trucks, it does offer a stocking program to dealers for these commodity vehicles.

Virtually everything else that it sells, however, is in some degree made to order, and much of Raymond's advertising is aimed at enumerating the options available to the customer. "Identify a want and turn it into a need; that's what advertising and promotion do," says Nenarella, who estimates that he spends 1.5% of sales annually for such activities.

Also implicit in this strategy is a concerted effort to keep the product line "niching up." This calls for continual development of product innovations that

enable Raymond to present its clientele with more sophisticated (and higher priced) equipment to meet their materials handling needs. The fastest-selling example of this is the swing-reach truck, which can handle pallets on both sides of an aisle without changing position. Scheduled for introduction this spring is the Model 88, a swing-reach refinement that enables the operator to ride up with the load so that he has more control of what he is doing. "When you are moving things 25 ft. in the air, many customers feel more comfortable having the man at load level," says Nenarella. For the privilege, users will probably pay about $5,000 more than they do now for one of Raymond's heavy-duty swing-reach trucks, which range from $50,000 to $60,000.

If Raymond's direction is to be upward and onward, does this pose problems down the aisle when it meets its larger competitors coming the other way? The company is already selling computerized systems that cost over $1 million, and that clearly is an area everyone is interested in jumping into. "We are all going to find ourselves more deeply involved in systems," says Hyster's Greer, "and Raymond may run into pitfalls as it tries to meet those demands with a specialized product line."

For the time being, Raymond is hedging its bets, relying on its basic products to earn money, and edging into systems where it is appropriate. Nenarella puts the matter succinctly: "We're in the truck business, and we are getting into systems only insofar as it helps us sell trucks."

Questions

1. *Explain the Raymond Corporation's overall corporate strategy.*
2. *The Raymond Corporation created separate sales and marketing divisions ". . . so they could work together." Discuss the apparent contradiction in terms of the company's sales and marketing problems.*
3. *Contrast the responsibilities of the Raymond field sales correspondents with those of a salesman for a consumer goods manufacturer.*

47

Strategies for Introducing Marketing into Nonprofit Organizations

PHILIP KOTLER

Is the marketing management process applicable to nonbusiness organizations? "Ivory tower" administrators in colleges and universities, hospital administrators, religious leaders, and government officials are increasingly employing marketing strategies to accomplish their goals.

In most societies of the world, economic activity is a function of the actions and interactions of a profit sector and a governmental sector. The American economy, however, contains an important third sector made up of tens of thousands of private, not-for-profit organizations ranging from The Society for the Preservation and Encouragement of Barber Shop Quartet Singing in America to major foundations, colleges, hospitals, museums, charities, social agencies, and churches.

This strong third sector constitutes a *middle way* for meeting social needs, without resorting to the profit motive on the one hand or government bureaucracy on the other. Third sector organizations tend to be socially responsive and service-oriented. They specialize in the delivery of social services that are not adequately provided by either business or government.

While Big Business is healthy and Big Government continues to grow, the third sector, unfortunately, is in trouble. Third sector organizations depend upon the support of private citizens and

upon grants from the other two sectors. Many colleges, hospitals, churches, social agencies, performance groups, and museums are increasingly feeling the pinch of rising costs and stable or declining revenues. Consider the following:

More than 170 private colleges have closed their doors since 1965, unable to get either enough students or funds or both. Tuition at Stanford and Yale is now over $6,000; if college costs continue to climb at the current rate, the parents of a child born today will have to put aside $82,830 to buy that child a bachelor's degree at one of the better private colleges (Pyke 1977).

Hospital costs continue to soar, leading to daily room rates of $300 or more in some large hospitals; many hospitals are experiencing underutilization, particularly in the maternity and pediatrics sections. Some experts have predicted the closing of 1,400-1,500 hospitals in the next 10 years.

The Catholic Church drew as many as 55% of all adult Catholics under 30 years of age to church in a typical week in 1966. By 1975 the figure had fallen to 39% and further declines in weekly attendance were expected.

Many performance groups cannot attract large enough audiences. Even those which have seasonal sellouts, such as the Lyric Opera Company of Chicago, face huge operating deficits at the end of the year.

Many third sector organizations that flourished in earlier years—the YMCA, Salvation Army, Girl Scouts, and Women's Christian Temperance

Source: Journal of Marketing, Vol. 43 (January 1979), 37–44. Reprinted from *Journal of Marketing* published by the American Marketing Association.

Union—presently are reexamining their mission in an effort to reverse membership declines.

In a word, these third sector organizations have marketplace problems. Their administrators are struggling to keep them alive in the face of rapidly changing societal needs, increasing public and private competition, changing client attitudes, and diminishing financial resources. Board members and supporters are asking administrators tough questions about the organization's mission, opportunities, and strategies. Unfortunately, many administrators are mere "Monday-morning quarterbacks" when it comes to strategic planning. At a time when these organizations face uncertain prospects, the lack of management depth poses a serious threat to survival.

Let us examine a major requirement for such survival: third sector administrators must begin to think like marketers. Ten years ago, Sidney J. Levy and I advanced the thesis that marketing is not just a business function—it is a valid function for nonbusiness organizations as well—and that all organizations have marketing problems and all need to understand marketing (Kotler and Levy 1969). The article created considerable controversy. Many academic marketers attacked it, saying that marketing made sense only in profit-oriented enterprises. However other marketing professors found the idea stimulating and, without necessarily agreeing that it was valid, began to study and experiment with it. Initial interest was confined to academia. The issue was of little concern to businessmen, and was largely ignored by administrators of nonprofit institutions.

More articles followed in the 1970s, reporting applications of marketing technology to such areas as college recruiting, fund raising, membership development, population problems, public transportation, health services, religion, and arts organizations.[1] Benson Shapiro's article in the

September-October 1973 issue of the *Harvard Business Review* elicited many favorable comments, published in the following issue of *HBR*. The only textbook on the subject, *Marketing for Nonprofit Organizations*, appeared in 1975 and has enjoyed a growing readership (Kotler 1975). Recently Gaedeke (1977) published a book of readings, Lovelock and Weinberg (1977) a book of cases, Lovelock (1977) a bibliography of over 100 cases, and Nickels (1978) a general marketing textbook giving equal attention to business and nonbusiness marketing. It appears that marketing for nonprofit organizations is an idea whose time has come.

How have administrators of nonprofit organizations responded? Are they interested or aware? Enthusiastic? Do they know how to use marketing? Is it making a difference anywhere? On this tenth anniversary of the idea's launching, we are in a position to supply some answers.

Enter Marketing

Of all the classic business functions, marketing has been the last to arrive on the nonprofit scene. Some years earlier, nonprofit managers began to get interested in accounting systems, financial management, personnel administration, and formal planning. Marketing lagged, except where the nonprofit institution experienced a decline in clients, members, or funds. As long as institutions operated in a sellers' market—as colleges and hospitals did throughout the 1960s—marketing was ignored, but as customers and/or resources grew scarce the word "marketing" was heard with increasing frequency, and organizations suddenly discovered marketing or reasonable facsimiles thereof.

Colleges

Colleges provide a good example of this development. By the mid-1970s, they were reading this grim scenario: (1) the annual number of high school graduates would decline from a peak of 3.2 million

---

1. A relevant 43-page bibliography lists over 600 references. See Rothschild, Michael L. (1977), *An Incomplete Bibliography of Works Relating to Marketing for Public Sector and Nonprofit Organizations*, Second Edition, Boston, MA: Intercollegiate Case Clearing House 9-577-771.

in 1977 to 2.8 million in 1982–83; (2) the proportion of high school students electing to go to college might decline; (3) a higher proportion of the college-bound students would elect to attend community colleges instead of four-year colleges; and (4) the absolute and relative future level of tuition would deter college-going in general and hurt private colleges in particular.[2]

What are college administrators doing about this? One group is doing nothing. Either enrollment hasn't slipped, or if it has, the administrators believe the decline is temporary. Many believe it is "unprofessional" to go out and "sell" their colleges.

A second group has responded with "marketing," which in too many cases means aggressive promotion unaccompanied by any real improvements in competitive positioning, teaching quality, or student services. For example:

The admissions office at North Kentucky State University planned to release 103 balloons filled with scholarship offers.

The admissions staff of one college passed out promotional frisbees to high school students vacationing on the beaches of Fort Lauderdale, Florida during the annual Easter break.

St. Joseph's College in Rensselaer, Indiana achieved a 40% increase in freshmen admissions through advertising in *Seventeen* and on several Chicago and Indianapolis rock radio stations. The admissions office also planned to introduce tuition rebates for students who recruited new students ($100 finders fee), but this was cancelled.

Bard College developed a same-day admission system for students who walk into their office and qualify.

Worcester Polytechnic Institute offers negotiable admission in which credit is negotiated for previous study or work experience to shorten the degree period.

The University of Richmond has spent $13,000 to create a 12-minute film for showings to high school students and other interested publics.

Drake University advertised on a billboard near Chicago's O'Hare Airport that "Drake is only 40 minutes from Chicago" (if one flies).

Duke University paid for a supplement in *The New York Times* to tell its story.

Promotional competition has not yet led to premiums given to students for enrollment (free radio, typewriter) or offers of "satisfaction guaranteed or your money back," but these may come.

In equating marketing with intensified promotion, there are several dangers. Aggressive promotion tends to produce strong negative reactions among the school's constituencies, especially the faculty, who regard hard selling as offensive. Also, such promotion may turn off as many prospective students and families as it turns on. Aggressive promotion can attract the wrong students to the college—students who drop out when they discover they don't have the qualifications to do the work or that the college is not what it was advertised to be. Finally, this kind of marketing creates the illusion that the college has undertaken sufficient response to declining enrollment—an illusion which slows down the needed work on product improvement—the basis of all good marketing.

Promotion alone doesn't always work. Briarcliff College, a long-established women's college, faced an enrollment drop from 688 in 1969 to 280 in 1973. The college president scrambled to find ways to "sell" Briarcliff to prospects, including advertising and more high school visits. He personally went on the road to talk up Briarcliff, managing to raise enrollment to 350. But his effort was too little and too late. Briarcliff's finances continued to deteriorate and the college finally closed its doors in 1977.[3]

A genuine marketing response has been undertaken by a relatively small number of colleges. Their approach is best described as *market-oriented institutional planning*. In this approach, marketing is recognized as much more than mere promotion,

2. See *A Role for Marketing in College Admissions,* New York: College Entrance Examination Board, 1976, 54 and elsewhere.

3. See "Rest in Peace," *Newsweek,* April 11, 1977, p. 96.

and indeed, the issue of promotion cannot be settled in principle until more fundamental issues are resolved. These issues are shown in Exhibit 1. By doing its homework on market, resource, and missions analysis, a college is in a better position to make decisions that improve student and faculty recruitment and institutional fundraising.

As an example, the University of Houston recently completed an intensive institutional audit using several faculty task forces. The final report presented recommendations on the university's mission, strategy, and portfolio. The portfolio section recommended which components of the university's "product mix" (schools and departments) should be built, maintained, phased down, or phased out. The criteria included: (1) the centrality of that academic program to the mission of the university, (2) the program's academic quality, and (3) the program's marketing viability. Thus, a department of women's studies that is marginal to the mission of the school, of low national reputation, and unable to attract an adequate number of students, would be slated for phasing down or out. A few other schools such as New York University, Northwestern University, and Kent State University are taking marketing initiatives to bring strategic planning and marketing into their operating frameworks.

Exhibit 1

Issues in market-oriented institutional planning facing colleges and universities

Market analysis

1. What important trends are affecting higher education? (Environmental analysis)
2. What is our primary market? (Market definition)
3. What are the major market segments in this market? (Market segmentation)
4. What are the needs of each market segment? (Need assessment)
5. How much awareness, knowledge, interest, and desire is there in each market segment concerning our college? (Market awareness and attitude)
6. How do key publics see us and our competitors? (Image analysis)
7. How do potential students learn about our college and make decisions to apply and enroll? (Consumer behavior)
8. How satisfied are current students? (Consumer satisfaction assessment)

Resource analysis

1. What are our major strengths and weaknesses in faculty, programs, facilities, etc.? (Strengths/weaknesses analysis)
2. What opportunities are there to expand our financial resources? (Donor opportunity analysis)

Mission analysis

1. What business are we in? (Business mission)
2. Who are our customers? (Customer definition)
3. Which needs are we trying to satisfy? (Needs targeting)
4. On which market segments do we want to focus? (Market targeting)
5. Who are our major competitors? (Competitor identification)
6. What competitive benefits do we want to offer to our target market? (Market positioning)

Hospitals

Hospitals are beginning to treat marketing as a "hot" topic. A few years ago, health professionals scorned the idea of marketing, imagining that it would lead to ads such as "This week's special—brain surgery, only $195." Hospital administrators also argued that patients didn't choose hospitals, their doctors did; so marketing, to be effective, would have to be directed to doctors.

Thus, it came as a surprise when a single and tentative session on marketing for hospital administrators, sandwiched between several other sessions during the 1975 convention of the American College of Hospital Administrators, drew about one-third of the 2,000 attendees. Perhaps they were tired of hearing panels on rising hospital costs and money collection problems, but more probably they were beginning to sense an opportunity, in marketing, to halt their declining occupancy rates.

As did many colleges, some hospitals rushed into marketing with more enthusiasm than understanding, believing it to consist of clever promotional gimmicks. For example:

Sunrise Hospital in Las Vegas ran a large advertisement featuring the picture of a ship with the caption, "Introducing the Sunrise Cruise, Win a

Once-in-a-Lifetime Cruise Simply by Entering Sunrise Hospital on Any Friday or Saturday: Recuperative Mediterranean Cruise for Two.''

St. Luke's Hospital in Phoenix introduced nightly bingo games for all patients (except cardiac cases) producing immense patient interest as well as a net annual profit of $60,000.

A Philadelphia hospital, in competing for maternity patients, let the public know that the parents of a newborn child would enjoy a steak and champagne candlelight dinner on the eve before the mother and child's departure from the hospital.

A number of hospitals, in their competition to attract and retain physicians, have added "ego services," such as saunas, chauffeurs, and even private tennis courts.

Fortunately, some hospitals are now beginning to apply marketing to a broader set of problems. Where should the hospital locate a branch or ambulatory care unit? How can the hospital estimate whether a new service will draw enough patients? What should a hospital do with a maternity wing that is only 20% occupied? How can the hospital attract more consumers to preventive care services, such as annual medical checkups and cancer screening programs? How can a hospital successfully compete in the recruitment of more highly trained specialists who are in short supply? What marketing programs can attract nurses, build community goodwill, attract more contributions?

The marketing naivete of the typical hospital is well-illustrated by a hospital in southern Illinois that decided to establish an Adult Day Care Center as a solution to its underutilized space. It designed a whole floor to serve senior citizens who required personal care and services in an ambulatory setting during the day, but who would return home each evening. The cost was $16 a day and transportation was to be provided by the patient's relatives. About the only research that was done on this concept was to note that a lot of elderly people lived within a three-mile radius. The Center was opened with a capacity to handle thirty patients. Only two signed up!

Not all hospital administrators launch new services without research and testing of market size and interest. An increasing number are now attending marketing seminars to learn more about marketing research and new service development. The Evanston Hospital, Evanston, Illinois, a major 500-bed facility, appointed the world's first hospital vice president of marketing. Recently, MacStravic (1977) published an entire book devoted to hospital marketing, and many articles are now appearing on health care marketing.[4]

Other Institutions

In addition to colleges and hospitals, other institutions are paying more attention to marketing. The YMCA is taking a fresh look at its mission, services, and clients in order to develop new services and markets for the 1980s. Major charities like the Multiple Sclerosis Society, the American Heart Association, and the March of Dimes are investigating marketing ideas that go beyond selling and advertising. Marketing successes have been reported by arts institutions,[5] family planning associations (Roberto 1975), and energy conservation groups (Henion 1976). It is likely that within 10 years, much of the third sector will have some understanding and appreciation of the marketing concept.

Implementing Marketing

The interesting thing about marketing is that all organizations do it whether they know it or not. When this dawns on a nonprofit organization, the response is much like Moliere's character in *Le Bourgeois Gentilhomme* who utters: "Good Heavens!

4. See, for example, the special issue on marketing of hospitals, *Journal of the American Hospital Association,* June 1, 1977.
5. See, Newman, Danny (1977), *Subscribe Now! Building Arts Audiences through Dynamic Subscription Promotion,* New York: Theatre Communications Group, Inc. This book deals primarily with the use of promotion as a marketing tool rather than with overall marketing strategy.

For more than forty years I have been speaking prose without knowing it." Colleges, for example, search for prospects (students), develop products (courses), price them (tuition and fees), distribute them (announce time and place), and promote them (college catalogs). Similarly, hospitals, social agencies, cultural groups, and other nonprofit organizations also practice marketing, wittingly or unwittingly; whether they do it well is a separate issue. For institutions which would like to improve their marketing effectiveness, I recommend consideration of the six steps shown in Exhibit 2. The "steps" really represent alternative approaches to the introduction of marketing into a nonprofit institution rather than a rigid sequence of steps.

Marketing Committee

As early as possible, the head of the institution should consider appointing a marketing committee to examine the institution's problems and look into the potentialities of marketing. In a college, for example, such a marketing committee might consist of the president, vice presidents of faculty and development, director of admissions, dean of students, and one or two school deans. The committee should also include a marketing professor and/or a marketing practitioner. The marketing committee's objectives are (1) to identify the marketing problems and opportunities facing the institution; (2) to identify the major needs of various administrative units for marketing services; and (3) to explore the institution's possible need for a full-time director of marketing.

Task Forces

The chief administrator should consider appointing task forces to carry out various phases of an institutional audit. The aim is to discover how the institution is seen by key publics, what its main constituencies want that institution to be, which

Exhibit 2
Approaches to introducing marketing in a nonprofit institution

1. Appoint a Marketing Committee
2. Organize Task Forces to Carry out an Institutional Audit
3. Hire Marketing Specialist Firms as Needed
4. Hire a Marketing Consultant
5. Hire a Director of Marketing
6. Hire a Vice President of Marketing

programs are strong and which weak, and so on. The task force's reports should adduce a consensus on institutional goals, positioning, and strategies. Even when task forces fail to find dramatic solutions, the members usually gain a deeper appreciation and understanding of the institution's problems and the need to work together to solve them.

Marketing Specialist Firms

From time to time, the organization should engage the services of marketing specialist firms, such as marketing research firms, advertising agencies, direct mail consultants, and recruitment consultants. A marketing research firm might be hired to survey the needs, perceptions, preferences, and satisfaction of the client market. An advertising agency might be hired to develop a corporate identification program or an advertising campaign. High quality marketing specialist firms bring more than their specific services to the client; they take a total marketing viewpoint and raise important questions for the institution to consider concerning its mission, objectives, strategies, and opportunities.

Marketing Consultant

As a further step, the organization should seek a marketing consultant to carry out a comprehensive *marketing audit* on the problems and opportunities facing that organization. The marketing consultant could be someone affiliated with the institution—such as a marketing professor, or a board member who is a marketing specialist. However, volunteers tend to give less attention than is necessary to the project, and often lack objectivity. It is usually preferable to engage a professional marketing consultant, one who has experience in that nonprofit subsector of the economy. In education, for example, several consulting firms have emerged specializing in college marketing and management. Alternatively, the institution could seek the services of a general consulting firm. In any event, the institution should make an effort to invite at least three proposals from which to select the best consultant. A contract should be written which specifies the objectives, the time frame, the research plan, and the billing. A liaison person within the institution should be assigned to work with the consultant, arrange interviews, read and comment on the emerging reports, and make arrangements for the final presentation and implementation of proposals.

The marketing consultant will interview representative sets of people connected with the institution. In the case of a college, he or she will interview the president, members of the board of trustees, major vice presidents, directors of admissions and public relations, several school deans, several department chairmen, several professors, several students, representative alumni, and outside opinion leaders. The marketing consultant would seek to answer the following questions for each *academic program* studied:

What is happening to student size and quality?
How successful is the program in attracting qualified students?
What are the main competitive programs and their positions in the market?
What is the image and reputation of this program?
What is the mission and what are the objectives of this program over the next five years?
What budget is needed to accomplish these objectives?
What fund raising potentials exist in the program?

What marketing problems face the program and what marketing activities are being pursued?
What useful services could a marketing director contribute to this program?

On the basis of this survey, the marketing consultant will develop and present a set of findings and recommendations regarding the institution's operations, opportunities, and needs in the marketing area. One of the recommendations will specifically deal with whether the institution is ready to effectively utilize a marketing director or vice president of marketing.

Marketing Director

Eventually the organization might become convinced of the need to appoint a director of marketing. This requires the development of a job description which specifies to whom this person reports, the scope of the position, the position concept, the functions, responsibilities, and major liaisons with others in the institution. Exhibit 3 presents a job description in a university context. The job is conceived as a middle management position, one in which the occupant primarily provides marketing services to others in the institution.

A major issue is where this person should be located in the organization and his or her relationships with kindred functions. Specifically, what is the marketing director's relationship to planning, public relations, and fund raising? A good case could be made for locating the marketing director within the planning office and therefore reporting to the vice president of planning. It would not make sense for the marketing director to report to public relations or fund raising because this would overspecialize the use made of marketing. The solution used by a large, eastern hospital consisted of appointing a vice president of institutional relations to whom directors of marketing, public relations, fund raising and planning reported.

Some public relations directors have been un-

Exhibit 3
Job description: Director of Marketing for a university

Position title: Director of Marketing

Reports to: A vice president designated by the president

Scope: University-wide

Position concept: The director of marketing is responsible for providing marketing guidance and services to university officers, school deans, department chairmen, and other agents of the university.

Functions: The director of marketing will:
1. Contribute a marketing perspective to the deliberations of the top administration in their planning of the university's future
2. Prepare data that might be needed by any officer of the university on a particular market's size, segments, trends, and behavioral dynamics
3. Conduct studies of the needs, perceptions, preferences, and satisfactions of particular markets
4. Assist in the planning, promotion, and launching of new programs
5. Assist in the development of communication and promotion campaigns and materials
6. Analyze and advise on pricing questions
7. Appraise the workability of new academic proposals from a marketing point of view
8. Advise on new student recruitment
9. Advise on current student satisfaction
10. Advise on university fundraising

Responsibilities: The director of marketing will:
1. Contact individual officers and small groups at the university to explain services and to solicit problems
2. Prioritize the various requests for services according to their long run impact, cost saving potential, time requirements, ease of accomplishment, cost, and urgency
3. Select projects of high priority and set accomplishment goals for the year
4. Prepare a budget request to support the anticipated work
5. Prepare an annual report on the main accomplishments of the office

Major liaisons: The director of marketing will:
1. Relate most closely with the president's office, admissions office, development office, planning office, and public relations department
2. Relate secondarily with the deans of various schools and chairmen of various departments

---

comfortable about the emergence of marketing directors, out of fear that they may eventually be reporting to the latter. Some public relations directors argue that marketing isn't needed, or that it is being done, or that they can do it. To the extent that marketing is thought to be aggressive promotion, public relations people feel they are best equipped to carry out this function. To the extent that marketing is seen to consist of market analysis, new services development, marketing strategy, product line evaluation, and so on, public relations personnel are not equipped insofar as their training is basically in the fields of journalism and communications, not economics and business analysis. However, public relations persons can, of course, take courses in marketing and attempt to promote the concept of a combined office of marketing and public relations.

Marketing Vice President

The ultimate solution is the establishment of a vice president of marketing position. This is an upper level management position which gives more scope, authority, and influence to marketing. A vice president of marketing not only coordinates and supplies analytical services but also has a strong voice in the determination of where the institution should be going in terms of its changing opportunities.

The vice president of marketing would be responsible for planning and managing relations with several publics. The person's title may be altered to that of vice president of institutional relations or external affairs to avoid unnecessary semantic opposition. Thus far, only a few nonprofit organizations have gone this route.

The top marketing job should be tailored to the specific institution. Consider the YMCA, often called "the General Electric of the social service business." The YMCA is in not one, but several "businesses:" recreation, education, camps, physical fitness, hotels, and so on. Central headquarters must wrestle with decisions on where to build new facilities, what new programs to introduce, what programs to drop, how to promote membership, and dozens of other matters. Were a vice president of marketing appointed, this person would be responsible for defining better ways to serve various constituencies. Reporting to the vice president would be functional marketing specialists (marketing research, pricing, promotion, and planning), product managers (recreational programs, educational programs, camps) and market managers (teens, young marrieds, senior adults). These people would design programs and offer services to the various YMCA units throughout the country. There is no question that marketing decisions are being made all the time throughout the YMCA system but they are made, unfortunately, without professional marketing expertise.

Let us assume that an institution decides to hire a marketing vice president. This person's contribution will be carefully scrutinized. The new appointee will have to develop a strategy to make marketing visible and useful.

The marketing executive is not likely to be immediately swamped with requests for services, because many administrators initially will not understand marketing. The marketing executive should spend the first few months meeting various groups within the institution to learn about their problems. For example, Evanston Hospital's new marketing vice president arranged separate meetings with senior physicians, residents, interns, senior nurses, and others. At each meeting he described his job position, explained the nature of marketing, indicated the kinds of problems he could solve and services that he could offer, and then opened the meeting to discussion. He sought suggestions of projects that he might conduct. At the end of two months, he found more than enough useful projects. His problem, in fact, was to set priorities for the many projects, and he did so by rating each potential project using the following criteria (on five-point scales): (1) the importance or centrality of the project to the future of the institution; (2) the magnitude of the improved service or cost savings that it might effect; (3) its probable cost; (4) the difficulty of carrying it out; and (5) the length of time it would take to complete. An ideal project was one that was very important, would effect great cost savings, would cost little to do, could be easily carried out, and could be completed in a short time. It became clear which projects went to the top of the list, and he concentrated his efforts in the first year on these projects.

The marketing executive will be expected to prepare an annual marketing plan listing major projects and a required budget. Much of the budget will go toward buying the services of outside marketing research firms and advertising agencies for needed projects. At each year's end, the executive will prepare a report summarizing levels of accomplishment and savings. Eventually, the nature of this position will become well understood within the organization and easy to assess its contributions toward institutional survival and growth.

Conclusion

At the present time, the marketing idea is beginning to attract the interest of administrators in the third sector. This is evidenced by the growing literature on college, hospital, and other third sector marketing, as well as by increased attendance at specialized marketing conferences for nonprofit organizations. Interest is not likely to abate; indeed, it is likely to increase as more administrators come to see their institution's future in marketing terms. For an institution, marketing offers a much richer understanding of what is happening and throws light on new opportunities.

Despite the growing interest in marketing, however, many nonprofit organizations still resist it. Many groups within these organizations see marketing as a threat to their autonomy or power. Eventually, out of necessity, marketing ideas will filter into these organizations. Marketing will initially be viewed as advertising and promotion rather than as a revolutionary new way to view the institution and its purposes. A few institutions will lead the others in developing an advanced understanding of marketing. They will start performing better. Their competitors will be forced to learn their marketing. Within another decade, marketing will be a major and accepted function within the nonprofit sector.

The issue that frightens some observers is not that marketing will be ineffective but that it may be too effective. They see funds and clients flowing to institutions that are willing to spend the largest sums of money on advertising and promotion. They fear that large scale promotional warfare will ruin the smaller institutions that cannot afford marketing, and will create a competitive stalemate among the larger institutions. This fear is based, once again, on the fallacy of viewing marketing as primarily promotional.

The real contribution of marketing thinking is to lead each institution to search for a more meaningful position in the larger market. Instead of all hospitals offering the same services, marketing leads each hospital to shape distinct service mixes to serve specific market segments. Marketing competition, at its best, creates a pattern of varied institutions, each clear as to its mission, market coverage, need specialization, and service portfolio.

Administrators and businessmen who have a stake in the third sector are beginning to recognize the contributions that marketing thinking can make. Marketing will lead to a better understanding of the needs of different client segments; to a more careful shaping and launching of new services; to a pruning of weak services; to more effective methods of delivering services; to more flexible pricing approaches; and to higher levels of client satisfaction. Altogether, marketing offers a great potential to third sector organizations to survive, grow, and strengthen their contributions to the general welfare.

References

Gaedeke, R. M. (1977), *Marketing in Private and Public Nonprofit Organizations: Perspectives and Illustrations*, Santa Monica, CA: Goodyear Publishing Co.

Henion, Karl E. (1976), *Ecological Marketing*, Columbus, Ohio: Grid, Inc.

Kotler, Philip (1975), *Marketing for Nonprofit Organizations*, Englewood Cliffs, NJ: Prentice-Hall, Inc.

———— and Levy, Sidney J. (1969), "Broadening the Concept of Marketing," *Journal of Marketing,* 33 (January), 10–15.

Lovelock, Christopher H., ed. (1977), *Nonbusiness Marketing Cases,* 8-378-001, Boston, MA: Intercollegiate Case Clearing House.

———— and Charles B. Weinberg (1977), *Cases in Public and Nonprofit Marketing,* Palo Alto, CA: The Scientific Press.

———— and Charles B. Weinberg (1978), "Public and Non-profit Marketing Comes of Age," in *Review of Marketing 1978,* Gerald Zaltman and T. Bonoma, eds., Chicago, IL: American Marketing Association, 413–452.

MacStravic, Robin E. (1977), *Marketing Health Care,* Germantown, MD: Aspen Systems Corp.

Nickels, William G. (1978), *Marketing Principles*, Englewood Cliffs, NJ: Prentice-Hall, Inc.

Pyke, Donald L. (1977), "The Future of Higher Education: Will Private Institutions Disappear in the U.S.?" *The Futurist*, 374.

Roberto, Eduardo (1975), *Strategic Decision-Making in a Social Program: The Case of Family-Planning Diffusion*, Lexington, MA: Lexington Books.

Shapiro, Benson (1973), "Marketing for Nonprofit Organizations," *Harvard Business Review*, 51 (September–October), 123–132.

Questions

1. *Develop a detailed outline of what you perceive to be your college's or university's marketing strategy and mix. Assess those marketing plans and recommend appropriate changes.*
2. *Kotler argues that most nonprofit organizations have been marketing—unwittingly. What marketing activities have been practiced by colleges? hospitals? churches?*

48

Marketing:
One YMCA
Attacks the Problems

JACQUELINE JANDERS

How can a nonprofit organization like the YMCA use marketing technology? The Milwaukee YMCA developed and implemented some marketing plans and found the experience very rewarding.

One of the earliest examples of marketing in the YMCA took place in New York City right after the Civil War. The original concept of the YMCA was a simple Association of young men united in Christ. Men used to meet regularly in religious reading rooms usually located above shops and stores.

The city was teeming with saloons and theatres and dance halls from which the Association wanted to attract the young men. One evening, as a group of YMCA members sat discussing how they could get more young men to join the Association, one of their number, businessman J. Pierpont Morgan, said, "If you want to attract the young men of today, you'll have to bring the YMCA down out of these upper rooms." That is just what they did and the first YMCA building was constructed in 1869.

Ever since the YMCA came down out of the upper rooms and began providing services for which dues and fees are charged, the YMCA has been in the "marketplace."

At its most elementary level a market exists whenever a buyer and a seller come together for a mutually beneficial exchange of a product, a service, an idea. Usually it is an exchange involving

Source: Perspective Magazine, May 1975, pp. 23–26. Reprinted with permission; *Perspective/Journal of Professional YMCA Directors*. © 1975: Association of Professional YMCA Directors in the United States.

money. Now, the YMCA has not thought in terms of buying and selling, but we do provide programs and services for which people pay dues and fees. Therefore in a sense there is a buyer and a seller and we have created a market.

As in the story above there is much more to marketing than that which takes place at the point of exchange. This article is about the value and the process of marketing in today's multi-service YMCA.

If we are indeed concerned with "being about our Father's business" and enriching the lives of people, we should use every management skill available to us. The most successful YMCA's are those which have truly thought they were in the "People Business" and have focused on satisfying the needs of people. Modern marketing can facilitate this process.

More Than Semantic

The problem with most discussions of marketing is that what gets emphasized is *promotion and selling*, not marketing. The difference is more than semantic. Selling focuses on the needs of the seller; the YMCA's need to enroll members and sign up participants. While selling is a part of marketing, marketing moves far back from the point of sale and focuses on the needs of the buyer; the potential member, the customer.

Marketing asks the questions: Who is the customer? Where is the customer? What are the customer's needs and wants? . . . And what value-satisfying programs and services can we provide that the customer will want to buy? I do not mean to imply that selling is unimportant. It is very important and I shall have more to say about selling later. But because marketing is a more complex and sophisticated management process, it often gets ignored.

Marketing is concerned with the identification of the needs and wants of potential members and the whole series of activities associated with the creation and delivery of programs and services which satisfy these needs. It is a concept which starts with top management and must become a way of thinking in every nook and cranny of the organization. YMCA directors are very program and operations oriented. Sometimes we think and act as if we were in the program business instead of the people business. Marketing is a management approach which is customer-oriented. The program or product is the consequence of the marketing effort not the starting point.

The Milwaukee YMCA initiated an in-depth Marketing Training Project in Fall, 1973 for all professional management staff. President M. Brutus Baker; Dick Protzmann, Vice President for Branch Operations; Larry Smith, Director of Manpower Development; and I were the Marketing Training Project Team for planning and implementation of the program. Professor Dick Berry, Management Specialist in Marketing from the School of Business and Management of the University of Wisconsin, was our co-planner, consultant and trainer.

The Marketing Training Project had two objectives:

A professional staff trained in the application of marketing principles and techniques to the end that these will be applied to the planning, development, packaging and promotion of YMCA programs . . . And because we are a results-oriented organization we established a measurable objective. . . .

Six useful marketing proposals for new or improved programs and creation of new markets to help achieve our corporate operating goals.

Briefly, the design of the training project was:

Selected readings, prepared by Berry to introduce us to the study of marketing as a modern management discipline.

A series of seminars and workshops for additional input, exploration and training in the many aspects of the marketing function.

Establishment of task teams to help internalize and put into practice learnings about marketing.

The content of the several workshops and seminars included:

Marketing strategy and the marketing-mix concept.

Marketing planning.

Customer orientation at contact point of front desk and telephone inquiry.

The role of the public relations program in marketing.

The application of counsellor selling techniques.

Telephone contact and sales.

Corporate planning and setting Branch unit objectives.

There were so many components to the Marketing Training Project that time and space here will not permit me to adequately report on all of them. Perhaps the concept of marketing and its dynamic implications for the YMCA can best be demonstrated by sharing with you the work of the marketing planning task forces and some of the results of their work.

Establishing the Marketing Planning Task Forces

As I have already suggested in the statement of objectives and the design of the training project the task forces had two purposes:

1. training: to be a vehicle for practicing and internalizing marketing principles and techniques.
2. results: preparation of 6 useful marketing pro-

posals that could be made operational in the Milwaukee YMCA.

The function of the task forces was Marketing Planning. The project team selected six program areas which we believed would best lend themselves to the experience; either because they were operated Association-wide and would be familiar to most staff, or because they were recognized problem areas, or because they were considered to be key market areas. It was decided to establish a marketing task force to develop a marketing plan for each of the following:

Health Clubs.
Tot Time preschool education program.
Y-Indian Guides—parent child program.
Family Program and Membership.
Camping.
Food Service.

Six professional marketing directors, laymen from business and industry, were recruited to serve as marketing consultants to the task teams. Each of these people agreed to meet with one of the task forces. Their function was to bring marketing expertise to the planning and an objective point of view to the program area. A Staff Chairman for each group was appointed to work with the various consultants and trainers, and to present the final marketing proposal.

Each of the 43 professional staff people in the Milwaukee YMCA was assigned to one of these task forces. Ideally, members of a marketing planning group should be selected for their creative ability, expertise in the program area, commitment to the task and influence in carrying out the resulting marketing program.

However, in this case because the primary purpose was training, *all staff were assigned*, across organizational lines, selected only partly for their interest, commitment or expertise in the particular program area.

After the task forces had met several times I was assigned to work with them. Obviously the success of each group depended upon the degree to which

full group interaction could be generated and sustained. My job was to help them pull together as a single creative unit building on each other's ideas and working toward a common goal.

At the same time I needed to keep before the groups all of the marketing concepts and methods Berry had given us in the initial 2 day seminar.

Marketing Mix

One of the most helpful tools provided during the first workshop was the concept of the "Marketing Mix." The marketing mix is the idea that there is a pattern of important elements or ingredients in every marketing plan. These elements are the 4-p's . . . product, place, price and promotion.

The mixing of these factors, which management controls, with external forces bearing upon the market, results in the formula for success which becomes the marketing plan. The external forces with which the 4-p's must be considered are consumer buying behavior, life styles, competition, the law, etc., which management does not control, but about which it must be thoroughly knowledgeable.

In order for the planning groups to properly mix all of the ingredients, Berry had stressed the importance of situation analysis and focusing on objectives. Roughly, the thought process and discussion from which ideas will flow and plans will evolve looks something like this:

Focus on objectives:
  What segments of the market are we dealing with?
  What are the needs of the customer?
  How can we satisfy these needs?
  What do we really want to do?
  Program or service objectives.
Situation analysis:
  Consider broad strategies.
  Consider corporate operating goals.
  Consider the customer viewpoint.
  Analyze strengths and weaknesses.
  What are the problems and opportunities?

Consider the product.
Consider the organization's resources.
Consider competition.

Mix all of the above . . . explore the resulting ideas . . . build on the best ideas . . . assess the minimum requirements to meet customer needs . . . identify features and benefits that will have the greatest customer impact . . . apply resources of time, money, staff and facilities. If workable, develop the idea and document the plan. If *not* workable, keep mixing alternative ideas.

The examples I will use to reveal the marketing planning process are taken from the experiences of the task forces. We were a-borning something new for the YMCA and there is no shame in suffering birth pains.

Overcoming Road Blocks

One of the problems all of the task forces initially encountered was the shift from marketing theory to practice. For example, the matter of setting objectives.

It was at first difficult for the groups to distinguish between identifying the objectives of the task team itself and the objectives of the program area they were assigned. In other words: What was indeed the task of the group and what was expected of them? And what were the objectives of the program category they were assigned? And again, what were the objectives of the marketing plan they would develop?

As you may imagine, some task force members wanted to set dollar and enrollment objectives similar to those they had already identified in the Branch budgets. These were the operators. Others who thought marketing means promotion leaped immediately to set promotion and advertising objectives. Others dealt with the ideal philosophical purposes of the YMCA and still others with the individual curriculum, program or fitness objectives.

The truth of the matter is that all of these are legitimate considerations in the marketing mix, but the group had another obstacle to overcome first. It was that of understanding and believing in their mission. A marketing planning group is essentially an invention or idea group. Our purpose was to identify new market segments, create a new program or improve an old one based on the needs of the market segment and to devise ways and means, including new promotion techniques, to deliver the program. Considerable time was spent in each group clarifying the above.

As each group began to analyze its marketing opportunities and group members were beginning to build on each other's ideas the following road blocks would also appear:

"We're already doing all we can." "We can't attract any more people until we get a new building." "It's really the price that's too high." "We tried that in my former Association and it didn't work." "No YMCA program should be self-sustaining." "People don't really want what they need." "That's P.R.'s job!"

Participatory management, the involvement of line managers in corporate planning and decision making, always sounds like a grand idea. However, the additional effort and responsibility it demands requires a lot of extra hard work. And who needs that?

If the work of the task forces was ever to get off the ground and become productive we had to clarify our mission and find a positive focus. It occurred to me that if the groups could picture the total corporate planning process and realize that they had been given the opportunity to participate in strategic planning for the Association it would clarify what we were doing.

They would see that this was a serious assignment, the results of which would greatly influence the future of the Milwaukee YMCA. A brief blackboard outline helped the groups see how strategic marketing planning fits into the total planning processes of the Association.

Further, they began to see that the kind of planning now required of them could serve their own interests later in the establishment and achievement of Branch unit objectives. These insights helped the groups gain confidence in their function as planners and we were able to move on.

Identifying the Program and Market Area of Exploration

The next step was to define and agree upon the program and market area in which the task force was to work. This may seem like a simple step in view of the assignments given. It really was not so obvious. For example, my first meeting with the family program and membership task force went something like this:

Minutes of three previous meetings were distributed which revealed that the group had done some homework. They had researched and discussed the philosophy of family program in the Milwaukee YMCA. They had compiled a list of physical and educational program offerings and membership statistics on the two family-serving Branches in operation at the time. They had also identified membership enrollment objectives for these two Branches for the coming year.

I asked the group which specific market they were interested in programming for. "Well, what do you mean? We're interested in selling memberships. We need to program for men, women, boys and girls . . . all of them, of course!"

This response demonstrated that we needed to get a better focus on the work of the task force if we were going to create any new markets or develop any new programs (the real work of the task force). We needed to narrow the perimeters of our work or time limitations and frustration would immobilize the team.

I rephrased the question, this time with a program emphasis. "What are the programs that you believe are most needed or wanted by families?" This resulted in some narrowing identification, mostly of physical programs, youth activities and health club services. Then one group member said, "Look, it's a package. Only Family Memberships are available, so when you buy a membership you get it all for the whole family—Mom, Dad and all the kids."

We were getting nearer to answering the original question so I asked, "Can we identify a YMCA family? Is it just any old combination of men, women, boys and girls?" There followed some discussion about how the young couple in the high-rise could be considered a "family," and that the teenager whose parents buy him a membership is certainly "part" of a family. Well, after several more hours and the aid of a "life cycle" chart and a close look at the characteristics of the families already enrolled, the group identified that the specific market segment we were most interested in was "young families, fathers and mothers with children between the ages of 6 and 12, living together."

At subsequent meetings we further defined the program and market by looking in depth at the needs, desires, problems and capabilities of the target families. We zeroed in on the developmental tasks of children in this age category. We discussed the predominant life style and family income and educational level of the families in the prescribed Branch service areas. We looked at the number and the concentration by neighborhoods of the target families.

We brainstormed about the real needs of families in this life cycle. Many of us personally recalled how we felt as children or parents at these ages. What were our desires, our needs, the normal problems of family life? How did or how could the Y have helped? We looked at how existing programs could help strengthen family life. In short, we conducted a total situation analysis of what we really wanted to do in relation to the needs of the families who were the target market segment we had identified.

By defining the program area in consumer terms and by focusing on the real needs of families the task force became more innovative. We began to deal more with family communications, values and relationships.

These, even more than physical fitness and leisure time activities, were seen as the real needs to be satisfied through family programming. New ways of appealing to couples and involving whole families were explored. New program ideas emerged. Women, with their changing roles, attitudes, self image and aspirations were identified as a whole new market on which to concentrate.

Outside marketing consultants were helpful. "You have to realize that people do not need the

YMCA to exist," one said. "However, as their basic needs are provided for, people begin to realize that man does not live by bread alone. The satisfactions the Y is concerned with are the intangible, though very real needs of most people. We have to first identify and then find ways of helping people recognize these needs; then we can satisfy them."

On another occasion during a heated discussion one of the outside marketing consultants said:

Look, you people act as if you're ashamed to charge a legitimate fee for your programs. If you believe in your basic service you know its value, and you want to make it available to as many folks as possible.

To keep the price of the basic service as reasonable as possible, you have to charge the full cost on the extra services that people want. It's a different market. In our company we know what our basic service is. It has to do with our purpose. Anything extra we offer we charge what we need to . . . so we can continue to provide our basic service to more and more people at a reasonable rate.

Bravo!

Compiling and Applying Background Material

Adequate preparation of information relative to the program and market subject area is absolutely essential to successful marketing planning.

A narrative description of each program category and some statistical data on existing programs had been prepared for each of the task forces at the time of assignment in order to get them started. To enable us to do a thorough situation analysis, considerably more research and documentation of facts had to be compiled as questions came up.

Most of this data was assembled by the task forces from existing information readily available in our own or other YMCA records or from published sources such as census tracts, etc. Generally no new market studies were undertaken by the task forces. The Health Club task force conducted one small survey to test "felt-needs" of potential members.

The information needed for each of the program areas we were considering included:

Market size and trends: number of people in the market segment, the number and size of families, were they increasing, decreasing or relocating in the service area? . . . mobility, income, life style, purchasing preferences, etc.
Competition: who and what is our competition? . . . visit it, collect samples of advertising and literature, compare prices and benefits, observe sales techniques, etc.
Technical program information: program resources available within the Y or in the field. Research or development already underway. Example: Havighurst's "Developmental Tasks and Education" was used by the Camping task force; Milwaukee Area Technical College tested Tot Time teachers' curriculum; National YMCA and other research in the field of family life education was reviewed.
YMCA policy or legal controls: The Tot Time task force considered State of Wisconsin standards for preschool programs. The Camping task force considered YMCA and American Camping Association standards.

Here are other examples of how the above information was secured and its usefulness to the task forces.

Market Size and Trends

The Tot Time task force compiled statistical population data on children under five years of age for each branch service area.

This information helped us identify that in some instances we were operating preschool programs in locations determined by where the facilities or teachers were available and primarily counting on these outside sources to provide enrollment. An examination of the statistics, by neighborhoods, revealed that the concentrations of very young families with children of this age were actually located elsewhere in the service area. These facts were certainly important in our "Place" considerations.

The statistics also revealed that the population under 5 years of age in the Greater Milwaukee area is approximately 100,000. Further, that of this number only 4,400 were enrolled in any kind of nursery program.

From the compiled information the Tot Time task force was able to identify and locate its target market segment and conclude that the growth potential for Tot Time programs was extensive for the next two to five years, based on the size and trend of the market.

On Competition

The Health Club task force members individually visited and filed reports on seven private and commercial competitive health clubs in the Greater Milwaukee area, and three successful YMCA health clubs in other cities. The most valuable learnings from these visits were:

The importance of quality: clean, comfortable, attractive, even posh facilities commensurate with the tastes of the market segment most likely to pay for these services.

Complete customer-orientation . . . use of counsellor selling. In every instance the potential customer was asked, "What do you want to accomplish?" Then the sales counsellor concentrated on showing how the health club membership could help the member achieve his personal goals.

The strength in the commercial clubs was the emphasis on sales.

Research indicated that their weakness is that there is only the most superficial attention to health and fitness programs and almost no expertise in this area. Whereas the YMCA has the expertise and the programs, our greatest weakness was in not having any kind of focus on sales.

An example of this fact came out in one of our counsellor selling workshops. During a role-playing exercise the professional YMCA director, upon meeting the prospect, conducted a tour of the facili-

ties. The overwhelming tendency was to talk only about the facilities. "This is our beautiful pool." "Here's our exercise room." "We have massage available, too."

Obviously, most of these facilities when they are seen speak for themselves as to what they are. We must translate our knowledge of the facilities into customer needs. An illustration:

With an electric drill in one hand and a block of wood with a hole in it in the other hand our trainer said, "Nobody has a need for this electric drill." Holding up the block of wood with the hole in it, he said, "What there is a tremendous need for is holes! We market the drill because it satisfies the customer's need for holes."

We market gyms and pools and exercise rooms to satisfy the customer's need for health, fitness, fun, fellowship, weight control, relaxation, etc.

Far more important in a tour of facilities is the communication with the prospect about who he/she is . . . how they happened to come to the Y . . . what it is they would like to accomplish . . . where they live . . . the family's interests . . . what kind of work they do.

All of these give us clues as to how a health club or Y membership can help satisfy the prospect's needs . . . but only if we do more listening than talking. When we talk about our program and facilities it must be in terms of benefits to the prospect.

If we have designed our program to meet customer needs instead of our own ego needs for a marvelous and highly technical program, and if we relate to the potential member in terms of his needs, it will become clear what he wants to hear about and what benefits and features to talk about.

Implementing the Marketing Plans

One of my favorite pragmatic friends holds a theory that "idea people" are great but ideas are a dime a dozen. "It's the implementors of the world who count," he says. "They get the job done." The Marketing Task Force approach is a way of getting the new ideas originated by the people who will be responsible for implementing them. Obviously, follow-through is essential.

Results

There is no doubt that the first objective for the formation of the task forces was achieved—that of training. The learnings which took place during the Marketing Training Project are evidenced in attitudinal changes that have influenced management decisions up and down the organization. The conscious application of marketing principles has affected manpower planning, training, program development and allocation of resources.

Customer-orientation and a focus on satisfying the needs of people has influenced volunteer involvement and support as well as enrollments. The marketing approach has subtly influenced day to day judgments. The staff have become better planners.

There is less resistance to charging appropriate fees. Better pricing and improved promotion efforts have resulted in increased earned income in 1974. Tot Time enrollments increased from 585 students in the fall of '73 to 704 today. Health Club membership has increased from 689 to 1228. The number of families enrolled in family-serving Branches has increased from 2,199 to 2,960.

There is a growing awareness of what happens in the non-profit market. For instance: You have designed a program and you have budgeted it with all the overhead to break even with an enrollment of 20 people. If, because you have overestimated the need, or inadequately promoted it, only ten participants are enrolled you not only have a no profit situation, you have a deficit . . . to which you must apply donor subsidy. This is poor management, not philanthropy.

Now on the other hand if we deliberately plan to subsidize a program, it is a different matter. Suppose we provide a program to meet a specific need and it is purposely planned, with a maximum enrollment, to be a deficit operation.

To increase the number of these programs is of course to increase the overall deficit . . . a point not often thought about outside of non-profit manage-

ment. If the reasons for operating this program at a deficit are sound, then this is where contributed dollars belong.

The YMCA is a non-profit organization. It should be non-profit by intent and good management not by accident and poor management!

The second objective for the formation of the task forces was substantially achieved with the completion and acceptance of four of the six marketing proposals. Each of the four completed proposals received a "go" decision from top management.

Within the framework of the organizational structure and the corporate planning system of the Milwaukee YMCA, the marketing plans are largely being implemented in the branches. This means that branch staff and boards of managers set branch unit objectives in the program area and develop action plans from the recommendations of the marketing proposals. Action plans include designation of staff responsibility, time schedules and budget requirements.

Several of the marketing proposals called for increased corporate staff and general office support in the form of more centralized direction or coordination of the program. Additional resources have been mustered to help implement the marketing plans. Examples:

Maintenance Reserve funds have been allocated to renovate the Central Branch Health Club entrance as recommended.

A highly skilled professional Health Club Director has been employed for this unit. Fifty percent of his responsibilities include conducting a training school for health club personnel for all branches with emphasis on massage and sales.

The Public Relations staff of the General Offices has been increased with the employment of a Director of Communications to aid in the development of interpretive materials and promotion of programs.

Increased coordination of the Tot Time program and the addition of YMCA Movement Education to the program were recommended by the Tot Time Task Force. One Branch Executive has taken the responsibility to get all Tot Time teachers, from across the Association, together on a regular basis for review of objectives, study, discussion and coordination of the recommended curriculum. Training in YMCA Movement Education has been added to the program under the direction of the Assistant Vice President for Physical Education. Standards for teacher credentials and salary ranges have been established.

Recruitment of a professional staff person to coordinate Y-Indian Guide programs for 3 or 4 Branches in a geographic district is underway. The revving up of an Association-wide Y-Indian Guide lay organization is being considered. The possibility of the Milwaukee Association hosting the 1979 National Longhouse Convention, 20 years after its last convention in Milwaukee in 1959, is under consideration.

A market study and analysis of population data for the Greater Milwaukee area, segmented by Branch service areas and neighborhoods was conducted. This information reinforced the decision to merge two Branches and helped gain acceptance of the merger. This information is also available to staff for planning in the Branches.

Because marketing is a management approach that grew out of the profit motivation of a free enterprise system many people have not seen what it has to do with the YMCA, a non-profit organization. I believe that marketing is a way of thinking and a management discipline that is as applicable to the YMCA as other management tools adopted from business and industry . . . from business office practices to Management by Objectives.

In business, the motivation for marketing planning is to satisfy customers and to make a profit. In the Milwaukee YMCA the motivation is to attract people to the Association to have an influence for good upon their lives . . . and to break even.

I believe that a marketing approach can help us achieve YMCA purposes. It is a new way of thinking about how to manage the People Business.

Questions

1. *What environmental and organizational factors contributed most to the success of the Milwaukee YMCA marketing efforts?*
2. *Select a nonbusiness organization in your community (for example, the local YMCA, a church youth group, or a civic club) and develop a marketing strategy and mix for that group.*

49

Ethics in an
International Business Context HANS SCHOLLHAMMER

Do U.S. marketers march to the beat of a different drummer when they enter foreign markets? Americans were shocked in the 1970s to learn that American corporations doing business abroad operated by a set of standards that were illegal or at least unethical in the United States.

Two and a half centuries ago, Daniel Defoe observed that "every degree of business has its invitation to do evil."[1] In recent months attention has focused on bringing to light the "evil deeds" of multinational corporations whose international business activities have become massive in the past fifteen years and continue to expand rapidly. It has been calculated that worldwide production by multinational companies constitutes about 15 percent of total world production, and that U.S.-based multinational firms alone—with foreign direct investments of about $140 billion at the end of 1975—account for about 10 percent of the aggregate gross national products of the world.

The continued rapid expansion of multinational corporations and the inordinate economic power they can bring to bear has brought their activities under close scrutiny. Some observers see in the multinationals the most efficient mechanism for the creation and distribution of wealth on a worldwide

Source: Hans Schollhammer, "Ethics in an International Business Context," pp. 54–63, *MSU Business Topics*, Spring 1977. Reprinted by permission of the publisher, Division of Research, Graduate School of Business Administration, Michigan State University.

scale and the only effective force to ameliorate a tide of nationalism in an increasingly xenophobic world.[2] Other observers see danger in the staggering accumulation of power among a relatively small number of global companies; they view these firms as fundamentally exploitative, detrimental to national sovereignty, and obstructive to legitimate social aspirations of the people of the world.[3] The widespread criticism of multinational corporations has been fueled by sensational revelations of unethical practices, such as undue political influence, bribery, and corruption committed by prominent multinational firms. Although relatively few multinationals have been implicated, their misdemeanors seem to affect the standing of all. As a result, the ethical standards of the multinationals are viewed with suspicion or apprehension by a wide spectrum of the public.

The Meaning of Ethics

Ethics are concerned with judgments of "what is right" (or moral) and "what is wrong" (or immoral), and conclusions are drawn regarding "what ought to be" instead of "what is." The term *ethical standards* is used to describe conformity to widely accepted modes of conduct. These, in turn, are governed to a large extent by customs, manners, and values that a particular society adopts as guidelines for regulating interpersonal behavior. Because of the range of societal values (be they religious, philosophical, or cultural), there are no absolute, universally accepted ethical standards. In fact, ethics and morals are subject to changing societal values as well as subjective interpretations which allow individuals to infuse ethical meaning into selfish aspirations and questionable actions. For these reasons, questions concerning business ethics in general are difficult to deal with, and those concerning the ethics of multinational companies are even more difficult because of the heterogeneity of societal values by which these firms are affected.

Although certain ethical norms such as honesty, integrity, self-discipline, loyalty, and compassion are widely proclaimed and are part of any civilization, adherence to these standards varies greatly among people. In dealing with ethical issues one is constantly confronted with apparent hypocrisy. In addition, one has to realize that there exists an inherent conflict between the economic imperative on the one hand, requiring "success" as characterized by business objectives (such as maximization of profits or a company's market share under competitive conditions), and ethical norms on the other hand. A study by Raymond C. Baumhart documents this dichotomy by pointing out an apparent "double ethic" which pretends that "general business behavior is quite different from the personal ethical attitudes."[4]

Ethics of Multinational Companies

In recent months, more than in any previous period, the public has had a glimpse of practices which raise grave questions about the moral standards and ethical behavior of major U.S.-based and foreign-based multinational firms. The exposures are due to investigations and charges by the Securities and Exchange Commission (SEC) involving about 200 such firms. In addition, the subcommittee on multinational companies of the U.S. Senate Foreign Relations Committee, under the chairmanship of Sen. Frank Church, has been following up on leads provided by the SEC and has extracted more of the gory details.

The SEC investigations began in 1974 with its probe of illegal corporate contributions to the re-election campaign of former President Nixon. These investigations brought to light similar secret political payments by the same companies overseas and an assortment of "special payments" (euphemistically referred to as agents' fees, consultants' fees, sales procurement commissions, and so forth) to influential foreign persons or other "bagmen." The SEC's main interest centers on ascertaining whether companies committed briberies or fraud or have broken rules requiring disclosures to shareholders. The investigations by Senator Church's subcommittee are primarily aimed at finding out what further legislation, if any, is needed to regulate the conduct and operations of U.S. multinational firms.

Among the firms which the SEC investigated or from which it received voluntary disclosures are aerospace companies such as Lockheed, Northrup, Grumman, McDonnell Douglas, and Boeing; oil companies such as Exxon, Phillips Petroleum, Mobil Oil, Gulf Oil, Ashland Oil, and Occidental Oil; and other companies in a spectrum of industries, including General Tire and Rubber, American Shipbuilding Company, United Brands (formerly the United Fruit Company), R. J. Reynolds, and Carnation.

For example, Lockheed admitted to paying about $25 million in overseas bribes and (since 1970) to having paid or obligated itself to pay $200 million in commissions and fees, which amounts to about 5 percent of Lockheed's foreign sales. Between 1963 and 1971, Exxon authorized—among other questionable payments—about $28 million in political contributions to ruling political parties and government officials in Italy. In addition, about $19 million in unauthorized payments were disguised in various ways, for example, as payments for goods and services never purchased. The SEC charges against General Tire and Rubber include illegal political contributions in the United States, overseas bribes, violations of foreign currency laws, unrecorded "slush" funds, overbilling of foreign subsidiaries for supplies, and a payment of $150,000 to Perco Establishment, owned by Adnan Kashoggi, a Saudi Arabian businessman, for help in getting General Tire and Rubber off the Arab boycott list. Robert Dorsay, chairman of Gulf Oil, tesitifed before the Church subcommittee that the political campaign managers of South Korea's ruling Democratic Republican Party extorted $4 million from Gulf Oil. In addition, he testified, the company paid bribes to minor government officials which were characterized as "low level tipping"; larger payments were classified as "entertainment expenses." United Brands paid $1,250,000 into a Swiss bank account in favor of a member of the Honduran government at a time when the company was trying to persuade that government to reduce its export tax on bananas. Subsequently, the tax was reduced from one dollar per forty pound box to thirty cents. R. J. Reynolds, the largest U.S. tobacco company, with significant other interests in container shipping and the petroleum industry, admitted to making more than $25 million in "questionable corporate payments to promote its business and political interests." More than $19 million was in the form of possibly illegal rebates by the company's wholly owned shipping subsidiary; in its statement to the SEC, Reynolds noted that "most shippers expected such payments and almost every foreign and domestic carrier paid them." Also, $5.36 million in questionable payoffs were related to Reynolds' tobacco business and went to low or middle level officials of foreign governments or government-owned companies.

Most of the recent exposures of questionable foreign payoffs and other corrupt practices have been attributed to U.S.-based multinationals. However, foreign-based multinational firms are not immune to these shady tactics, although less is known about their dealings. For example, Imperial Chemical Industries (ICI), Great Britain's second largest company, admitted having made questionable payments amounting to £1.35 million over a four-year period starting in 1971. With one exception ICI stated that all payments were made to grease the bureaucratic machinery in developing countries. Another firm based in the United Kingdom, Tate & Lyle, has recently been accused of bribing government officials in various countries. In a case involving the French aircraft manufacturer Dassault, Piet Dankert, a member of the Netherlands parliament, declared before a court in Amsterdam that the Office Français d'Exportation de Material Aeronautique had offered him approximately $50,000 in commissions if his government

would order the French-made Mirage F-1M53 instead of General Dynamics' F-16. One of the largest Japanese companies, Marubeni, is implicated as conduit in the Lockheed payments in Japan, and a former Japanese prime minister, Kakuei Tanaka, has been indicted as a major recipient of some of the Lockheed payments. All these payoffs involved sizable amounts, but even relatively small multinationals may make questionable payments. For example, the chief executive officer of a Japanese subsidiary with a small production facility in a racially mixed, low income community of Southern California revealed that, for the sake of harmonious working relationships in the plant, the company hires only Mexican-Americans as production workers. The company is compelled to make sizable financial contributions to local leaders of black groups to avoid trouble over the firm's hiring practices.

These few examples represent less than the tip of the iceberg. There is evidence of a global morass of bribery and corruption, and it is difficult to judge whether individual executives and the companies they manage are the culprits or the victims of practices that reach back to earliest civilizations. Polybius, the Greek historian living in the second century B.C., summarized Carthage's decline in a single sentence: "At Carthage nothing that results in profit is regarded as disgraceful."[5] During the Renaissance, corruption was rampant, and business historian Jacob van Klaveren suggested that sixteenth- and seventeenth-century Europe should be characterized not as the age of mercantilism but as the age of corruption.[6]

Multinational Companies as Culprits or Victims?

In a recent article on business payoffs abroad, Peter Nehemkis stated firmly that "bribery is an institutionalized fact of international business life."[7] This echoed a cynical characterization by Walter Goodman, who observed that "businessmen are as ethical as they can be and as unethical as they need to be."[8] In judging the global palm-greasing, it seems important to distinguish whether the payoffs are demanded by the recipients as a form of blackmail, or are offered in expectation of favors that should not be rendered because they are illegal or otherwise contrary to stated regulations. On the basis of available information, one can conclude that corrupt payments are far more often asked of than offered by multinationals. These firms seem to be more the victims of a social practice that is particularly pervasive among many of the developing countries of Latin America, the Middle East, Africa, and Asia.[9]

In many of these countries business firms are confronted with a chaotic entanglement of red tape maintained by poorly paid yet status conscious technocrats and politicians. To accomplish anything, be it, for example, the issuance of a required permit or the clearance of a shipment through customs, requires a "token of appreciation" or a lubrication bribe to start the bureaucratic wheels rolling. These relatively small payments to unfreeze a bureaucracy are in many parts of the world so common that they are treated as general business expenses.

A more aggravating problem is posed by the occasional demands for exorbitant bribes from high ranking government officials. The Lockheed payoffs abroad throw a particularly harsh new light on the potential for high level corruption among national leaders, as the accusations against Japan's Tanaka and Prince Bernhard of the Netherlands show. The Donner Commission's Report to the Netherlands government on the prince consort's involvement with Lockheed provides evidence of barefaced financial solicitations by Prince Bernhard, who in 1974 asked for a secret "commission" of 4 percent on complete aircraft and 8 percent on parts sold to the Dutch government. Lockheed executives estimated that, considering the magnitude of the deal, the "commission" would cost the company between $4 million and $6 million. Lockheed offered only about $1.3 million, which, according to an agent's statement, the prince accepted. Soon afterward, however, the Netherlands government decided not to buy the Lockheed (Orion) aircraft, and the "commission" never went through.

Multinational firms are vulnerable to extortive demands by high ranking officials—a situation that can only be characterized as blackmail. Many firms are susceptible because of intense interfirm competition or because of the vulnerability of their local investments. In the latter case, any payments extorted from a multinational firm under adverse circumstances are more in the nature of protection money than bribery since the main purpose is the protection of local interests from harassment, discrimination, or the capriciousness of local bureaucrats and politicians. Intense competitive pressure is frequently the major reason corporate executives take the initiative in offering corrupt payments in the hope that they might effect a desired outcome. It is not surprising that some companies in a quasi-monopolistic market position, such as IBM, RCA, or Kodak, seem to be relatively immune to these dubious payoffs. Firms that get caught up in these payments find it necessary to develop elaborate systems of concealment. If the secrecy breaks, the companies are faced with prosecution, shareholder actions, and embarrassment.

Considering the available evidence on corrupt practices leads to the conclusion that multinational firms are both victims and culprits. It takes two to bribe, and any moral judgment must necessarily take into account the motives of the donor and the recipient. At the root of this malaise is human greed fueled by an increasing materialism and a generally decreasing commitment to moral values or traditional religious values. This situation is aggravated by the frequently intense jockeying for competitive edge among multinational firms.

Remedial Actions

The widespread awareness of corruption and unethical behavior in international business has led to extensive discussion and to proposals for remedies. Corrective steps in progress involve five approaches:

international agreements on corrupt practices,
unilateral restrictive legislation,
regulatory measures by administrative agencies,

corporate codes of conduct as affirmation of company policies on ethical issues, and intergovernmental agreements on codes of conduct.

International Agreements

During the past three decades many global problems have been dealt with through international agreements. For example, tariff and nontariff restrictions to international trade repeatedly have been lowered through the offices of an intergovernmental association known as the General Agreement on Tariffs and Trade (GATT). Most Western and some Communist countries are members. In essence, GATT is the institution that sets and regulates the code of international trade conduct. Similarly, the proliferation of nuclear weapons has been checked by an international treaty, ratified by more than eighty countries. In July 1972 the United Nations Economic and Social Council adopted a resolution requesting that the UN secretary-general appoint a group of eminent persons to study the role of multinational corporations and submit recommendations for appropriate international actions. The request led to a report containing a series of recommendations, one of which deals specifically with ethical issues: [10] "The group recommends that host countries should clearly define the permissible public activities of the affiliates of multinational corporations and also prescribe sanctions against infringements. The financial contributions of multinational corporations as well as of others to interest groups should be regulated and disclosed." [11] The report also recommended the formation of a UN Commission on Multinational Corporations; this was implemented in 1975. The U.S. government instructed its delegate to the second meeting of this commission to call for an intergovernmental agreement on corrupt practices. Such an agreement would require from each ratifying country a commitment not to tolerate corruption and to establish criminal penalties for practices such as bribes and the request or acceptance of payoffs. In addition, the agreement as proposed by the U.S. government would include provisions for intergovernmental co-

operation on the exchange of information between law-enforcing agencies concerning corrupt practices and a uniform set of procedures for their disclosure.

It is felt a UN-sponsored intergovernmental agreement would go a long way toward reducing incidents of bribery and extortion involving large payments. It would probably have little initial impact on the petty palm-greasing that is a widespread practice with a long tradition and strong roots in the sociocultural conditions of many countries. But to the extent that an intergovernmental agreement would lead to greater openness and more information on the existence of this societal malaise, it would cause embarrassment to those governments that up to now have been tolerant of these practices; they would eventually have to make an effort to curb this petty corruption.

Unilateral Restrictive Legislation

On 14 June 1976 the U.S. government announced that it will seek legislation requiring disclosure of payments by U.S.-controlled firms made with the intent of influencing directly or indirectly the conduct of foreign government officials. This legislation also would make it unlawful for any person to falsify any record or account concerning payments by U.S. firms. In announcing this proposed legislation, former President Gerald Ford stressed that the number of U.S. firms implicated in corrupt payments abroad is relatively small but that the pattern of improper behavior cannot be tolerated. If it were allowed to continue it could badly erode public and international confidence in U.S. business and institutions.

Some members of Congress—among them Sen. William D. Proxmire—suggested that the proposed legislation should be more stringent and that it be made a crime, rather than merely an action requiring disclosure, for U.S. corporations to make payoffs to foreign officials. Regardless of the laws that eventually may evolve, the proponents of these measures believe that restrictive legislation will help executives of U.S.-controlled firms ward off extortion demands and will deter them from initiating bribes.

The efficiency of legislating ethical behavior can be questioned. Even the most stringent disclosure requirements could do little to eliminate questionable payments to "agents," "consultants," or "charitable organizations" that have been used as recipients or conduits for unethical payments. The most that can be expected is a possible reduction in the amounts actually paid, not in the payments as such.

In contrast to the initiatives of the U.S. government, European governments have done little to restrict unethical practices of firms under their jurisdiction; in general, they take the line that nothing useful can be done to curb corrupt practices in international business. To the extent that non-U.S. multinational firms would not be encumbered by restrictions similar to those proposed by the U.S. government, the situation could conceivably cause competitive disadvantages for U.S.-based corporations.

Regulatory Measures

Governments need not introduce legislation to deter corrupt practices. Instead, they can use their regulatory powers on transactions that require government approval. For example, under the Foreign Military Sales Program, business transactions between U.S. defense contractors and foreign governments must be approved by the Department of Defense and the Department of State. These departments are now stipulating that foreign governments that buy from U.S. defense contractors must be informed of all agent fees, commissions, or other contingent fees included in the purchase price. If a foreign government decides that all or part of these fees are unacceptable, the Department of Defense then informs the producing company that the amount in question is not an allowable expense. The rationale of this regulatory measure is obvious: The U.S. government does not want to be an accessory to questionable agents' fees abroad. The efficacy of the measure is, however, doubtful. A com-

pany might still decide to pay agent or consulting fees to foreign "experts" without disclosing them as separate cost items in a contract under negotiation. More troublesome than such an evasive strategy is the possibility that U.S. firms might lose sales to foreign manufacturers of military equipment that are not affected by restrictive regulations.

Under existing conditions, the unilateral imposition of legislation or restrictive measures by the U.S. government will most likely create competitive disadvantages for U.S.-based firms. On the other hand, there is a possibility that foreign purchasers, knowing the restrictions imposed on U.S. firms and thus being reasonably certain that they will not be embarrassed by future disclosures of corrupt payments, will actually prefer to buy from U.S. companies.

Intergovernmental agreements, legislation, and specific regulatory measures designed to cope with unethical business practices cannot be viewed as substitutes for a commitment to and enforcement of clear ethical standards on the part of each company. For this reason, potentially the greatest contribution to an improvement of business morality in an international context can be expected from adoption and enforcement of codes of conduct.

Codes of Conduct

The increasing frictions between multinational companies and government agencies of host as well as home countries have led officials and executives to postulate certain behavioral norms that constitute the essence of "good corporate citizenship." Similarly, the spreading awareness of illegal or unethical acts committed by executives of multinational firms has further spurred the demand for constructive and realistic standards of international business conduct. These standards are to serve as guidelines for judging the appropriateness of specific corporate activities in the pursuit of international business interests as well as of governmental actions affecting the operations of multinational firms. Two approaches to code development are being pursued:

Several international organizations are in the process of devising mutually agreed upon and enforceable guidelines for appropriate conduct by multinational firms; and

a growing number of these companies are promulgating their own in-house codes of conduct designed to affirm explicitly a company's commitment to ethical standards and good corporate citizenship worldwide.

Involvement of International Organizations

Efforts at codifying proper business behavior by means of international or intergovernmental agreements have a long history.[12] Concerning multinational business operations, the United Nations Conference on Trade and Development (UNCTAD) adopted a resolution in 1968 which set in motion a series of studies, among them a particularly noteworthy report from "a group of eminent persons."[13] A major recommendation of this report was the establishment of a permanent Commission on Multinational Corporations, under the auspices of the UN Economic and Social Council. This recommendation was approved and the committee was charged

"to explore the possibility of concluding a general agreement on multinational corporations, enforceable by appropriate machinery, to which participating countries would adhere by means of an international treaty" and

"to evolve a set of recommendations which, taken together, would represent a code of conduct for Governments and multinational corporations to be considered and adopted by the Economic and Social Council, and review in the light of experience the effective application and continuing applicability of such recommendations."[14]

Such a code of conduct is envisaged as an instrument of moral persuasion, strengthened by the authority of international organizations and the support of public opinion.

The UN Commission on Multinational Corpora-

tions has not yet suggested any specific proposal for such a code of conduct; its deliberations are in progress. The eventual results of these deliberations will probably show close similarity to the "Guidelines for Multinational Enterprises," on which the 24 member governments of the Organization for Economic Cooperation and Development (OECD), comprising the most industrialized countries in the Western world, reached agreement in mid-1976 after 18 months of negotiations.[15]

The OECD guidelines are essentially aimed at keeping the alleged powers of multinational companies in check and at making them more responsive to the interests of the host countries and to government policies in general. In turn, the governments of the OECD member countries committed themselves in principle not to discriminate between domestic- and foreign-controlled enterprises; if the latter are to be treated differently, the government concerned must inform the OECD within thirty days. The OECD will then review this discrimination with other interested parties. The OECD guidelines comprise nine general policies and focus on six sets of issues dealing with

the disclosure of information,
interfirm competition,
financing of business operations,
taxation,
science and technology, and
employment and industrial relations.

The general policies prescribe for multinational firms norms and behavior patterns which are frequently summed up under the "good corporate citizenship" label.[16] For example, multinational corporations are exhorted to take into account the aims and priorities of the host countries, particularly those concerning a country's social progress, its economic development, the creation of employment opportunities, the promotion of innovation, environmental protection, and cooperation with local business interests.

Concerning ethical issues, the OECD guidelines specify that multinational firms should not render—nor should they be expected to render—

any bribe or other improper benefit to holders of public office. In addition, the guidelines specify that unless it is legally permissible, multinational firms should not make contributions to political parties or to candidates for public office, nor should they become involved in local political activities in an improper manner.

Although the Guidelines for Multinational Enterprises are the result of an intergovernmental agreement among the 24 OECD member countries, they do not constitute a treaty, nor are they offered as a basis for specific legislative programs to be adopted by the individual countries. Instead, they are purely hortatory, and since many of the stated concepts are vague or ill-defined, there is considerable room for interpretation. For these reasons the practical value and the impact of these guidelines for improving the ethics of multinational firms are open to question. The guidelines simply spell out some of the controversial issues and make certain recommendations, but it remains to be seen whether the governments and the multinational companies will do much more than pay lip-service to their validity.

Considering the approaches suggested for dealing with ethical issues in an international business context, one comes to the conclusion that the most convincing measure is the commitment to a company-specific code of conduct that affirms the ethical standards that the individual firm wants to uphold.

Corporate Affirmation of Standards

During the National Foreign Trade Convention in November 1975, Lee L. Morgan, president of Caterpillar Tractor Co., stressed his view that the commitment to and implementation of self-imposed ethical standards for a firm's worldwide operations constitute the "principal root issue before the international business community."[17] He argued that such corporate guidelines should rank at the top of the agenda of leaders of multinational companies everywhere. Other corporate leaders have taken a similar position,[18] and a growing number of mul-

tinationals are adopting or refining codes of conduct for worldwide business activities.

For the articulation of a workable code of ethics the individual firm can use three approaches. It can develop a code that is essentially *prescriptive,* that is, stating what a company feels are proper practices and what behavior it expects from its employees. It can adopt a code that is essentially *restrictive,* that is, specifying what not to do. Finally, it can use a *combination* of the restrictive and prescriptive approaches. In general, the prescriptive approach is preferable since it emphasizes in a positive way what a company stands for rather than simply enumerating what it considers improper.

Formalizing principles and policies for a firm's international business conduct creates several benefits. First, it provides consistent guidelines for ethical business behavior of the firm's employees wherever they work. As such, a corporate code of conduct is an internal communication device concerning basic company beliefs. Second, a code can be used as a control instrument to reemphasize periodically the company's commitment to ethical and socially responsible actions; for example, some companies are now demanding that their managers sign annual pledges that they have upheld the principles and policies affirmed in the company's worldwide code of conduct. Third, once the company has adopted a code, it can make it available to the public, documenting and explaining the firm's commitment to ethical business conduct; in this manner, the code becomes a public relations instrument.

Most companies that have already adopted a code of conduct agree, however, that the greatest benefit results from the process of developing it. If corporate executives take this task seriously, the discussions on the substantive content of the code force executives to crystallize company policy and specify the principles that guide their actions. Although the initiative for a corporate code of ethics must come from the top leadership, its development should involve a broad segment of the firm's management.

A particular problem in the development of a multinational company's code of conduct is the temptation to adopt a concept that is frequently referred to as "situation ethics," that is, the application of different ethical standards in different parts of the world. It has been argued that since ethical standards are culturally derived, they are subject to variations, and the individual firm should adapt to the prevailing ethical standards of a society. Such an approach is, however, likely to create severe conflicts. A multinational firm should, therefore, strive for a uniform, worldwide code with the highest ethical standards as the common denominator for all operations.

Cynics may point out that in the absence of any guarantee that corporate executives will actually abide by code standards, the adoption of a corporate code during a period of widespread public criticism of corporate misbehavior is simply a defensive maneuver and window dressing. Such a characterization would be justified if the leadership of a multinational firm were not truly committed to enforcement of the firm's code. The credibility of a code is thus put to the test when management has reason to suspect the code has been violated. If the suspicion is correct, the corporate leadership must act immediately and in a punitive manner; by doing so, it gives notice that it will not tolerate corporate wrongdoing and that its code of ethics is operative and not a mere statement of good intentions.

Conclusion

Since "every business has its invitation to do evil," most business executives are necessarily confronted with an ethical dilemma. Assertions of low business morality are by no means new, but recent revelations about widespread corrupt practices implicating a remarkably large number of multinational firms have provided evidence that briberies, falsification of business records, collusive agreements, and similar improper actions have proliferated to an intolerable extent. The available evidence also suggests that many multinational companies are initiators of unethical activities as well as vic-

tims of high and low level extortion. In order to cope with this ethical issue various measures such as restrictive legislation by individual governments, intergovernmental agreements on operations and behavior of multinational firms, and exhortations by international agencies are under consideration. Although it has been pointed out that business people generally change their practices only under pressure,[19] the impact of these externally imposed measures on improving business morality in an international context is still likely to be limited. It can be argued that the only really effective way to improve business morality is for the individual firm to develop and enforce a uniform, worldwide code of conduct as a guideline for all of a firm's employees to do what is right and not what seems to be expedient. Only to the extent that the international business community succeeds in this endeavor will it be able to combat the widespread public distrust and increasingly restrictive regulations affecting the future growth and success of international business operations.

Notes

1. Daniel Defoe, *The Complete English Tradesman* (London: D. Rivington, 1727), II, p. 21.

2. See, for example, Neil H. Jacoby, "The Multinational Corporation," *Center Magazine* 3 (May 1970): 37–55; and Howard V. Perlmutter, "The Multinational Firm and the Future," *Annals of the American Academy of Political and Social Science* 403 (September 1972): 139–52.

3. See, for example, Richard J. Barnet and Ronald E. Müller, *Global Reach: The Power of the Multinational Corporations* (New York: Simon & Schuster, 1974); Robert Gilpin, *U.S. Power and the Multinational Corporation* (New York: Basic Books, 1975); Harry Magdoff and Paul M. Sweezy, "Notes on the Multinational Corporation," and Theotonio Dos Santos, "The Structure of Dependence," both in *Readings in U.S. Imperialism,* edited by K. T. Fann and D. C. Hodges (Boston: P. Sargent, 1971), pp. 93–115 and 225–36; and Hugh Stephenson, *The*

Coming Clash: The Impact of Multinational Corporations on National States (New York: Saturday Review Press, 1972).

4. Raymond C. Baumhart, "How Ethical Are Businessmen?" *Harvard Business Review* 39 (July–August 1961): 19; see also, by the same author, *Ethics in Business* (New York: Holt, Rinehart and Winston, 1968).

5. Quoted by Baumhart in "How Ethical Are Businessmen?" p. 8.

6. Jacob van Klaveren, *Europaische Wirtschaftsschaftsgeschichte* (Stuttgart: Kohlhammer Verlag, 1960), 51.

7. Peter Nehemikis, "Business Payoffs Abroad: Rhetoric and Reality," *California Management Review* 18 (Winter 1975): 7.

8. Walter Goodman, *All Honorable Men: Corruption and Compromise in American Life* (Boston: Little, Brown & Company, 1963), p. 99.

9. See, for example, Ronald E. Wraith, *Corruption in Developing Countries* (New York: Norton Publishing Co., 1964); and Louis Turner, *Multinational Companies in the Third World* (London: Allen Lane, 1974), pp. 126–27.

10. United Nations, *The Impact of Multinational Corporations on Development and on International Relations* (New York: 1974).

11. Ibid., p. 46.

12. See, for example, USA-BIAC Committee on International Business and Multinational Enterprise, *A Review of Standards and Guidelines for International Business Conduct* (New York: the Committee, 1975).

13. United Nations, *Impact of Multinational Corporations*.

14. Ibid., p. 7.

15. Organization for Economic Cooperation and Development, *Declaration of OECD Members on International Investment and Multinational Enterprises* (Washington: OECD Publications Center, June 1976).

16. Multinational companies are frequently urged to behave as "good corporate citizens" in host countries. The term is vague but is generally used to prescribe an agglomeration of traits or behavioral norms that include promotion of local personnel to positions of responsibility, local participation in ownership, respect for national laws and cultural values, restraint in the exercise of corporate power, actions in support of the host country's socioeconomic priorities, and so forth. See, for example, International Chamber of Commerce, *Guidelines for International Investment* (Paris: 1972).

17. Lee L. Morgan, *Worldwide Business Conduct*, address before the 62nd National Foreign Trade Convention, New York, New York, 18 November 1975, published by the Public Affairs Department, Caterpillar Tractor Co.

18. See, for example, Carl Burgen et al., "How Companies React to the Ethics Crisis," *Business Week*, 9 February 1976, pp. 78–79; and W. M. Blumenthal, "Business Ethics: A Call for a Moral Approach," *Financial Executive* 44 (January 1976): 32–34.

19. Victor Obenhause, *Ethics for an Industrial Age* (New York: John Wiley & Sons, 1967).

Questions

1. *"When in Rome, do as the Romans do." Should this be the major policy guideline for U.S. corporations in business dealings in other nations?*

2. *What should be the limits of corporate ethics in international business dealings? Should U.S. corporations live by U.S. law, by their own set of corporate ethics, or by the "law of the business jungle"?*

3. *Discuss the appropriateness of each of the five approaches reviewed in this article for minimizing corruption and unethical behavior in international business.*

50

When Levi Strauss
Burst Its Britches

PETER VANDERWICKEN

Although Gillette found foreign markets to be a bed of roses, Levi Strauss found these markets to be fraught with thorns. The Levi Strauss policy of national manager autonomy cost the company dearly in its European operations in the early 1970s.

Along with Coca-Cola, jazz, and the automobile, the humble but hardy garment known as jeans ranks as one of America's major contributions to global culture. Over the past decade, jeans have become not only the new rage among the young but also a ubiquitous emblem of unfashionable fashion and probably the world's most widely popular trouser.

In the competitive and chaotic apparel industry, no company has stitched together a sturdier performance from the craze for jeans than their original maker, Levi Strauss & Co. Outstripping the growth of all its competitors, the company has multiplied its annual sales volume ninefold to $653 million, a compound annual growth rate of 24 percent. Its profits kept pace, and its return on investment was consistently better than that of its rivals. That record has helped the company to acquire an enviable reputation for managerial prowess.

Until last year. Then, with the suddenness of a summer storm, some marketing blunders dealt a blow to both profits and reputation. The setback occurred in Europe, where Levi's had been growing the fastest; its sales there leapt from $8 million in 1965 to $100 million in 1973. In achieving such hectic growth, the company committed a number of classic management errors, and so stumbled into that familiar booby trap: an excess of inventories. To make matters worse, it took months before top company executives realized that they faced a serious problem. And it required a full year of ever more costly price cutting to dispose of the goods.

The debacle cost Levi Strauss at least $12 million and left the company with a deficit of $7,244,000 in the fourth quarter of last year, its first quarterly loss since the Depression. With that painful setback, Levi's earned only a meager $11,856,000 in its fiscal 1973, which ended November 25.

The unexpected loss was an embarrassing blow to the credibility of the proud men who run Levi's. The company had reluctantly gone public in 1971 to raise $45 million of capital to finance expansion. And only a few months before the fiasco Levi's top executives had dismissed warnings of impending trouble brought them by Wall Street analysts. Chairman Walter Haas Jr., fifty-eight, calls the European episode "a traumatic experience." His fifty-five-year-old brother Peter, the president, puts it even more bluntly. "Obviously," he says, "I'm in the same situation Nixon is—I'm either a knave or a fool. We should have known and didn't, or we didn't know as accurately as we should have."

Shirtsleeves for the Fourth Generation

The lapse has only temporarily dampened the company's ebullient operating style, which is almost as

Source: Fortune 87 (April 1974), 131–136, 138. Reprinted from the April 1974 issue of *Fortune Magazine* by special permission; © 1975 Time, Inc.

original as its principal product. Levi Strauss's main office for most of its 124-year existence has been in the same block of Battery Street in downtown San Francisco. Lately the company has occupied a funky old building filled with littered desks, rock-music posters, and cluttered memorabilia. Its casual, offbeat atmosphere attracts lots of bright young M.B.A.'s, who twirl their mustaches, devise wildly imaginative marketing programs, and wear—of course—Levi's.

By any measure, Levi Strauss is also one of the country's most socially responsible corporations. It takes pains to hire the handicapped, contributes generously to charities, and aggressively seeks black and Chicano workers. Thirty-eight percent of its U.S. employees, including 11 percent of its executives, are members of minority groups.

The company clearly reflects the manner and the concerns of the brothers who run it. Though born to wealth and social position, and schooled at the University of California and the Harvard Business School, both Haases are informal outdoorsmen who enjoy camping and horseback riding at their ranches north of San Francisco. They work in shirtsleeves and encourage all employees—even including sewing-machine operators—to call them by their first names. For years, both have devoted a substantial chunk of their time to civic causes, notably national and local efforts to fight social inequities. Both are pillars of the city's business establishment. Walter is, among other things, a director of the Bank of America and a trustee of the Ford Foundation; Peter is a trustee of Stanford University.

The Haases form the fourth generation of family management at Levi Strauss. They are great-grand-nephews of the company's founder, Levi Strauss, an immigrant from Bavaria and a life-long bachelor, who began selling dry-goods and equipment to the gold miners who flocked to California in the early 1850s. When a prospector asked for some pants that would withstand the rugged environment, Strauss made the first Levi's from canvas intended for tents and wagon covers, but soon switched to the familiar blue-cotton denim. Cowboys, too, discovered that the indigo-dyed denims were comfortable and durable on the range, and the virtues of old Levi's pants entered the folklore of the West. More than a century later, their design changed only by the removal of a few copper rivets; they are still the company's basic product.

Worn and Torn, At $25 a Pair

By a wide margin the world's largest manufacturer of pants, Levi Strauss last year turned out some 25 million pairs of blue jeans. Its brand name has long since been adopted as a worldwide synonym for the product, and the distinctive "Levi's" tag—always sewn on the outside of its pants—is a familiar sight on rear ends from Belgium to Borneo.

Even so, blue jeans nowadays account for only a quarter of the company's business. Last year Levi's also made more than 75 million pairs of corduroy jeans and slacks. It is becoming a large manufacturer of shirts, and has a fast-growing line of blouses and slacks for women. Two years ago it bought a belt company, and it is looking for other acquisitions.

Most of its growth, however, has been internal, achieved by broadening its product line and entering new geographical markets. Today Levi's is a multinational business, with manufacturing plants in twelve countries and sales subsidiaries in twenty-five.

Until last year, the very idea that the company might run into trouble in Europe would have seemed ridiculous. As the craze for jeans and corduroy pants swept over the Continent, every youth seemed to want several pairs. Entrepreneurs shipped crateloads of used and discarded Levi's from the U.S. to Europe and sold them for double the price of new pants. In Paris boutiques, worn and torn Levi's sold for an outlandish $25 a pair. Both small European manufacturers and Levi's major U.S. competitors, H. D. Lee Co. (now a division of VF Corp.) and Blue Bell Inc. (which makes Wrangler jeans), scrambled for shares of the exploding market.

Levi's had begun exporting to Europe on a small scale in the early Sixties, and formed a subsidiary called Levi Strauss Europe (L.S.E.), as part of its international division, to coordinate its growing operations there. But even in 1969 L.S.E. consisted only of a dozen employees based in Brussels and a warehouse in Antwerp, through which pants were imported from Levi's factories in the U.S. and Hong Kong and sold to independent distributors throughout Europe.

All Out for Market Share

Levi's international business was run with what the company calls "total autonomy," and the man who ran it was Vice President Edward Combs, who was thirty-four when he took over in 1964. The Haases regarded him as their most aggressive executive, and many in the company considered him heir apparent to the presidency. As the European demand for jeans began to soar, Combs made a crucial decision—with Peter Haas's full concurrence. He decided that Levi Strauss should expand rapidly in Europe to grab as large a market share as possible. Only later would the company impose its usual financial and management controls.

It was a risky strategy, but Combs reasoned that it would be much easier to gain a position in the market before competitors became entrenched. If Levi's expanded with its customary caution, it would have to fight well-established rivals later. Moreover, Levi's executives regarded their denim and corduroy jeans as basic garments not subject to the changing whims of fashion. Since demand was far outrunning supply, there seemed to be no pressing need for inventory controls.

In August, 1969, Combs sent thirty-six-year-old Carroll Robinson, Jr., who had been the company's advertising manager for four years, to Brussels as the general manager of Levi Strauss Europe. His appointment reflected the company's emphasis on marketing. An energetic and engaging man who wears rumpled suits and chain-smokes Viceroys, "Bud" Robinson had masterminded many of the adroit campaigns that had helped Levi's jeans become *de rigueur* with American youth.

In Europe, Robinson got his first crack at operating responsibilities. He began frantically hiring people, ordering goods from Strauss plants in the U.S. and elsewhere, and buying factories to start

European production. The demand for pants seemed insatiable. In 1970 L.S.E.'s inventory turned over seven times (about four is normal for apparel) and the main warehouse in Antwerp had to be fully replenished an incredible nineteen times.

Learning that a shipment was arriving, distributors would send trucks to Antwerp and buy anything they saw. "Trucks and cars were backed up outside," Robinson recalls. "We had a table there and our customers would start fighting over the goods. Pretty soon they'd be sneaking around the table into the warehouse. They'd drive away with pants flapping out the back of the truck."

To improve Levi's distribution within Europe as quickly as possible, Robinson took another crucial step. Rather than bring in Levi Strauss salesmen who were experienced in domestic apparel markets but unfamiliar with marketing in Europe, he acquired the firms that had been L.S.E.'s national distributors in ten countries and turned them into sales subsidiaries. Close relationships between manufacturers and retailers are vital in the apparel business, and Robinson believed that L.S.E.'s distributors and their salesmen would provide that tie, enabling Levi's to keep attuned to changes in each national market.

Acquiring the distributors gave L.S.E. a large organization within Europe. In four years its staff increased to nearly 3,000, its subsidiary companies from one to thirteen, its plants from one to nine, its warehouses from one to twelve. But meshing the acquired firms with L.S.E. proved to be unexpectedly difficult. Their presidents were long-established businessmen in their own countries, and they resisted changing their methods. In Britain, Willie Gertler, of F. J. Gertler Co., bucked proposals for warehouse consolidation and other managerial changes so hard that the company shifted him into another job.

The Figures Were Out-of-Date

In keeping with well-established Levi Strauss policy, each national manager retained full autonomy and profit responsibility. At first, L.S.E. received only quarterly balance sheets—outdated information. Moreover, each new subsidiary operated differently, with its own accounting and inventory-control systems. Only Attias Ets. & Cie in Switzerland was computerized, and its system didn't fit with L.S.E.'s.

Worst of all, several of the firms did not have accurate information about their inventories. Their reports to Brussels—and L.S.E.'s reports to San Francisco—were often so lacking in details (about sizes and styles, for example) as to be meaningless. But for a while, Levi's fast sales growth obscured the problem.

While Robinson was struggling to reshape L.S.E.'s European distribution, he was also attempting to reduce its heavy dependence on imports. L.S.E.'s supply line stretched literally around the world. In 1971 and 1972, almost three-quarters of the pants the company sold in Europe were imported from other Levi Strauss plants in the U.S., Puerto Rico, Mexico, and Hong Kong. L.S.E. had to order its denim and corduroy materials, generally from the U.S., have them shipped to a manufacturing plant, usually in the U.S. or Hong Kong, wait for production to be scheduled and carried out, then ship the finished goods to Antwerp. At best, this process took eight to twelve weeks, but often there was as much as six months' delay. Frequently only half of an L.S.E. order arrived when it was due.

Once goods did reach Europe, L.S.E. couldn't keep track of where they were. Management failed to realize that by buying the distributors it had multiplied the inventory-control problem by twelve. Moreover, the ever increasing volume of pants, in various fabrics, styles, and sizes, flowing through twelve warehouses, overwhelmed the efforts of clerks to keep adequate records of the movements. As a result, warehouse workers often did not know where to find goods stacked in the bins. Incredible as it seems, if a retailer returned a shipment, L.S.E.'s warehouses had no means of reentering the goods into inventory. The company had never encountered more than a trickle of returns and such a system had not been considered.

The Perils of Promotions

Throughout 1971, L.S.E.'s main problem involved getting enough goods to sell. Confident that they could sell everything available, sales subsidiaries routinely ordered more than they had sold to retailers. The retailers gratefully accepted shipments that were months late. Only late in the year, thanks to rapidly expanding European production and still climbing imports, did the shortages begin to ease. Unfortunately, L.S.E.'s chaotic and out-of-date records gave its managers no inkling of the change.

Just at this point the two men who knew the most about Levi's European business, and who might have sensed the change, were promoted to new jobs. Combs became executive vice president, responsible for the day-to-day operations of the entire company (he died in a plane crash last April). Robinson succeeded him as vice president-international, moved from Brussels to San Francisco, and began dividing his attention between Europe and Levi's fast-growing activities in Canada, Latin America, and the Far East.

Peter Thigpen, thirty-two, took over as general manager of L.S.E. A former Marine with an M.B.A. from Stanford, Thigpen had been with L.S.E. only three years, most recently as marketing director. Still, he was the most experienced American executive on the scene.

When Fashion Turned Fickle

Simultaneously, European tastes in jeans underwent a surprising and rapid change—a phenomenon that Levi Strauss had not hitherto encountered. A French apparel manufacturer, New Man, soon joined by half a dozen others in West Germany, Britain, and Belgium, began making jeans in wild colors and far-out styles, using such fabrics as upholstery and velvet. They became fast-selling items of high fashion—at fancy prices. Europeans began demanding their ordinary jeans and corduroy pants in a variety of styles and colors.

Up to this point, Levi's had sold little else in Europe but its basic straight-leg blue jeans and corduroy pants. With those long lead times and a complex distribution network, the company could not readily shift its output to conform with such swings of fashion. Despite this handicap, Thigpen and his colleagues decided to compete in the high-fashion business with faster-moving local rivals.

It was, he now says, "a crucial marketing mistake." The demand for Levi's traditional jeans was still growing vigorously. But in its zeal for still more sales growth, the company plunged into a high-fashion market for jeans that it was ill equipped to handle. The new lines sold well, but they enormously compounded L.S.E.'s growing problem of controlling inventories.

A Vogue for Patch Pockets

Levi's European managers had ignored some early warnings of trouble. "Demand was so fantastic," says Robinson, "that no one believed it would ever taper off."

In late 1970 the French Distributor, Ets. Frenkel, S.A. (which Levi's was unable to buy), sharply reduced its orders for the standard scoop-pocketed jean and requested nothing but patch-pocket jeans for the spring of 1971. There was no demand for patch pockets elsewhere in Europe, and L.S.E. declined to produce them. So a Frenkel partner, Maurice Jablonsky, flew to Hong Kong and ordered two million pairs from the Levi Strauss subsidiary there. By mid-1971 patch pockets were the rage in Europe, and L.S.E. belatedly began making them in its European factories.

In the spring of 1972, retailers in England wanted to drop straight-leg blue jeans—Levi's bread-and-butter product—in favor of bell-bottom jeans. Levi's had been selling 250,000 pairs of straight-leg jeans a month in England; they were made in the U.S. and Hong Kong and took four months to deliver. The retailers warned that if Levi's would not provide bells promptly, they would buy from local manufacturers, who could deliver quickly.

Levi's shifted some production in the U.S. and France to bell-bottoms as rapidly as it could, but it continued to produce large quantities of straight-

legs, which were selling well elsewhere. Within weeks, however, the bell-bottom craze swept through Europe and demand for straight-leg jeans dwindled. Levi's had millions of them in its supply line, and when they arrived in Antwerp, virtually all of them remained in the warehouse.

Bell-bottom corduroys became popular throughout Europe about the same time, and in addition to making straight-leg cords in twenty-seven colors, L.S.E. started making bells in twenty-five colors. When its marketing men tried to drop the straight-leg corduroys, retailers insisted they be retained because the straight-legs were still selling. But in midsummer, just as Levi's plants were reaching full production on belled cords, the market for all corduroy pants shriveled as consumers switched en masse to the new bell-bottom denims. In mid-1972, 65 percent of all pants sold in Europe were corduroys. A year later, the figure was only 15 percent.

Trying to Stop "The Big Steamroller"

Belatedly aware of the upheaval in fashion, the young L.S.E. managers tried to decrease their immense imports of suddenly unfashionable pants. They canceled huge orders for corduroy fabric from the U.S. But the very size of "the big steamroller," as Peter Thigpen calls Levi's, made it slow to respond to Europe's suddenly changed market. A firm corporate policy at Levi Strauss, in keeping with its sense of social responsibility, is to avoid layoffs. The company tries to provide year-round employment for the thousands of women working on its sewing-machine lines. That policy forced L.S.E. to curtail its orders to the foreign plants gradually so that other divisions could take up the slack. For at least six months, L.S.E. continued both to import and to manufacture pants that were hard to sell.

Not until January, 1973, did Robinson and Thigpen begin to realize that they faced a serious problem. L.S.E's year-end figures showed an inventory of eight million jeans, pants, and shirts, double the level of a year earlier and enough for more than six months' sales. Moreover, inventories were still increasing, and the two men realized that rival manufacturers, including Blue Bell and Lee, had begun three months earlier to cut prices in order to unload excessive stocks. L.S.E. asked its subsidiaries to take similar action.

Once again, those independent-minded national managers resisted. Never before had they had enough inventory and they couldn't believe they did now. Ironically enough, the strongest objections came from an executive who had worked for Levi's for twenty years. Alex Kolb, general manager of Levi Strauss Germany, insisted that the sales slump in corduroys and straight-leg blue jeans was temporary and that other manufacturers were destroying themselves and their markets by panicky markdowns.

He and others contended that Levi's relationships with retailers, and the entire apparel market, would be devastated if the company began aggressively dumping its massive inventories. They also argued that when the spring selling season began in a few weeks, fashions might change again and the overstocked pants might be sold at full markup. Thigpen was reluctant to press too strongly against such firm advice from his own men closest to the customers. As a result, little action was taken for several weeks.

All News to the Controller

About the same time, Levi's top management in San Francisco began to take notice of the situation. Though aware of the figures that disturbed Robinson and Thigpen, Peter Haas did not yet consider European inventories to be a significant problem. "We felt that even though they were too high," he says, "they were in denims and cords, which at that time we called 'stable.' "

Some securities analysts were less sanguine. When Margaret Gilliam, of Dominick & Dominick in New York, learned of the inventory figures, she flew to San Francisco to question management about them. She found some executives still unaware of the situation; Paul Deihle, the corporate controller, first learned about it from her. She concluded that the Levi's executives were refusing to face up to the inventory problem and changed her investment recommendation from "buy" to "sell."

Gilliam's visit aroused concern, and in February top management intervened directly for the first time in L.S.E.'s affairs. In effect abrogating the autonomy of the European operation, the executive committee directed L.S.E. to reduce its inventories by the end of fiscal 1973 to below their level at the end of fiscal 1972. Even so, Levi's executives believed the problem could easily be solved by judicious markdowns, without seriously affecting profits.

"My Kamikaze Dive"

Responding to the executive-committee directive, Robinson cut back orders at Levi's far-flung factories for jeans for Europe. But he could not override the policy of keeping those plants busy, so his drastic production cuts didn't take effect until June. In Europe, Thigpen began what he calls "my kamikaze dive" to unload the inventory glut by cutting prices. It took him a while to achieve momentum, partly because competitors had moved sooner to reduce *their* inventories, so that Levi's had to offer larger discounts to retailers than expected.

Through the spring, Levi's executives believed the inventories were shrinking satisfactorily. Sales again were picking up, and now-fashionable goods—bellbottom jeans and casual slacks—were selling well. At the company's annual meeting in April, Peter Haas repeated his belief that the inventory problem was a minor one. Most of the goods were in staple lines of denim and corduroy pants, he said, and were "less vulnerable to large markdowns compared with high-fashion items."

In fact, the company had scarcely begun to overcome its difficulties. Most European managers, inexperienced in closing out inventories, sold their best and most easily salable goods first—the exact opposite of accepted retailing practice. Moreover, the European retailing industry is unequipped to handle large sales of discounted, out-of-fashion goods. Since there are few bargain basements or discount stores, it was difficult to find outlets for such goods, especially in Levi's huge quantities. All summer, salesmen for the sales subsidiaries continued to press their regular customers to buy unfashionable trousers; it was the only way they knew to get rid of them. Some subsidiaries tried to dump pants in one another's markets, and Thigpen repeatedly found himself arbitrating the resulting disputes.

Under normal marketing conditions, a markdown of 5 to 10 percent from the wholesale price is sufficient to unload unwanted inventory. But by late spring, the European apparel markets were reeling from manufacturers' months'-long struggle to dump inventories, and prices were tumbling. A pair of Levi's straight-leg corduroy pants, for example, sold in Germany for $6 wholeslae in 1972. By March, 1973, the price had dropped to $4; by June, it was $3.50. The worst still lay ahead: by August the price fell to $2.75; and by November, to $1.50. Retail prices dropped accordingly, from $10 to $3.

Left with the Cats and Dogs

By late spring—midway in that price plunge—it was apparent even in San Francisco that L.S.E. was not resolving its problem. Finally concerned, top management began sending experts to Europe to help out. Several marketing specialists and the corporate manager of inventory control were transferred there on a permanent basis.

Once more, Levi's top command misread the evidence. The European inventories declined in July and August, and executives in San Francisco concluded that the rescue efforts were paying off. In mid-September, Bud Robinson confidently told Levi's executive committee that the inventory liquidation was proceeding successfully and would be completed, with no major additional markdowns, by the end of the fiscal year.

At the same time, he routinely asked each Euro-pean subsidiary to submit a pro forma year-end financial statement. Those figures, combined with the results of the annual physical inventory taken the previous month, would be used to estimate the company's year-end results.

When the figures arrived in San Francisco two weeks later, Robinson and Edmund Pera, controller of the international division, were stunned. The physical inventory, which had been conducted by Levi's outside accounting firm, Arthur Andersen & Co., showed that L.S.E.'s inventory consisted mainly of a mishmash of hard-to-sell odd sizes and unusual styles. "All we had left," Robinson discovered, "was cats and dogs."

The financial projections were equally disturbing. The value of the European inventory was declining so swiftly that the European operation would surely suffer losses. The rest of Robinson's international division was doing so well, with sales in some regions well above planned levels, that he hoped the division could meet its profit target for the year despite the European loss. Nevertheless, he decided to fly immediately to Brussels with Ed Pera for a close look.

Bad News on the Blackboard

They finally discovered the true magnitude of the debacle. In a stuffy, crowded conference room in L.S.E.'s headquarters, they spent half a day with the manager and controller of each subsidiary, going over their inventories item by item. They demanded to know how much each company had received in the last ninety, sixty, and thirty days for each item being marked down, how much the subsidiaries expected to have left by year-end and what price it might be worth by then in the demoralized market. Robinson, Pera, and Thigpen took turns at a blackboard, chalking down the prospective financial impact of the bad news that had so long eluded them. Suddenly, says one participant, "a lot of young men began to look very old."

The tense sessions began at 8:00 A.M. and stretched on till 9:00 P.M. Then, says Pera, "we'd go out and get half-snockered. We couldn't believe it.'' The executives in San Francisco had no idea that prices had fallen so fast, or that the European inventories were of such poor quality. It was clear that with the markdowns approaching 80 percent, European losses would be enormous. And vast numbers of jeans still remained unsold in the warehouses, their value declining by the day.

A few managers remained optimistic about selling their inventories at full markup. But this time Robinson and Pera demanded larger reserves for markdowns and conservative inventory valuations. They ordered new pro forma statements, based on the newly accepted valuations, and returned to California.

Skeptics on a Junket

When the new statements arrived in late October, the consequence was clear: The European loss would not only wipe out the international division's profit, but would cause a large fourth-quarter loss for the entire company. Had the 16 million pants sold in Europe last year brought full prices, sales there would have totaled $115 million. But half of them, or eight million, had to be sold at discounts, and the receipts totaled only $99.5 million. Instead of earning a profit, the European operation lost $12 million.

When the company disclosed its fourth-quarter loss, the shock reverberated on Wall Street. In a single day's trading on the New York Stock Exchange, Levi Strauss common dropped from $29 to $21.50. By unhappy coincidence, that blow fell barely a week before the beginning of a three-day, $65,000 company junket to San Francisco for some forty securities analysts. The trip was intended to improve Levi's image in the investment community. But instead of being able to crow about the company's considerable achievements, Bud Robinson spent four hours aboard a chartered jet from New York explaining the European loss to the critical guests. Many of them went home from San Francisco still skeptical about the agility of Levi's management.

Though plainly shaken by the European fiasco, the Haases vow that Levi's will never again get too big for its britches. "We've done a lot of soul-searching," says Walter Haas. "Peter and I were unpopular for years with some of our people because domestically this company could have grown much faster. We have been behind the market every year. But we wanted to grow within our resources, both financial and management. Our European operation didn't do the same. It will never happen again, I can assure you that."

Toward that end, Levi's far-flung subsidiaries will operate with considerably less freedom. The virtues of allowing each manager to run his own business have yielded to the need for accurate information and adequate control in Brussels and San Francisco.

The Haases contend that their troubles in Europe are over. The glut of inventory has been cut to a manageable 5,362,000 pairs of pants, about a four-month supply. Accounting methods and forms used by the sales subsidiaries are being standardized. The subsidiaries' controllers will soon begin reporting to the L.S.E. controller, not to the president of their subsidiary—an adaptation of the famous I.T.T. control mechanism.

The European warehouses are being consolidated from twelve to three, and Levi's inventory-control experts are designing computerized primary and back-up inventory-accounting systems. This year 70 percent of the goods L.S.E. sells will be made in Europe, shrinking those long supply lines to about six weeks.

"I Guess They Feel Deceived"

After what must have been the most painful soul-searching of all, the Haases are replacing Bud Robinson as vice president–international, effective this month. His successor, Robert Grohman, the former president of B.V.D. Co., has had years of foreign experience. Robinson wanted to stay in a line job, but instead was made vice president for corporate marketing—a staff position he feels offers little challenge. So he has been looking for a job outside Levi's. "I'm the guy who's responsible for international, and I guess they feel deceived by me," says Robinson. "I feel a bit had, if you want to know the truth."

Levi's stockholders may feel much the same way. Still, as expensive as Levi's European inventory debacle was, the company nevertheless did capture the No. 1 share of the Continent's market for jeans. That achievement might have taken longer, and therefore been even more costly, if the company had taken time to install all its controls first. Probably the biggest cost of the whole affair has been the damage to Levi's image. It will take quite a while for Levi Strauss to recover its old mystique.

Questions

1. *Specifically, what were the factors that led to the unexpected Levi Strauss Europe debacle in 1973?*
2. *Assess in retrospect the Levi Strauss strategy of rapid market share expansion in Europe during the 1960s. What factors might have led the Levi Strauss executives to make the risky decisions they made?*

Cross-Reference Table*

Text Author(s), Title, Edition	1	2	3	4	5	6	7	8	9	10	11
Pride and Ferrell *Marketing: Basic Concepts and Decisions* Second Edition, 1980	1	2,3	4,5 6,7 8	9	10,11	12,13 14,15 16	17,18 19,20	21,22	23,24	25	26
Bell *Marketing: Concepts and Strategy* Third Edition, 1979	1		2,3 10,43	9		10,11			12,13	5,17 18,19	
Boone and Kurtz *Contemporary Marketing* Second Edition, 1977	1,2 3	37,39 40,41	4,5 6,7 8	10,11	9	12,13 20	14,15 16,17 18,19	23,24	25	26,38 43	27,28 29
Cundiff, Still and Govoni *Fundamentals of Modern Marketing* Second Edition, 1976	1,2 11,37	3	9,11	10			4,5 6,7 8	12,14 15,16 17,18 19,26	13	24	26
Enis *Marketing Principles* Second Edition, 1977	1	2,3	10	37,38 39,40	43,44 45,46	9	9,10 11	4,5 6,7 8	12,13 14,15 16,17 18,19 20	30,31 32,33 34,35 36	23,24 25,26 27,28 29
Gwinner et al. *Marketing* First Edition, 1977	1	37	2,3	43	12,13 14,15 16,17 18,19 20,21 22	23,24 25,26 27,28 29,30 31,32 33,34 35,36	37	25,26 27	38	49,50	9,11
Heskett *Marketing* First Edition, 1977	2,3	1	9,10 11,20	7,8 12,13 14,15 16,17	21,22	30,32 33	31,34 35	23,24 44,38	25	25,27 28,29	4,5 6,18 19
Kotler *Marketing Management* Third Edition, 1976	2,3	1	9,10 11,20	7,8 12,13 14,15 16,17	21,22	30,32 33	31,34 35	23,24 44,38	25	25,27 28,29	4,5 6,18 19
Lack and Ferrell *Marketing Strategy and Plans* First Edition, 1979	1,43	2,3 12,13		7,8	4,6 10	9,10 16,37 38,39 40,41 42	15	14,30 31,32 33,34 35,36	21,22	23,24 25,26 27,28 29	18,19 20
McCarthy *Basic Marketing: A Managerial Approach* Sixth Edition, 1978	1,47 48	2	3	37,38 39,40 41,42	37	9		11	10	12,13 17,18 19,20	14,15 16
Stanton *Fundamentals of Marketing* Sixth Edition, 1979	1	2,3	4,5 6	7,8 10	9,11		46	5,12 17,18 19	13,20	14,15 16	21
Wentz *Marketing* First Edition, 1979	1,2 3	43,44 45,46		9,10	11	14,15 16,17 18,19	12,13 20	23,24	25,27 28,29	26,38 44	30,31

column header: Text Chapter Number (spans columns 1–11)

* This table correlates the articles in Robicheaux, Pride, and Ferrell,
Marketing: Contemporary Dimensions, Second Edition, with chapters
of selected introductory marketing texts.

12	13	14	15	16	17	18	19	20	21	22	23	24	25	26	27	28
27,28 29	30,31	32	33,34 35,36	37,38 39,40	37	41,42	43,44 45,50	46	47,48	49,50						
23,24 25,26	27,28 29	30	31,32 33	34,35 36	21	21	44,15 50	4,5	6,7 8,18 19		37,38 39,40 41,42	47,48 49,50				
30	31,32 33	34,35 36	21	22	37,42 45,47 48,49											
23*	24	27,28 29	30,31	34,35 36	30,31 32,33	21	22	37,38 39,40 41,42	43,44 45,46 47,48 49,50							
21,22	43,44 45,50	46,47 48,49														
10,42	39,40	2,44 45	41		49		47,48	37,38								
43,44 45,46 47,48 49,50	36	50	49,37 38													
43,44 45,46 47,48 49,50	36	50	32,33	14,30 31	34,35 36		4,6		49,50	37,38 39,40 41,42						
5,17	46		44,45 47,48 49	50												
20	23,24	26,38 44	25	27,28 29	30,32 33	34,35 36	31	21	22	22	43,44 45	50	49,50	6,7 8	50	37,38
22		24,26 38,44	23	25	27,28 29	30	34,35 36	31,32 33	48	49,50	41,43 44,45	39,40 42	37,38 47,48			
32	34	35,36	33	21	22	4,5 6	7,8	39	40		37,38 47,48 41,42	49,50				